DESERT

HUMANITIES

Series Editors: Ron Broglio and Celina Osuna

Also in this series:

The Belly of the Whale:
Bilingual Edition
by Claudia Prado; translated by Rebecca Gayle Howell

Sand, Water, Salt:
Managing the Elements in Literature of the American West, 1880–1925
by Jada Ach

WILD WEIRD WEST

ESSAYS ON ARID AMERICA

GARY REGER

TEXAS TECH UNIVERSITY PRESS

This book is typeset in EB Garamond. The paper used in this book meets the minimum requirements of ANSI/NISO Z39.48-1992 (R1997). ⊗

Designed by Hannah Gaskamp
Cover design by Hannah Gaskamp

Library of Congress Cataloging-in-Publication Data

Names: Reger, Gary, author. Title: Wild, Weird, West: Essays on Arid America / Gary Reger. Description: Lubbock, Texas: Texas Tech University Press, [2024] | Series: Desert Humanities / series editors, Ron Broglio and Celina Osuna | Includes bibliographical references and index. | Summary: "A wide-ranging collection of essays on multiple aspects of the Southwestern American deserts"—Provided by publisher.
Identifiers: LCCN 2024031781 (print) | LCCN 2024031782 (ebook) |
ISBN 978-1-68283-228-8 (paperback; acid-free paper) | ISBN 978-1-68283-229-5 (ebook)
Subjects: LCSH: Deserts in literature. | Deserts—West (U.S.) | Ecocriticism. | LCGFT: Essays. | Literary criticism.
Classification: LCC PN56.D477 R44 2024 (print) | LCC PN56.D477 (ebook) |
DDC 809/.9332154—dc23/eng/20240830
LC record available at https://lccn.loc.gov/2024031781
LC ebook record available at https://lccn.loc.gov/2024031782

24 25 26 27 28 29 30 31 32 / 9 8 7 6 5 4 3 2 1

Texas Tech University Press
Box 41037
Lubbock, Texas 79409-1037 USA
800.832.4042
ttup@ttu.edu
www.ttupress.org

For Edie, Alison, and Caroline

CONTENTS

ILLUSTRATIONS

PREFACE

My fascination with deserts began when my parents retired to Sun City, Arizona. To escape the stultifying regimentation of this suburb in the sands—designed, constructed, and marketed by Del Webb, whose company had earlier built the Poston Japanese-American internment camp—I sought refuge in hikes and drives in the Sonoran Desert, often accompanied by my brother Greg, who shares my enthusiasm for desert landscapes. Unconsciously, these excursions seeded new academic projects that began coming to fruition years later. In 2010 I taught a course called "Writing the American Desert" at Trinity College in Hartford, Connecticut—about as far from the desert as you can get in America. The then-director of the American Studies program, Lou Masur, welcomed this intrusion onto his territory. A few brave and enterprising and very smart students—one of whom confessed she only took the course because Lou urged her even though she had no idea what she'd signed up for; she ended up performing brilliantly—enrolled. We read classics by writers like Edward Abbey and watched a documentary on Burning Man. (An early scene showed a woman having her pubic hair sculpted; several students who watched it at 8 a.m. in the library kept looking nervously over their shoulders to see whether any passers-by happened to glance in.) I only had one chance to teach that course, but it was foundational for my later work.

In 2012 I discovered the Western Literature Association (WLA) and attended my first annual meeting that year in Lubbock, Texas. I will be forever grateful for the very warm welcome afforded me by the membership, especially by Melody Graulich, who invited me to dinner and was generous enough to laugh at my jokes. There I read a very early and less than terrific version of chapter 5 below. Since then, till the pandemic, and now again afterwards, the WLA meetings have seen me every year; many of the essays in this book were conceived as papers for the WLA, as noted in the notes to each such chapter.

Four chapters here (3, 4, 6, and 9) have appeared before in published versions; I have revised them, sometimes quite radically, to take account of new scholarship (or scholarship

I had missed), clarify my argument, capture shifts in my understanding, and correct minor (or major?) lapses. The original publications and/or presentations are cited in a note attached to the titles (always note *). Chapters 2, 5, 7, and 8 are quasi-new, as very different and much shorter versions were presented at meetings of the WLA, except for chapter 7, which I read at the 2018 meeting "Celebrating the Sonoran Desert—A Tri-National Symposium." I am very grateful to the organizing committees for these conferences for accepting my papers and to the audiences at each for incisive and helpful commentary. I have tried to incorporate all critiques and suggestions offered orally and in writing; I regret that for the former I usually did not note the names of my interlocutors. Please forgive me! Chapters 1 and 10 are completely new, written to tie the essays in the book together, set background, and tease out the themes that these disparate explorations of the American desert imaginary share. There is some repetition from chapter to chapter, especially regarding biblical and European tropes about deserts. These passages appeared originally because the chapters had been written as stand-alone essays. After some hesitation I have let the repetitions stand, both as reminders to the reader and to enable the chapters to be read independently. I trust the repetition will not be too annoying to anyone reading the book straight through.

It's probably important to confess that my own academic training—in Greek and Roman history—prepared me in no particular way to tread in the fields of literary studies. The techniques of literary analysis and approaches to extracting meaning from fiction were largely foreign to me. Readers will no doubt pick up on my deficiencies as they parse my approach to novels like *Fruit Out of Rock*. However, history and literature share an abiding commitment to close reading and deep analysis; readers will also surely note the historical inflection of my approach to various questions in chapters that follow. The liberal arts are allies; I expect my new colleagues will pardon my infelicities and hope they will welcome whatever new insights or ideas I may present.

At the same time, I have trekked far and wide in the chapters that follow, often deep into territory where I lacked both map and compass. It is inevitable that I have made mistakes, missed important literature (for many topics, the secondary material is vast), and no doubt offered naïve or simplistic arguments. All I can offer by way of defense is that I have gone where my interests nudged me and done my best to dredge up (and understand) specialist literature and try to be cautious in my interpretations. But I would also say that in this age of growing academic specialization it has been an unusual pleasure simply to follow where the trail has gone, without undue worry that I may have wandered off it into some prickly byway. I hope my readers will be understanding, even when they vigorously disagree.

A few *caveant lectores* follow.

NATIVE AMERICAN MATTERS

Throughout the book I've had occasion to discuss various aspects of Native American culture and religion. These discussions include analysis of some words and phrases in various languages referring to physical features in the desert landscape, mythology, stories, and contemporary fiction and poetry. My knowledge of the languages of Indigenous groups, of which there are scores in the desert Southwest, is quite limited. I have relied on the treatment of secondary sources and, for some languages, dictionaries and grammars to help me; they are cited in the notes as appropriate. When I quote a word in an Indigenous language, I use the transcription provided in my source. For most languages there have been changes in the ways sounds are represented, but rather than transpose earlier versions into currently accepted representations (which might have imposed new errors), I have thought it better to leave words as my sources give them, for the ease of readers who may want to check the sources. For California languages, a convenient treatment can be found in Victor Golla's comprehensive *California Indian Languages*. For example, the usual proper spelling of the name of the Indigenous people Anglos call the Mohave (their name for themselves is 'Aha Makhav, "Water People") is with an "h"; the alternative, with a "j," is the official spelling for names of places and physical features ("Fort Mojave," the "Mojave Desert"). However, these spellings are not always consistent; the tribal reserve near Needle, California, is called the Fort Mojave Indian Reservation and its residents the Fort Mojave Indian Tribe. In Harry J. Winters's *'O'odham Place Names* he puts glottal stop marks before and after the first O. Except where I refer to his book, I have preferred the standard orthography without the first mark, which is also that used by the Tohono O'odham nation.

I have made liberal use of ethnographic studies too. There are many difficulties in using older ethnographies—the anthropologists who compiled them were often burdened by racist biases; many ethnographers were amateurs without formal training; work was often done under severe restrictions of time and under less than ideal conditions; in general the ethnographers did not know, or knew only very imperfectly, the language of the group they studied and so had to rely on translators, whose renditions into English could not be checked; in many cases the ethnographies we have were directed by A. L. Kroeber, who imposed a template on his students and researchers that sometimes makes for a rather formulaic and dry rendering of a complex culture;[1] and some ethnographies were written and published many years after the fieldwork on which they are based. Nevertheless, for all too many Indigenous groups, the early ethnographies are the only surviving account of lifeways that have disappeared, or are deeply attenuated. (Some groups, like the Tohono O'odham and Diné (Navajo), however, have managed to retain their language and culture relatively intact.) I have not had access to contemporary, living representatives of the cultures I have discussed, and I am only too aware that my interpretations are several degrees removed from firsthand. In regret I offer a proleptic apology to any Native Americans who may read my chapters and find my work inadequate or mistaken. Let it be known that I have tried my best to treat my material with sensitivity and respect. I welcome any corrections or suggestions that can be incorporated into later work.

There has been in recent years an efflorescence of Native American writing in prose and verse and an accompanying secondary scholarly literature on it. For the desert Southwest, much of this creative work has been in poetry; discussions are sprinkled throughout the chapters. Especially resonant have been poems of Ofelia Zepeda (Tohono O'odham) and Simon Ortiz (Acoma); now-classic fiction like N. Scott Momaday's (Kiowa) *House Made of Dawn* has been invaluable. But I have made no effort to undertake a thorough review of this vast and growing literature. That would be a project for another book. I am only too alive to the errors this may have led me into, and that this project would surely have been richer had I the time to pursue that literature. (As it is, work on these chapters has spanned many years.) Perhaps I should mention that I have not used the abundant work of Tony Hillerman. His Indigenous *bona fides* have been questioned; I take no position.

In the very first sentence of the prologue to her study of ecotourism and Indigenous peoples across the globe, Alison M. Johnston writes, "This book is not intended to speak on behalf of or in the place of Indigenous Peoples."[2] So too my treatment here of Indigenous matters, which I offer with all due humility and respect.

Secondary literature poses its own problems. For some of the authors and books I have studied, the scholarship is enormous and always growing: for example, Bret Easton Ellis, Mary Austin, and Joan Didion, whose recent death has unleashed a new mass of reflections on her own wide-ranging output. For others, like Frances Gillmor, the field is largely barren. When it comes to UFOs (Unidentified Flying Objects), the central topic of chapter 8, there is a bifurcated literature: academic studies that try to situate the phenomenon in its social context or offer psychological explanations especially for the abduction narratives that proliferated after 1966 (and continue, although at a reduced rate, today), and "popular" expositions that more or less accept the reality of UFO sightings and abduction experiences. Since my interest is in the crux of UFOs, alien encounters, and the desert, I have often dipped into the latter. The recent US government release of video of supposed UAPs (Unidentified Aerial Phenomena, now the official preferred designation; I have retained the old and much more familiar UFO) has unleashed a new debate about the reality and nature of the phenomena; I take no position.

TRANSLATIONS

Except where noted and when I have used a translated version of a work originally written in another language, all other translations are my own. (There aren't many.) I am grateful to Sara Kippur for advice on some gnarly passages in French.

SPANISH-LANGUAGE LITERATURE AND THE MEXICAN DESERT

From the Pacific Ocean in Southern California to El Paso and Juarez, the Mexico-US border is nothing more than a line in the sand, an artificial boundary that marks no or few changes in topographic, ecological, cultural, or social reality, except for the national language. East of El Paso the Rio Grande forms the border, but neither is there substantive difference between the two sides of the river. The US states of California (the southern region), Arizona, New Mexico, and Texas in the west and the northern Mexican states of Sonora and Chihuahua form a cultural *koine*, whose history—and prehistory—reach deep into the past.

A comprehensive study of the southwestern desert world would, then, encompass also the Mexican Northwest: both sides of the line as if it did not exist, except for its effects on politics and language. Literature that could be comprised in such a broader context might include the rich trove of Spanish explorers' and priests' accounts, like those of the Coronado expedition or Father Kino's detailed journals of his many years traveling in Pimería Alta (today's northern Sonora and Southern California and Arizona) and ministering to the

Indigenous populations.[3] The literature produced by Mexican authors set in the deserts of northwestern Mexico is likewise rich and important; to give just two examples, one might consider Emma Dolujanoff, whose *Cuentos del desierto* ("Tales of the Desert") are set in Sonora, or the stories of the Chihuahuan author Jesús Gardea, collected in translation in *Stripping Away the Sorrows of the World*. In Gardea's story "Above the Water," for example, his protagonist Jimena is driven crazy by the heat and drought:

> The stones burst in the sun. The drought will leave us with nothing at all, not even our sanity. They say the resurrected souls of animals roam the plain. Their bones are all in place, stepping solidly on the earth. So many years without water, they're ready for anything. Spooks and ghosts. . . . What suffocating heat.[4]

The language and imagery echo those of the desert tropes we will see throughout the book. The drought and the death of animals are reminiscent of Elmer Kelton's *The Time It Never Rained*, set in a devastating drought in southwestern desert Texas in the 1950s; the "spooks and ghosts" call up the hauntings Cordelia Barrera has recently recounted in her *The Haunted Southwest*.[5] This brief passage gives just a hint of the richness in complementarity and expansion that the literature I have set aside could offer. Like the Indigenous literature, the Spanish-language literatures of colonial Spain and national Mexico deserve a place in any examination of writing the southwestern deserts, and I regret the lack of time that prevented me from bringing them in.

ACKNOWLEDGMENTS

For the book as a whole, I am very grateful in first and last instance to Edith Folta and Jada Ach for ongoing advice, encouragement, and careful critical reading of several chapters, especially 1, 2, 8, and 10, that greatly helped me shape my arguments. Caroline Reger deployed her skills as an archivist to provide some essential long-distance bibliographic aid. Several individual chapters benefitted from the help and advice of friends and colleagues. Katherine Bergren and Sara Kippur read and commented on an early draft of chapter 3; their critique improved it immensely. I am also grateful to Laura Ance of Éditions Grasset in Paris for facilitating permission to publish translations of passages from Yves Berger's *La pierre et le saguaro*. Chapter 4 owes much to Fiona Hobson and Damien Kempf, who organized the conference at the University of Liverpool where it was first presented. Fiona and the reviewer for the version published in *Cultural History* offered many useful comments that materially improved the paper.

For chapter 5, Lisa Tatonetti proved to be a crucial commentator. Her expertise saved me from much foolishness and pushed me to return to *Fruit Out of Rock* with an eye open to erotics, which I found in abundance, and to reconsider the role of gender. Chapter 6 went through being both a conference paper and an essay published in *Boom California*. The former editor of *Boom*, Jason Sexton, and an anonymous reader helped me hone my argument. For chapter 9, Mike Levy, the editor of *Extrapolation*, where an earlier version appeared, not only made substantive comments but also was willing to take on a manuscript that violated the word limits by which the journal normally abides; likewise, the anonymous reader suggested numerous revisions that I happily adopted. Chapter 10 owes a great deal to Lisa Tatonetti and Cordelia Barrera, who generously sent me a copy of her *The Haunted Southwest*, which plays a central role in that chapter's argument.

The final version of this book was written in Las Cruces, New Mexico. I am very grateful to Elizabeth Horodowich and Mark Cioc, current and former chairs of the History Department at New Mexico State University, for granting me a visiting faculty appointment that allowed me to use the university's interlibrary loan services. Likewise, the Interlibrary Loan Department at Trinity College in Hartford, Connecticut, facilitated my work on the chapters as they developed into articles or presentations.

I owe a great deal to the two reviewers who read a preliminary draft of the book for Texas Tech University Press. I took their comments and criticism seriously and have made many changes and additions meant to address them, although probably not to their full satisfaction. One of the readers revealed himself to me, so I can thank Aidan Tynan by name. He also shared with me unpublished work, for which I am likewise grateful.

The staff at Texas Tech University Press has been absolutely delightful to work with. My editor Travis Snyder was enthusiastic about the book from the beginning. Christie Perlmutter copyedited the text with speed and aplomb and caught many errors; the book would not be as clean as it is without her hard work. Senior designer Hannah Gaskamp produced four fun covers; choosing which to go with was not easy. Hannah also typeset the text with celerity and care. John Brock, marketing manager, has worked hard to get the book into the hands of readers, for which I am extremely grateful.

For the figures, I owe thanks to many folks who facilitated permissions and provided images. Michaela Buenemann took time out of her duties as chair of the New Mexico State University Department of Geography and Environmental Studies to draw Figs. 1-1, 1-2, 1-3, and 8-1 for me. Thanks to Barbara Buhler Lynes, the anonymous owner granted permission to reproduce as Fig. 3-1 Georgia O'Keeffe's "Part of the Cliffs" after Barbara's illustration in her catalogue of O'Keeffe's work (*Georgia O'Keeffe: Catalogue Raisonné*). The photograph in Fig. 3-2 was taken by Herb Lotz; he and the Georgia O'Keeffe Museum in Santa Fe, New Mexico, gave permission to use it—and I am very grateful to Marcella Sandoval of *Pasatiempo* in Santa Fe for putting us in touch and to Rana Chao and Kira Randolph at the museum for their crucial help. The photograph in Fig. 4-6 belongs to the Imperial Irrigation District; Robert Schettler, Information Officer for the Imperial Irrigation District, kindly granted permission for me to use it for free. Fig. 4-8, which shows Harold Bell Wright at work, is in the archives of the Pioneers' Museum of the Imperial County Historical Society; Tyler Brinkerhoff, museum archivist, wrangled it for me. Fig. 7-2 reproduces the map that accompanies A. L. Kroeber's publication of "A Mohave Historical Epic"; David Yokoyama provided the permission for the University of California Press, and the high-quality scan was made by John Turkle of Big Picture in Las Cruces, New Mexico. The map of the Domínguez-Escalante Expedition route in Fig. 7-3 is used with the kind permission of the University of Utah Press. Glenn Steckling of the Adamski Foundation provided Fig. 8-2 at no charge. At the Integratron in Landers, California, Rose Acquino-Fliegel and her husband Michael Acquino let me in to take photos (Fig. 8-3) even though the site was closed for a private event; Michael also gave me a map that enabled me to find George Van Tassel's Giant Rock residence. (The Integratron is now owned by the Karl Sisters.) Fig. 8-6 is used with permission of Princeton University Press. Bill Hillman kindly granted permission to use Fig. 9-1 from his online Edgar Rice Burroughs collection. Figs. 9-2a-b by the late Frank Frazetta are reproduced with the kind permission of his son Bill Frazetta. For Fig. 9-3 I am very grateful to J & M Davey for permission to reproduce James Cawthorn's splendid drawing of Dejah Thoris and for providing an excellent scan. Fig. 9-4 originally appeared in the *Extrapolation* article that is now chapter 9; Rosemary Barrow gave me permission to use it for that article, but when I tried to contact her for her okay to do so again, it turned out she had died at a tragically young age. (Johns Hopkins Press, which publishes the journal Barrow's article appeared in, disavowed any copyright over the image.) I thank her again for her kindness. The three figures from Stratton's account of the *Captivity of the Oatman Girls* (1858) were all made with great care and precision by Richard Ring and Henry Arneth of the Watkinson Library at Trinity College, in Hartford, Connecticut.

It would be churlish of me not to end with a big thank-you to all the wonderful members of the Western Literature Association and the contributors to *Reading Aridity in Western American Literature*, which Jada Ach and I co-edited. The subjects of this book lie very far from my own academic training, and it was only thanks to the generosity and encouragement of the Western literature people that I dared to enter their field, stay there, and eventually produce the essays that comprise the chapters that follow. Undertaking a new scholarly arena is no easy task, but it has been a real pleasure thanks to the folks who have become colleagues and friends. Despite their support, it goes without saying—but I'll say it—that any dumbness to be found herein is entirely to be laid to my account.

WILD WEIRD WEST

CHAPTER 1

INTO THE AMERICAN DESERT

The deserts of the American Southwest take on a multiplicity of roles in literature set in or about or making use of their landscapes. Their alterity as opposed to the wet American East, the Cis-Mississippi world of farms and cities, grants them a status unique in our imaginary. Vast empty landscapes, a harsh, arid, hot environment, endless fields of irrigated crops that would wither and die without stolen water, landing sites for UFOs, tension between a sense of the sacred and a sense of the blasted, a masculinist challenge redemptive for effeminized Eastern males but also reconfigured by manly action into a femininized agricultural space, a realm where tourists conjure themselves in stagecoach Westerns, a landscape transferred to Mars where manliness can be enacted in a society of naked natives and a colonialist project pursued and consummated, and not least home to an Indigenous population that has worked out its own imaginary of the desert space they simply live in—all these and more are elements of the ways the southwestern American deserts play out in novels, travel narratives, poetry, film, and Native American epics in which deserts serve as stage and, sometimes, actor.[1]

In this book I have collected eight essays that address various aspects of the elements of the literary desert listed above. Originally written as conference papers or as contributions to collected volumes or journals, they have been revised to reflect new scholarship and especially new thinking or rethinking on my part about the questions they raise. As a whole, they are intended to serve as entrées to a wide variety of approaches to the southwestern American deserts. The material they take for their subjects ranges from a Mohave epic recorded in 1902, through fiction and travel narratives by American and French writers, to Edgar Rice Burroughs's fantastic Mars. The fundamental idea that unites these diverse chapters is that exploring the ways that deserts function in some literature can provide meaningful insights into a wide range of attitudes we have about not only deserts as landforms but about cities, gender, sacrality, the power of names, artistic representation, masculinity, settler colonialism, and the environment. These issues have been explored by others, of course, and references to plenty of earlier scholarship can be found in my notes. My work expands on and, perhaps, enriches the studies on which I rely. But there are two other matters that run like a thread through all the chapters: what is—if there is at all—a "desert literature," and can we see deserts as active agents, a nonhuman feature of the Earth's surface that has the power of agency? I return to these two questions in chapter 10. The various themes that weave in and out of the chapters cluster around the literary approaches of ecocriticism and the new materialism—a branch of posthumanism; it is insights from these contemporary critical approaches that help bind the chapters together, despite their diversity of topic.

A brief introduction to ecocritical and new materialist critical approaches may be useful here for some readers. While ecocriticism has a long pedigree, first bruited in the 1970s and now well established in the literature, it has tended not to be applied to desert environments. New materialism is a newer development, which likewise has seen less application to deserts. (There are, of course, notable exceptions to both these generalizations; references to much of this literature will be found in the notes throughout the book.) As deserts comprise a large proportion of the landscape of the American West and a great deal of literature has been written about them or set in them, however, it seems imperative to deploy ecocriticism and the new materialism in thinking about our western deserts, the literature about them, and broader instances of human-desert interaction. Ecocriticism and the new materialism can help illuminate desert-human interactions along the many dimensions that weave in and out of the chapters below, ranging from manliness and nudity through redemption and healing to space aliens, sexuality, erotics, and beyond.

Ecocriticism helps to illuminate several aspects of human-desert interaction that emerge in the chapters that follow, including the gendering of deserts, a primary theme in chapters 4 and 5, environmental degradation, which is the driver of the ecological disaster at the heart of the novel *Fruit Out of Rock* (chapter 5), and, in chapter 6, the deleterious impact of the desert Santa Ana winds on human behavior in Los Angeles. (This too intersects with the question of desert agency.) In chapter 3, an ecocritical approach helps to explicate the reaction of French visitors to the Southwest as they experience its aridity, emptiness, and just plain strangeness through sensual interaction. In these themes and topics, ecocriticism affords insight into intersections of desert environments with human beings, both those living or traveling in deserts and those outside deserts but who are affected by desert environments nearby (as in the case of Los Angeles). Because desert environments have often been depicted as hostile to humans, dangerous and threatening, regarding them through an ecocritical lens that accords the desert as much standing as the human serves to rebalance our attitude toward the deserts themselves and the interrelation between them and us.[2]

The new materialism affords a complementary approach that emphasizes especially the agency of the nonhuman:

> Reworking received notions of matter as a uniform, inert substance or a socially constructed fact, new materialism foregrounds novel accounts of its agentic thrust, processual nature, formative impetus, and self-organizing capacities, whereby matter as an active force is not only sculpted by, but also co-productive in conditioning and enabling social worlds and expression, human life and experience.[3]

Whether explicit or implicit, these kinds of questions run through the chapters that follow. Especially indebted to new materialism is the matter of desert agency—the exercise by the desert landscape of transformations on the people who experience it, a matter that I return to in chapter 10. This exercise plays out notably in the sacrality of the desert, explored from different angles in chapters 2, 3, and 8, from the desert as a source of power to Native American healers to the messages of Space Brothers and Sisters accorded to the UFO contactees of the 1950s. Desert sacrality operates bidirectionally, as the desert affects those who traverse it or live in it and they, in turn, leave their mark on its materiality, inflecting the people who experience it and taking from its inhabitants and visitors their own sense of the sacredness they experience and reinforce by their actions, rituals, and stories. These marks can be read clearly in the practice of naming, examined in chapter 7; the nature of different people's relations to desert space comes out in the rules by which they assign names to physical features of the desert and the meaning those names carry socially and culturally.

The aspect of a new materialist approach to literature and the environment—and more broadly, to people and the environment—that is most relevant to my work here is the role of agency. In all the chapters of the book, the desert expresses in one way or another, whether clearly and explicitly or subtly and implicitly, an agential effect on the people who encounter it. It deploys its agency along multiple axes: so, on the one hand, its physical characteristics of heat and aridity impel people to behave in particular ways; on another, its sacrality demands respect and the observance of ritual and actions that, if neglected, cause it to impose punishments on us (see especially chapters 2 and 6). Agency of nonhuman actors is a central focus of new materialist thinking; it is therefore especially potent in uncovering and explaining desert agency, treated explicitly in chapter 10.

Perhaps, finally, it might be useful to consider two other modes through which desert landscapes evoke reflections that can be viewed through these literary critical lenses. Desert sacrality is especially resonant here, since it operates with powerful bidirectionality. The sacrality of deserts imposes demands on people who interact with them, through rules about behavior, secrecy, and ritual, but also depends on people to maintain that sacrality by their appropriate actions. This sense of the desert as sacred plays out even in the encounters between UFO contactees and the Space Brothers and Sisters who, as if divinities, come bearing messages about how we must live our lives and warnings about nuclear weapons.

Colonialist interaction with the deserts provides a second example. Two great colonialist powers imposed themselves on the southwestern deserts: first the Spanish, whose presence began in the early sixteenth century, and then the Americans, whose trickle in the 1820s and 1830s swelled first with the migration to California for the Gold Rush and then with the seizure of the greater Southwest after the Mexican-American War. Both colonialist powers confronted long-established Native American populations whose relationships with their desert environments were fundamentally different from the colonialists', who brought with them proto- or fully developed capitalist approaches to the land; the Spanish also carried a religious imperative—Catholic Christianity—that saw Indigenous ideas about sacrality as sacrilegious. The impact of the colonialist legacy comes out distinctively in the renaming of the deserts' physical features, explored in chapter 7, but even serves as the grounding for Edgar Rice Burroughs's Martian fantasies (chapter 9). There, too, thrums the question

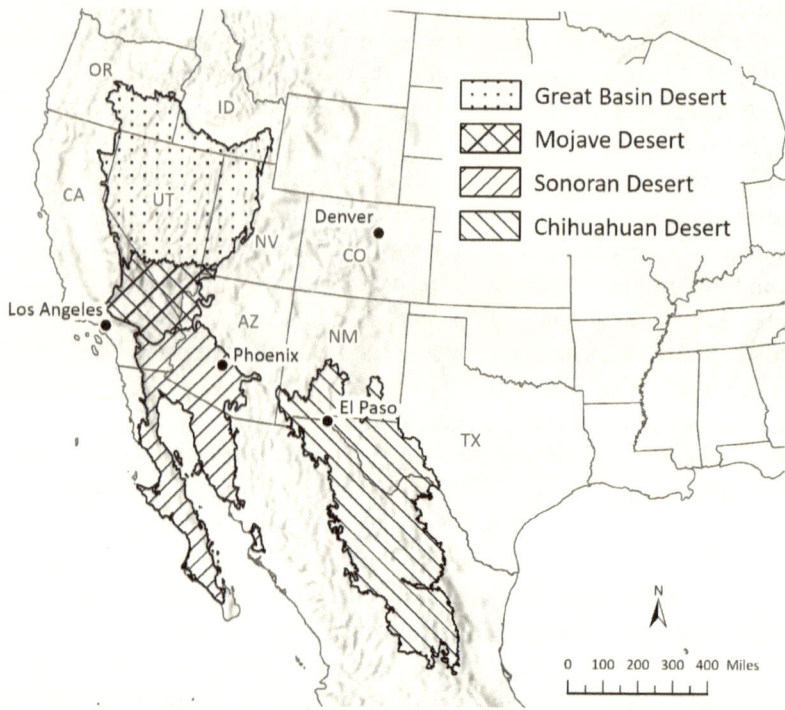

Figure 1-1: Deserts of the American Southwest. (Compiled by Michaela Buenemann, Department of Geography and Environmental Studies, New Mexico State University.)

of manliness—crucial in nineteenth- and twentieth-century thinking about the degrading effects of urban environments on white men and the redemptive role wildernesses, including deserts, could play in restoring their manliness.

Deserts contribute to ecocriticism and the new materialism and the environmental humanities generally because they pose a sort of limiting challenge to interpretation—they are landscapes that, it seems—but isn't so!—are uninhabitable by people, lacking our basic need, water, and presenting far too much of heat, sun, emptiness, tracklessness, and hostility. As we will see, ecocriticism and the new materialism help us move away from these stereotypical presuppositions about deserts and help make tangible the influences they exercise, as environments and through their nonhuman agency, on their inhabitants and their visitors.

These comments, I hope, will have served to provide a general sense of the critical approaches that have helped me in my treatment of the diverse subjects of the chapters to come. First, however, we need to consider what a desert consists in—that is, the simple geophysical fact of the desert landscape: how is it produced and what are its reigning characteristics?

WHAT IS A DESERT?

The American West hosts four or five major deserts, depending on how the geography is cut: the Great Basin Desert, which covers much of Nevada and eastern Oregon and Washington;

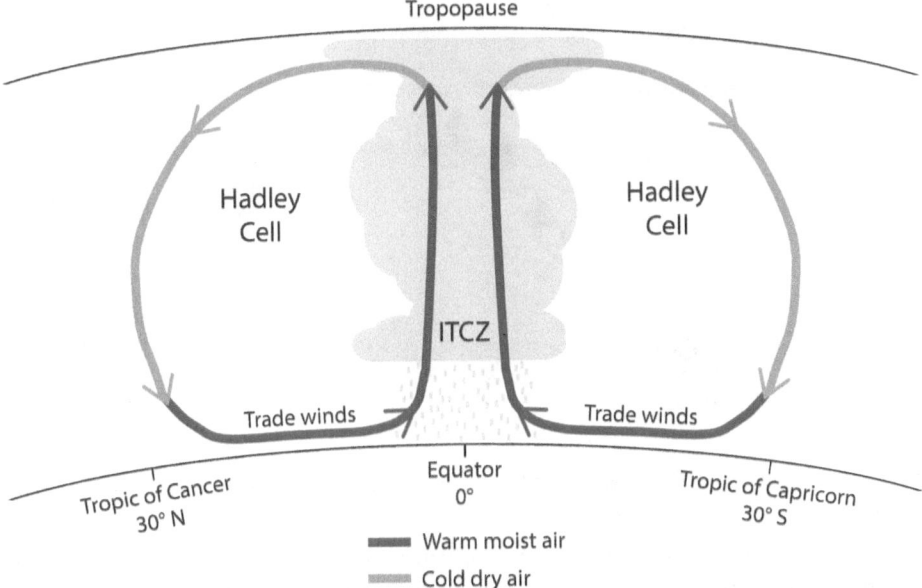

Figure 1-2: Hadley Cell Circulation. (Compiled by Michaela Buenemann, Department of Geography and Environmental Studies, New Mexico State University.)

the Mojave Desert, which takes in southern Nevada and a good portion of southeastern California, including Death Valley; the Colorado Desert—sometimes subsumed under the Mojave, but better seen as part of the greater Sonoran Desert—which stretches west of the Colorado River as it flows between Southern California and Arizona; the Sonoran Desert, which begins with the Tinajas Altas Mountains of Western Arizona and extends to Tucson in the west and Phoenix in the north, reaching also deep into the Mexican state of Sonora; and the Chihuahuan Desert, which comprises southern New Mexico and southwestern Texas, and likewise penetrates deep into the Mexican state of Chihuahua (Fig. 1-1).[4] Within these vast regions are desert subdivisions, like the Anza-Borrego in Southern California, or the Lechuguilla Desert in Arizona.

Each of these deserts has its own characteristic landforms, climate, fauna, and flora. The Great Basin in Nevada is marked by its basin-and-range topography and cold winters and in the Great Salt Lake holds the largest salt lake in the United States (although as I write it is rapidly shrinking) trapped in a closed basin. The Colorado Desert has a gravely surface (see Fig. 4-2) and contains the largest dune field in the United States (see Fig. 4-9), lending it a physiognomy (at least there) that evokes the classic desert stereotype of *Lawrence of Arabia*. The Sonoran Desert hosts the emblematic saguaro cactus, often appropriated as *the* marker of "desert" for American viewers of Westerns (even when set in locales where it does not grow); it is also notably arid in its western stretches, while on its eastern reaches, around Tucson, which receives a mean annual rainfall of about 12.3 inches (312.42 mm), just over the desert cutoff, it is practically lush. The Chihuahuan landscape of New Mexico is highly degraded after decades of intensive cattle grazing, and today often supportive of nothing more than mesquite.

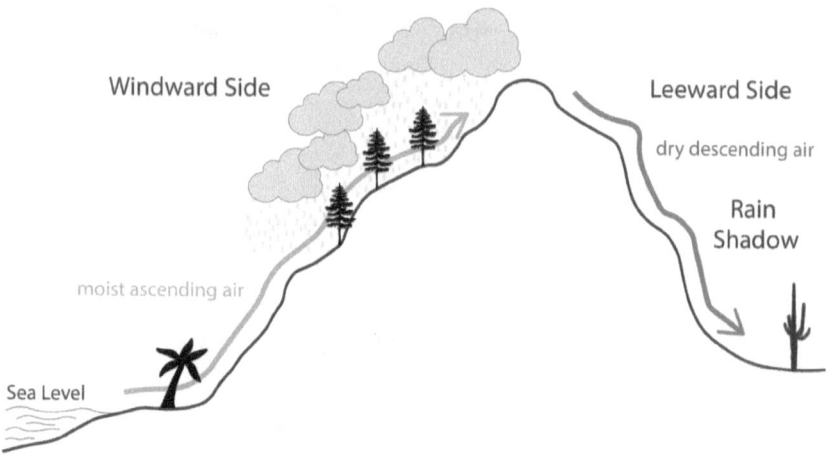

Figure 1-3: Rainshadow Desert. (Compiled by Michaela Buenemann, Department of Geography and Environmental Studies, New Mexico State University.)

In the American Southwest there are two main mechanisms that produce desert conditions. On a global level, atmospheric circulation carries warm, wet air upward from the equator toward the Tropic of Cancer (and, south, the Tropic of Capricorn). This air, having reached an altitude of about 6.2–9.3 miles (10–15 km) and now drained of its moisture and cold, descends along a line more or less defined by 30° N. This circulatory pattern is called a Hadley Cell (Fig. 1-2). As the air mass reaches the ground, now drastically desiccated, it brings high pressure to bear. Under these conditions precipitation is rare and the sky clear, thus exposing the ground to the unblocked radiation of the sun. The result is a desert. The Colorado, Mojave, Sonoran, and Chihuahuan Deserts are all wholly or partially the consequence of Hadley Cell circulation.[5]

The other driver of desert conditions in the Southwest is rain shadows (Fig. 1-3). When prevailing winds strike a high mountain range, like the Sierra Nevada in California, they are driven up along the slope. As they rise they cool; as they cool they are less able to hold moisture, and so they dump it in the form of rain or snow. The heavy snowpacks typical of the western slopes of the Sierra Nevada before the advent of climate change were precisely the result of the collision between wet westerlies coming off the Pacific and the extreme, sharp relief of the mountains. As the air masses breach the ridge of the mountains and descend the other side, they warm; largely devoid of moisture, their relative humidity drops as they approach the landscape on the east, in the case of the Sierra, and create desert conditions. The Great Basin Desert of (mostly) Nevada and the parts of the Mojave shouldered up against the eastern foot of the mountain chains east of the Sierra proper are rain-shadow deserts. Death Valley is an extreme and excellent example. Badwater Basin is 282 feet (86 m) below sea level at its lowest point; a mere 11 miles (17.7 km) away stands Telescope Peak, the highest point of the Panamint Range: 11,049 feet (3,368 m). The relief between the two is 11,331 feet (3,454 m); they are separated by only about 15 miles (24 km) by foot.[6] Death Valley gets about 2 inches (50 mm) of rain per year and continues to hold the world record for highest accurately recorded temperature of 134° F (57° C), despite some controversy.

Such are the geophysical definitions and characteristics of the southwestern deserts whose literature is the subject of this book. But any entrée into the southwestern desert world would be woefully incomplete without consideration of the interaction of human beings with the desert world; it is that interaction that has of course produced the literature of the desert. And those interactions have been strongly conditioned by a congeries of tropes about deserts carried into the deserts by settler colonists from Spain (via Mexico) and the Cis-Mississippi East of the United States, both ultimately dependent on European and biblical ideas about deserts.

DESERT TROPES IN THE EURO-AMERICAN IMAGINARY

Euro-American notions about deserts owe more to the Bible than to any other source. Biblical accounts of the nature of Middle Eastern deserts embrace virtually all the presuppositions about desert environments that Euro-American colonists carried, along with their cultural baggage about landholding, ownership, and private property, as they slogged west beyond the Mississippi River or north from Mexico. The tropes and stereotypes they brought tended to be widely applied to the western deserts without a great deal of discrimination among the desert environments they encountered, in contrast to the views about the land held by the Indigenous peoples, who had lived on, with, and off desert homelands for longer or shorter periods.

"Strange, wonderful, and scary"—such are the adjectives with which Diana K. Davis adorns the title of her chapter on biblical, Greek and Roman, and mediaeval European ideas about deserts.[7] The basic attitudes toward desert space articulated in the Bible—especially the Hebrew Testament—consist in a pair of diametrically opposed conceptualizations about the character of the desert. On the one hand, the desert is a space where people go to meet God. While captive in Egypt, Moses fled into the desert in the land of Midian to escape the Pharaoh's wrath; there on Mount Horeb he finds a burning bush out of which God speaks to him, appoints him as leader of his people, and promises to guide the Israelites out of Egypt into the Promised Land. For forty years they wander in the desert; God provides manna as food and grants Moses the power to draw water from rocks. It is also in the Sinai Desert, on the mountain of the same name, that he colloquies with God and negotiates out the Ten Commandments (and a bevy of other rules and regulations) during a forty-day sojourn on the mountain top.[8] The prophet Elijah, chastened by the Israelites, fled into the desert of Judah; there an angel provided him food and God appeared to him as a gentle whisper as he stood on a mountain. Hosea has God remind the Israelites that "I cared for you in the desert, in the land of burning heat." This positive attitude toward the desert thanks to the closeness to God the Israelites enjoyed during their long desert exile was reinforced by the prophets when they compared their own contemporary corrupt society with that of the Exodus.[9] This desert trope emerges most distinctly in chapter 8, as I explore the desert as the locus for visitations by Space Brothers and Sisters; Dana Howard's encounters with Diane from Venus, discussed there, bespeak this role of deserts as holy ground especially neatly, in her experiences along the eastern slopes of the San Jacinto Mountains, looking across the wide Mojave Desert.

The desert also, though, acts as a locus of punishment and cleansing, where sins can be expiated and unfaithful Israelites returned to godliness. Hosea makes this explicit in a speech he puts into God's mouth:

I will make her [i.e., the untrue mother, who stands for Israel] like a desert, turn her into a parched land, and slay her with thirst. . . . I am going to tempt her, I will lead her back into the desert and speak tenderly to her. There I will give her back her vineyards.

Uwe Lindemann reads Hosea's model of the desert for Israel as a four-part journey: the sojourn in the desert out of Egypt, during which the Israelites are close to God; the settlement in Canaan, when they fall into false worship of Baal; a second expulsion into the desert, which serves as punishment and cleansing that results in a return to the right relationship with God; and the blossoming of the desert into settled agricultural land (he sees this as a return to cultivated land, but that is not quite what Hosea says) with permanent return to God's good graces. In laying out the terms of his covenant with the Israelites, God threatens to render "[t]he whole land . . . a burning waste of salt and sulfur—nothing planted, nothing sprouted, no vegetation growing on it" if they dare contravene the agreement—to render it, simply put, a desert.[10]

Linked to this trope in the Hebrew Testament is that of making the desert bloom. In Hosea God remarks that finding Israel—which the prophet is condemning for its unfaithfulness—was like finding grapes in the desert.[11] This idea finds its most explicit expression in Isaiah:

The desert and the parched land will be glad.
The scorched land will rejoice and blossom . . .
Water will gush forth in the wilderness
and streams in the desert.
The burning sand will become a pool,
the thirsty ground bubbling springs.
In the haunts where jackals once lay,
grass and reeds and papyrus will grow.[12]

The desert can also serve as a refuge. In Revelation, the woman who gives birth to the man who will rule the nations is persecuted by Satan and flees on wings of an eagle "into the desert (*eremos*), where she has there a place (*topos*) made ready by God" and is fed and protected.[13] Chapters 4 and 5 are especially concerned with this trope, particularly in the way that a blossoming, tamed desert, converted to agriculture, is gendered female in the American imaginary. Running parallel with this gendering, a complex phenomenon that plays out differently in different times, cultures, and places, is a desert eroticism: perhaps surprisingly, an ability of the landscape to charge erotic desires and behaviors, in apparent contradiction with the desert's "masculine" harshness and silence—although of course masculinities have their own erotics. These matters come in for consideration in chapters 4 and 5.

But the desert is also the realm of demons and devils, a blasted landscape God has abandoned. Jesus undergoes a series of tests in the Palestinian desert, a space where Satan has free rein to try his resistance to temptation. In Egypt the earliest Christian ascetics retreated to the deserts in imitation of Jesus to encounter demons and hone their souls; the earliest and best known, Antony, sparked legions of followers. These contradictory ideas about deserts inflected European experiences of the southwestern desert world; to give a single example, the forty-niners who struggled across the Great Basin Desert, the Mojave Desert, and the Colorado Desert in search of gold in California expressed in their memoirs the horrors of the blasted desert.[14] This trope persists in American writing about the desert. In Bret Easton Ellis's *Imperial Bedrooms*, a quasi-sequel to his first novel, *Less Than Zero*, the narrator Clay "rents" a girl and a boy and takes them to a ranch house in the movie colony of Palm Springs. There he brutally rapes, beats, and humiliates them. These acts play out in the desert context:

> At night the moon would hang over the silver-rimmed desert and the streets were empty and the girl and boy would get stoned by the fire pit and sometimes dogs could be heard barking over the wind thrashing the palm trees as I pounded into the girl and the house was infested with crickets and the boy's mouth was warm but I didn't really feel anything until I hit him, always panting, my eyes gazing at the steam rising from the pool at dawn.

The house sits near the base of the San Jacinto Mountains; the girl, by the end of this horrendous weekend, admits, looking up toward the hills, that they were "the crossing place. . . . This," she adds by way of explanation, "is where the devil lives."[15]

Complementing these conceptualizations about desert space is a set of tropes about what deserts are like. These tropes include *aridity, heat, emptiness/tracklessness, danger*, and *violence*. Aridity is of course the fundamental fact about deserts as climatological phenomena: the very definition of a desert is a region where precipitation is thin and evapotranspiration high. There are several formulae geographers and climatologists use to delineate the line between a true desert and a semi-arid region, but in general precipitation under ten inches (254 mm) per year serves as a handy rule of thumb.[16]

However, while aridity serves as a fine yardstick for identifying a desert landform, as such it is not what directly determines how we interact with the desert. For us, the question is the *availability* of water.[17] In the Sonoran Desert—before the hydroengineering of the twentieth century—several permanent streams meandered through the desert: the Salt and Gila Rivers, rising in mountains in northeastern Arizona and west-central New Mexico; the Bill Williams River; and the Colorado River, flowing down from the Rocky Mountains in Colorado. Water was always sufficient—sometimes over-sufficient—for people living on or traveling along these streams. Oases pocked the Mojave Desert, like Palm Springs, and the Mojave River, although intermittent, provided water for part of the year. The real issues for people were knowing where to find water, when it would be available, how much would be present, and how to carry enough between one source and the next. When in the great Mohave Historical Epic the gambling boy Nyītše-vilye-vave-kwilyêhe returns home through the desert, he stops at a place called Aqwaq-haθêve: "There was water there and he thought: 'I will drink. It may be the only water. I will be thirsty if I do not find any.'" The next day he comes to a place where he knew there would be water and drank.[18]

With enough water, heat is survivable—up to a point, in any case. Determined to follow the Camino del Diablo in the Sonoran Desert from Ajo to Yuma, Arizona, which runs for

130 miles (209 km) just north of the Mexico-US border, in August, John Annerino estimated he'd need one gallon of water for each 8- to 10-mile stretch. He and his two companions each consumed three to five gallons (11.4–19 liters) of water between water holes. They walked at 3 miles/hr (4.8 km/hr), a brutal pace in August Sonoran heat, which reached a maximum temperature of 108° F (42° C). Both Annerino's companions collapsed of dehydration at different points on the trek. At the end of the route, where it descends from the Tinajas Altas mountains—whose name means "high waterholes," because pools up by the ridgeline almost always hold water—into Yuma comes a 40-mile (64 km) waterless stretch. Despite packing six gallons each (22.7 l), which weighed 50 pounds (22.7 kg), they drained their containers 10 miles short of the end; only because they hiked at night could they complete the trek.[19]

While Annerino's trek ended happily, if only by the skin of the waterskin, other journeys along the Camino del Diablo did not. Grossly underprepared and misled by their coyotes, who abandoned them, twenty-six migrants crossing from Mexico to Arizona in May 2001 succumbed to heatstroke and, except for a few, died miserable deaths in the desert heat, which reached 110° F (43.3° C) at its highest. It is lack of water combined with heat that makes deserts dangerous.[20]

Aside from aridity and heat, deserts are also regarded as lonely. So the 1950s UFO contactee Orfeo Angelucci speaks of "[t]he lonesomeness of the eternal desert," which encompasses both the sense of isolation and of the desert's unchangeableness.[21] Much earlier, the pioneering Christian ascetic Saint Antony sought out ever deeper and more remote locales in the Egyptian desert to avail himself of its empty loneliness. This loneliness, the isolation from normal human society, forms a fundamental component of the ascetic life—of which a crucial self-deprivation is the avoidance of women.

Luis Alberto Urrea's *The Devil's Highway* deploys a number of these tropes to express the hostility and alienness of the desert to the migrants whose dreadful fate he tracks. Tracklessness and emptiness afflict them once they are lost: "Names are forgotten. Locations are nebulous, at best, since none of them, not even the Coyotes, even knew where they were. Nameless mountains loomed over them, nameless stars burned overhead, nameless demons gibbered from the nameless canyons."[22] I return to the matter of namelessness and names in chapter 7.

THE AESTHETIC TURN

The tropes about desert danger and desert ugliness were predominant in the American imaginary about the western deserts throughout the nineteenth century. They represent brilliantly the principle, just stated, that we bring to deserts our own presuppositions, seeing them as conditioned even before we arrive by the tropes that we carry, whether we know it or not. The converse occurrence, of course, happens when those tropes are overthrown and our presuppositions about the desert world take on a completely new coloring. This, it is often claimed, is exactly what happened to Americans' understanding of their desert country—or at least, some elite Americans—when the former Rutgers University art historian John C. Van Dyke published *The Desert* in 1901.

In 1897, having sired a child on the wife of a colleague, Van Dyke resigned his post at Rutgers University and his club memberships and fled to his brother Theodore Strong Van

Dyke's ranch near Daggett, California. His many boasts of his desert exploits in *The Desert* and subsequent writing were virtually all fraudulent; his experience of the desert landscape was acquired mostly by gazing out the window of a railroad club car, and his tales of fighting off rattlesnakes and wandering through the desert on a horse (he does not say whether it had a name: see chapter 7) were gleaned from stories regaled by his brother's ranch hands. Nor was his re-envisioning of the desert world as beautiful, colorful, and desirable new. He was an acolyte of the Art for Art's Sake movement, whose precepts framed his response to the desert. The emphasis of the Art for Art's Sake movement lay on beauty and aesthetics; indeed, it was sometimes referred to as Aestheticism or the Aesthetic Movement. Central to Van Dyke's recasting of the desert Southwest was precisely the insistence on the desert's beauty.[23]

Van Dyke's ideas about the desert were widely influential. His book sold very well and was positively reviewed.[24] Moreover, his appreciation for a natural world (apparently) untrammeled and unmodified by man fit nicely into the conservationist and preservationist movements that were gaining adherents and power in late nineteenth and early twentieth century America.[25] Of the desert, Van Dyke insisted:

> We have often heard of "Sunny Italy" or the "clear light" of Egypt, but believe me there is no sunlight there compared with that which falls upon the upper peaks of the Sierra Madre or the uninhabitable wastes of the Colorado Desert.... Once more ride over the enchanted mesas of Arizona at sunrise or at sunset, with the ragged mountains of Mexico to the south and the broken spurs of the great sierra round about you; and all the glory of the old shall be as nothing to the gold and purple and burning crimson of this new world.... The love of Nature is an acquired taste. One begins by admiring the Hudson-River landscape and ends by loving the desolation of the Sahara.[26]

Van Dyke can't quite evict "waste" from his discourse, but the thrust of the passage sets the wasteland narrative insistently aside in favor of "[t]he love of Nature" that impels the sensitive soul—particularly one well-prepared by the study of art for art's sake—to embrace the desert as a desirable and desired aesthetic space.

Although there's no question about the widespread influence of *The Desert* on American conceptualizations of the desert—at least in some circles; as we will see throughout the following chapters, older tropes, both negative and positive, persist—his contribution to a "turn" in American thinking was not original. As just noted, Van Dyke's academic work, before his unceremonious departure from Rutgers, focused particularly on the Art for Art's Sake movement that had taken hold among European artists and critics in the later nineteenth century. In 1893, years before his Mojave exile, Van Dyke had published *Art for Art's Sake: Seven University Lectures on the Technical Beauties of Painting*, which he had delivered to audiences at the Metropolitan Museum in New York City. His central aim in these lectures was to analyze changes in attitudes toward landscapes in painting and argue for a new, modern sensibility superior to romantic visions of the immediate artistic past. He explicitly evoked the desert. In romantic painting, he asserted, "the desert existed not so much for its white light, rising heat, and waving atmosphere, as for the home of the roving lion, or the treacherous highway of the winding Bedouin caravan." In complete contrast, the modern landscape painter sought "beauty in the forms and colors and lights of nature aside from man and his doings"; he aims "to portray by means of emphasized form and color this essence of nature." This approach, however, is far from mere representationalism: to capture the viewer, the artist must transfuse through "poetic fire" the "facts of nature," which are "newly wrought in the crucible of the painter's mind."

> Thus in a landscape the relief of an object by its light and its shade may not be sufficient in itself to render the picture attractive and pleasing, although it may be absolutely true to nature and realistic enough for an exclamation point. A stretch of desert in the sunlight, with never a tree nor mound nor building to cast a shadow, may be nature itself; but if we should look upon either the original, or its counterfeit presentment on canvas, we should be dazzled, and perhaps annoyed, by its garishness, its bewildering light, its monotony. The eye could find no relief in such a scene, and necessarily it would not be attractive.[27]

The development of this new artistic vision, which Van Dyke seized on and expounded, can be traced back to French artists and writers who started visiting the northern Sahara Desert in the 1840s and 1850s, not long after the French had captured Algiers and began the 70-year process of bringing the western and central Sahara under their imperial aegis. I will examine one of these painters and writers, Eugène Fromentin, in chapter 3. Another was André Gide,[28] who in 1900 was extolling the color play in a desert much harsher than the American Mojave that inspired Van Dyke. In a travel journal in which he preserved his impressions of a trip from Biskra to Touggourt in Tunisia in 1900 and published in 1906, he writes:

> And now the dawn: from the night's still-cold azure to the red rim of the sands occurs a prismatic analysis of daylight, more delicately and more subtly nuanced, but also more precisely detailed, than that of a perfect rainbow; and on the awestruck earth, a resurrection of colors. All with a total absence of art, with a beauty purely and solely natural.[29]

Gide's observation of the play of light is at least as precise and admiring as Van Dyke's, and he has also, strikingly, given the prize to the beauty of desert light over the most spectacular natural exhibition of color in middle climes, the rainbow, product of that atmospheric superabundance of water whose absence serves as an unmistakable marker of the desert world. Van Dyke, in his turn, reaches likewise for the rainbow, not as a shadow or simulacrum of desert color, but as the epitome of prismatic vision accorded us only occasionally in the humid East but always there in the desert: "Rainbows by day and rainbows by night!"[30]

In his reflections on desert light, Gide turns almost immediately to the implications for art of the special ways it works in a desert atmosphere:

> There was a time when I dared not to admit to myself how little refuge and sustenance art finds on this land. I needed to claim it was lovely in order to admire it so passionately.

That was when I was still quite ready to confuse art and nature. Now, what I love in this country is—I can tell—its actual hideousness, its inclemency: what constrains any art *not* to exist . . . or to take refuge elsewhere. . . . In the desert, you must learn to be content with the education—I mean the exaltation—it proposes, then discover how to counterpoise it. This is precisely what a Monet would have acquired here, I imagine: the analysis of his craft, of his eye; the simplest knowledge of each tone in itself, of its relationships and its possible importance; the disappearance of all planes, the vanishing of reflections, the lack of variegation, the nakedness of the milieu. And, returning home, he would have acquired—from the interactions of the tones themselves, from the resources of each, from the readiness of surfaces to reflect, from the ambience itself—a comprehension both more knowing and more spontaneous, a kind of revelation.[31]

What Gide is arguing here is not a return to the conceit of desert ugliness (despite its "hideousness") but rather a much stronger and more radical claim for desert beauty and desert necessity: that the desert so decomposes and recomposes light in its purest form, without planes or reflections, in a pure nakedness, that it provides the only stage on which an artist can actually learn what light and color mean. The desert's hideousness for Gide is situated precisely in the impossibility, he suggests, of there being "art" here; nature cannot be reconfigured or improved upon by the artist. In other words, we cannot use art in the desert to mediate our relationship with the landscape, for art cannot teach us anything about seeing the desert, in the way that Monet's *Water Lilies* helps us see a pond in a Parisian park in a new and striking way. Rather, Gide's Monet must go home to apply the lessons of exaltation the desert would have taught him, back to a world where the best nature can do is the rainbow. In this regard it seems to me that Gide's embrace of desert light and color is far more radical than Van Dyke's. Gide accepts the desert as an absolute arbiter, whereas Van Dyke looks to redeem the desert as a better place to see than "sunny Italy." Van Dyke, too, stressed "the beauty of the ugly." Neither Van Dyke's nor far more (I would suggest) Gide's evocation of hideousness is an aesthetic of decadence, claiming to find "beauty" in the face of Medusa, but rather a recognition that desert immensity and simplicity cannot meet human-scaled standards of beauty; they evoke a different reaction, a beauty in "ugliness," that must be learned. Van Dyke insists, "The weird solitude, the great silence, the grim desolation, are the very things with which every desert wanderer eventually falls in love."[32]

The addition of a conceptualization of deserts derived from Van Dyke's funneling of the Art for Art's Sake movement from its French sources and an American modernist movement into an American intellectual imaginary did not replace the old, dichotomous biblical ideas about deserts, nor the tropes of emptiness and danger (Van Dyke's lions), but rather added another mode through which to see our southwestern desert landscapes. Different writers might come to these landscapes imbued with one or more of these modes and might switch the mode through which they perceived the desert even while gazing on it, or later. The result is a complex, never fully coherent, deeply human set of impressions, claims, arguments about the desert landscapes—and we will find all these tropes, from the oldest biblical to the newest preservationist, playing out in the literature explored throughout this book.

There are two more, related, attitudes toward the deserts of the Southwest that I explore in this project. One that was held about the whole West—we will see it especially in chapter 9—is that exposure to their harsh, demanding environment could work a transformation on men weakened by contamination by the non-white, urban, immigrant, and female predominance in the decadent cities of the East Coast. Theodore Roosevelt's call for western experience to toughen and reinvigorate American manliness was nothing new; as Richard Slotkin has shown, the anxiety about decadence and the wilderness cure was already thrumming in books like *The Last of the Mohicans.* Jane Tompkins has observed that this practice of manliness echoes the asceticism of early Christians who retreated to the desert:

> The hero almost never has sex, and when he does it's only implied, not shown, the denial of sex being central to the kind of deprivation the Western finds essential for the exemplary life. Like the absence of greenery, it is a turning away from fertility, fluidity, propagation, and an affirmation of what is hard and dry and takes a long time to come to fruition. For the desert itself is the great exemplar of ascesis. The hero imitates the desert's fierceness in his hard struggle to survive, its loneliness in his solitary existence, and its silence in his frugal way with language. Gnomic, carved out of life experience, compressed and delivered under pressure, the sayings of cowboy heroes, by their brevity, acknowledge, as do the saying [*sic*] of the desert fathers, the importance of things that cannot be said.[33]

Precisely these elements of the desert Tompkins has elucidated here come out in the treatment of *The Winning of Barbara Worth* by Harold Bell Wright in chapter 4 and Frances Gillmor's *Fruit Out of Rock* in chapter 5.

But what did the reinvigorated manly man do, once in the West? He brought "civilization," which, of course, trailed behind itself the very contamination he was seeking to escape. But if he was lucky, or persistent, or rich, or endowed with good contacts, he had another option: the capitalist development of the western landscape. Mining and ranching, as we will see in chapter 5, supported by eastern and British capital, combined the best of both worlds: you could remain a manly man, riding the range or extracting gold, and become rich (or richer, as the case may be). These two linked ways of seeing the desert shared an instrumentalist attitude: the desert was there *for* men to *use*, whether for self-redemption or self-enrichment.[34]

This aesthetic of the desert, such as it is, has, however, more complicated inflections than those just canvassed. As Aidan Tynan argues in his excellent, dense recent book, *The Desert in Modern Literature and Philosophy: Wasteland Aesthetics*, the collision of desert tropes with Modernism has confected a "desert [that] often functions . . . to suggest how modern society devastates life and meaning through a homogenising disenchantment of space, but also how these devastated spaces, in their very strangeness and solitude, may offer a re-enchantment and revivification." This conceptualization of desert space echoes through not just literature directly concerned with deserts, but rather how deserts' "affects of wonder and joy or disgust and terror . . . constitute a crucial but largely ignored component of our global imaginary." Deserts emerge, Tynan shows, in a wide range of literature that may seem at first to have nothing at all to do with deserts.[35] My aim here is to expand on our sense of the "desert imaginary" which, following Tynan, sits at the center of our understanding of the world we inhabit, whether we are conscious of it or not.

Finally, though, we need to consider yet another congeries of ideas about the desert—ideas much older than art for art's sake, indeed as old as, perhaps, the biblical notions that we know about thanks to their having been written down. These are the concepts that the Indigenous inhabitants of the southwestern deserts had about their homelands. Fundamental to these ideas, as we will see in chapter 2, is *sacredness*: the conviction that the landscape is saturated with the sacred, and human interactions with it must be governed by a recognition of this sacredness and knowledge about the proper ways to approach and revere it. In turn the landscape *gives back*: it provides sustenance, water, housing, and, perhaps most important, *power*. The gift of power comes through dreams, which are sometimes regarded as having come from the landscape itself or a feature in it. This desert is an agential desert, a view sometimes shared by Anglos, as we will see in chapter 10. There are both intersections and contradictions between the notions Euro-Americans brought to, or developed about, the southwestern deserts with those of the people they found there. The unraveling of some of these is a basic task in the chapters that follow.

PART 1

THE DESERT
SACRED

CHAPTER 2

SACRED DESERT, PROFANE DESERT, GENDERED DESERT IN THE AMERICAN IMAGINARY*

NOTHING IS SACRED, UNLESS WE AGREE: NOT LIFE, NOT EVEN THE LAND.[1]

[M]OUNTAINS WILL GENERALLY BE CELEBRATED AS PLACES, NOT OF BELONGING, BUT OF ENCOUNTER WITH THE OTHER.[2]

There has always been a tension in the western Euro-American imaginary between the desert as a sacred space and the desert as a "profane" one. Moses met God face-to-rear end in the Sinai desert; in the Egyptian desert, Saint Antony faced down Satan in the guise of a lascivious woman. Edward Abbey vacillated between celebrating a spiritual desert (an "ecomystical" locus, in a recent analysis) and a dump for discarded beer cans. Hari Kunzru set his contactee cult in the Mojave Desert (like George Adamski's "Nordic" aliens); the desert brought redemption for a "fallen woman" in Zane Grey's *Shower of Gold*, while heartless capitalists scooped up the ranches of indigent (and Indigenous) owners to build a desert town of the future. (In Zane Grey's *The Light of Western Stars* it's a golf course that redeems a desert mesa in the New Mexican Chihuahua.) Richard Francaviglia traced out a spiritual geography in the Great Basin Desert of Nevada, in the territory that nineteenth-century railroad travel guides presented as forlorn and ghost-ridden and that was enlisted in the 1950s as a national sacrifice zone for nuclear tests.[3] In a book on sacred mountains, Edwin Bernbaum offers a romantic, sublime account of the nature of the sacred:

The sacred is profoundly mysterious, not just as the wholly other, but as an embodiment of the unknown itself. It is the aura of mystery, of something beyond our ken, that attracts us. We are drawn to the sacred precisely because it is unknowable—something that remains mysterious even when we are in its presence. . . . The unknown also possesses a darker, more

---

* A very different and much shorter version with a somewhat different title was presented at the annual meeting of the Western Literature Association on September 23, 2016.

dangerous side: instead of our salvation, it may hold our damnation.... As an expression of ultimate power and reality, what we regard as sacred possesses ultimate value and meaning. It embodies whatever we cherish above everything else, whatever stirs our deepest feelings and awakens our highest aspirations.[4]

In this chapter I'd like to trace the ways that these opposing but intertwined themes of desert sacrality and desert "profanity"—which, as we will see, is more complicated than this word captures—play out in some literature, both fictional and not, across time and space. My guiding question focuses on what sacredness and profanity mean projected onto a landscape which, in fact, has no "meaning"—it is simply itself. Why then, do we feel such power in desert landscapes?

WHAT IS SACRED? WHAT IS NOT?

Notions of desert sacredness entered the Euro-American imaginary through biblical tropes that go all the way back to Genesis and Exodus, where desert space offers encounters with God and the purgation of sin accumulated in a land of exile through trial and suffering. Some early Christians took up this trope eagerly, following the model of Saint Antony in his retreat to the desert, the better to fight his demons. For the first Euro-Americans to penetrate the desert Southwest, it was the trope of deserts as blasted, abandoned space, dangerous and hostile, that dominated most reaction. For some, there was a feeling that travel through the desert-imposed hardships cleansed and prepared a traveler to be accepted into the Promised Land of California, and so in a sense there was a sacrality to the landscape, though of a brutal and unforgiving character. These matters are explored in more detail in chapters 1, 3, and 5. At the same time, as the southwestern deserts came to be settled by Euro-American colonists who were eager to exploit the riches buried there—whether crops induced to sprout by irrigation or minerals to be mined—a capitalist attitude toward the landscape, shorn of any numinousness, took hold. The land became, for many, secular or neutral. But as exploitation dominated attitudes toward the land, there emerged a reaction. Preservationism and environmentalism argued that the land should be protected, left in a "pristine" state—a view that tended to erase the former and current presence of Native Americans on the land and their views about it. Recently Native American groups have become more insistent on their rights in the land and have found support among some Anglos; in southwestern Nevada, local communities have banded together with Fort Mojave and Chemehuevi peoples to advocate for designation of the sacred mountain Avi Kwa Ame as a national monument. The tribes had been pushing for such recognition for decades.[5] This heady mix has determined notions of sacrality and its opposites with respect to the southwestern deserts, and continues today to foster a complex, sometimes contradictory attitude toward the extensive deserts of the Southwest.

The semantic range of a word in one culture that's translated as "sacred" may often have a very different range of meaning from the English word. For example, the Māori of New Zealand draw distinctions between everyday sites and *waahi tapu* sites. *Tapu* is generally rendered as "sacred," so "sacred site." But the range of meaning for the Māori is much broader than the English word; it "transcends mere sacredness." And the various subdivisions of the

Māori regard different places as having different values of *tapu*.[6] Jane Hubert has extracted a general definition, however, of the features of a sacred site:

> The concept of sacred implies restrictions and prohibitions on human behaviour—if something is sacred then certain rules must be observed in relation to it, and this generally means that something that is said to be sacred, whether it be an object or site (or person), must be placed apart from everyday things or places, so that its special significance can be recognized, and rules regarding it obeyed.[7]

This definition sits at a very high level of abstraction; an example or two may help render it more concrete. Burial sites often are seen as sacred sites. A website devoted to sites in the Mojave Desert lists rules to obey while visiting pioneer cemeteries: do not walk on graves; do not remove anything left at or on the graves; do not enter at night; do not conduct seances, use Ouija boards, or do paranormal investigations without permission of the cemetery officials; do not photograph or film "irreverent scenes." These rules are contextualized as needed to show respect, but they clearly flow from the sense that the sites are sacred, hedged around therefore with regulations that reflect that sacrality.[8]

Hubert further notes that:

> In the context of sacred sites and sacred places the prohibitions on behaviour that exist define the relationship between god or gods and the people. Gods can protect and assist, but they can also punish and destroy, and therefore there is always some degree of danger involved in offending a deity, who must be placated and assuaged.[9]

Among the Paviotso, a Paiute group living in Western Nevada and far Eastern California when the Spanish arrived, a certain cave was regarded as a very powerful and sacred place; people retreated there to seek power to become healers. Strict rules oversaw the acts a petitioner had to undertake: s/he had to sleep inside, during which dreams would come to her/him of animals and people doctoring; later a crack in the rock opened up (analogous to Moses's experience in Exodus), out of which emerged a man who gave the petitioner explicit instructions to reify her/his healing power. But one Paviotso, called Happy Dave, although eager to acquire power, could not bring himself to enter the cave. After an unpleasant night outside, an owl came to him and "told him that he had not done the right thing and was wasting his time. He told Happy Dave that he should go home." The owl then enjoined Dave to bathe in the river and apply white paint to his horse "[to prevent the sickness that would result from his improper conduct in relation with supernatural spirits]."[10]

But the sense of sacrality of a place, particularly of the desert, can be at once vaguer and broader. In *Topophilia*, Yi-Fu Tuan extolls the desert he first experienced in Death Valley as a Chinese graduate student in 1952. After a night sleeping out:

> the sun had risen high enough to throw its rays on the range of mountains across the valley and presented me with a scene, totally alien to my experience up to that time, of such

unearthly beauty that I felt transported to a supernal realm. . . . The desert, including the barren parts and (I would even say) especially those, appeals to me. I see in it a purity, time-lessness, a generosity of mind and spirit.[11]

Tuan also stresses the appeal of the desert as a locale for ascetic practice, which can be read as a process that lends sacrality to the site where it is undertaken.[12] Similarly, assessing Americans' response to wilderness, John Brinckerhoff Jackson insists that "the wilderness experience is not mystical, for the relationship revealed is not with the divine but with unspoiled nature; but its effect is to subdue the omnipresent clamor of the ego and to reveal to us that we, along with all living things, are inseparable parts of the cosmic order."[13]

It's something of a cliché to note that the land was and is sacred to Native Americans. "[M]any native peoples' religions," write David Carmichael, Jane Hubert, and Brian Reeves,

are cosmotheistic; they believe that all natural parts of the world have a humanlike force. In such a belief system, plants, animals, rocks, etc. are conscious and willful; they must be treated with proper respect. The source areas for plants, animals, and earth materials may be considered powerful or sacred, as they are by the Mescalero Apache.[14]

Knowing what is "sacred" and what it means to say something is "sacred" are, however, com-plex problems. There have been several efforts to define the sacred from a Native American viewpoint. R. S. McPherson summarized the sense of the Diné (Navajo) about the Four Corners region:

The earth is not just a series of dramatically poised topographic features that incite the wonder of man or beckon for exploitation, but rather a living, breathing entity in an ani-mate universe. The land with its water, plants, and animals is a spiritual creation put into motion by the gods in their wisdom. These elements are here to help, teach, and protect through an integrated system of beliefs that spell out man's relationship to man, nature, and the supernatural.[15]

This notion of the sacrality of the land corresponds, more or less, with the stereotypical view that Indigenous peoples saw the land as sacred, but it is also more than just that, for it also expresses a relationship between the land and its inhabitants: sacrality is not just a *state* or *condition*, but an active interaction between the land and the people who occupy it. The National Council of American Indians defined sacred sites as "places that are sacred to practitioners of Native Tradition religions and [such] sacred places include land (surface and subsurface), water and air; burial grounds, massacre sites and battlefields; and spiritual commemoration, ceremonial, gathering, and worship areas." Another definition, enshrined in a 1996 presidential Executive Order (no. 13007), identifies as sacred "any specific, discrete, narrowly delineated location on Federal land that is identified by an Indian tribe, or Indian individual [meeting certain requirements], as sacred by virtue of its established religious significance to, or ceremonial use by, an Indian religion." It's apparent there's a degree of circularity to these definitions. Moreover, they embrace a static view of sacrality: they do not allow for changes over time in the idea of the sacred, whether a given site is regarded as sacred, or whether the nature and/or degree of its sacrality may change over time. Who attests to a site's sacrality also matters; the Executive Order permits only testimony from an "Indian individual determined [by whom?] to be an appropriately authoritative representative of an Indian religion."[16] Ethnographers whose accounts I explore below relied on informants who were willing to talk to an Anglo—so sometimes these may not have been the best informed, and may have had their own reasons for providing an inquisitive white man with an account of a sacred site.

Deward E. Walker Jr., who had studied Indigenous religions for more than three decades, offers a broader and more flexible account of the sacred in Native American religions. He came to the view that Native Americans have "[a] special sense of the sacred that is centered in natural time and natural geography." While accepting Émile Durkheim's abstract definition in which the sacred are "things set apart and forbidden," Walker regards Indigenous sacrality as "more founded on the idea that it [the sacred] is an embedded attribute of all phenomena." It is, he argues, "'access points' or 'portals' to the sacred" that dot the landscape, sites which "are often impossible to know before the dreams or visions reveal them." His account also allows for change over time, as in the Southwest, where the "introduction of corn, beans, and squash had profound [religious] consequences."[17] We will see that Walker captures important aspects of the sacred in the imaginary of at least some Indigenous peoples.

Moreover, the multiplicity of Indigenous groups that lived in the desert Southwest before and after the intrusion of Europeans—especially after the Spanish *entrada*, intent as they were on eradicating "demonic" Indigenous beliefs and imposing Catholic Christianity—held a wide variety of religious beliefs.[18] One example of the assumption of a uniform system made by some academics is the view that all, or almost all, rock art in the Southwest represents the trance visions of shamans. This view has come in for serious criticism, to which I turn briefly at the end of the chapter. But if we are to honor and understand the sacrality of an Indigenous landscape, we must be sensitive to variability over time and space. And we must admit from the very start that, absent emic informants for the deep past, our efforts are often at best no more than reasonable hypotheses, back-projections from the present or very recent past, or even sheer speculation.[19]

Across the globe and below the equator, analogous problems crop up in Australia. Efforts there to define the sacred in the complex context of Indigenous land claims, ritual secrecy, intergroup conflict, mining demands, and development efforts have been explored in some detail by Ken Gelder and Jane M. Jacobs in their excellent book *Uncanny Australia*. Starting from the classic study *The Elementary Forms of Religious Life* by Émile Durkheim, originally published in 1912 and relying heavily on anthropological reports about Australian Indigenous religious practices, they distill a broad, largely functionalist, definition, in the Australian context, of the sacred: "Something is sacred because its significance exceeds what it is. . . . Uluru is an example . . . it is much more than just a 'rock' or a 'monolith.'" At the same time, however, a sacred site bears an uncanniness in that it embodies a contradiction:

[A] site which is claimed as being both significant and sacred is always an exclusive thing: only certain people know about it, sometimes its precise location is known only by a select few, and usually the specifics of its content are guarded. But in modern Australia a secret sacred site is never entirely exclusive or intangible. For the special status that secrecy confers upon a place to be understood—for it to confer the significance it is intended to—there needs to be at least some level of disclosure and spread of information. In some cases, in fact, large numbers of people need to know that this is a secret place meant only for a few, in order to protect that place from inappropriate uses and visitations.[20]

Similar issues bedevil the sacred sites of American Indigenous people, who must, like their Australian brethren, reveal details about them in order to argue for their protection. And assertions of sacred rights can become grounds of dispute, as in the Bears Ears National Monument, where government officials under the Trump administration downplayed or dismissed Indigenous claims. Gelder and Jacobs detail the same sorts of conflicts in several case studies of Indigenous claims to sacred sites in Australia. Indeed, in a further swirl of complexity, even a museum housing sacred objects—often stolen from their rightful owners—may become a sacred site, as Indigenous keepers agree to let the museum house them, as happened with the South Australia Museum.[21] The sacred is, then, not simply turned on or off, like a light; it can be a far more complex phenomenon, entailing the physical landscape, the traditional rights of its guardians, secrecy, processes of revelation and concealment, and change over time.

On the other side of the dichotomy, "profane" is typically defined simply as the opposite of sacred. Indeed, in some analyses the two are seen as an indispensable pair, a view that can be traced back to Durkheim's definition in his 1912 *The Elementary Forms of Religious Life*, in which he argued that the exclusionary polarity sacred-profane was "the bipartite division of the universe, known and knowable, into two genera that include all that exists but radically exclude one another."[22] Many scholars have followed Durkheim. In his own study of the sacred, called, tellingly, *The Sacred and the Profane*, Mircea Eliade insisted on a strict dichotomy between sacred and profane space; the former was, in his view, heterogeneous and centered on a fixed point, while the profane was "homogeneous and neutral," without any "qualitative differentiation and, hence, no orientation . . . by virtue of its inherent structure."[23] Richard H. Jackson and Roger Henrie likewise expressed this connection clearly many years ago:

[Sacred s]pace is sharply discriminated from the non-sacred or profane world around it. Sacred space does not exist naturally, but is assigned sanctity as man defines, limits and characterizes it through his culture, experience and goals. "Sacred" space exists for all people, for a truly profane world would consist of completely homogenous space with no point within it having any value over another. This is not the case because all people endow some space whether it be home, birth place or fishing hole with a qualitative value. The common discrimination is between profane space and sacred space, but it is impossible for an individual to view the world as truly profane space since he discriminates in some sense between space.[24]

Jackson and Henrie's dichotomy, like Eliade's, is too strict, since people assign profane space value, often, in our capitalist society, on the basis of revenue that can be extracted; a hill laced with auriferous veins of quartz has a differentiated value as opposed to a gravelly bajada studded with saguaros. But the larger point they make, of the interdependence of sacrality and profanity, in mutual conversation, remains.

This analysis, perhaps good as far as it goes, however ignores a problem with the notion of the "profane." Like a maypole, the pole opposite the "sacred" sprouts a collection of ribbons that are all nonsacred but hardly the same. First, land that is nonsacred can be, as it were, evil, or obstreperous, or uncooperative. In Kiowa N. Scott Momaday's *House Made of Dawn*, Abel, living in Los Angeles, recalls for his girlfriend Milly his father's struggles against his farmland:

> *Daddy plowed and planted and watered the land, but in the end there was only a little yield. And it was the same year after year after year; it was always the same, and at last Daddy began to hate the land, began to think of it as some kind of enemy, his own very personal and deadly enemy. I remember he came in from the fields at evening, having been beaten by the land, and he said nothing. He . . . knew that he had tried everything and failed, and there was nothing left to do but sit there in wonder at his enemy's strength.*[25]

Abel's father's land is endowed with the kind of agency and animacy sometimes attributed to a sacred place,[26] but instead of hosting spirits or recalling a mythical past, it operates as a malevolent force, grinding down the man who's trying to wring a living out of it. The father's land is "profane" in the sense of nonsacred, but it is at the same time an active agent. That vibrant malevolent land is then one kind of "profane."[27]

Another type of nonsacred land is land simply without spirit—neutral land: for example, a vacant lot in a Phoenix suburb, perhaps once destined to contain a house but now abandoned and purposeless except, maybe, as a locus for children's games. In a larger sense such a patch of land has no meaning. But this kind of neutral nonsacred land might also have a commercial, profit-making purpose: the land a mall stands on, or a cotton field outside Yuma, Arizona, in the desert. Finally, there is land that has been desecrated or violated. Here I am thinking of land that has been taken as military reservations, bombing ranges, large-scale open pit mining operations, or any other end that deeply scars and damages the land. We need different terms to differentiate these categories of the "profane," so different as they are.

In Euro-American practice, there are procedures that can flip a site back and forth between the various poles. In Christian, Jewish, Muslim, and other religions when a new church, synagogue, mosque, or temple is built, the officiant must undertake a ceremony to consecrate it. At the other end, a sacred building that is no longer needed can be deconsecrated and then devoted to secular use; I've seen churches converted to coffee bars and dance clubs. In 2011, the Anglican cathedral in Christchurch, New Zealand, damaged by an earthquake, was deconsecrated in a ceremony in which the bishop declared: "I do remit this building, and all objects remaining in it, for any lawful and reputable use, according to the laws of this land. This building, having now been deconsecrated and secularized, I declare to be no longer subject to my canonical jurisdiction."[28]

How, then, can we sum up this rather complex nexus of "sacred" and "profane?" If a sacred space is one dedicated to the holy or spiritual, set aside and hemmed in by rules of human behavior in its presence and ritual performance, its apparent opposite, the profane, turns out to have a multiplicity of manifestations that need different language to identify. The simple opposite, it seems, is the neutral/secular—space that has no spiritual element. (For people like Native Americans, such space does not exist.) But also opposite the sacred is space that is dedicated to evil, for want of a better word, space that is malevolent; we might say such space is also sacred, but in a negative sense from a Christian point of view, such as a space devoted by a witches' coven to enacting ceremonies to conjure up the devil or the desert as a realm abandoned to demons. Then there is also space that has been violated, desecrated, subject to a sacrilegious action—that might be space that was formerly sacred but has been violently mistreated, like Yucca Mountain in Nevada, honeycombed with tunnels intended for the storage of nuclear waste, or a bombing range like the Naval Air Weapons Station China Lake. Neutral space, however, can also be so mistreated: from the viewpoint of the Department of Energy and the Pentagon, the Nevada Test Site was not "sacred," but it surely is now a violated space, contaminated with radionucleotides and littered with the fragments of bombs. The best language I can think of to capture these different conditions of non-sacrality are, then, neutral/secular, malevolent, and violated.

But when we leave aside structures like churches or the huts the Mescalero Apache construct for their Girls' Puberty Ritual (which sacralizes and then desacralizes a space),[29] it is land, its physical features, in which sacrality, neutrality/secularity, malevolence, or violation resides or does not reside. How these conditions are expressed and the emotional and intellectual ties between human beings and the land are the basic ways that we can trace and differentiate ideas of sacredness and its opposites as seen by different cultures.

EURO-AMERICANS AND THE DESERT SACRED AND PROFANE

French intellectuals—at least, some French intellectuals—love the deserts of the American Southwest. Michel Foucault famously took acid, we are told, in Death Valley; Bruce Bégout devoted a book to the *Zeropolis* he found in desert Las Vegas; Jean Baudrillard ended his trans-American pilgrimage in Los Angeles after travels through the great American deserts. Less familiar than these figures—perhaps because his books have not found their English translators, except for *Le fou d'Amérique*, published as *Obsession: An American Love Story* by Putnam in 1978—is Yves Berger, who died in 2004. In 1990, in Paris, Berger published a little book, not even 150 pages, called *La pierre et le saguaro* ("The Stone and the Saguaro"), in which he recounted his encounters with our desert Southwest, after travels in New Mexico, Arizona, and Nevada.[30] What, exactly, Berger wrote is up for discussion; are his ostensible travelogues creative nonfiction or something else, some combination of autobiography and travel literature infused with fantasized episodes or pure lies, perhaps not unlike Eve Babitz's *Slow Days, Fast Company*, whose narratives she labels with the ambiguous designation "tales" and with whom Berger shares a fascination with Los Angeles?[31]

The French literary critic Michel Gueldry cut to the heart of Berger's motifs in both his fiction and his travel writing. Berger's "experience of the landscape," Gueldry writes, "ends in a geography of the imagination [*une géographie de l'imaginaire*], penetrated by spirituality."

> In other words, if words incarnate the essence of things, the writer must become those things to guarantee himself an omniscient eternity: to get rid of characters, situations, intrigue, in consequence all the traditional elements of the novelistic form, becomes a necessity, if one wants to approach the world of elements, the only source of health. The overlapping of images of the days of travel replace novelistic developments because they lead to a shamanistic experience in which the poet becomes the world by the deployment of the verb and, simultaneously, transmits his visions through the trance of language.[32]

In essence, I think, this erasure of everything but the images of daily events transmogrified into a "shamanistic" blossoming of language captures precisely what is both irresistibly attractive to Berger in the desert and what renders it a space of the sacred for him. For it is the very *emptiness* of the desert, its *absences*, not presences, that lend it a numinosity, a glow, as it were, of the divine.

Berger's desert imaginary is replete with these tropes of absence. "From the solitude," he writes, "came to us a kind of exaltation." Thus from the absence of people (and, often enough, anything else) arises a quasi-mystical experience; note, too, that Berger has personified exaltation: it comes of its own accord to the desert traveler, who simply stands and receives, in awe. Mirage, hallucination—the visionary impulse of the desert, which makes of even "[t]he voyage of Coronado . . . that of a hallucination"—represent another kind of absence or emptiness, of reliable sensory experience of actual physical things. Being in the desert brings on a sense of being at the end of the world, a place where time and space slip into a whirl of confusion. "We advance in a confusion of things," he writes of his passage through a ghost town, for "[i]n the desert, everything ends with the desert." A day in silence teaches Berger "the superiority of the discourse of magic (or religion) to the scientific. The goddess is indeed stronger than the law, dry and dreary." (Note the unironic inversion: typical attributes of the desert—aridity and dreariness—are transferred to its "opposite," the law.) Indeed, in the end, the desert escapes all perception, all definition: "the desert, equal to itself, flat and naked in the immensity of its space lost to view."[33]

Berger draws part of his stock of imagery from American movies about the West, as he admits openly. The confession is a bit of a letdown, after his magical invocations of a sacred desert space. Still, the movies aren't real, either, and perhaps it barely matters that his perceptions are filtered through the screen. For the images in the Westerns from which Berger learned much are themselves often infused with precisely these same tropes of emptiness, silence, desolation, which the sense of desert sacredness demands.[34]

Berger is hardly alone in his vision of desert emptiness as the carrier of its sacredness. Bill Kennedy Shaw, one of the coterie of British officers in Egypt in the late 1920s and 1930s who explored the Libyan Desert and then founded the Long Range Desert Group in World War II, found the attraction in a space clean of people, and there are many dirty ones, in every sense of the word, in the Middle East: clean of flies: clean sand instead of clay or of limestone dust. Also because it was quiet, at times so silent that you found yourself listening for something to hear. And it was so beautiful too, not at midday when the hills look flat and lifeless, but in the early morning or late evening when they throw cool, dark shadows and the low sun makes you marvel at the splendid symmetry of the yellow dunes. A psychologist would say, perhaps, that to take pleasure in deserts is a form of escapism, a surrender to the same impulses which made hermits of the early Christians, a refusal to face the unpleasant realities of modern life. He may be right.[35]

Aside from the racism, throughout this language—and that of far too many writers to name—echoes the call of the austere, the clean, the stark: notions of a "sacredness" not always expressed in such blatant terms, indeed sometimes denied—the "Nordic" aliens George Adamski claimed to have met in the California desert were, like us, mortals, even if a somewhat cynical reader might rather call them "gods"; for Edward Abbey, the desert exerts "spiritual appeal. . . . There is something about the desert"[36]—but always there, standing in implicit or explicit contrast to the corruption and profanity of city life, or, perhaps, even tamed landscapes of agricultural abundance and deep human imprint.

"There is something about the desert." For Berger, for Shaw, and for many others, that "something" is, at least in part, the "emptiness" that can feel clean, pure, untainted. A desert landscape first glimpsed by a European eye—so accustomed to the managed, wet, humanized landscape of the European world—can come across as a perfectly pristine space, unchanged since the creation of the world. (Indeed, William Manly, who crossed Death Valley on his way to California in the Gold Rush, admitted that the desert was God's handiwork, although he confessed he couldn't see why God had bothered.) And that sense of unchanged, original purity lends itself easily to the idea that the desert is closer to God than a landscape transformed by human agency. This notion stems in part from many episodes in the Bible, both Hebrew and Greek, in which encounters with God come most easily in the desert: in Egypt, Moses goes out into the desert beyond the Nile with his people to worship, because there is his God, and later, it is in the Sinai desert that he has his encounter with God's backside.[37]

This sense of desert spirituality is also basic to much of the 1950s contactee literature that we will consider in chapter 8; for now, here's a single example. Orfeo Angelucci, who claimed to have met his aliens in Los Angeles and then later in the Mojave Desert near Twenty-Nine Palms, said that he was accosted in a diner there by a man who identified himself merely as Adam. Dying of cancer, Adam asserted that he had come to the desert in a kind of spiritual quest; he was soon enough taken up to Venus, where he learned many secrets of the universe from the inhabitants of Alpha Centauri sojourning there. But before his space adventure, he was imbued with a sense of the desert as a sacred place: "the entire desert valley around me," he told Angelucci in prelude to a narrative of his time on Venus, "seemed to become a place of mellow things. . . . Even the most blase [sic] and indifferent person seems to feel a soft spell of some kind here. I cannot name it. . . . You feel momentarily the very square yard of sandy ground under your feet can carry you away to the stars." Later he avers, "The ground seemed to have become conscious, pulsating in its harmonic communion with every part of Creation unto infinity." It's in this reverie that a UFO comes to sweep Adam up into space.[38]

This is the desert sketched by David Jasper in his book *The Sacred Desert: Religion, Literature, Art, and Culture*, and which recurs again and again in all kinds of contexts.[39] Here's an example, from a rather cynical and sometimes snide look at desert sacredness. In a memoir recounting an exploration of "the New Age in the American Desert," as the subtitle puts it, Melanie McGrath meets early on a juice-bar attendant, and a little colloquy ensues as the attendant asks:

> "Have you been out to the desert yet?"
> I shake my head.
> She opens her eyes in mild surprise, as if offended by my unconventional behavior.
> "You *must* go! The life force there! I mean, the whole desert energy thing roots you into this amazing consciousness of your interconnectedness with all beings."[40]

This theme finds expression in deeper and more sympathetic ways in Richard V. Francaviglia's sensitive and layered exploration of the Great Basin Desert of Nevada. "Some people," he writes at one point, "transform emptiness into meaning by searching for—and finding—inspiration here [in the desert] amid 'complete desolation,' as a truck driver once characterized the entire Great Basin from Salt Lake City to Reno."[41]

What, then, about the multiple opposites of the sacred? How can this clean and pure desert of spirituality be also, or become, a locus of pollution, a violated space, one of a multitude of profanities? Answers are perhaps multiple and ambiguous, but I would like to consider two modalities: the effect of human acts, and the inversion of the "nature" of the desert.

If human transformation of a landscape can remake its relation to the divine and the human, then surely also human intervention in the desert can uncouple the land from its spirituality. In a desert world, which, as God promises more than once in the Bible, should be made to bloom, such transformative intervention can be read as turning wasteland into productive, purposeful fields and farms. Oliver Wozencraft offers an early example. A physician who left his home in Louisiana to slake gold fever in the California fields of 1849, Wozencraft and his companions got lost west of Yuma crossing the Algodones dune field in the southern Colorado Desert in California. Exhausted, dying of thirst, Wozencraft suddenly spied "an enchanting vista to the farthest horizon. Limpid water flowed through a land of plenty. Cool green fields bordered cottonwood-shaded canals. Fat cattle grazed on the rich grass. The inviting odor of fresh-cut alfalfa was in the air." This was, he knew for certain, no mirage or hallucination, but a vision of the future. He prayed in thanksgiving, and then spent the rest of his life trying to bring water to what would later become the Imperial Valley—a massive, capital-intensive, labor-exploitative farming operation that, literally, obliterated the desert.[42] Here his sense of the sacred not only leads to, but in fact blesses the reconfiguration of a desert: making the desert bloom an act of sacred duty.[43] Of course, once the desert is a farm, the likelihood that God will be visiting may fade away; the spirituality that aridity and emptiness enabled is gone. But that seems to be okay: the terrors of the desert that God meliorated have evaporated, washed away, and he's not really needed anymore.

However, in other cases the change is not regarded as so benign. In Zane Grey's *Shower of Gold* (originally published in 1913 in a bowdlerized form—Grey's original text only appeared in 2007)[44]—greedy capitalists invade the desert realm, bringing construction, land-grabbing, money-grubbing, and the termination of a ranching life that had respected the desert's character. Valerie Kuletz, who grew up in the militarized deserts of Southern California, recounts the blasts, bombs, waste disposal, and toxic sludge that have transformed a pristine landscape into a *Tainted Desert*. The photographic testimony of Richard Misrach in *Bravo 20* shows how striking desert features were progressively obliterated by aerial bombing attacks, while abandoned bullet- and bomb-riddled school buses hunker by craters stagnant with orange water. In the American context, perhaps no single desert transformation more starkly renders the desecration of the sacred than the decision, made in the 1950s, to sacrifice large sections of the Mojave and Great Basin Deserts to nuclear testing. For this "ultimate defilement," as it were, let's turn now to Frank Bergon's desert novel, *The Temptations of St. Ed and Brother S*.[45]

St. Ed is a visionary. Dissatisfied with the regulations of monasteries he has tried, he breaks out into the Great Basin Desert of Nevada to found a monastic community determined to reproduce the lifeways of the great desert monks of Late Antique Egypt. St. Ed's rules, however, are too harsh for most aspirants; in the years he has been out in the desert, only a single adherent, Brother S, has stuck it out. Things look bleak, for his bishop wants him to abandon the desert monastery and move into town where, as a priest—for he is ordained—he can serve a small Catholic community. Then serious disruption comes in the form of Amy Chávez, a Bureau of Land Management officer who was stranded in the desert and almost died while investigating the mysterious deaths of wild horses.

To make a long story short, it turns out that officials of the Nevada Test Site—the home of US nuclear testing—have their eyes on St. Ed's monastery and much surrounding land belonging to Native Americans to construct a nuclear waste facility. (The obvious inspiration here is the Yucca Mountain project.) These intrusions drive St. Ed to violate his own rules: to admit women to the monastery, to allow changes in the rhythms of life, and, worst of all, to engage with the secular world—all leading to disaster and, finally, death.

The themes we've explored up till now come together in complex and many-layered ways in another French-language text set in the southwestern desert, this time though not Parisian but Québecois. Nicole Brossard's *The Mauve Desert* purports to be a translation by one "Laure Angstelle" of the tale of an Arizona girl named Melanie and her adventures with a certain Angela Parkins and "the long man," who turns out to be J. Robert Oppenheimer.[46] The first part of the novel focuses on Melanie and her drive across the desert trying to escape her mother and her oppressive life in the run-down motel she (the mother) runs. The desert is omnipresent. The first sentence proclaims, "The desert is indescribable." And the second: "Reality rushes in there, rapid light." At once, then, Melanie's desert is genuine, and it has too an air of magic about it, encapsulated in the way that its aridity makes her hair spark when she runs a comb through it. Soon enough, though, as Melanie hopes for a dawn "forgotten by civilization," its sacredness is violently disrupted by "the men who came to the desert to see

their equations jump like humanity." And yet Melanie also insists that "the desert is civilization"; "I never panic," she avers, "in the desert." This lack of fear comes, it seems, because in
the desert "fear is precise," it is "real": "wind, thorns, snakes, tarantulas, animals, skeletons."
And yet again, Melanie's desert can be a dump, a "tainted desert": along a ramshackle street
where you "pass motels, motor homes, sheet-metal shacks, telephone poles, carcasses of autos,
piles of tires. That's the desert. I bought myself a can of Coke, I drink without stopping. I'm
thirsty. Reality makes me thirsty."

What I have quoted is only a small sample of the images of the desert in Brossard's novel;
they interplay in complex dances of meaning and interrelations, sometimes reinforcing, sometimes contradictory. In fact, of course, every image is seen through Melanie's fifteen-year-old
eyes; it is her emotional state, which changes radically from scene to scene, that determines,
in large part, how we perceive her desert: as sacred, as profaned and polluted, as reality, as its
opposite, or something else entirely.

Like Berger, Melanie has at her disposal an armory of desert tropes. There is, however,
one constraint, or at least one major constraint, on the breadth of her vision and the lability
of her interaction with her desert space, and that is "the long man," the one who has brought
to the desert something novel, something whose presence marks the imposition onto the
desert something wholly new and wholly inescapable: the nuclear bomb. Melanie does not
quite understand what the long man's mission means, but we do; and, at least to a certain
degree, the defilement of the desert by motels and piles of rotting tires and the abandoned
carcasses of automobiles pales as defilers in comparison to the bomb.

Finally, let's consider the problem of "desert inversion."[47] In the Bible, both Hebrew
and Greek, the desert can be depicted as a realm of demons. Most famously, Jesus spends
his forty days in the desert to undergo Satan's temptations; the desert is here figured
as Satan's special space, where his powers are greatest. This trope echoes in literature
about the American desert. In *Amnesiascope*, the dystopic science fiction novel of Steve
Erickson, the protagonist, escaping Los Angeles at the end of the book, hopes that the
demons that have dogged him will abandon him for their natural home as he passes
through the desert. In *Ask the Dust*, by John Fante, Camilla Lopez, worn out and down,
vanishes into the Mojave, never again to be seen—Arturo Bandini's great loss. Again
and again in Los Angeles fiction the Santa Ana winds carry desert demons into the city
and drive ordinarily sane people to acts of depravity or criminality.[48] So the desert can
be in and of itself also a malevolent space, without the intervention of human misuse:
indeed, in one sense, the desert is *the* proper place for waste and nuclear weapons—as
government officials argued when they withdrew thousands of square miles of western
desert as "national sacrifice zones."

Obviously, there are other momentous questions here, not least those of environmental
justice; the desert spaces "withdrawn" by the US government had all long been occupied
and claimed by Native American groups, for whom the land was indeed sacred, as we have
seen and will see shortly. A full exploration of these issues, which would be crucial to a
more nuanced understanding of the interaction of human beings with our western deserts,
is needed to open a window on a very different way of "seeing" the desert, something true

elsewhere on Desert Earth where Europeans (under whom I include also Anglo-Americans) have brought their biblically sourced tropes as means of "understanding" desert spaces.[49]

PETROGLYPHS, PICTOGRAPHS, SACRED AND GENDERED LANDSCAPES

As noted above, the sacrality of the land is central to all Native American thinking. The details, however, for groups living in the desert Southwest are more complicated than a simple declaration of sacrality and are also imbricated with gendered notions about specific locales in the desert landscape that are interconnected with gendered material culture and social traditions (I delay treatment of gender to chapters 4 and 5.) They also vary from group to group. Native American views about the desert add a deep and complex component to consideration of the desert as sacred space. There are three main sources for unraveling this congeries of ideas: testimony of Native Americans themselves, ethnographic literature (much produced in the late nineteenth and early twentieth centuries), and the rock art that abounds across the Southwest.

A clear statement about the sacredness of land for the Zuni people, whose homeland now is a mesa in New Mexico, was offered by Jim Enote in a collection of Indigenous "Voices of the Grand Canyon," collected by the Grand Canyon Trust:

> The Grand Canyon, especially from Lees Ferry to Phantom Ranch, is dense with Zuni sacred places. Some that are really important are near what is called Supai Man, where there is a directional marker carved into a slab of stone pointing towards Zuni and a path out of the canyon. At Unkar Delta there are ceramics and water control features exactly like the ones we have here in present-day Zuni. Along the river and throughout the canyon there are many springs, where we still gather water to bring back to Zuni for ceremonies. There are dozens of places in the canyon, where we collect salt, willows, reedgrass and other plants, as well as mineral pigments.[50]

It's notable that Enote seamlessly interlinks the sacrality of sites in the canyon with not just ceremonial/religious activities but also with what might seem in the Euro-American imaginary as ordinary, nonsacred undertakings, like the collection of salt and, especially, the control of water. This inextricability of water use and the sacred is emphasized too:

> Water is life. Water is the giver and sustainer of life. Water is a sacred and spiritual element to the Tribes of the Partnership. The Creator instilled in the First Peoples the responsibility of protecting the delicate, beautiful balance of Mother Earth for the benefit of all living creatures. The Partnership will embrace and own the stewardship of the Colorado River and lead from a spiritual mandate to ensure that this sacred water will always be protected, available and sufficient.[51]

As Paul A. Formisano observes in his recent study of literature linked to the Colorado River, "this position [of the tribes] also infuses river management with spirituality." This spirituality intertwines the "natural" and "cultural" worlds—really, they are inseparable—and discharges in an attitude of stewardship: a term itself perhaps too Euro-American, for it still presupposes both a divide between the natural world and us and a position of superiority, as among the Christian environmentalists who argue that God's charge to humanity in Genesis is a duty to stewardship—but leaving us at the top of the scale.[52]

The Chemehuevi, who spoke a Uto-Aztecan language,[53] lived on the west bank of the Colorado River next to the Mojave, whose territory skirted the river, in the Colorado Desert. Their landscape is very much a basin and range topography, with jagged mountain chains separated by flat, wide valleys. These mountains were interconnected by the Chemehuevis' Mountain Sheep Song, which bound everything into a "sacred tetralogy of man, song, mountain, and game animal." These mountains include *Mug^wiyagaiv^ya*, today called El Dorado Mountain; *ʔAagah*, Spirit Mountains, whose highest point is today's Mount Newberry (the Mojave's Avi Kwa Ame, treated below); *Timpisagwagatsitci*, meaning "Green Stone," today's Providence Mountains; and *Yuvisaavittci*, the "Greasy Substance Lying Mountains," which are evidently the Dead Mountains with a continuation lying west of Needles, California, on the Colorado River. The Mountain Sheep Song that embraced and sanctified these mountains marked out strips of hunting territory that ran from the top of one range to the next. This was called a *cuukutiiravi*, a derivative of the Chemehuevi word for "desert," *tiiravi*. Carobeth Laird cites a few verses of the song:

My mountain canteen
will go swinging like a pendulum
swing like a pendulum
my mountain canteen
will go bouncing up and down
will go bouncing up and down
my mountain canteen

"Like a pendulum" is a gloss; the Chemehuevi, *wa'yuk^waa'gaiv^ya'*, literally means "will go along swinging back and forth."[54]

Sites sacred to Indigenous populations were everywhere in the desert Southwest. The Chemehuevi knew a mountain called Bone-Gray Peaks where spirit-animals dwelled, so named because of their color. Ice Mountain, *Pariʔasikaiv^ya*, home to the bat spirit animal, has usually been regarded in contrast to Bone-Gray Peaks as mythical, but it may have been an actual place. At least two actual caves were known to the Chemehuevi as "places of great power and mystery," one called *Kwin^yacváh*, located in Arizona near the confluence of the Big Sandy and Santa Maria Rivers, the other, whose name has not been recorded by ethnographers, somewhere in mountainous Nevada. Both were places to which men and women adverted for songs and power. For the Mescalero Apache, caves generally were sacred sites of power because they provided access into the underground realm of the spirit world. (Springs held the same power because they too were flowing out from underground.) The Akimel O'odham held similarly that the spirits their healers called on for help in diagnosing

Figure 2-1: Baboquivari Peak.

disease lived on mountains in the landscape of spirits: the healer's voice "will go where the mountains are standing, and inside of them is something [spirit], or some kind of thing . . . that gets caused to show up" to assist a healer in his diagnosis of disease. A sacred place the Akimel O'odham called *Hâhâtesumiehĭn* or *Hâhâtai s'maihĭsk*, "Stones Strike," may have been a pre-contact Hohokam shrine and so a sacred site of great antiquity. In southern New Mexico, the deep recesses of caves sometimes served as "dark area shrines," where, it seems, ritual activity and deposition of offerings took place. Examples include Chavez Cave north of Las Cruces, which was in use probably 700–900 CE, Surratt Cave in central New Mexico, likely in use from c. 1350–1450 into the 1500s CE, and U-Bar Cave in the Alamo Hueco Mountains in the New Mexican bootheel.[55]

The most sacred site in the homeland of the Tohono O'odham is the great peak Baboquivari (Fig. 2-1), whose Tohono name is Vav Giwulik.[56] The eastern boundary of their Nation runs along the crest of the mountain; near the top is a cave in which the Tohono O'odham culture hero 'I'itoi lived. The Tohono poet Ofelia Zepeda celebrates the sacrality of the mountain in several of her poems:

> Passing below the sacred peak,
> here prayers signified by rosary beads are futile.
> Calling on the Virgin Mary is useless.
>
> Instead, one must know the language of the land.
> One must know the balance of the desert.

In another poem, reflecting on driving off the Tohono O'odham homeland, she finds solace as the blacktop on which she travels "whispers, 'You will always see Waw Giwulik / In your rearview mirror.'" The poem "Do'ag Weco" recounts a pilgrimage to the base of Baboquivari: "From the tops of mountains come memories / of stories, songs, names of plants, / animals we have long forgotten." A prayer for strength, health, goodness, and the justifications for these requests is addressed to the mountain, which holds in its memory Tohono O'odham cultural and historical knowledge. More generally, mountains radiate sacrality in Zepeda's work. In the poem "Music Mountain" she intones the names of six, ending with Baboquivari, and then explains:

It has been said before,
these mountains will not listen
if we simply speak words to them.
They will only hear us
if we come with melody, rhythm,
pitch, and harmony.
To these circling mountains
we must speak with voices
in songs, rhythmic speeches, orations, and prayers.
We must be prepared with repetition,
a singular, undisturbed beat.
That is the way of the mountains.
This is what they want to hear.[57]

The Diné (Navajo) poet Luci Tapahonso reports a conversation with a medicine man at the Gila River Arts Center in which he related a tale about a mountain near Phoenix. "We've always been told not to climb it, and we don't," he averred, and explained:

> Actually, spirits live on that mountain, and some of our most sacred places are there. At certain times, the medicine people will make offerings or go to receive blessings atop the mountain. They're the only ones who are allowed to go there. The kids know this, and while they might not understand why it's forbidden, they know it's a place to be respected and even to be feared.

A white man the medicine man met asked about the mountain and insisted on climbing it. Warned it was dangerous, he nevertheless went ahead. "A few days later" the medicine man ran into him again and he was on crutches. He'd slipped and injured his ankle. It is not made explicit, but the implication is clear: the white man was punished by the mountain spirits for his violation of its sacrality.[58]

For the Mohave, Chemehuevi, Yuma, and some Southern Paiutes, one of the most sacred spots in the Mojave Desert is the mountain Avi Kwa Ame. Now part of a national monument in Nevada that includes the Spirit Mountain Wilderness (Spirit Mountain being Avi Kwa Ame, topping out at 5,639 ft [1,719 m]; the Anglo name for the mountain is Newberry Peak), Avi Kwa Ame was made and named by the Mohave culture hero Mastamho and served as his retreat once his teaching tasks were done. He built a house on the summit which he named Avi-nyamaθam-kuvatše and then declared that "Men who are not doctors will call [the mountain] Avikwame, but some of you will dream about me and they will call it avi-nyamaθam-kuvatše."[59] This highly sacred mountain then became the site at which, through dreams, Mohave, Yuma, and other Colorado River peoples' doctors attained their skills.[60]

A detailed account of the acquisition of power through dreaming about Avi Kwa Ame was recounted by the Yuma doctor Tsuyukweráu (known in English as Joe Homer) as a preface to and assurance of his true knowledge of a Yuma creation story, narrated to John Peabody Harrington toward the start of the last century. Accounted the "best dreamer" among the Yuma, Tsuyukweráu related the origins of his powers and knowledge:

> Before I was born I would sometimes steal out of my mother's womb while she was sleeping, but it was dark and I did not go far. . . . Every good doctor begins to understand before he is born, so that when he is big he knows it all. . . . When a little boy, I took a trip up to Avikwaame Mountain and slept at its base. I felt of my body with my two hands, but found it was not there. It took me four days and four nights to go up there. Later I became able to approach even the top of the mountain. At last I reached the willow-roof in front of the dark house there. Kumastamxo was within. It was so dark that I could hardly see him. He was naked and very large. Only a few great doctors were in there with him, but a crowd of men stood under the willow-roof before the house. I tried to enter, but could not.

As a boy Tsuyukweráu ate leaves of jimsonweed plucked from the west side of the plant to improve his dreaming. Eventually he attained "the power to go to Kumastamxo any time, to-night if I want to. I lie down and try hard and soon I am up there again with the crowd. He tells me everything I want to know, and it takes only a little while to go there." Son of Kwikumat, the Yuma's culture hero, and a naïve young woman, Kumastamxo was the first child ever born, conceived when Kwikumat taught the young woman how to have sex. He took over many culture-teaching duties from his father.[61] Dreams that take the dreamer to a sacred site to acquire knowledge and power are standard among the peoples of the Colorado River region. As a sacred space Avi Kwa Ame joins the other mountains mentioned above as central to the sacrality of the desert landscape, linked as it is both to the origins of culture and the conferral of doctoring power.[62]

Finally, I'd like to mention a recent instance of the links among dreaming, mountains, and power. In her book *Oak Flat: A Fight for Sacred Land in the American West*, Lauren Redniss recounts the efforts of the San Carlos Apache of east-central Arizona to reclaim a sacred space dedicated to girls' menstrual onset ritual, the Sunrise Ceremony. Oak Flat had been appropriated by copper mining conglomerates for a vast open pit mine. (See Fig. 4-5 for a sense of what such mines do to the landscape.) During the struggle against the mine and the federal government, a San Carlos woman named Theresa Nosie began dreaming about a mountain calling to her husband Wendsler. Answering the call, he drove to Mount Graham—*Dził Nchaa Si An* in Apache—and climbed to the peak. The mountain expressed its power by materializing as his climbing companion a white girl, who vanished when he reached the summit, and a massive thunderstorm, whose formation warned of the approach of spirits and insisted Wendsler needed to get down as fast as he could.[63]

There is writing *about* the desert landscape, and tropes embedded in that writing, but there is also writing *on* the desert landscape itself. In the southwestern deserts it has been estimated that there are more than 30,000 panels of rock art, whether painted pictograph or pecked petroglyph; on the Coso Mountains of southeastern California, located mostly within the Naval Air Weapons Station China Lake, are preserved over 100,000 discrete images.[64] The meaning of these images has been debated by ethnographers, anthropologists, and archaeologists for decades. Some seem to be simply directional markers of one kind or another or boundary markers of tribal territories, while petroglyphs in the Coso Range of the Mojave Desert have been seen (debatably) as records of shamanic vision quests. At the other extreme, the extraordinary White Shaman Mural on the Pecos River in Texas has been read as a detailed evocation of an ancient peyote collection ceremony, which connects with myths about the creation of the world and the daily cycle of sun, moon, and planetary movements.[65] The connection between rock art and sacred space is twofold: the sites of this art are themselves often regarded as sacred, and the art itself is often said to depict the visions Native Americans received in "trance" as they sought power.

For most, if not all, southwestern desert Indigenous peoples, the fundamental bond between humans and the divine is that acquisition and maintenance of *power*. In much ethnography, the word used for persons who enjoy such a connection is "shaman." Among the Piipaash and Halychduum, together constituting the Maricopa, the word often translated as "shaman" is *gwĭsicœ*, which comes from the root meaning "power" and so is better glossed as "a person with power" (and see also *gwĭsiœi'k*, "one has power," a verb construction).[66] The O'odham *ma:kai* is rendered "medicine man, doctor" in the Saxon, Saxon, and Enos dictionary, but as "shaman" in Bahr, Gregorio, Lopez, and Alvarez's study of the staying sickness, a class of non-transmissible disease to which only the Akimel O'odham are subject. According to Frank Russell, however, this is but one of three classes of "shaman." The *si'atcokam* treated disease by magic, while the *hai'-itcottam*, who are not strictly shamans, undertake cures by medicinal treatment. In this threefold scheme the *ma:kai* were regarded as also having power over crops, weather, and war.[67] In Chemehuevi the word is *puh^waganti*, a combination of *-aganti*, "having," and *puh^wa-*, "power to doctor," while Shoshone and Paiute Numic peoples of the Great Basin Desert and adjacent regions called their specialists *poɩagunt*, "one having supernatural power," and rock art sites *poɩaghani*, "house of supernatural power."[68]

The acquisition of power occurred in most cases in the context of "dreams, or by solicitation in specified places,"[69] as we've just seen with Tsuyukweráu. In many cases dreams inviting the dreamer to attain power came unbidden and so might occur anywhere; the dreamer did not need to be in some explicit site of thrumming power. Petitioners who actively sought power, however, might betake themselves to a site known to hold and confer power, again, though, through dreams. Among the Cocopah, whose original territory straddled the Colorado River delta region but who today reside in the Colorado River Indian Reservation, the content of the dream was standard and involved transportation to a sacred mountain, typically Feather Mountain, *wi čawal*, an island at the head of the Gulf of California, or Mayor Peak, *wi spa*, a prominence west of the confluence of the Colorado and Hardy (New) Rivers in Baja California.[70] These two sacred sites were essential to acquiring power. For other groups, the person hoping to attain power needed to present himself at a sacred site and undertake his dream experience there—as unhappy Happy Dave, as we have seen, failed to carry through.

Caves, usually loci of strong sacredness and gendered female,[71] often played a vital role as sites for accessing power. Among the Piipaash and Halychdum (Maricopa), the commonest route was to have a dream, or rather a series of dreams, that conferred the power. Such

Figure 2-2a: Tlaloc image at Three Rivers Petroglyph Site, New Mexico, with prominent goggle eyes.

dreams almost always came unbidden and were rarely purposely sought out. If, however, a Maricopa intentionally hoped to attain power, only two caves could confer it. In one, called *kukupu'rniva*, a seeker who "wished to be rich or to become a shaman, or have crops prosper, be a good runner, or have many girls about him" would sit deep in the cave with his hand out and pray. A strong wind from inside would grant the wish, which would be energized only after some ritual performances in the next few days. There is no trance or travel to a supernatural world; sometimes people took jimsonweed (*Datura*), but only to dream.[72] Once obtained, power can be put to many uses, but most commonly it is deployed to heal.

Another congeries of sacrality on the landscape that reaches into the deep past is linked to the inducement of rain. Sometime, probably, between 900 and 1000 CE the Mesoamerican god Tlaloc migrated from his central Mexican home into present-day New Mexico, eastern Arizona, and northern Chihuahua. Among his attributes was control of rain. Tlaloc's locus of worship in the Aztec world where he originated was Mount Tlaloc, a 4,000-meter-high (13,124 feet) mountain east of Tenochtitlan, the Aztec capital, in the sierra that includes the famous volcano Popocatépetl. Tlaloc's iconography is highly distinctive, marked especially by his set of large goggle eyes, which, displayed on rock art, pottery, and textiles (see Figs. 2-2a-b), serve as a constant distinguishing feature.[73]

Tlaloc's association with mountains was linked to the belief that mountains were bringers of rain; Tlaloc was also associated with caves, springs, and rivers, because rainwater was believed to originate underground. Mountains are repeatedly attested as sacred sites linked to rain-making in the desert Southwest. The Tewa, who occupy a pueblo on the Rio Grande,

Figure 2-2b: Tlaloc image at Three Rivers Petroglyph Site, New Mexico; body and right hand.

have a rain-making shrine on Mount Tsikomo, one of their four sacred mountains. The Zuni's rain-making deities are said to dwell on Mount Kor'koshi. An especially resonant site is

Hueco Tanks in western Texas, a little north-northeast of El Paso. These eminences, replete with *kachina* images—*kachinas*, which appear around 1300 CE, are derived from Tlaloc and take on his rain-making prowess—serve as perfect exemplars of rain-filled mountains, pocked with *tiñajas*, that usually contain water year-round.[74]

Caves on mountains were an especially favored locale. When Tlaloc's worship migrated north, into the deserts of present-day New Mexico and Arizona, the same topographic features attracted him, and we find them linked to Tlaloc as sacred sites in the Sonoran and Chihuahuan Deserts. The wall of the sink that leads to Surratt Cave in central New Mexico bears a large face with the goggle eyes typical of Tlaloc; the cave may have been associated with rain-making rituals (which fits neatly with Tlaloc). Tlaloc figures appear also at Chavez Cave in southern New Mexico. U-Bar Cave in the New Mexican bootheel was clearly used for religious-ceremonial ends, perhaps related to hunting. A cave on Mount Taylor, a very prominent feature west of Albuquerque, was used as a kiva or shrine—again, a sacred mountain site.[75]

Tlaloc, *kachinas*, and the landscape features in which they were embedded belong to a "Mesoamerican rain-making conceptual system" that spread deep into the southwestern desert world.[76] It is abundantly apparent that this conceptual system was tied firmly to sites on the landscape that were sacred and often hosted ceremonies that asked the gods who oversaw rain to bring the precipitation crucial to agriculture in a desert environment. Mountains and caves were prominent in this mélange of sacrality and, as we have seen, served as sacred sites for a multiplicity of purposes. Caves' power derived in particular from their ability to link the ordinary, everyday world with the supernatural world underground; this connection is sometimes illustrated by figures, like snakes, depicted as emerging from and/or entering cracks in the rock walls of caves.[77]

FINDING MEANING WHERE THERE IS NO MEANING

The desert, in and of itself, is, really, meaningless. It is simply *space*. It is human beings, interacting with it, *performing* it, rethinking it, projecting onto it, reacting to it through the filters of their cultural optics, who bestow a *meaning*, and thereby render what was *space* into *place*.[78] Berger gets this exactly right when he asserts that it is precisely the desert's emptiness to Euro-American eyes that forms its essential quality, or perhaps better said, non-quality; Melanie plays it out as her emotions flip her from mood to mood in her desert drive; Wozencraft projected his vision of a blooming future onto a space that contained, evidently, only the promise of dry, and imminent, death; McGrath's New Age dreamers haunt a desert of perfected spirituality; and aliens bringing peace, love, and understanding fill, for George Adamski, a vacant landscape. The desert is *empty*, so that it may be *full*. What fills it, we bring, whether we know it or not. As Eris Williams Reed remarks, "[L]andscapes were not inherently sacred but rather created through worshippers' repeated engagement with them."[79] But, at the same time, as explored in chapter 10, the desert may express an *agency* that reflects back on us as we move through or inhabit it. In other words, the filling of the desert, especially the discovery and maintenance of its sacrality, depend on the interplay between the landscape's agency and ours, and the ways in which each feed and reconfigure the other.

ROCK ART AND SHAMANISM

The theory that rock art represents visions attained in trance has a long and contentious history. To examine the debate in detail would take us far from the question of sacrality of the southwestern desert landscape; a few words will have to suffice. The basic claim, put forward in its most vigorous form by David Lewis-Williams and T. A. Dowson, asserts that shapes depicted in rock art represent "entoptic" visions universally experienced by humans in a state of trance, which could be induced by repetitive dancing, chanting, drumming, and/or hallucinogenic drugs. David Whitley and his colleagues have vigorously argued this view for southwestern rock art. In my view, this theory has been pretty thoroughly debunked by various opponents, notably Paul G. Bahn.[80] However, rock art need not be trance-induced to be sacred—and, I think, largely, we should indeed see sites of rock art as additional locales of special power.

Finally, a word or two about "shamanism" and "shamans." As alluded to above, the Native American words that describe persons endowed with power have often been translated as "shaman" and their practices designated "shamanism."[81] The words in Indigenous languages whose translations have all been collapsed into "shaman" typically refer to the possession of power, which is the fundamental attribute of persons who exercise ritual healing, deploy curses, or otherwise manipulate the supernatural world. In older literature these words are often rendered "medicine man" or even "doctor"—and although the former carries a flavor of condescension, it is surely closer to Indigenous realities than "shaman." "Healer" doesn't quite capture everything the practitioners do, but it is closer to their prime social function and doesn't bear the condescending connotation. In any case, shaman and shamanism come from the very different cultural context of indigenous Siberian peoples; their means of acquiring power and their practices differ widely from those of southwestern Native Americans.[82]

FRENCH TRAVELERS IN THE ARID SOUTHWEST*

The desert world of the American Southwest has exerted a magnetic attraction on many French travelers. From Simone de Beauvoir, who visited in 1947, to Bernard-Henri Lévy, who published his recapitulation of Alexis de Tocqueville's American journey in 2005, French intellectuals have believed they found in the American deserts a key to unlocking the American character. In this chapter my interest revolves around the impact of the experience of the sere desert landscape—so different from their home in France—on their understanding of the American world.

The centrality of landscape and the travelers' reactions to it cry out for an ecocritical look at just how French travelers understand the American desert. Much of their writing has gone essentially unnoticed in the ecocritical literature, at least as far as I have been able to determine. While this neglect no doubt stems from many causes, two stand out for me. First, our French visitors have written initially not for an American but a French audience. Second, because they are *French*, their work has not fallen under the umbrella of American literature. Ecocritics dealing with literature about America, then, seem unintentionally to have excluded these writers just because they are not typically subsumed under "American literature."

This chapter tries to remedy, or at least address, these problems by situating several French travel writers, two novelists, and one film into an American literary context, to argue that they deserve incorporation into a greater American literature, and to explore how ecocritical approaches can elucidate the ways they represent and understand arid America. The travelers I have chosen to treat all stand in various French intellectual traditions of the mid- and later twentieth century.[1] I have chosen them in large part because their goals in coming to the United States embraced, in whole or in part, an effort to find meaning in this country—a project not unrelated to that of the first classic French explicator of the American scene to his compatriots, Alexis de Tocqueville. Their reactions to the arid Southwest shaped their

---

* Originally published in *Reading Aridity in Western American Literature*, eds. Jada Ach and Gary Reger (Lanham, MD: Lexington Books, 2020) 243–71.

cultural work and prompted them to reflections on the landscape and its characteristics like heat, aridity, and emptiness in ways that can be easily read through an ecocritical lens. The fundamental ecocritical move is to bring into conversation the southwestern desert world as an agent creating experience with the subjects who absorb, react, and ultimately express this interaction. The deserts captivated French travelers in part because the landscape seems to capture something distinctly American—a physical manifestation of the exceptionalism that has figured in French thinking about America since Tocqueville.

In all the works that I will examine, the desert exerts a power and appeal that come out of its own ecological characteristics. The human artifices, as Jean Baudrillard calls them, like roads and motels, do not make the desert friendlier or easier to understand in the universe of these works; they are rather contrivances implanted in a landscape perfectly fine without them—indeed, perhaps violated by their presence. From an eco-oriented new materialist perspective, the desert is a landscape that speaks for itself, and sometimes in a language human beings cannot grasp—the desert does not care. Because the southwestern deserts are spaces where it is not easy to live for the non-Indigenous, steeped in aridity and heat, they demand that visitors take them on their own terms. Trying to sort out what those terms are, and why these sere landscapes so appeal to French men and women coming from a temperate and damp European world, is one of the central projects in all these cultural products. For Jean Baudrillard, the desert *is* America, and his elision of the two in the end may obscure his response to the desert itself; our other visitors, especially Simone de Beauvoir and Yves Berger, have senses better attuned, and therefore may seem to enjoy something that may seem like an "unmediated" experience.[2]

One unifying theme of all these works is the experience of Death Valley as the *ne plus ultra* of the American desert. Many other thematic elements also link these works, and can be traced back to, or at least root themselves in, French experiences much earlier in a different desert world. And taking an ecocritical approach to unpeeling the intertexualities of both the works and the human-environment nexus can, I hope, clarify my claim that these French works can be read more expansively as American literature.

THE TRAVELERS

The French I have chosen to examine here visited the United States starting soon after the end of the World War II. The 1940s through the 1980s were decades of considerable intellectual and political ferment in France, as its intellectuals (and others) confronted French collaboration with the Nazi occupation, the wars in Algeria and French Indochina, France's place in the world, and the new global power of the United States, all mixed up with experimentation in literary forms and topics.[3] Their feelings about America were often conflicted, even contradictory. What they saw in the American desert—its physicality, heat, aridity, colors—lodged powerfully in their memories and helped fashion an imaginary of America that emerged in book and film. Reading their work from an ecocritical perspective will, I hope, help elucidate the bonds between the physical world and the emotional and intellectual recreation of the desert experience and its meaning for French understanding of Americanness.

Simone de Beauvoir (1908–1986), the earliest of my travelers, was a dominant figure in the French intellectual world of the 1950s and 1960s, and her influence now is probably the greatest of the travelers I am studying, thanks to her position as a founding figure in later twentieth-century feminism. However, except, perhaps, for her affair with Nelson Algren, whom she met in Chicago, her journey through the United States has received relatively little attention.

It was the America on the cusp of Camelot that Michel Butor (1936–2016) saw whirring by on the highways and packaged in his 1962 novel *Mobile*. Despite his fame, *Mobile* was greeted in both France and, after translation, in Anglophone countries as a disaster of a book; the admiration of critics was a long time coming. Its epigrammatic, allusive style and jarring typography (not reproduced in the translation) put readers off.[4] His America-wide journey took him through the desert Southwest, but the organization and approach of his book separate widely brief reactions to the desert spaces he sees.

Jean-François Lyotard's (1924–1998) short novel *Le mur du Pacifique* ("The Wall of the Pacific") presents itself as a strange amalgam of discovered text framed by Lyotard's commentary.[5] The post-modernist and post-structuralist Jean Baudrillard (1929–2007), perhaps best known for his study of simulation and hyperreality, focused *America* largely on the West Coast and desert Southwest. In effect, *America* can be read as a sort of case study of Baudrillard's theories of hyperreality and simulation: the consummation, so to speak, of human and historical development toward a final end.[6] Yves Berger (1931–2004), who spent his working life as the literary director of the major French publishing house Éditions Grasset, developed a lifelong passion for the United States after childhood reading of Jack London and James Fenimore Cooper. He wrote several novels set there and promoted in France translations of Dee Brown, Vine Deloria, and N. Scott Momaday. Having visited America, and especially the Southwest, many times, he encapsulated his experiences in *La pierre et le saguaro*.[7]

Bernard-Henri Lévy (born 1948) is another major figure in French philosophical tradition. His work both as an academic and a journalist has made him a prominent and sometimes controversial public intellectual in France. In the first decade of the twenty-first century, he decided to recreate Alexis de Tocqueville's (1805–1859) exploration of the United States.[8] The result was *American Vertigo*, which enlarged Tocqueville's scope by embracing the West and Midwest, territories not yet incorporated into the United States when Tocqueville visited in 1831. Finally, there is the 2015 film by Guillaume Nicloux, *Valley of Love*, set and filmed in Death Valley, whose centrality for my project here lies not only in its setting but, as we will see, the fact that it is a *film*.

Several themes recur in all the works I want to examine: the notions of *the void*, *solitude*, and *emptiness*; the *desert sublime*; the impact of *painting and film* on French perceptions of American deserts; the desert as a *sensual space*; and the very American insistence on the fundamentality of *mobility and constant movement*. Together, these themes construct the imaginaries of the American desert embodied in the works I am examining. They come directly or indirectly out of a human-environment interplay, especially in the context of movement, that turns out to be a consequence both of the physical world's impact on the observer and of the refractions of perception that the lenses of cultural preconditions—notably the impact of Georgia O'Keeffe's painted representations of the New Mexican desert on Berger—impose on the viewer.

THE FRENCH AND THE DÉSERT AFRICAIN

The French have a long colonialist history of experience in deserts. Starting with the invasion of coastal Algeria in 1830, French military forces—followed by colonists—penetrated the northern Sahara south of the Kabyle and the Saharan Atlas Mountains; by 1900, the French presence stretched from Morocco and Senegal to the present-day boundaries of Chad and South Sudan. This experience inflected French perceptions of the Sahara and helped set the parameters of French imaginary of deserts in general and is reflected in the reactions of French visitors to the deserts of the American Southwest. Exploring this background would take us far from the focus of this chapter, but a brief excursion on a nineteenth-century French painter and a turn-of-the-twentieth-century essayist may provide some useful background.[9]

As early as the 1840s and 1850s artists like Eugène Fromentin (1820–1876) had begun to capture the Saharan landscape on canvas in paintings that both limned the desert's stereotypical features of emptiness, loneliness, and silence and asserted a stark beauty in its muted colors and vast prospects. Fromentin celebrated his Saharan experiences in *Un été dans le Sahara* ("A Summer in the Sahara," first edition 1857, third edition 1874), a record of his travels in 1853. (He had already visited before in 1846.)[10] On desert colors, he writes:

> What was totally incomparable, was the sky: the sun was going down and turning golden, purple, coating with fire a mass of little clouds detached from a great black curtain drawn above our heads, and lined up like a fringe of foam on the edge of a troubled sea. Beyond began the azure; and then, at depths that had no limits, across unknown clarity, we perceived the heavenly country of blue.[11]

Here already, on the edge of the Sahara in the middle of the nineteenth century, we have a French commentator expatiating on the incomparable colors of the desert. But Fromentin's theory of seeing the desert and capturing it in art was more complicated than simply reproducing the colors with a passionate vividness. He insisted on the difference between the *view* of the landscape, captured in the sketch, and a *vision*, which could only be expressed in painting.[12]

André Gide, whom we met in chapter 1, insisted on the special appeal of the Saharan dawn's "prismatic analysis of daylight" which imbued the "awestruck earth [with] a resurrection of color."[13] Gide traveled in the Sahara in 1900 and wrote up the journal he kept for publication in 1906. The positive views of the desert of French travelers, linked especially to an appreciation of its play of colors, contrast markedly with the very negative tropes that dominated American ideas about the desert well into the twentieth century. A standard story of the American turn, which begins with *The Desert* by John Van Dyke, published in 1900, and finds its apex in Edward Abbey's account of his desert years in *Desert Solitaire* (1968), requires reconsideration, and has been challenged by a number of scholars. I've discussed this in chapter 1.[14] But the French take cannot be attributed to the transformation in

American thinking about American deserts: the positive feelings were long before embedded in a French intellectual tradition (which, of course, was also saturated with a romanticism apparent already in Fromentin).

INTO THE VALLEY OF DEATH

Over four months in 1947, from late January to late May, Simone de Beauvoir embarked on a cross-country college lecture tour in the United States. A highlight of the tour was a road trip she took with her friend Nathalie Sorokine Moffat (called "N." in her account), a French woman married to a Hollywood screenwriter, following a great circle from Los Angeles to San Francisco and Reno, Nevada, and back. On March 10 they left Lone Pine in the Owens Valley for Death Valley. Moffat's husband and another male friend joined them, which reassured Beauvoir; Death Valley was "[d]angerous for men, it's also hard on cars . . . and N. and I congratulate each other that we are not venturing there alone."[15]

"After we leave Lone Pine," Beauvoir averred, "the desert begins again." They passed what was probably the poor remnants of Owens Lake, "half-dried," where salt-extracting workers were "shut in between the implacable sky and a petrified earth. Heat, salt, and boredom: this place, so picturesque to pass through, must be a regular little hell on earth." Anticipating Death Valley, the next stop after Lone Pine, Beauvoir expected to "find the salty heat of the desert."[16] She then recounted her impressions as the road took them down into Death Valley itself and "winds across the mountain,"

> where ochres mingle with bright purples. We discover a valley. . . . A dry, bluish grass covers the bottom. . . . In this place that is so hostile to man, the road is a moving affirmation of humanness. . . . Scott's castle stands amid sand dunes reminiscent of the Sahara. . . . Even in this season [March] the heat is overwhelming; we are all sweating. In about two hours we arrive at the place called Furnace, which the pioneers considered the very heart of hell.[17]

Beauvoir's desert impressions combine virtually all the themes we will find in her later compatriots. The colors are striking and almost unnatural, ochres and purples, a characteristic desert palette. The landscape's emptiness reads as hostility, and a road becomes a human-made mark in an unwelcoming natural setting.[18] Dunes, the emblematic stereotype of the desert, link Death Valley to the Sahara—two deserts in fact quite different in almost every way, except, of course, for the heat, which evokes the very center of Hell.

In the fall of 1975, a few months after the publication of *Surveiller et punir: Naissance de la prison*,[19] Michel Foucault visited California to give a series of talks at the University of California at Berkeley. During his stay, Simeon Wade, then a lecturer at the Claremont Graduate School, invited him down to Southern California to give a talk, meet students— and, most centrally, to travel to Death Valley and experience the sere desert landscape on LSD, which Wade called "a powerful elixir, a kind of philosopher's stone." After some hesitation, Foucault embraced the invitation, and the plan, with enthusiasm. Wade warned Foucault that "[t]he landscape alone is likely to have something of a magical effect upon you. It is a kind of Shangri-la, protected from microwave radiation and other kinds of pollution."[20]

Unfortunately, much of the surviving description of Death Valley during Foucault's trip comes from Wade's own impressions rather than Foucault's. He depicts a view of the valley from a high pass as "a gigantic mass of slate and limestone bisected by two enormous mountain ranges" at the bottom of which "Death Valley bored into the earth like a solar plexus." After Foucault dropped the LSD, he and his companions "walked deeper into the Artist's Palette, which glittered in the beam of the setting sun like a mosaic tomb illuminated by an excavator's torch." As the acid took effect, "The brightly colored strata of the canyon walls fluttered like streamers in a parade." About to head off to Zabriskie Point, Foucault objected (according to Wade): "'Leave!' Foucault said in amazement. 'How can we leave such beauty? Why don't we just stay here. I cannot imagine finding a more lovely place.'"[21]

Wade recounts his own drug-induced visions:

> As we motored along the Artist's Drive, I felt I was on a carnival ride through the grotto of Leonardo's *Madonna of the Rocks*. Each object was clear and distinct. Everything seemed artificial. I was experiencing the phenomena on many levels simultaneously, as if my mind were an eight-track tape, each sensation with multiple channels of its own. I could speak, think, desire, hear, see, feel, imagine on many discrete levels that connected to marvelous effect. Unimaginable synesthesia, immense worlds of delight, Proustian paradise found.[22]

The artificiality Wade, and evidently Foucault too, experienced through the carnival mirror of LSD rises for some visitors out of the desert landscape itself, absent the infusion of chemistry— or perhaps conjured by the chemistry of the desert, as we will see.

At the virtual center of *America*, Jean Baudrillard situates a few lapidary pages on Death Valley. Just as for Beauvoir, "everything human is artificial. Furnace Creek is a synthetic, air-conditioned oasis." But Baudrillard leaps immediately to the "violent, electric juxtaposition" between Death Valley and Las Vegas, contraposing the "sterility of wide open spaces" with "gambling, between the sterility of speed and that of expenditure." Speed, as we will see, is a fundamental feature of Baudrillard's reaction to the desert space; its ecology, for him, demands velocity.[23]

About thirty years later, the French director Guillaume Nicloux placed Isabelle Huppert and Gérard Depardieu, as a divorced couple whose son Michael, living in San Francisco, recently committed suicide, in the same Death Valley landscape. Isabelle and Gérard (the characters bear the actors' names) are there, despite unfinished animosities, because Michael sent them letters in which he promised to appear to them in Death Valley during a certain week after his death. The two protagonists oscillate between a sweltering resort (the Ranch, part of the Oasis at Death Valley, located at Furnace Creek) and drives and walks in the desert itself. The plot plays on multiple dimensions with Jesus's mission in the Bible, most especially in the desert setting where he was tempted (see Matthew 4:1-11): it is in this desert where the faith of Isabelle and Gérard is tested. Death Valley, then, serves for these French travelers as the *ne plus ultra* of the desert, the encapsulation of the American desert at its most extreme and most typical.

THE VOID: SOLITUDE AND EMPTINESS

"The desert," Yves Berger avers at one point in *La pierre et le saguaro*, "had eaten the azimuths."[24] That is to say, one's sense of direction goes wrong; there's "nothing but sand, sky, and, what's choked us, the horizon, the horizon."[25] For Lyotard, the "desert horizons [are] enjambed along the long sinusoidal highways."[26] Earlier, Berger writes of "so much solitude, aridity, and savagery . . . resignation to an empire sweltering in the sun, poverty and misery . . . so much forever impassable space."[27] For Baudrillard, all America, encapsulated in the desert, is a void.[28]

The sense of desert emptiness comes out in Berger's imagined vision of "the Valley of Death" even before he has seen it, "its legend . . . heightened in me signals of danger, images of sterility, of isolation, of solitude, of death. Images of powerlessness."[29] Elsewhere he writes of how colors conceal the desert's endlessness: "The cliffs marked with iron red of sandstone, where lichen formed blue splotches, hid from us the extensiveness of the desert . . . the desert equal to itself, flat and naked in the immensity of its space lost to view." Or again: "Sometimes we roll on a perfectly flat plain, without anything before us but the emptiness [*vide*] before us and with nothing on the horizon but the horizon far from us."[30]

This vacant desert, as Berger, Baudrillard, and Lyotard describe it, is ripe for capitalist exploitation: a place which has nothing requires, in the catechism of growth, *something*. So in Lyotard's reading Los Angeles bleeds into a desert void imprinted and filled up with the empty brands of commodification; in a sense, the void remains, simply disguised under row after row of houses and strip malls themselves empty, even when brimming with people and things.[31] Simone de Beauvoir, crisscrossing the country, driving several times through the southwestern deserts, sees the empty space in quite a different mode. For her, an early passage through northern New Mexico provoked the sense of "an endless desert of pink stones . . . great plateaus of flaming color." In March, Beauvoir, headed for Lone Pine, writes "the road crosses a desert—a desert of stones and red grasses at the foot of snowcapped mountains." On the road descending to Lone Pine,

> [t]he landscape is stunningly beautiful. It's a sun-drenched desert, as arid as Andalusia or Africa, but with a veil of snow filtering through the burning colors. The white mountains belie the menace of a scorching earth. . . . We're crossing a single desert and can see it all in every glimpse. We are even more lost than [driving] on the [California] coast, where at least the sea defined the limits of the land. Here, all around us, lines stretch to infinity and the horizon is so vast it's dizzying. Not a trace of anything human.[32]

The desert hardly figures in Lévy's chapter of *American Vertigo* called "Desert Vertigo," but driving side roads from Grand Junction, Colorado, he admits of the landscape he encounters, "*Desert* isn't the right word, since we're in the mountains, but it's a kind of desert. It has the same feeling of sparseness, desolation, and infinity as the California scrubland."[33]

Our French travelers hail from a land that, for them, is full. France is a landscape of thousands of villages and towns, pocked with bigger and smaller cities, occupied and made human by thousands of years of transformation. Emotional reactions to this cultivated environment may vary from love through nostalgia and yearning to boredom or even anger at a monotony of peopledness—but France lacks a desert.[34] So it is perhaps no surprise that for French visitors the vastness and apparent ecological emptiness of the American deserts, combined with the repeatedly observed absence of people, take on an emblematic meaningfulness, indeed for Baudrillard *the* meaning, of America. As Amy Clary has argued, for Mark Twain in *The Innocents Abroad*, the decisive difference between the American and Middle Eastern deserts—the feature that made the former appealing and the latter repulsive in the global imaginary, despite their shared aridity—was precisely the emptiness of the former and the long populated, human-impactedness of the latter.[35] The void, the emptiness, exert a deep emotional—*affective*, in the terminology of affective ecocriticism[36]—pull on our French visitors. This emotional response often plays out in an experience of the desert as a sublime space.

THE DESERT SUBLIME

Ideas about "the sublime" go back to the Greeks and Romans, who saw sublimity in language and in landscape, but the development of a later idea of the sublime came with European writers of the later eighteenth and earlier nineteenth centuries, in books like Immanuel Kant's *Observations of the Feelings of the Beautiful and Sublime* and, in a more refined form, in his *Critique of the Power of Judgment*, Edmund Burke's *A Philosophical Inquiry into the Origins of Our Ideas of the Sublime and the Beautiful*, and the essays of Joseph Addison.[37] Briefly, a sublime landscape instills in its viewer a complex stew of emotions that combines fear and awe with a sense of immensity and the nonhuman. Wild alpine landscapes felt sublime to Europeans of a Romantic bent, but deserts counted, too. Berger expresses his own sense of the sublimity of the southwestern desert landscape:

> I never leave for the United States . . . without delivering myself into a transaction that consists of plunging into "immensity" and a "loss of sight" . . . The American sky . . . The American space . . . The clouds of America . . . The settings and risings of the sun over there . . . The night over there . . . The quivering water of a fever overwhelms me and, after a period of incubation, I see "immensity" and "loss of sight" as a kind of youth, as the first morning of the world.

When Berger "crosses the frontier that [New Mexico] has with Utah, Colorado, Arizona, and Texas," he always recites in homage to New Mexico some lines from D. H. Lawrence, especially Lawrence's assertion that "[as] for the sublimity of beauty, I know nothing which can compare with what I have experienced in New Mexico."[38]

As often in his pronouncements, Baudrillard's evocation of the sublime tends toward the totalizing. For him, "[t]he desert is a sublime form that banishes all sociality, all sentimentality, all sexuality." He does, however, allow that Death Valley, no matter how "beautiful the deserts of Utah and California . . . is something else again—something sublime."

> The preternatural heat haze that enshrouds it, its inverse depth—below sea level—this landscape with its underwater features, its salt surfaces and mudhills, the high mountain chains

surrounding it, making it a kind of inner sanctuary—a gentle, spectral place of initiation. . . .
A fragment of another planet . . . where another, deeper temporality reigns, on whose surface
you float as you would on salt-laden waters.[39]

The features of the Death Valley landscape that Baudrillard counts in his inventory of sublimity may, perhaps, not resonate quite directly with those of the standard, Romantic European evocation of the sublime, but they certainly present the strangeness, the nonhumanness, the vague hostility to human beings interwoven with beauty and compellingness that make, say, the mountainscapes of *The Mysteries of Udolpho* simultaneously repulsive and enticing to Emily St. Aubert. At Livingston, Texas, Butor's narrator asks, " *What are you afraid of?* The sea at night" and " *Tell me, what are you afraid of?* The desert at night."[40] For the sublime scene is more frightening in the dark, and the identification of sea and desert is as old as the ancient Egyptians.

The tension between the human and the desert sublime comes across clearly in contrasting shots in *Valley of Love*. Scenes of broad, empty desert landscapes, seen sometimes through the windscreen of Isabelle and Gérard's car, sometimes as still views from Dante's View or Zabriskie Point, alternate with tight frames of the two main characters perched on folding stools, with a scraggy white cliff behind them. The first type of shot emphasizes the desert's nonhumanness: there are no houses, buildings, signs, shacks, abandoned cars, none of the detritus of American life, only the brush and gravel and mountains and sky, and one human feature, the road. Where the road goes, whether it ends, are impossible to say. This desert bears its sublimity in its unreadability, and the emotions of fear and fascination draw the eye toward it. The more intimate scenes serve as the loci of Gérard and Isabelle's conversations and arguments, their very human interaction, disconnected from their environment aside from Gérard's incessant, sweat-infused complaints about the "fucking heat."

A sublime landscape must be qualitatively different from the ordinary world we know from day to day. The tamed France of farms and villages offers no taste of the sublime; it's wild mountains, deep, dark, and dank forests, scenes of disaster, revolt, pain, and deserts that take the viewer out of the ordinary. But as a mode of reacting to a harsh landscape, the sublime is embedded in Western European thought about the natural world. It is therefore no surprise that a sublime read of the southwestern deserts comes naturally to many French observers. Sublimity serves as a filter through which to grasp a landscape that, on its own, seems impenetrable, even unseeable. The great expanses, the void, of the American desert radiate sublimity in a back-and-forth conversation between viewer and viewed, filtered through cultural tissues of long-standing importance in the European imaginary.

The sublime plays out in another way in the experiences of our French travelers in the American Southwest. As Dean MacCannell has noted, the impact of sublimity on tourists can be profound. MacCannell alludes to the so-called Stendhal syndrome, first described by Stendhal in recounting his exposure to great works of art in Italy, in which the viewer swoons in the face of the overwhelmingly beautiful. MacCannell extends the experience to other tourist sites, including being "in the presence of breathtaking scenery."[41] Berger, Beauvoir, Foucault, and all our Franch travelers experience the thrilling sights of the southwestern deserts, so very different from their native France. This is a reminder that our Franch travelers are, essentially, tourists, experiencing the Southwest not just through the window of their vehicles but with the sensory organs of the tourist.

THE DESERT THROUGH THE FILM OF PAINTING, THROUGH THE LENS OF FILM

Perhaps the most compelling feature the southwestern deserts present which contributes to their sublimity is their colors and light, often read, along with the landforms themselves, through the media of painting and film. In this intertexuality of art and land lies a basic ecocritical result: it is not simply the viewer who reads the land, but the land that reads back, through the eyes of the artists like Fromentin in the Sahara who are themselves transformed by the land they depict in their paintings, which then condition the way the viewer infused with the representations of the art "thinks" the desert before experiencing the actual landscape—and even then, of course, the viewer's response to the scene before her is inevitably shaped, to a greater or lesser degree, by the representations taken from the art.

For Berger, mesas stand as the most emblematic and representative features of the southwestern desert landscape, with their steep sides, level tops, and seductive array of colors.[42]

> The mesas—all the mesas—which, when the fire in the sky fades out in the evening, all become rose, then all blue, then all violet, then all black all along the extent and height of their masses, soon indistinct, soon just a barrier to which are reduced space and the horizon, properly snapped up—night and day and the world which issue there, in the disappearance of the mesas for the glory of the mesas!—then, the next morning, they . . . resume the colors by resuming the path, the opposite trajectory. With, if it's possible, other colors, as if the day were richer than the night: browns, beiges, yellow-roses, oranges, deep blues at different places in the palette, at different moments of time.

A cloud passes, colors change, then five minutes later, they change again, "provoking our ecstasy. . . . The light plays in a ballet in which the mesas figure as immobile dancers." In the end, Berger exclaims, "geology is beauty!"[43] Likewise Baudrillard extols the desert's minerality, a place where "the mineral, the organic, salt desert, sand dunes, rock, ore, light, heat, everything the earth has been, all the inhuman forms it has been through, gathered together in a single anthologizing vision."[44] In his discussion of French intellectuals' engagement with America, Jean-François Mathy remarks, "[T]he mineral realm will serve to symbolize, through the recurrent motif of the desert, the disorienting and purifying effect of the American experience on the foreigner's mind."[45] Nothing could capture Baudrillard's reactions more precisely. The role of minerality in human reactions to and interactions with the desert comes across powerfully also in Kyoko Matsunaga's study of Kyoko Hayashi's exposure to the Trinity Site, where the first atomic device was exploded, and trinitite and Leslie Marmon Silko's fascination with turquoise.[46]

Berger's splendid desert is celebrated for him most emblematically by his "great lady of the desert, the desert's sublime painter," whom "I love, I venerate." It is not Georgia O'Keeffe's vulvic and phallic flowers, the favorite of many admirers, that Berger has in mind, but rather

Figure 3-1: "Part of the Cliffs," Georgia O'Keeffe. (After Lynes 1999, 1, 580–81 no. 931. Used with permission.)

Figure 3-2: The Cliffs. Herbert Lotz, Ghost Ranch Landscape, 1999. (Source: © Georgia O'Keeffe Museum. Used with permission.)

her desert landscapes. Berger writes of "leaving the road or the trail" to follow "beaches of salt" where he can encounter "the sharp, enthusiastic memory of her paintings and find, one time, at least one time, that one who, a half-century ago rambled the desert of New Mexico in the New World and whose disappearance is, for me, who feels himself at home with Georgia O'Keeffe, a heartbreak."[47] Berger then dishes up a lengthy quotation from O'Keeffe (without citation) in which she recounts her first impressions of the New Mexican landscape.[48]

Berger mentions only one of O'Keeffe's paintings, which he calls "Cow's Skull with Red 1931–1936."[49] But it is not hard to read in his verbal descriptions of the mesas a casting into words of her visual representations. By this I do not mean to say that Berger did not "see" and seek to capture the landscape in front of him, the mesas turning through a palette of colors as the sun set. Rather, I want to suggest that his admiration for O'Keeffe's work strongly suggests that her recasting of the desert landscapes into painted images gave him a frame within which to experience and understand the formations he admired.

Perhaps most resonant with Berger's evocation of the shifting colors of desert mesas are two paintings of the same subject—"Part of the Cliffs" (1937, Fig. 3-1) and "Untitled" (1940)—which refigure a classic mesa with signature oranges, reds, and greenish-grays that spill down the lower half of the formation like bajadas, and level strata on the top half marked out in yellows and gray. A photograph of the actual formation that O'Keeffe was capturing in paint (Fig. 3-2) illustrates how she reimagined and intensified the natural colors of the stone.[50] Analogously, O'Keeffe's paintings shaped the *hibakusha* (atomic bomb survivor) Kyoko Hayashi's expectations about the New Mexican desert, with a resonance remarkably like that of Berger's.[51]

Berger's description of the shifting coloration of his mesas as the sun sets and rises has a cinematic quality which at first blush seems very different from the static depiction of a scene in a painting, but O'Keeffe's returning to the same scene to paint more than once can be read cinematically too, as if viewing individually frames on a reel. Film also influenced Berger's vision of the landscapes of parts of the southwestern deserts not painted by O'Keeffe. He lays its impact out in a long passage:

> We went toward them [sites not catalogued in tourist guides] bearing the images of the westerns, in our mind whose visionary nature we conjured up, that we sought out in ourselves, and it was as if we had been gifted with an interior eye suited to re-watch the films. On the roads in Utah that took us to Kimball Junction, in the Wasatch mountains, then another day at Fairfield and on the road in New Mexico toward Pine Springs, I have taken, in another life, the Overland Stage Line, the Pony Express, a Butterfield stage. . . . I close my eyes . . . when the eye inside opens and I see myself, I am watching myself on board the Butterfield, we spin through the great natural corridor made by the Delaware Mountains to the south, the Guadalupes to the north and one day, one time we enter, at two thousand four hundred meters high, El Paso. . . . Around 1880. Perhaps a bit before—I see myself, I am watching myself.[52]

What is perhaps most remarkable here is the divorce from the landscape in front of Berger; he transports himself into an imagined landscape taken from westerns and imposes on the actual physical world before his eyes his fantasies of film. The desert becomes nothing more than the setting for an almost mystical transportation into a Hollywood production.

Musing on Death Valley, Simone de Beauvoir declares, "[W]e discover California through movie images." She lists the "[c]owboys, sheriffs, herds of buffalo, galloping horses, wild mountain passes, villages with wooden houses" that populate the frames she's watched roll by on screens in Paris. In Pecos, Texas, "[i]n the middle of the desert, close to the Mexican border," she drinks in the sight of cowboys "all young, manly, and handsome, like Tom Mix. Once again, we think we're in the movies." Death Valley itself "is where von Stroheim made the final scenes of *Greed*." But to actually stand in the place, in the landscape where the images were captured, instills in her a terror film's alchemy never conjured, a heady mix of fantasy, reality, and the sublime, for

> no landscape ever seemed to me as overwhelming on screen as these plates of salty earth, cut by deep crevasses and stretching to infinity between walls of fire. I never even dared to dream of touching them, yet I am touching them, and in the startling truth of the setting, the drama itself becomes real: I believe in the agony of von Stroheim's heroes. The depth of this valley frightens me.[53]

But it is Baudrillard who most consistently and insistently connects his desert visions with film. Indeed, he starts *America* with an evocation of film as the only way to recapture and comprehend his desert road trip:

> We'd need the whole film of the trip in real time, including the unbearable heat and the music. We'd have to replay it all from end to end in a darkened room, rediscover the magic of the freeways and the distance and the ice-cold alcohol in the desert and the speed and live it all again on the video at home in real time. . . . The unfolding of the desert is infinitely close to the timelessness of film.[54]

His evocations of cinema come repeatedly. "The desert you pass through," he writes, "is like the set of a Western."[55] But it is not just the desert that is a film. Writing about Hollywood, he insists that cinema resides not in the sound stages but "all around you outside, all over the city, that marvelous, continuous performance of films and scenarios" for "[i]n America cinema is true because it is the whole of space . . . life is cinema."[56] This omnipresence of cinema is central to Baudrillard's deserts, for the entirety of America for him is a desert, both a real, physical desert and (perhaps at the same time) a metaphorical one, so that the viewer is no more in the presence of the essence of America than when standing before an empty, hallucinatory desert. Yet at the same time the scene is a movie: everything is a movie, and so in the end Baudrillard's vision erases the eco-reality as an entity separate from the human: for it is *all*, in fact, a creation of us. America's unique physical, ecological *reality* dissolves into the *reel*.

MOBILITY AND ENDLESS MOVEMENT IN *AMERICA DESERTA*[57]

Butor called his novel of America *Mobile*, happily the same in French and English. Indeed, a leitmotif of all the writers I am discussing is *mobility*, the *movement through space in the limitless American desert*. For Baudrillard, who ploughs "the tyre tracks of Jack Kerouac," it is America's "desert speed" that he seeks, because "[s]peed is simply the rite that initiates us into emptiness."[58] In several scenes in *Valley of Love*, the camera looks out from the back seat of Gérard and Isabelle's car toward an endless highway with desert shrubs and gravel spreading deep into a horizon framed by desert mountains. The desert both enables and compels movement.

Indeed, and simply put, every one of the works treated here is structured as a classic American road trip. Isabelle arrives from France at Furnace Creek where Gérard meets her in a big rented SUV; they drive the desert, argue, keep silent, sweat, Gérard stops to pee. Beauvoir takes bus or car from Los Angeles to Death Valley to Las Vegas to Santa Fe, over long western highways; there is nothing in her peregrinations in New York City or the South to match the rhythm of the road. Lyotard's most explicit mention of the desert involves the horizon seen from the highway.[59]

The road trip calls up a troubling ecocritical contradiction, for the *viewer* in the automobile is connected to the landscape primarily by *the gaze*: the natural world of rocks, cacti, gravel, mesquite, pock-marked hills, exists only through the mediation of the window and, perhaps, the vibration of the tires on pavement, gravel, brush. Desert silence, Baudrillard avers, is a "product of the gaze that stares out and finds nothing to reflect it."[60] For Lyotard's alter ego Vachez, one of the elements "moving softly" against each other in his experience of the Pacific wall is "the desert horizons enjambed along long, sinusoidal highways."[61] Here, perhaps, is where the point of his equivalence between the desert and Las Vegas becomes clear: just as Las Vegas is a largely mediated, air-conditioned environment, seemingly cut off from the burning desert in which it sits, so the passenger in the SUV is cut off from desert heat, desert smells, in the sealed-up automobile. Even empty hotels in the midst of the desert have their air-conditioners whirring away.[62] Perhaps this is why Isabelle resists air-conditioning in her sweltering resort room—perhaps she wants the immediacy of sensual contact with the desert that A/C denies. Berger, who of all our French visitors figures himself closest to a presumptively "unmediated" experience of the desert, never mentions A/C: his road trips, one imagines, featured an open window. But in fact, *automobility* is central to the desert experience of every one of our French visitors: they interact with the landscape, in whole or in part, through the window of a vehicle.[63]

THE SENSUAL DESERT[64]

"The pure wonder" of the desert, Berger writes near the beginning of his book, "is the feeling of never being seen it gives to each sight of it."[65] For our French visitors, it is sight, the sense of vision, that marks the first and strongest reaction to the desert landscape, as in the role of the gaze just noted. An absence of signs—not road signs but markers in any sense—prevents the voyager from seeing where town ends and desert begins. Berger feels the same when he approaches Monument Valley, where

> El Cápitan . . . commands the valley . . . then an entire avant-garde of stones in the immense plain. The plain lost to view. Punctuated by stunted trees and spiny plants as far as the limits of the space, down on the horizon which seems to defend a formidable empire of clouds, limits that aren't, that never are, of space, but always of the eye which, for a moment, can no longer see (it is too far) and, literally, is extinguished.[66]

But our response to an environment is not captured in the single sense of sight, even if vision seems often to be the dominant mode by which the desert impinges on our consciousness and emotions. Hearing, smell, taste, and touch play their roles too. Berger, for instance, reverts repeatedly in his book to the odors of the desert. During time spent in Diné (Navajo) country, in the vicinity of the Canyon de Chelly, during "a day in silence and the air charged with the odor of pines and cedars" (note too the absence of sound), he comes to "understand the superiority of the discourse of magic (or religion) to the scientific." Later, driving through the desert, he inhales the aromas of "wormwood, juniper, *tumbleweed* . . . mesquite, the chaparral that comprises the bushes and undergrowth, and that odor of sage, of dust and dry grass that is that of the desert. Which is the only odor of the desert, its dry air dissolving everything, except its own." Indeed, the desert confronts Berger with "an air so charged, mingled with odors that we could hardly tell them apart."[67] The desert exercises part of its potency through odors that penetrate and compel responses in the visitor of its own volition, regardless of whether or not the visitor wants to respond.

Since our emotions are embodied, they connect immediately to and mutually affect our sensual experiences. Baudrillard bemoans "the general cryogenization of emotions" he finds in his America.[68] This embodiment of emotion, a topic of great interest both to ecocritics and psychologists, mediated through the senses, accounts in great part for the ways that the natural world affects us as a space of agency independent of ourselves. We can see its effects in the literature I've studied here—the heat and aridity, most obviously, which can shift the emotional setting of a person in the desert, but also the shifting colors of a mesa under the sun, which mesmerize Berger. Early in *Mobile* Butor quotes a guide to the Southwest which asserts that "[d]espite the bigness of the Southwest, little things—sights, sounds, and smells—often create the most lasting impressions." A list that follows cites, among other things:

> —*strings of scarlet chili drying against adobe walls,*
>
> . . . .
>
> —*heady aroma of campfire coffee*
>
> . . . .
>
> —*musty odor of creosote bush after rain*
>
> . . . .
>
> —*juiciness of thick steak broiled over mesquite coals*
>
> . . . .
>
> —*tang of enchiladas smothered in chili sauce*[69]

Odors, tastes, sights—sensual experiences make the most lasting impressions, impressions that embed themselves in the memory and shape emotional responses not only in the presence of the desert, but in its recall. Except for *Valley of Love*, which as a film purports to present an immediate experience to the viewer, secretly shared in real time (of course, a confection), all the works here were composed in retrospection.

All our French visitors attest to the power of the desert to shape their reactions to and memories of it. The desert ecology they encounter works its influence on them, in a fundamentally ecocritical fashion; that is to say, the sensual effusions of the desert do not act simply as neutral presences whose interpretation depends entirely on the activity of the human consciousness they touch. Rather, desert sensuality works its way into the bodies of the visitors and fashions, agentially, the nature of the experience the visitors take away. The sublime reaction to deserts carries the same charge: the experience of sublimity acts directly on our emotional machinery, bypassing our consciousness and reasoning faculties, to reframe the way we feel about the landscape before us. Here both ecocriticism and the new materialism can clarify the complex interaction of the human and the desert world. Because deserts are so stark, so different from built and humid eastern—and indeed, France's—environments, these effects become especially sharp and obvious. This is one of the ways that the study of deserts and the literature associated with them contributes to expanding, nuancing, and reinforcing the arguments of new materialism and ecocriticism—a project that, as we have seen in this chapter, gains additional power when seen through the eyes of Europeans for whom the American deserts are a true *terra incognita*.

FRENCH LITERATURE, AMERICAN LITERATURE?

What, many readers may have been wondering, is an essay about French writers doing in a collection of studies of *American* literature and *American* experience dealing with the arid West? That the southwestern American deserts exercised an alchemical fascination on Berger and his compatriots goes without saying; the lenses through which they regarded—and the noses through which they smelled, the ears by which they heard, the fingers under which they palpated—the sensual effusions of the desert, so different from temperate and wet France, were borrowed from sources as different as American films and art, the Bible (as so many of our desert tropes), and nineteenth-century French experiences in the Sahara. Be that as it may, however, these writers wrote in French, for (initially) a French audience—in what sense might their work deserve to be seen in the company of American literature?

It seems to me that several angles of vision can shift our optics to bring Beauvoir, Berger, and others into the scope of a wider "American" literature. The long-standing paradigm under which only works written in English could count has been undermined, especially by scholars of western and southwestern literature, by the insistence that Latin@ and Chican@ writers, including those writing in Spanish, deserve consideration as contributors to American literature. Code-switching in these literatures has, for example, attracted attention, and in a recent study Rosina Lozano has offered a powerful case for regarding Spanish as a language native to the United States.[70] Many Latin@ and Chican@ American writers like Gloria Anzaldúa, Sandra Cisneros, Gustavo Pérez Firmat, and Rudolfo Anaya (to name just a few) have written in Spanish or incorporate Spanish into predominately English-language literature. It would seem terribly arbitrary to embrace their English-language work as "American literature" while exiling their Spanish-language writings into some other, nebulous category. While the embrace has yet to be fully consummated, there have been calls to see Spanish-language literature produced in and about the Sonoran and Chihuahuan Deserts as part and parcel of the literary production of the great arid Southwest—or Northwest, seen from the south side.[71] The hardening of the border, an effort by the metropoles (especially the one in Washington, DC) to demarcate the line between them and us as hard, fast, and impenetrable, is likewise a relatively recent phenomenon; much fiction of an earlier date presupposed the porosity, or even nonexistence, of a separation.[72]

More broadly, the study of American culture has been undergoing a "transnational turn" neatly encapsulated in Shelley Fisher Fishkin's 2004 address to the American Studies Association. Likewise, in the introduction to *Shades of the Planet* (2007), a collection of essays treating American literature as world literature, Wai Chee Dimock undermines the "exceptionalism" of American literature and calls for seeing it in a global context.[73] The turn has also been reflected in new academic outlets, like the *Journal of Transnational American Studies*, founded to provide a forum for scholarship seeking precisely to burst the "American" bounds of American studies. In a special forum in volume 8 (2017), the journal explored "*La Florida française*: Florida, France, and the Francophone world," with articles that recovered not only the long-gone sixteenth-century French colony in Florida but ways that a French past intertwines with a French present in culture, history, and literature.[74]

Perhaps most important, however, is the simple fact that the construction of America has never been a project belonging exclusively to Americans. As Susan Weiner has observed, writing of Baudrillard's *America*, it is precisely because France and America were "two cultures . . . each closed systems that happened to be uncanny inversions of each other" that French observers could see and explicate America's practical character with a clarity denied to Americans themselves.[75] Alexis de Tocqueville remains the touchstone: his account of his visit to the United States in its toddlerhood has achieved classic status as one of the best analyses of what it means to be an American.[76] If some, perhaps much, of his discussion is now superannuated, as some claim, to read him even today is often to stare into a mirror, and he casts a deep shadow over even the most recent French explications of America—in both Lévy and Baudrillard.[77] Obviously, Tocqueville never visited the desert Southwest, which was still in Mexican hands in 1831—New Orleans was as far west as he got—but his analysis of the American character as shaped by democratic egalitarianism resonates with the myth of the western hero. In Max Lerner's formulation: "Every man becomes his own center of intellectual and moral authority. He is constantly in motion, so that there is no chance for him to come under the sway of traditions."[78]

Here is the very portrait of the stereotypical independent, libertarian westerner, indeed Elmer Kelton's Charlie Flagg or Owen Wister's Virginian.[79] Tocqueville also saw clearly the tensions between this independence and egalitarianism which generated loneliness and alienation (not of course his word), "how socially disintegrating the passion for autonomy can be"[80]—precisely the bind Flagg finds himself in as his world falls apart. Who would say to anyone hoping to understand ourselves that she should not read Tocqueville just because he wrote in French for the French? And why should we not embrace *Democracy in America* as a foundational component of American literature?

Interwoven with the tension between individualism and egalitarianism in Tocqueville's reading of America is also the notion of American exceptionalism—our long-standing celebration of ourselves and our country as somehow exempt from the old rules that directed the course of European history. A powerful strain in recent ecocritical study, indeed in American studies more generally, has been to challenge this motif, this "prison of American exceptionalism."[81] The roots and branches of this exceptionalism are many and complex, but when you dig down, almost all lead to or intersect with Tocqueville, who argued more cogently and at greater length than any other observer of the early American scene that the United States was not like any country in Europe: it was truly something new under the sun—an exception.

And while this leitmotif was taken up with delight by many later American commentators, whether they knew their Tocqueville or not, it was also in France that the conviction of American exceptionalism became just as thoroughly embedded. Often enough, especially in the anti-American sentiment in leftist French circles after World War II, it could be deployed not to praise but to damn America: an exceptionalism made up of power without morality, consumerism, shallowness, anti-intellectualism; these were themes one could excavate out of Tocqueville too, whose very first sentence in *Democracy in America* asserts that no country practices philosophy less than the United States. But no matter which way you go, the base of the case remains an assertion of exceptionalism.[82]

Where, then, does this leave the ecocritic? I hope to have shown that an ecocritical reading of Beauvoir, Butor, Lyotard, Baudrillard, Berger, and *Valley of Love* uncovers fundamental, shared ways that the southwestern deserts affected these French visitors. In turn, an ecocritical reading of their impressions of the desert unveils the agency, the activity, and the vibrancy the desert exerted on them, to help concoct the emotional and memory responses that shaped their writings about the desert, a matter to which I return in chapter 10. Finally, inasmuch as the American landscape has been viewed by many commentators as central to the articulation of an American character, often situated in a site of exceptionalism, we can see the ways that French visitors, imbued with their Tocqueville and their own intellectualized—and Orientalized—traditions of seeing the colonial Sahara, contributed to and in some manner sharpened the project of mythologizing an American identity.

PART 2

THE DESERT
GENDERED AND
EROTIC

CHAPTER 4

MAKING THE DESERT AMERICAN*

[T]HE LANDSCAPE DOES NOT EXIST OUTSIDE THE CULTURALLY TRAINED
MIND AND IMAGINATION OF THE OBSERVER. . . . THE HISTORICAL EVO-
LUTION OF WESTERN LANDSCAPE PERCEPTION AND REPRESENTATION
DEMONSTRATES THAT THE SUBJECTIVE PROCESS INVOLVED IN MEN-
TALLY ORGANIZING OUR BIOCHEMICAL VISION INTO COHERENT AES-
THETIC IMAGES ARE IN THEMSELVES RESULTS OF SOCIOCULTURAL
DEVELOPMENTS.[1]

Landscapes, as Heike Schaefer states clearly, do not simply exist; they arise from a process of cultural construction in which an observer's personal encounters are blended,
molded, and shaped by a congeries of past experiences, the history embedded in the
landscape, and a collection of cultural and social tropes about the land. The feelings a landscape evokes—love, revulsion, indifference—are, in part, the creation of this process. In their
encounter with the New World, Europeans passed through a dizzying series of sometimes
contradictory reactions to the land before them, all freighted with long familiarity with both
the landforms and the metaphorical, even mythical, understandings of that land. To the
Atlantic coast of what would later be the United States they applied especially metaphors
of a gendered landscape, a female land ripe and ready, needing only men to bring it to its
useful fertility, like a virgin needing only penetration to be delivered to her proper end.
This way of understanding the landscape worked well until the Europeans, pushing west,
passed into space more and more arid, until at last they encountered the desert Southwest.
There the tender, female gendering of space, which had defined much of their emotional
interaction with the young United States, collapsed. Groping for other metaphors, many
travelers reached into the Bible, which offered a rich series of tropes to account for a
landscape decidedly unfeminine. In a sense, their encounter with the desert became an
encounter not with a physical but an imaginary landscape—a landscape at violent odds
with the "America" they had left. But, starting around the mid-1880s, and gathering pace
thereafter, some visionaries began to imagine ways to transform that desert into a landscape
more in line with the female East—a landscape not of travail, harshness, danger, and death,
but a landscape burgeoning with farms, sweet with water, obedient to man and plough.
It is a small corner of this complex historical and cultural process that I would like to
explore here, first in more general terms and then by focusing on one desert-set novel that

* Published in a very different version in *Cultural History* 2 (2013) 165–81, a revised version of the paper read at
the conference "Envisioning Landscapes: Adaption and Renewal," at the University of Liverpool, June 22, 2012.

encapsulates the themes.

"THE LAND AS WOMAN"[2]

From the first, Europeans arriving in the New World reached for metaphors of sexuality and womanhood to limn the landscape. Christopher Columbus declared it "a land to be desired, and seen, it is never to be left." For Sir Walter Raleigh in 1595, Guiana was "a countrey that hath yet her maydenhead." In 1609, Robert Johnson declared himself "ravisht with the . . . pleasant land," adorned with "valleyes and plaines streaming with sweete Springs, like veynes in a naturall bodie" and "hills and mountaines making a sensible proffer of hidden treasure, neuer yet searched." For Robert Mountgomry just over a century later, America presented a *Paradise* with all her Virgin Beauties." Thomas Morton apostrophized New England in 1632 as "Like a faire virgin, longing to be sped / And meete her lover in a Nuptiall bed." In 1705 Robert Beverley, describing the colony of Virginia, exclaimed of denizens' impressions, "Here all their senses are entertain'd with an endless Succession of Native Pleasures. Their eyes are ravished with the Beauties of naked Nature."[3] Indeed, the new American land seemed so bountiful, so brimming with good things, that some believed God had purposefully withheld it from the Europeans till they were spiritually ready; Loren Baritz remarked of this Promised Land that "God had hidden the New World until men were equal to its promise." Because the Pilgrims "saw themselves as the anti-type of the Israelites, the Promised Land of the Exodus becomes the American wilderness itself, transformed as it will be, into the Kingdom of God . . "[4] and as F. Scott Fitzgerald wrote, Americans see their land as the "fresh, green breast of the new world."[5] Centuries before, but in the midst of the passionate embrace of this New World, John Donne deployed the metaphor to charged erotic effect in "To His Mistress Going to Bed":

> License my roving hands, and let them go
> Before, behind, between, above, below.
> O my America, my new-found-land!
> My kingdom, safeliest when with one man manned,
> My mine of precious stones, my empery,
> How blest am I in this discovering thee!

Or, as Ralph Waldo Emerson insists in his essay "Nature," the natural world—which he always apostrophizes with the feminine pronoun, "she" or "her"—exists precisely to lay before *man* a vision of beauty designed to refresh and satisfy. "Does not the New World," he remarks, "clothe his form with her palm-groves and savannahs as fit drapery? Ever does natural beauty steal in like air, and envelope great actions."[6]

And to cite just one more example, the Acoma poet Simon Ortiz compares a sleeping woman—surely his sex partner, dozing after intercourse—to the land:

> I see the gentle move [*sic*]
> ment of your valleys,
> the undulations of slow turnings.

Opening my eyes,
there is a soft dark
and beautiful butte
moving up and down
as you breathe.[7]

It's not hard to see in her "valleys" the curves of her hips and in the "beautiful butte" her breasts. The living woman is the living land; the imagery plays into the long-standing identification of the land, and more broadly, Nature, with woman.[8]

From Robert Johnson to Jay Gatsby and Simon Ortiz, Americans repeat "what is probably America's oldest and most cherished fantasy: a daily reality of harmony between man and nature based on an experience of the land as essentially feminine—that is, not simply the land as mother, but the land as woman, the total female principle of gratification." So Annette Kolodny in her classic study, *The Lay of the Land*.[9] This fantasy or trope or metaphor served to mediate, consciously or unconsciously, the relationship of Americans to their landscape in a manner deeply satisfying to an agrarian, expansionist society. The passive, female land required the vigorous action of the male principle, Thomas Jefferson's yeoman, to bring her to productive fertility; the unexplored landscapes of the West were virginal territories, waiting for those vigorous men to discover, domesticate, and fructify them. As Kolodny emphasizes, the trope carried its contradictions, not least that by seeing the land as all women, both virgin and mother, it ran the risk of incest. But in various ways, Americans negotiated these challenges, and altogether found the trope a compelling and satisfying means of understanding the landscapes of the new American world.

THE DESERT AS A BIBLICAL LANDSCAPE

Americans first encountered a landscape reluctant to conform to the figure of a woman when the federal government dispatched a series of expeditions to explore the vast new territory that had come into American possession with the Louisiana Purchase of 1803. A key line emerged at the 100th (or, according to some, 99th) meridian, west of which rainfall dropped below the minimum required for dry agriculture. Two separate parties under Zebulon Pike and Stephen Long passed within a few years of each other through the increasingly dry plains east of the Rocky Mountains and south of the Missouri River (more famously tracked by Meriwether Lewis and William Clark); horrified, they declared the Plains "the Great American Desert" and predicted they would remain forever uninhabited.[10] But Americans' first widespread experience of real desert came with the Gold Rush of 1849–1850. Of the thousands of hopefuls who struggled through the Great Basin Desert, the Mojave Desert, the Sonoran Desert, and the Colorado Desert, the clearest and most thorough account came in the memoir of William Manly. Guide to the Bennett-Arcane party who got trapped in Death Valley (Fig. 4-1), Manly and a companion found a way out of the desert to the California coast, collected supplies, returned to their charges, and led them to safety. Reflecting, forty-five years later, on his final escape in March 1850, Manly expostulated:

Figure 4-1: Bennett-Arcane Camp, Death Valley.

> We were out of the dreadful sands and shadows of Death Valley, its exhausting phantoms, its salty columns bitter lakes and wild, dreary sunken desolation. If the waves of the sea could flow in and cover its barren nakedness, as we now know they might if a few sandy barriers were swept away, it would be indeed, a blessing, for in it there is naught of good, comfort, or satisfaction, but ever in the minds of those who braved its heat and sands, a thought of a horrid Charnel house, a corner of the earth so dreary that it requires an exercise of the strongest faith to believe that the great Creator ever smiled upon it as a portion of his work and pronounced it "Very good."

It would be hard to find a franker expression of the desert wasteland trope, and the same idea recurs throughout Manly's reminiscences.[11]

This trope of desert as wasteland comes straight from the Bible, which provided it and a second, complementary, way of seeing the desert. The second trope represents the desert as a realm of testing: a barren, hostile space, given over by God to Satan, where faith can be steeled. The archetype of this trope occurs in the story of the Israelites' forty years' wandering in the Sinai desert—only after enduring thirst, heat, emptiness, and the constant temptation to reject God may they finally pass into the Promised Land of milk and honey. The appeal of this trope to California immigrants was irresistible; just like "the Israelites while marching to the land of Canaan," they too had to struggle through an unforgiving desert wilderness to earn a place in the Promised Land of, first, abundant gold. It is quite clearly one of Manly's chief themes that the only possible purpose of this "purposeless desolation"[12] is as a test of those virtues and moral strength. The Bible was the most common book the forty-niners carried on their trek, and some forty-niners expressed explicitly how its desert tropes provided a way to understand the landscape they experienced.[13]

These tropes that governed the seeing of the desert landscape in the mid-nineteenth century stood in apparently irremediable contradiction to the feminine landscape that sustained American expansionism farther east. This was a wholly masculinized landscape, uncompromising, harsh, dry, unfeeling. It was, simply, un-American—neither mother nor lover. And aside from Death Valley, the most hostile southwestern desert straddled the Colorado River, in southwestern Arizona and southeastern California (Fig. 4-2). Nineteenth-century travelers were largely unanimous in their assessment of the Colorado Desert as "a desolate, barren

Figure 4-2: Colorado Desert.

waste, which can never be rendered useful to man or beast, save for a public highway."[14] So Frederick Law Olmstead, designer of Central Park, who passed through the desert in the 1850s. Twenty years later James Fowler Rusling echoed and amplified Olmstead's views:

> Here we struck the southern California or great Colorado Desert . . . we might as well have been adrift on the Great Sahara itself. . . . As we approached the Desert . . . the very genius of desolation seemed to brood over the landscape. This was now the Colorado or Yuma Desert in earnest, without bird, or beast, or bush, or sign of life anywhere—nothing, in fact, but barrenness and desolation.[15]

In 1877, Josephine Clifford wryly observed that the Colorado Desert belonged to the state of California, "though why," she smirked, "California should feel any desire to claim the wilderness of sand and rattlesnakes lying between Vallecito Mountain and Fort Yuma, I cannot see." Harold Bell, early resident of Los Angeles, declared it a "basin of burning sand" fashioned when "nature was certainly in a very bad frame of mind . . ." and quoted a poem by Albert Fennel Kercheval (1829–1893) describing travelers' first glimpse of the Colorado Desert from the eastern bank of the Colorado River:

> On the river's farther shore,
> Desolation spread before,

There the desert's fiery breath,
Furnace-fanned and fraught with death,
Ever casts its withering spell,
Dark as sin and hot as hell.[16]

CHALLENGES OF THE ARID WEST TRANSFORMED

The nineteenth century did see some efforts to reconfigure the arid West in ways that would permit it to be seen as traditionally feminine. John Wesley Powell gained his fame as the first Anglo known to have passed safely through the great canyons of the Colorado River, and this achievement led eventually to his appointment as the second director of the United States Geological Service, which he had conceived. In 1878 Powell presented recommendations on the settlement of the West. Insisting that aridity obviated the centuriated principles of land distribution that had governed the Northwest Territories, Powell urged instead the division of the West into geographically determined hydrological basins, properly surveyed to determine their carrying capacity, and limited in the numbers of settlers allowed. Powell saw in careful science and irrigation the only road toward reaping fertility and agricultural wealth from the West, but in the scrim of politics his proposals were rejected.[17]

But another, far more powerful strain of change had been setting the stage for undermining the biblical view of the southwestern American deserts—a revolution in the way travelers experienced the desert landscape.[18] By 1881, the Southern Pacific Railroad—the "octopus" of Frank Norris's muckraking novel—had pushed track along right-of-way secured originally by the Texas and Pacific Railway from San Diego, California, through the Colorado Desert and over the Colorado River to Yuma, Arizona, across the dreaded Forty Mile Desert to Phoenix, south to Tucson, through the New Mexico–Arizona borderlands once the domain of the Chiricahua Apache to Deming, New Mexico (Fig. 4-3). Train travel delivered comfort and ease, promoted relentlessly in the travel literature the railroads distributed. The *Pacific Tourist*, the travel guide issued in 1881 by the Union and Central Pacific Railroads for passengers bound to San Francisco, touted the revolutionary experience of passing by train through the Great Basin Desert of Nevada, in explicit contrast to forty-niners like Manly and his party: at Ogden, Utah, passengers traveling west "board a train of silver palace cars, in the evening . . . and will soon be whirling away across the Great American Desert." Starting at Ombey, Utah,

> [f]rom the frequent views of the Great American Desert which the traveler can obtain while passing over this portion of the road, he can form some idea of its utter barrenness and desolation, and the great sufferings of those who have attempted to cross it without adequate preparation, and the consequent burning thirst they and their animals have endured."

(Just a few years before, one of the engineers who mapped out the route for the Central Pacific through the Great Basin had condemned the landscape as "this infernal region of Salt & desolation.") The Atkinson, Topeka and Santa Fe Railway, the Southern Pacific's chief competitor on the southern transcontinental route, contracted with Fred Harvey to plant luxurious way

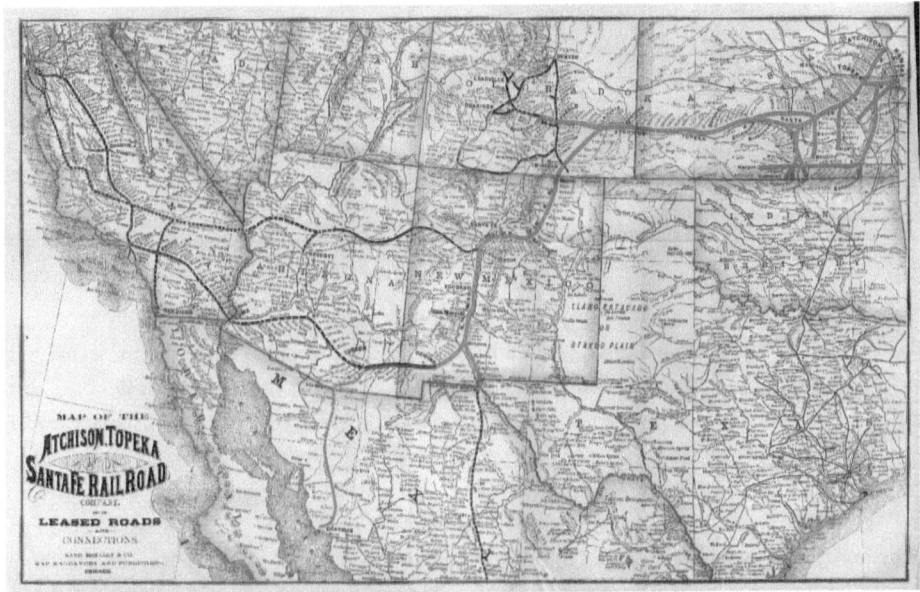

Figure 4-3: Atchison, Topeka and Santa Fe Railroad Line, 1891. (After Rand McNally.)

Figure 4-4: Kelso Station.

Figure 4-5: Lavender Pit.

stations with quality restaurants, ice cream, accommodations, and good-looking waitresses whose virtue was guaranteed by the contracts they signed, in godforsaken patches of desert wilderness. The Southern Pacific likewise built happy oases for their employees in the midst of desert wilderness, like the stop at Kelso, in the Mojave, which has recently been lovingly restored (Fig. 4-4). No one would be dying of thirst and heat exhaustion here.[19]

Through-tracks like the Southern Pacific tell only part of the railroad tale. Southern Arizona and northern Sonora, Mexico, saw a boom in railroad construction in the same period; railroad ties represented new commercial and social opportunities on the border-lands, and completion of new lines occasioned international celebrations.[20] This building boom was driven by another major change in the desert landscape—the intrusion of masses of Eastern and British capital into the borderlands to exploit the copper boom. Demand for copper had risen radically with Thomas Edison's decision to use it for electric transmission, and as the electrification of Eastern cities proceeded apace, the traditional American sup-plies from Upper Peninsula Michigan proved wanting. The huge ore bodies in Southern Arizona and northern Sonora drew industrial-scale mining, employing hundreds of workers and stimulating the construction of railroads and a supporting infrastructure, as in Bisbee, Arizona (Fig. 4-5).[21]

Finally, the 1880s had seen the elimination of a human threat—Native American, and especially Apache, resistance to ever-tighter government control of the land and promotion of Anglo in-migration. This desert danger was encapsulated in the lurid tale, amplified in the telling, of the 1851 slaughter of the Oatman family in the Sonoran Desert of Arizona, the capture of two young girls, and their sale into "sexual slavery" by the Indians (but the older daughter, Olive, married a Mohave and had children; she resisted "rescue" and by all accounts lived an unhappy life in Anglo society). The bloody wars of the 1870s, which had made the desert frontier a terrifying place for so many Anglos, ended with the surrender of Cochise in 1872 and the capture of Geronimo in 1886. By the time of the copper boom, Cochise was dead and Geronimo was living in Oklahoma, farming and hawking Apache wares to tourists.[22] By 1900, not only was the desert no longer a landscape of privation and testing, a space through which one suffered to prove, like Manly, one's worthiness to enter the Promised Land, it was rather a couple days' worth of curious landforms, regarded from the comfort of a club car, and, what's more, a space where a person could get rich prying the goods out of Mother Earth. The desert had lost its dangerousness.[23] The possibility might

Figure 4-6: Colorado River Breakthrough. (Used with permission of the Imperial Irrigation District.)

now open up for the transformation of the American imaginary of the southwestern deserts from a masculine—and so un-American—landscape into one that could be properly feminized. The railroad, the mining boom, safe, swift travel, and the elimination of the Native American challenge to government power were preconditions necessary, but not sufficient, to effect this change. For that, one final, transformative act was needed: irrigation, which alone could "make the desert bloom."

Meanwhile, it had not escaped the notice of perspicacious travelers that the basin of the Colorado Desert lay below the level of the river (and indeed it was later realized that the basin was, at its low point, well over two hundred feet below sea level).[24] Various schemes were floated to turn the river water west into the desert, to recreate a tropical paradise some argued had flourished there in the distant past. These plans, none of which even came close to fruition, drew inspiration from a general movement in the arid West to reclaim desert landscapes by irrigation, championed notably by William Ellsworth Smythe, and which issued, eventually, in the creation by the federal government of what became the Irrigation and Reclamation Service. Smythe and his acolytes insisted that—as the Mormon efforts in Utah were said to prove—the desert lacked for a fertility to match the Cis-Mississippi United States only water: that, in other words, the desert could be made to disappear under a bursting world of happy and prosperous agriculture.[25]

And in fact this vision was finally applied to the Colorado Desert. I cannot here trace the long and rather sordid process, which involved land fraud, violation of Mexican sovereignty, battles between land developers and the Southern Pacific Railroad, and underfunded, poorly designed water diversion schemes, that issued in the tremendous flood in 1905–1906 by which the present-day Salton Sea was created (Fig. 4-6 and 4-7).[26] But by 1910 what had been the heart of the Colorado Desert, with 200,000 acres under irrigation, was well on its way to being transformed into the agricultural paradise that was renamed the Imperial Valley. This transformation, I suggest, made possible a reconceptualization of some desert spaces under the feminine image of the American landscape—a domestication, a synchronization

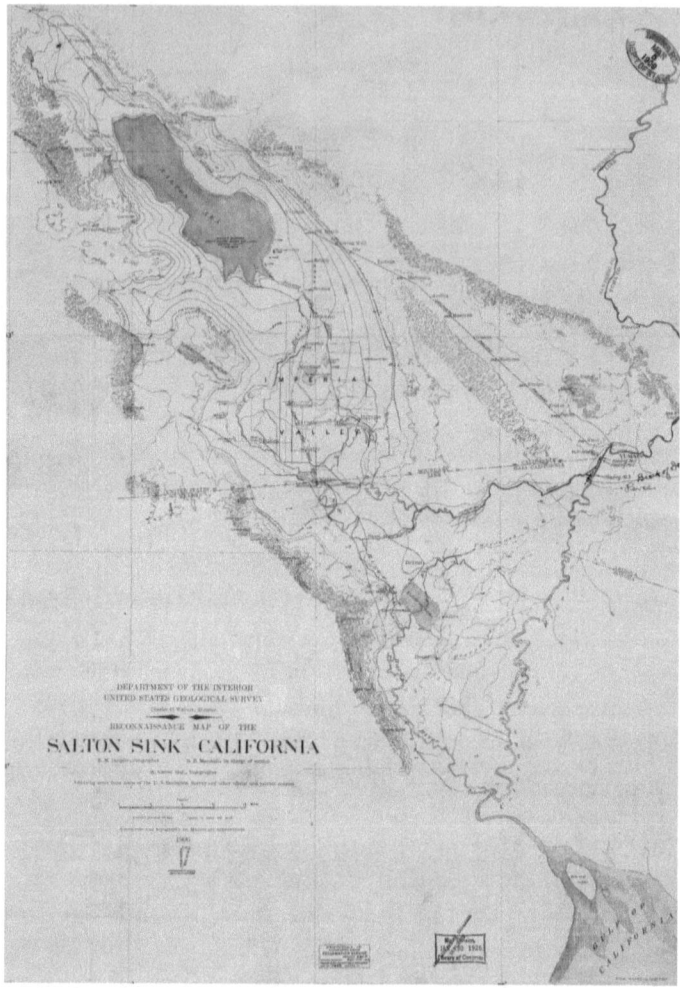

Figure 4-7: USGS Map of the Salton Sink, 1905.

of what had been a wasteland to a happier, more "appropriate" relation between Americans and this miscast land.

THE AESTHETIC TURN

Alongside the transformations just surveyed, which set the stage for a reconceptualization of deserts—or at least some parts of some deserts—another change operated, which also effected new modes of looking at desert landscapes. I've explored this change in chapter 1, but it's worth revisiting here. In 1897 John C. Van Dyke, scion of a well-to-do family from Brunswick, New Jersey, professor of art history at Rutgers University, popular lecturer, and confidential advisor to Andrew Carnegie, abruptly resigned his academic posts and club memberships to head out west, to the desert. He moved in with his brother in Daggett, California. Four years later he published a series of essays about his desert experiences under the title *The Desert: Further Studies in Natural Appearances*.[27] As we saw in chapter 1, unlike most of his American contemporaries, who "regard a desert as a thing to be avoided if possible and to be got through, if needs be, with all expedition,"[28] Van Dyke championed a new aesthetic of the desert that emphasized its colors, light, beauty, and function as the breathing spaces of the world. He provoked a shift in attitude toward the desert away from the wasteland narrative that had prevailed.[29] The persisting impact of Van Dyke's vision can be seen in a passage from Frederick Turner's epic poem *Genesis*, about the terraforming of Mars, published in 1988. The desert redeemed is colored in:

> this new terrain of the northern plains
> Where gently undulating country glows
> With the soft fire of a thousand pigments.
> Here the next stages of ecogenesis
> Has reached its climax in a magic carpet
> Of golden furs and powdery crimsons,
> Spore-yellows, saturated browns and blues,
> Purples shot with greens, and fleshy pinks,
> Open mild glitterings of slimes and foams.[30]

Van Dyke's alternative view, which purported to take the desert on its own terms, did not, however, modify the gender of the desert—his desert remains relentlessly male: dangerous, powerful, uncompromising, stark, austere. Indeed, it required a fully masculine sensibility, a Van Dyke or a Theodore Roosevelt, to appreciate its aesthetics on its own terms. These two new desert sensibilities, the female version seeing the desert as space just awaiting men to bring it to its natural but stymied fruition, and the male version demanding we accept and appreciate it as it is, passed into the twentieth and twenty-first centuries as two models for Americanizing the desert. But these models, though gendered opposite, need not be wholly contradictory. Van Dyke's encomia of the desert insisted on the landscape's *beauty*: the play of colors, the subtlety of its appearance, its changeability as the light passes from dawn through noon to dusk, the cool nights adorned with brilliant stars and glowing moon. Van Dyke's descriptions of the desert refute the wasteland narrative not by proclaiming the desert as useful—which, in the end, is the central motif of feminized redemption—but as a good in and of itself. The good professor was, in fact, a fraud, his desert exploits invented or stolen from his brother's friends, and his aesthetics not born of a desert experience but borrowed from the European Art for Art's Sake movement, of which he was one of the principal champions in the United States. A positive aesthetic of the desert had been worked out decades earlier by European artists and explorers, especially from France, in the Sahara. But Van Dyke's remarks in his extremely popular and well-received book worked headily on his American readers, who knew nothing of either his fraudulence or the disreputable drivers that sent him west.[31]

These streams of desert revisionism, the transformation to the feminine of a formerly harsh, masculine landscape, and its aestheticization, which also contributed to the project

Figure 4-8: Harold Bell Wright at work, probably in his outdoor writing workshop at Quiet Hills Farm near Escondido, California. (Used with permission of the Imperial County Historical Society Pioneers' Museum.)

of feminization, come together neatly in *The Winning of Barbara Worth*, a novel published in 1911 by Harold Bell Wright, who lived part of his life in the Imperial Valley (Fig. 4-8). To this I now turn.

THE DESERT MADE WOMAN

> To look at Barbara Worth was a pleasure;
> to be near her was a delight.[32]

Wright's *The Winning of Barbara Worth* presents a complete account of the conversion of the potentially female desert space into woman—thus creating a landscape that can be treated as fully American within the context of the attitudes I have explored, a landscape that can be tamed, fructified, and farmed.[33] Before the coming of Barbara, Wright's Colorado Desert displays all the characteristics of unredeemed wasteland. It is "a dreadful land where the thirsty atmosphere is charged with the awful silence of uncounted ages," distinguished by "only a rude trail—two hundred and more hard and lonely miles of it—the only mark of man in all that desolate waste and itself marked every mile by the graves of men and by the bleached bones of their cattle."[34] Men see it as "the divil's own land," a "land of lean want, of gray death, of gaunt hunger, and torturing thirst."[35] This is the very opposite of the nurturing mother or fecund virgin Americans had been accustomed to see in the Cis-Mississippi landscape. Here again is that masculinized, biblical wasteland, the desert trope that had dominated American understanding of its landscape west of the 100th meridian, and particularly of the great southwestern deserts, as we have seen.

Figure 4-9: Algodones Dunes.

With the coming of Barbara, the reading changes. She is, as Wright makes abundantly clear, identified with the desert. Jefferson Worth and his party find her in the midst of the Algodones Dunes (Fig. 4-9) after a dreadful sandstorm; she is the sole survivor of a pioneer family caught in the storm. She is miraculously completely unhurt. Worth finds her when her cries for water and "Mama!" cancel out the howls of coyotes, "the triumphant cry of the Desert itself."[36] When next we meet Barbara, she's a grown young woman, just returned to town after a ride in the desert:

> As she stood now on the sidewalk laughing and chatting with a group of friends . . . her beautiful figure lost none of the compelling charm that made her, on horseback, so good to look at. Every movement and every gesture expressed perfect health. The firm flesh of her rounded cheeks and full throat was warmly browned and glowing with the abundance of red blood in her veins. Though framed in a mass of waving brown hair under a wide sombrero, her features were not pretty. . . . But something looked out of her brown eyes and made itself felt in every poise [*sic*] and movement that forced one to forget to be critical. It was the wholesome, challenging lure of unmarried womanhood.[37]

This is practically the very model of the female landscape, ripe and ready to be ploughed. That Barbara is not pretty follows, I would suggest, from her relation with the desert—it too is not "pretty" in any conventional or recognizable sense (as Van Dyke himself admitted);

but, as Wright is at pains here to emphasize, while her face may not be pretty, her *body* is compellingly beautiful—the word "figure" draws attention to her shape and curves, evokes images of ample breasts and full wide hips.[38]

Wright lards *The Winning of Barbara Worth* with plenty of transparent allusions to her identification with the desert. One of her girlfriends remarks, "Could anything on earth induce you to give up your horse and your desert, Barbara?" When Barbara goes riding in the desert, its entire physiognomy is transformed in her eyes. Before her the "King's Basin [Wright's name for what became the Imperial Valley] lay, a magic, constantly changing ocean of soft colors . . . ahead were the hills, brown and tawny . . . the dry air was invigorating like wine and came to her rich with the smell of the sun-burned, wind-swept plains." Adjectives that before would have evoked desert desolation—"sun-burned, wind-swept"—transmogrify into charms. Barbara herself "breathed deeply. Her cheeks glowed—her eyes shone." Just in case a sliver of doubt should persist in the mind of the obtuse reader, Wright takes no chance of being misunderstood:

> Particularly did the King's Basin Desert interest her. She felt that, in a way, it belonged to her; that she belonged to it. It was *her* Desert. Its desolation she shared; its waiting she understood; something of its mystery colored her life; something within her answered its call. It was her Desert; she feared it; hated it; loved it.

There is no doubt, Barbara is the desert—and Barbara is a nubile, sex-starved young woman. Her fear and love of the desert follow from her own as yet unadmitted sexuality, her need and yearning for a fecundizing partner. And that she is a woman, despite her boyish attire and riding skills, becomes perfectly clear when, while she is out riding in her desert, her horse stumbles and falls, she is struck unconscious, and must wait to be rescued by a young surveyor named Willard who happens to be exploring nearby.[39]

For what, precisely, do Barbara and her desert wait? Her closest relationship throughout the book is not with her adoptive father Jefferson Worth, whom she finds cold and off-putting, but, after her stepmother, rather with a personage Wright calls "the Seer."[40] An engineer who helped build the first railroad across the desert, he enjoyed Barbara's "full confidence and trust." His chief ambition lay in Reclamation—in the great project championed in the late nineteenth and early twentieth centuries by such figures as William Ellsworth Smythe, to turn water in tremendous quantities onto the desert landscapes and make them bloom. Barbara fully identifies with this dream. As she talks with the Seer soon after her rescue, she feels "the very air . . . electric with the coming of a mighty age when the race would direct its strength to the turning of millions of acres of desolate, barren waste into productive farms and beautiful homes for the people." "'I wish,' she said wistfully, 'it was *my* Desert that you and Abe were going to survey.'" The Seer assures her that "'Some day, perhaps, that, too, will come,'" and she answers, "'I know it will.'"[41]

Barbara and the desert wait for precisely the same thing: for a man to come along and, with his active masculinity, fertilize them. Barbara yearns for the desert to be irrigated as a metonym

Figure 4-10: Field Under Cultivation in Imperial Valley, Westmoreland, California.

for her own fervent sexual desires, and, after several hundred more pages of capitalist intrigue, changing of allegiances, pulsing but unexpressed desire, and man-made disaster—when the Colorado River floods out the basin, thanks to greed and ignorance of the ways of the desert[42]—the reclamation project is consummated, farms replace desert desolation, Barbara is delighted, and the man who brings water to her desert in a manner to fructify, not flood, marries her. Barbara and her desert enjoy their consummation virtually simultaneously. In her desert now

> were beautiful scenes of farms with houses and barns and fences and stacks, with cattle and horses in the pastures, and fields of growing grain, the dark green of alfalfa, with threads and lines and spots of water that, under the flood of white light from the wide sky, shone in the distance like gleaming silver.
>
> Gazing on this scene with Willard, Barbara asks, "'You like my Desert?" . . . coming closer to his side—so close that he felt her presence as clearly as he felt the presence of the spirit that lives in the desert itself. And Willard avers, "'Barbara! . . . Don't you *know* that I love you? Don't you know that nothing else matters? Your Desert has taught me many things, dear, but nothing so great as this—that I want you and that nothing else matters. I want you for my wife.'"[43]

With this, and the kiss Wright shies from describing, the desert conundrum is resolved—feminized, the desert can now be a genuine American landscape, brought, by the power of man, to its proper role—and her proper role—as sexual partner and fruitful mother (Fig.

4-10). As Louise Westling says, "at the heart of American pastoral" we find "a sentimental masculine gaze at a feminized landscape and its creatures that masked the conquest and destruction of a 'wild' continent."[44]

But—there is a tension, if not a contradiction, in Barbara's identification with the unredeemed desert. She and it are both "waiting" for, obviously, the man (and men) they need to transform into fertile fields of baby-making and lettuce-growing. But Barbara's own behavior, before Willard comes into her life, is not strictly gendered feminine. She rides alone in "*her* Desert"; she dresses like a cowboy; her girlfriends upbraid her, gently but unmistakably, for her unladylike behavior. The Chicana poet Pat Mora has remarked, "The desert is no lady,"[45] and neither, in many ways, is Barbara. She acts more *as if* gendered male. As we will see in the next chapter, of the multiple genders recognized by the Indigenous peoples who dwelt along the southern stretches of the Colorado River—Mohave and Cocopah, to mention only two—the man-woman is one such gender: the biological woman who identifies as gendered male, taking on the cultural trappings of that gender. (Sexual behavior is more complicated; some persons so gendered married women, some men.) That is to say, aside from the sexual desires her desert arouses—Wright offers no hint they may have been directed to women, not surprisingly, given the era in which he wrote and his own deep conservatism—in Barbara is also at play a more complex erotics expressed not in sexuality but in her gendered behavior. In the following chapter, built around another novel in which sexual and gender expression seem on the surface entirely conventional in a Euro-American sense, I elaborate on these problematics of desert sexuality, gender, and erotics.

CHAPTER 5

DESERT AND CANYON, FRUIT AND GOATS

Sexual Topography in Frances Gillmor, *Fruit Out of Rock**

I n chapter 4 I explored the interplay of sexuality and the reigning Euro-American heteronormative gendering of the desert landscape. Barbara Worth's sexual awakening is
linked to her hopes for the fertilization of "her" desert—a project that begins after the
great Colorado River flood with the domestication of the river's water, channeled through
irrigation ditches to fructify what becomes known as the Imperial Valley. But there is a
strange tension in Barbara's emotional condition, for she responds to an erotics that is,
unexpectedly, bound to the desert, a space rendered in Harold Bell Wright's imaginary as
infertile and anti-female; moreover, Barbara's own gendering is ambiguous. In this chapter
I turn to another novel in which the interplay of sexuality, gendered landscapes, and erotics
plays out under, perhaps, a brighter light. Hopefully an investigation of Frances Gillmor's
only work of fiction and a digression into Indigenous gendering and erotics of the desert will
help elucidate the complexities of this congeries of sexuality, desire, and the desert.[1]

Fruit Out of Rock (Fig. 5-1), published in 1940, tells the story of Amanda Margison,
daughter of a fruit-grower in the Aravaipa Canyon in the high Sonoran Desert northeast of
Tucson, Arizona.[2] Amanda, aged about twenty, must shoulder responsibility for running the
family fruit orchard after her father dies and her brother John, bored with farming, leaves for
a job in a nearby mine and life in an unnamed town. Amanda gets help from her neighbor
Abel Bane, the first Anglo settler in the canyon and its most fervent protector. But a serious
challenge awaits her in the form of Stephen Ross, a young wanderer from New Mexico who
is hired by another neighbor, Davis, to run a herd of goats up on the desert plateau above the
canyon. Amanda falls hard for Stephen and he for her, even though they stand at opposite
poles on the role of the canyon: Amanda, loyal to the orchard and Bane's vision of the canyon

---

* A shorter preliminary version was read at the annual meeting of the Western Literature Association on
November 6, 2012.

Figure 5-1: Cover of *Fruit Out of Rock*.

as a fruitful, peaceful oasis of agriculture, knows that Stephen's commitment to goats would spell the destruction of the canyon should he bring them down to feed. Stephen sees his plans to buy up a farm in the canyon to convert to a goat ranch of his own as the key to economic security and a future with Amanda. The tension between Amanda's love of a person and love of a place forms the central conflict of the novel.[3]

At least from the publication of Annette Kolodny's now classic book *The Lay of the Land* we have understood how Anglo settlers in the United States deployed tropes of gender and sexuality to color the landscape. In the wet, mild territory east of the Mississippi, the land's easy conversion to agricultural fertility reinforced notions of land as female, notions that had a long history in European thinking about nature.[4] All that was required, it seemed, was the addition of activeness and potency attributed to the male to bring the land to its natural fertility. The West, however, and most especially the desert Southwest, posed problems. Its aridity mocked notions of female fertility, long linked to wetness as an essential female trait. Tropes about desert landscapes embedded in European thought from biblical exempla figured deserts as male, not female. Efforts to resolve these contradictions appear in many places in the later nineteenth and twentieth centuries;[5] Gillmor's novel plays with these tropes in a gendered, sexualized, and erotic landscape to mirror the challenges her characters, and especially Amanda, struggle to work through in the course of the book.

The Aravaipa Canyon, where Amanda was born and has lived her whole life, is clearly figured in the book not only as female but explicitly as an analogue for vulva, vagina, cervix, and womb. From a distance it resembles "a shadow slashing the range." The stream at its bottom flows without fail. The "mouth of the canyon" opening onto the plain below recalls a vulva, whose "brown foothills" surrounding the opening conjure up labia. The canyon, unlike the desert plateau above, supports a rich complex of productive fruit orchards. When Amanda leaves the canyon to make runs to town, she passes through this landscape in a state of high sexual excitement. Indeed, the canyon and its features that conjure up female reproduction serve both as the site of and the stimulus to the awakening of Amanda's own sexual needs.[6]

The link between the canyon and Amanda's awakening personal sexuality comes across explicitly in many scenes and remarks throughout the book, but perhaps the most graphic occurs early in the novel and reinforces the female figuring of the canyon landscape. Amanda walks up the canyon, beyond Abel Bane's place and the last irrigation ditch, and passes through a tight constriction—a "narrowed box"—into a grotto where the water runs deep and narrow. There "she began to take off her clothes, letting them drop around her feet. She stood for a moment naked, feeling the sun warm on her body." She lowers herself into the stream.

> Above her head her hands clung to a boulder, holding her against the downstream pull. The water ran cool and strong, down her arms, over her shoulders and breasts, along her half-lifted body, along her thighs and legs. . . . [She emerges from the water and] at the edge of the stream stood for a minute, running her hands over her body, waiting for the sun to dry her. . . . Loose and effortless, she felt her arms and body swing to her stride. . . . She was neither happy nor unhappy; she was hardly thinking; she was walking and alive.[7]

The sensuality of this scene prepares us for the stirring of Amanda's sexuality that is to come. But it also figures the upper canyon as a womb: the constriction is a cervix that opens into a grotto, a uterus, where cottonwoods flourish, fertility is rife, water pools, and Amanda can feel unabashedly female and sexual. Later—but before she and Stephen have sex—she takes him to the grotto, which, he remarks, "you never showed me . . . before!" Amanda, responding, "It's almost a secret cave, isn't it, Stephen?", had kept its existence from him earlier in their relationship but always knew she'd take him there.[8] This foreshadows both their later intercourse and, even more pointedly, Amanda's pregnancy. There could be no clearer marker that the grotto symbolizes the womb.

The desert plateau above, Stephen's realm, figures in contrast as linked to Euro-American heteronormative constructions of "the male," just like Barbara's desert in *The Winning of Barbara Worth*. It bakes under a "hard, hot sky," a "hard sky—under the high, hot morning." It is a "sun-silenced desert," a "brown desert," a "high land of sun and silence," shaped by its aridity. Stephen's endless worry up on the desert plateau is finding enough grazing for his goats; the landscape is stingy with nourishment, and Stephen's panic rises across the course of the book as hoped-for rains fail to arrive. Gillmor drives home repeatedly the contrast between unproductive ("masculine") desert and the fructified canyon; it was Abel Bane's great achievement, as the first Anglo settler, to turn desert to garden, and other characters in the novel, including Amanda's mother, recognize this contrast between sterile desert and fertile canyon.[9] And yet, as we will see, the desert's imaginary is rather more complicated.

There are multiple elements in these descriptions that evoke a long-standing set of tropes in thinking about the desert and the sown that go back at least to the Hebrew Testament. The contrast between the wet and the dry underlies many of these tropes. In Greek medical theory (to cite just one example), women were seen as wet and cool, men as dry and warm. Female wetness, demonstrated unequivocally by their monthly need to discharge excess fluid, was linked to their fertility; by metonymy, this association between the wet and the fertile and the female was easily transferred—as Kolodny has shown—to landscapes. On the macroscopic scale, this distinction appeared in the contrast between the wet, fertile East and the dry, desolate desert West, which I treated in chapter 4. In *Fruit Out of Rock*, the same contrast is drawn in microcosm between the canyon itself and the desert plateau above.

It is also no coincidence that Stephen is a goatherd. Watching a herd of goats caper by, Father Latour in Willa Cather's *Death Comes for the Archbishop* recalls goats as "the symbol of pagan lewdness." In European thinking goats have long represented a randy, sexually indiscriminate hypermasculinity, driven not by the "natural" and proper desire to fertilize and reproduce but the urge to satiate lust. In Greek and Roman mythology, Pan and Silenus (companion to Dionysus) both bear goat features, goat hoofs and goat horns, markers of their dangerous sexuality; both figures are involved in rape and the uncontrolled, passionate, and dangerous sexuality of the drunken orgy. In mediaeval European mythology about witchcraft, women are initiated into the diabolical world through intercourse with a goat. In general, the goat carries a charge associated with the dangerous outside, the dangerous "other": the "beast without" that stands for the "beast within," in David Siddle's memorable formulation.[10]

And indeed it is in Stephen's desert landscape of masculine sexuality that Amanda's own sexual desire grows most urgent, decoupled from any sense of its reproductive function. Visiting Stephen up at his "little cliff house" Amanda yearns for the day she could come up and stay with him, a "happy dream": "'That I'll come to you,' she whispered, 'and never be hungry again.' 'With both of us hungry, Amanda—,'" Stephen whispers, and they come within an ace of having sex; when they stop themselves, Stephen says bluntly, "'You don't know how it is, Amanda. All day alone, herding goats. All night alone'" and she responds, "'I know.'" But up in the desert where the sexual urge bites especially hard, resistance is, in the end, futile, Amanda soon embraces her desire and she and Stephen succumb, his "touch gentle on her hair, on her breast, his body strong against hers."[11] Amanda is a full and willing participant in this act, which she thoroughly enjoys, but her initial eager consent is also colored for her by her rising fear that Stephen plans to bring his voracious and indiscriminate goats down into the canyon in search of food. She knows they will eat everything in sight and with the disappearance of ground cover the canyon will be poised for catastrophic flooding should rains come.

Men in *Fruit Out of Rock* misfire in the face of the female landscape; as the desert, masculine, is sterile, so for Stephen the grotto-womb of the canyon cannot be treated properly.

Stephen sees the canyon as nothing more than an opportunity—first for economic success, by buying up property in the canyon where he could establish a goat ranch, and then, more urgently, as a fearsome drought presses on his goats, as a reservoir of grazing provided by its fertility. Very much against Amanda's vigorous pleas he finally drives his goats down into not just the canyon but its very womb, the grotto itself, where, after they have stripped the ground bare, he cuts down the cottonwoods so they may devour their branches. This rape—for that is clearly how Amanda sees this act—brings down precisely the expected disaster; when the rains finally come, a terrific flood devastates the canyon, killing Stephen, his goats, and Abel Bane. Goats, markers, as we have seen, of hypermasculinity, randy, pleasure-driven, selfish sexuality, come not to impregnate but to take. That is why goats "belong" up in the desert; indeed, Amanda's recognition of the link between Stephen's sexual needs and his goats drives her at one point to keep him out of the canyon, up on the desert rim.[12] But now, when the canyon succeeds in flushing out its assailants and "purifying" itself, it is also at the cost of its fertility, for the fruit orchards are likewise destroyed.

Stephen simply fails to grasp the "appropriate" male role; he is hypermasculinized, and his hypermasculinity blinds him to the proper relationship he should have with the canyon. His goats do not "put [the] land under ditch and fence" to nurture its fertility; rather, they consume everything they find and rob the land of the very features that enable its fertility. (What the canyon may have been like under its dispossessed Indigenous Apache occupants is another matter, to which I return below.) Abel Bane, Amanda's neighbor and mentor, denounces Stephen's plan to buy up a neighboring property and convert it to a goat ranch: "It was desert," Bane declares, and, with goats, "It would be desert again!"[13] Perhaps the purest evidence of Stephen's failure to understand the right relationship with the canyon comes in his violent argument with Abel Bane over Stephen's right to cut canyon trees to feed his goats. Stephen has cut, and plans to continue to cut, trees in the grotto above Bane's orchard. When Bane insists Stephen has no right, Stephen demands Bane produce a title: "That's the thing," he asserts. Stephen agrees to pay for the trees, if Bane "can prove ownership of this property." Bane, in turn, claims that his work bringing the canyon fertility is all the title he needs; he rejects any notion that money could substitute for trees and fertility.[14]

Stephen views the canyon through the lens of commodification and colonization. Land is meant to be owned, with a piece of legal paper to prove ownership. For those like Bane who see the land instead as a feminine entity whose passive fertility must be awakened by the active action of a man with the correct attitude—a sexuality aimed not at pleasure but at fruitfulness—this view is anathema. Bane works respectfully with the land as a humble steward, sensitive to its needs and capabilities; the land in return actualizes the fruit he plants—he and the canyon, its soil, its water, and the sun, work in partnership. Ownership, a hierarchical relation, is completely different. A theme opposed to the capitalistic seizure of the land is present in other writers of earlier twentieth century, for whom Mary Austin may, perhaps, stand. Her critique comes out clearly in the essay "My Neighbor's Field" in *The Land of Little Rain*, where the language marching through her discussion of men's dispute over a little plot of land—*master, owned, market, kept, security, money, possession*—makes absolutely clear her rejection of the masculinized, colonialist commodification of the land that the men take as a given.[15]

Amanda's brother represents another failed male response to the female landscape. From the start, John hates the canyon; he wants what he sees as the "freedom" represented by the outside world. But it's obvious that John rejects the sexual power of the canyon: whenever he leaves the canyon to buy supplies, it is "as if with the falling away of the canyon walls he stood erect."[16] He finally makes his permanent escape by securing a place in a nearby, recently reopened mine (a purely commodified space, run by foreign—English—capital, intent only on making money). When Amanda visits him on the Fourth of July for a great dance party thrown in the shaft of the mine itself, she encounters a false, sterile vagina and womb—made by men, not nature, devoid of water and fertility, lit not by the sun but by artificial illumination. She needs alcohol to stir up fake sexual feelings that discharge in a meaningless kiss with a nonentity she meets there (even her brother, who works with him, knows nothing about him). It is the opposite of the genuine sexuality of the canyon, and a crucial step in Amanda's admission to herself of the power of her sexual needs; it is not long after the dance, and the kiss, that she sleeps with Stephen. The mining culture brings jobs, but the "[g]ood times" that accompany them are the mendacious satisfactions of prostitution and befuddlement with marijuana; money earned by this violence against the earth engenders corruption, sterility, and the social violence of the police.[17] John cannot be a "real man" to the vaginal canyon; he seeks refuge in the excavated vagina of the underground mine. The product of John and his fellow miners with this pseudo-vagina is not fruit or a baby but molybdenum[18]—an element in sudden great demand because used to strengthen steel, surely wanted as US industry was ramping up in preparation, proleptically, for World War II.

Despite having abandoned the orchard for the mine and now living in town, John works to patrol the boundaries of Amanda's normative, white heterosexuality. He disapproves of her driving into Tucson by herself to sell the crops; he thinks at the very least a man should accompany her. When he leaves, she cleans out his room in the house for Miguel, the Yaqui farmhand Amanda employs, who, to John's disapproval, takes John's place both in his room and at his place at the table. And in the incident at the July 4 dance in the mine, when Amanda, slightly drunk, kisses a man whom John admits he doesn't really know, John is nevertheless approving: the partner in the kiss is obviously a straight white man, so potentially an appropriate mate for Amanda in John's gendered world. John fails in all these efforts to keep his sister confined in his approved female roles: she dismisses his complaints about driving, keeps Miguel on and even works side by side with him in the orchard, and rebukes herself for her intoxicated kiss, for which she feels shame and revulsion the next day.[19]

An effective male response to the canyon appears in the figure of Abel Bane, the first Anglo to settle the canyon. Abel shares his house with a wren, for which he has cut an opening in his door to let her go in and out on her own, and a bull snake that keeps mice down. We're repeatedly told that "Trees grow for him," and in a centrally important chapter, he shows Amanda how to set a new orchard, lovingly scooping pits for the infant trees and directing water from the Aravaipa River onto them. Bane started, evidently, by mining (at least he had a claim that he had worked) but his real passion was fruit. Having his choice of sites, he settled as far up the canyon as you could go and still plant;[20] beyond lay the grotto where Amanda had bathed.

A crucial interaction between Amanda and Abel occurs when he helps her plant the Margison family's last patch of land that had not yet been planted when her father died. With Miguel, the three work side by side digging holes for the planting, "the time measured by the shove into hard earth, the weight of earth turning, the holes at last, regular and in line, with earth loose in the bottom, waiting the young trees."

> Amanda, working beside him, was quietly happy in the day. She felt herself in her own place, doing her own work, which had been her father's before her. Joy flooded the day, and life was a strong current on which she rode.[21]

The "strong current" recalls Amanda's naked bathing in the stream of the grotto and reconnects her with the erotics and sexuality she experienced there. But here the sexuality is muted; she does think of Stephen as she works, but only in the context of the hard work he faces up on the desert, caring for his goats. Abel's almost mystical connection with the canyon, his ability to plant and fructify, spills over into Amanda too. Both together breathe the erotics of the orchard they are making.

Bane serves as the male power properly in tune with the canyon/vagina and absolutely essential to bring it to its consummate purpose, fertility. He is, so to speak, the penis to the canyon's vagina. As in passionate sexual intercourse, he positions himself as deep up in the canyon as he can, bumping right up against the entrance to the grotto/womb where Amanda first feels her unfettered female power. His abandonment of mining for agriculture marks his recognition that to dig into the canyon for its mineral wealth is a form of violence, a rape, that he explicitly rejects.[22] He has no wife or companion because he is in fact married to the canyon, engaged with it (her) in an endless act of sexual intercourse that brings forth the peaches and figs that pass through its vulva in a kind of birth, to feed the population down in the Gila Valley and as far away as Tucson. It seems at first glance that in Gillmor's vision of the relationship between people and the female canyon it cannot unfold its potential fertility, however great that may be, without the active cooperation of the male, and that this problem is precisely the conundrum that Amanda is caught in as a woman: she apparently needs a man to complete her, to actualize the sexuality and consequent fertility that have shaped her from the moment she bathed naked in the Aravaipa's fertile stream. It is her choice of a man that forms her tragic mistake; but even so, she ends the book ready to restore the canyon—and to have Stephen's baby. But it's more complicated than that, for after her sexual interlude with Stephen she resumes the role she had before he appeared—her activity as a fruit-grower, content and (re)productive. In other words, Amanda can serve as the actualizer of the canyon's fertility: she can adopt a "male" gender role, as Bane has taught her in helping her plant. Her relationship with the canyon rejects the Euro-American conceit that only men can fertilize women, male the female. Both she and Bane himself disrupt the gender stereotypes their culture seeks to impose. The stereotypical judgment of Bane's gender-bending is expressed early on when, after a description of the domestic practices he undertakes that ought to be a wife's, putting up fruits and vegetables and making candles, Gillmor writes: "'He's queer,' they said of him."[23]

To read the canyon's topography as a metaphor for female genitalia, however, poses one considerable problem of correspondence: while there are obvious analogues for the vulva, vagina, cervix, and womb, there is nothing to represent the clitoris.[24] A cave, as an enclosed opening, would better suit the metaphor, it would seem; there's a good example in Willa Cather's *Death Comes for the Archbishop*, in which bishop Latour takes refuge from a storm in a cave with a "fetid odor, not very strong but highly disagreeable," whose opening consists of "two rounded ledges, one directly over the other, with a mouth-like opening between. They suggested two great stone lips, slightly parted and thrust outward." An "orifice" gives access to a "lofty cavern" lit only by the "narrow aperture" of the stone lips. The bishop instinctively feels an "extreme distaste for the place." There's no doubt this cave and its opening should be read not just "as both the symbolic mouth and vagina"[25] but also a cervix and womb: a complete analogue for the female reproductive system. In a prose comment on his short poem "The Expectant Father," the Acoma poet Simon Ortiz describes a cave to which he'd hiked, with a shallow pool in which "tiny water beings" lived. The context compels seeing it as a metaphor for the womb. In "The Poet" he writes "there was another cave. A woman was moaning, / and later she was laughing"—an obvious cave as vulva and vagina and sexual intercourse.[26] Now, the parallels between these other organs and the canyon are not necessarily precise and exact; notably the vaginal canyon is also not enclosed. But the absence of a correspondence to the clitoris seems a serious matter demanding some explanation.[27]

Gillmor's Aravaipa Canyon is not the only canyon in literature to symbolize the vagina.[28] In a study of novels by the Spanish writer Juan Goytisolo, Kessel Schwartz has remarked on his representation of a "vaginal journey" as "a kind of sacred grotto, and also [as] the yawning chasm or canyon." In Kiowa N. Scott Momaday's *House Made of Dawn*, Angela Martin St. John, an Anglo refugee from Los Angeles, finds sexual awakening with the Pueblo protagonist Abel in the house she's rented in a canyon; even before they have sex, she feels burblings of sexual frisson whenever she is in the canyon.[29] Perhaps the best-known example is Panther Cañon [*sic*] in Willa Cather's *The Song of the Lark*. Like Amanda (but with the sexual overtones a bit muted), Thea bathes naked in the canyon stream, in a canyon she describes as a "cleft in the world." Martha Cutter read the topography unambiguously as a "vulva-like gorge." Some years ago, Ellen Moers had already examined what Freud called the "complicated topography of the female genital parts" written by women writers onto the landscape. In *Mill on the Floss*, Maggie Tulliver has sex with Stephen in the Red Deeps, where, Moers argues, the bank, hollow, and mounds are unmistakable sexual symbols; Maggie has sex but feels only affection, not physical desire. In Mary Wollstonecraft's *Mary: A Fiction*, there is the "Temple of Solitude," a "cavity of a rock" surrounded by shrubs and from which a stream flows. In *The Falling Woman* (1992), an Australian novel by Susan Hawthorne about the desert travels of two lesbian lovers, a V-shaped canyon is linked to the womb and birth. And Moers declares Panther Cañon to be "the most thoroughly elaborated female landscape in literature."[30]

So it is quite clear that canyons can be read vaginally despite the missing clitoris-analogue. In the case of Gillmor's canyon, the function that is emphasized is not sexual pleasure but reproduction. The center of the canyon lies in the fertile grotto beyond the cervix-like narrowing; it is the destruction of this space that precipitates the disastrous flood that forms the central event of the novel. In parallel, Amanda's own single sex act with Stephen results in conception; again, it is her fertility, her ability to bring new life into the world, that is the obvious, greater point of her sexuality and the true goal of her desire (even if she did not understand that at the moment she and Stephen make love).[31] Moreover, clitoris or not, Amanda experienced deep satisfaction and pleasure in her intercourse with Stephen: in the afterglow "[a] wave of tenderness swept through her, and she turned, pressing her face against his shoulder. The night was quiet—and all the struggle within her was gone."[32]

This view may be reinforced by the "false vagina" of the mine. There is no possibility of conception in the mine, which lacks a womb; and so the only possible "use" for this vaginal space is meretricious pleasure or profit (as the prostitutes the mine's reopening attracts). Gillmor does not offer a description of the entrance to the mine detailed enough to know whether she consciously thought of it as possessing a stand-in for the clitoris, but the contrast between sterile, morally reprehensible pleasure associated with the mine and the positive, morally justified sexuality of the canyon in its devotion to reproduction, is clear—and suggestive—enough. The mine, then, also represents a colonialist rape of the landscape, standing in opposition to Indigenous ideas about the proper relationship between the land and human beings, as we saw in the exploration of the sacred in chapter 2. Amanda and Abel Bane too reject this colonialist exploitation of the land—which was Bane's own first effort to wring a living from the canyon—as a one-way street on which only the exploiter benefits and the exploited is left damaged, uglified, and worthless.

And yet—neither Bane nor Amanda herself fully escapes the colonialist attitude toward the land. As Suzana Sawyer and Arun Agrawal have argued, the gendering of the land—and, more broadly, "nature"—as female has served the Euro-American colonialist project. In the colonialist encounter with sub-Saharan Africa and South America, "torrid" zones of unrestrained fertility, the land was seen as female, thrumming with potent sexuality. It was on this female landscape that Euro-American colonists exercised their power, taming and controlling it. As female, the land was "ripe for exploration and conquest."[33] In effect, Bane and Amanda too adopt just this relation with the canyon: it is a passive female on which they impose their vision of Edenic improvement. Their motivations may be benevolent—at least in their minds; they seem oblivious to the changes they exercise on the preexisting canyon ecology, the flora, fauna, water, and soil they must disturb or displace to transform canyon into orchard—but they nevertheless treat the land in ways less violent but still analogous to those of the miners. Unlike them, however, it is the potential sexuality and fruitfulness of the land that preoccupies Bane and Amanda; this was foremost in Euro-American colonialist minds, whether as a dangerous and terrifying sexuality demanding domestication and control or as a passive nature, ready to play its female role, if only the male power should undertake its active, fructifying task.

In this context it may be worthwhile to speculate a little bit about Gillmor's own sexuality, for her personal experiences may shed some light on Amanda and Stephen. Gillmor never married. While doing graduate studies at the Istituto de filosofía y letras in Mexico City she met a Norwegian expatriate named Ola Apenes. Their letters leave no doubt that she was in love with him and he with her; they traveled together on ethnographic tours in Mexico and she was heartbroken when, as a volunteer in the Royal Norwegian Air Force, he died in 1942. In commenting on *Fruit Out of Rock* Sharon Whitehill suggests that the "surprisingly sexual focus on Frances's part, appropriate enough to her story, also reflects the awakening to love in her personal life"[34] since she completed her final draft of *Fruit Out of Rock* after she had met Apenes.

Possibly; but Whitehill reports two other possible love affairs in Gillmor's life. As an undergraduate at the University of Arizona at Tucson, she dated a fellow student named Dick Shaw. One time they drove out together, alone, and "parked in a lover's lane" on a hill overlooking San Xavier del Bac south of Tucson, where, perhaps, they engaged in "some spooning." Shaw asked Gillmor to marry him several times during the course of their relationship but was refused.[35]

The third instance is for our purposes the most resonant. Beginning in April 1930, Gillmor and her mother lived in a cabin in the real Aravaipa Canyon for several months. The place made a strong impression on her. In a letter she called the canyon an "incredibly lovely spot" where "one comes suddenly up out of the desert into canyon with its clear cold stream roaring down over gravel and boulders at the foot of high honey-yellow cliffs. At the foot . . . herds of white goats with little bells tinkling. Farther up are fruit ranches raising oranges and grapefruit and peaches and pecans."[36] It is obvious that she transposed the topography of the real Aravaipa directly into the book. But the resonance of the canyon may well have resulted from more than just a compelling topography. It was during her time there that she met Joe Buzan, son of the woman who owned the land the cabin stood on. A neighbor who ran an orchard in the canyon recalled that he often saw Gillmor and Buzan

> walking together up the canyon. In those days it had a sandy bottom, and you could walk barefoot a long distance from the Buzan ranch. . . . Each day I'd go up and sit on a rock and try to do watercolors or photography, and Frances and Joe would come along. Frances was riding a horse one time, and Joe was walking. They said hello and went on past.

We do not know whether Gillmor ever had sexual relations with any of these men (Apenes would probably be the best bet), but she was already 26 or 27 years old when she had her "brief summer romance" with Buzan; her friend of 35 years, LaVerne Harrell Clark, believed Gillmor and Buzan enjoyed a "romance."[37] Aravaipa Canyon must have carried for Gillmor a heavy sexual charge even if she and Buzan never consummated their relationship. I think this goes a long way to explain the choice of the canyon as the site of Gillmor's most explicitly sexual book, the symbolism of the canyon as vaginal, and, perhaps, the incomplete correspondence between its topography and the body for which it stands.

In her brief discussion of *Fruit Out of Rock* Vera Norwood makes the pregnant observation that Gillmor remains well within the bounds of normative female sexuality in the novel. Gillmor's take focuses not on sexual satisfaction in the sense of orgasm but on fertility and reproduction as the ends toward which Amanda's sexual urges push her. This distinction is apparent in a number of ways. First, Amanda's relationship with the canyon—taken, as I have argued, as a metaphor for the female reproductive system—is entirely about fertility and reproduction. She is a fruit-grower; we see her planting new orchards, harvesting, driving her crop to town. She derives genuine satisfaction from her tasks, but they are *work*—they involve energy and time, and she is tired and worn out when they are finished. Reproduction here is not about pleasure. Second, the pleasures she does gain from the canyon are not sexual in the sense of being passionate and consummative. Her pleasures come from walks, bathing in the stream, watching the sunset and changing sky. These are pleasures of calmness and peace; perhaps analogous to pleasures she might feel after sexual consummation, as her contentment after her intercourse with Stephen, but there are none in her relationship to the canyon that are analogous to orgasm. Rather, Amanda's pleasures fall clearly under Audre Lorde's conceptualization of the erotic, which "is not a question only of what we do; it is a question of how acutely and fully we can feel in the doing."[38] Already at the start of the book, when Amanda emerges from the stream in the grotto,

> the taut weariness had slipped from her. Loose and effortless, she felt her arms and body swing to her stride. Even the troubled half-consciousness of unhappiness had slipped from her. She was neither happy nor unhappy; she was hardly thinking; she was walking and alive.[39]

Amanda's deepest relationship with the canyon is precisely conditioned by her acute and full feeling—it is fundamentally erotic in the all-encompassing sense that Lorde champions.

Amanda has something of the same relationship with the desert landscape above the canyon's rim. One day she goes out riding to visit Stephen for the first time up at his camp in the desert:

> She rode through a silence of sun, broken only by the creak of saddle leather and the steady sound of her horse's hooves on rock. The voices of all the desert birds were stilled. A hawk circled high above her. . . . [Then w]ith caught breath she pulled her horse in and listened, gathering the moment to her. The small sounds of the desert came to her then: the fine hiss of wind through the spines of a giant cactus above her, the high whisper of insects. . . . She moved on in quiet contentment, conscious of the smell of sun on leather and horseflesh and creosote bushes, of the blaze of light on high desert, conscious of the cool breath of night coming on as the shadows of the suguaros [*sic*] lengthened.

But this eroticism isn't fully self-contained like that Amanda experienced during and after her time in the grotto pool: this eroticism is colored by Stephen's as-yet half-detected sexual gravitation: "Stephen was somewhere in this wide top country," and when she spied his goats, "Her heart lifted; Stephen would be somewhere near."[40] In Amanda's response to canyon and desert we have two different erotics, one that represents just a relation between the young woman and the landscape, and the other—which might once have been identical to that Amanda has with the canyon—shifted, or perhaps better, overlain, with a straightforward heterosexual tension. Amanda can still feel the desert, but she feels it with the presence of a man.

Third, and perhaps most telling, comes her reaction to her one sex act and her pregnancy. She displays no surprise or shock or embarrassment or shame at all. Reflecting on her one night with Stephen, "She wondered that she had no feeling of having broken with all her childhood teaching. 'A week ago, I should have said it was wrong,' she said to herself. 'And today it is right.'" For Amanda pregnancy is the right, expected outcome of sexual intercourse. She tells her mother matter-of-factly, while they are surveying the damage after the flood and death of Stephen and Abel Bane:

> "Next year,' said Amanda quietly, "I'll have Stephen's child to think of."
> Her mother looked at her speechlessly.
> "That's why I say we go on with what we have. I'm looking forward Mother, not back—"

She turned to her mother suddenly, her voice breaking.

> "Mother—be happy for me. Don't you see? I want this baby so much—Stephen's baby."[41]

She expects to go on as she has, running her farm and raising her child. Her sorrow at Stephen's death—which Stephen partly redeems right at the end, by trying to help Bane stem the flood, which finally sweeps them both away—is tempered by her recognition that his plans for the canyon would have destroyed it. And she seems not to express any sense at all of sexual loss. Indeed, her future, such as we are invited to imagine it, includes no husband or lover; she is complete with canyon, ranch, and child. She has still her erotic connection with the canyon, which she had before Stephen arrived and which continues to sustain and satisfy her.

Here, I think, the "normative female sexuality" that struck Norwood plays out. The goal is reproduction: once achieved, the need for sex goes away. This is not to say that Amanda did not welcome and want sex—she clearly did, and felt no guilt about it. But once her sexual needs were met, fertility and pregnancy, not romantic, coupled heterosexual love, were the lasting outcome. Earlier she had wanted marriage with Stephen,[42] but after his death she experiences no regret that she cannot attain this Euro-American good. She will be content with baby and farm, even if she did not realize that consciously when she slept with Stephen.

At the same time, though, Gillmor has Amanda pushing at the boundaries of women's gendered place in other ways. Amanda takes on the duties after her father's death that her brother should have assumed (but in fact was not man enough for; he deceived himself into believing he could make enough in the mine to hire a working man so Amanda wouldn't have to drive the fruit into town herself). She learns, and loves, the skills needed to be an effective grower; she is indeed the fructifier of her farm, a task that by rights should belong to a male, and a potent one, like Abel Bane. She works not in the house exclusively but outdoors; she drives her truck, alone, to the mild scandal of her neighbors, into town to sell her fruit. She lives way out in the countryside without a man to protect her. She rejects vigorously the implication that as a woman without a man way up in the canyon she ought to be afraid; she refuses to be like her neighbor Maren Johnson, who's "afraid of everything—afraid from the day she came to the canyon." On many dimensions Amanda's behavior challenges the "female normative" of her world. She doesn't conform to the rules and regulations that ought to shape the woman in the Euro-American culture she comes from.[43]

Gillmor's vision takes long-standing, stereotyped tropes about landscape, gender, and nature and uses them to frame her story, shape her characters, and drive her plot. It's clear she favors the female side of her landscape; the canyon wins in the end, though temporarily ruined, the canyon is where orchards can thrive once again, and the canyon is where Amanda, as a woman, finds her place. She will raise her child without Stephen in the warm embrace of the canyon, surrounded by the new orchard she has already begun to plan by the end of the book. Her burning sexuality has been tamped down because satisfied by pregnancy; at the very end, Amanda's mother, surveying with her daughter the destruction of the flood, remarks sadly, "It's a heavy end to loving him, Amanda," but Amanda retorts, "No. ... It's what goes on—even if all the rest is finished."[44] Now that Amanda is pregnant, her need for a man seems to melt away; she can both have and raise a child by herself *and* tend to the canyon. Gillmor's vision seems to assert the superfluousness of a man once that act of fertilization has been accomplished—and the self-sufficiency of a woman and her canyon to carry on, perfectly adequately, by themselves.

Quite strikingly, in fact, both the fully sympathetic characters in *Fruit Out of Rock*— Amanda and Abel Bane—refuse to conform to the heteronormative couplehood that especially configured the "yeoman farmer," the type both represent. Amanda and Bane are perfectly content to live and work without a sexual partner, fully occupied with their orchards. And this brings us back again to eroticism: for, as already noted, the connection they have with the canyon rests on an erotic relationship; they enjoy ongoing, complete erotic fulfillment in planting, tending, harvesting, and marketing the fruit they and the canyon grow in cooperation. I'd now like to widen our lens, to consider gendering and landscape erotics in a broader view.

GENDER, EROTICS, AND THE MEANING OF THE DESERT

In this chapter and the previous I've considered gender and the landscape in a dichotomy between male and female and quite broadly. Stretches of desert landscape "become" female, I've suggested, through the activation of fruitfulness. What was a barren desert turns into a fruited plain when active men direct a generative fluid onto and into it. That is, the metaphor is blatantly sexual; it rests on the reproductive capacity of women and men in their different but complementary ways, although the maleness of the desert depends on its harshness, independence, silence, and aloofness. This congeries of male traits is highly American in its content; it is an expression of the basic stereotype of masculinity that colors much of our literature, imposing a form of manliness that we see in advertising, politics, and all over in the American scene.[45]

But gender and the land can interrelate in more complex, even contradictory, ways; indeed, land that once was gendered can even be stripped of its gendering, transformed into a kind of neuter or nonbinary space in which neither male nor female arise.[46] Moreover, there are other ways to mark gender than through purely reproductive, dualist modes. A brief consideration of gendering and Native American views about the desert landscape and its rock art can serve as an example and an entrée into a more complex, and sometimes more subtle, gendering. Finally, gender is not a simple male-female dichotomy, either in the Anglo-European social world—although there have been and continue to be powerful forces striving to confine gender to precisely that dichotomy—or in the cosmologies and societies of many desert Indigenous peoples.[47]

Many Indigenous peoples of the desert Southwest have expressions of gender quite different from those of the Euro-American culture that raised Amanda. For instance, among the Utes rattlesnakes are gendered male after the sacred rattlesnake (/tuu-kʷ-ua=pi/) who controls the Underworld, but they are associated with women. They are regarded as ideal spirit-helpers for girls undergoing puberty initiation and dominate rock art connected with such rituals. They are used as decorations on baskets, which are quintessentially female-gendered both because they were made by women and association of the basket with the womb. The vaginas of mythic women were guarded by skirts of rattlesnakes.

Rock art sites—especially those associated with healing and spirits, as we examined in chapter 2—tend also to be gendered female, a view expressed in a number of ways. The Bell Bluff site, for example, was called *choishishiu*, "female dog"; the inversion is expressed both by the site's use by a male healer named Jim Hangton and by the fact that male dogs were often regarded as spirit helpers. (The term *pusin tinliw*, "male dog cave," points up another inversion: as we have seen, caves in Anglo thought are often regarded as female.) Other names for rock art sites with female gendering include *pachki*, "red," alluding to menstrual blood, and *taiwan*, "woman's gambling basket."[48] Other parts of the landscape, however, bore male gendering. High places tended to be gendered masculine, so mountain peaks' names might end in a termination meaning "penis, erect penis." Such peaks, especially the highest within one clan's range, were typically believed to be where the world was created and loci of great power. Low places—springs, valleys, and so on—were seen typically as female.[49]

The female aspect of rock art sites is also expressed in ways other than naming. The sites were guarded by rattlesnake spirits, which, as we have seen, were frequently associated with women. Vulva forms were often present, or landforms with rock art were interpreted as vulvas; a notable example is at Painted Rock in the Carrizo Plain in California, seen as a huge vagina. At the top is a painting of figures in a Chumash canoe: among them, "getting in a canoe" is a euphemism for having sex. Many rock art sites are treated as if vaginas—entryways to another world.[50] Another instance of gendered landscapes, but having both female and male aspects, appears in the abundance of "yoni" (vulva) and penis formations in Southern California, especially in the territory that belonged to the Kumeyaay people, and extending into the Anza Borrego and Mojave Deserts. These sites exploited natural slit- and penis-like shapes, often enhanced by intentional reshaping, as retreats for childless couples who hoped to stimulate their fertility. In her exploration of the landscape of yonis in Kumeyaay and others' territories, Charlotte McGowan identified twenty-one sites each bearing a plethora of vulva-yonis, some wholly natural formations, some manipulated to increase their resemblance to female genitalia.[51]

These few examples point up several important qualifications about the desert and its gender. While some gender assignments of landscape features clearly rest on rather obvious analogies between them and male- or female-identified sexual organs—mountains and penises, caves and vaginas, slits in rocks or standing pillars[52]—other aspects of gendering depend on cultural readings. The complementarity of male and female is also present in Indigenous societies, but not necessarily expressed in the same ways as among Anglos. In some cases, this gendered complementarity was expressed in quite specific ways. Among the Akimel O'odham, for example, men alone built houses (the *ki*), but among the Northern Paiute who lived near Pyramid Lake in the Great Basin Desert of Nevada, men were responsible for erecting the internal supports of a house while women applied the covering of brush or matting. Such gendered tasks—which are performed on the basis of a person's gender, *not* biological sex—are found repeatedly. Nikki Cooley, a member of the Navajo/Diné nation, regards

> the big Colorado River as the male river, the raging, big, and intimidating figure. And the smaller rivers, like the Little Colorado River and the San Juan River, are considered the female rivers. They're the soft, gentle, calming counterpart. But in general, all waters are referred to as being female as they give and sustain life. The confluence is where the male and female rivers meet, and together, they go downstream to nourish the rest of the canyon and its residents, the flora and fauna.[53]

Cooley genders the rivers on the basis of characteristics of male and female perfectly in line with Euro-American gender stereotypes, which may reflect a mix of both Indigenous notions and Anglo ones, but her move also points up the difficulty of adducing a simple formula to explain Indigenous gendering of the land.

Further gendered aspects of the desert landscape flowed out of mythological times. For the Chemehuevi of the desert Southwest, the origin of the Earth was attributed to the creative deity Ocean Woman. She made land by masticating shed skin and stretching it out in all directions. Her action imprinted a female gender on the landscape. Later, as the creative period closed, she and two other, male creative figures, Wolf and Coyote, departed: Ocean Woman went south, Wolf and Coyote north, thus lending respective female and male genders to these directions. The gendered world unfolds in ever-expanding complexity:

> Among the Southern Ute and others, stars and flocks of birds are considered to be females.... Similarly, lice are regarded as women. These share the characteristic of uniform size and diffuse distribution, appropriate metaphors for women of the Basin. The sun and large mammals, regardless of biology, are considered to be males because, like men, they are solitary and larger. In all, Man refers to pronounced parts of the environment and Woman to open, even expanses.... The metaphors of promontory/plain are especially appropriate for Basin topography where rows of broad valleys are divided by sawtooth mountain ranges.[54]

For its Indigenous inhabitants the desert landscape with its animals and plants is then not a single gendered space—it rather presents a mosaic of differently gendered places, intermixed and mingling. Moreover, the gendering of place is deeply imbricated not only as an echo of human male-female gender but also with cultural, social, and religious practice. Gendering that runs against the apparent grain of the "biological," like regarding all mammals as male no matter an individual's biological sex or assigning rattlesnakes to women, reflects the complexity of the cultural imperatives that attribute gender to the physical world. Clearly, Native Americans' interactions with their homelands played out through a gendering much more complex than the simple male-female dichotomy I explored in chapter 4 in the re-gendering of part of the Colorado Desert into the Imperial Valley, the rendering of Barbara's desert into a feminized landscape by the activation of Barbara's own female gender, or the canyon-desert female-male dichotomy of *Fruit Out of Rock*—which, as we have seen, is undermined by the relations Amanda and Abel have with the canyon.

The considerations I've just outlined invite further reflections on the matter of gender among our southwestern desert peoples. The fact of the matter is that the majority of these peoples recognized one or more genders alongside "male" and "female." In *Written by the Body*, Lisa Tatonetti's recent, detailed, and brilliant elucidation of Indigenous gendering, she tracks nonconforming masculinities (which would seem to evoke George Devereux's women-men in his study of Mohave "homosexuality"), nonconforming femininities (with Devereux's men-women), Two Spirit persons, trans, lesbian, and other expressions of gender. In a bibliographic study published over three decades ago, Will Roscoe catalogued twenty-two groups in the Southwest and Great Basin for whom ethnographers had documented the presence of men-women and women-men. In the desert world that we've been studying, these include the Cocopah, Yuma, and Mohave on the Colorado River; the Hopi on their Four Mesas and their neighbors the Zuni; several Rio Grande Pueblos, including the Isleta, and the farther west Laguna and Acoma; along the Gila River and on both sides of it the Akimel O'odham, Tohono O'odham, Piipaash and Halychdum (Maricopa), Yavapai, and Walapai; the Diné (Navajo), whose vast but deeply impoverished reservation occupies most of northeastern Arizona; and, in the Great Basin Desert, the Northern and Southern Paiute, Shoshoni, Ute, Washoe, and Koso.[55]

Let's take the Mohave as a well-attested example. Among them, a person gendered a woman-man, an *'alyha*, might marry a man, have intercourse with him, perform the typical duties of a wife, and even feign menstruation and pregnancy. A man-woman *hwame* might likewise marry a woman and hunt, plant, and undertake other male-gendered behaviors. But both genders might also sometimes marry or have sex with persons of the "opposite biological" sex: so an *'alyha* with a woman and a *hwame* with a man.[56]

But this neat schema of four genders doesn't always work. In the Mohave Historical Epic, which I treat in more detail in chapters 7 and 10, the great hero Hipahipa, who had been living alone in the middle of the desert, undertook leadership of the Mohave who had been displaced from their Colorado River homeland. Under his aegis they marched back out of the desert and after a series of battles retook the Mojave Valley. Hipahipa was killed in heroic battle with fleeing enemies. The Epic makes clear Hipahipa's heroic stature. He's clairvoyant, knowing how many men his enemies have mustered; he consumes vast quantities of food; he probably bewitches the Mohave to come to him in the desert; the Mohave expelled from their riverine homeland "turned sharply E[ast] into inhospitable mountain desert, which they might well have avoided, because Hipahipa had charmed them, as on other occasions he charmed the antelope"; he can scalp without incurring miasma; he foretells his own death. A. T. Hatto calls him "[t]he Rattlesnake-shaman Hipahipa with his superior powers." But there are things about him that do not seem manly. He has neither wife nor children, indeed he seems never to have had sexual relations with anyone. He abhors rabbit, rats, and jackrabbit, the standard fare of desert-dwellers (he does eventually come to accept them as palatable) in favor of an exclusive diet of rattlesnakes. He hunts them by day and then wears not the standard male accoutrement of a loincloth but rather a skirt—composed of the rattlesnakes he's captured and will be dining on at breakfast. Rattlesnakes are associated with women, especially as guardians of the vulva; Hipahipa's rattlesnake skirt would seem to recall this link to female rather than male genitalia. Among the Mohave a man wearing a skirt is marked as an *'alyha*, a male-bodied person who performs a female gender. When Hipahipa dies he proves to have no female relatives to perform his rites; four unrelated women constitute themselves as adoptive kin to do the business.[57]

Do his practices, then, mark Hipahipa as an *'alyha*? Not according to his own account of his youth:

> I think none of you know me. Do you not know me? You have seen me before. I was at Kohôye [near Barstow, California] with you. I was a young man then, and a bad man. I kicked and ran and fought. I dreamed that way: that is why I did it. I could not help it. I was young then. My name was Noise-unruly-night. Now I am called Hipahipa.[58]

Hipahipa clearly states he was a man in his youth, presumably *'iipa*. The calling of a male-bodied person to third-genderhood came typically in intrauterine dreams; the attraction to female toys and behavior and friendship with girls appeared in childhood; adherence to the third gender was tested around puberty. Once it was clear that the pubescent was indeed destined to be an *'alyha* he underwent a ceremony that publicly established his status.[59] Hipahipa seems then to be ambiguous: he does male things, especially warfare, but he also engages in behavior markedly female. His status as a hero places him outside normal society, and his mixture of male and female, but not *'alyha* (or *hwame*), reinforces his position in a heroic world. Gender-mixing helps mark him as unique.[60]

The multiplicity of genders among Indigenous human beings raises the question of whether there were landforms gendered woman-man or man-woman, two-spirit, or otherwise. As far as I have been able to see, there is little evidence except two telling instances. The Piipaash and Halychdum (Maricopa) believed that a woman-man spirit dwelt in the Sierra Estrella (see Fig. 7-1 in chapter 7). The mountain was called *Vii 'Alyha*, according to Harry J. Winters, Jr. The Yuma had a mountain with the same name that likewise housed a woman-man. If in dreams the mountains appeared as young girls, the dreamer was then destined to transform into a woman-man. "The signs of the transformation came early in childhood," just as with the Mohave.[61] If there were two mountains of third gender, then it is highly likely there were others of third or fourth, unknown to the ethnographers who researched among the groups.

AMANDA, ABEL, AND BARBARA IN A
GENDERED LANDSCAPE

Before Abel Bane, the Margisons, and other Anglos occupied the Aravaipa Canyon, it was home to the Aravaipa Apache people. They are attested to have recognized four genders, woman-man and man-woman along with male and female. We also know a fair amount about their treatment of the landscape as gendered space. In one version of the Apache creation myth, the Mountain Spirit Yusn brought them out from the Earth. Displeased with their misbehavior, he departed but left the Gahns to guide them; again they were recalcitrant and the Gahns "retreated to their sacred mountains." For the Apache the physical world around us is but a shadow version of the spiritual world, where resides *diyi'*, power. This power is accessed at points of intersection between the two worlds: in general, anywhere they seem to connect, like sacred mountains—four marked the boundaries of the Mescalero Apache homeland: the Guadalupes, Salinas, Capitan, and San Augustin—caves, and springs.[62] It is obvious even without explicit testimony that the Aravaipa Canyon, and especially the spring that fed the pool where Amanda bathed, must have been a site of high sacrality and power for the Aravaipa Apache.

There's a striking parallel in the fantasy novel *Kynship: The Way of Thorn and Thunder*, Book One of *The Kynship Chronicles* by Daniel Heath Justice. As Lisa Tatonetti has insisted, streams of sexual and erotic power, *wyr*, that arise from the land, flow through the book. In a crucial scene, the protagonist Tarsa approaches the Eternity Tree in a "physical, emotional, and spiritual encounter . . . [by which] sexual colonization and its attendant shames can be overcome." Tarsa entrusts herself to the pool that embraces the Eternity Tree and "felt [the water] caress her body. Her clothing dissolved; there was no barrier between her flesh and the rippling touch of the water." Tarsa exits the pool naked and transformed, charged with ancient Indigenous knowledge and now assumed into a "web of relationship and responsibility by the erotic power of the *wyr*."[63]

Places too for the Apache carried erotic charges. At Widows Pause for Breath (*'Istaa Hadaanáyolé*), three sisters who'd succumbed with their husbands to sexual desire before a raid (when sexual contact was prohibited) mourned the husbands' death in the expedition. At Trail Extends Across a Red Ridge (the color is significant) With Alder Trees a boy was warned he should avoid intercourse with his new wife when his grandmother, who was visiting, was menstruating. He pressured his wife anyway and she relented. The boy got sick, his penis swelled, it hurt to urinate. After a friend cured him he was told simply not to "bother your wife when her grandmother comes to visit." We have seen other examples of a sexual charge in places, as at Coarse-Textured Rocks Lie Above in a Compact Cluster. These sexual links with a place all contain, as most Western Apache toponyms do, a warning about self-control. Keith Basso concludes: "Knowledge of places is therefore closely linked to knowledge of the self. To grasping one's position in the larger scheme of things, including one's own community, and to securing a confident sense of who one is as a person."[64]

The shifting and ambiguous gendering of Hipahipa surely calls to mind the ambiguous gendering of Abel. He fertilizes, he knows trees, but he also hangs around the kitchen canning and making candles. He combines tasks of both male and female genders, but the latter components do not erase his power as a male. Nor is he dissatisfied with himself, ashamed or anxious. He is perfectly content—except when Stephen's goats threaten the canyon.

And so too Amanda, as we saw above. In her case the strength of gendering is even more pronounced, for her ability to conceive a child with Stephen does not in the least override the "male" duties she undertakes with complete success. Indeed, when her father dies, Amanda at once assumes his male-gendered duties toward orchard and canyon. Both characters break through the cultural barriers of heteronormative, male- and female-gendered couplehood.

There is one last matter about Aravaipa Canyon we must note: it is a place of ominousness, a realm of ghosts, what Cordelia Barrera would call a haunted landscape. In April 1871 a group of Apache was camping in the canyon. Their campsite had been moved up-canyon, to near the spring that fed the river, when late spring weather reduced the flow. Their name for the Aravaipa Creek was The Water Flows with the Cane. They were supplied grain, beef, blankets, and other material from nearby Fort Grant under a treaty negotiated in the 1850s, after the Gadsden Purchase had brought under American control Arizona south of the Gila River and up to the Mexican border (which had not yet been firmly established). Over the next two decades, conflicts among the Aravaipa Apache, other Indigenous groups, Hispanics, and Anglos played out in and around the canyon. The tensions and a history of conflict between Apache and other nations discharged on the last day of April 1871 in a horrific slaughter in the canyon. One hundred forty-four Aravaipa Apache were killed, almost all women and children, twenty-nine captured, their homes set ablaze, and the corpses left "sprawled along the creek." The killers included Hispanic settlers, Americans, and Tohono O'odham. The massacre was organized by a rancher living near Tucson, Jesús Elías, and his brother.[65]

Maren Johnson's fear of everything, which Amanda disdains, has its roots in this haunted past. Visiting the Margisons, gazing into the cabin's burning stove reminds Maren of "Apache fire on de mountain . . . down de mountain." Amanda's mother reassures her, "No, Maren. There aren't any Apache fires now. The Apaches don't come down into the canyon at all. . . . They aren't there at all, Maren." Yet as

[t]hey sat by the hot stove while the wind stirred the branches of the tree against the roof . . . beyond the mountain darkness the people of the past years moved in far light as if in the half-remembered patterns of a dance.

None of those who had lived in the canyon or on the height of cliff, and gone again—none of those who had moved in a day of light and left a memory faint as the whispers of the sun-silenced desert. Of the old people all that remained was a circle of stones that had been a house, only a drawing on a smoked rock, and a piece of broken pottery on hard ground.[66]

Under this elegiac language throbs memory of the massacre, of the Indigenous peoples whose home the canyon was, till they were virtually exterminated. This memory, baked into the very soil, serves as a painful, cruel counterpoint to the sexuality and erotics that Amanda and Abel derive from their daily contact with the earth. Gillmor never mentions the massacre, although it is apparent she knew about it, despite the highly oblique language she recounts it in.

And finally, these hints of past violence evoke the abiding guilt of colonialism. It was the massacre that emptied the canyon so that Bane, the Margisons, and the other Anglo settlers could move in, treating it as if it were virgin territory, virtual *terra nullius*, even if they acquired a vague, faint knowledge of the death and destruction that had cleared the way for them. The land of the canyon, then, infuses Amanda and Bane with a complex, contradictory stew of emotions and powers: sexual desire and fecundity, an erotics of the landscape and agriculture, an appreciation of its beauty, a fierce impulse to protect it from destructive outsiders like Stephen and his goats, and a legacy of settler colonialism that shadows every moment they live there, every move they make, just as in the title of Karl Jacoby's book about the massacre, *Shadows at Dawn*. Aravaipa Canyon and its desert rim are potent landscapes, replete of memory and ancient power, throbbing with sexuality and erotics, gendered in colors as mixed as a gay pride flag—and, it would seem, charged too with agency, able to inflect the lives of the people who have lived there.[67]

EURO-AMERICAN GENDER AND THE SOUTHWESTERN DESERTS

In *Reinventing Eden: The Fate of Nature in Western Culture*, Carolyn Merchant frames the relation between human beings in a Euro-American context and the "natural" world in the practice of Recovering Eden exercised on a landscape gendered typically as female. I have argued in this and chapter 4 that the desert Southwest came across to the white American settler-colonists who explored and settled this space in the nineteenth and twentieth centuries as male—harsh, tough, arid, dangerous, debilitating, daunting, dispiriting, deterring, a picture of deserts dependent on biblical depictions, especially in the traverse of the Sinai after the Israelites fled Egypt. It was the process of irrigation and the imposition of agriculture that, for parts of the Southwest, effected the transformation of the landscape into a female-gendered space, analogous—but hardly identical—to the humid, welcoming, flowering, fertile East. Merchant traces the trope of Recovering Eden back to the Greeks and into a series of branching recovery narratives: the mainstream, the conservationist, the preservationist, the feminist, the American; some stand in contradiction to one another, others intersect.

For the West, as Merchant rightly notes, it was the diversion and manipulation of water that engineered the transgendering of the land.[68] The settler-colonists were hardly the first people to repurpose the few reliable southwestern desert rivers to settled agriculture, however. For instance, the Hohokam (c. 800–1400 CE) of the Salt and Gila River Valleys of what is now the greater Phoenix region in Arizona cut hundreds of miles of canals fed by diversion dams on the waterways and carefully designed to deliver water to fields that often lay above the level of the rivers. The founder of Phoenix, Jack Swilling, who opened the first modern canal in 1867, was inspired by the remnants of Hohokam canals he'd noticed.[69] Water, gently flowing, fecundating, was the instrument in the hands of the energetic Adam crucial to feminizing the deserts; water has been associated with the female at least since Greek medical writers, who saw menstruation as proof that women suffered from a superabundance of fluid, which had to be discharged regularly.[70] But water in the desert is not always the passive, cooperative element of the transformative imaginary. The vast discharge of water from the "womb" in Aravaipa Canyon wreaked havoc on the feminized landscape of fruit orchards below; examples of the destructive power of desert water abound—although the Aravaipa flood can also be read as an act of cleansing, the canyon's obliteration of the transformation humans had wrought, leaving an empty space into which a former ecology might return. Indeed, the feminized landscape of the southwestern deserts was often enough not a passive, obedient woman but a raging figure, resistant to the restraints imposed by men with their dams, weirs, headgates, canals, flow meters, the complex of industrialized instrumentation of control. This too, however, is another stereotypical trope about the female, as governed by ungovernable emotion, enslaved to passion, impervious to reason. (A view that, again, goes back to the Greeks.)

In other words, gendering the desert is a complicated and fraught project. The simple dichotomy between female and male landscapes operates on a highly abstract level, dependent on stereotypical tropes about these two genders embedded in a long history of Euro-American thinking about the body, the mind, and the application of concepts based on them to entities that in fact have no gender and do not behave in properly gendered ways. Further, as we have seen, gender does not work conceptually in non-Western cultures in the same ways as for Euro-Americans, and so when applied to deserts—as indeed to other landscapes—generates contradictions and complexities unaccommodated in Euro-American thought. At the same time, applying a gender (or genders) to deserts entails rules about how one treats the land: as an unruly female in need of masculine authority, which will then be obedient and fecund, or as a separate, agential entity deserving the same respect one accords to one's fellow human beings? As a masculine space that must be transformed into a feminine one in order to serve the needs of men, or as a partner that can work with us in cooperation but can still sometimes be terrifying and dangerous, best avoided lest one incur its wrath? These matters are also wrapped up with the question of material agency, to which I revert in chapter 10.

PART 3

KNOWING THE DESERT

THE DESERTS OF LOS ANGELES

Two Topologies*

"Night falls quickly in Los Angeles," observes the narrator of Alison Lurie's *The Nowhere City*, "as in the desert which it once was."[1] "The desert" looms over much fiction set in Los Angeles, from Raymond Chandler's detective novels to Bret Easton Ellis's decadent rich of *Less Than Zero* or the quasi-future city of Steve Erickson's *Amnesiascope*. The desert figures powerfully too in nonfictional treatments of the city, like Carey McWilliams, *Southern California: An Island on the Land*[2] or Mike Davis, *City of Quartz*. These invocations of the desert might strike a positivist geographer as strange. The Los Angeles Basin is not arid enough to count as a real desert. The greater Los Angeles region lies nestled in the clasp of mountains: the Santa Monicas north and west, beyond which lurks the little paradise of Santa Barbara; the San Gabriels, just north of the city, which link up, across Cajon Pass, with the towering San Bernardinos, culminating at their east end in the 11,503-foot (3,506 m) peak of San Gorgonio; to the southeast, the basin-and-rangy ridges of the Santa Anas; and, beyond the Perris Valley, the San Jacintos sheltering Palm Springs, with the Santa Rosas to their south (see Fig. 1-1). Beyond those mountains—north of the San Bernardino Mountains, east of the San Jacintos—the great Mojave and Colorado Deserts roll across an arid countryside all the way to Las Vegas, and beyond.

Cultural snobbery aside, then, Los Angeles is no desert.[3] By the standard definition of geographers, deserts receive annual rainfall under ten inches (c. 254 mm); Los Angeles's average yearly accumulation of about 14.77 inches (c. 375.2 mm) situates the city safely out of the arid fold.[4] Of course, interannual variation is considerable; across the 139 years for which records exist, Los Angeles has experienced a desert-level shortage thirty-nine times, or about one year in 3.5. Anton Wagner insisted many years ago that microvariations abound; although the semi-arid steppe climate of the Köppen-Geiger BS classification predominates,

---

* An earlier version was published in *Boom California* in the May 24, 2017, issue at https://boomcalifornia. com/2017/05/24/the-deserts-of-los-angeles-two-topologies/, accessed September 20, 2023; a still earlier version was presented at the 2015 annual meeting of the Western Literature Association.

topographical variation, coastal influences, and the sea all conspire to impose different climatic regimes across the broad LA basin.[5] Sober observers have long known that Los Angeles isn't desert. Los Angeles occupies, Carey McWilliams observed, "this fortunate coast walled off from the desert by the great arch of mountains."[6] But the pull of the image is powerful, and fiction need not be bound by the strictures of the geographer. For many writers LA *is* a desert, not only metaphorically but also in physical fact. LA as desert clearly has had deep meaning, literal or metaphoric or both, for writers seeking to evoke something of the feel of the city.[7] The desert carries multiple, sometimes opposing, valences, both derived in Western thinking from tropes in the Hebrew Bible. It is on the one hand a space of austere purification, where sins are atoned and the purified can see the face—or at least, hindquarters—of God, and on the other a vile, useless wasteland; other tropes come out of, or are related to, these two oppositions.[8]

These two valences, I suggest, may explain, in part, the pull of the desert in writing about LA. On the one hand, the desert out east or north, the Mojave of Huxley's Antelope Valley home or movie stars' Palm Springs, may represent an escape from LA to something "realer" or "purer" (and see already the contrast between corrupt Hollywood and revivifying country in *The Girl from Hollywood* by Edgar Rice Burroughs, although his rural setting is the mountains, not the desert).[9] Clay of *Less Than Zero* may be seeking something like this when he turns in memory to family time in Palm Springs (although in fact his family life there is as corrupt and nihilistic as in Beverly Hills, as in Norman Mailer's *The Deer Park*). Nathalie Vincent-Arnaud sees the desert in Ellis's novel as a contradiction, both a refuge, a *locus amoenus*, and a no man's land; but for Clay its more important function is as a place where his "escapes . . . in the desert, outside this space of total confusion [Los Angeles], are presented . . . as an escape which possesses no other finality than the retaking of a lost memory."[10] On the other hand, seen as plopped down in a desert, LA can be figured merely as the gaudy disguise of a desert wasteland, ready to reassert its hideous uselessness and, in fact, unable to foster anything genuine ("nothing means anything here" is the refrain of *The Nowhere City*)—watered by stolen moisture, it is but an urban Imperial Valley, a faked landscape.[11]

These two topologies stand in dialectical opposition to each other. They demand from a writer a representational choice: is the relation of Los Angeles to the desert one of geographic distance and distinction, such that they occupy two different spaces that only come into conjunction through the movement of characters (whether physically or mentally) or the invasion of the space of Los Angeles by the desert itself or its representatives (the Santa Ana winds, in particular); or is the relation one of superposition, of a Los Angeles *on* a desert, a unique ecological and ideological phenomenon such that its intrusion into LA may come at any moment, in any place, *here* but not *here*, or indeed may shape the whole personality of the city by an invidious but invisible and irresistible presence below the surface? In what follows I would like to explore the play of these tropes, and others, in some fiction and nonfiction set in Los Angeles. Obviously far too much has been written about the city to treat even a modicum of this writing,[12] and the themes I hope to elucidate hardly exhaust the ways the desert has been used in stories about LA. (I have left film and television completely aside.) But I hope that even such an incomplete, fragmented, and selective exploration may contribute to how we understand the ways the presence of the desert has shaped writers' conceptualizations about this complex, alluring, frightening city.

THE DESERT IN THE AMERICAN IMAGINARY

Broadly speaking, American ideas about desert space derive from tropes deeply embedded in the Bible. These tropes do not form a coherent picture of desert space; rather, they facilitate a multiplicity of attitudes, some contradictory. In brief, biblical tropes frame the desert first as a blasted, dangerous place, abode of demons and death, abandoned by God. But the biblical desert also figures as a space where one, like Moses, can meet God; the desert can be a visionary place. The biblical desert can also be a ground of testing and purification, a necessary preliminary to entry into the Promised Land; or it can be a refuge, a safety zone for people escaping persecution or simply seeking a godly life. Finally, the desert can be a landscape of redemption, both for fallen people and as a ground that, with care and God's help, can be made into—or returned to a preexisting—paradisiacal state, a garden in the desert. This cache of tropes served Americans to help make sense of the deserts they encountered as they moved into the arid West. To them was added, in the early twentieth century, by reaction, an insistence on desert beauty, a view that fed into the environmental movement around wilderness preservation.[13]

First Topology—The Desert Out There

The first topology is the desert out there: beyond Los Angeles, to the east and north, the desert one must cross and endure to reach the Promised Land, and to which one may escape or be exiled, whether to find a place of purity and cleanliness opposed to the corruption that has overtaken the Promised Land, or to serve out a punishment and (hopefully) find redemption. As with deserts generally, it can also be a site of danger and death; in Bret Easton Ellis's *Imperial Bedrooms* the narrator's friend Kelly Montrose's body is found "hung from a bridge, [in] a bleak desert lined with scrub brush beneath it." This desert sends its demonic emissaries into the city, borne especially on the Santa Ana winds.[14]

One important and complex role the "desert out there" plays is as a barrier or escape hatch. This theme links to the biblical tale of the Israelites' passage through the Sinai Desert to the Promised Land, an analogy so blatantly apt to the travails of overland immigrants who suffered the Mojave and Colorado Deserts to reach California that it became a cliché. In this role the desert as barrier or boundary pairs nicely with the Pacific to the west, thanks especially to the ancient trope of ocean as desert. So in 1897 Frank Norris bracketed San Francisco as between: "to the west the waste of the Pacific, to the east the wastes of the desert." As another put it, "[t]he blinding blue desert of the Pacific." Remember ("Mem") Steddon, heroine of the 1922 Hollywood novel *Souls for Sale*, takes a madcap drive with another actor along the coast highway, north of Hollywood, "'on the rim of the world' with desert on one side and the whole Pacific sea on the other." Rose, the main character of Kate Braverman's *Lithium for Medea* (1979), meditates on the boundaries of LA, desert and sea; Cynthia Kadohata's *In the Heart of the Valley of Love* (1992) begins with a lapidary reference to "the black desert, beyond reach of Los Angeles." The "long haul across the deserts" prevents good theatrical companies from playing Los Angeles, and passage over the desert—by airplane—brings F. Scott Fitzgerald's last tycoon out of the rest of the country and into the inimitable LA.[15]

For a forty-niner like William Manly, whose exploits in escaping Death Valley in 1849–50 and returning to rescue immigrants stranded there were immortalized in his autobiography, those deserts were a challenge and a test, but they can also serve LA as a protective barrier or a release valve, a safety hatch. The hero of Steve Erickson's *Amnesiascope* longs for a thousand-mile-wide Mojave to keep crazy Eastern evangelicals out of his city. Later, he escapes Los Angeles through that same desert, which, he hopes, will reclaim as its own during his desert passage the "evil spirits" that have bedeviled him. Rose of *Lithium for Medea* finds in the desert beyond Los Angeles her refuge, her escape, a desert theme found much earlier in John Fante's *Ask the Dust*. Indeed, for Mem of Rupert Hughes's *Souls for Sale*, crossing the desert west to east marks a return from the unreality of Los Angeles, that "terrifying city" (yet, simultaneously, "a restoring fountain of health and hope and ambition"), to a realer, and certainly duller, world; indeed, departing, "[s]he had a little of the feeling Eve must have had as she made her last walk down the quickest paths of Eden toward the gate that would not open again." Mem's train is even figured as the serpent. It spends two days passing through the desert—a space that, Mem admits, "had its charms" and stands for the world she has left: a long, flat vista of "dead platitudinous levels [that] made going easier," for "[p]latitudes were labor saving and you went faster and safer over them."[16] This desert is a metaphor for the life Mem left behind, stultifying and ambitionless, cramped, ruled by a rigid father, for the fountain of hope and happiness she found in her Hollywood successes.

In John Gregory Dunne's *True Confessions*, Desmond Spellacy is exiled to the desert in Twenty-Nine Palms outside Los Angeles in permanent penance-making after he's caught up in scandal. Priest and advisor to the Cardinal of Los Angeles, Des had a long relationship with Jack Armstrong, one-time pimp and later corrupt contractor who did most of the building work for the Church. In an act of revenge by Des's dishonest policeman brother Tommy, Armstrong is framed for the gruesome murder of Lois Fazenda, the "Virgin Tramp"—based on the actual "Black Dahlia" murder of 1947.[17] In Dunne's dark vision, everything and everyone in Los Angeles is both corrupt and not what they seem: police detectives work as bagmen, nice girls service their bosses in back rooms, upstanding married barbers like to shave prostitutes' pubes—and kill them.

The desert by Twenty-Nine Palms doesn't know this corruption. To a naïve parish priest trying to fix his car, Des's brother Tommy conveys the trick of adding pepper to a defective carburetor learned in the used-car business. Parishioners' problems run to dysfunctional bowels and young nuns vocationally confused; Des's housekeeper avers "she had never been in a man's room alone"—unlike virtually every other woman in *True Confessions*. (Tommy's wife, Mary Margaret, is chaste, but she's also insane.) For Des, the twenty-eight years he spends in desert exile (a little joke on the name of his desert town) provide an opportunity to reflect on his sins, to recognize the role played in his life and career by his lust for power and control—sins far worse than those of the flesh, as Des's former confessor had known. The Egyptian desert fathers knew this too—they struggled against sexual desire but were perfectly aware that, as sins go, it was hardly in a league with pride, power, and arrogance. It is living in the desert that helps Des not merely to see his own sinfulness—he has already been thinking about it throughout the novel—but to confront it and, as it were, make peace with it. This would have been impossible in Los Angeles; the contrast between the desert out there and the city could not be greater.[18]

The desert's proximity, in other words, offers some writers about Los Angeles a convenient locale for the performance of contrition for sins committed in, and often abetted by, the city. In deploying the desert in this way, writers are playing right into that powerful trope of "the desert" in Western imagination, the desert as a locus for punishment and expiation. It seems not excessive to propose that the degradation of Los Angeles, depicted in so much of the fiction set in the city as worse by orders of magnitude than that of other cities, should be counterbalanced by a harsh environment suited, in this conceptualization, only to wear away the accumulated filth of the sinful soul. Polar opposites on the moral and environmental meter stand shoulder to shoulder, ready on the one hand to foster husband killers, daughter rapists, and all manner of unspeakable human atrocity,[19] and on the other to redeem, through suffering and deprivation, the souls so befouled.

Another powerful contrast between desert and city plays out in John Fante's *Ask the Dust*, recently praised as "perhaps the most seminal work in the literary history of Los Angeles." Here the articulation between desert and city runs through the figure of Camilla, the object of Arturo Bandini's lust, envy, anger, despair. Her sometime boyfriend Sammy, a would-be writer whose stories Bandini trashes, lives out in the Mojave Desert 150 miles from Bandini's Bunker Hill hotel. Camilla moves back and forth between Sammy's desert shack and Bandini's dark urban landscape, but she is, in fundamental ways, in her sexuality, her shamelessness, linked to the desert, not unlike another desert woman, Barbara Worth of Harold Bell Wright's *The Winning of Barbara Worth*[20]—although Barbara's sexuality is expressed indirectly and her morals unimpeachable. The ironies in *Ask the Dust* are more subtle than in Dunne's novel, for Camilla's behavior violates—apparently—rules of "civilized" behavior—she sleeps around, she smokes pot, she returns to an abusive boyfriend—but in many respects she is a more genuine person, truer to herself, than Bandini and his city. In the end she abandons herself to the desert, walking off into the Mojave and vanishing over a ridge; her body is never found, and *Ask the Dust* ends with the startling image of Bandini inscribing a copy of his first book to her and heaving it out into the desert—an admission at once of love, loss, and defeat.[21]

Fante's biographer Stephen Cooper suggests that in fashioning Camilla, Fante took features of his sometime girlfriend, the Mexican Marie Baray, and "combined [her] smoldering beauty with the edgy borderline instability of Audrey, the flamboyant waitress from Main Street's Liberty Bar." But Camilla's character and behavior bring to mind another woman from the distant past with deep links to the desert. Mary of Egypt, who lived in Late Antiquity, renounced her parents at the age of twelve. She ran away from home to Alexandria, biggest city in Egypt and the capital of the Roman province. There she pursued a life of utter depravity and dissolution, acting as a quasi-prostitute—"quasi" because she often didn't even bother to charge her clients, even those who offered to pay, due to her uncontrolled and insatiable lust for sex, which drove her to accept as many men as she could. When, however, she was barred from entering a church in Palestine by an invisible force, she renounced her promiscuity and retreated to the desert east of the Jordan River. There, much later, she met a monk named Zosimas to whom she related her story. After she was done, "she ran off again into the depths of the desert." For Mary, the desert serves as a space of repentance and purification, in contrast to the city, an abode of endless sin. But the desert acts in another register on Mary: when Zosimas encounters her, she is naked, but so desiccated by her years in the desert that she is practically unrecognizable as a woman.

> Her figure is imprinted with the charisma of the wild landscape of which she has become part. The desert has turned Mary's female weakness into masculine resolution and ascetic capacity; for wilderness blurs not only the boundaries between human and nonhuman, but also gender boundaries.[22]

Fante was raised as a devout Catholic and attended a Catholic high school; it's not at all unlikely that he'd heard of Mary, although I know no evidence. She's celebrated on April 1 in the 2004 revision of the Catholic martyrology. In any case the parallels are striking, and the impact of the desert as both a redemptive space and a gender-bending one we've explored already in chapters 1, 4, and 5.

The external desert can, of course, invade Los Angeles, too. In Aldous Huxley's *Ape and Essence* its desert dunes blanket the concrete of the city streets, like Sahara sand concealing the monuments of ancient Egypt; indeed, in this post-apocalyptic LA, the desert has spread everywhere. In *The Day of the Locust* Nathaniel West's narrator Tod Hackett, gawking at a speaker at the "Tabernacle of the Third Coming," muses that he "was probably just in from one of those colonies in the desert near Soboba Hot Springs where he had been conning over his soul on a diet of raw fruits and nuts. . . . The message he had brought to the city was one that an illiterate anchorite might have given decadent Rome."[23]

Perhaps no dangerous desert intrusion into Los Angeles has resonated more with many of its writers than the Santa Ana winds, emblem of "the terrible hot season from June to September when a fiery wind blows from the desert and the sky turns blood red."[24] An early version of their impact appears in *On the Lot and Off*, the last novel of George Chester and his wife Lilian Chester, published in 1924:

> Shrieking and moaning, the wind swept in from the desert to take its eerie part in the life of Hollywood, to wield its mysterious influence on the fourth or fifth or whatever largest industry in the United States. It was one of those summer days rare to the Pacific coast, but poignant, when through the yellow sunlight there sift vague phantom shapes of impalpable dust which bite the skin and smart the eyes, and are the prickling forerunners of a three-day withering heat from out of the very heart of the vast shadeless inferno up yonder in the waste places. It was such a day as lowers the vitality and depresses the spirit and sets the nerves on edge, and when vitality ebbs and depression reigns and nerves are aquiver, both men and women do things which they might otherwise not have done; so no one knows what

tremendous extent of folly and of tragedy might be chargeable to this same shrill, shrieking, moaning, sobbing wind from the deadly desert.[25]

The Santa Ana winds serve more or less as a *deus ex machina*, for they effect the *dénouement* of the plot by driving several characters to actions they might otherwise have abjured, even sometimes against their own best interests.

On the Lot and Off has a potboiler of a plot, but the central thrust is just the efforts of the protagonist Izzy Iskowitz to gain control of his own motion picture studio. For this to happen, many unpredictable, evidently impossible things must occur, and it's the Santa Ana winds that do the trick. So, for instance, the winds cause the owner of the Producer and Distributors Trust Company to place his wholly incompetent son Tennyson in charge of the bank at the very moment that the financially toppling Sam Black of Luna Pictures is begging for an extension on his loan:

> but at that moment an exotic gust of wind from right out of the blistering pit of the dust whistled around the corner and between the classic gates and through the leaded-glass windows of Sam Black's office, and smote him hip and thigh and blue-tipped nose with such an excruciatingly shivering blast that he yelled into the phone—insulting Tennyson and sealing his fate.

Later, in a crucial move in his plans, Izzy gets his boss David Schusshel to buy Luna, and again the wind is key: "On a cooler, less enervating day, David might have withstood. . . . But outside howled the desert wind, and through the screens there blew a steady stream of hot, enervating air, and David's resistance was low; and he fell." And Prudence Joy, the actress Izzy loved but could not marry, in thrall to a no-good husband and desperately in need of money, swallows her pride and begs Izzy for advice, sitting in his office "perfectly motionless while that gale from the desert shrieked and moaned and shrilled its mournful dirge outside, while the stinging heat which came from it seemed to dry up the very life in her." The winds are determinative—except for Izzy, who's immune to their effects.[26]

The Chesters don't call their "desert wind" specifically the Santa Ana, but that's clearly what they meant. In any case, these winds then howl through much subsequent LA fiction, especially what evolves into the *noir* detective story in the hands of James M. Cain, Raymond Chandler, and others. Chandler's own most famous description of the Santa Anas, which appeared in 1939 in the story "Red Wind," has taken on an emblematic role, thanks in part to Joan Didion's citation of it in her essay "Los Angeles Notebook." Two years later Erle Stanley Gardner, writing under the pseudonym A. A. Fair, cooked up an even more "extraordinary two pages" on the winds:

> In the spring and late fall southern California has peculiarly violent desert windstorms known as "santanas," sometimes called "Santa Anas." For hours before such winds start, the sky will be clear and dustless. The air will be warm, listless, devoid of life. The details of objects can be seen with startling clarity. Silk or rayon garments will crackle with static

electricity.

Then suddenly a blast of wind comes sweeping down from the east and north, a hot, dry wind which churns particles of dust so fine they filter between dry lips, grit against the surfaces of teeth. As a rule, those storms blow for three days and three nights. Those sections which are protected from the wind itself nevertheless feel the dehydrating effects of the dry, hot air. People's nerves get raw. They are listless and irritable. Perspiration is sucked up by the dry air so the hot skin becomes gritty with dust. . . .

One look at the star-studded sky, and I knew a santana was coming. Stars blazed down with such steady brilliance the heavens seemed filled to overflowing. The air out of doors seemed as close as it was in the study—warm, dry, devitalizing air that made one's nerves stand on edge. . . .

When I had finished the third chapter [of the book he was reading], the wind struck. It struck with the force of a solid wall. The house swayed with the force of that first terrific gust. All over the place I could hear doors slamming, could hear people running, and the sound of closing windows. . . .

My nerves are always on edge during those windstorms.[27]

The effect of the Santa Anas—both the physical impact of dusty, obscured vision, a "dryness [that] is fairly stinging, like a slightly sour amphetamine," and the psychological disorientation they bring—match well the mood of noir; "the evil," Norman Klein notes, "is still in the atmosphere."[28]

In Frederick Kohner's *Gidget*, it is "one of those icky desert winds we call the Santa Ana" that sparks "real drama" in the plot, "that very important element labeled by [Gidget's high-school English] teacher Glicksberg as the 'clincher' or climax." Gidget has earned herself a back-handed invitation to a luau on the Malibu beach, despite warnings that it would be an "orgy" (a word she has to look up in the dictionary). During the party "a creepy wind was blowing . . . like something coming right out of a furnace." This Santa Ana, rushing down from the mountains and the desert and out to sea, turns back on the land and whips sparks carelessly spread by the revelers onto the sagebrush beyond the highway, fanning up a great roaring brush fire. The desert-spawned fire serves as a blatant metaphor for Gidget's own raging but misdirected sexuality, for in the confusion, as police and fire trucks swoop down to contain the blaze and enlist the help of the partying surfers whose drunken carelessness caused the fire, Gidget cannot get home and ends up seeking shelter in the Kahoona's beach hut. On his return he insists that it will be impossible for her to pass the cordon of police cars and fire trucks before morning; she can, he offers, sleep in his bed, while he takes the chair. Gidget, out of a mix of guilt—after all, he's exhausted, having just spent several hours battling the flames while she dozed in his hut—and desire, voices a daring invitation: "'Maybe you're not comfortable in that chair. There is room enough in the bed for both of us here.'" He accepts, and Gidget reckons "this was the moment I had been waiting for. Now it would happen. He would make me a woman." Instead, like the sudden rains that had just doused the brushfire, the Kahoona douses Gidget: "'[W]hen it happens between you and a man it must be beautiful. . . . And it must be all for love, Franzie.'" (He uses her real name—a marker that this is serious.) "'The time must be ripe. When the time is ripe—you'll know. You'll be trembling the way you tremble now—but it'll be right. This isn't.'" The desert brings a whirlwind of endangered virtue; luckily, a good patriarchal figure is there to protect Gidget from herself.[29]

In one of the "tales" called "Sirocco" in Eve Babitz's collection *Slow Days, Fast Company*, her narrator[30] repudiates the trope of the evil Santa Ana winds. "From earliest childhood," she insists, "I have rejoiced over the Santa Ana winds. . . . Every time *I* feel one coming, I put on my dancing spirits." As with Gidget, the Santa Anas spell for Babitz's narrator a potent sexual compulsion—but unlike with Gidget, there's no "grown up man" around to hit the brakes. The narrator recounts two experiences, both connected with her "just friend" William, both involving other women, both prompted by the Santa Anas, however much she "hate[s] blaming things on the weather."

The first, narrated with a certain coyness, revolves around an Italian named Isabella Farfalla, "bored with the ancient decadence that her own country provided" who, "like the Santa Anas" "was a devastating force. . . . [I]t was her nature to interject chaos at the very time things had about ossified." At the opening of a new club, Isabella and the narrator engage in some heavy petting:

> "You two really looked beautiful," William sighed about me and Isabella, "kissing each other like that."
>
> "Well, at least we looked beautiful," I said. "*Now* what do I do?"
>
> "Maybe you really like women better," he suggested. "Maybe that's been it all along."
>
> "But what does one *do* with women?" I said, imagining at once exactly what one would do. "It was probably just the Santa Ana," I said.
>
> "You never kissed *me* like that," he replied.

Her second experience came later, in October: "It was a Sunday and the Santa Ana had been afoot since the night before. It was so dry that the bougainvillea, picked, would embalm in the heat and last forever like Japanese paper flowers." She gets a phone call from a friend, Day Tully, and invites her over; in the Santa Ana aridity Day's "brown hair crackled from the lightning in the air." The narrator suggests a walk to William's; Day agrees, but cautions: "I hear this wind changes people into maniacs." Indeed—soon after arrival at William's and the consumption of "freezing-cold, green jigger glasses of vodka," the narrator

> was the first to pounce. What I wouldn't do with Isabella, who knew what she was doing, I now smoothly instigated between Day and William and myself. Passion from boredom and vodka flashed through my veins, passion and fanned curiosity toppled us, Santa Ana-ed, down upon William's bed. Only not William. I wouldn't let William touch me, and we almost tore poor Day in half.

For Babitz's narrator—or shall we drop the pretense and just call her "Eve"?—the Santa

Ana madness brings happy release: "if we didn't have the Santa Anas," she concludes, "how straight we would all be."[31]

The Santa Anas continue to work their malevolence today. In *Strip Tees*, Kate Flannery relates their impact on her when she migrates from Philly to LA just a few years ago. She meets Ivy, who apparently wanders LA looking for young women to entice into working for American Apparel:

> Ivy found me at Little Joy, a dive bar on Sunset Boulevard I discovered on the night the Santa Ana winds arrived. They roared like a supernatural force, knocking out the power in Echo Park, and I thought it might be spooky to explore my neighborhood like that, out there in the blackness with the sounds of swaying palm trees creaking overhead. The night *felt* electric, it crackled with possibilities. Winds like these just didn't exist in Philly.

The bar emerges out of the dust and chaos of the winds: "I was just about to give up on my walk through the Santa Anas—the wind was warm like bathwater but stung my bare legs with grit—when I saw the Little Joy ahead." Kate accepts the job, even though its premise—that she'll be a "spokesmodel" for the brand by wearing their clothing as she works—violates her own feminist convictions: she needs the money. American Apparel turns out, of course, to be a dreadful place to work, founded by a serial rapist.[32]

In her celebration of the Santa Anas as a blatant catalyst for sexual experimentation Babitz plays a field she has mostly to herself—unless Kate Flannery's "The Year I Fucked Everybody,"[33] which comes later in her job, is a delayed haunting. But the underlying trope remains the same; there's no questioning Day's observation that the winds change folks into maniacs—they do indeed for Eve too, and fundamentally, she's really no different from Gidget: both open themselves up to sexual experience under the influence of the winds, both indeed welcome the cover the Santa Ana mania grants to do something they have been wanting for a long time. And neither sees anything *wrong* with what they want—the swirling desert invitation to sexual adventure outside the bounds of marriage or heterosexual coupled conformity.[34]

The Santa Ana winds, then, bring *in* the desert: a dangerous, unpredictable, socially destructive or disruptive force of nature. They are emblematic of the "dangerous desert" trope that sits at one of the two poles of desert imaginary discussed in chapter 1. Corrosive, corrupting, disorienting, debilitating, the winds block thought, dissolve morals, wreak devastation; they are, so to speak, Satan and his desert demons embodied in a howling rush of air.

There's another way the desert comes into Los Angeles, a gentler way in which the desert is reproduced, welcomed, or remembered. Kiowa N. Scott Momaday's *House Made of Dawn* alternates between scenes set in New Mexico and scenes in Los Angeles. During his time in Los Angeles, Abel—who has recently returned from a foreign war—feels alienated and estranged, even though he has a girlfriend, Milly, with whom he enjoys Sunday picnics on Santa Monica beach and shares confidences. His war trauma has tracked him to Los Angeles and gets all mixed up with his relations with Milly, to the point that his trauma intrudes even into their lovemaking. He drinks and cannot hold a job. Abel meets one Tosamah, Priest of the Sun, who runs a "Holiness Pan-Indian Rescue Mission." Tosamah conducts a peyote ceremony that ends with an evocation of the four directions, a marker that "something holy was going on in the universe."[35] The peyote ceremony doesn't cure Abel, but it brings into the circle that Tomasah creates the flavor of Abel's desert home, the natural world in which he grew up. The imported desert is reassuring, calming, and healing, mediated through the peyote and the Native American companionship during the ceremony. Unlike the desert of the Santa Anas, the peyote-infused desert brings relief to Abel, alienated and confused in the white world of Los Angeles.

In the poem "Many Farm Notes," the Acoma poet Simon Ortiz evokes a Navajo girl:

> The L.A. kid was a city child
> and a Navajo rodeo queen,
> who said she'd seen me on the road
> coming out of Window Rock,
> said her friend had said,
> "I think that was him,
> we just passed him up,"
> and felt so bad,
> said she was born in L.A.
> but wasn't really a city girl
> and visited her homeland
> every Summer, and said
> her mother was from Lukachukai.[36]

Even though the nameless girl was born in Los Angeles, she remains at core a desert girl, a denizen in soul if not in reality of the high desert of the Navajo Nation in northeastern Arizona. She returns every summer to recharge her desert self and bring it back to the city where, I imagine, it keeps her and protects her and shapes her identity—an identity bound up with the specific place, Lukachukai, a settlement on the Nation in the shadow of the Lukachukai Mountains, in Arizona, that birthed her mother. For both Ortiz's anonymous Navajo girl and Silko's Abel, grounding in the desert is crucial to enable them to survive in Los Angeles.

The Second Topology—"Underneath It All"[37]

In his 1939 novel, *Ask the Dust*, John Fante writes of the desert underneath the city of Los Angeles:

> Here was the endlessly mute plasticity of nature, indifferent to the great city; here was the desert beneath these streets, around these streets, waiting for the city to die, to cover it with timeless sand once more. There came over me a terrifying sense of understanding about the meaning and pathetic destiny of men. The desert was always there, a patient white animal, waiting for men to die, for civilizations to flicker and pass into the darkness. Then men seemed brave to me, and I was proud to be numbered among them. All the evil of the

world seemed not evil at all, but inevitable and good and part of that endless struggle to keep the desert down.[38]

Here, then, is an early and lapidary statement of the second topology, the desert below, lurking silently and patiently underneath the concrete and hamburger stands and tract houses for its inevitable opportunity to reclaim the landscape people have appropriated, improperly and arrogantly, from its arid sands.

This second topology clashes with a beloved trope about Los Angeles: that it is a paradise, an Eden set in a bedizened landscape; as such, the city becomes a sort of "Ellis Island of beauty" where people flock to join the American dream. This is the LA of the promotional literature churned out by the ream by California boosters in the nineteenth century (and in a recent series of California tourism ads starring celebrities) in which Los Angeles figured not as desert but as an Edenic landscape, a paradise on Earth: "if not the original Eden, then a simulacrum that excelled the model." Berthold Brecht, writing in his journal during his sojourn in LA, saw through the falsity, or so he thought—through the glittery surface of palm trees and hydrangeas, Art Deco office buildings and iconic hamburger stands, Hollywood back lots and ribbons of freeway; because Los Angeles sat on an original desert, he averred, it was not only an ecological wasteland but also intrinsically hostile to culture and art: "as for culture: it decays unbelievably fast (like California's artificial flora, planted on desert ground, when not watered)," for "all this greenery is wrested from the desert by irrigation systems, scratch the surface a little and the desert shows through." Or, as Eve Babitz remarked, apropos a graffito, "In Los Angeles it's hard to tell if you're dealing with the real true illusion or the false one."[39] This works, of course, because of an environmental trope about Los Angeles itself in contradistinction to the desert underneath: that it sits in an arena of bountiful good health, beneficent climate, and easy living. Many years ago, Carey McWilliams encapsulated this trope in a few lapidary pages of *Southern California* he called "The Folklore of Climatology." Boosters like Samuel Storey, writing in 1889, believed they'd "found a Paradise on Earth" where "lungers"—sufferers of tuberculosis—found relief, flowers and fruits proliferated, and the only fear possible was enervation from living in paradise.[40]

This trope developed early in the city's history. A proleptic Los Angeles as paradise appears already in Horace Bell's 1881 memoir *Reminiscences of a Ranger: Early Times in Southern California*, retrojected deep into the Spanish past. He imagines a trio of Spanish soldiers perched on a hill, enchanted by the scene below:

> The plains and rolling hills had discarded their mantle of green and donned their sere robes of summer. Gazing toward the sun, which had now marked the first segment in the circle of its journey, plains, hills, forests, lakes, rivers, valleys, and towering mountains in a splendid panorama met their wondering vision. To the rear of where the three warriors sat . . . lay in silent beauty the shimmering waters of a beautiful lake sheltered from the rude blasts of the ocean by a rampart of kind and protecting hills. To the left for leagues could be traced the serpentine windings of the river. . . . Obliquely to their rear and looking southward to the sea the waters of the Porciuncula [River, later the Los Angeles River] swept by like a silver

stripe in a ribbon of green, shaded by the umbrageous white-armed sycamore and the more verdant cottonwood, under whose protecting shades gamboled countless herds of deer and antelope, while still beyond are to be seen rocky islands in the ocean posted like knights in armor guarding the portals of Paradise.

One of the soldiers, shaking off his bedazzlement at "this vision of beauty," thanks his commanding sergeant for "shar[ing] with us this foresight of Paradise." It is, of course, the site of the future Los Angeles, chosen by "our Blessed Lady, the Angel Queen" herself.[41]

Standing in fervent opposition to this happy talk is what J. U. Peters has called "The Los Angeles Anti-Myth," well represented by Dunne's *True Confessions*. This Los Angeles of corruption, violence, fornication, debasement, and falsity Peters traces to the city's decenteredness, its agglutination of suburbs, a "spatial disorder" that "suggests a deeper spatial implication: the jarring and dehumanizing shock of sudden displacement which the characters in many novels undergo."[42] Indeed—but another contributor to this condition surely is also the "false tinsel" that lurks below: "Los Angeles was a desert to begin with" and remains part of "this western desert."[43] Remarkably similar language in novel after novel evokes the desert qualities of the Los Angeles scene: its "hot sun" in *True Confessions* or the "hot dry air" of *Less Than Zero*; the "parched and arid heat of Los Angeles" in Carolyn See's *Golden Days*, a "heat like a flat pan in the High Desert." In Huxley's *After Many a Summer Dies the Swan*, the Englishman Jeremy Pordage first perceives LA as "mountains—ridge after ridge as far as the eye could reach, a desiccated Scotland, empty under the blue desert sky." Ross MacDonald's cynical Lew Archer sees LA simply as "an urban wilderness in the desert." And when an economic recession grips the film industry, "[t]he garden of Los Angeles had reverted to the desert."[44] Not, be it noted, *a* desert, but *the* desert: the desert that had always been lurking there.

The Los Angeles desert frames Gavin Lambert's 1954 novel *The Slide Area* from the first pages. Introducing his Los Angeles, Lambert's narrator—a Hollywood scriptwriter—stresses the city's "impression of unreality," reinforced by the "neurotic" "behavior of the air." In fact "nothing belongs except the desert soil. . . . Because the earth is desert, its surface always has that terrible dusty brilliance." The city rests on "land dried and crusted into desert . . . a quagmire under a hot sun"; it is, he insists, "difficult to settle in a comfortable unfinished desert" where "buildings lie around like nomads' tents in the desert" and a motel stands "solitary in the desert of its parking lot." Lambert isn't completely consistent in seeing LA as built on a desert, for sometimes he remarks on the role of the "gritty mountains" in separating the city from "the dry Mojave desert," and he starts and ends his tale with electrical storms "near Palm Springs . . . out over the desert." The predominant theme, though, is certainly Los Angeles *as* desert, and the desert fact of the city, its aridity, original emptiness, sterility, shape the stunted lives of the novel's characters. The link is explicit in Lambert's narrator's description of his friend Mark's beach house after he has left for the South Pacific: it presents "[a] little desert of emptiness and stillness that people seem instinctively to avoid."[45]

This theme is especially prominent in See's *Golden Days*. The protagonist Edith Langley grows up "in the parched and arid heart of Los Angeles." Returning after a sojourn in New York, she imagines LA as a plant in the desert, its extension from downtown "a thin stem, the Santa Monica freeway, heading due west and putting out greenery, places in this western desert where you'd love to live—if things went right." Desert vegetation is tough, thorny, resistant to drought and abuse, but likewise not easy to approach—perhaps, in contrast to Edith's initial impression, not so easy to live with. The house she buys on her return is tucked deep up Topanga Canyon, the "Old Canyon," which "[s]ome people say . . . is the *desert* part"—although, in fact, "Los Angeles was a desert to begin with." Yucca grow, taller than Edith's daughters; there are rattlesnakes, neighbors warn, and Edith later watches two boys wrangle over possession of a three-foot-long snake—but surely no rattler—that had unwisely slunk into the neighborhood market. The canyon bakes in 120-degree heat, and, like all southwestern deserts, is subject both to flood and fire. The desert of LA impinges even on Edith's wardrobe, as she switches from flannel shirts to silk blouses, "raw silk" being, she supposes, "the flannel of the desert."[46] In other words, the desert does not simply frame See's LA, offering a counterpoint out east, or north, over the passes, to serve as a locus for redemption or despair; the desert *is* LA, and living in the city becomes, for See's protagonists, an adaptation to a desert world. In ways both blatant and subtle, the desert compels her characters to react to it—be it by shedding flannels for silk (the same projected persona, a different skin) or, eventually, by adapting to a nuclear-devastated landscape, a final act of desertification performed on a desert wasteland.[47]

While the deserts of Los Angeles barely inflect *After Many a Summer Dies the Swan*, Aldous Huxley's first LA novel, in his second novel written in California and set in Los Angeles, *Ape and Essence*, the desert does not merely serve as a setting but plays a central role in both plot and message. Two screenwriters, Bob Briggs and Huxley's narrator, discover a rejected script in a movie producer's slush pile submitted by a certain William Tallis. Intrigued, they travel out to see the author, a recluse living "on the southwest fringe of the Mojave desert." Huxley draws a contrast between the "tough ascetic lives of the desert" and the cottonwoods and willows along irrigation ditches, "clinging precariously . . . to another, easier, more voluptuous mode of being." Huxley's desert outside LA immediately evokes the tension between the city itself, which can only exist by importation of water and thus promotes a morally corrupt way of life (already evident in the scripts Bob and his partner paw through), and an ascetic, and so purer, desert life—a framing that evokes also the role of the desert in Dunne's *True Confessions*. Then, as Bob and the narrator approach Tallis's house:

> Out there, on the floor of the desert, there had been a noiseless, but almost explosive transformation. The clouds had shifted and the sun was now shining on the nearest of those abrupt and jagged buttes, which rose so inexplicably, like islands, out of the enormous plain. A moment before they had been black and dead. Now suddenly they had come to life between a shadowed foreground and a background of cloudy darkness. They shone as if with their own incandescence.
>
> I touched Bob's arm and pointed.

"Now do you understand why Tallis chooses to live at the end of this road?"[48]

Tallis's script imagines a Los Angeles in 2108 after combined disasters of nuclear war and environmental catastrophe have devastated the United States.[49] LA, "the great Metrollopis [*sic*] is a ghost town . . . what was once the world's largest oasis is now its greatest agglomeration of ruins in a wasteland. . . . Dunes of sand have drifted across the concrete." The plot of Tallis's movie revolves around the arrival in Southern California of an expedition from New Zealand that includes a botanist named Poole. Captured by the gang that rules the ruined city, he meets a young woman named Loola; they fall in love, but strict eugenics rules imposed by the gang forbid their relationship. Eventually Poole and Loola escape into the desert, across the San Gabriel Mountains, headed north for a supposed paradise where love is free and children can be conceived; to do so, they seek refuge and invisibility in the "enormous expanse of the Mojave desert," the desert beyond the desert of Los Angeles.[50]

Thus the desert plays a multiplicity of roles in *Ape and Essence*: it is at once the "desert underneath," the ecological reality of Los Angeles concealed—only temporarily, and always precariously—by an overlay of water and fakery; it is that ecological reality not created but simply revealed by the nuclear bombs and other crises that stripped away the "false tinsel"; and it is also a more genuine ecology "out there," where Tallis lives and through which Poole and Loola escape; it is refuge. Perhaps we are invited to imagine a better LA had its desert never been gussified with Hollywood falsity, or perhaps the desertified Los Angeles tyrannized by the Archimandrite and his acolytes is what it deserves. In any case, the "natural" desert is clearly the better place, even if it is tough and unforgiving. Poole and Loola, in the end, must serve an apprenticeship of suffering and purgation during their desert trek north, sore feet, little food, and thirty miles and more of painful walking. It is the desert as *test*, another desert sojourn to reach the Promised Land—California, love, happiness, children. *Ape and Essence*, then, may stand for a type—prefigured almost presciently in Philip Wylie's 1945 short story "The Paradise Crater," which government officials feared represented a leak in the Manhattan Project—scenarios of the Los Angeleno apocalypse, especially those predicated on nuclear annihilation, which evoke a return of the repressed when the LA underlying them has been figured as masked desert.[51]

In *After the Bomb*, young Philip Singer, his brother, and his brother's girlfriend Cara survive a thermonuclear blast over LA because they happened to be lounging in an old bomb shelter in the brothers' backyard. The book tells the story of Philip's efforts to save his badly burned mother while moving through a ruined, post-nuclear landscape. The desert of *After the Bomb* bears, however, two valences, opposite and ironic. On the one hand, the Santa Ana that launches the plot adumbrates the desert-like destruction of the hydrogen bomb to come; on the other, it, and the desertification of the bomb itself, strip away the falsity of Los Angeles: Philip's apparently omni-competent brother Matt proves hopeless, clueless, and almost useless after the catastrophe, while Matt's girlfriend Cara, whom Philip had hoped to snag for himself before his brother lured her away, now sees who's really reliable in an emergency. In the end Matt is redeemed, more or less; whether Cara will switch brothers remains undisclosed. But fundamentally it's the falsity of the LA world that had worn Philip down in his ordinary life that's stripped away by desert wind and desertifying bomb—LA both invaded and revealed.[52]

The fundamental falsity of the desert materializes—deceptively—in its mirages, and Los Angeles is all mirage. So when Paul, a protagonist of Lurie's *The Nowhere City*, drives through an LA cityscape "for once swept clear of smog by the desert winds"—the Santa Anas, as Lurie's allusion to the season makes clear—"[t]he city shimmered in the dry, warm air, every detail sharp, but all colors bleached out by the intensity of the light, like a mirage." Paul fears lest this mirage "wasn't the harmless decorative sort, but one of those false visions that hover just above the horizon of the desert, luring travelers on to exhaustion and despair."[53] So too people: in Chandler's *Farewell, My Lovely*, "Helen Grayle"—in fact Velma Valento—started life as a sexually promiscuous chorus girl, but after eight years has succeeded—it seems—in burying her sordid past. The reinvented Helen is a "true product of Los Angeles, a city of resplendent surfaces"; she is "a figment, inspired by a culture that glorifies illusion."[54] That is to say, Helen is a mirage: that deceptive, fatal emanation of the desert, a confection of shimmering air with no more tangible reality than a passing breeze. This image suits perfectly Hollywood, that emblem of Los Angeles in so much fiction, whose primary function (that is, aside from coining profits for its studios) is simply to deliver a gullible public confected falsity as if it were something real.[55]

SOME FINAL RUMINATIONS AND UNANSWERED QUESTIONS

The whole congeries of desert imagery and Los Angeles fiction was captured succinctly in an essay by Charles Crow, who, evoking Joan Didion's *Play It As It Lays*, writes of

> the desert, that vast and troubling presence which most Angelenos would like to ignore. The paradox of Los Angeles, geographically, is that it is both a seacoast and a desert city. . . . [T]he ecology of the city is so fragile that it cannot hope to survive very long; at some point the aqueducts that are its arteries will fail... and the city will disappear. . . . The desert, lurking in the east, is the city's doom. Out of the desert blow the Santa Ana winds, drying the hillsides and spreading the brush fires. . . . Deserts have always been places of prophecy and truth-seeking, and the message of this desert, "the hard empty white core of the world," is annihilation, nothingness . . . [a place where] a man walked into the desert seeking God and was killed by a rattlesnake.[56]

Which is not to say, of course, that the man in question failed to find God; he may just not have found the God he thought he was looking for.[57]

Desert redemption, desert evil, the desert out there, desert demons borne into town on the Santa Anas—desert barrier, the desert below, the desert remade in nuclear annihilation, desert truth, desert falsity, abhorrence, fascination, attraction—so many deserts shape the city, in its fiction; without the desert, indeed, there is no fictional Los Angeles. Before I conclude, however, it behooves us to consider, briefly, some nonfictional treatments of Los Angeles, although the desert tropes—whether "out there" or "below"—seem often less prominent in such works. A certain tension between Los Angeles as desert and not-desert features in Mike Davis's two dense and remarkable books about the city. The earlier *City of Quartz* starts with a tour of the desert ruins of the utopian community of Llano del Rio, which Davis explicitly calls "desert"; here and there in the book the notion recurs, although without much emphasis, yet with implicit approval. Everything has changed nine years later in *Ecology of Fear*, which begins with a stark rejection of the desert trope as a self-serving notion designed to justify the continuing theft of water from the Colorado River and the Owens Valley. Instead, the Los Angeles region is seen as a Mediterranean climate (which is accurate)—although, again, Davis sometimes reverts to the possibility of desert resurfacing or desert invasion, as when he notes that the last 150 years have been "anomalously mild, and therefore atypical"; the desert, we are warned, encroached on what is now Los Angeles during the "epic drought periods" of the Middle Ages. This Mediterranean trope—which we also touched on above in a passage from Harold Bell's book—is abundantly clear in the booster literature of the later nineteenth and earlier twentieth centuries, in which Southern California in general is depicted as a land of abundant good health, sunshine, and pleasure. Much of this literature figured Southern California as "our Mediterranean"—a view captured explicitly in the title of Peter Charles Remondino's 1892 encomium, *The Mediterranean Shores of America: Southern California: Its Climatic, Physical, and Meteorological Conditions*.[58]

Of course, Davis is right in *Ecology of Fear*, as were the old-time boosters: Los Angeles sits not in a desert but in a Köppen-Geiger BS climate, a steppe, as I noted at the start of this chapter, and as Glen M. MacDonald argued cogently in a recent contribution to *Boom*.[59] Why, then, have the desert tropes of "out there" or "underneath" exercised such a magnetism on so many writers of fiction about LA?[60] I have no definitive answer to the question, which would require a much longer discussion than can be accommodated in a few words at the end of this chapter. It does seem to me, however, that at least three drivers may be at work.

First, there is *moral coding*. Since LA is so often figured as corrupt, decadent, and unnatural, the desert, whether a space "out there" or a hidden underbelly to the city, can be figured as a moral opposite. The long-standing trope of desert redemption and purity, seen perhaps most blatantly in *True Confessions* of all the books studied here, can then serve as a space of purgation and moral repair. This moral opposition, however, can work in another way too: the desert can come into or rise up from underneath the city and sweep away its corruption, sterilizing an urbanscape subject to vile putrefaction. So *Ape and Essence*, much of the "LA holocaust" literature, *Golden Days*, and even Claire Vaye Watkins's recent *Gold Fame Citrus*. (Of course, in Eve Babitz's perverse reading, the desert exercises just the opposite force when its Santa Ana winds sweep in: they enable repressed behavior by wiping out the strictures of bourgeois morality.)

Not unrelated, perhaps, is the sense of the desert as an *escape hatch*—a refuge, a place to escape the city, to find a more genuine life, or at least a chance to start over. This driver seems connected with a very powerful sense of the West in general as a place to "start over," where you can shed old identities and baggage and become a new person; and certainly this notion is fundamentally intertwined with the myth of California itself, as a Promised Land where the new covenant can be struck.[61]

And then there is the *simple distaste for Los Angeles* as a city—a kind of revulsion that seems to infect an extraordinarily large proportion of literature about the city. Reyner Banham observed some decades ago that Los Angeles "gets attention, but it's like the attention that Sodom and Gomorrah have received, primarily a reflection of other people's bad consciences," abused by the "pedestrian litterateur who finds the place 'a stinking sewer' and stays only long enough to collect material for a hate-novel." It would be easy to draw up a lengthy catalogue. For such writers there may be no better fate for Los Angeles than desert-ified obliteration; for, even a desert, repulsive as it may be, is still better than Los Angeles.[62]

This is all rather speculative and certainly incomplete. I have begged other important questions, too. Desert spaces (and the West more generally) have figured often in the American imaginary as emplaced on our continent for the express purpose of "white redemption": the white male, emasculated or in danger of emasculation thanks to his exposure in urban space to dangerous "others," especially the racially or ethnically different (not to mention women), may find his hope of recovery of his masculinity by lighting out for the desert, whose harshness tests, refines, and redeems him, themes well explored by Richard Slotkin and David Teague, and to which I revert in chapter 9. The "whiteness" of this narrative trope brings up another unexplored question: the degree to which the whole framing of LA and the desert is entirely, or mostly, a white and/or upper-middle class preoccupation.[63] Finally, there is the matter of "nature." The desert trope carries an implicit dichotomy between urban LA as "not nature" and the desert as "nature." But of course this whole construction—of the "wild," the "natural" in opposition to the human "artificial"—has been thoroughly challenged by scholars as diverse in their interests as Roderick Nash, William Cronon, Carolyn Merchant, and for Los Angeles itself Jenny Price, in her now-classic essay "Thirteen Ways of Seeing Nature in L.A." In other words, much of the literature I've examined here (and no doubt much I have missed) rests and depends on an opposition itself a confected dualism—not unlike the dichotomy of "desert out there" and "desert underneath" that I have suggested form the two topologies of the desert in LA.[64]

CHAPTER 7

KNOWING BY NAMING*

[A] PLACE NAME IGNITES MEMORY, ETIQUETTE,
RELATIONSHIPS, FONDNESS, AND SADNESS.[1]

BUT THE FIFTH WORLD HAD BECOME ENTANGLED
WITH EUROPEAN NAMES: THE NAMES OF THE
RIVERS, THE HILLS, THE NAMES OF THE ANIMALS
AND PLANTS—ALL OF CREATION SUDDENLY HAD
TWO NAMES: AN INDIAN NAME AND A
WHITE NAME.[2]

I'VE BEEN THROUGH THE DESERT ON A HORSE WITH NO NAME
IT FELT GOOD TO BE OUT OF THE RAIN
IN THE DESERT YOU CAN REMEMBER YOUR NAME
'CAUSE THERE AIN'T NO ONE FOR TO GIVE YOU NO PAIN
—AMERICA, "A HORSE WITH NO NAME"

So sang the folk-rock band America in 1972 (or 1971, if you happened to be living in Europe) in a bridge that quickly spawned jokes ("You're in the desert! There's nothing to do! Name the horse!"). Despite a certain silliness, these lines do point up the importance of naming—that of the poor unnamed horse, but even more that of the singer, who, it seems, needs the emptiness, sun, and heat of the desert to recover his own lost name.

Names are crucial to our individual identities, and we as humans are compelled to assign identities also to the nonhuman features of the world around us. Discussing the Indigenous Australian Kangaroo clan, Émile Durkheim insisted that "identity in name is presumed to entail an identity in nature" because, "[f]or the primitive, the name is not simply a word . . . it is part of the being and, indeed, an essential part." For Ernst Cassirer "the god acquires full individuality only through his name and image."[3] The same can be very much true of a toponym. Taken from an event, a myth, or the physical features of a site, or borrowed from a saint or a wealthy local landowner, a place name can stand for power and bear deep meaning for those able to interpret it. But different cultures approach the assignment of names to physical features in very different ways, under differing, sometimes indeed contradictory, and

---

* A much shorter and very different version was presented at the 2018 conference "Celebrating the Sonoran Desert—A Tri-National Symposium," in Ajo, Arizona.

often flexible and ambiguous, rules. While naming is important everywhere, in the desert, where landmarks are crucial (in days before paved roads, automobiles, gas stations, and GPS) for orientation, names take on special significance. And, as we will see, the two great colonial projects exercised on the southwestern desert world, the Spanish and the American, left their potent traces on the landscape in the form of old names erased (or simply ignored) and new names imposed.[4]

The assignment of new names that had nothing to do with either the topography of the landscape or preexisting Indigenous names was a basic component of the European colonial project globally. In North America the large island off the southwest coast of present-day British Columbia was christened Vancouver after George Vancouver, the head of the expedition that mapped the coast in the 1790s. The same province's Fraser River took its name after Simon Fraser (who also has a university named after him), in 1808 the first European to run the river—he and his companions, however, depended on local Indigenous knowledge to guide them through the river's treacherous canyon.[5] Pikes Peak in Colorado stands on land traditionally occupied by the Utes. Their name for the mountain was *Tabakaiv* or *Tabatzkaiv*, which means "Sun Mountain." The name comes from the fact that it is the first mountain in the Front Range struck by rays of the rising sun; it was one of the Utes' most sacred mountains. The Spanish named it El Capitán, after the leader of their expedition. Pikes, of course, comes from Zebulon Pike, who led the American exploratory expedition through the middle of the Louisiana Purchase and "discovered" the mountain that now bears his name. In miniature here is the tale of multiple overlays of colonial naming on top of an Indigenous name—colonial names not derived from natural characteristics or a local story or myth, but from the men who brought new colonial rule. An analogous process can be seen in the Texas border town of Laredo. Its original saint's name, Villa de San Agustín de Laredo, granted in 1755, was shortened to Laredo by 1848 (much as Los Angeles's long original Spanish name has also been curtailed in practice). The town's original street names reflected physical features of the site or evocative designations: Chacon, after a creek; El Tropezon, "Big Stumble;" Cantaranas, croaking frogs. By 1869, however, Laredo's streets had been renamed after Mexican and American heroes, like Washington, Zaragoza, Lincoln, and Matamoros. As Cordelia Barrera comments, "Newcomers to the region routinely named and renamed towns, places, and sacred spaces."[6] This process recurred repeatedly throughout the desert Southwest (not to say the rest of what is now the United States), burying or erasing Indigenous names.

For both the Spanish and the Americans, the desert world of the Southwest presented a strange, bizarre, unfamiliar, desolate, and frightening landscape. Although the Spanish had come to the New World from a country that had its own desert landscapes, notably the Tabernas Desert in the Almería, and portions of the southeast coast of the Iberian Peninsula (and parts of the Canary Islands), the more immediate origin of the invaders who penetrated the southwestern deserts was tropical or semitropical Mexico. The deserts of the Southwest—and here we should also include the deserts of the present-day Mexican states of Chihuahua, Sonora, and Baja California, no different for the Spanish from the Southwest, for the border line is new and artificial—posed disturbing challenges. Moreover, the Spanish imperial project was infused with an insistent, sometimes forcible and violent, evangelizing that stamped Christianity not only on the Indigenous inhabitants but also on the landscape itself. A saint's name on a place marked the spot, and by extension the territory, both as recovered for Christ and as irrevocably a possession of the Spanish crown. And the saints' names wiped out the Native American sacrality embedded in the land.[7]

For the late-coming Americans, a similar imperial urge operated to rename and occupy the land. But the American settler-colonists functioned under different social rules, framed by a strict regime of private ownership and capitalist exploitation, a system ratified and bolstered by the federal government's Homestead Act of 1862, General Mining Act of 1872, and Desert Land Act of 1877. It thus made eminent sense for a landowner to stamp his land with his name. Likewise, prominent men, capitalists and politicians, imposed their names on the land to commemorate their power and contributions to bringing civilization to the desert.[8]

INDIGENOUS NAMING PRACTICES

Generally speaking, the Indigenous peoples of the desert Southwest followed two broad practices in bestowing names on features of the landscape. In many cases names reflected physical or topographic characteristics of the feature named. In others the name captured an event or meaning associated with the place, such as a mythological or historic occurrence; the special case of the Western Apache is reviewed below. Carobeth Laird expresses clearly the functions toponyms served and the ways they were derived among the Chemehuevi of desert Southern California:

> Some Chemehuevi placenames were borrowed from foreign languages, predominantly from the Mohave in the area along the lower reaches of the Colorado River. Others commemorate events, mythological, legendary, or historical, but never the name of a person who actually lived. A few names are obscure in origin and meaning. However, the great majority of these names, even those which are quite poetic, are vividly and concisely descriptive. Obviously a descriptive placename had a practical value: it enabled a man traversing a route he had learned about simply by word of mouth to know precisely where he was. This was of prime importance to persons going on foot across a country of great heat and great distances, where life itself depended upon knowing exactly how to get from one precious watering place to the next.[9]

This analysis of Indigenous toponyms can be transferred with confidence—though also with modifications—to the practices of other precolonial Indigenous peoples of the desert Southwest, who all faced the same exigencies of landscape as the Chemehuevi.

Some examples of Chemehuevi topological nomenclature will illustrate the point. Two islands on the Colorado River toward the north end of the Chemehuevis' range were called *Saw'wiivy*a, Round Island, and *Muuvi'a*, Cottonwood Island. Two other locales bore extremely vivid, evocative names: *Timpiwi'anana'ats*i and *Tava'awi'anana'ats*i, respectively Stone Penis Growing Up (or Stone Penis Erected) and Chipmunk Penis Erected. Today they are Pyramid Rock and Monument Peak. Some peculiar-looking adobe hills were called

Figure 7-1: Estrella Mountain, Phoenix, Arizona.

Wiyaan⁷nikʸaati, Adobe Hanging Like Tears. An historical incident is commemorated in *Nagwᵃipapiayaya* (also attested as *Nagwᵃipatigah*), whose component parts mean "They Clubbed Each Other a Long Time Ago." Another place, "an overhanging bluff with a small layer of white clay near its apex," took its name, "One Who Carried White Clay on His Back," *⁷Avinyootsi*, from the memory that "in very ancient times a man travelling with a load of white clay on his back died there, and his body became the bluff." Two peaks a few miles from the Bill Williams River are called *Nayiipiyanagumatsi*, Brother and Sister Married Pair. The name derives from a Mohave myth about a brother and sister who engaged in an incestuous marriage and were turned into rock.[10]

The Piipaash and Halychdum (Maricopa) people, who occupied the territory south of present-day Phoenix, Arizona (and after whom Maricopa County is named), recognized four important mountains or elevated features in or near their territory. They included Pima Butte near Sacaton (on the current Akimel O'odham reservation), called *Vii Vakii V'aw* or *Vii Vaav*, which means "Mountain Standing at Home" or "Mountain Standing Back Home;" *Vii 'Alyha*, "Male Homosexual Mountain" (Leslie Spier writes *Vialy̆ xa'*, with the translation "third-gender" or "two-spirit mountain"), the present-day Sierra Estrella (Fig. 7-1), encompassed in Estrella Mountain Regional Park south of Phoenix (the word for a third-gender or two spirit person is *elxa*, syncopated as the last element of the mountain's name); *Vii Kw'ahaas* (*Vikwa̱ xa's* in Spier), "greasy mountain," today's Salt River Range, more commonly known as South Mountain; and *Haak Shvadoo*, "Pushed/Moved Out of the Way" or "Pushed/Moved to One Side, which stands near the junction of the Salt and Gila Rivers. "Greasy mountain" took its name from myth; it was where Coyote wiped his greasy hands after eating the Maricopa's culture hero's heart. Two names are clearly descriptive of the topography; Estrella Mountain had a woman-man living inside it and so marks the gendering of the feature with the third gender that the Piipaash and Halychduum (Maricopa) recognized. Dreaming of this mountain turns the dreamer into a man-woman.[11]

The names the Akimel O'odham bestowed on their landscape around the Gila and Salt Rivers were sometimes different from the Piipaash and Halychduum (Maricopa)'s. South Mountain was Greasy Mountain for them (*Muhadag*). They may have borrowed the Spanish *sombrero* as *Wonnum* to name a mountain whose location is unknown. The descriptive *kok chut*, "curled up," a mountain near the Casa Grande ruins of late Hohokam date by Florence, Arizona, and mentioned in one of the stories about the expulsion of the Hohokam, is *Ku'ukchelik*, meaning "curved upward," now Sawtooth Mountain. The Akimel O'odham called Estrella Mountain "broad [mountain]," *Komatk*, a nicely descriptive designation (Fig. 7-1). When the Hohokam retreated in the face of the O'odham invasion, they sought refuge at "Big Mountain," *Ge'e Duag*. The color of the Colorado River—whose name is Spanish, meaning "Red River"—also induced the Akimel O'odham's name: *Wik Akima*, "red river" (unless the name is a back-formation from the Spanish, as seems likely with *Onk Akimel*, the Salt River, Rio Salado in Spanish, and which may be likely since in Mohave the Colorado is *'Aha Havilly*, "water river"). After providing the Mohave and several other Colorado River groups with the fundamentals of their material and social culture, their culture hero Mastamho turned himself into a bald eagle on the mountain called *Avi-kutaparve*. This mountain "is now white in one place," a feature surely reflecting the white head of the eagle Mastamho had become. "[A] dry lake bed . . . about fifteen miles east of [the town of] Mojave, wide, level, entirely without vegetation, and surrounded by mountains" was named *Hayekwire-nye-matätre*, Rattlesnake's Playground, a very evocative moniker indeed.[12] The Shoshoni people who occupied Death Valley called today's Telescope Peak, the highest point in the Panamint Range, *Mugudoya*, *mugu*, "point," and *doyavi*, "mountain."[13] These names illustrate nicely the practices of Indigenous naming that derive names for physical features either from their appearance and resources—especially water, as we'll see shortly—or historical or mythical events that took place there.

The Mohave Historical Epic recorded by A. L. Kroeber offers a bounty of toponyms located along both sides of the Colorado River.[14] The Epic also provides incidental insight into Mohave acts of naming. The Epic starts with a migration out of the Mojave Valley on the river toward present-day Barstow, California. Finding two places along (probably) the Mojave River that had no names, the migrants called them *Katšoak-kunüve* and *Amat-kohóye*; *'amat* means "land, ground."[15] Later the "gambling boy" Nyītše-vilye-vave-kwilyêhe exiled himself to the desert after a series of gambling losses, in the last of which he had bet his body and his opponent scalped him. Eventually he decided to return to the Colorado River Valley. As he journeyed through the desert to the east of the river, he encountered several places without names (at least as known to him). He remarks to himself, "This place has no name. I want to give it one so all will know it. I will call it Inyil-owaiǒve." After his fourth night on his desert march he awoke and said to himself, "This place has no name. I will give it one. I call it Kusmǒm'uva, so that all will know." Finally, he named a third locale, although the Epic does not give his designation.[16] It is important to note that Nyītše-vilye-vave-kwilyêhe's motivation in each case is to make sure that people know the place thanks to the name he gives.

Nyītše-vilye-vave-kwilyêhe's journeys out into the desert from and back to the Colorado River can be traced in detail, and the names of some of the places he stopped provided a vivid description of the sites.[17] The sites he passed or stopped at can be traced on Kroeber's map (here Fig. 7-2), the outbound ones marked E, the return F.[18] His first stopping point, E1, is called *Amat-ku-tara'alye*. He spent his first night out at the foot of the mountain *Akake-humi*, sacred to the Mohave, for their culture hero Mastamho rescued them by setting them on

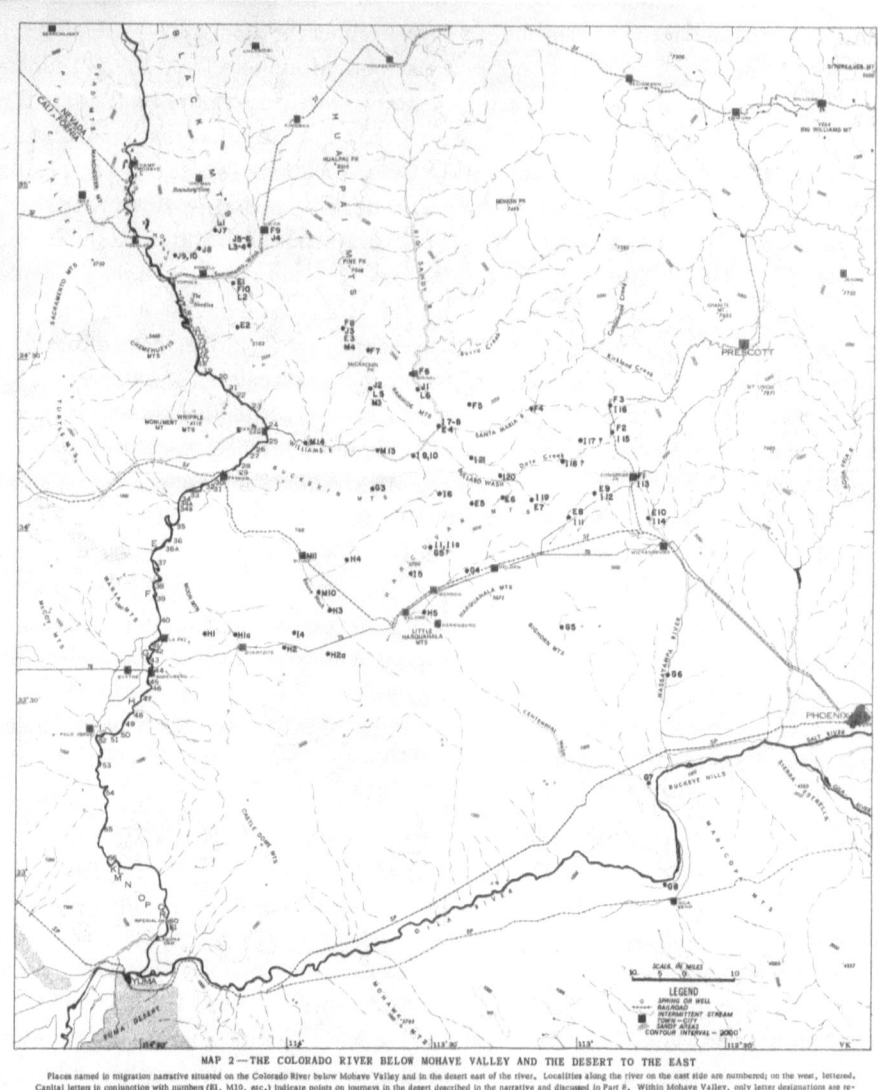

MAP 2—THE COLORADO RIVER BELOW MOHAVE VALLEY AND THE DESERT TO THE EAST

Places named in migration narrative situated on the Colorado River below Mohave Valley and in the desert east of the river. Localities along the river on the east side are numbered; on the west, lettered. Capital letters in conjunction with numbers (E1, M10, etc.) indicate points on journeys in the desert described in the narrative and discussed in Part 8. Within Mohave Valley, only letter designations are repeated from map 1, for orientation.

Figure 7-2: Movements of the Mohave in the "Mohave Historical Epic." (After Kroeber 1948–1963, figure opposite page 176. Used with permission of the University of California Press.)

the peak during the flood. *Humi* means "high, tall," appropriate for an eminence that rises to 5,102 ft (1,556 m).[19] Several of the sites he stopped at contain elements in their names that assure the presence of water—emphasizing the crucial importance of this resource for travelers in the arid desert. *Aha-atši* (E3 = F8), "fish spring," and *Aha-nye-viðutše* (E7) both contain the word *'aha,* "water." The name(s) of an uninhabited site, *Ah'a-kuvate* or *Ah'a-ɵampo* (F3), both begin with *'ah'a,* "cottonwood," and *Iðo-ka'ape* (F1) starts with the word for "willow"—cottonwoods and willows grow along watercourses in the Sonoran Desert. A site at the confluence with the Santa Maria River of an arroyo Nyĩtše-vilye-vave-kwilyêhe had been following likewise has willows: *Iðo-ʻikwe-tšavaðukwe* (F4). Finally, *Kutpama* (E4), which stands by the confluence of the Santa Maria and Big Sandy Rivers to form the Bill Williams River, was also known as *Ikwe-nye-va(tše)*, "floating cloud(s)."[20] Nyĩtše-vilye-vave-kwilyêhe's travels and naming practices bespeak the need in the desert for toponyms that reflect the nature and qualities of a place, names that help travelers find what they need—water to drink or fish to eat—and make physical features easy to identify. Getting lost in the desert isn't hard; names that speak the landscape offer welcome aid.

Harry J. Winters Jr.'s comprehensive catalogue of O'odham toponyms provides a bounty of Indigenous names, many still in use by the inhabitants of the O'odham lands in Arizona. The application of the same descriptive words to different features of the landscape reveals clearly how the O'odham assigned names to emphasize physical features. The O'odham word *komalik* or *komaḍk* expresses the shape of a feature, particularly mountains, ridges, and buttes. In general, the word captures an appearance of flatness or thinness. So *Chuk Komalik* on the Barry M. Goldwater Air Force Range presents a distinctive flat-topped appearance; *chuk* means "black," and indeed the (volcanic?) rock making it up has a dark cast. *Toa Komalik* in Sonora has a sharp ridge, a "thin crest," in Winters's description; the range is called Sierra Blanca in Spanish, echoing the O'odham name, which means "white thin" mountain. A third instance is *Vashokam Komalik* in the Tohono O'odham reservation; its name means "flat [mountain] at a pasture."[21]

Another very common word embedded in many names of physical features is *gakolik* or *gaokoḍk*, meaning "leaning, bent over." A mountain simply called *Gakoḍk* illustrates the usage vividly: its isolated peak forms a rough cylinder bent over or leaning over. *Weg Gakoḍk* displays almost the same shape. *ʼAʼai Gakolik* in the Ajo Mountains, whose ridge forms the eastern boundary of Organ Pipe Cactus National Monument in Southern Arizona and the western boundary of the main unit of the Tohono O'odham reservation, has a profile with two projections on either end of the ridge, each leaning out. *ʼAʼai* means "on each side" here.[22] The western end of the Superstition Mountains east of Phoenix is known as *Viʼikam Gakoḍk*, "survivor bent" or "leaning" mountain (the profile is less clearly *gadoḍk* than in the other mountains cited). This name neatly combines both a physical description and a myth:

> The name comes from the O'odham story of the great flood which covered the world and destroyed most of humanity. Some O'odham took refuge on top of the ridge in the western Superstitions as the flood waters were rising. After some time they sent a dog to see if the waters were still rising. The dog came back and they asked him what was happening. When he started to tell them, they turned to stone. Those who turned to stone can still be seen as pinnacles along the top of the mountain.[23]

A remarkable function of place names occurs in the practices of the Western Apache, which incorporate both the meanings of toponyms we've seen generally in Indigenous names and a vivid pattern of naming that both describes a place so that it can easily be recognized and also commemorates an event. (Another function I return to below.) For instance: *Tsée*

Biká' Tú Yaahilį'né, "Water Flows Down on a Succession of Flat Rocks" or *Tséé Hadigaiyé*, "Line of White Rocks Extends Up and Out." Historical tales are also evoked through place names that stand for the story, the social world of the Apache grounded in topography. Here are two examples. The toponym *T'iis Cho Naasikaadé*, "Big Cottonwood Trees Stand Here and There," triggers this historical story:

> Long ago the Pimas [Akimel O'odham] and Apaches were fighting. The Pimas were car-rying long clubs made from mesquite wood; they were also heavy and hard. Before dawn the Pimas . . . attacked. The Pimas killed the Apaches with their clubs. An old woman . . . thought [the noise] was her son-in-law because he often picked on her daughter. She cried out. . . . Because the old woman cried out . . . the Pimas came running to the old woman's camp and killed her. . . . Only a young girl who ran away and hid survived. It happened at Big Cottonwood Trees Stand Here and There.

In another case, a man conceived sexual desire for his stepdaughter. When she was alone he tried to molest her, but her uncle happened by, killed him, and dumped his corpse into a storage pit at *Tséé Chiizh Dah Sidelé*, "Coarse-Textured Rocks Lie Above in a Compact Cluster." When the girl's mother came home her daughter related the whole story; later the people who owned the pit disposed of the body. No funeral rites were held for the offender.[24]

As Keith Basso, who recorded and analyzed these toponyms, remarks, they are rich in information about places, events, morality, cultural identity; as the two examples illustrate, too, the toponym may recall an important historical event, like a raid in which everyone was killed but a young girl, or an individual transgression. But the point of evoking a story by reciting a toponym is also "almost always promoted by an individual's having committed one or more social offenses to which the act of narration, together with the tale itself, is intended as a critical and remedial response." If the target of the tale takes it to heart and "resolves to improve his or her behavior—a lasting bond will have been created between the individual and the site or sites at which the events in the tale took place."[25] Here, unlike for the Spanish and Americans, naming serves not as a mark of appropriation and ownership but as a means of preserving the memory of a story. Further implications of this practice are treated below.

In an interview published in 2000, James A. Goss emphasized the importance of tra-ditional names for the topography of Indigenous lands in supporting Native American claims to recover or assert sovereignty over traditional territories. Such claims, he noted, "hinge very much on their ability to demonstrate, for example, that they have traditional and ancient names for the places within their territories."[26] Thus naming for Indigenous groups served multiple purposes, some shared among most cultures, some peculiar to a few, or just one. Guides to travel and information about resources at stopping points, recollections of mythical or historical events, easily recognized descriptions of the physiog-nomy of topographic features, moral tales, claims to possession: Indigenous names carry all these tasks and more.

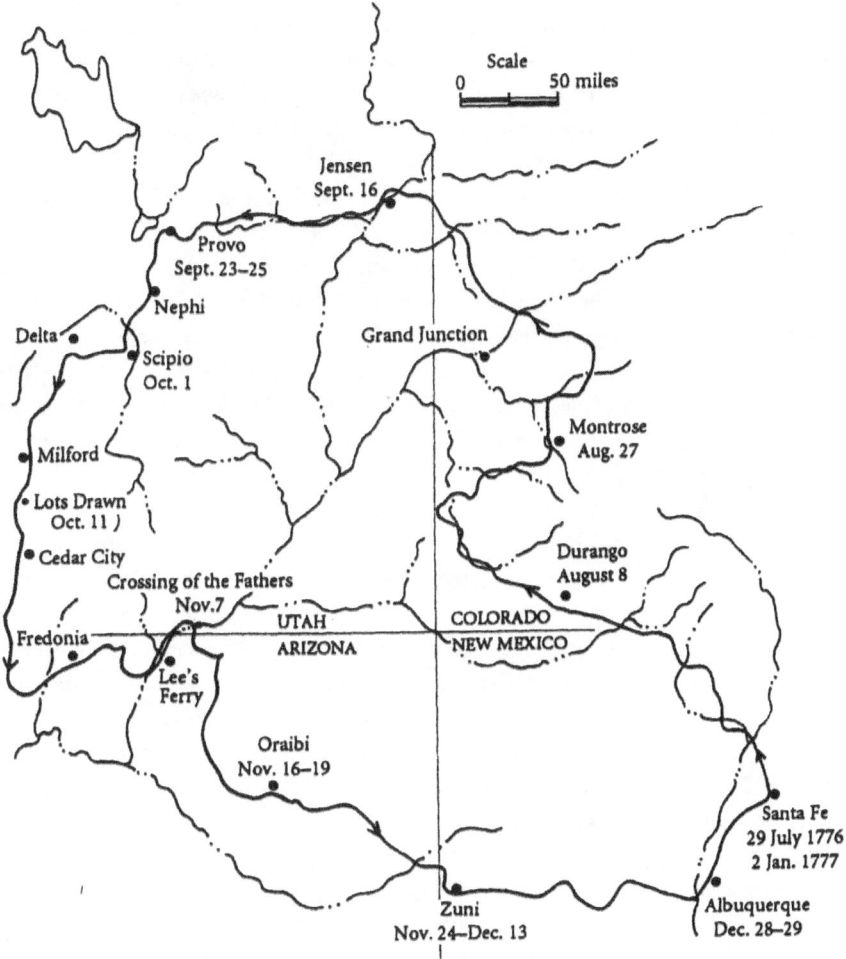

Figure 7-3: Domínguez-Escalante Expedition route. (After Vélez de Escalante 1995, map facing title page. Reprinted courtesy of the University of Utah Press.)

COLONIZING NAMING 1—THE SPANISH

The Southwest underwent two major periods of post-Columbian colonization.[27] The first brought Spanish *conquistadores*, padres, and settlers north from Mexico. They established a string of missions along the California coast, explored north as far as the Colorado Plateau, settled in Southern Arizona—the Pimería Alta—and moved up the Rio Grande as far as present-day Santa Fe and Albuquerque. In New Mexico they were expelled in 1680 by a coalition of Pueblo peoples; the Spanish returned ten years later, after internal dissension weakened the Pueblos. After 1822 the territory north of the present Mexico-US border fell to Mexico. But only a couple of decades later the United States stripped Mexico of this land, taking Texas, California, and the deserts in between. A second wave of colonization, this time of Americans, preceded and followed annexation. These waves of colonization were marked by many changes, not least of which was a gross revision of naming practices of desert features.

For the Spanish, "[n]aming geographical features did not mean describing them . . . much less putting their position on a map. Naming in Spanish practices was a ritual speech, like the Requirement, the ritual declaration of war announced in a speech." This practice "of taking possession often involved renaming places with appelations [sic] derived from the realm of the sacred—saints . . . and sacraments . . . and that of nature."[28] The day-to-day record of the Domínguez-Escalante Expedition of 1776—which famously stumbled upon the Grand Canyon—offers an excellent example of just this practice (Fig. 7-3). On August 3 they entered a small valley they called Santo Domingo and christened three small mountains La Sanctissima Trinidad. Two days later a site near the confluence of the Navajo and San Juan Rivers was called Nuestra Señora de las Nieves, "Our Lady"—that is, Mary—"of the Snows." On August 7 they named a meadow San Antonio and their campsite La Vega de San Cayetano ("The Meadow of St. Cayetano"). A few days later they halted at a site christened San Bernardo. The names roll on: El Paraje de San Luis, El Paraje de la Asuncíon, El Río de Dolores, El Río de San Francisco (today's Uncompahgre River), pastureland called Santa Mónica, on and on and on. These names, it will be noted, all come from saints; the names of campsites, in particular, tend to be borrowed from the name of the saint on whose day the expedition stopped there.[29]

Spanish explorers also honored members of their expeditions by fastening personal names onto the geography. Don Bernardo Miera y Pacheco's name was granted to the Laberinto de Miera because he was the first to negotiate its tortuous turns. Present-day Horse Lake was named after Lorenzo Olivares. A "copious spring of good water" received the name El Ojo de Laín, after Don Joaquín Laín. Robledo Mountain in Doña Ana County of southern New Mexico in the Chihuahuan Desert was named after a member of the 1598 Oñate expedition who died nearby.[30]

Even when the Spanish learned the Indigenous name for a place, or a contorted version, they nevertheless often renamed the site with a Spanish name. The soldiers of the Coronado expedition renamed Taos (which they seem to have known as Braba or Ubara or Yuraba) Valladolid, perhaps from a vague resemblance of the pueblo to the Spanish city. Even in a list giving Indigenous names, Pedro de Castañeda, chronicler of the Coronado expedition, designated three villages by the Spanish Aguas Calientes ("hot waters").[31] Spanish explorers could also, of course, assign names based on the physical characteristics of the landforms they saw or to commemorate events that took place at the location. Vélez de Escalante, who recorded the advance of the Domínguez-Escalante Expedition of 1776—and lent his name to the Escalante River—gives the name of a canyon as El Cañon del Engaño, "the Canyon of Deceit," "on account of a certain incident," which he declines to relate; a river gets named Río de las Paralíticas ("River of the Paralyzed Women") due to the camp of three women so suffering there. Two water sources were called Agua Tapada, "covered water"—we don't know why—and Agua Escondida, "hidden water," so called because it was concealed within a dense copse. A narrow and steep valley was called La Cañada Hondo, "the deep valley."[32]

Nyĩtše-vilye-vave-kwilyêhe's trek through the desert east of the Colorado River finds its echo in the journal of Eusebio Kino. Kino was a Jesuit priest seconded to the Pimería Alta—today's northern Sonora and Southern California and Arizona, named after the Spanish name for the O'odham, the Pimas—to explore and evangelize. In 1700, having determined that no sea ascended as far north as the confluence of the Colorado and Gila Rivers, Kino and his party set out on October 7 from his riverine camp, which he called the Camp of the Sandías owing to the watermelon growing by the bank of the river. He proceeded over the next several days to a *ranchería* on the Colorado River he named San Pedro, then to San Dionisio; he took a siesta at La Tinada, a waterhole; then another waterhole, El Carrizal; and another *ranchería* which he designated as San Marcelo del Sonoydag.[33] Unlike Nyĩtše-vilye-vave-kwilyêhe's stopping places, these names—mostly taken from Catholic saints—offer no guidance whatsoever to the character of the topography or the presence of water; only La Tinada, "the tank," promises the latter, but the name betrays not a clue as to its location. It was far more important to Kino to mark his procession by the saints of his church than to offer guidance to subsequent travelers. They would have to rely on the maps the Spanish explorers drew and the advice of Indigenous informants. But the saints' names on the landscape proclaimed the new religion—and the new masters.

Despite some names that reflected the look of the features that bore them, the vast majority of Spanish names impressed on the southwestern landscape would have been absolutely useless as guides to navigation. In a perceptive essay, George English Brooks has argued that the naming practices of the Domínguez-Escalante Expedition flow from an insurmountable tension, if not contradiction, between the goals of the expedition and the landscape it encountered:

> [T]he expedition struggles to reconcile its Christian, imperial, and human endeavors and expectations with its immediate environment and actual circumstances through naming, imagining, and casting its own projections over the places and peoples it encounters. As the expedition makes its way farther into unfamiliar lands, these place-names . . . provide indices to the degree and kind of transformation the party undergoes on its 1,700-mile journey. . . . The group finds the viability of its objectives shaken nearly to the breaking point not only by the physical difficulty of the terrain but also by its inexorable strangeness.[34]

This insistence of imposing foreign, Christian names on an entirely unknown landscape represents at the same time a statement of imperial power, of taking the land for Spain, an assertion of the presence now of a new, "true" religion to replace the "pagan demonism" that dominated the unreconstructed New World (conversion was intertwined with conquest as the twin goals of the Spanish in the Americas), and an effort to "normalize" this topography, so deeply foreign, by bringing its names into the fold of the Old World. The radical contrast between Indigenous naming practices and the proliferation of saints' names utterly incomprehensible to the Southwest's inhabitants not only attempts to erase the Native American landscape, as Brooks writes, but also aims to alienate the Indigenous inhabitants from their own homeland. However, Brooks further argues, the deeper the expedition penetrates into unknown and strange lands, the greater the draw to "merge projective Christian nomenclature with a more descriptive and adoptive attitude." The tension here is expressed in part in the recording of not only Spanish toponyms but also Nahuatl and Ute when it reaches the Timpanogos Valley in Utah.[35]

COLONIZING NAMING 2—THE AMERICANS

Naming topographic features after prominent—or, sometimes, not so prominent—people was a common practice among American settler colonists.[36] Names open a window onto what the namers regarded as important, valuable, and meaningful, as we've already seen with Indigenous names that, among other things, help guide travel safely through the desert. A series of examples from Arizona will illustrate the point. Barnes Butte, in Maricopa County, was named after Will C. Barnes, a local cattleman, legislator, and soldier. Oatman Flat commemorated the site of the Oatman massacre. Wasson Peak, also known as Amole Peak, in Pima County, took its name from a newspaper publisher who had also been a close advisor to the Arizona territorial governor A. P. K. Safford (1869–1877). Diaz Peak in Organ Pipe Cactus National Monument marks the site of the death of Melchior Diaz, a participant in the Coronado expedition, while Gadsden Peak, also in the monument, was so renamed in 1953 on the one-hundredth anniversary of the Gadsden Purchase, which conveyed territory south of the Gila River in Arizona and the southwestern bit of New Mexico from Mexico to the United States; the US ambassador to Mexico, James Gadsden, negotiated the transaction. Several businessmen had features named after them, including Masters Peak, after a president of the Maricopa and Phoenix Railroad, and Mount Wrightson, after a manager of the Salero Mining Company, killed by Apaches. The Baker Peaks and Tanks, now in the Goldwater Range, commemorate a rancher who settled by the tanks around 1870. The Growler Mountains in Organ Pipe Cactus National Monument are named after a prospector, John Growler. There is even a mountain said to have been named after a prospector's mule: Muggins Mountain in Yuma County.[37]

A Yuma County mountain once called Coronation Peak has a rather peculiar nomenclature history. Its current name is said to be derived from its appearance, its peaks, when bathed in twilight sunlight, said to resemble a glowing golden crown. John Russell Bartlett sketched it in 1852 during his ill-fated service on the U.S. Boundary Commission and called it Pagoda Mountain, because it reminded him of "Hindu pagodas." It received its present name, Klothos or Clothos Temple, in 1900, assigned by an artist after one of the Greek Fates.[38]

American-imposed names in or near the Chihuahuan Desert in New Mexico share Arizonan practices. Chatfield Peak in the Sacramento Mountains was named after a local rancher; the origin of the range's name, which is Spanish, is unknown. Cookes Canyon, Cookes Peak, and Cookes Spring in Luna County all took their names from Captain Philip St. George Cooke, the commander of the Mormon Battalion that passed through the region in 1846–1847. Nearby Massacre Peak, a flat-topped mountain, was supposedly used by the Apache as an observation point to plan attacks on passing Anglos; its name commemorates in particular a confrontation in 1861 between the secessionist Emmett Mills and six companions, fleeing California, and an Indigenous force under Cochise and Mangas Coloradas.

Dog Canyon, which had been a favorite Apache camp, was so named because US troops found only a dog there when they seized an abandoned camp.[39] There are many other analogous examples.

Naturally enough, some American-assigned names reflect the physical appearance of a feature or recall a metaphorical resemblance. The former mining town of Gunsight, now abandoned, took its name from a nearby butte "with a striking resemblance to a gun sight with the 'barrel' of the gun being formed by a ridge." However, because the gunsight also recalls a man's head and shoulders, it is also called Montezuma Head. Tortilla Mountain seemed to look like the food. The Sand Tank Mountains west of Phoenix and now a unit of the Sonoran Desert National Monument were named after the local moniker for the *tinajas* (pools) nestled in depressions in the rock. Antelope Wells, on the Chihuahua–New Mexico border, received its name from the herd of antelope at its water hole; this name recalls Indigenous practice, while Camel Mountain in Luna County is thought to resemble a—camel.[40]

It must be noted, however, that today's desert nomenclature forms a palimpsest—the final colonial thrust treated the naming of the landscape in a complex way. In some cases an Indigenous name was kept, even if, typically, distorted for American tongues and ears. Spanish names imposed either in the Spanish colonial period or later—the Hispanic population of the Southwest is big—have been retained too. And then on top of these two layers of naming, each itself having many substrata, are those easily pronounced Anglo names taken from people, events, or impressions of the camel-like appearance of a mountain ridge line.

Present-day nomenclature on the southwestern deserts, which I have just barely touched on here, presents, then, a complex stew of Indigenous, Spanish, and American names. Leafing through the excellent compilation of names in the borderlands by Bill Broyles, Luke Evans, Richard Stephen Felger, and Gary Nabhan, and the books of Will C. Barnes and Robert Julyan, yields a cornucopia of names of dizzying variety. It would be misleading to suggest that *all* Indigenous naming, *all* Spanish naming, and *all* American naming conformed to one single dominant pattern. My point here is rather that there are ways of naming each culture followed that *typify* something important about the relation each cultivated with the desert landscape, ways of naming that tell us something important about how each conceptualized the land it occupied, or, as the case may be, conquered.

Crucial to the argument I am proposing here is that the naming practices I've examined are in the desert. Settler colonists in the wet East likewise imposed nondescriptive names on many physical features, although in many cases, like Connecticut and Massachusetts, Indigenous names were adapted.[41] So, to give just a few random examples, the tallest peak in the White Mountains of New Hampshire is called Mount Washington; a river in Connecticut is the Thames (after the English river of the same name); the great New York river is named after Henry Hudson. Nomenclature in the East is complicated, of course. There are toponyms derived from physical features or aspects of the land, like the Great Dismal Swamp of Virginia or the Smoky Mountains of North Carolina. There is no hard-and-fast rule. But what matters about the desert is the dry fact that it is a difficult environment, in which knowledge about the location and nature of resources can spell the difference between life and death. The Indigenous naming practices often record precisely information needed for survival, whereas Spanish and American practices often abjure this in favor of names that mark possession. (Again, that is not to say that *no* Spanish or American names serve the same ends as Indigenous ones.) In other words, names and the desert interact in ways that can matter crucially to the people who live there—but can convey very different categories of information.

In *Writing Colonisation*, her comparative study of Australian and Italian literature through the optic of colonialism, Sabina Sestigiani devotes three chapters to an extended exposition of the impact of naming on the land. She finds her starting point in essays by Walter Benjamin and Maurice Blanchot. Benjamin's essay, originally published in 1916, argues, from the creation story in Genesis, that when God created the world he brought it forth by a kind of speech. God's naming is an act of creation, and "The absolute relation of the name to recognition [of a created thing] exists only in God, because it [the name] is in its most inner being, identical with the word that creates." The natural world had its own sort of "speech," but a speech without sound. When Adam was given the task of naming the animals, he used a language with which he spoke out loud a true name, that linked the animals to God's creative effort through him. But after the Fall human languages splintered into hundreds of incompatible varieties and the new names given to the world were then mere "blather," *Geschwätz*: "To be named [under these conditions] . . . was perhaps always a premonition of sadness. . . . How much more to be named not from the language of Paradise of names, but from the hundreds of human languages, in which the name already decays. . . . Things have no proper name except in God." The result is an "over-naming," *Überbenennung*.[42]

Blanchot goes farther. He asserts—"argues" would be too strong—that a thing's name deprives it of its being while granting humans mastery over it; indeed, "speech," he remarks, "is the murderer of existence."[43] It is from Blanchot's position in "Literature and the Right to Death" intermixed with Benjamin's argument about the falsity of over-naming and the ironic duty God gave humans to name (corrupted beyond correction by the Fall) that Sestigiani extracts her very strong position:

> The act of naming has helped us to organize our dwelling place: the earth. This act commanded by God has prompted us to interpret and read aloud a given, strange world. To name is thus a form of violence that provokes death: the destruction of a thing in its carnal or physical existence in order to grasp the idea of its spiritual essence. We aspire to reach beyond what is beyond our phenomenal world through our knowledge. Naming the earth is killing the earth. We kill and create, but the idea that is created in naming is a lie.[44]

The relevance of this position to my concerns in this chapter is both patent and confusing. Sestigiani's interest focuses almost exclusively on acts of naming by colonial powers, whether invaders and conquerors or settler-colonists or both. These powers are both European: the English and the Italians. Her argument, then, is entirely embedded in long-standing European ideas about naming that start with Genesis and are filtered through two prominent twentieth-century European theorists. In cases where a feature of the landscape is christened with the name of a politician or explorer or saint, thus irredeemably detached from the landscape it sits in—as we have seen—her argument has its point. The mountain no longer called by a name that evokes its physicality has in a sense been "killed"—although of course it is still there, a fact that Blanchot admits himself, in passing.[45] And the link Sestigiani draws between these acts of naming and colonialism illustrates yet another way that colonialism rejects, demeans, and expropriates land once belonging to Indigenous peoples.

But when we turn to names that evoke the physical features of a landform, the situation is perhaps different. They serve, or try to serve, a different master, which in some cases can verge on the ways that Indigenous names often provide information crucial to travelers in the desert. Sestigiani, however, goes rather farther again in talking about Indigenous naming in Australia: "The heavenly linguistic state of humans in the Garden of Eden is perhaps the closest to that of Aboriginal people before they encountered colonialism. At that time, they experienced a direct connection between language and place"; she then quotes Ken Gelder and Jane M. Jacobs in support. However, her first quotation from them—"Aboriginal people inscribed their language, their signifiers, directly on to their place, as if the one was as real as the other"—presents not their view but that of Stephen Muecke in his *Textual Spaces*, which Gelder and Jacobs immediately substantiate with a long quotation from him. The second quotation attributed to Gelder and Jacobs—"Aboriginal languages never had to put up with the notion of the arbitrary signifier-signified relation"—is, except for the first two words, actually another quotation from Muecke.[46] Gelder and Jacobs, it must be said, do not cite Muecke in approbation, as Sestigiani supposes, but to criticize his views.

These details, however, aren't really what has drawn my attention here. Rather, it is the much broader question of what naming does to the landscape. As we have seen, there is a strong contradiction between names that evoke the physicality of a feature on the land, that inform a desert traveler about what she may expect there, and those that commemorate a colonial erasure of that physicality in favor of honoring a landowner, politician, or saint. In between rests, somewhat uneasily, names derived from the appearance of a feature—like Gunsight Mountain—but that are tied to a specific cultural element that is not, or cannot be, shared beyond the culture in which it is embedded; gunsight is meaningless to anyone who doesn't know what a gun is. (Many Indigenous names, as we have seen, embody information anyone could use; the same is true of some colonial names.) Rather than "killing" the landscape, naming tied directly to the physicality of a feature, or that provides the desert traveler with useful, even life-saving, information, seems to do just the opposite: to bring out the physical reality and direct human experience of the place. If this is right, then the real contrast resides in the contrast between principles of Indigenous and colonialist/Euro-American naming. To name a place after a Catholic saint simply because an explorer happened to camp there on that saint's day obliterates the physical reality of the place; in a sense, the place no longer "exists" in the landscape, for it has been extracted and incorporated into a sacred calendar entirely foreign to the cultural world where the place sits. In this way, it seems to me, Sestigiani's "killing by naming" offers a powerful tool for grasping the implications of colonialism on the names on the land.

A related argument is presented in JM Arthur's *The Default Country*, which considers the ways Australia was viewed by British settler-colonists in comparison with their homeland.

She illustrates the erasure of Indigenous names by the colonists, a process that does not even recognize that the land had already been named: to name a place, she notes, is not called "re-naming" but simply "naming," as if the site had been nameless and naked before a European arrived to bring it into knowledge by the imposition of a name. "Part of knowing," she writes, "is the act of naming." In other words, for European colonists, even when they recognized that a place had an Indigenous name, that name provided no knowledge of the place—it was opaque to them. At the same time, the imposition of a "new" European-derived name robbed the Indigenous inhabitants of their knowledge of the place. When James Cook christened a mountain in New South Wales Mount Dromedary because it reminded him of the hump of a camel, the Indigenous name *Gulaga* disappeared, and the sacred significance it has for Indigenous women is denied. The image in Cook's mind when he named it was, of course, completely meaningless to the people who actually lived there.[47] Colonial renaming in the deserts of the American Southwest wreaked exactly the same arrogant havoc on the landscape there. Creating colonialist knowledge of the landscape by naming often, then, demanded ignoring and denying preexistent Indigenous knowledge of the same places. Arthur offers a succinct description of the relation between colonization and naming:

> Colonisation is a process in geographical space. The perspective of knowledge is thus one of "here" and "there"; at first of distinguishing between spaces that have been colonised and those which have not, and then between those which have been brought more closely into the sphere of colonial knowledge. The act of colonisation, the act of crossing the landscape, was not only a physical event but a conceptual one; the landscape experienced by the colonists, and the landscape not yet experienced or brought into the frame of knowledge, were understood differently.[48]

In an interview, the Australian novelist David Malouf avers he "has always been fascinated, in all the books I have written, by that business of naming, of making the thing by speaking its name. But here [in Australia] we spoke the name, and what appeared was something entirely unexpected."[49] The colonial name spoken imports colonial notions about the landscape and the ways of naming; erasing or overriding the Indigenous name, the new colonial appellation's unexpectedness is, often enough, an assertion of power, control, and authority of the colonialist.

THE WAYS OF NAMING

What distinguishes Indigenous naming from colonial naming in many—but certainly not all—instances is the tendency for Indigenous names to pick out physical features of the location named or to give a name that evokes an incident, whether mythological or historical, associated with the site. As we have seen in the case of Nyĩtše-vilye-vave-kwilyêhe's travels through the desert, this practice served to help wanderers navigate through the landscape and be confident that a site would have crucial resources, especially water and food. The naming practices of the Western Apache in Arizona, beautifully elucidated by the anthropologist Keith Basso, play a different but culturally central role. The names evoke a story that has a moral; one can invoke the moral—and make a point to one's interlocutor—simply by stating the name.

Basso recounts a hot afternoon when he's lounging with three Apache cattlemen under a grove of trees. A fourth, younger man named Talbert arrives. He's been despondent after the collapse of a love affair, drinking, propositioning women, but has now sobered up and wants to come back to work. The first three cowboys mention the Trail That Goes Down Between Two Hills and remark that Talbert has evidently gotten tired of walking back and forth and smelling burning piss. Talbert laughs and admits, "For a while I couldn't see!"

The toponym Trail That Goes Down Between Two Hills describes nicely a spot with "two wooded knolls of similar size and shape with a footpath passing between them that descends to a grassy flat on the west bank of Cibecue Creek"; a big cottonwood stands near the stream. Basso is puzzled; what has the mention of this place name to do with Talbert? The answer, it turns out, is a tale with a moral. At this very spot a certain Old Man Owl, notorious for his concupiscence, was teased by two beautiful sisters. They had positioned themselves on the tops of the hills, and called out in turns as he passed by "[C]ome here! I want you to rub me between my legs!" Old Man Owl trundled back and forth from hill to hill as the sisters called in counterpoint. On another occasion one climbed the cottonwood and exposed her vulva to him. His poor vision induced him to think the tree was a woman and set it on fire to bring it home, but the girl urinated and twice extinguished the flames—and rained urine on poor Old Man Owl.

Talbert got the message: he'd been acting like Old Man Owl—who was nearly blind, so mistaking a woman for a tree, and hence Talbert's confession that "For a while I couldn't see!"—chasing women who didn't want him. He'd stopped, and his friends, by the simple allusion to Old Man Owl's adventures at Trail That Goes Down Between Two Hills, both reminded him of his foolishness and praised him for reforming himself. Now ready to resume work, Talbert has been reintegrated into the community.[50] This name, Trail That Goes Down Between Two Hills, holds a multitude: it evokes a very particular place, well described, that can be distinguished even by an outsider; as such, it might serve as a marker for someone moving about in the countryside. The presence of a stream and cottonwood assures the presence of water. But it also embodies a story that can be used, indirectly but effectively, for admonishment and moral instruction. In effect, it is a geophysical toponym that also embeds a historical tale with moral content. There are many such toponyms in the country of the Western Apache.

The point of this excursion into Western Apache place naming is to emphasize, again, the complex and diverse social and cultural practices that may underlie and confer power on the apparently simple, straightforward act of granting a place a name. While far from monolithic in its rules—indeed, to write "Indigenous naming" implies a consistency among different Indigenous groups that did not necessarily hold—Indigenous naming often served a very practical aim in the desert, this world of little and impermanent water, great heat, the danger of getting lost, mendacious mirages, and death. But for the Indigenous peoples the desert was also home, a world whose character they well understood and respected (see chapter 2 on the sacrality of the land), an everyday substrate on which they built their lives.

The Mohave Historical Epic likewise illustrates both the challenges and the mundane reality of living in the desert.

Yearning for Romeo, kept from her by his Montague appellation, Juliet soliloquizes, "What's in a name? That which we call a rose / By any other name would smell as sweet."[51] In Verona, perhaps. But the desert is different. Strip the Indigenous name off a feature and replace it with the moniker of an American landowner, and you lose all the associations that the original name bore—the site of water, or an event from history or mythology, or an edifying moral tale. As Lois Rudnick remarked, Native American names typically "express the land's natural characteristics rather than the individual discoverer's ego."[52] You also commit a gross offence, as Basso learned when he excused himself for mispronouncing a place name by saying he'd practice it later and for the nonce, "It doesn't matter." One of his companions rebuked him, in Western Apache, through another:

> What he's doing isn't right. It's not good. He seems to be in a hurry. Why is he in a hurry? It's disrespectful. Our ancestors made this name. They made it just as it is. They made it for a reason. *They spoke it first, a long time ago!* He's repeating the speech of our ancestors. He doesn't know that. Tell him he's repeating the speech of our ancestors![53]

When the names the ancestors gave are erased, the map of the landscape that Nyītše-vilye-vave-kwilyêhe followed and added to slips away. I do not mean to suggest that Indigenous names are better than Spanish or American ones in any absolute sense, nor that settler-colonists never fixed places on the landscape whose names carried meaning; Punta de Agua, once the spring from which the Santa Cruz River began, and Peroxide Well both promise water, if the latter perhaps infused with a nasty flavor.[54] The point is that the three societies we've examined here recreated their map of the southwestern deserts to fit their own cultural expectations and cared about those names with different passion and understanding. They read the desert in different ways, and through their different readings the desert becomes a different place, a "cultural landscape" befitting the people for whom it is home.[55]

At the same time, though, there is that one crucial element that distinguishes Spanish and American naming from Indigenous: colonialism. In a study of the second part of Castañeda's *Relación* of the Coronado expedition, Maureen Ahern has pointed out the ways in which his account of the pueblos the Spanish met as they moved up the east coast of the Gulf of California and into the Southwest "were regions of the globe that needed to be placed under the rational power of measurement and mapping." She cites Barbara Mundy's lapidary phrase, "naming is the heart of mapping," and we have seen how this plays out in the names the colonialists imposed on a landscape already rich with names. The Coronado expedition's naming practice was often multilayered; they sometimes learned and recorded Indigenous names, but then lay over them a Nahuatl name—using the Indigenous language of the Aztecs that was predominant in New Spain to the south—and then a Spanish name, often, but not always, as we have seen, derived from a Catholic saint. This complex palimpsest of names, in which the colonial names were both the latest and the dominant, served as a mechanism for bringing a new and strange world under the crown's authority—and making it "real" as opposed to the mythical land of the Seven Cities of Cibola under which it had been sub-sumed before.[56] American practice, as we have seen, was imbricated both with a colonialist project and a settler-colonial one framed by a capitalistic model of landholding; that model encouraged the use of owners' names on the desert landscape. In both cases, though, it was colonialism that drove naming; even when an Indigenous name was retained, it was typi-cally modified for ease of pronunciation by Spanish or American tongues. Its meaning, too, was lost, and so too the link with the landscape so important to Indigenous populations. Naming was, and remains, not only a form of knowing but also a claim to possession.[57] As Tzvetan Todorov put it, succinctly, many years ago: "[N]omination is equivalent to taking possession." Renaming is central to the colonial project. And, especially for the Spanish, this renaming constituted an act of giving the renamed landscape "the *right* names"—names derived from the calendar of Catholic saints and God himself, Jesus, and Spanish royalty, a practice taken up by Columbus as soon as he penetrated the Caribbean.[58]

But colonial possession of the desert does not come easily, and surely not through the sim-ple imposition of a name. The wet, fertile, female-gendered (in a Euro-American sense) East lay open to the colonial powers from across the sea; the language of early British colonialists reviewed in chapter 4 emphasizes the land's passivity, its openness to the imposition of male colonial power, "safeliest when with one man manned," as Donne put it. The desert, in stark contrast, is hard, harsh, unrelenting, and unforgiving: it resists the colonists with its heat, its aridity, its emptiness, its apparent tracklessness.[59] While its Indigenous inhabitants know it intimately, as Nyītše-vilye-vave-kwilyêhe knew how to pass safely from water source to water source, as Hipahipa intuited the approach of the Mohave exiles toward his desert outpost, the Spanish and the Americans faced a landscape of unutterable alterity and alienness. By naming they tried to familiarize it, domesticate it, under the banner of Catholic saints or capitalist landowners. The desert, nevertheless, refused—only with railroads, diverted water, air conditioning, automobiles, electrification, all the appurtenances of modern life have the deserts around a Phoenix or underneath an Imperial Valley been rendered "livable." Desert refusals render visible the landscape's *agency*. The desert acts on the people who intrude and settle; it is not some passive object lying out there beyond the meridian, waiting, powerless. I return to the question of material agency in chapter 10, where the matter is imbricated also with the large question, adumbrated in chapter 1, of in what a desert literature consists.

PART 4

THE AMERICAN DESERT ELSEWHERE

THE FLYING
SAUCERS HAVE
LANDED

Desert Landscapes and Alien Contact in the American Imaginary*

"THIS IS AN ALIEN LANDSCAPE, SAND AND DEATH STRETCHING FOR MILES
IN EVERY DIRECTION."[1]

"SHE TELLS THE SAME OLD STORY TO EVERYONE THAT SHE KNOWS,
SHE'S JUST SITTING IN HER ROOM READING BOOKS ABOUT UFOS."[2]

I n the 1950s, out in the deserts of the American Southwest, beings from other worlds began to contact humans receptive to their visitations.[3] The most famous of these "contactees," as they are known, were probably George Adamski (1891–1965) and George W. Van Tassel (1910–1978). Both experienced their first encounters with alien beings in the Mojave Desert. But other contactees also had their interactions with aliens in the desert, including Daniel William Fry, Dana Howard, Truman Bethurum, Wayne Aho, and Orfeo Angelucci. The message brought by these Space Brothers and Sisters, which we'll explore in more detail later, was both a warning about the damage being done to Earth and the universe by our irresponsible exploding of atomic bombs and a promise, if we reformed our ways, of the opportunity to join them in a cosmic family of love and peace. As, however, encounters shifted away from the desert world, which was especially suitable for spiritual interaction with our Space Brothers and Sisters, the nature of the encounters also changed—as we will see.

---

* A much shorter version was presented at the 2017 annual meeting of the Western Literature Association.

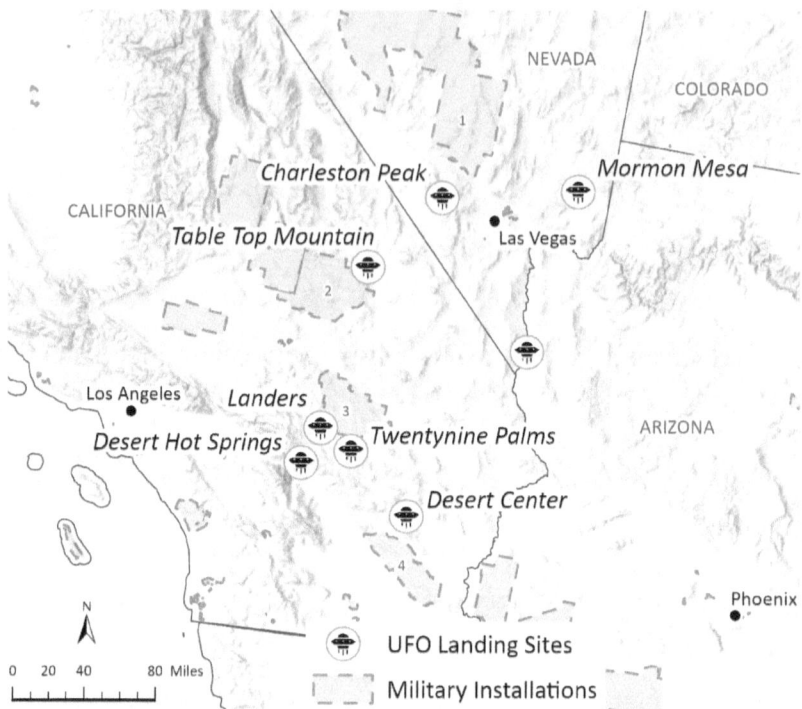

Figure 8-1: Contactee Sites. Compiled by Michaela Buenemann, Department of Geography and Environmental Studies, New Mexico State University.

GEORGE ADAMSKI, "THE ULTIMATE CONTACTEE"[4]

Saturated in theosophical ideas and long obsessed with aliens and saucers, Adamski started to hear in 1951 and 1952 about strange landings out in the desert. Then, on the "[m]emorable November [t]wentieth," he had his own first encounter in the desert 10.2 miles from Desert Center, California, in the direction of Parker, Arizona (see Fig. 8-1).[5] Adamski had already been traveling to places in the desert where, he had heard, saucers had been landing. For the excursion that ended in his first encounter, he called on friends who were also enthusiasts; this move helped assure that he had witnesses to confirm his experience. His narrative set-up of his encounter emphasizes the desert nature of the locale. He and his companions stop about eleven miles from Desert Center, at a place "not as sandy as one usually expects on deserts. Instead, strange and interesting rocks . . . covered the earth. . . . They were sharp and jagged." Flora consisted of "[s]mall bushes of silver-white desert Holly . . . [a]nd a few other desert scrub growths. . . . But all plant life was conspicuously sparse. . . . A strong gusty wind was blowing, and it was quite cold compared with the heat of the sun's rays when the wind temporarily subsided." Adamski continues:

> The sky was beautiful and clear with little wispy clouds forming here and there, only to float away into nothingness. And although we knew most of the mountains in the background were miles away, they appeared quite close in the deceptive atmosphere of the desert.[6]

© Adamski Foundation

Figure 8-2: George Adamski and Orthon. (Used with Permission of the George Adamski Foundation.)

After lingering off the main road and observing planes flying over the nearby mountains, Adamski and his companions spotted "a gigantic cigar-shaped silvery ship" that hovered nearby. It departed, but Adamski had a feeling events were not over. He had one of his companions drive him closer to the mountains. Within minutes of being dropped off, he spied a second, smaller craft that landed in a dip in the mountains. As he took pictures, he hoped he might meet its occupant—and indeed there soon appeared a figure wearing pants like ski trousers and long hair. It was, Adamski suddenly realized, "a human being from another world!" Adamski approached and the two engaged in a conversation facilitated by sign language and telepathy. Adamski hoped to be permitted inside the saucer, but this hope was dashed, and soon, after impressing the soles of his shoes into the sand, Adamski's interlocutor entered the ship and it departed. One of his companions made plaster casts of the footprints; another sketched the spaceman after watching through binoculars.[7]

Adamski's second encounter with the Space Brothers—including the Venusian he called Orthon (Fig. 8-2)[8]—began in Los Angeles, where he was drawn mysteriously to a hotel he had stayed in before. There, at night, two men came to him and invited him to go for a ride. At one's touch, Adamski experienced "a great joy"—"[t]he signal was the same as had been given by the man I had met on the desert on that memorable" night he first met a Space Brother. They passed out of the city and after an hour and a half or more "were entering desert country."[9]

The desert setting is obviously central to Adamski's representation of his experiences. It is not merely that the touchdown sites are remote, although, as we will see in other, similar accounts, the choice of a remote, unpopulated site figures in the aliens' calculations about where to land. It is also the character of the desert itself, refracted though a long-standing imaginary about this landform, that makes it an ideal choice for alien-human contact. Adamski's descriptions, particularly of his first encounter, emphasize the isolation and strangeness of the desert: plants that grow scruffily and do not resemble those with which he's familiar, wispy clouds that mysteriously evaporate in the sky, the striking contrast between cold wind and hot sun, the strange rocks, the illusions of distance—all these features stress the differentness of the desert, its inversion of ordinary human experience, its strange mixture of allure and vague fear. These desert qualities play up precisely the topography's numerousness—the sense that here is a special place, a liminal place, where contact between humans and others can happen.[10]

THE OTHER GEORGE—VAN TASSEL

Born in Ohio but relocated to California at age 20, George Van Tassel got to know a prospector named Frank Critzer who was living in a sort of cave called Giant Rock near Landers, California, in the Mojave Desert. In 1947, after Critzer's death, Van Tassel secured a lease from the Bureau of Land Management to reopen an airstrip at the Rock; he also started a café and moved his family into the cave. One night in 1951 Van Tassel was meditating out in the desert when a UFO, hovering far out in orbit, translated him in astral form to meet with the Council of Seven Lights, a body of Space Brothers. Thereafter he received messages from various aliens that conveyed information ranging from weather reports to warnings about nuclear war. Van Tassel started a Giant Rock Spacecraft Convention in 1953; lasting till 1965, it attracted at its height more than 10,000 conventioneers and hosted talks by Truman Bethurum, Orfeo Angelucci, and Adamski. According to James Mosley, who remembered attending a convention in 1970, the original "gentle, new age crowd" to which Van Tassel catered was overwhelmed by "hard-ass bikers." Van Tassel's acolytes included Bob

Figure 8-3: Integratron, Landers, California.

Short, who saw saucers and met their occupants there in the desert (with his wife) and went on to start a UFO ministry in Arizona.[11]

Van Tassel never recounted his experiences in a UFO with anything like Adamski's detail (recounted below). In his first book, published in 1952, *I Rode a Flying Saucer*, he merely states, "I rode a flying saucer!"; his communications with his space beings occurred instead after learning "how to separate the true vibrations from the discords" through "scheduled meetings, at regular times, *to consolidate our effort, in unity*, to add more *power*, to make the *receptivity* more sensitive and easier to control." The messages from his space beings, which account for the majority of the book, reassure Van Tassel that they come in peace and cannot be stopped. The chief warning to Earthlings, as with Adamski, is about the bomb: "[M]any of your fellow beings will *suffer prolonged illness* from an experiment to be conducted next week. This folly in the use of atomic power for destruction will rebound upon the users."[12]

Van Tassel's chief legacy—aside from his books—is a structure he built near Giant Rock under the direction of his alien guides (Fig. 8-3). This Integratron, which is still standing and now used for "sound baths" said to foster "deep relaxation, rejuvenation, and introspection," was constructed without the use of metal (no nails) and supposedly concentrated certain geomagnetic forces to promote cellular rejuvenation.[13]

TRUMAN BETHURUM AND HIS SPACE SISTER

Eleven times between July and November, 1952, Truman Bethurum (1898–1969), who worked first on road construction near Overton, Nevada, at Mormon Mesa and later on Davis Dam on the Colorado River, was invited into a spaceship from the planet Clarion.[14] The saucer settled down during these visits onto various sites in the desert, usually on or near Mormon Mesa.[15] To his shock, the captain of the "scow" (for so the saucer was called[16])

Figure 8-4: Aura Rhanes.

proved to be a ravishing woman named Aura Rhanes (see Fig. 8-4). She had "smooth skin . . . a beautiful olive and roses" color, with a "brown-eyed flashing smile" that made "her complexion appear more glowing." She sported "a black and red beret," "a bodice . . . of fitted material . . . like black velvet," and a skirt "of the most radiant red material" Bethurum had ever seen. On the ninth visit, Aura dressed differently, in "a light gray slack [*sic*] outfit" in which "she looked very chic indeed . . . with her fully developed figure set off by the slacks, which appeared almost as if painted on her, so snugly did they fit." As one of his fellow workers remarked, after Bethurum confessed his encounter, "'Leave it to old Tru to find a good lookin' dame in the middle of the desert!'"[17]

The locale of the desert is clearly crucial to Bethurum's experiences. Typically to access the landing place, he must "hit out across the desert, bumping along over the rough terrain, plowing over scrub brush," often very late at night, under only the illumination of a "bright desertlight [*sic*] night." At one point, Bethurum muses about the environment in which he finds himself:

> In the west the night was creeping away over the purple mountains and the east the marvelous sky began to flame in glory as the sun rose up over the horizon. I could feel its heat already and I knew the day would be another scorcher. All around me as I drove to the shop was the parched desert with its yellow sands and dried out colorless student [*sic*] shrubbery already beginning to quiver with heat waves.

At one point he wonders whether "I was seeing things that weren't there? Had the desert heat got me? Was I nuts?" Aura Rhanes even explains the attraction for her of desert spaces as landing places:

She mentioned the extremely large desert area and added that it was especially adequate for landing their scow without endangering anything or anyone. She also added, with a small one-sided smile on her lips, that in a remote area such as this there would be no molestation efforts from earth men, or attempts at restraint.

In a later encounter, the desert formed an explicit topic of Bethurum and Aura's conversation.

We talked a bit about desert spaces, the extreme heat, even at midnight, the lack of foliage, the scarcity of water, and she made a remark which startled me.

"I expect to be around for thousands of years, but the water in your deserts will mostly be tears."[18]

Aura speaks of the deserts in blatant biblical terms. Describing her home planet Clarion—of which Bethurum exclaims at one point after a long description of its wonders, "'Clarion sure sounds like heaven'"—where all inhabitants "know what is right and want to do it," Aura insists:

The same could be true on your earth. God has been liberal in His blessings, and there is no dearth. Your peoples could amalgamate and act in unison instead of constantly warring upon each other, and then you'd find your earth living upon. Your deserts and plains could be transformed into gardens that would be like heaven. The substance and effort and life spent each year on your wars would bring an abundance of water into your deserts . . . [a]nd you'd have a very paradise in which to build your homes and rear your children.

She ends with a repetition of her tearful prediction: "'But so far as I can see into the future of this planet, the water in your deserts will be mostly tears.'" These comments, on which Bethurum later excogitates, are a direct echo of Isaiah (40:3–5):

A voice of one calling:
"In the wilderness prepare
the way for the Lord;
make straight in the desert
a highway for our God.
Every valley shall be raised up,
every mountain and hill made low;
the rough ground shall become level,
the rugged places a plain.
And the glory of the Lord will be revealed,
and all people will see it together.
For the mouth of the Lord has spoken."[19]

DANA HOWARD

Perhaps the clearest instances of the link between the desert and the spiritual elements of contact occur in the meetings between Dana Howard (I have not been able to track down her birth and death dates) and her Venusian sister Diane. Howard first encountered Diane in June 1939 after she and her fiancé Stephen crashed in the Superstition Mountains and Dana was transported by "a beautiful rocket-shaped ship" to Venus.[20] The Venusian stayed away until April 29, 1955, when she materialized again in a séance held in a church in Los Angeles, as an ectoplasmic figure over eight feet high. But Diane seems to have far preferred to meet her earthly contactee not in the crowded confines of urban LA but the open deserts outside the city, "the cactus-studded desert," as Howard insists, "where I love to roam." Her re-encounter with UFOs (after her earlier flight to Venus) occurred in August 1952, when she was driving "out on the desert near Cabot's Old Indian Pueblo, Desert Hot Springs, California." Both Howard and Diane herself explicitly praise the desert as the appropriate setting for transmitting and receiving high spiritual messages:

> Many spiritual leaders have found inspiration under the desert's white moon. The desert wastes are alive with spiritualized energy. God planted his choicest seeds on the desert that they might spread and grow, feeding and nourishing those who came in search of His Treasures.

Indeed, Diane insists, referring clearly to Jesus, "Your master found His great strength on the desert sands."[21]

Howard meets Diane in Desert Christ Park, set "high in the beautiful Yucca Valley of California," where a local sculptor had fashioned statues of Jesus and the disciples. Howard's visitation comes on "one of those mid-March days when the desert is idyllic with unseen rays and the waxen blooms dotted here and there over the consecrated earth seemed to stem from some long past antiquity." Or, on another occasion:

> It was high noon, and the rugged desert canyon I loved so well had come alive with the outbreathing [sic] rays of the Universe. Kim, my adorable little black-and-white terrier, followed at my heels, for this spot on the desert was her special place, too. She seemed to sense the nature spirits, playful little people invisible to the sight of humans, but who danced and played on the desert sands, perhaps to the merry tunes of aerial music.

Howard's dog Kim can recognize Diane even before she materializes. But Howard too is attuned to the radiance of the alien cosmos:

> It was early morning and the golden sands of the desert were breakfasting on the first glow of the sun's actinic rays. I loved to walk at this hour when all the unseen little people were gay—filled with the spirit of the new-born day. I could see them now in my mind's eye as they danced with the rhythm of abandonment, tuned with the orchestration of the *spirit of life*.

Making my way over the wind-swept sand dunes drinking in inspiration for my day of work, I came to a sudden halt. It had happened many times of late—a tingling sensation in my body—bells ringing from afar—the fragrance from beautiful flowers—strains of melody floating in from out of nowhere.

A patch of soft sand beneath a sprawling greasewood bush beckoned to me. It was an ecstatic moment... then a merging with an "alien" something as though I were being hooked up with all the main lines of the Cosmos.[22]

And then Howard is in contact with Diane, who proclaims, "[I]t is with the spirit of gladness I greet you this day out on the clean desert sands." Venus too, she avers, has "the same clean sands" which led the Venusians to "the throne of God." The role of the desert is the same on both planets, for, Diane insists, "Out where the wilderness is wild, you too will come to know the meaning of God." And again: Diane calls to Howard while she is sleeping outside on one of the "balmy summer nights" when "the starry heavens . . . created a giant canopy over the desert wastes." On yet another occasion, Howard recounts her time at "The Altar in the Wilderness Shrine," which is set "in a secluded idyllic canyon, a sacred plot of earth" opposite "the tall cliffs of the San Jacinto Mountains." Here, in this "valley of destiny" where Howard experienced "the electric fluids of the cosmos flowing through my body" and "[t]he clean desert air caressing my senses," Diane materialized as a "wraith-like shadow" "behind a misshapen Indigo Bush."[23]

According to Howard, the desert has a long history in Venusian contact. She tells us that the Egyptian pharaoh Ich-na-ton (i.e., Akhenaton, 1353–1336 BCE), "perhaps one of the greatest psychics who ever lived," went each day "out into the blazing, sun-clad desert" to receive "his divine instructions" from his Venusian guides. "Day by day, true to his visions, he continued his trek into the lonely desert for moments of sacred quietude with his God," Aton. Much like Ich-na-ton, Howard was instructed to fashion an "Altar in the Wilderness Shrine," located "in a secluded idyllic canyon" on (it seems) the eastern slopes of the San Jacinto Mountains, facing the Mojave Desert. The shrine sat above a spring of curing waters that had been known to the Cahuilla Indians, on a "plot of earth [that] should serve as a focal center for healing consciousness. Here blind and stumbling humanity would one day be led out of its chaos into the promised land of the New Tomorrow."[24]

At one of Diane's appearances at this shrine, she predicted that "right here on this hallowed ground long-dead centuries will be revived. On this sacred earth the veil between worlds is very thin, so thin it is difficult to separate the material from the divine." Then she quoted Isaiah (40:3), which Aura Rhanes also echoed: "'Prepare ye the way of the Lord; make straight in the desert a highway for our God.' Here on these singing desert sands humanity will listen to the sounds of the soul."[25]

Elsewhere Howard writes of "[t]he desert's iridescent tints"; "the sunshine of the desert canyon" where she "perched . . . on a smooth desert rock" while awaiting one of Diane's visitations. Regan Lee, one of the few who has paid serious attention to Howard, explicitly compared Diane to manifestations of the Virgin Mary—thus setting Howard's experiences in a fully Christianized context, although without noting the central importance of the desert setting (which has not been a general feature of Mariological manifestations). But Howard also attributes the births of Islam and Judaism to desert settings, the one "under the desert's white moon" and the other in "the desert wilderness, seeking for the Promised Land."[26]

Typically, the aliens so often contact people only in remote areas and at night because "most people are not prepared to meet these beings face to face."[27] The aliens themselves resort to this explanation. As we saw above, Aura Rhanes told Bethurum she chose remote desert locales as landing sites to avoid prying eyes. This answer is also a predominant one among the conspiratorially minded who believe the US government knows all about UFOs but shields the general population from the truth because we would panic if we knew.[28] But Howard holds a quite different view. "Our deserts are the last recognized frontiers of hope," she writes, adding in another passage:

> Those who love the desert love it with a passion they cannot explain. At night there is an endless tune from the melodies of nature—voices and sounds from the desert's own soul . . . brilliant by day with its billions of granules of golden sand, by night the spacious filament alive with twinkling stars. It is all on the threshold of new experience, for if diseased "thought forms" are to be broken up, humanity must be far removed from the din and noise of the city. People must be concentrated and nucleated.

Deserts are simply, she avers, "hallowed spots on the earth's surface . . . points of ingress and egress from earth to higher planets."[29]

Many lesser known contactees also met their Space Brothers and Sisters in the desert. Daniel William Fry, who worked at the White Sands Proving Ground, stumbled upon an unstaffed UFO during an evening walk on July 4, 1950, and was taken on a flight to New York City and back. During the excursion a disembodied voice offered a potted history of a nuclear war between Lemuria and Atlantis and the standard warning about nuclear weapons: "[I]t should always be remembered that 'An ounce of understanding is worth a megaton of deterrence.'"[30] A certain Adam, whom Orfeo Angelucci met in a diner, related his encounter with a Space Sister named Vega, who took him for a spin to a gigantic spaceship circling Venus.[31] And Wayne Aho, who lived in Washington state, was summoned to a desert locale for his meeting with aliens.[32] Orfeo Angelucci, whose first contacts took place in urban Los Angeles, later moved to the desert in Twentynine Palms, California, finally taking up his original plan on moving to Los Angeles from New Jersey to dwell in the desert. There his sense of alien presence was sometimes almost overpowering: "There is a cosmic spell over the desert most of the time, but tonight the mystery was less distant and intangible; it was close and pulsating." "It was," as his friend Adam declared, "the call of the desert."[33] Howard would surely have agreed.

CHANGES IN CONTACT AND MESSAGING

As the 1950s passed into the next decades, shifts in the nature of contact and the content of messages occurred that have been well explicated by Aaron Gulyas and John Rimmer.[34] Physical contact, conversation, and trips on board actual flying saucers as recounted by

Adamski, Bethurum, Howard—all grounded in actual physical encounters with material beings and objects—retreat in the face of "channeling"—psychic, nonphysical communications inserted directly into the minds of the receivers by space beings with names like Ashtar (who first communicated with Van Tassel) and Hatonn. Elements of "channeling" were already present in the telepathy by which many contactees interacted with their aliens, like Adamski with Orthon during their first encounter. The desert too recedes into invisibility, as virtually all the channeling experiences occur in urban or suburban environments.[35] There are also transitional incidents, like George Menger's interview with a perfectly material female alien in woods near his suburban New Jersey home. With this change comes also a significant shift in the nature of the messages, in many cases, to address political matters and threaten dire consequences if humans do not obey the dictates of extraterrestrial organizations like the Intergalactic Federation Council on Earth Transition.[36] This technology of transcendent interplanetary communication had deep roots in Europe in the late nineteenth century, as we will see below.

But a more menacing new form of encounter emerges too: the abduction, given its model by the tale of Betty and Barney Hill, whose experiences were recovered from their lost memory by hypnosis,[37] but which really took off in the 1980s and 1990s.[38] And, as we will see, even more ominous events are percolating.

CONTACT GOES AWRY

The experiences of the contactees stand at the polar opposite of "alien abductions," which began to emerge in the 1960s and gripped the imagination of much of the public; they have continued to feed popular culture, including science fiction TV series like *The X-Files*. One very notable difference between the contactees and the abductees is that the latter rarely experience encounters in desert space. The abductees may be taken, like Betty and Barney Hill, from their car on a lonely New Hampshire road, or, like Whitley Strieber, from his bedroom in an upstate New York cabin or his apartment in Manhattan. Another fundamental difference is the nature of the experience: contactees' aliens are human in appearance (sometimes, indeed, too human) and benign; the abductees face strange, emotionless little "Grays" and insectoid or reptilian monsters whose intentions often seem the opposite of benign and who often induce pain and crushing fear. In many cases sexual abuse, the involuntary extraction of ova and sperm, often by mechanical means, rarely by ordinary human intercourse, forms the central event of the abduction, in striking contrast to the thrumming sexuality the contactees feel. The aim is the production of alien-human hybrids; the Grays seem to care little, if at all, for the pain and humiliation they cause their abductees.[39] None of these features figure in the desert visitations; in them, for Adamski, Bethurum, Howard, and their compeers, the encounters are benevolent, warm, inviting, welcome, safe, even if at times seductive, and, above all, aimed at helping humanity face the terrible problems bedeviling our civilization.

More broadly, the abduction narrative fits into larger, more terrifying developments that emerge in the 1970s and 1980s and that take us back again to the deserts of the Southwest. In this complicated and convoluted view, Earth is the locus of a galactic-wide struggle among different alien species. The violent and hostile "Reptoids," who control the Grays, are in league with American military and spy agency elements. Their headquarters are buried under

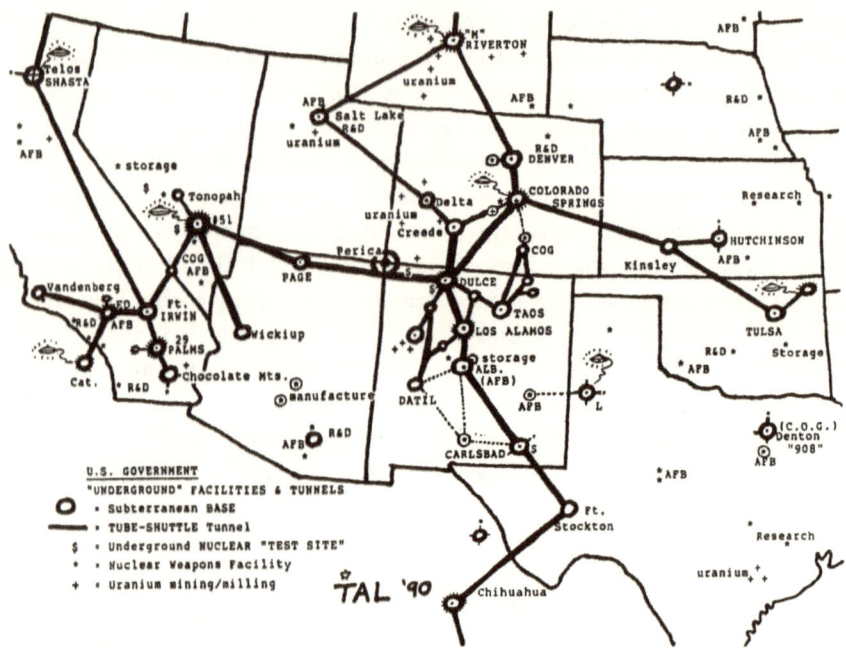

Figure 8-5: Underground UFO bases. (After Hamilton 1991, 102.)

Archuleta Mesa near Dulce, New Mexico, on the Jicarilla Apache reservation, and linked by underground tunnels to satellite bases all over the desert Southwest (see Fig. 8-5); the base of their opponents lies somewhere under Death Valley. The abductions, whose primary purpose is the creation of hybrid human-alien beings and the insertion into the skulls of the victims control devices (for an instance, see chapter 10), are just one component of a plan ultimately to eliminate most of the human population of our planet to make way for alien settlement; a small cadre of the Bavarian Illuminati who have been working with the Reptoids will be granted dictatorial authority over the human remnant.[40] In this new version of the purpose of alien visitation, all the benevolence of the 1950s Space Brothers and Sisters and their compassionate concern for our happiness have evaporated.

THE MESSAGES OF THE SPACE BROTHERS AND SISTERS

What, then, did the contactees' aliens, the Space Brothers and Sisters, bring to their human contactees? The basic themes of their messages in the 1950s were essentially the same. First and foremost, they brought warnings of the dangers of nuclear testing. In Adamski's first meeting with his Venusian guide, after establishing the visitor's Venusian origin and a few other preliminaries, Adamski (naturally) asked why the aliens were coming to Earth. At that point the two communicated by gesture and telepathy rather than language:

He made me understand that their coming was friendly. Also, as he gestured, that they were concerned with radiations going out from Earth.

This I got clearly since there was a considerable amount of radiation of heat waves rising from the desert. . . . Such as the waves that are often seen rising from pavements, and highways on hot days.

He pointed to them and then gestured through space.

I asked if this concern was due to the explosions of our bombs with their resultant vast radio-active clouds?

He understood this readily and nodded his head in the affirmative.

My next question was whether this was dangerous, and I pictured in my mind a scene of destruction.

To this, too, he nodded his head in the affirmative. . . .

Adamski adds his own interpretation:

[I]t has long been known by scientists of Earth that the cosmic ray, as it is called, is more powerful in outer space than it is in the Earth's atmosphere. And if this be true, is it not just as logical to assume that the radio-active force from the bombs being tested by nations of Earth could also become more powerful in space, once leaving the Earth's atmosphere. Logical deduction supports the statement of this space man.

The two continued their conversation of gesture and thought, until finally the alien "pointed to the Earth itself, and with a wide sweep of his hands and other gestures [indicated] that too many 'Booms!' would destroy all of this."[41]

Other guides reinforce Orthon's message. The "desert tears" of which Aura Rhanes spoke to Bethurum carry an allusion to the horrors of testing bombs in the Nevada desert, which had not begun in 1952 but started the next year, in March, with the Upshot-Knothole series (he would of course have known about the bombing of Hiroshima and Nagasaki and the Pacific tests). Diane warned Howard about the dangers of "trying every sort of magic in an attempt to short-circuit thinking," something that did not work very well with the atomic bomb. Zuhl—one of Adamski's later guides—while explaining the operation of unmanned scouts, notes:

"It was by means of disks like these . . . that we first became alerted to the abnormal conditions building up in the fringe of your atmosphere—a condition constantly increasing with every atomic or hydrogen bomb that is exploded on Earth."

"Men of your Earth," one of Adamski's "Martian ladies" declares, "know the terrible power sealed within the bombs they are piling up for use against one another. Yet they blunder on ever nearer to the brink of an unthinkable world-wide slaughter." George King's Aetherius devoted a lengthy discourse to the dangers of thermonuclear explosions, which included the spread of strontium-90 and "etheric distortion." Orfeo Angelucci is told, "Already man's material knowledge has far outstripped the growth of brotherly love and spiritual understanding in his heart."[42]

This remark overlaps with a second basic theme: humans are warlike and violent, self-destructive, and deeply misguided. Diane expostulates at length on the horrors of human history:

> "Look down on the long road of earthman's stumbling past, my daughter. You will be sickened by the nauseating stupidities of all human-kind on earth. You will look askance at the greed-built structures. To these earthman must light the fires of destruction that he may not be forced to look upon the monstrosities he has created. . . . Earthman of today has shown but little more mercy than the feudal overlords of days gone by. When he sees himself in the rôle of the master, whip in hand, ready to lash out at the least provocation, he will then realize that his ignoble urges are no different from the master and slave precepts born and bred into the childhood of the cycle."

In a coffee shop, Ramu, another Space Brother, recounts for Adamski a much longer and more detailed history of Earth, which "was the slowest planet in our system to reach the stage where it was capable of maintaining human life."[43] I return to this tale below, for it provides, I think, a key to tracing one possible source of the contactee vision.

The explanation for our defects is simple: we do not recognize the one true "Eternal Father" who created and rules the universe. Orthon insisted to Adamski that humans know virtually nothing about the "Creator of All," for we have lost contact with the divine. Our perversions include "unholy prayer" offered up when we are at war, asking "your Divine Father to bless your efforts to gain a victory over your own life-brother, even to the extent of destroying him." From, or thanks to, this great divine being who oversees the universe, the whole of creation is infused with a single "force" that sustains it and brings life, which abounds everywhere, on every planet. As one of the "Masters" explains, "In the endless vast Infinite are many forms. . . . These vary in size, from infinitely small dust particles, invisible to the human eye, to the largest planets and suns without number. All are bathed in the sea of One Power, supported by the One Life." To Howard, Diane insisted, "Venus is not a fantastic utopia. The Venusians . . . are a perfectly balanced people who have sought beyond man-created systems for their enlightenment. They believe there is but ONE and all things are created by HIM."[44]

When scholars of contactees look for the roots of their tales, most point to Theosophy, the religion created by Helena P. Blavatsky in the late nineteenth century, and spiritualism.[45] There's no question that Theosophic practices of contact with Ascended Masters through mental transmission of teachings over great distances parallels the accounts some—but not all—contactees reported, and that spiritualism in its focus on nonmaterial, mind-to-mind contact, or ectoplasmic manifestation forms the core of some UFO groups' practices. However, Adamski and his cohort insist on actual, physical encounters with their Space Brothers and Sisters (even if later communication, as with Van Tassel, took place by telepathy). I would like to suggest another possible component. In 1938 the British scholar of mediaeval and Renaissance literature and noted Christian apologist C. S. Lewis (1898–1963) published *Out of the Silent Planet*, the first volume of a "space trilogy" completed by *Perelandra* (1943) and *That Hideous Strength* (1945). In the first volume, an Earthman named Elwin Ransom is kidnapped by Weston and Devine, two unscrupulous schemers (a physicist and an investor) who believe he's to be offered as a human sacrifice on Malacandra, Lewis's inhabitants' name for Mars.[46]

Lewis's Mars echoes strikingly the planet expounded in many books, articles, and lectures by Percival Lowell. A Boston Brahmin well set with money and time, Lowell spent some years in Japan before turning his interests to the planets. Learning that Mars and Earth would be in apposition in 1892, he scouted desert locales for a suitable site to erect an observatory. He settled on a mountain outside Flagstaff, Arizona, and installed a refractor telescope there in time to begin observations. Inspired by the Italian astronomer Giovanni Schiaparelli, Lowell soon mapped out hundreds of canals crisscrossing the planet. Changes in coloration over the course of a year seemed to him evidence of water transport from melting polar icecaps via the canals to feed by irrigation fields otherwise impossible on an extremely arid, desert landscape; both he and visitors to his observatory drew the obvious analogy with Arizona's Sonoran Desert, already being brought into fruition by canals dug near Phoenix. Lowell spun out a grandiose theory of an advanced, peaceful, more or less socialist, globe-spanning Martian civilization; faced with disaster as their aging home desiccated, the Martians banded together and eliminated interstate competition and war to create a scientifically based culture that assured their survival.[47]

Lewis admitted years after the publication of *Out of the Silent Planet* that he knew, when he wrote in the 1930s, that Lowell's Mars was a fantasy—indeed, the Boston Brahmin's observations and inferences had already been thoroughly demolished even as he was expounding them.[48] But Lewis nevertheless took up Lowell's Mars as the setting for Ransom's adventures. His Mars, it turns out, is a blasted desert landscape because of a titanic war between the forces of good and evil that raged millions of years before throughout the Solar System. The Martians, having suffered the brunt of the fighting, carved out and retreated into canyon-like canals, where there was enough water and air to survive. Despite their suffering they stayed firm in their allegiance to the good forces—simply put, God and the angels—while Earth, abandoned to the defeated evil one—Satan—was embargoed by the rest of the Solar System, to live out its dreary days in silence, isolation, and ignorance. Earth is, as Angelucci's informant declares, "'the accursed planet', the 'home of reprobate, fallen ones.'"[49]

The possibility that Lewis's vision of the solar system served as a source for contactees' ideas comes across most clearly in a lengthy speech given by the aliens Ramu and Firkon to Adamski in a coffee shop in Los Angeles. Planets are constantly being created in the universe, and all are populated by volunteer colonists once a fresh planet is ready for habitation. Earth, "the slowest planet in our system to reach the stage where it was capable of maintaining human life," received its colonists in due course, but then "something unexpected" affected the atmosphere, rendering its future "unfavorable." Most colonists abandoned the planet, and "the few who chose to remain had permitted themselves to deteriorate amidst the lush beauty and abundance of this new world. . . . Gradually, they became content to live in natural caves and were eventually lost in the annals of time."

Time passed, and Earth was again ready, but the atmosphere had not improved. However, the rest of the universe, although largely living in peace and harmony, suffered from "here and there a few" humans distorted by "personal ego and aggressiveness," and it was decided to ship these miscreants to (among other planets) Earth. They received no tools or other aids and were forced to "use their knowledge and start with nothing more than what nature provided." These settlers are, in fact, the Bible's "fallen angels." The Space Brothers came from time to time to assist, but the Earthlings "were a haughty and defiant lot, and did not welcome the help." Still, they managed to create a life, and the Earth became in fact a Garden of Eden. Then disaster: these settlers "ate of the fruit of the tree of 'knowledge of good and evil,'" and division, violence, ambition, conflict, war, nations, religious differences, and all the other evils of our present existence arose.

Earth, then, differs from every other planet in the solar system. We—for it is us, descendants of those haughty settlers—turn our energies toward self-destruction. Satan is not a separate being but the result of our opposition to "the Divine principle"; once we reform ourselves, Satan will become an angel of light. Further, Earth functions at a "low frequency," which further impedes our development and prevents our understanding of our past lives. Our "low frequency" likewise accounts for our slow maturation, our eighteen years of childhood as opposed to two on other planets. At the same time, this phenomenon—which is entirely our fault, since the frequency at which a planet pulsates is a function of its inhabitants, nothing else—speeds up old age and deterioration. Such, then, are the defining features of our benighted home.[50]

Lewis's space trilogy is an allegory about the Fall and redemption. Earth is under the sway of Satan, whose rebellion precipitated disaster on Mars and a disruption of the order of the Solar System, separating Earth from the other planets and their inhabitants. Christian theology, often distorted or revised, runs through the messages of the Space Brothers and Sisters more or less explicitly. For George King, Jesus was a Master who came to Earth from Venus "to save it from catastrophe."[51] Howard's Diane speaks likewise openly of the Master who is clearly Jesus. Adamski and Van Tassel too receive admonitions saturated with Christianity.[52]

There is yet another element that may well have played a role in the articulation of the contactees' visions. In the late nineteenth and early twentieth centuries many mediums, notably in Europe but also in the United States, experienced in séances, in which they shifted into states of transcendence, visions of, or even visits to, other planets. Perhaps the most famous— because subject of multiple lengthy studies—was "Hélène Smith" of Geneva, Switzerland. Smith, whose real name was Catherine-Elise Müller, expounded long tales of her past lives in India and as Marie Antoinette, but for our purposes her most important visions related to Mars. In 1894 and 1896 her spirit-guide Léopold (also known as Joseph Balsamo, count of Cagliostro) conducted her to the Red Planet, where she saw

> carriages without horses or wheels, emitting sparks as they glided by; houses with fountains on the roof; a cradle having for curtains an angel made from iron with outstretched wings,

Figure 8-6: Hélène Smith's Martian Painting. (After the cover of Flournoy 1994. Used with permission of Princeton University Press.)

etc. What seemed less strange, were people exactly like the inhabitants of our earth, save that both sexes wore the same costume, formed of trousers very ample, and a long blouse, drawn tight about the waist and decorated with various designs. The child in the cradle was exactly like our children . . .

On another occasion Smith stood

on the border of a beautiful blue-pink lake, with a bridge the sides of which were transparent and formed of yellow tubes like the pipes of an organ, of which one seemed to be plunged into the water. The earth was peach-colored; some of the trees had trunks widening as they ascended, while those of others were twisted. . . . The women wore hats which were flat, like plates. . . . On the bridge there was a man of dark complexion (Astané), carrying in his hands an instrument somewhat resembling a carriage-lantern in appearance, which, being pressed, emitted flames, and seemed to be a flying-machine. By means of this instrument the man left the bridge, touched the surface of the water, and returned again to the bridge.

She also articulated a "Martian language" that was nothing other than a modified French. Surprisingly, perhaps, even though she'd participated in lively conversations about the canals when not in trance, they do not appear in her accounts.[53] She later produced paintings of the Martian landscape (Fig. 8-6). In contrast, one "Mireille," another medium who visited Mars in 1894, dutifully reported plenty of water, attested by clouds that obstructed her view, shining seas, and "canals of an enormous length ... [that] had been dug across the continents by the Martians who, although amphibious, preferred to live in water and used them to go from one sea to another."[54]

Plenty of others had similar visions. The astronomer Camille Flammarion, whose two-volume study of Mars served as an encyclopedia of observations on the planet, also dabbled in mediumistic visions: he published his account of the satellites of Uranus and their spirits in 1908. The American psychic Mrs. Smead's visions of Mars seem to have been inspired by reading Théodore Flournoy's account of Smith and various articles on Mars. A certain Machner painted Martian plants and flowers and may have depicted "flying saucers" in one of his works, although they could be lenticular clouds (the reproduction I have seen is too poor to allow a determination). "Stellar songs" were dictated to a group at a séance in Paris. The painter Fernand Desmoulin signed his paintings and watercolors "Astarte." Transportation to Jupiter provided Victorien Sardou with the subjects of his work. Gérard de Nerval traveled to a distant planet where he was vouchsafed visions of the germs of creation, gnosis of the origins of the universe. As W. Deonna has pointed out, even further back stood the opium-induced visions of Edgar Alan Poe, Thomas de Quincey, and Thomas Coleridge.[55]

The visions of these mediums may have fed into notions about extraterrestrial life in several ways. Simply put, these early visionaries attested via their trances to the existence of life on Mars, Jupiter, and other planets; to the advanced civilizations there ensconced; and to the possibility of communication with their inhabitants, who could reveal the secrets of the universe and help Earthlings advance to a higher plane of spiritual existence. What changed between a Hélène Smith and a George Adamski was the UFO. In Smith's day, there was no widespread notion of visitations by the Space Brothers and Sisters.[56] The arrival of the UFOs—in which, as we have seen, Adamski took a keen interest—offered a new, up-to-date, technological mechanism for the very same type of interaction: aliens could actually visit *us*, because they deployed super-advanced technology; they could whisk us away to their planets, if they wished, where we could see their civilizations; and we could enjoy these experiences even if we lacked the skills of a Hélène Smith to shift into a trance and put ourselves into the hands of a spirit-guide.

Of course, there were also people imagining a technological form of visitation in the late nineteenth century. H. G. Wells had his Martians arrive in canisters shot from massive Martian cannons; in *Auf zwei Planeten* ("On Two Planets") by Kurd Lasswitz, Martians had established a listening post above the North Pole and employed fast ships to sail the empty space between planets.[57] So there was, perhaps, no lack of notional physical (as opposed to spiritual) contact in the years the mediums we have examined were operating; and it is worth remembering that from 1892 Percival Lowell was vigorously and vociferously arguing that Mars hosted not merely a civilization but an advanced socialist society of peace, planet-wide government, and prosperity.

NATIVE AMERICANS AND UFOS

Long before the start of the "modern" UFO phenomenon—and discounting the reports of the 1890s, many if not all of which were hoaxes—what is now the United States had been visited by beings from the stars: the "Star People" who appear in many Native American traditions, both among peoples living in deserts and elsewhere on the continent. There have been a number of studies or, perhaps better, recountings of contemporary encounters by Native Americans with Star People and accounts said to have been passed down from earlier generations. In the instances recorded in *Star Ancestors* and *Space Age Indians* by Ardy Sixkiller Clarke, many of the encounters are benign or even helpful. In *Space Age Indians*, she collects fifteen accounts of interactions with Blue Men, a number of which occurred in Vietnam during the war, who save humans from disaster or death or heal them of life-threatening injuries or chronic conditions or warn them of danger. Wilson, for instance, who lived in Hawaii and was a vet, was warned to avoid Diamond Head "because I was in danger." UFOs also healed the sick and in one case levitated a car to remove it from an oncoming train. In several cases the UFOs deliver messages about Earth's isolation in the universe due to its "war-mongering mentality." These aliens are peaceful and benign.[58]

Several of Clarke's interviewees insist on the historical depth of Native encounters with Star People. Blue Otter, a Cherokee elder, told her the Cherokee met the Blue People after the Cherokees arrived in what is now Tennessee; these people lived underground then. An informant tells her, "The Star People had always interacted with our people. Our ancestors knew them, our grandfathers knew them.... [W]e had all heard star ancestor stories that the ancestors watched over us and protected us."[59] A Cherokee informant insists, "The prophecies speak of ancient scientists from the sky rescuing Indian people from a sinking Atlantis and instructing them to make their migration. Mainstream America calls these scientists *extraterrestrials*. Indians call them Star Beings, Sky Guardians, Star Ancestors, or simply 'deities.'"[60] There is, however, a radical difference in the aims of different species of Star People. While some are benign, the Reptilians are not. "The reptile men," one informant insists, "have one purpose in mind and that is to kidnap victims and do their horrendous experiments." The Grays, in contrast, "are interested in reproduction."[61]

Several of Clarke's informants maintain "[t]here is a difference between the Star People of my grandfather's day and the star visitors I have met." Today's visitors, this informant says, engage in experiments that create half-human, half-mechanical beings and use mind control on their victims. The reptile men, remarks another, are not "the Star People of our elders. They are a different race; not human-like."[62] It is apparent that the versions of contact Clarke has collected are syncretized with the tropes of post-1947 Anglo stereotypes of aliens. On the one hand, some are concerned with the health of individuals and the Earth as a whole, worried about war, environmental degradation, and nuclear weapons. Others, however—typically the Reptilians—conduct cruel experiments and abduct their victims, who may report "missing time" typical of abduction events since Betty and Barney Hill. Underground bases and cattle mutilation also occur. Grays who conduct genetic experiments with government connivance are not helpers.[63] The alignment of these accounts of the reptoid Star People with the horrific visitors recounted in Branton's account of Dulce Base, noted above, is obvious, and likewise the shift from benevolence to malevolence. It's clear there has been leakage between some Native American and Anglo notions about Star People.

For a brief report in *The Masterkey* for 1950, Mark Harrington interviewed a Shoshone informant about some rock art by Charleston Peak near Las Vegas, Nevada, a highly sacred site. He was told the art had been drawn by a "little devil about so high," indicating with his raised hand about three feet. Other Native American informants attributed rock art to spirits and claimed the figures in them depicted the spirits themselves.[64] The Mojave Twins, a large land art sculpture near Fort Mojave, Arizona, were believed by some Native Americans to represent a pair of twins who had come from the sky for a temporary visit.[65] Stories of "elves" abound in Native American mythology. In an exhaustive catalogue, John E. Roth amassed thousands of instances of "little people" known from ethnographic sources. Some of these entities bear resemblances to space aliens. I note here only some examples from desert peoples of the present-day Southwest. The Ute knew of "dirty little star gods" who may have been humanoid in appearance. The Paiute, Chemehuevi, and Taracahitan knew a figure called Takwish who was a wife-stealing meteor; this creature was also known to the Hokan and Takic peoples. The Havmusuvs "flew in silvery, winged whirring canoes. They held a small tube that stunned their enemies, causing lasting paralysis and a pain like being pricked by many needles," while Takwis was for the Takic and Tubolilabal peoples "a night man-eater meteor linked to ball lightning, meteors, and thunder." Another creature was said to consume part of a corpse's shoulder so that the heart could become a star, and one Tokwite "stole Serrano souls until shot in the penis by Coyote. His spirit escaped to become a meteor." The Lipan Apache and Navajo were afflicted by a sheep-mutilating creature with an ape-like face and five-inch footprints. Among at least two peoples, petroglyphs were said to be made by these creatures.[66] Here, then, we have instances of abduction, whether of the bodily person or the soul, animal mutilation, travel in flying ships, and generally association with stars, meteors, and the sky. Many of these stories were collected by late nineteenth or early twentieth-century ethnographers, thus long before they could have been contaminated by post–World War II alien and UFO tropes.

Star Beings figure prominently in Leslie Marmon Silko's memoir *The Turquoise Ledge*. While living near Tucson on the edge of Saguaro National Park, Silko decided in 2005 to return to her early love of painting. Almost at once "something from the reading I'd done earlier in 2005 suddenly came back to me. Many indigenous tribes in the Americas and Australia have ancestral stories about stars that came to Earth. The Star Beings came to contact human beings; or perhaps we are their descendants." Silko reviewed photos she'd taken of petroglyphs which she realized recorded visitations by the Star Beings in the deep past. As she sketched the photos, it came to her that the Star Beings wanted her to paint their portraits; "[t]hey insisted I use the largest canvases possible and that their portraits must always be hung at a height that dwarfs the human viewers in order to intimidate them."[67]

There ensued a long, silent colloquy between Silko and her Star Beings. They insisted she accept an invitation to an arts festival in Ciudad Chihuahua in 2006 to learn things her portrait painting needed. She received "thought communications" from them that guided her portraiture. She came to realize they'd contacted her long ago, when she was contemplating a star map including the Pleiades and Orion on a Navajo shield; she'd been chosen because she'd seen petroglyphs as a child and, later, was impelled to draw maps of the Pleiades, Orion, and Scorpio. She struggles with the nature of the Star Beings: do they experience emotions? Do they disdain us? Why do they keep coming back to Earth? Do they really look like us or do they don a disguise when we see them? Do they care that we slaughter one another? They seem to have no compassion. They also forced Silko to write poetry in Nahuatl, a language she did not know; she bought dictionaries to work through, and discovered Nahuatl words for star, *citlalin*, full of stars, *citlalloh*, and, remarkably, spaceship, *cictlalpuzacalili*.[68]

Silko's chapters on the Star Beings interweave with reflections on the natural world, especially rattlesnakes that live under her house and turquoise that she finds on her walks in a nearby arroyo. She grows *Datura* (jimsonweed) to enjoy the hawk moths that feed on their flowers. The Aztec rain god Tlaloc is an incarnation of the Star Being called Venus-Eyed Rattlesnake (see Figs. 2-2a and 2-2b); he appears, she says, on a cliff painting at Hueco Tanks in Texas.[69] Summer rains in 2006 are especially abundant. Silko suffers financial troubles, but the Star Beings refuse to let her sell their portraits to make money.[70] In other words, Silko's relationship with the Star Beings is at once deeply personal and impersonal. She never meets any face-to-face, like a contactee; they do not talk to her or convey information about the universe or warnings about destructive human behavior. At the same time, they interpolate themselves into every aspect of her life; they are always watching, present, silent, keeping her on the track they have laid out for her. Her experience with her Star Beings seems far distant from both Anglo and Native encounters with UFOs and their occupants—it seems rather like a natural relationship hardly different from her relations with the rattlesnakes that reside under her house. Perhaps she has sought to evoke a relationship meant to appear more traditional, in line with a precolonial interaction with beings at once deity-like and corporeal.

But a recurrent theme in some of the Native American accounts aligns with the contactees' aliens' insistence that we are endangering ourselves, the Earth, and even extraterrestrials with our nuclear experiments, widespread damage to the Earth, and disavowal or forgetting of the secrets the aliens conveyed long ago. The Earth, an informant explains, "is in a state of domestic violence." One Richard Hoagland, who claimed he'd worked for NASA, explored Indian legends of travel to Mars and "discovered" the "Face on Mars," which, he claimed, perfectly reproduced a monument at Silbury Hill in England. He argued Mars had had an advanced civilization that had destroyed its atmosphere; the Martians escaped to Earth, where they have now put our planet on the same self-destructive course. Although Indians are said to have signed a covenant with Grays (who some say were created in lab experiments by the Nordics), Nordics, Katsinas, and Angelics, some extraterrestrials have manipulated us "into believing in a primitive way." There is a galactic war ongoing between good and evil aliens; "[t]here are a lot of [alien] species who come to Earth and, as part of their recreation, create a vicious event using humans. They experience vicariously someone else's anger, love, passion, and they feed on that emotion. That is their entertainment."[71]

Much in these accounts is clearly syncretism of some long-standing Native American legends with recent Ufology and Christian apocalypticism. So we hear of "soul abduction" alongside of benign abductions; egg and sperm harvesting and use of women as incubators;

telepathically conveyed information about the Rapture and Tribulation; and material clearly drawn from Revelation. The Star People's imminent return echoes claims about Jesus and the Millennium. There is even borrowing from Immanuel Velikovsky's *Worlds in Collision* with the claim that Venus was born as a comet passing through our atmosphere in 3113 BCE.[72] And as Susan Lepselter has observed, there is a tight linkage between some aspects of alien abduction, New Age spirituality, and a confected and commodified "Indian" experience of UFOs:

> [S]ome UFO experiencers talk about the fact that long ago, space aliens came first to visit Indians in a kind of annunciation. Those aliens who came through space or time to the Indians weren't these clinical, cold abductors. They did not experiment on human bodies. They did not steal our vital, physical bounty, the birthright of our natural selves. Those aliens who visited the earth *back then* before the Europeans arrived are sometimes said to have been wise and spiritual, sharing secrets of the universe with a worthy people.
>
> People sometimes talk about how space aliens can be found in ancient cave drawings, how Indians know the truth. . . . In UFO talk, as in New Age discourses, Aboriginal peoples of the world can become a sign of potential recovery, of freedom from the captivities of modernity. . . . It is of course a vast trope of guilt and desire.[73]

Simmering below the surface of much of the discussion of alien visitations, abduction, galactic war, and so on is a nervousness about colonialism. The topic is right up front in H. G. Wells's *War of the Worlds*, whose premise is that the Martians intend to conquer us and take over our planet; Kurd Lasswitz's *Auf zwei Planeten* delivers an ironic warning about supposedly "benevolent" European colonialism, which all too often descends into racism, violence, and genocide. (Lasswitz had before him the example of German East Africa, where a horrendous colonial war had been prosecuted but a few years before he wrote.) Native Americans, of course, had only too much experience with colonial powers (see chapter 7 for one aspect of this history), but even for the Anglos who encountered visitors from space, the potentiality of conquest and subjugation lay just under the surface. The dire warnings delivered by a Diane or Orthon carried the implication that, if we do not mend our ways, they just might have to intervene, if only to protect themselves from the effects of our nuclear weapons. And, of course, the deserts of the Southwest had themselves served as the locus for multiple colonial projects, from the first *entradas* of the Spanish *conquistidores* in the early 1500s to the seizure of vast tracts of desert territory for military bases and bombing ranges. We—by which I mean we Anglos—might end up as victims of a colonial project, directed at us from outer space, exploiting our remote, useless deserts as the base from which to carry out their schemes.

BACK TO THE DESERT

Finally, we may return with Carl Jung to the desert. Part of his explanation for UFO sightings is compensation theory: the notion that people who have "lived sufficiently long in the solitude and silence of deserts, seas, mountains, or in primeval forests" may experience "spontaneous psychic phenomena." Especially subject to such visions are ascetics and anchorites, whose yearning for food, sex, wealth, company conjures up "loaded dishes and flagons and luscious meals . . . seductive and voluptuous beings [who] yielded themselves to their pent-up sexual desires, riches and worldly power . . . and bustling crowds, noise, and music [that] enlivened the intolerable silence and loneliness."[74] Deserts, as Jung observes, present just the environment of reduced sensual stimulation that we may compensate for with visions. And so, perhaps, UFOs and their occupants?

The desert locale for the 1950s contactees on whom I've focused here seems to be fundamentally important precisely because of the close links between the desert and the physical manifestation of spiritual beings and the use of (although not exclusively) human vocal communication to transmit messages of deep spiritual and global importance. It is this congeries of elements that makes the situation of contact in the desert so resonant with the long-standing tropes of the desert as a place of spiritual encounter that informs Western traditions about deserts and religion.[75]

Another trope links the contactees to the desert. Jesus went to the desert east of Jerusalem for forty days to test himself against Satan's temptations; naturally, he resisted, and that success gave him some of the authority and confidence he needed to preach his message. The contactees likewise revert often to Jesus; we have already seen that Dana Howard set up an altar to Christ in the desert, and Diane frequently refers to him as "your Master." A contactee can even seem to be identified with Jesus. Orfeo Angelucci is warned that as the Space Brothers' emissary on Earth, he "must act! Even though people of Earth laugh derisively and mock you as a lunatic, tell them about us!"[76] He seems at once Jesus and the apostles.

The choice of a desert as the place to reveal messages may seem prosaic or practical: prying eyes are unlikely to be lurking nearby when a saucer lands; debunkers find it harder to prove a negative (that no ship landed and no Space Brother or Sister stepped out) since no one was there but the designated contactee; lots of empty, unused space offers plenty of choices for the actual spot for landing and communication. George Van Tassel took to the desert simply because he "was sold on the clean air, the intense quiet nights and outdoor living in the desert" where he "learned to *feel* the freedom of living with nature"; his desert dwelling did, however, help prepare him to receive communications from his aliens. But a deeper and more important significance of the desert resides in its ability to validate the encounter thanks to the very long, deeply embedded tradition of deserts as sites for direct, physical encounters between people and supernatural beings. God's manifestation to Moses as a burning bush in the desert stands as the type-instance; many, many more followed.[77]

And it is probably also not wholly coincidental that so many of the 1950s contactees who experienced physical encounters in the desert lived in Southern California, especially Los Angeles. The region—and notably the City of Angels—already had by the 1930s a reputation as a cauldron for brewing new and sometimes strange religions, ranging from Amy Semple McPherson's Temple of Light to the bizarre, Alistair Crowley–inspired cult of the Cal Tech (and later Jet Propulsion Laboratory) scientist John Parsons, and, starting in 1950, the enduring Dianetics/Scientology movement of L. Ron Hubbard, which still enjoys a central base of support in the Hollywood community.[78] To this cultural receptivity I would add LA's lucky proximity to the Mojave and Colorado Deserts and the notion, already embedded in fiction about the city by the 1920s, that LA itself sat on a desert—something not geographically true, but extremely powerful as a trope about its weather and the character of its inhabitants.[79] This cluster of circumstances may help explain the emergence of the contactee phenomenon in Los Angeles and Southern California in the 1950s.

The desert locale of the experiences we've reviewed links also to broader interpretations of the significance and meaning of the contact experience for the contactee. It is, fundamentally, transformational:

> [T]hrough the experience of encounter with these superior beings, one feels that one has come in contact with something divine or transcendent and that, consequently, one has undergone a developmental change in one's spiritual condition. In other words, the contactee experiences a religious growth and acquires a status or prestige that surpasses that of other humans, who have not been fortunate enough to have been approached by aliens in their flying saucers. The contactee becomes a person set apart, which may explain, to some degree, why he or she enjoys popularity and/or succeeds, on occasion, in attracting a following. Moreover, contactees can acquire a sense of duty, destiny, and mission, which further sets them apart and, in typical prophetic expression, usually evokes ridicule and/or persecution.

In addition, the contact experience effects a change in lifestyle; contactees may "experience a rebirth, a transformation, or a new beginning, at times leading to a career change and to the adoption of a different worldview that is more concerned with modern issues, like war, ecology, and nuclear energy."[80]

Indeed, Hilary Evans has argued that the abduction experience serves, in effect, as a kind of contemporary initiation experience. The six features by which he defines an initiation experience include four that resonate with the contact experience: that the encounter is *solitary*, or, in rare cases, shared with another person in intimate emotional connection; that it occurs in an *isolated locale*, which obviously the desert answers to superbly; that the alien encountered is a *wise and superior being*; and that *light*, often without an obvious source, accompanies the experience. The emphasis on light recurs, for instance, in Howard's connection of "morning light streaming in my window" with her "view reaching across the wide expanse of desert [which] helped me hook up with the subjective domains—to extend the dimensions of my mind."[81] Evans's first two characteristics, the solitude of the experience and its remote location, both cohere nicely with the other themes of the desert trope that we have seen in this chapter and throughout this book.

The encounters of contactees with Space Brothers and Sisters and, more broadly, the Native American stories about entities that can be treated as a category of extraterrestrials return us again to the desert sacrality explored in chapter 2. As we have seen here, the standard Western tropes about deserts as isolated, forbidding, and strange combine with the likewise old notion of deserts as sites of spirituality—most obviously in the case of Dana Howard, but more or less occluded in other contactees' tales—to infuse the southwestern deserts outside Los Angeles and farther east with the *frisson* that makes them perfect sites for alien contact.

Although never made explicit, the use of the eastern Mojave in Nevada as the locale for above-ground nuclear testing in the 1950s adds to the appropriateness and urgency of desert landings and communication, since it is nuclear weapons against which the Space Brothers and Sisters warn most fiercely. While not all contacts occurred in deserts—not even for the classic desert contactees—it is nevertheless the desert environment that sets the stage for the most resonant and meaningful encounters, its special character that puts contactees into a state of receptivity for the astounding events they experience.

The Mars fiction of Edgar Rice Burroughs, the subject of the next chapter, plays out as a kind of inversion of the contactee experience. Rather than Space Brothers and Sisters floating down to Earth in their Martian or Venusian ships (or "scows"), ripe with advice and warnings about ending war and abolishing atomic weapons, John Carter, a Virginian gentleman and plantation owner who lost everything and migrated to Arizona after the Confederacy's defeat, is translated to desert Mars. There he exploits his skills as a swordsman, his paternalistic views of women, and the physical advantages the weaker Martian gravity confers on him, to impose peace on the warring Martian races and install himself as the planetary emperor. Carter's encounter with the Martian desert serves to revitalize his lost manliness, just as the deserts of the Southwest had done for generations of American men degraded and feminized by the urban East. In contrast to the fears of invasion and colonization that emerge in the 1970s and 1980s, Carter's project is a one-man colonial enterprise that brings not exploitation but benevolent rule by a wise, superior being.[82] And this regeneration, deeply dependent too on the violence that Richard Slotkin saw as basic to recovering manliness, occurs in the context of one of the most persistent tropes about wild spaces, including deserts: that the uncivilized natives go about *naked*.

CHAPTER 9

NAKED ON THE
DESERTS OF MARS*

When in *Princess of Mars* John Carter, hero of the first three books Edgar Rice Burroughs set on the Red Planet, meets Dejah Thoris, his first real Martian woman, she is, he can't help but notice, "destitute of clothes . . . save for highly wrought ornaments . . . entirely naked, nor could any apparel have enhanced the beauty of her perfect and symmetrical figure." The "maid" Thuvia, whom Carter meets later in *The Gods of Mars*, is equally "entirely unadorned"—that is to say completely naked, lacking even "highly wrought ornaments" because she was being held as a slave. In another context Carter noted "the perfect lines of Thuvia's glorious figure, which the harness of a Barsoomian princess accentuated rather than concealed."[1] Dejah and Thuvia's nakedness is no fluke; every woman Carter encounters—that is, every woman in shape and appearance essentially indistinguishable from the ladies he left behind on Earth—cavorts in complete nudity, "save for [her] highly wrought ornaments." Indeed, we discover that, once Carter and Dejah enter onto talking terms, she finds clothing "strange, unsightly," disfiguring, and "grotesque." What are we to make of this bold female nudity, far too bold for the covers of the magazines the stories originally appeared in (Fig. 9-1) or the producers of recent films from the books to show? The renowned SF illustrator Frank Frazetta did depict Dejah mostly nude from the front, with only a small triangle of cloth covering her pubes (Fig. 9-2a), or fully nude from the rear (Fig. 9-2b), and James Cawthorn produced an accurate rendition of the Barsoomian princess in her encounter with the Thark Tal Hajus (Fig. 9-3).[2]

The decades before Burroughs first published "Under the Moons of Mars" in serial form in the pulp *All-Story Magazine* in 1912 (it appeared in book form in 1917) saw European and American culture struggling in multiple, complex ways with the idea of female nudity outside the bedroom (or the brothel). As an object of male gaze, the naked woman was often, of course, regarded as an invitation to sex, but the nude female body accumulated other valences as well, often in tension with each other.[3] Naked or partly-naked women "discovered" in the American West or sub-Saharan Africa or the South Pacific provoked long and nervous discussions about sexual morality, the nature of the "primitive," and the

---

* Published as "Naked on the Deserts of Mars," *Extrapolation* 57 (2016) 305–37; an earlier version was presented at the 2013 annual meeting of the Western Literature Association.

Figure 9-1: Thuvia, Maid of Mars. Cover of *All-Story Weekly*, April 8, 1916. (After http://erbzine.com/mag2/0223.html. Used with permission.)

persistence in far-off places of fragments of an Edenic world where nudity was not yet permanently sexualized. Anthropological investigation of human races justified in the name of

Figure 9-2a-b: Two drawings of Dejah Thoris by Franz Frazetta. Fig.9-2a: after ffdej2.jpg (496×598) (erbzine.com); Fig. 9.2b: after ffdej3.jpg (351×788) (erbzine.com). (Used with permission of Bill Frazetta.)

science the collection of archives of photographs of naked "natives," on whom an anthropological gaze was perfectly innocent. (*National Geographic* published its first photograph of a bare-breasted woman, a Zulu bride, in 1896.)[4] The London stage experimented with virtual nudity, displaying actresses in costumes so tight-fitting and flesh-colored that they could easily be mistaken for completely naked; in middle-class parlors hostesses presented *tableaux vivants* under the guidance of handbooks of party entertainment that advised poses and costumes that verged on nudity while insisting on the educational and moral value of the scenes. And some especially daring feminists even embraced female nudity as a natural display of female power, clothing as the artifice whereby fearful men sought to contain and deny a power they themselves neither understood nor possessed.

An exploration of this complex congeries of attitudes toward the naked female operating in the cultural world Burroughs inhabited may, I hope, lead to a deeper and more nuanced understanding of how we might read nakedness of the deserts of Mars. Along with issues of sexuality and display, tropes of nudity intruded on American (and European) thought through exploration, which unveiled societies where nudity was accepted (at least for the white male gaze); feminism and assertions of female power, which some commentators associated explicitly with nudity and the display of women's sexual organs; the movement of Anglos into the Trans-Mississippi West, with the combined expectation that Western toughness could "save" white masculinity and fear of "going native"; and Edenic tropes of

Figure 9-3: Dejah Thoris and Tal Hajus by James Cawthorn. (Used with permission of J & M Davey.)

nudity as a prelapsarian ideal recoverable, perhaps, in distant places—or on Mars. We may begin with the most obvious matters: sexuality, display, and the male gaze.

STRAIGHTFORWARD NAKEDNESS: TITILLATION AND AROUSAL

Readers of pulps like *All-Story Magazine*, virtually exclusively male,[5] no doubt found Burroughs's naked Martian women titillating, a marker, on first blush, of easy sexual accessibility; and there can be no doubt that Burroughs surely had this effect first and foremost in his mind when he decided to deprive his Martian women of clothes. He was, however, restrained in his description; while offering up plenty of details he never quite describes the naughty parts. Consider the full passage in which Dejah is introduced. She presents:

a slender, girlish figure, similar in every detail to the earthly women of my past life. . . . Her face was oval and beautiful in the extreme, her every feature was finely chiseled and exquisite, her eyes large and lustrous and her head surmounted by a mass of coal black, waving hair, caught loosely into a strange yet becoming coiffure. Her skin was of a light reddish copper color, against which the crimson glow of her cheeks and the ruby of her beautifully molded lips shone with a strangely enhancing effect. She was as destitute of clothes as the green Martians who accompanied her; indeed, save for her highly wrought ornaments she was entirely naked, nor could any apparel have enhanced the beauty of her perfect and symmetrical figure.[6]

Burroughs confines his vivid description to the features no proper American woman of his day would have blushed to display in public: Dejah's face, eyes, hair, skin color, cheeks, lips. Of the rest we get only a vague "slender, girlish figure . . . perfect and symmetrical." So although Burroughs is insistent and unambiguous about her nudity, he leaves the details to our imagination. Burroughs's vagueness here points up an important difference between literary depictions of the naked body and visual ones, which we explore below (and which, as I mentioned above, filmmakers and illustrators have largely eschewed). Even when coy or crafted to conceal rather than reveal, pictures may bear a different, sometimes more potent, resonance than words. Nevertheless, for his first readers, Burroughs's literary Martian nudity may well have seemed "needlessly and shockingly indecent," to borrow a phrase from a different context,[7] and has, as we will see, connections with other literary and indeed visual depictions of nudity in late nineteenth- and early twentieth-century Euro-American culture.

It is quite true, as Richard Mullen has observed, that after the initial description Burroughs rarely reverts to the nudity of his Barsoomian women. But this silence, or relative silence, need not be attributed to a sort of "prudish prurience."[8] Burroughs is perfectly aware that no reader will forget that Dejah and the other women John Carter meets are naked. And even though Burroughs usually veils any obvious or even indirect implication of sexual attraction Carter might feel toward his naked princess, the urges are there and occasionally peek through despite the Southern gentlemanliness that precludes open expression of improper feelings or even remarks on her state of undress. For: "As my arm rested on her for an instant," Carter confesses at one point, when he throws a silk over her shoulders to protect her from the cold, "I felt a thrill pass through every fiber of my being such as contact with no other mortal had even [sic] produced." Carter had, he admits, "loved her since the first moment that my eyes had met hers." This awakened desire is, as Diane Newell and Victoria Lamont have observed, part of the formula of popular historical novels whose shape *Princess of Mars* closely reproduces. "In countless novels of this type," they write,

the story begins with the hero languishing in the tedium of established civilization, until the opportunity to involve himself in some colonial exploit, usually involving Civil War in a foreign land and the rescue of the princess of the more righteous of the warring tribes, regenerates his under-tested masculine virtues. Burroughs' plot follows this pattern almost exactly.[9]

So Dejah's nudity serves a wholly predictable end: to stir up some salacious feelings in the reader. It is worth reflecting a little further on how this stirring-up works. Dejah is the object of Carter's gaze and the reader sees her through his eyes, as he is the first-person narrator of the books. The reader depends on Carter's decisions about how much to say and when to say it to construct an image of Dejah (and other Martian women in the books). Carter's reticence about sexual details—nothing about her breasts or stomach or hips or thighs or mons veneris—leaves the reader with a frustratingly incomplete picture of this supposedly stunning, naked woman. Of course, Dejah and other Martian women can be constructed by the reader according to his own fantasies (as in the illustrations various artists have offered: see again Figs. 9-1, 9-2a-b, and 9-3), but as far as the text itself is concerned, Carter withholds some of the most basic information. Since, "[a]s is now widely recognized, romance beauty is regularly expressed in terms of availability to the dominant, aestheticizing gaze"[10]—a gaze gendered, naturally, male—and since the reader identifies with Carter, his reading of Dejah as a sexually exciting woman is constrained precisely by not only the visual image Carter offers but also, and even more powerfully, by Carter's presentation of Dejah's attitudes (for which, of course, we must wholly rely on Carter's reporting) and his own.

Carter's self-reportage seeks to present himself as a proper Southern gentleman. Throughout the books he refrains from any improper actions, comments, or, mostly, even thoughts. Indeed, Carter's almost complete silence about Dejah's nudity after that first encounter reflects an ability to ignore what ought to be a rebarbative shamelessness. (This complicated matter comes in for further discussion below.) The hero's virtue intact (a virtue that, of course, is essential to his eventual winning of his princess), the reader is invited too to feel an analogous moral smugness: however charming the image of that naked Dejah Thoris cavorting on the Martian deserts, both Carter and his reader retain a wholly proper attitude toward her.

Now, as Newell and Lamont remarked, the princess in the popular historical novels that *Princess of Mars* and its sequels echo is supposed to spur the degenerate male hero to revitalize his failed masculinity. Dejah certainly plays this role. *Princess of Mars* begins with Carter facing failure and despair. Once a Southern plantation owner and master of slaves, an officer in the Confederate Army, he was left impoverished and aimless after the defeat of the South. His chivalry finds no outlet anymore. He wanders west, to the Arizona Territory, where he teams up with another wanderer to prospect for gold in the desert. When they find their trove, everything goes wrong as Apaches kill Carter's partner and trap him in the cave from which he translates to Mars. Carter presents as a perfect image of the type, the lost demasculinized male, ripe for desert redemption.

Dejah, however, is a little more complicated. Richard Slotkin, whose analysis lies behind Newell and Lamont's, casts the Dejah-type as the regenerative barbarian, the "fully sexualized woman" a hero like Carter requires as his "rescue-object" to reawaken his ability to fight and breed. This is not a role a white woman can play—a matter to which I return below.[11] Dejah, both demur and haughty, takes a while to get to that "fully sexualized woman." At their first meeting, when Carter fails to respond to a hand signal she gives (she too is a prisoner of the Tharks), "the look of hope and renewed courage which had glorified her face as she discovered me, faded into one of utter dejection, mingled with loathing and contempt." It soon becomes apparent, however, that Dejah has feelings for Carter—feelings completely opaque to him, in part because of his ignorance of "love-making on Mars"—but the sexuality of these feelings seems muted. Carter certainly desexualizes Dejah in many instances; she is for him "all that was virtuous and beautiful and noble and good." At the same time, Carter and Dejah both undercut this proper relationship with clear expressions of passion and sexual desire, which come out notably at the end of *Princess of Mars* when, thinking Carter dead, Dejah accepts a marriage proposal from a man she does not love. Carter wins her back, and finally they may express fully their feelings: "'Kiss me, John Carter,' she murmured. "I love you! I love you!' . . . As I pressed her dear lips to mine the old feeling of unconquerable power and authority rose in me. The fighting blood of Virginia sprang to life in my veins." Here, then, is the consummation of regeneration that completes Carter's recovery—with an image whose blatant sexuality Burroughs's coy phraseology can hardly conceal.[12]

It is important not to overlook the power, passive though it may be, that Dejah's nakedness and sublimated sexuality afford her. Dejah falls into the hands of the Tharks when they shoot down her airship; they and her red race have been enemies for ages. Soon after their first meeting, Carter figures Dejah as a woman in need of a protector. Perhaps he reads her nakedness as vulnerability,[13] although he does not explicitly say so. But there is no doubt that he sees in Dejah a beautiful woman threatened with death and, before that, the fate worse than death—("[B]efore the torture you shall be mine for one short hour," the evil Tal Hajus promises in a later scene [see Fig. 9-3])[14]—desperately in need of a powerful man. It's far from apparent, however, that Dejah saw herself in the same light. When Carter sees her for the third time, "she gave me one haughty glance and turned her back full upon me." Carter reads her action as the "womanly" act of someone with "human instincts of a civilized order," but that seems wishful thinking. Taken before the Thark council, Dejah replies to their hostile questioning with defiance: "Why, oh why," she cries,

> will you not learn to live in amity with your fellows, must you ever go on down the ages to your final extinction but little above the plane of the dumb brutes that serve you! A people without written language, without art, without homes, without love; the victim of eons of the horrible community idea. Owning everything in common, even to your women and children, has resulted in your owning nothing in common. You hate each other as you hate all else except yourselves.[15]

A woman willing to speak so haughtily to captors who plan first a rape and then a painful execution does not come off as someone in obvious need of protection.

Dejah's ability to fulfil a regenerative role for Carter is imbricated with her mixed racial identity. Dejah belongs to the Martian "red race," result of miscegenation among the various "pure" races of Mars many centuries earlier.[16] Mulattoes, of course, carried a highly sexualized and dangerous charge in late-nineteenth and early twentieth-century America. Paradigmatic is Cleo in Thomas Dixon's notorious *Sins of the Father*, published in 1912 (the same year that "Under the Moons of Mars" appeared). She is depicted as extraordinarily beautiful, sensual, and alluring, features that conjured for the ingenuous young white man who falls into her trap "a temptation so fierce that yielding could only be a question of time and opportunity." As an antebellum Southerner, Carter will have been perfectly familiar with the dangers of miscegenation and the lure of the mulatto. Dejah escapes the stereotype in part because she is a princess, not a commoner like Cleo, and in part because of the prissiness with which Carter constructs her.[17]

So far well and good and, notably, Dejah's nudity does not tip the balance toward the rapacious sexuality of a mulatto like Cleo. There are, I think, more resonances to female nudity in Burroughs's time that nuance and, to some degree, normalize public female nudity; that, while accommodating, indeed promoting and justifying, the male gaze behind which a sexual pleasure lurks, nevertheless seek to impose a different reading on the publicly naked female body. One venue in which to find practiced this erotic but masked male gaze on women was the *tableaux vivants* that were a popular form of middle-class parlor entertainment until replaced by photography and film. These performances, which began in the late eighteenth century, purportedly provided educational entertainment by reproducing high art or scenes from Greek and Roman history in frozen displays of people dressed in appropriate costume and set in appropriate scenery. *Tableaux vivants* served as both private home entertainments and attractions on the Victorian stage, notably in London.[18] One early American proponent of the *tableau vivant* as suitable home entertainment insisted in 1858 that:

> The Tableaux Vivants may be new to many of our readers, although they have been popular for some years, in polite society, both in Europe and this country, and especially in the South. These Tableaux are easily understood and arranged by persons of taste, and form one of the most refined recreations that a mixed party can indulge in.[19]

No discriminating hostess need fear; her *tableaux*, she may be sure, are "refined" displays perfectly suitable for a "mixed party" comprised of "persons of taste." It is not hard to see the nervousness rippling below the surface in this reassuring paragraph.

Such manuals as the one just quoted, after quelling any anxieties, instructed hostesses on how to confect an effective *tableau vivant*, by

> [r]ecommending revealing clothing such as "delicate white gauze robes," "robes cut loose in the neck," and "loose flowing garments" as costuming for female characters . . . [and] focus[ing] almost exclusively on material signs that could betoken the moral qualities possessed by the ideal woman. "Purer thoughts" and "taste," then, become almost exclusively linked with male appreciation of the female body, as the primary sign of virtue. What emerges in the scenes these manuals describe is an erotic tension between male "persons of taste," who are bearers of the look, and female signs of "the beautiful," who are their object.[20]

These home entertainments, then, afforded men (and women) the excuse to gaze without embarrassment on women displayed in ways that emphasized their bodies and sexual appeal, and even verged on nudity. Even though the power of the gaze and the embedded sexual

Figure 9-4: Actress in Flesh-Colored Body Stocking, c. 1900. (After Barrow 2010, 222, Fig. 3. Used by permission of the author.)

interest remain, the surface read becomes uplifting, educational, proper even for a proper lady's parlor.[21]

Something analogous was happening on the London stage. There *tableaux vivants* became a central element in the programs of prominent and popular theaters like the Palace. Again, the scenes chosen for display focused on replications of high art featuring female nudes, often with a classical theme, and on incidents from classical history that likewise required naked female bodies. Like the homestyle *tableaux vivants*, those on the London stage did not engage in actual female nudity. But costumes were deployed that came as close as possible: tight-fitting body stockings of a single flesh color (often white) that emphasized the shape of the body beneath (see Fig. 9-4).

The effect did not escape disapproving observers. Michael Ryan, a theologian commenting on stage costuming already in 1839, condemned stage "dresses as white as marble, and fitting so tightly that the shape of their bodies could not be more apparent, had they come forward on the stage in a state of nature." Some observers in the 1890s saw, or thought they saw, "exposed breasts, protruding nipples, and scantily covered genitals." Costume designers in the 1890s worked hard to achieve an "illusion of actual nudity." Mary E. Phillips, a social reformer, linked these displays explicitly to the primitive: "more [of] what one sees [on the stage is] like the bends of savages than anything else."[22]

The sexualized, powerful, and frightening mulatto and the *tableau vivant* as a socially acceptable venue for offering women to the male gaze come together rather nicely in Louisa May Alcott's 1866 novelette *Behind a Mask or a Woman's Power*. When the heroine, Jean Muir, illegitimate daughter of an aristocratic woman who ran off with a Scottish minister, decides to seduce one of her charges—she is a governess for a wealthy family—she arranges a biblical *tableau vivant* representing the assassination of the Assyrian general Holofernes by Judith. In preparation, she

> had darkened her skin, painted her eyebrows, disposed some wild black locks over her fair hair, and thrown such an intensity of expression into her eyes that they darkened and dilated till they were as fierce as any southern eyes that ever flashed. Hatred, the deepest and bitterest, was written on her sternly beautiful face, courage glowed in her glance, power spoke in the nervous grip of the slender hand that held the weapon, and the indomitable will of the woman was expressed.[23]

Jean sees quite clearly the power she can exercise by arranging this display. It excuses her appearance—she is trying to seduce, but she cannot be accused of seduction—and invites men to look and imagine. Jean's power may be a thin reed, shaped by the limited options women had for either expressing their own sexuality or simply having power in a patriarchal society. Other women, however, read female nudity in a very different, indeed daring, if not shocking, way.

Céline Renooz, an ardent feminist and prolific writer, was blunt. "The primitive woman," she wrote in 1897,

> proud of her femininity, long defends her nudity, which ancient art has always represented. And in the present life of the girl, there is a moment when she feels, by a secret atavism, *the*

pride of her genitals [*la fierté de son sexe*], she intuits her moral superiority and does not understand why she must hide the reason. At this moment, suspended between the laws of Nature and social convention, she does not know whether the *nude* should frighten her, or not. Indeed, a sort of confused atavistic memory, recalling to her the time before clothing, displays the habits of this time as a paradisiacal ideal. . . . It is at this moment in life when a young man is dominated by shame at his genitals [*sexe*], while the young girl feels herself seized by pride in her own. The man hides himself, the girl reveals, the man covers up, the girl uncovers. And among savage peoples missionaries fail to get girls to wear undergarments.[24]

Here is a statement about public female nudity that celebrates women's sexuality and endorses their unabashed display of the organs of their sexual power in public places. Dejah, of course, would not have seen things this way; her sexual morality is in many ways remarkably conservative. But there are elements in Renooz's analysis that point to further venues for exploring attitudes toward female nudity. Especially resonant is her insistence on the "primitive woman." It is "the laws of Nature" that impel her to favor a nakedness that it would be wrong to call shameless, because for her there is no shame in overt display, just the opposite. The same view—that the primitive woman prefers her natural nakedness—recurs in accounts of missionaries and some other explorers who encounter naked women who resist the imperative of clothing.

John Williams, who evangelized in Tahiti and Samoa for the London Missionary Society in the early nineteenth century and trained Tahitian converts as Christian teachers to be assigned evangelical duties in the South Pacific, complained that Samoan women, given fabric,

liked the cloth very well to put around their middles but they [the Tahitian missionaries] could not induce them to cover their persons of which they are exceedingly proud especially their breasts which are generally very large. They are continually wishing the teachers [*sic*] wives to lay aside their garments & "fasamoa" do as the Samoa ladies do, gird a shaggy mat around their loins as low down as they can tuck up the corner in order to expose the whole front & side of the left thigh anoint themselves beautifully with scented oil, tinge themselves with turmeric put a string of blue beads round their neck & then faasiara walk about to show themselves.[25]

In their different ways, both Renooz and Williams see in the female nudity they either celebrate or abhor the lure of the primitive: women before civilization did not see the need to cover themselves. With this in mind we may turn now to another element in the fabric of Burroughs's Martian nakedness: the role of the primitive and the construction in particular of the fictional American western frontier as a primitive space.[26]

NAKED WEST OF THE HUNDREDTH MERIDIAN

It has often been observed that Burroughs's Mars bears all the marks of the fictional American West transferred to space.[27] This fictional West, as a space of frontier, continues to depend on Frederick Jackson Turner's "frontier thesis," first articulated in a paper titled

"The Significance of the Frontier in American History" delivered in Chicago before the American Historical Association during the World Columbian Exhibition. (Perhaps no discredited idea on historical change has continued to exercise authority in other fields as much as Turner's thesis.) I sketch here briefly the defining features of Turner's frontier that shaped much American science fiction. First, perhaps, comes character. The frontier American is self-reliant, silent, suspicious of government, tough; he—for he is almost always a "he"—finds in the frontier an opportunity for heroism, for self-reinvention, for the chance to become almost anything he wants—it is, as the Germans sometimes say of America, *das Land der unbegrenzten Möglichkeiten* ("the land of unbounded possibilities"). The Western space itself is unformed, wild, in need of taming and control, a space where nature rather than civilization rules, "a romance setting that panders to the power fantasies of American males."[28] Within this Western space, it is violence—a violence necessary for the hero, the only proper and sufficient response to a world without law—that offers a regeneration, as Richard Slotkin has memorably put it, a mode of action through which the hero self-actualizes and becomes, finally, himself.

The irony is that the very act of "taming" the frontier also destroys the very features that made it a frontier; the wistful, elegiac mood that colors much Western fiction and the science fiction born of it comes from the realization that a regenerated hero spells the end of the frontier. This frontier space is situated at a distance from the reader, a distance that imposes challenges to cross and separates strictly the frontier "there" from the civilized, literate "here." The chief difference between the Western frontier and the science fiction frontier is that "science fiction projects the frontier into the future and documents its reality by means of scientific extrapolation."[29] Yes, in general—but Burroughs's Mars sits squarely in John Carter's present; the real distinguishing feature in this case is the distance, crossable only by an inexplicable translation. No railroad or stagecoach delivers Carter to his Martian frontier.[30] Finally, the frontier is deeply imbricated with American racial fear: fear of the impact of mixing with inferior races (that irresistible lure of the more-than-willing mulatto), fear that the white race has gone "soft"—and hope that the experience of the tough Western world, especially the desert (for Burroughs's Mars borrows many elements from Percival Lowell's desiccating planet), may offer the place where the white race can find the challenges it needs for reinvigoration and reinvention. These racial anxieties find reflection in Burroughs; his Mars becomes the stage where Carter, lost and purposeless after the defeat of the South in the Civil War (and, by implication, I suppose, the elevation of blacks to the same level as whites), can recover his white manliness.[31]

The general setting of *Princess of Mars* and its sequels fits the Western stereotype, but just in case that weren't enough, Burroughs sprinkles his text with direct references to the *topoi* of frontier Western literature. Contemplating the threat that Dejah will be raped by her Thark captor, Carter advises that "we save the friendly bullets for ourselves at the last moment, as did those brave frontier women of my lost land, who took their own lives rather than fall into the hands of the Indian braves." Mars has "an enormous tract of arid and semi-arid land," just like the desert West. The thoats Carter and the Martians ride are just analogues for horses; they even require "saddle trappings"; a cavalry force he encounters is mounted on thoats whose "trappings and ornamentation bore such a quantity of gorgeously colored feathers that I could not but be struck with the startling resemblance the concourse bore to a band of the red Indians of my own Earth."[32]

Before he found his footing as a writer, Burroughs had tried his hand at various vocations, including several months spent as a regular soldier in the US Army. He enlisted in 1895 and was dispatched to the Arizona Territory and stationed in Fort Grant. Little Western adventure awaited him; he engaged in some desultory, unsuccessful campaigns to capture the so-called "Apache Kid"[33] and writhed in his bunk afflicted with dysentery. He eventually convinced his father to arrange a discharge, and he returned to Chicago in 1897. But he now had some direct experience of the still partly wild West, which found expression not just in *Princess of Mars* but also in two standard, Indian-themed Western novels, *The War Chief* (1927) and a sequel, *Apache Devil* (1933).[34] Burroughs therefore had direct exposure to the frontier West; it is no surprise that its tropes colored his fiction.

Female public nudity or near-nudity was, for many Eastern observers, a remarkable and noteworthy component of Western "differentness." Passing in March 1849 a group of white men living with Mexican women on the banks of Cibolo Creek in Texas, George Evans remarked, "These women were dressed in the very cheapest manner, having generally nothing but a chemise and skirt to hide their charms, and this dress often failed of its desired object, being in rather dilapidated condition. However, blushes were scarce in the faces of these almost nude damsels" and, later, on a visit to a Mexican *ranchero*, he noted "ladies . . . dressed in the usual custom of chemise, wide around the breast and consequently open, over which they wore a skirt. A scarf served the double purpose of bonnet and shield for the breasts." The trapper James Pattie and his companions, traveling in the 1820s, "gave [some Indian women] some old shirts, and intimated to them as well as we could, that it was the fashion of the women to cover themselves in our country, for these were in a state of the most entire nudity," a gesture toward decency probably to be laid to the account of Pattie's editor and collaborator the Reverend Timothy Flint. Pattie also enjoyed an affair with the daughter of the governor of Nuevo México.[35] This casual nudity or near-nudity in the presence of men is picked up in fiction set in the West by Burroughs's contemporaries. In Zane Grey's *Heritage of the Desert*, published in 1910, a young woman and her man escape near drowning in the Colorado River; when she emerges from the stream, her "wet buckskin blouse and short skirt clung tightly to her slender frame." She laughs off the situation, observing the desert heat will soon dry her off. Another Zane Grey novel, *Wildfire*, ends in a highly sexually charged scene with a girl tied naked to a horse, chased to be rescued by hero through blazing fire.[36]

An essay published in 1907 by Frederick Monsen in *The Craftsman*, one of a series, extolled the "natural life" of the Hopi Indians through their custom of going naked; their nudity, Monsen insists, their "hardy, vigorous life and freedom from all physical restraint [by which he means clothing], has fashioned beautiful, strong bodies that are absolutely natural and . . . suited to the circumstances of their lives and environment." Monsen illustrated his article with a collection of photographs of mostly naked prepubescent children, typically posed, or at least shot, to cast a shadow over their genitals; often their sex cannot be determined. The Hopi adults, he claimed, "were as unconscious of the need of clothing or the lack of it as were Adam and Eve prior to the apple episode."

Monsen thus constructs the "primitive" Hopi practice of nudity (as he sees it) as wholly innocent, natural, empowering, and Edenic. His final commentary on the practice, and the reaction of the Euro-American observer, is worth quoting in full:

> Although, if you have lived long enough among the Hopi for them to feel thoroughly acquainted and at home with you, they may sometimes go around without clothing as comfortably and unconsciously as with it—you feel no sense of shock as at the sight of nakedness, for your experience is precisely like that recorded by the explorers and travelers in Africa and among all dark-skinned races;—it is not the lack of clothing but the sight of the white skin that is startling. A brown skin seems in a way to be a sort of clothing like the fur of an animal and excites no more attention after once you are used to seeing it undraped. You note only the extreme beauty of color, form and movement, and after a while, begin to realize something of the innocence, freedom and childlike joy of living that we like to think prevailed among all men in the morning of the world.[37]

This passage could serve as a guide to and commentary on Martian nudity in Burroughs. Like the Hopi in Monsen's reading, Burroughs's Martians are completely unconscious of their nakedness, except when confronted with the bizarre and rebarbative practice of wearing clothes; it is their natural state. Like Monsen himself, Carter is at first rather shocked at the nudity of his Martian princess but very soon gets over it and hardly comments on it afterwards. Monsen's appeal to skin color as the key to why Hopi nudity soon fails to trouble finds its reflection in Dejah's own skin color: she is a member of the red Martian race and, as Carter notices on his first encounter, has "skin . . . of a light reddish copper color."[38] It is only the white Martians Carter meets much later who, like the white race of Earth, wear clothing. The quasi-animality linked explicitly to dark skin color that Monsen attributes to his Hopi was a widespread view about primitive nakedness in the nineteenth and early twentieth centuries; it recurs in contexts as various as Monsen's essay, colonial India, and the island of Bali.[39]

But the matter of dress/undress goes still farther, for public nudity could stand as a mark of cultural and racial inferiority. This interpretation was another pole of the complex magnetic field within which European colonial powers struggled to understand, and denigrate, the undress they found in the "primitive" world.[40] This distinction is surely implied in James Pattie's offer to his completely naked Indian women of shirts to cover themselves in the Eastern fashion; if this hint of decency should be attributed not to Pattie but Flint, the point accrues even more salience. Later Pattie paused with another group of Indians, whose "woman and children . . . like the other Indians we had seen, were all stark naked." (These women, with Pattie's help, induced one of his companions to strip naked so they could examine his body: "they came one by one and stood beside him; so as to compare their bodies with his.") Euro-American commentators on the O'odham peoples of present-day Arizona and Sonora, starting with Juan Manje in 1694, described the Hia-Ced O'odham who lived in the deep desert as "walking about naked"; an American in 1882 called the Papago (Tohono O'odham) women "better dressed than most Indian women"—Papago being regarded as among the most civilized of tribes. The chronicler of the Coronado expedition to the Southwest claims that in the pueblo of Cicuye "virgins also go nude until they take husbands, because they say that if they do anything wrong then it will be seen, & so they do not do it. They do not need to be ashamed because they go around as they were born."[41] This trope extends far beyond the American Southwest. As Charles Sturt pressed into the desert interior of Australia in 1844–1845, he repeatedly noted whether the men he encountered were circumcised or not—an observation dependent on their nudity. Dixon Denham, who with Hugh Clapperton and Walter Oudney explored the regions around Lake Chad in 1822 and 1823, reports repeatedly on the dress of the women he sees; the farther south he goes, the more deeply he penetrates unknown, wild territories, the less the women wear, until he receives accounts of the women of Adamowa, who go around completely naked.[42]

Burroughs exploits this presupposition of clothed marking the civilized, naked marking the barbaric. Mars is a dying planet, condemned to the inevitable secular death that the nebular hypothesis of planetary formation compelled. As it dried up, the great Martian civilizations of the deep past died out, racial mixture prevailed, and the pure white race that had reached great heights of culture disappeared (though later Carter finds remnants). In an ancient, ruined city of this past, Carter and Dejah come upon wall paintings depicting light-skinned people wearing "graceful, flowing robes." Later, their son Cathoris and "the maid" Thuvia discover a lost valley inhabited by the Lotharians "clothed in flowing robes." In both cases, in contrast to standard Martian nudity, clothing forms—with light skin, beardlessness, and blond hair—the guarantee of a civilized race.[43]

Primitive nakedness could also be read as innocent and Edenic. Adam and Eve's recognition that they were naked, and the sense that they should somehow be ashamed, came only after the consumption of the apple infused them with knowledge. So too observers in the South Pacific, who came with attitudes different from the missionaries', might see nudity as an Edenic marker. Having jumped ship in the Marquesas Islands, Herman Melville and his companion Toby encountered two locals, "a boy and girl, slender and graceful, and completely naked, with the exception of a slight girdle of bark, from which depended at opposite points two of the russet leaves of the bread-fruit tree." Soon they were established in a village as guests of a local dignitary, and Melville made acquaintance of the young Marquesan woman who would become his lover, Fayaway, who

> for the most part clung to the primitive and summer garb of Eden. But how becoming the costume! It showed her fine figure to the best possible advantage; and nothing could have been better adapted to her peculiar style of beauty. On ordinary occasions she was habited precisely as I have described the two youthful savages whom we had met on first entering the valley.[44]

A crucial element here is the failure of the women—and of the men around them—to

THE CAPTIVES AT THE INDIAN CAMP-FIRE.

Figure 9-5: Oatman Girls Captured. "The Massacre." (After Stratton 1858, 85. Scan by Richard Ring and Henry Arneth of the Trinity College Watkinson Library.)

realize how improper their condition is. This "obliviousness" resonates with the fact that Carter quickly accepts female nudity as normal and unremarkable in his Martian setting. After his first encounter with Dejah, he rarely refers to women's dress. In this, Carter plays a role quite at odds with the South Pacific missionary, who, as a carrier of civilization, must compel the natives to understand how completely inappropriate their nudity is, to adopt Western dress and standards of modesty, and to recognize the inherent superiority of the civilization (and religion) they bring.[45] The resonances with the Spanish colonial enterprise in the deserts of the Southwest are obvious.

Several of these tropes come together in a notable way in the third edition, published in 1858, of R. B. Stratton's *Captivity of the Oatman Girls. Captivity*, originally published in San Francisco in 1857 under the less captivating title *Life among the Indians: Being an Interesting Narrative of the Captivity of the Oatman Girls*, told (and partly fictionalized) the tale of the Oatman family, attacked in February 1851 by (probably) Tolkepaya Indians in what is now southwestern Arizona, during an ill-advised crossing of the desert toward Fort Yuma. While a son escaped, the parents were killed and the two Oatman daughters, Olive and Mary, were taken captive; later, they were sold or traded to Mohave Indians with whom they lived till Mary died and Olive was "recovered" in 1856. For the new edition, intended for circulation on the East Coast, Stratton and his publisher added a new and amplified series of illustrative

Figure 9-6: Oatman Girls in Indian Dress (no caption). (After Stratton 1858, 155. Scan by Richard Ring and Henry Arneth of the Trinity College Watkinson Library.)

ARRIVAL OF OLIVE AT FORT YUMA.

Figure 9-7: Olive Oatman Restored. "Arrival of Olive at Fort Yuma." (After Stratton 1858, 272. Scan by Richard Ring and Henry Arneth of the Trinity College Watkinson Library.)

woodcuts. When the girls are depicted with their family, and even just after the massacre, they are dressed in typical mid-nineteenth-century girls' clothing: long frocks reaching their ankles and fully covering the bosom; frilled caps concealing most of their hair (Fig. 9-5).

But the illustrations that show them with the Indians put them in "Indian" clothing: no head covering, naked to the waist with breasts clearly depicted and navel exposed, and a short loincloth not even covering their knees (Fig. 9-6). Their appearance is identical to that of native Indian women also in the illustrations. Only once rescued and back in "civilization" does Olive (Mary being dead) don again an appropriately modest dress (Fig. 9-7).

In other words, in the mind of the illustrator (who is anonymous), the Oatman girls revert to the primitive: they perforce dress like the Indians with whom they live and display no embarrassment or modesty about their state of more than semi-nudity. This depiction contrasts markedly with Stratton's text, in which he tries to drive home again and again that the girls have not "gone native" but cling to the modes and practices, insofar as they can, of white civilization. From beginning to end, they are always contemplating escape (why they fail to try is never explained); they practice white agriculture in the Mohave village, so superior to the Indians' ways; and when little Mary finally expires, Olive insists on and gets her a proper Christian burial, not the cremation the Mohave practice and had planned. There is not a single reference in the text to their clothing except at the very end when, returned to Fort Yuma, "Olive, with her characteristic modesty, was unwilling to appear in her bark attire and her poor shabby dress among the whites." She refused to be seen until "a noble-hearted woman . . . sent her a dress and clothing of the best she had" (Fig. 9-7).[46] Stratton here is sedulous in stressing that it is the shabbiness of Olive's habiliment, not her nudity, that provoked her modesty. Without the illustrations the reader is invited to suppose Olive wore the dress in which she was captured for the next five years. It seems as if the pull of the trope of nudity was too much for the illustrator to resist, even if his woodcuts clash with the picture of the girls Stratton wants to draw.[47]

THE NAKED MAN

I mentioned above Burroughs's two Apache novels. The very first word in *The War Chief*, the earlier of these books, is "Naked." The paragraph ends with "naked arms and legs." The word "naked" is repeated a few paragraphs later, still on the first page of the edition I have used, and then again and again: "almost naked," "[a] naked warrior," "almost naked" (twice more), and so on.[48] But in contrast to Dejah, the person to whom all this nakedness is attributed is not a woman but a man, and a warrior at that. That is to say, it's not possible to explore the trope of nudity on Burroughs's Mars without recognizing that *everyone* on Mars is naked, including Carter himself.

Carter had arrived on the planet, by that mysterious translation Burroughs never explains, completely naked. Indeed, his nakedness begins even before he's left our planet. Coming to in the Arizona cave, after the Apache have fled in terror, he finds himself looking down at his clothed body but himself standing above it "naked as at the minute of my birth." Moments later he is lying under a noonday Martian sun, its "heat . . . rather intense on my naked body." Carter seems completely unfazed by his condition; he wanders about the desert until he meets the first of the several races on Mars, the green Tharks—who are also the only Martian race not human in appearance, but of course are also entirely naked. Eventually Carter wins weapons and a Martian harness, but as we know, that does nothing to cover the body.[49] Moreover, and more important, Carter's nudity seems perfectly commonplace to Dejah Thoris, who displays neither surprise nor embarrassment when he appears before her naked for the first time.[50]

Carter's effortless acceptance of his own nakedness, Dejah's, and everyone else's right from the start, without even much reflection (he never asks, "Why am I naked?"), serves as a crucial signal as to who Carter is. He is, in Richard Slotkin's memorable phrase, a "man who knows Indians."[51] The man who knows Indians is a liminal figure, whose prototype, in Slotkin's analysis, is Hawkeye in James Fenimore Cooper's *Last of the Mohicans* (1826), whom Cooper modeled on Daniel Boone. He—and he is almost always a "he"—acts as the protagonist in the myth of the frontier, which Slotkin sees as a basic structural feature of American self-identity; he "must cross the border into 'Indian country' and experience a 'regression' to a more primitive state and natural conditions of life so that the false values of the 'metropolis' can be purged and a new, purified social contract enacted." Such figures can move easily between both worlds, white and Indian, civilized and savage; they understand the social and cultural rules under which the Indians operate, and even have sympathy for the applicability of such rules in the natural world the Indians inhabit. Indeed, they can "pass": they can act like an Indian, think like an Indian, almost be an Indian, without losing the privilege that their whiteness confers.[52]

Burroughs sets Carter up carefully as a man who knows Indians well before he meets Dejah. Once captured by the Tharks, he quickly learns their language, grasps their customs and values, and uses his superior skills and knowledge to beat them at their own game. He kills two Tharks in single combat, in the approved fashion, one even before he knows the cultural rules—he seems to grasp them intuitively, in part because they share much with Southern chivalry. Put under the guard of a Thark woman, Sola, Carter quickly penetrates to the core of her personality, discovering that she does not share her tribe's bloodthirstiness, and acquires his first Martian friend. Sola sets Woola, a Martian watchdog, to keep an eye on him, a creature that "waddled on ten short legs . . . [and] was about the size of a Shetland pony, but . . . the jaws were equipped with three rows of long, sharp tusks." Soon enough Carter figures out the animal's patterns of behavior and escapes, but later it rescues Carter from attack by a "white ape," almost losing its life in the act. Carter saves it from euthanasia, and it becomes his lifelong friend, or, as Carter puts it, "my devoted slave." Like Slotkin's emblematic "man who knows Indians," Carter can operate deftly in their cultural world without offending them or losing touch with his own, superior civilized deportment. Dejah's nakedness, for Carter, can be regarded as another strange Indian custom, not to be tolerated in proper white society, but understandable and excusable in its own context—if the observer understands the Indian.[53]

Here, I would suggest, is part of the explanation of the puzzle of Martian nakedness. On the one hand, Mars is a primitive society—Barsoomians fight with swords (they have firearms, but it is shameful to use one in a fight), honor is the overriding social good, they travel largely on thoats (horses) or on foot. As befits the most advanced race on Mars, Dejah's red race controls the highest technology: the airships lifted by the "eighth ray" and powered by radium motors, their guns, wireless radio, and sighting devices, and their responsibility for running the atmosphere factory.[54] But romantic rules govern courtship, friendship, and warfare. Carter's Southern heritage serves him perfectly; it enables him to know these Indians almost instantly, and to leverage that knowledge—and the advantage having grown up in Earth's greater gravity confers—to marry the princess and become lord of the planet.

At the same time, Barsoom is the fictional frontier West. Carter knows these rules, too. He has been a prospector in the Arizona desert; he has spent weeks alone with his partner in an unforgiving wilderness; he has seen the violence and remorselessness of the Apache. This is a world Burroughs too knew, in a way, having spent just under a year in the Army stationed at Fort Grant. This West demands a man who knows Indians, and Carter's past experiences and personality fit him ideally to the job.

Let me add one last element. I have referred several times to the Edenic trope, in which prelapsarian nudity is constructed as innocence. The Collegiate Church of San Isidoro at León, Spain, preserves a mediaeval reliquary that shows, among other scenes, God, Eve, and Adam at the moment the first couple are expelled from Eden. Adam's nakedness has already been covered, but Eve resists as God tries to force a tunic over her head. In a nuanced analysis, Giorgio Agamben has argued that Eve's resistance marks her rejection of the new obligation to be clothed: Eve is seen as "an extraordinary symbol of femininity. This woman is the tenacious custodian of paradisiacal nudity." (Céline Renooz, of course, would read Eve's resistance quite differently: as a refusal to surrender her female power.)

Agamben goes on to suggest that Edenic nudity represents sinlessness, a state in which Eve wants to continue, hence her refusal to dress; for us, post-Eden, nudity is a condition marked by the removal of clothing: for Eve (and Adam too) it was instead a persistent state.[55] These considerations open another window on Martian nudity. Burroughs's Martians are not Christians. They never dwelt in paradise, disobeyed, were expelled and forced to live in sin and suffering. They had no, and needed no, Jesus Christ—unless it now be *John Carter*, as Slotkin has suggested.[56] Like Renooz's "savage peoples" or Melville's Fayaway, they stand outside Euro-American cultural-religious strictures about the body and sin. That is, the Martians live in a permanent prelapsarian condition in which their nakedness bears none of the shame that afflicts the world from which Carter has come.

OPENING A WIDER OPTIC

We have come a long way from Carter's first encounter with Dejah Thoris's naked body. Burroughs's Martian nudity reads in multiple ways across the books. On a most obvious level it is meant to titillate the male reader, whose imaginary gaze takes in Burroughs's naked women cavorting across the Martian deserts. But female nudity is also a metonym for the still-uncivilized Western frontier. Naked Indigenous women form part of the expectation of frontier narratives; they mark the absence, for the moment, of the imposition of cultural rules that will, once imposed, convert frontier to settled territory. And they bespeak racial inferiority: it is only women of a racially inferior category—Indians, Mexicans, blacks, slaves— or women of mixed racial ancestry whose bodies can be exposed without shame. Needless to say, that inferiority likewise legitimates the claim of white European men to the use of those bodies—as in James Pattie's episodes of "pleasant fornication"[57] and access even to the daughter of the Mexican governor of Nuevo México, as well as the uncounted Southern men whose rape of their women slaves led to the "shame of Dixie." Carter's reaction to the nudity of Dejah and other Martian women reinforces his manly, Southern character. As a good antebellum Virginia gentleman whose slaves "fairly worshipped the ground he trod," Carter would undoubtedly have slept with slave women.[58] But on Mars he resists the advances of Phaidor (and other Martian women he encounters), and Dejah's status as a princess for him outweighs both her racial inferiority and the nudity that marks it.

In the end, Carter triumphs over every adversary, wins Dejah as his wife, becomes the supreme ruler of Mars, the "Jeddak of Jeddaks," and reigns with his queen in the city of Helium. But in assuming planetary leadership Carter, unlike triumphant missionaries, does not impose civilized sartorial standards on his subjects. They remain naked—and so does he.[59] Indeed, transported back unwillingly and unexpectedly to Earth, he yearns to return and take up again his Martian life and Martian wife. Carter becomes the man who not only knows Indians but goes over to their side; he is a renegade. In uniting all the Martian races, ending their enmity, and bringing peace to the planet, he nevertheless does not civilize. The nakedness remains on the deserts of Mars.

It may be appropriate to end with a few thoughts about possible implications for and uses of this study more broadly in science fiction literature. Public nudity as a practice seems relatively rare in science fiction, but Burroughs's Martians do not stand entirely alone.[60] Two examples, very different, occur to me. In *Trouble on Triton* (originally published in 1976 as *Triton*), Samuel R. Delany's "heterotopic" novel, public nudity is presented as an acceptable social choice. Because not everyone in Triton's society goes naked, the choice provokes comment from Delany's characters; it plays a different social role from the nudity of Burroughs's Martians. *Nude on the Moon*, on the other hand, a low-budget movie from 1961, posits a woman-only society on the Moon in which everyone is nude all the time (although film conventions of the time required the actors to wear rather ridiculous flesh-colored costumes covering their hips, and shots of their breasts tend to be gauzy and ill-focused). *Nude on the Moon*, of course, was intended entirely for titillation, as a kind of under-the-radar quasi-pornographic production disguised as a legitimate film. What makes it interesting for our purposes is the notion that its setting in an "alien," science fiction world somehow legitimates what would otherwise be—and was advertised as—an exercise in voyeurism.[61]

This last observation may serve to introduce a penultimate reflection. Much science fiction is about world-building: trying to imagine societies constructed on rules different from, and sometimes antagonistic to, those that govern the Euro-American cultures that, for a long time, were the chief producers and consumers of the genre. In this work, science fiction shares many interests and techniques with anthropology, sociology, and ethnography. Burroughs's Mars is a prime early example of precisely such world-building, and the nudity of its inhabitants one of the most strikingly different features of its culture. As such, the study of Martian nudity and its relation to the social world in which Burroughs and his contemporary readers were embedded may make a modest contribution to our efforts to analyze and understand the ethnographies of science fiction.

BACK TO THE DESERT

Finally, we must return to the desert: what role, if any, does it play in the trope of nudity in *Princess of Mars* and its sequels? The clue to a response, I think, can be found in the character of all the spaces where nudity is—or is claimed to be—practiced and accepted, whether Mars, the American Southwest, the desert Australian outback, the islands of the South Pacific, or equatorial Africa. These spaces are all *heterotopias*—that is to say, they are fundamentally and qualitatively different from the temperate, "civilized" spaces of Europe and eastern America, and deserts stand in the most heterotopic relation to these latter (see chapter 4). It is not surprising that people who inhabit such exotic spaces engage in social practices bizarre or indeed repellant to "civilized" Euro-Americans. Deserts release people from the restrictions imposed by ordinary Euro-American social rules: they may go naked, they may enjoy some "pleasant fornication" with the unmarried daughters of their hosts, they may pursue an Edenic life in oases surrounded by desert aridity and heat. The climate may legitimate shedding of clothing, but that's really only an excuse. It is rather the qualities of the desert as a strange, nonconformative, heterotopic space that invites the cultural practice of nudity. Both on Earth and on Mars, the inhabitants of the deserts embrace a sartorial posture that seems utterly natural and unremarkable in a place where heat, aridity, and otherness reign.

And this imperative, if that's right, to shed clothes in desert environments bespeaks once again the question of material agency. Of course, many desert inhabitants do just the opposite of going naked. The Bedouin of the Saudi Arabian Peninsula and the Tuareg of the deep Sahara cover their bodies from head to toe; the natives of Arrakis, the desert planet of Frank Herbert's *Dune*, adapted too the sartorial practices of the earthly desert dwellers on whom they were modeled. But for John Carter, and maybe the Martians he encounters, the impulsion of desert Mars ran in the other direction: to wear just their skin against the desert. To Carter it seems "right" to go naked on Mars—but who has made his nudity "right?" Himself, his Martian companions, or the desert in which they all dwell?

WRITING AND RE-WRITING THE AMERICAN DESERT

SO BY THE WILL OF FORTUNE (*TYCHE*)
EVERYTHING HAS CONSCIOUSNESS.
—EMPEDOKLES[1]

From a *horror vacui* to redemptive peace, from a realm of demons to a home for God, from a wasteland to a natural preserve, from a brittle, hard, arid, hot masculine to a yielding, soft, wet, cool feminine, from an almost uncrossable wilderness to tourist haven, from ugliness to beauty, from repulsive to sublime—the deserts of the American Southwest have played multiple and sometimes incoherent roles in our imaginary about the spaces we acquired after the Mexican-American War in 1848. For decades they were mostly a landscape in the way, the purgative space that had to be conquered before entrée into the Promised Land of auriferous California. Later, the miracle of irrigation wreaked a transformation; the doctrine of Art for Art's Sake reconfigured perceptions of the desert; preservationism and environmentalism tried to erase the wasteland trope. Through all these changes, which never eliminated the old notions about the desert that, as we have seen, are deeply rooted in the Bible, people visited and wrote about the deserts. Is there a common thread in writing the American desert that we can tease out and follow in the literature that treats it? Is there, to put the question differently, a *desert literature* with lineaments and conventions that distinguish it from other genres? To that question I now turn.

WHAT IS—OR IS THERE—A DESERT LITERATURE?

Now that we have looked at a wide variety of literature relating in one way or another to the southwestern American deserts (and beyond), it's appropriate to widen our optic and consider whether there is such a thing as "desert literature." It seems to me that there are three broad categories we can consider: literature merely set in a desert but which could be transferred to another setting without or with only minor modification to plot and characters; literature for which the desert setting is essential; and literature in which the desert acts as a character—where it has "vibrancy" or "volition," even, as, for instance, in the "pulsating" desert of Adamski or Angelucci.[2]

The Chicana poet Pat Mora, from El Paso, Texas, depicts an animate desert in her poem "Unrefined":

> The desert is no lady
> She screams at the spring sky,
> dances with her skirts high,
> kicks sand, flings tumbleweeds,
> digs her nails into all flesh.
> Her unveiled lust fascinates the sun.[3]

In other poems her desert speaks: "The desert says: feel the sun / luring you from dark, sad waters / burst through the surface / dance" and a *curandera* finds her power to heal because "she listens / to the desert, always the desert."[4] Perhaps Mora's active desert could be read as just personification: not a representation of the desert as active *in fact*, but only as poetic metaphor. After all, the desert doesn't dance, it has no skirts, it doesn't scream, unless you count the howling spring winds that roar through the Chihuahuan Desert landscape of southern New Mexico and El Paso or the raging Santa Anas in LA.

An example of the first category—literature merely set in a desert—can be found in the mystery novel *Desert Cat*.[5] The plot revolves around Penelope Warren, who owns a bookstore in the fictional town of Empty Creek, Arizona—which seems modeled, perhaps, on Cave Creek—and becomes entangled in a murder investigation when a corpse appears on the doorsill of the bookstore. Central to the shape of the plot is the fact that Empty Creek is a small town, where virtually everyone knows everyone else. The characters meet up in the local saloon, and Penelope's bookstore is also a central gathering place. The geographic setting is the northern Sonoran Desert, but the desert plays virtually no role in the plot. The only local geographic element important to the story is Superstition Mountain, where further murders occur. Otherwise, the story could have been set in any small town. If *Desert Cat* is desert literature, it is so only on the thinnest of margins.

At first glance Ron Felber's *Mojave Incident* may seem to require its desert setting. A young couple, Tom and Elise Gifford (pseudonyms), who are having some marital problems, leave Los Angeles for a weekend camping trip in the Mojave. Tom hopes to bag a big buck; Elise wants to visit a cavern. Arriving late at the campground where they'd planned to stay, they find it full and instead park their pickup with its camping shell in an isolated spot overlooked by Table Top Mountain (see Fig. 8-1 for the location). Elise has been apprehensive since before they departed, and, it turns out, with good reason. A mob of miniature craft, hundreds, appear in the night sky, swarming toward them. They become little creatures, gremlin-like, with glowing red eyes. Then a massive mother ship settles down in the valley between their campsite and Table Top. The gremlins press against the camper, two "monitors" appear, and then a white, ghostly figure whom they identify as a female "comforter." The aliens—for of course that is what they are—invade their minds, force them to act against their will partly in order to explore emotions, since the aliens have none, and finally abduct them, their pickup, and the ground it sits on into the big UFO. Elise's body is violated; she fears they have lost time. Tom remembers an earlier encounter, when he was a teen; Elise suffered a rape as a child. They feel strange bodily sensations. Back home, the aliens reappear in their house as shadowy figures, terrorizing them and watching as they force Tom and Elise to have sex; she gets pregnant. Whenever they sense the aliens' invisible or shadowy presence (as "watchers"), they demand answers to their questions, but get no replies. Later, under hypnosis, they discover they have been probed and prodded and Elise fitted with a tracking device, Tom probed anally. The couple comes to believe they have been chosen for some mission and their daughter born of alien-compelled sex will grow up to be a sort of intermediary between the aliens and the human race.[6]

The Giffords' experiences mostly follow the standard plot and themes of the classic abduction event. Susan A. Clancy offers a brief summary of some elements of this standard plot:

> [A]liens come in the night. When they approach you, you cannot move. You feel terrified and helpless. You levitate, feel vibrations running through your body, see shadowy figures.... [The a]liens leave strange marks on your body, such as bruises or scoop marks . . . UFOs are seen at night from solitary cars on wooded roads . . . when you've had an encounter with extraterrestrials, you're unable to account for a period of time.... Afterward you feel anxious or depressed, different from other people and from your former self.[7]

To her summary must be added sexual experimentation and bodily invasion with quasi-medical instruments; the emotionless affect of the aliens even as they perform "tests" that sometimes cause great pain; ongoing trauma; the presence of "screen memories"; continued post-abduction observation by "Watchers" with all-seeing black eyes. Hypnotherapy is needed to penetrate screen memories or recover events in lost time. And the aliens are completely in control of the experience—"[Y]ou cannot initiate a contact with them," Adam had reminded Orfeo Angelucci decades earlier. "They do the contacting."[8] The Giffords' abduction includes all these standard details.

The model for the abduction experience was set in 1966 with the publication of *The Interrupted Journey* by John Fuller, noted already in chapter 8.[9] Fuller reported on the recovered memories of a couple, Betty and Barney Hill, who, it seemed, had been abducted by aliens on a lonely stretch of New Hampshire road late at night in 1964. They had been undressed, prodded and poked; a long needle was inserted into Betty's stomach as, she supposed, a pregnancy test. They suffered unexplained psychological disturbances until the whole narrative of their abduction tumbled out in a series of hypnosis sessions. But—and this is crucial for us—their encounter did not transpire in a desert. And many, if not all, of the subsequent abductions that followed the Hills' pattern likewise took place almost anywhere *but* in a desert.[10] In other words, although the Giffords' abduction happens in a desert, the pattern their experience tracks has no need whatsoever of a desert to occur. As we saw in chapter 8, this translation out of the deserts constitutes a central element in the development away from the classic contactee experience of the 1950s.

However, the desert is not entirely irrelevant to the Giffords' encounter. It intrudes into their experience along two chief dimensions. Even before the aliens arrive, Elise confesses her anxiety once she and Tom have entered the Mojave: "It's just these mountains, I guess," she tells Tom. "The desert. So far from everything. So strange looking. Kind of gives me the creeps." Later, she remarks on the noisiness of the desert, which clearly unsettles her. Several times the sacrality of the desert region where they camped arises. Elise does some research in a book called *Mystic Places*, which "said that the local Indians considered this part of the desert sacred; a place where the deities came to show themselves to tribal priests." She recounts petroglyphs and the Mojave Twins, "a huge ground drawing that can only be recognized from planes passing high over the desert"—or, one imagines, UFOs. A week after the encounter, as they return to the site hoping to learn something about what happened, Tom reflected on

> why Indian tribes such as the Piutes [*sic*] and Mojaves considered this ground sacred. Truly, it
> appeared other-worldly: its stark, desolate terrain heightened by macabre volcanic formations
> that gave testimony to the violent turbulence that seethed beneath the surface.[11]

Elise's initial reaction to the desert landscape—she had never visited the Mojave before this trip and had been reluctant to go out there—would seem to be a screen for a deeper worry, the anxiety she felt about going on the trip from the start. The notion that "Indians" saw the desert area where the Giffords camped as "sacred" strongly suggests aliens had been landing there for centuries and were regarded as gods. The Mojave Twins, like the Nazca lines in the Atacama Desert in Chile, presumably would have been made by or for the aliens, who could see them from above in their ships.[12]

In sum, the role played by the desert in *Mojave Incident* is not central to either the plot or the characters. The desert more or less stands for, on the one hand, fear and anxiety ultimately linked to the aliens, and, on the other, ideas of Native American sacrality of land—also linked to visitations by aliens. So *Mojave Incident* is a bit closer to "desert literature" than *Desert Cat*, but not much; and far more important to the book than the desert is the standard pattern of alien abduction, which can—and typically does—occur far from the desert.

In March 1902, A. L. Kroeber, indefatigable anthropologist of Native cultures in California, spent six days listening to Inyo-kutavêre, an elderly Mohave, recite a "great telling," *itš-kanavk*, a lengthy tale of Mohave expulsion from and return to their Colorado River homeland. Inyo-kutavêre told the tale in Mohave; Kroeber's interpreter Jack Jones (Kwaknialka) rendered it into English, and Kroeber wrote it down. Inyo-kutavêre died before he could bring the tale to completion; many years later Kroeber published it with extensive commentary. Although Inyo-kutavêre's "great telling" is said to be the longest preserved Native American story, it has received remarkably little scholarly attention; to the best of my knowledge, there are only a handful or articles and one monograph devoted to it. An excerpt appears in an anthology of Indigenous California stories.[13]

The telling consists of two apparently unrelated stories. The first revolves around a brash young man named Nyĭtše-vilye-vave-kwilyêhe. Humiliated after losing a bet—he had bet his life, but his winning opponent was satisfied just to scalp him—he retreated into the desert in present-day Arizona, just east of the Colorado River. There he lived for four years with a desert-dwelling group. Afterwards he returned to a less than enthusiastic reception among the Mohave.

The other story deals with Hipahipa and the return of the Mohave under his leadership to their riverine homeland. When we first encounter him, he is living in a Potemkin village of fake huts and wells. He displays superhuman powers: he subsists only on rattlesnakes that he captures and suspends, alive, from his belt; he is also clairvoyant, sensing the Mohave who come to beg his help before they have arrived. After some resistance he agrees to help recover their river territory; like many epic heroes, after astounding achievements in battle, he is killed in the final, decisive fight.

These two stories—which might have been linked up had Inyo-kutavêre lived to complete the telling—rest on ideas about human relations with deserts quite different from stereotypical Euro-American notions, which often see deserts as spaces where manliness can be challenged, enhanced, and restored, as we have seen repeatedly (notably in John Carter's Martian adventures recounted in chapter 9). In the Mohave Historical Epic, human relations with deserts are instead multifaceted, whether teaching a better way to live or serving as a refuge for someone who doesn't fit in. The Epic, simply put, offers a different way to understand deserts and how we might live with and in them, a story that challenges the stories Anglo-Americans tend to tell themselves about these great spaces. The Epic also presents the deserts not as exotic, strange space but as a familiar landscape, complementary to the rich river bottom but not frightening or hostile; they are space where one can live, although the lifeway they demand is different from that the river requires.

Two ecozones comprise the settings for the Mohave Historical Epic. The Mohave homeland lay in the Colorado River Valley, roughly between present-day Fort Mohave, Nevada, and Cibola, Arizona; the present Colorado River Indian Reservation, shared by members of the Mohave, Chemehuevi, Hopi, and Navajo (Diné), occupies a reduced stretch of this territory. Before the construction of dams and diversions the Colorado regularly flooded the bottomland, which the Mohave, who lived in fixed settlements, planted in corn, beans, squash, and other crops; the rhythm of regular floods, the narrow valley, and agricultural abundance reminded many Euro-American observers of the Nile. This lifeway was taken up by the invaders who expelled the Mohave and is nicely illustrated by an incident at Atšqāqa, on the river at the south end of Mohave territory. There, Umase'āka, one of the leaders of the invaders, instructed his followers, "When the river flood goes down, let us plant where they [the previous inhabitants he had expelled] did and see how it will grow." He and his people lived for two years there on the crops. Later, he ordered them to burn the brush to make fields where they could plant.[14]

The other ecozone where the Epic is set is the desert. Here a contrasting lifeway was imposed: hunting and gathering provided food; people lived not in nucleated settlements but in small, dispersed groups under a headman; and they moved every few years, as the local resources were exhausted. Living on the edge of resource depletion, they were suspicious of newcomers. When a leader of the expelled Mohave named Maǝkwem-tšutšām-kwilyêhe, having failed to recover the Mohave homeland, turns east from the river into the desert, he comes upon the residence of two desert-dwelling Mohaves. They feed the refuges rabbit and mescal—typical desert foods—but object strongly to Maəkwem-tšutšám-kwilyêhe and his people's settling nearby in the desert: "We are scattered over the country: we have taken all the springs: there is no place for you to stay."[15] The relation of the desert-dwellers to their environment consists in a simple understanding of the limitations of its resources and its carrying capacity. The desert isn't hostile or dangerous; it simply can't support as many people as the river bottom, and so Maəkwem-tšutšám-kwilyêhe must be turned away.

The desert serves the Epic as a locus of both self-exile and refuge. When Nyĭtše-vilye-vave-kwilyêhe, having bet his body, loses in his fourth and final gambling contest, his opponent Umase'āka forbears killing him in favor of just scalping him. Wretched with shame, Nyĭtše-vilye-vave-kwilyêhe betakes himself across the Colorado River and deep into the desert in the east. He spends six years there in exile. Before he had been haughty, duplicitous, "wantonly willful, petulant, quarrelsome, abusive of hospitality, thankless to his friends and followers." He had blamed his people for making him lose in gambling by cheering him on and so distracting him; after his first three losing contests he had abused some friends who, sympathetic to his plight, took him in by stealing the door to a house, blocking a chimney hole to fill another house with smoke, and spilling stored grain on the floor of a third. When he emerges from the desert, though, he is a different person. He returns to Umase'āka's settlement and, rather than bear a grudge, brings presents which he distributes to Umase'āka's people. He then travels up to his home, where he listens abashed as his wife explains in no uncertain words why everyone hates him: "When he was here, he always made trouble for us," she reports as the common opinion. "It is well: he is dead."[16]

Nyĭtše-vilye-vave-kwilyêhe's desert exile was transformative. When first arrived at the desert settlement where he will stay six years, he refuses to take responsibility for his situation. "My family did wrong," he insists, "and I lost everything." But the local leader Lying-on-dust nevertheless welcomes him and elucidates his people's lifeway:

> "Tomorrow morning we will go hunting and the women will go out to look for seeds. At sunset we eat. We live on those things. Soon you will learn all that. Here are water and fire ready. Go and make a fire. You know where water is, and we have water jars: you know how to get water to drink. Thus we live. You had better stay."

Nyĭtše-vilye-vave-kwilyêhe learns how to collect firewood; he is given a bow and arrow to hunt rats and rabbits for himself; he's supplied with clothing and moccasins and a blanket. After four years, he comes to realize he is happy.[17] The exigencies of a desert life, in which Nyĭtše-vilye-vave-kwilyêhe must learn to take care of himself, invert his personality: whereas before he was self-centered and troublesome, now he is self-sufficient and content. The desert can wreak this change because life in the desert strips away all but the basic necessities and refocuses the mind and body on the simple requirements of food, warmth, and shelter.

For Nyĭtše-vilye-vave-kwilyêhe the desert also serves another purpose: as a refuge. He hides his shame at being scalped, his skull exposed, his hair and skin stolen, by retreating into the desert landscape east of the Colorado River. Until he arrives at Lying-in-dust's camp, he is by himself; only a certain Kunyiɵe, residing at the first settlement he encounters, witnesses his humiliation. Not only does Nyītše-vilye-vave-kwilyêhe not stay with Kunyiɵe, even though invited, he also perpetrates another abuse of hospitality, the same selfish behavior that has been his standard before.[18] It is notable that Lying-in-dust, who will have seen Nyītše-vilye-vave-kwilyêhe's disfigurement, makes no remarks on it; it is as though in the desert Nyītše-vilye-vave-kwilyêhe can be accepted as he is, without judgment. As long as he adheres to the desert's rules about acquiring his own food and conveying his own water, he can live unmolested—and, eventually, admit to himself that his desert life has made him happy. Nyītše-vilye-vave-kwilyêhe's previous behaviors, selfish and cruel, might be tolerated in the Colorado River settlements, but the desert cannot abide them; its demands call for a personality of an entirely different character, and his life in the desert indeed changes him for the better.

Hipahipa, the great hero of the Epic, likewise pursues this desert lifeway, but to an even greater extreme. When he appears, he is living by himself far out in the desert east of the Colorado River. His residence straddles a waterless arroyo, with ten houses and ten wells on each side—uninhabited, the "wells" in fact dry; the aim is to make it look like there's a village. He subsists entirely on rattlesnakes, which he captures live by day and hangs from his waist, head up and rattle down. He cooks and consumes them in the morning. To dissuade intruders, he magically changes the shape of his feet to leave footprints of men, women, and children. Nearby live two leaders, Cut-blood-knee and Ha-yeɵa-yêɵwa, who, like Hipahipa, live on typical desert fare obtained by hunting: rats, rabbits, and jackrabbits.[19]

And in the case of Hipahipa, the impact of the desert may have had another effect on him aside from the way of life it imposed. As we saw in chapter 5, he seems at some point to have undergone a shift from a male-bodied male, an *'iipa*, to a mixed personality, exhibiting both male and female characteristics, although not quite a complete male-bodied female, an *'alyha*. Where and when this change was effected is not made clear in the Epic, but Hipahipa performs his female practices in the desert; perhaps it was his move into the desert that brought out this aspect of his makeup, or perhaps it was the emergence of it that drove him into the desert, which, again perhaps, may have been more receptive to a personality as complex and ambiguous as his. In any case, Hipahipa seems free to perform his genuine self on the ground of the desert.

The desert and the challenges it presents are constant presences in the Epic. People worry daily about finding enough food. Water is a persistent concern: the central question in Nyītše-vilye-vave-kwilyêhe's travels is where he will find water, and whenever he does, he drinks, as we've seen. After the battle between Nyītše-vilye-vave-kwilyêhe's and Umase'āka's people, the latter undertake an eight-day trek through the desert; at least five of their eight camps were at water. Another group marching through the desert, ordered to carry water at the outset, followed the Colorado River and then turned east, stopping at two springs at least along the way.[20]

It is clear that the desert plays an active role in the Epic; it is as much a character in the story as Hipahipa or Nyītše-vilye-vave-kwilyêhe. Moreover, its functions can be illuminated through the lenses of both ecocriticism and the new materialism. From an ecocritical point of view, the desertscape serves as the inescapable ground on which the action of the Epic occurs; it demands that the Mohave who encounter it adhere to the stipulations on their lifeway that it imposes. Furthermore, the desert exercises agency: it compels Nyĩtše-vilye-vave-kwilyêhe to transform precisely in order to meet those stipulations. The Epic works neatly as an instance of desert literature, for its plot and characters would be inconceivable as depicted in any setting other than the desert; indeed, we are accorded the contrast with the river ecozone, where Nyĩtše-vilye-vave-kwilyêhe can be an entirely different person from the Nyĩtše-vilye-vave-kwilyêhe of the desert.

In the search for desert agency, *Molly* by Kevin Honold starts promisingly. The first-person narrator, Raymond, who's looking back on his childhood under the care of the eponymous character in a trailer perched on a New Mexico mesa, avers of his uncle that "The desert is hard on restless souls like his." More vividly, of "that road running through the desert" evoked in the novel's first sentence, he later muses,

> A desert highway will begin to vanish if you watch it long enough. Up close it seems a proper token of industrial enterprise, triumph of the machine age, seemingly ineradicable. One can observe how the earth has been leveled and graded, two layers of asphalt laid and tarred at the seams and hems, all of it nicely bedded, a changeless thing in a changeless desert.

This road, then, seems at first an emblem of human agency imposed on a "changeless" landscape with neither volition nor agency of its own. This picture is that of human will enacted on inert material. "But," Raymond reflects a little further,

> follow with your eyes as the road ascends the bajada and wends through the benched hills into the mountains. It soon acquires the appearance of something makeshift and provisional. As perspective widens, it becomes clearer that the desert determines the highway, and not otherwise.

Raymond goes on to compare the road to a "strip of tape like surveyors might nail to the desert floor,"[21] but the damage has been done. Raymond's desert has been conferred an agency; it, not the surveyors or the construction engineers or the asphalt layers, has imposed its will on the road, set its path through the landscape. But this theme is soon enough dropped in *Molly*; when the desert recurs later in the book, it is a mere landscape through which the characters move without being affected by it.

Arturo Islas's *The Rain God* revolves around the figure of Miguel Chico. An apparently successful professor at a prestigious university, he is haunted by his family's past, the overbearing figure of his grandmother Mama Chona, and his own chronic medical suffering and homosexuality. When he returns to his hometown on the southwestern Texas borderland, near El Paso in the Chihuahuan Desert, he's forced to face these demons. In his struggles, the desert plays an active, indeed determinative, role. It "is a space of warring ideologies that mirrors Miguel Chico's own unease with his body" that also "[a]lthough . . . associated with death, graveyards, terror, and bodily horrors . . . signifies a rupturing place of freedom tied to ancestral connections."[22]

The desert acts on Miguel repeatedly throughout the novel. Early on, under treatment for his intestinal disease, "the desert was very much in his mouth, which was already parched by the drugs." He recalls his godmother's "fear of being buried in the desert" and feels the ice chips his brother feeds him to provide relief instead as "grains of sand scratching down his throat." His body feels like "the desert on a cold, clear day after a snowfall." Miguel drives through the desert, and his own sadness and sense of betrayal emerge from the endless landscape. A particularly striking and explicit instance of desert agency for Miguel comes as he contemplates the death of his uncle Felix:

> [G]azing out at the California dusk settling on the leaves of the birch tree and turning them blue, Miguel Chico felt the sadness of that time of day. There are no sounds in the desert twilight. On very cold or very hot days, the land and its creatures breathe in that dry acid air of the space between day and night and, as the first stars appear, resume their activities in one long exhalation.

Miguel recalls Felix's love of twilight quiet "as much as the smell of the desert just before and after a thunderstorm," the sky "fresh with the fragrance of the mesquite, greasewood, and vitex trees." The smell, his cousin had said, announced the coming of "[t]he angels. . . . The ones in the sky." Felix, murdered by a young soldier whom he'd hoped to have a homosexual encounter with, died in a desert canyon.[23]

The pull of the desert, however, is more ubiquitous and powerful than it seems at first in passages where it is explicated evoked. Miguel "longs to return to the desert," but not simply to reconnect with his family or recover a childhood; the desert's magnetism is rather "an urgent, ambiguous, and often phantasmagoric demand emanating from his own sick body." There is, as Cordelia Barrera cogently observes, a Gothic quality to the novel, in which "a menacing desert landscape parallels the repressed psychological states and ambiguous relationships" that bind the characters together. But the desert does not simply reflect—or refract—these conditions; it also draws them out, into Miguel's consciousness, and forces him to face facts about himself and his family long repressed. One of his greatest challenges, which he ultimately overcomes, is to throw off Mama Chona's disgust for the family's Indigenous heritage; to embrace it means to accept too the desert. The Rain God rules the desert, a space that depends on the annual monsoon to sustain its hardy, arid-adapted life. He is part of the active agency of the desert that works on and through Miguel and drives the narrative and psychological trajectory of the novel. Thus, "The desert unites the novel's six separate segments . . . [and] encapsulates the central strategy by which Miguel Chico learns to read the story of his culture's past correctly and meaningfully."[24]

The role of the desert varies considerably in the texts I've examined, ranging from virtually without importance (as in *Desert Cat*) to the vibrancy of the desert in *The Rain God*. There has, in recent years, been discussion in the secondary literature about the matter of nonliving objects' "agency," "vibrancy," and "animacy," as briefly mentioned above. It's clear, I think, that in literature in which the desert is of central importance the desert exhibits precisely this kind of activity—it works on the people who live in it, as an active agent. In the Mohave

Historical Epic, the desert plays this role because it is one of the two ecozones in which all the action takes place, and the exigencies of living in a dry, resource-poor landscape—or perhaps better put, a landscape where resources are scattered and sometimes unreliable—determine almost everything about how people live: the endless worry about water, the need to shift location as resources are depleted, the pressure to keep population low. Further, the Native American conceptualization of the landscape as a sacred space, in certain locales having concentrations of power, lends it a virtual consciousness. This sense of a vibrant, living, agential landscape is not confined to Native Americans. In an introduction to the songlines of Aboriginal Australians, Margo Neale writes evocatively and with insistence:

> Everything starts and ends with Country in the Aboriginal worldview. Yet there are no endings in this worldview, nor are there any beginnings. Time and place are infinite and everywhere. Everything is part of a continuum, an endless flow of life and ideas emanating from Country, which some refer to as the Dreaming.
>
> In the Dreaming, as in Country, there is no separation between the animate and the inanimate. Everything is living—people, animals, plants, earth, water and air.[25]

It is in *The Rain God*, as we've seen, that desert agency comes forward powerfully and clearly. Such agency recurs in several of the texts we've examined. In some of the literature set in Los Angeles the desert plays a crucial active role. The Santa Ana winds bring desert agency into the heart of Los Angeles in *On the Lot and Off*, *Gidget*, and several of Eve Babitz's tales. In the journal of the Domínguez-Escalante Expedition, George English Brooks reads an "agency of the places it seeks to subdue" as the landscape resists, as it were, the imposition of European names.[26] The sense of sacrality of desert landscapes explored in chapter 2 implies, if it does not express, a sense of agency. Yves Berger's response to the desert—so too Simone de Beauvoir's—surely also entails an action by the landscape on these French travelers. Ofelia Zepeda, Simon Ortiz, and Pat Mora's poetry all resonates with implied agency. While it is not present in everything we've studied, agency hovers over the desert again and again. We need, then, to consider how this may come to be.

COMING TO TERMS WITH AGENCY

"[G]iving nature a 'voice' . . . has nothing to do with anthropomorphizing the non-human world."[27]

Several modes have been proposed to describe the agency of non-animate objects like the land. In his early study of Edgar Allen Poe's "Fall of the House of Usher," D. H. Lawrence insisted on the agency of all things: "Usher," he wrote,

> thought that all vegetable things had sentience. Surely all material things have a *form* of sentience, even the inorganic; surely they all exist in some subtle and complicated tension of vibration which makes them sensitive to external influence and causes them to have an influence on other external objects, irrespective of contact.[28]

A better and more explicit expression of the notion of inanimate agency could hardly be imagined. "Animacy," for which Mel Y. Chen has argued, is a concept borrowed from linguistics. Many languages distinguish among the degrees of agency possessed by various classes of referents set in a hierarchy of animacy, often ranging from adult males at the top to the inanimate at the bottom. Chen revisits the concept through examination of two inanimate elements, lead and mercury, whose activity on the human body poses "a potential threat to valued human integrities. They further threaten to overrun what an animacy hierarchy would wish to lock in place." Lead, Chen argues, claims an animacy that allows it to "invade" consumer products and, through them, bodies, which its activity damages: "By its very definition, the toxin, as much as it may have been categorized as inanimate, is more than mere matter, for it has a potency that can directly implicate the vulnerability of a living body."[29]

Chen does not address potential animacy of landscapes, and their theory seems, perhaps, ill-suited to elucidating the questions I am addressing here (although in general their claims about the intrusion of the low hierarchy animacies into human bodies has an appeal). Another, related approach, Jane Bennett's "vibrancy" or "vitality," may be more directly relevant.

> By "vitality" I mean the capacity of things—edibles, commodities, storms, metals—not only to impede or block the will and designs of humans but also to act as quasi agents or forces with trajectories, propensities, or tendencies of their own. My aspiration is to articulate a vibrant materiality that runs alongside and inside humans to see how analyses of political events might change if we gave the force of things more due. . . . [A]n actant [a term she borrows from Bruno Latour] is a source of action that can be either human or nonhuman; it is that which has efficacy, can *do* things, has sufficient coherence to make a difference, produce effects, alter the course of events. . . . I want to highlight what is typically cast in the shadow: the material agency of effectivity of nonhuman or not-quite-human things.[30]

Bennett's interest lies especially in ecology and the politics of dealing with our vast ecological problems; she doesn't treat matters like deserts, or landscapes in general. But I would argue that her analysis transfers easily and effectively to precisely the question of agency in the land.

A landscape's agency might be expressed through Bennett's "assemblages,"

> ad hoc groupings of diverse elements, of vibrant materials of all sorts.
>
> Assemblages are living, throbbing confederations that are able to function despite the persistent presence of energies that confound them from within. They have uneven topographies, because some of the points at which the various affects and bodies cross paths are more heavily tracked than others, and so power is not distributed equally across the surface. . . . The effects generated by an assemblage are, rather, emergent properties. . . . Each member and proto-member of the assemblage has a certain vital force, but there is also an effectivity proper to the grouping as such: an agency *of* the assemblage.[31]

A desert virtually begs to be treated as just such an assemblage. A desertscape is not a simple space but a complex agglomeration out of which the desert *qua* desert emerges. In chapter 1 we saw how Hadley Cells and rain shadows create the conditions under which aridity arises. But these atmospheric and geophysical elements are not simple and uniform. Hadley Cell circulation is the consequence of global patterns of solar radiation, airflow, humidity, the Coriolis effect—itself created by the Earth's rotation—among other factors. Rain shadows are a conspiracy of wind and relief, again elements whose existence depends on other factors, some in the deep geologic past (see Figs. 1-2 and 1-3). But a desert is also an ecological construction, and the individual components of its ecology contribute each in their own varying ways to constitute the desert. Mesquite provides shade that allows animals to shelter from the sun, and as nurse plants tend the sensitive sprouts of, say, saguaro cacti. The mineralized surface known as desert varnish, host also to a multitude of bacteria, provides the tablet on which Indigenous petroglyphs are scratched. The monsoons of summer in the Chihuahuan and Sonoran Deserts transform the desert landscape with an infusion of moisture that triggers the blossoming of millions of flowers and the emergence to mate of the desert toad. The agency that spins out of the desert assemblage exhibits precisely the changeability, the emergent properties, of Bennett's phenomenon.

Val Plumwood has articulated another, parallel approach to uncovering agency in nature. She argues that the concept of a "cultural landscape"—landscape: a word I've used repeatedly—has blocked our ability "to recognize the services and agency of the natural systems that support us." In her view, the structures of knowledge that we use when we look at nature impose "hegemonic concepts of agency in the land and natural systems." As a result, we are blinded to the agency in the natural world and attribute whatever agency we may see to our own intelligence or mind or reason acting on an uncreative and separate material substrate. She critiques the term "landscape" as a consequence of this position in her case; landscapes are precisely those territories formed by our own agency and imposed on the land. She argues for experiencing land through all our senses to create "a dialogical kind of story that sees the land as a field of (product of, outcome child/offspring of) *multiple interacting and collaborating agencies* which can include humans but is never exhausted by them."[32]

Plumwood sees as foundational the nonhuman components of the land, whose agencies make possible an overlay of human cultural features, which in turn often obscure or conceal the crucial roles those natural agencies play in making possible a human cultural landscape in the first place. In the desert we might count the presence and absence of water and food resources; the regime of precipitation (or lack thereof); seasonal changes; the contrast between night and day; and the geophysical and atmospheric agents that create the desert in the first place. To get to a proper account of natural agencies, Plumwood insists we must "start from our ecological context, taking account of what is valid in the indigenous, anti-dualist, and skeptical critique of nature and discarding the idealist and human-centered elements."[33]

Plumwood never quite explains how agency arises in nonhuman (or nonconscious) materialities. Her case seems to presuppose such agencies exist; the problem she sees is the way our dualistic thinking has obscured or completely hidden the natural agencies of material congeries, which seems very much like Bennett's assemblages. But where does this agency come from? How, precisely, does it operate? How can we put it into words that make sense to us as humans without betraying the character of agencies that are, evidently, fundamentally different from our own?

In one of a series of lectures delivered in 2013 and published in revised form in 2017 as *Facing Gaia: Eight Lectures on the New Climatic Regime*, Bruno Latour devotes much of a chapter to this problem of understanding agency in nonhuman materialities. His argument is complex. He begins from what he sees as the artificial distinction between "nature" and "culture"—a distinction as old as the *physis* versus *nomos* debates of the Greeks. This dichotomy, he argues, has allowed us to deprive the nonhuman material world of agency—it's just "nature" operating under immutable "natural law"—in a process he designates as *deanimation*, and thus conversely to assign all agency to people. Latour shows that in fact there is a swirling, dynamic interface in which all elements on Earth interoperate, affecting one another continuously, unpredictably, in a space he calls the *metaphoric zone*, which "is *a property of the world itself.*"[34] Here the agencies of all the participants, whether human, animal, plant, environment, geology, or atmosphere, interlace with their various abilities and intentionalities to create an outcome that is the totality of the world in which we live moment to moment. Latour's metamorphic zone sounds a lot like Bennett's assemblage.[35] Latour's defense of nonhuman, material agency, which he elaborated even more forcefully in two earlier essays, is preparatory to his rehabilitation—if that's the right word—of James Lovelock's Gaia, which forms the main topic of the lectures. Here we see, then, yet another way, though related, that nonhuman agency has recently been defended; indeed, Latour insists that we *must* accept the agency of all the components of our world: "One of the great enigmas of Western history," he observes, "is not that 'there are still people naïve enough to believe in animism,' but that many people still hold the rather naïve belief in a supposedly deanimated 'material world.'"[36]

This does not present a problem for Native American accounts of the natural world. They often simply presuppose the agency of the world around them, a view that Plumwood notes and marks as important. For instance, the title poem to Ofelia Zepeda's collection *Ocean Power* contrasts the relation between the Tohono O'odham and the desert they know well and their confusion and uncertainty upon first seeing the ocean.

> Words cannot speak your power.
> Words cannot speak your beauty.
> Grown men with dry fear in their throats
> watch the water come closer and closer.

She evokes the desert which the Tohono O'odham understand:

> Why did they bring us this way?
> Other times we crossed the desert floor.
> That land of hot dry air
> where the sky ends at the mountains.
> That land we know.

The problem confronting Tohono O'odham who see the ocean for the first time is fundamentally that they lack the spiritual and cultural tools to interact with the ocean's vibrancy.

> We are not ready to be here.
> We are not prepared in the old way.
> We have no medicine.
> We have not sat and had our minds walk through the image
> of coming to this ocean.
> We are not ready.
> We have not put our minds to what it is that we want to give to the ocean.
> We do not have cornmeal, feathers, nor do we have songs and prayers ready.
> We have not thought what gift we will ask from the ocean.
> Should we ask to be song chasers
> Should we ask to be rainmakers
> Should we ask to be good runners
> or should we ask to be heartbreakers.
> No, we are not ready to be here at this ocean.[37]

The ocean has a power—what Bennett might call a "thing-power"—that the Tohono O'odham visitors sense immediately as they approach the shoreline—and they are also immediately aware that they lack the tools necessary if they were to have a proper relationship with that power. In the desert they grasp the land's vibrancy, the interchange between its agentic activity and their human condition; there they know what they can ask of the land and how to ask it. Zepeda's visitors, in contrast, are at such a loss in the face of the ocean's power that they can only imagine asking of its vast waters gifts they are used to receiving from the desert.[38] In a way, the route Zepeda takes around the agency problem is to interrogate not the agency of the natural itself but rather the appropriate human approach to the natural which has an agency. She isn't really concerned with how Baboquivari or the ocean exercise agency; her worry is whether she and other Tohono O'odham have the knowledge needed to appeal to the mountain or the sea and receive the benefits each can, by their agencies, bestow.[39]

This acceptance of the agency of the nonhuman extends far and wide among Indigenous peoples across the Earth. In their introductory essay to the collection *Ecocriticism and Indigenous Studies: Conversations from Earth to Cosmos*, Joni Adamson and Salma Monani canvas Indigenous statements about the natural world from a variety of Indigenous populations through "The World People's Conference on Climate Change and the Rights of Mother Earth," which took place in April 2010. Out of this conference came a "Universal Declaration of the Rights of Mother Earth" which rests on the idea that "Mother Earth is a living being." (The resonance with James Lovelock's Gaia, discussed below, is obvious.) The Declaration includes a lapidary point: "The term 'being' includes ecosystems, natural communities, species and all other natural entities which exist as part of Mother Earth." All these entities are "persons" and must be treated as such. Adamson and Monani conclude that from the Arctic North to the Antarctic South, Indigenous understandings of "you" [addressed to the Earth] or "sentient creator beings," suggest a cosmos of relations that speak to complex entanglements of the human with the more-than-human that must be creatively and thoughtfully negotiated.

They add that the essays in their collected volume "reveal how many Indigenous cultural traditions throughout the world imbue their worlds with agential 'persons.'"[40] The natural acceptance of the agency of deserts and their landforms that we see among southwestern desert Indigenous peoples, then, sits comfortably in a worldwide sense of that agency. Indigenous peoples would be puzzled, if not amused, by the struggles of Euro-Americans to grapple with the notion that entities other than themselves are agential.

A broad sense of objects' agency operates too in taboos, which, Mary Douglas has observed, "depend on a form of community-wide complicity." She adds:

> The implicit theory [in societies that have taboos] is that physical nature will avenge the broken taboos: the waters, the earth, animal life and vegetation form an armoury that will automatically defend the founding principles of society, and human bodies are primed to do the same.[41]

In her waters and earth Douglas comprises the land, though without here explicitly talking about agency, and she does not return to the agential question later. (This quotation is from the preface to the 2002 reprint of *Purity and Danger*.) But it is quite obvious that agency is implied in her remark—a reference to agency in the context of non-Euro-American cultures. And indeed a broad sense of material agency resides, Pueblo peoples would insist, in images placed on the land, for "images are perceived as having inherent power, or agency" so that "textile/pottery designs replicated in the open landscape [as rock art] can be viewed as vehicles for communicating with, pleasing to, and even commanding the attention of cloud spirits" to discharge rain.[42] This is a splendid instance of agency inhering in a nonconscious, nonliving object—a fine case for the new materialism.

Much the same relation between human beings and agential places comes out in Keith Basso's study of Western Apache place names, which we had occasion to consider from a different angle in chapter 7. "[P]laces," he observes in what could be read as a fine commentary on agency that the desert by El Paso exercised on Miguel Chico, "possess a marked capacity for triggering acts of self-reflection. . . . Place-based thoughts about the self lead commonly to thoughts of other things," to networks of interrelations among people, the present, the past, other places, such that "[t]he experience of sensing places . . . is both thoroughly reciprocal and incorrigibly dynamic." Ultimately, "places come to generate their own fields of meaning."[43] Basso calls the relation between people and places "interanimation," which arises because places' "significance and value [are] found to reside in (and, it may seem, to emanate from) the form and arrangement of their observable characteristics." Basso, however, in the end shrinks from recognizing an agency residing in place independent of human beings. He insists that "such voices as places possess should not be mistaken for their own. Animated by the thoughts and feelings of persons who attend to them, places express only what their animators enable them to say."[44]

Here I think Basso underplays the power of the place. In his interpretation, places' ability to evoke feelings, moral lessons, networks, works only because the human observer brings to the places his/her own memories, cultural knowledge, and ability to link the tales embedded in the places with aspects of their own lives. For him as an Anglo anthropologist, presumably, the sites are silent, since he does not bear the baggage necessary to grasp their information. But what changes when he knows the story? The place then does talk to him; he gets the moral tale. And it is the *place* that is crucial: the tale has its impact because it comes out of the place to speak to Talbert; would the story of Old Man Owl have had the same effect on Talbert if his friends had simply told it to him over beers in a bar? I think not. The power flows from being in the place where the events occurred, and this is part and parcel of the agency Trail That Goes Down Between Two Hills exercises (see chapter 7).

It will surely be objected to the imputation of agency to the desert landscape that in fiction and poetry we are simply anthropomorphizing. The desert may be called "no lady," its mountains may be treated as carriers of myth, history, and power, but these attributes shouldn't be reckoned *really and truly* to inhere in the physical space; it's all just "poetic talk," so to speak. This is not a trivial objection. And I might be accused of inconsistency: I've argued here and there in this book that the desert is simply *there*, and it is human interaction, or perhaps even mere presence, that assigns it attributes like sacrality or gender.

In a brief "Note on Anthropomorphism," Bennett defends the practice as providing a key to "catalyz[ing] a sensibility that finds a world filled not with ontologically distinct categories of beings (subjects and objects) but with variously composed materialities." She insists further that

> [i]n a vital materialism, an anthropomorphic element in perception can uncover a whole world of resonances and resemblances—sounds and sights that echo and bounce far more than would be possible were the universe to have a hierarchical structure. We at first may see only a world in our own image, but what appears next is a swarm of "talented" and vibrant materialities (including the seeing self).[45]

There appears to be an unanswered problem in this formulation: that present is not only anthropomorphism, but also anthropocentrism. Our only experience with agency or vibrancy is our own as human beings; when we seek agency or vibrancy or any of their synonyms in a material object like a landscape, are we not inevitably impelled to read that agency as like our own? Yet, must that be so? How can we avoid the trap of seeing the land as a reflection of ourselves, a problem that arises too in the gendered and sacred landscape, and which I have tried to escape by asserting that gender (and erotics) is something we *impose*, not an inherent quality, of the desert or the sown (see chapters 2 and 5)? When, however, we see agency in a landscape (or any other analogous object), we cannot squirm out of the problem as easily.

It seems to me that there are moves that writers have made to try to assert an agential landscape without having to articulate precisely what it is or how it works. In *The Rain God* the desert surely is meant to be seen, as Barrera remarks, as agential; it is crucial to Miguel's transformation, but Islas implies rather than expresses explicitly its activity. Somehow or other, Miguel is affected; we can see how he changes; but the deepest agent, the desert, remains masked. As we saw in chapter 5, for the Piipaash and Halychduum (Maricopa) and Yuma Native Americans a mountain bearing third gender transmits dreams into the sleep of young men who will undergo a gender transformation; its agency is expressed by a medium that both tribes recognize as deeply meaningful and that can be understood in human terms; but how the dreams are projected, how the mountain decides whom to transform, is completely opaque. So one way to grasp the agency of a landscape is through the humanly recognizable effects it engenders; the mechanisms and nature of its agency may be left, as it were, a mystery.

There have been attempts to describe the actual agency of a material object. One way is to imbue the object with a living consciousness that embodies the will that acts. (This seems to be an approach that would arouse Plumwood's suspicions.) Animism, the belief that every-thing is alive, takes this route; many Native American tribes too, in seeing the land as sacred, imbue it with a living force. This move is hardly confined to Indigenous Americans: the Greeks and Roman saw nymphs in pools of water, satyrs in the woods, a whole bevy of active, conscious, willful agents that interacted with human beings. In T. H. White's *The Sword in the Stone*, the goddess Athene takes young Arthur ("Wart") on a tour of the nonhuman world, in which he finally encounters rocks, which turn out to have a consciousness, but for whom time moves so slowly that they appear inert to us.[46] An objection to this solution, however, is that it could be seen as simply a projection of our own conscious agency onto nonhuman things, the famous "pathetic fallacy."[47] Rather than describe a truly nonhuman agency, it presupposes that everything is *like us*, with the same affect, thought-processes, and so on.

Two other modes occur to me. James Lovelock and his followers insisted that the Earth should be seen as an integrated system, a view that shifted easily to a claim that the Earth is an agential entity, an enormous living organism comprised of its fauna, flora, bacteria, viruses, atmosphere, tectonic plates, oceans, and so on: everything. This huge system is alive and acts agentially; it is formed by "the whole of life on Earth within the older and more general framework of geology." The first of the "three of Gaia's principal characteristics" and "[t]he most important property of Gaia is the tendency to keep constant conditions for all terrestrial life." It reacts to the acts of human beings and, when we cause damage, responds with self-protective actions that may not be terribly welcome by us.[48] Gaia's agency, which is not human, has a clear intentionality: to protect itself and the conditions that allow life to flourish. Bruno Latour has rehabilitated Lovelock's Gaia—which came in for vigorous criticism when the theory originally came out—arguing that his concept of a living, agential Earth offers an excellent mode for grasping what is often called the Anthropocene, linked to anthropogenic climate change.[49] Gaia, then, may be the best example of an agency nei-ther conscious (perhaps!) nor human, a Bennettian assemblage, and a precise instance of Plumwood's "*multiple interacting and collaborating agencies* which can include humans but is never exhausted by them."[50]

The other instance that occurs to me is in the extraordinary science fiction novel *Solaris* by Stanislaw Lem.[51] Humans have discovered a planet circling two distant stars, whose surface consists almost entirely of a gel-like "ocean." A station has been placed 500–1500 yards (457–1372 m) above the surface of the ocean to study it. Opinions about the nature of this ocean are all over the place; there is no agreement:

> Du Haart [a scientist who'd studied Solaris] was the first to have the audacity to maintain that the ocean possessed a consciousness. The problem, which the methodologists hastened to dub metaphysical, provoked all kinds of arguments and discussions. Was it possible for thought to exist without consciousness? Could one, in any case, apply the word thought to the processes observed in the ocean? Is a mountain only a huge stone? Is a planet an enormous mountain?

The ocean "was engaged in a never-ending process of transformation, an 'ontological autometamorphosis.'" (In a tour de force, Lem describes the extraordinary forms the ocean auto-generates, none of whose purposes or meaning can be explained.) Even if the ocean is sentient, all efforts to communicate with it have failed. Kris Kelvin, Lem's narrator, remarks that

> any scientist who devotes himself to the study of Solariana has the indelible impression that he can discern fragments of an intelligent structure, perhaps endowed with genius, haphazardly mingled with outlandish phenomena, apparently the product of an unhinged mind. Thus was born the conception of the "autistic ocean" as opposed to the "ocean-yogi."[52]

Kelvin, a psychologist by training, has arrived at the station hoping to be more successful in unraveling Solaris's mysteries. But an unauthorized experiment, in which Solaris was bombarded with high-energy X-rays, has provoked a reaction: simulacra ("Phi-creatures") start to appear on the station, derived from troubling events in the scientists' pasts; Kelvin sees and is haunted by a simulacrum of Rheya, a former wife who committed suicide after he left her.[53]

The nature of Solaris, the composition of its agency, indeed whether it is in fact "sentient" in any human sense, are never figured out. The planet remains a complete mystery except that somehow it is excavating trauma from the scientists' memories and transforming them into agglutinations of neutrinos with—at least in Kelvin's case—the shape and consciousness of human beings. Solaris provides a prime example of nonhuman —maybe even nonconscious—agency. Its deep, impenetrable alienness defeats every effort by its human researchers to wrest from it an account of itself, yet it undeniably exercises an agency on those very researchers. Through Kelvin Lem insists repeatedly throughout *Solaris* that none of the multifarious theories about the ocean has cracked the problem; this prepares us to see, at the end, that Snow's—he's one of the other two original occupants of the station—new theory is surely also just more pointless speculation.[54] The ocean remains an impenetrable agent, an agential object that is fully nonhuman.

Many of the elements in the problematics of agency come together neatly in a recent interview with Kim Stanley Robinson by Ezra Klein in the podcast he does for the *New York Times*.[55] Robinson talks about his experiences with LSD when he was in university and refers to "brain scientists" who claim LSD "actually does change you." The effect, he suggests, is in part cognitive estrangement: a condition brought on by the molecule that makes the world seem strange by stripping away our ordinary perceptions of it, and this estrangement leaves the experiencer permanently changed. While neither Robinson nor Klein say so explicitly, this effect is obviously readable as a kind of agency, an interaction between our complex neurochemistry and the molecule working together in a Bennettian assemblage. Robinson describes the action as "a relationship between our biochemistry and the outside world."

In connection with Robinson's latest book, *The High Sierra: A Love Story*,[56] he and Klein talk about the notion of psychogeology. Essentially, this idea is that landscapes have character, if not personality. Robinson insists:

> [mountains] have their characters. And I say this even about the Sierra—basins have characters. Why should that be? It's just rock and empty space in particular patterns. And yet, at least to my mind, they coalesce into a particular feeling. Like in the Ionian Basin, you're going to feel scared and oppressed and like something's wrong. You can try to explain it, but it's more of a gestalt. And that's psychogeology.[57]

Robinson also invokes Bruno Latour's Actor-Network Theory and gives as an example the notion that when Louis Pasteur was working on his cures "amongst his collaborators were the bacteria he was working on." Another such collaboration, Robinson notes, is that between us and the bacterial flora that inhabit our bodies, which "are part of our self and our mind and our consciousness." Anticipating Robinson, Bennett also alludes to Latour's thinking, although without explicitly evoking his Actor-Network Theory. This idea, which is closely related to Bennett's assemblage, in my view, urges us to see the agential interconnections and interweavings among all the actors in a given situation.[58] As Robinson notes, the theory has been criticized on the ground that it attributes agency to actors that do not have agency. But "we often miss," Robinson remarks, "that we are being changed by things, even if the things are not intending to change us." This comment grates against another observation, that Actor-Network Theory usefully encourages us to attend to the world around us "even if we take the corrective, that a lot of the actors in these theories don't have agency in the sense that maybe they are inanimate, maybe they cannot choose, maybe they don't have free will, maybe they're subjugated." There is considerable tension between these two remarks and even within the second itself, for how is it we can call something an "actor" if it does not have agency? Like some other observers, Robinson seems torn between the vitality of Actor-Network Theory and the materialist criticism of nonhuman agency that Bennett and Plumwood reject.

The preceding paragraphs have given but a glimpse into a vibrant—if I may say so—project of exploring the idea of nonhuman and even nonliving agency. A potent argument for agency of the nonhuman, inanimate world appears in Jeffrey Jerome Cohen's remarkable book *Stone: An Ecology of the Inhuman*. The claim of agency for stone serves as the framework of his argument, which runs from mediaeval texts to the present, and leans heavily on Latour's work on Actor-Network Theory (among other things).[59] Clearly, study of the southwestern deserts and the literature that evokes them has a lot to contribute to this project. Deserts' alterity may especially highlight the agency they effect on humans who visit them; we also have, as we have seen, a good deal of information about how Indigenous inhabitants interacted with these desert spaces, which give us a means by which to reflect on the Euro-American tropes that still inflect Anglo visions of desert space.

What we have in the end, then, are two modes of agency. In fiction or travel narratives or film, or even art, the desert can be agential—without having to face the question of whether such agency exists, or is even possible, in the real world. Fiction and its compatriots indeed may claim and illustrate desert agency, as *The Rain God*, Berger's saguaros and stones, Angelucci's shimmering desert, or any of the other work we have studied.[60] The other mode is the assertion that agency of nonhuman, nonconscious, and even nonliving things can exist and act on us and the world around us, as Gaia or Kim Stanley Robinson's High Sierra landforms. It is not for me here to answer definitively the questions these matters raise. I will only say that the recognition of agencies outside us and the animals we regard as conscious and self-activating fits comfortably with an ecocritical and new materialist approach to the literatures of the desert Southwest. This view finds support in the arguments of philosophers like Bennett, Chen, Latour, and others.[61]

The new materialist approach to agency, however, has been subjected to a vigorous critique recently by Timothy Clark. Clark argues that this notion of agency applied to nonhuman entities, and especially nonanimate ones, rests on an obvious fallacy: that it has been thought that they do not have agency, and the discovery of agency by the new materialists is neither new nor groundbreaking. Clark insists that they have agency because "[e]ver since someone dodged a falling branch or built a wall, it has been obvious that material objects *do* things, *change* things, have 'tendencies of their own,' and *have agency* in a basic, widely used sense of the word."[62] It seems to me that Clark's critique misses the point by attacking what is basically a straw man. Agency is not simply *"do*[ing] things" but rather imbricates *intentionality*. A falling branch is not the consequence of an agential decision on the part of a tree in Clark's construction; it happens because, say, the wood is rotten and a strong wind comes along. As we've already seen, ideas of sentience and intentionality in the material world are central to the new materialist construction of agency and are fundamental to the ways that Native Americans have seen and continue to see the world they inhabit. This agential intentionality or intentional agency plays out in new materialist readings of fiction—something Clark evades in his analysis. Moreover, Clark confines his critique largely to nonfiction applications of agency via the new materialism, but as we have seen, it's a potent tool for analyzing fiction, like *Solaris* or *The Rain God*, and Native American literature like the Mohave Historical Epic. So, I'd suggest that what Clark seems to see as a devastating critique in fact doesn't address the basic ideas behind the play of agency in new materialist thought. The agency of new materialism and Bennett's assemblages, then, retain their explanatory power.

But a problem remains that can be unfolded by considering a simple question: what is agency? In ordinary life when we think of agency, we associate it with conscious human decision-making or action. I express agency when I decide to have a coffee or go for a walk. People who lack agency, wholly or partly, seem less than fully human or deprived in some way often regarded as impermissible: so slaves' agency is highly curtailed by their "social death," as Orlando Patterson argued; women unable to choose whom to marry or open a bank account are likewise seen as robbed of the agency that human beings ought to enjoy.[63] These two states, however—enslavement and oppression—open up a wider lens. For their restricted agency is a result of *social conditions*, and that leads to the realization that no act of agency can be completely dissociated from the social world in which it occurs. That is to say, human agency takes place within a social context that may constrain choice or direct it toward one possibility rather than another.

When we talk, then, about the agency of the inanimate—if that's the right word—the agency of a landscape, of the desert, are we talking about an agency that, like ours as human beings, functions within some kind of context that at least partially prescribes the parameters within which it must exist? The new materialism posits a capacity for agency in nonhuman entities, even, as I've noted already, nonliving ones. In fact, as the epigraph starting this chapter plainly demonstrates, the idea that agency infuses everything is hardly new; the Sicilian philosopher Empedokles, who lived in the fifth century BCE, had already insisted on it, and the anthropologist Philippe Descola, categorizing the ways people see their relation to the environment, counted as one animism, whose fundamental characteristic, in Descola's view, lies precisely in seeing a continuity from us to the natural world, all infused with spirit.[64]

But nothing, not even the desert, acts outside a context. The parameters of the agency—or agencies—within which deserts affect us, and we them, are set by broad but definable limits. For instance, the aridity of the desert acts on the human body, drying it out, impinging on the functions of our organs, demanding that we consume water in quantities far beyond what our bodies would require in the humid East. The yearning for rain that runs below the surface of *The Rain God* is precisely such an action on the characters in the book. But the context of agency is surely far more complicated than that. Bennett's assemblage is a grouping of multiple elements, each bearing its own agency, whose interactions are constrained, limited, defined, and impinged upon by one another; the final—if there is a final—agential action the assemblage exercises is an amalgamation of all the sub-agencies of the elements of the assemblage. It seems right to hold that desert agency, like all other agencies, does not exist outside a framework but rather acts only insofar as its boundaries permit. Even Solaris, whose makeup remains utterly opaque to the scientists who study it, works within its limits: the ocean's ability to materialize people drawn from the memories and emotions of the scientists ends at some point in space as one withdraws from the planet. (What other limitations may exist are a mystery.) The presence in nonhuman agencies of this machinery of constraint has yet another effect: it brings nonhuman agency into closer conversation with our own. The agency of a stretch of desert, while perhaps mysterious in its aims and operation, nevertheless remains, like our own, contained. In a sense, then, this brings us too into the new materialism; we too are material objects, functioning in contexts just as the nonhuman world does. We return to nature, as it were.

CODA—WALKS IN THE DESERT

In March 2003, I was on a backpacking trip in Organ Pipe Cactus National Monument and the Cabeza Prieta National Wildlife Refuge in Southern Arizona, nestled up against the Mexican border. To reach our campsite in the Cabeza—which we could only enter after signing a hold-harmless agreement with the federal government in case we should be blown up by an unexploded bomb, as the refuge had previously been part of the Goldwater Range—we had to drive along the track of the Camino del Diablo, a section of the old Spanish colonial route leading from Chihuahua Ciudad to California. (The same route John Annerino and his companions trudged, as described in chapter 1.) Federal environmental law passed to keep vehicles out of the Cabeza had been suspended to permit the US Border Patrol to operate on the unpaved, dusty, rut-ridden road; we passed several of their trucks on the way in.

We had to haul our equipment, food, and especially water from the turn-off where we'd parked our vehicle to a campsite a couple of miles from the road. There we slept under a crystalline night sky radiant with stars and the Milky Way; by day, slathered with sunscreen, we hiked through a rough, volcanic landscape, over razor-thin quartz ridges of the basin and range mountains, with views deep into the Mexican Sonoran Desert and glowing sand-yellow formations all around us, dominated by the black volcanic cone, the "Black Head," from which the Cabeza Prieta took its name. Midafternoons we crawled under creosote bushes to garner a little shade against the gleaming sun, to nap or read or write notes or simply to gaze out mesmerized at a landscape apparently asleep under a pearlescent sky. We never saw another person once we'd left behind the Border Patrol agents in their white truck loaded with detection equipment.

This landscape presented all the conundrums of the desert I'd read and thought about for some years and had contemplated far off in the wet East with small groups of students. It was easy to conjure up the travails of the early Spanish and the more recent human disaster chronicled in Luis Alberto Urrea's *The Devil's Highway*. You could imagine the figure of a ragged, bearded, filthy, emaciated Moses clambering up one of the ridges to meet God from the rear. But the desert also displayed an ethereal beauty, colors and shapes as magical as Van Dyke tried to capture in his prose. Edward Abbey is buried somewhere out there, perhaps in the Growler Mountains along the boundary between the Cabeza and Organ Pipe Cactus National Monument. And both reserves exist to protect rare and fragile ecologies—the Cabeza in particular as home to desert bighorn sheep. They have benefited from the preservationist movement once it saw that desert scrublands were just as deserving of our care as the High Sierra of Kings Canyon or Yosemite.

To cut down on weight I didn't carry a camera; to avoid interruptions from the bustling outside, I left my phone in storage. (A few years earlier I had been hiking alone in Organ Pipe, buzzards circling my head, when my cell phone rang. I learned my lesson.) So I have no photographs except those stored in my skull. I can't share them here, but they sustain me in my love of our southwestern deserts, along with my indelible memories of the heat on my skin, the smells of the creosote, the wind, the night skies, the exquisite pleasure of lying down to sleep with joints loose and muscles sore after scrambling up and down desert ridges.

Our peace was broken from time to time by the roar of jets based at Luke Air Force Base outside Phoenix, whose pilots practiced their bomb runs in the Goldwater Range to our north and often penetrated the airspace above the Cabeza. Eerily, on the morning of March 19, 2003, we were met with utter silence—not a plane in the sky. When we came out a few days later and stopped at a Mexican restaurant in Wellington, Arizona, a newspaper headline confirmed what we already knew: the Iraq War had begun that March 19. We were reminded of another use to which we have put our desert spaces: as national sacrifice zones where we practice the art of rendering death. It is a ruinous abuse of a fragile beauty, of the lungs of the planet.

NOTES

PREFACE

1. See Isabel Kelly's apology for "the telegraphic style, adopted at the time by the Department of Anthropology, at Berkeley" (Isabel T. Kelly, *Southern Paiute Ethnography*, Anthropological Papers 69 [Salt Lake City, 1971], iii); by "at the time" she refers to the time her study was drafted, in 1933 and 1934; it was finally published only 37 years later.
2. Alison M. Johnston, *Is the Sacred for Sale? Tourism and Indigenous Peoples* (London: Earthscan, 2006), xii.
3. The Coronado expedition is treated briefly in chapter 7. Father Eusebio Francisco Kino, *Kino's Historical Memoir of Pimería Alta: A Contemporary Account of the Beginnings of California, Sonora, and Arizona*, 2 vols., trans. and ed. Herbert Eugene Bolton (Cleveland: The Arthur H. Clark Company, 1919). One trip of Kino's, however, is examined in chapter 7.
4. Emma Dolujanoff, *Cuentos del desierto* (Hermosillo: Gobierno del Estado Sonora, Instituto Sonorense de Cultura, 2016) (digital edition of the original 1959 publication); Jesús Gardea, *Stripping Away the Sorrows from this World*, trans. Mark Schafer (Colonia del Valle: Editorial Aldus, S.A., 1998), 13.
5. Elmer Kelton, *The Time It Never Rained* (Fort Worth: TCU Press, 1984) with Quinn Grover, "Aridity, Individualism, and Paradox in Elmer Kelton's *The Time It Never Rained*," in *Reading Aridity in Western American Literature*, eds. Jada Ach and Gary Reger, 45–66 (Lanham, MD: Lexington Books, 2020); Cordelia E. Barrera, *The Haunted Southwest: Towards an Ethics of Place in Borderlands Literature* (Lubbock: Texas Tech University Press, 2022).

CHAPTER 1

1. As Celina Osuna has reminded me in conversation, it's important to think not about "the desert" but "deserts"—they are different in many ways. I write about "the desert" when I am thinking about tropes and stereotypes that collapse deserts into a single type-entity.
2. For a recent review of developments in ecocriticism, see Timothy Clark, *The Value of Ecocriticism* (Cambridge: Cambridge University Press, 2019).
3. Susan Yi Sencindiver, "New Materialism," in *Oxford Bibliographies* (2019), accessed August 15, 2023, https://www.oxfordbibliographies.com/display/document/obo-9780190221911/obo-9780190221911-0016.xml.
4. See Thomas T. Warner, *Desert Meteorology* (Cambridge: Cambridge University Press, 2004), 104–15, and Julie Laity, *Deserts and Desert Environments* (Oxford: Wiley-Blackwell, 2008), 37–43. Both subsume the Colorado Desert under the Sonoran and Mojave Deserts; I have kept it separated out since much of the literature I discuss treats it as a separate landform.
5. Warner, *Desert Meteorology*, 27–33; briefly, Laity, *Deserts and Desert Environments*, 2–4. There are various mechanisms that moderate Hadley Cell deserts, some of which—particularly monsoons and orography—operate in the desert Southwest.
6. Warner, *Desert Meteorology*, 33–44. The Atacama Desert in Peru and Chile and the Namib Desert in Namibia are the result of very cold currents moving just offshore in very deep water; very little moisture is taken up by the winds passing over the ocean, and so there is little precipitation. The Atacama is the driest desert in the world after Eastern Antarctica. See Warner, *Desert Meteorology*, 46–53.

7. Diana K. Davis, *The Arid Lands: History, Power, Knowledge* (Cambridge: MIT Press, 2016), 23–47. See also Laura Feldt, "Wilderness and Hebrew Bible Religion—Fertility, Apostasy and Religious Transformation in the Pentateuch," in *Religion and Society, Wilderness in Mythology and Religion: Approaching Religious Spatialities: Cosmologies, and Ideas of Wild Nature*, eds. Laura Feldt, Gustavo Benavides, and Kocku von Stuckrad, 55–94 (Berlin: De Gruyter, 2012), and Gary Reger, "Greeks and Romans in the Sahara Desert: Ideology and Experience," *Global Environment* 12 (2019): 26–30.

8. Exod. 3:1–7; Exod. 16–17:1–6; Exod. 19-34; forty: Exod. 16:35, 24:18, 34:28; there are many other instances of forty in the Hebrew Testament, making clear the sacrality of the number. There are several words in the Hebrew Testament that can be translated as "desert" or "wilderness," the commonest of which by far is *midbar*. See Nogah Hareuveni, *Desert and Shepherd in Our Biblical Heritage*, trans. Helen Frenkley (Keot Kedumin: The Biblical Landscape Reserve in Israel, 1991), chapter 1, and Philipp Enger, "Eine Wüstenwanderung mit Israel," in *Was Ist eine Wüste? Interdisziplinäre Annäherungen an einen interkulturellen Topos*, eds. Uwe Lindemann and Monika Schwitz-Emans (Würzberg: Verlag Königshausen & Neumann, 2000), 30–31. See Uwe Lindemann, *Die Wüste: Terra incognita, Erlebnis, Symbol: Eine Genealogie der abendländischen Würstenvorstellungen in der Literatur von der Antike bis zur Gegenwart* (Heidelberg: C. Winter, 2000), 64–68, on the desert in the Bible.

9. 1 Kings 19:4–15; Hosea 13:5. The word in both passages for desert is *midbar*; I have changed The New International Version of the text of Hosea from "wilderness" to "desert." Lindemann, *Die Wüste*, 65.

10. Hosea 2:3 and 14–15 in the New International Version, slightly modified ("wilderness" in verse 14 into "desert," as in verse 3; the word is *midbar* in both). In the Hebrew text the verse numbers are different: 2:5 and 16–17. Lindemann, *Die Wüste*, 65. Deut. 29:23.

11. Hosea 9:10, *midbar*.

12. Isaiah 35:1, 6–7, New International Version, slightly modified ("scorched land" in place of "wilderness"); Lindemann, *Die Wüste*, 65–66. See also Ezekiel 20:35 and 34:25.

13. Rev. 12:6 and 14.

14. Matt. 4:1–11; Lindemann, *Die Wüste*, 69–79. See especially the remarks of Manly recounted in chapter 4.

15. Bret Easton Ellis, *Imperial Bedrooms* (New York: Alfred A. Knopf, 2010), 157–58. On the nature of this novel, see Georgina Colby, *Bret Easton Ellis: Underwriting the Contemporary* (New York: Palgrave Macmillan, 2011), 165–71. A good summary of the contradictory biblical tropes about deserts outlined here can be found in Veronica Della Dora, *Landscape, Nature, and the Sacred in Byzantium* (Cambridge: Cambridge University Press, 2016), 120–37, with a somewhat broader focus on "wilderness."

16. For some of the formulae, see Laity, *Deserts and Desert Environments*, 7; M. A. Chandler, "Depiction of Modern and Pangean Deserts: Evaluation of GCM Hydrological Diagnostics for Paleoclimate Studies," in *Pangea: Paleoclimate, Tectonics, and Sedimentation during Accretion, Zenith, and Breakup of a Supercontinent*, ed. George D. Klein (Boulder: Geological Society of America, 1994), 120–21, 129. The problem of definition arises acutely in the case of Los Angeles: see chapter 6.

17. Consider East Antarctica, the most arid desert on Earth: there is plenty of water everywhere—you just need to chip it out and melt it.

18. A. L. Kroeber, "A Mohave Historical Epic," *University of California Publications: Anthropological Records* 11 (1951), 84 F 59 and F 60. For more detailed discussions of the Epic, see chapters 5, 7, and 10.

19. John Annerino, *Desert Survivor: An Adventurer's Guide to Exploring the Great American Desert* (New York: Four Walls Eight Windows, 2001), 16–18.

20. Luis Alberto Urrea, *The Devil's Highway: A True Story* (New York: Back Bay Books, 2004). The story is told *passim*. A map with narrative at xviii–ix gives the day-by-day events, including temperatures, the highest on May 23.

21. Orfeo Angelucci, *Son of the Sun: The Secret of the Saucers*, ed. Timothy Green Beckley (New Brunswick: Global Communications/Conspiracy Journal, 2008), 157, cf. also 215. The contactees' desert experiences are examined in chapter 8.

22. Urrea, *The Devil's Highway*, 108.

23. John C. Van Dyke, *The Desert: Further Studies in Natural Appearances* (New York: Charles Scribner's Sons, 1901); Peter Wild and Neil Carmony, "The Trip Not Taken: John C. Van Dyke, Heroic Doer or Armchair Seer?" *Journal of Arizona History* 34 (1993): 65–80; David W. Teague and Peter Wild, *The Secret Life of John C. Van Dyke: Selected Letters* (Reno-Las Vegas: University of Nevada Press, 1997); Peter Wild, "Introduction," in Dix Van Dyke, *Daggett: Life in a Mojave Frontier Town*, ed. Peter Wild (Baltimore-London: Johns Hopkins University Press, 1997), 8–10. Subsequent desert essays: John C. Van Dyke, *The Open Spaces: Incidents of*

Nights and Days under the Blue Sky (New York: C. Scribner's Sons, 1922). His lectures appear in John C. Van Dyke, *Art for Art's Sake: Seven University Lectures on the Technical Beauties of Painting* (New York: Charles Scribner's Sons, 1893). The French conquest of the Sahara began with the capture of Algiers in 1830 and was essentially complete by the end of the nineteenth century. John's brother Dix wrote a memoir of his life in Daggett: Dix Van Dyke, *Daggett: Life in a Mojave Frontier Town*, ed. Peter Wild (Baltimore-London: Johns Hopkins University Press, 1997). For a study of the origins of the Art for Art's Sake movement, see Elizabeth Prettejohn, *Art for Art's Sake: Aestheticism in Victorian Painting* (New Haven: Yale University Press, 2008), esp. 1–9.

24. For instance, Anonymous, "The Desert" [review of Van Dyke, *The Desert*], *New York Tribune*, February 8, 1902.

25. For an early exponent, George Perkins Marsh, *Man and Nature: Or, Physical Geography as Modified by Human Action*, ed. David Lowenthal (Cambridge, MA: The Belnap Press of Harvard University Press, 1965) (originally published in 1864); Richard H. Grove, *Green Imperialism: Colonial Expansion, Tropical Island Edens, and the Origins of Environmentalism, 1600–1860* (Cambridge: Cambridge University Press, 1995) and Chad Montrie, *The Myth of Silent Spring: Rethinking the Origins of American Environmentalism* (Berkeley: University of California Press, 2018) on the early development of environmentalism.

26. Van Dyke, *The Desert*, ix–x.

27. Van Dyke, *Art for Art's Sake*, 26–27, 31, 96–97.

28. Lindemann, *Die Wüste*, 175–86.

29. André Gide, *Amyntas: North African Journals*, trans. Richard Howard (New York: The Echo Press, 1988), 45. Gide made six trips to North Africa between 1893 and 1903: Lindemann, *Die Wüste*, 354n5.

30. Van Dyke, *The Desert*, 105.

31. Gide, *Amyntas*, 49 and 52–53 (first ellipsis in the original).

32. Van Dyke, *The Desert*, 19. I follow here the trenchant analysis of Sylvie Mathé, "Méditation sur le désert: figures et voix," in *Mythes ruraux et urbains dans la culture américaine*, ed. Serge Ricard (Aix-en-Provence: Publications de l'U de Provence, 1990), 137–38 (citing Van Dyke but not Gide). So Arla Bay, British protagonist of Lawrence Clark Powell's *El Morro*, on first seeing the Grand Canyon: "I don't know if what I feel is liking. It calls for a new vocabulary" (Lawrence Clark Powell, *El Morro* [Santa Barbara: Capra Press, 1984], 16). This representation of the desertscape edges into the sublime, on which see chapters 3 and 10.

33. Jane Tompkins, *West of Everything: The Inner Life of Westerns* (New York: Oxford University Press, 1992), 84.

34. Richard Slotkin, *Regeneration through Violence: The Mythology of the American Frontier, 1600–1800* (Norman: University of Oklahoma Press, 1973), *The Fatal Environment: The Myth of the Frontier in the Age of Industrialization, 1800–1890* (Norman: University of Oklahoma Press, 1985), and *Gunfighter Nation: The Myth of the Frontier in Twentieth-Century America* (Norman: University of Oklahoma Press, 1998). See also Tompkins, *West of Everything*, 76–85, on masculinity and the western landscape and 145–49 on Anglo-Saxon superiority; R. W. Connell, *Masculinities*, 2nd ed. (Berkeley: University of California Press, 2005) on masculinities in general, and 185–99 for a brief, rather superficial review of the development of Euro-American masculinities from c. 1500 CE to the present.

35. Aidan Tynan, *The Desert in Modern Literature and Philosophy: Wasteland Aesthetics* (Edinburgh: Edinburgh University Press, 2022), 7; see also his comment that the desert "resonates with a modern sense of dislocation" (94). It is perhaps only worth noting in a footnote that my book, like Tynan's, deals exclusively with Euro-American deserts and ideas about deserts. Deserts are global phenomena and hundreds if not thousands of human populations live in or around them and have their own views about what a desert is and how one relates to it. As I am about to note, in the Southwest there are plenty of Indigenous populations whose ideas about their space can be radically different from those of the Euro-American colonists who invaded their deserts. I'll deal with some aspects of this matter in the chapters that follow.

CHAPTER 2

1. Terry Dowling, *The Complete Rynosseros*, vol. 2 (Hornsea: PS Publishing Ltd., 2022), 572.

2. Kate Rigby, *Topographies of the Sacred: The Poetics of Place in European Romanticism* (Charlottesville: University of Virginia Press, 2004), 139, referring to European Romanticism. As we will see, mountains often embody sacrality for desert Native Americans.

3. Exod. 33:20–23; Athanasius, *Vita Antoni* 5, 5–6; Hari Kunzru, *Gods without Men* (New York: Alfred A. Knopf, 2012); George Adamski, "December Thirteenth: The Return Visit," and "The Memorable November Twentieth," in *Flying Saucers Have Landed*, eds. Desmond Leslie and George Adamski, 217–22 and 185–216

(London: Werner Laurie, 1953), also in George Adamski, *Inside the Space Ships* (New York: Abelard-Schuman, Inc. 1955), 55–60 and 23–54; Zane Grey, *Shower of Gold* (New York: Dorchester Publishing Co., Inc., 2007), and *The Light of Western Stars* (Rockville: Phoenix Rider, 2009); Richard Francaviglia, *Believing in Place: A Spiritual Geography of the Great Basin* (Reno: University of Nevada Press, 2003). For a discussion of desert tropes and changes in ideas about the desert in the Euro-American imaginary, see chapter 1.

4.   Edwin Bernbaum, *Sacred Mountains of the World*, 2nd ed. (Cambridge: Cambridge University Press, 2022), 6, 7, 9.

5.   Alex Schechter, "'The Place Where Shamans Dream': Safeguarding Spirit Mountain," *New York Times*, January 24, 2023.

6.   See T. Sole and K. Woods, "Protection of Indigenous Sacred Places: The New Zealand Experience," in *Sacred Sites, Sacred Places*, eds. David L. Carmichael, Jane Hubert, Brian Reeves, and Audhild Schanche (London: Routledge 1994), 342.

7.   Jane Hubert, "Sacred Beliefs and Beliefs of Sacredness," in *Sacred Sites, Sacred Places*, ed. David L. Carmichael, Jane Hubert, Brian Reeves, and Audhild Schanche (London: Routledge 1994), 11.

8.   https://www.thedesertway.com/cemeteries-etiquette/, accessed September 18, 2023.

9.   Hubert, "Sacred Beliefs," 13.

10. Willard Z. Park, *Shamanism in Western North America: A Study in Cultural Relationships* (Evanston: Northwestern University Press, 1938), 27–29, quotation at 29, bracketed phrase is Park's gloss.

11. Yi-Fu Tuan, *Topophilia: A Study of Environmental Perception, Attitudes, and Values* (with a new preface by the author) (New York: Columbia University Press, 1990), xi.

12. Ibid., 51–52.

13. John Brinckerhoff Jackson, *A Sense of Place, a Sense of Time* (New Haven: Yale University Press, 1994), 87.

14. David L. Carmichael, Jane Hubert, and Brian Reeves, "Introduction," in *Sacred Sites, Sacred Places*, ed. David L. Carmichael, Jane Hubert, Brian Reeves, and Audhild Schanche (London: Routledge 1994), 6; see also Deward E. Walker Jr., "Protection of American Indian Sacred Geography," in *Handbook of American Indian Religious Freedom*, ed. Christopher Vecsey (New York: Crossroads, 1993), 101: "Clearly sacred geography is a universal and essential feature of the practice of American Indian religions." On the Mescalero Apache, see David L. Carmichael, "Places of Power: Mescalero Apache Sacred Sites and Sensitive Areas," in *Sacred Sites, Sacred Places*, ed. David L. Carmichael, Jane Hubert, Brian Reeves, and Audhild Schanche, 89–98 (London: Routledge 1994).

15. R. S. McPherson, *Sacred Land, Sacred View: Navajo Perceptions of the Four Corners Region* (Provo: Brigham Young University, 1992), 11.

16. See https://sacredland.org/tools-for-action/, accessed May 18, 2022. This site, run by the Sacred Land Film Project, provides a much more extensive "Operational Definition" crafted in 2008, which calls sacred a "place in the landscape, occasionally over or under water, which is especially revered by a people, culture or cultural group as a focus for spiritual belief and practice and likely religious observance. In addition, to satisfy this stem definition and reflect its wide and rich variety, a sacred site must also have one or more of the following nineteen characteristics found under the headings: Descriptive, Spiritual, Functional and Other. Having more or less of these characteristics does not imply that the site is more or less sacred, but it may usefully reflect the complexity and rich variety of its sacred qualities." A list of the nineteen criteria follows. The Executive Order can be found at https://www.doi.gov/pmb/cadr/programs/native/Executive-Order-13007, accessed May 18, 2022. I cannot restrain myself from quoting a statement about sacred land from an Australian "lost race" novel of 1891 by W. Carlton Dawe: the protagonists, about to bury a dead companion, choose a place under a tree where the lost explorer Ludwig Leichhardt had carved his initial. "The spot," the narrator says, "seemed not so desolate as another, for there the white man had stood, that fact alone making the earth more sacred" (W. Carlton Dawe, *The Golden Lake: or, the Marvellous History of a Journey through the Great Lone Land of Australia* [Melbourne: E. A. Petherick Co., 1891], 103). In a landscape sacred from end to end to the Indigenous, this comes across as outrageous, racist blasphemy. In her study of UFOs and religion, D. W. Pasulka, *American Cosmic: UFOs, Religion, Technology* (New York: Oxford University Press, 2019), 76, writes: "The sites in New Mexico function as sacred sites for a new religion of the UFO event and . . . the religion of technology."

17. Walker, "Protection," 102–4, 101; Émile Durkheim, *The Elementary Forms of Religious Life: A Study in Religious Sociology*, trans. Karen Fields (New York: Free Press, 1995), 44 (Walker cites the 1915 translation by Joseph Ward Swain at p. 62).

18. In what is now California alone there were probably about 500 ethnic groups speaking almost ninety languages

belonging to twenty-three or more language families: Donna L. Gillette and Mavis Greer, "Spirituality in Rock Art Yesterday and Today: Reflections from the Northern Plains and Far Western United States," in *Rock Art and Sacred Landscapes*, eds. Donna L. Gillette, Mavis Greer, Michele Helene Hayward, and William Breen Murray (New York: Springer, 2014), 266; Victor Golla, *California Indian Languages* (Berkeley: University of California Press, 2022). Park, *Shamanism*, 2, stresses the "quite striking differences" in the character of shamanism throughout the Great Basin Desert. I treat briefly the problematics of "shamanism" below.

19. However, see the work of Christopher Ehret, *Ancient Africa: A Global History, to 300 CE* (Princeton: Princeton University Press, 2023) in reconstructing the deep African past, without written records, using archaeology, linguistics, oral tradition, ethnography, rock art, and other sources.

20. Ken Gelder and Jane M. Jacobs, *Uncanny Australia: Sacredness and Identity in a Postcolonial Nation* (Melbourne: Melbourne University Press, 1998), 116 and 120. Durkheim, *Elementary Forms*, drawing heavily on Walter Baldwin Spencer and Francis James Gillen, *The Native Tribes of Central Australia* (London: Macmillan and Co., Limited, 1899) and *The Northern Tribes of Central Australia* (London: Macmillan and Co., Limited, 1904), among others. Durkheim's basic argument is that the sacred, by its excessiveness, provides the glue that holds a society together. "Sacred objects," write Gelder and Jacobs, in a statement applicable to places too, "are otherwise ordinary things . . . which are marked in certain ways. Those markings are special. . . . The important point is that this significance always exceeds what it represents" (*Uncanny Australia*, 99). On Uluru, see Barry Hill, *The Rock: Travelling to Uluru* (St. Leonards: Allen & Unwin Pty Ltd., 1994); Tom Lynch, "From Handback to Landback: Lessons from Uluru," in *Storied Deserts: Reimagining Global Arid Lands*, eds. Celina Osuna and Aidan Tynan, 195–213 (London: Routledge).

21. Gelder and Jacobs, *Uncanny Australia*, 67–81 on Bula and 128–32 on Hindmarsh Island; 89–96 on the South Australia Museum, with additional examples.

22. Durkheim, *Elementary Forms*, 38, and 303 for "sacred beings" vs. "profane beings."

23. Mircea Eliade, *The Sacred and the Profane: The Nature of Religion*, trans. Willard R. Trask (New York: Harcourt, Brace World, Inc., 1987), 22. Eliade's analysis is marred by an uncompromising rigidity and bipolarity.

24. Richard H. Jackson and Roger Henrie, "Perception of Sacred Space," *Journal of Cultural Geography* 3 (1983), 94.

25. N. Scott Momaday, *House Made of Dawn* (New York: Harper Perennial Modern Classics, 2010), 108, italics in original.

26. On land as possessing "animacy," "vibrancy," or "agency," see chapter 10.

27. The desert in Melissa Broder, *Death Valley* (New York: Scribner, 2023), seems strikingly malevolent, too: the protagonist gets lost because the hiking trails she follows appear to change direction and aim; these transformations all but lead to her death.

28. Hubert, "Sacred Beliefs," 14; https://anglicantaonga.org.nz/news/tikanga_pakeha/130_years_on_chch_cathedral_ceases, accessed June 2, 2022.

29. Carmichael, "Places of Power," 93–94.

30. Yves Berger, *La pierre et le saguaro* (Paris: Bernard Grasset, 1990). Almost all of Berger's many books reflect his fascination with the American West: *Le Sud* (1962), whose protagonist dreams of a perfect American past in antebellum Virginia; *Le fou d'Amérique* (1976), with the 1978 translation noted above, which depicts a French doctor visiting the United States who falls passionately in love with an American woman and through her learns about the fate of the Indians; *Les matins du Nouveau Monde* (1987), built on an identification of the Allies in World War II with the Confederate Army of the Civil War, and the Axis with—the North of Lincoln (!); *L'attrapeur d'ombres* (1992), in which a possibly invented Nez Percé Indian surfaces to guide Berger through five national parks on a trip from Los Angeles to Salt Lake City; *Immobile dans le courant des fleuves* (1994); *Le monde après la pluie* (1997); and *Santa Fé* (2000); and a basketful of essays and photo albums, many dealing with the United States. For a brief but incisive critical discussion of his oeuvre through *L'attrapeur d'ombres*, see Michel Gueldry, "Yves Berger: de la quête poétique à la disparition du roman," *French Review* 68 (1995): 615–25. Chapter 3 examines Berger and some other French travelers in the American Southwest in more detail and from another angle.

31. Perhaps most notorious is the claim, made at the end of the book, that Berger participated in the burial of Abbey. As Gregory McNamee notes in his introduction to his English translation of these pages, Berger admitted to the editor of the *Journal of the Southwest* that he made it up: McNamee in Yves Berger, "The Burial of Edward Abbey," trans. Gregory McNamee, *Journal of the Southwest* 35 (1993), 357. A friend of mine who did in fact help bury Abbey dismissed Berger's confection with a succinct assessment: "bullshit."

32. Gueldry, "Yves Berger," 621, 623, 624.

33. Berger, *La pierre*, 80 (exaltation), 69 (Coronado), 66–68 (end of world), 63 (confusion), 62 (advance), 52 (silent day), 42 (immensity).

34. The role of film in shaping Berger's response to the desert is further explored in chapter 3.

35. Saul Kelly, *The Lost Oasis: The Desert War and the Hunt for Zerzura* (Boulder: Westview Press, 2000), 65, quoting, I think, a 1932 set of notes by Shaw preserved in the Harding Newman Papers at the Imperial War Museum, London. In Alexander MacDonald, *The Lost Explorers: A Story of the Trackless Desert* (London: Blackie and Son Limited, 1907), 246, however, a protagonist complains of "flies abusing his face."

36. On Adamski see chapter 8; Edward Abbey, *Desert Solitaire: A Season in the Wilderness* (New York: Simon and Schuster, 1968), 240 and 242; so also Ann Ronald, whose desert offers "a sanctuary for the human soul" (Ann Ronald, *The New West of Edward Abbey*, 2nd ed. [Reno: University of Nevada Press, 2000], 96). See the excellent essay of Laura Smith, "Resurrection after the 'Blue Death': Literature, Politics, and Ecological Redemption at Glen Canyon," *Western American Literature* 51 (2016): 45–46, 51–52.

37. Exod. 33:20–23; see chapter 1.

38. Angelucci, *Son of the Sun*, 114–15. See further in chapter 8 on deserts, space aliens, and UFOs. Pasulka, *American Cosmic*, 51, preparing to visit the site of an alleged UFO crash (perhaps Roswell?), confesses, "I had the uncanny feeling that the place was somehow conscious I was there." See further in chapter 10.

39. David Jasper, *The Sacred Desert: Religion, Literature, Art, and Culture* (Malden, MA: Blackwell, 2004), 75.

40. Melanie McGrath, *Motel Nirvana: Dreaming of the New Age in the American Desert* (New York: Picador, 1995), 15.

41. Francaviglia, *Believing in Place*, 123.

42. Oliver Wozencraft, "Through Northern Mexico in '49," *Californian* 6 (1882): 421–26, as retold by Edward Maddin Ainsworth, *Beckoning Desert* (Englewood Cliffs: Prentice Hall, 1962), 63–68 (quotation at 63); see William T. Vollmann, *Imperial* (New York: Penguin Books, 2009). The same illusion (delusion?) was experienced in the Australian desert by Charles Sturt, who fervently believed in an "inland sea" and saw in mirages confirmation of its existence: Charles Sturt, *Narrative of an Expedition into Central Australia, Performed under the Authority of Her Majesty's Government, during the Years 1844, 5, and 6* (London: T. and W. Boone, 1849), vol. 1, 24, 258, 272, 317–18, 323–24, 363, 382; vol. 2, 13, 63; cf. Edward John Eyre, *Journals of Expeditions of Discovery into Central Australia and Overland from Adelaide to King George's Sound, in the Years 1840–1* (London: T. W. Boone, 1845), vol. 2, 132–33, with Roslynn D. Haynes, *Seeking the Centre: The Australian Desert in Literature, Art, and Film* (Cambridge: Cambridge University Press, 1998), 70–71.

43. See chapter 4 for some aspects of this matter.

44. See Jon Tuska's introduction (at p. 3) in Grey, *Shower of Gold*.

45. Grey, *Shower of Gold*; Valerie Kuletz, *The Tainted Desert: Environmental and Social Ruin in the American West* (New York: Routledge, 1998); Richard Misrach, *Bravo 20: The Bombing of the American West* (Baltimore: Johns Hopkins University Press, 1990); Frank Bergon, *The Temptations of St. Ed and Brother S* (Reno: University of Nevada Press, 1993).

46. Nicole Brossard, *Le désert mauve* (Montreal: Typo, 2010) was translated into English by Susanne de Lotbinière-Harwood and published by Coach House Books in 2002. The original French version, which I have used, appeared in 1987, although I have consulted it in the 2010 reprint by Typo. All translations are my own; I was unable to consult Lotbinière-Harwood's translation.

47. Steve Erickson, *Amnesiascope: A Novel* (New York: Henry Holt and Company, 1996); John Fante, *Ask the Dust* (Santa Rosa: Black Sparrow Press, 1980). This inversion plays out in a different key in chapter 6 on Los Angeles.

48. Chapter 6, below.

49. See chapter 1.

50. https://www.grandcanyontrust.org/advocatemag/fall-winter-2020/voices-grand-canyon, accessed September 23, 2023. Paul A. Formisano, *Tributary Voices: Literary and Rhetorical Explorations of the Colorado River* (Reno: University of Nevada Press, 2022), 181–82, also cites this statement. He attributes to Enote the idea that the "petroglyphs on Zuni lands to the east and within the Grand Canyon . . . reaffirm the people's deep connection to these sacred places" (181). Surely true, although Enote does not explicitly say that, except for mentioning the "directional marker."

51. United States Bureau of Reclamation and Colorado River Basin Tribes Partnership, *Colorado River Basin Ten Tribes Partnership Tribal Water Study Report: Final Report* (Denver: U.S. Department of the Interior, Bureau of Reclamation, 2018), accessed September 21, 2023, https://usbr.gov/lc/region/programs/crbstudy/

tws/finalreport.html. 1, inset, "Vision Statement"; also quoted by Formisano, *Tributary Voices*, 176.

52. Formisano, *Tributary Voices*, 177 (quotation), 162–64. The superior relation of humans to the natural world infuses also the colonialist residue in environmental discourse that figures nature as a weak female in need of our protection—from dangerous dark races: see Suzana Sawyer and Arun Agrawal, "Environmental Orientalisms," *Cultural Critique* 45 (2000), 88–93.

53. Margaret L. Press, *Chemehuevi: A Grammar and Lexicon* (Berkeley: University of California Press, 1979) provides a grammar and lexicon of Chemehuevi, although her word-list is incomplete; briefly, Golla, *California Indian Languages*, 176–77. See also Kenneth M. Stewart, "A Brief History of the Chemehuevi Indians," *Kiva* 34 (1968): 9–27.

54. Carobeth Laird, *The Chemehuevis* (Banning, CA: Malki Museum, 1976), 119–22, 11–14 for the Mountain Sheep Song, 331 s.v. wa'yukʷaa'gaivʸa'. On names, chapter 7. For the songs of the Chemehuevi band at Twenty-Nine Palms, California, see Clifford E. Trafzer, *A Chemehuevi Song: The Resilience of a Southern Paiute Tribe* (Seattle: University of Washington Press, 2015).

55. Laird, *The Chemehuevis*, 33, 32, 38–39. Carmichael, "Places of Power," 92–93. Donald M. Bahr, Juan Gregorio, David I. Lopez, and Albert Alvarez, *Piman Shamanism and the Staying Sickness (Ká:cim Múmkidag)* (Tucson: University of Arizona Press, 1974), 184, Text 29; Frank Russell, *The Pima Indians*, re-edition with introduction, citation sources, and bibliography by Bernard L. Fontana (Tucson: University of Arizona Press, 1975), 254; Thomas C. O'Laughlin, "A Possible Dark Area Shrine in Chavez Cave, Doña Ana County, New Mexico," in *Climbing the Rocks: Papers in Honor of Helen and Jay Crotty*, eds. Regge N. Wiseman, Thomas C. O'Laughlin, Cordelia N. Snow, Helen K. Crotty, and Jay Crotty, 137–46 (Albuquerque: The Archaeological Society of New Mexico, 2003); John Greer and Mavis Greer, "Dark Zone Pictographs at Surratt Cave, Central New Mexico," in *Forward into the Past: Papers in Honor of Teddy Lou and Francis Stickney*, eds. Regge N. Wiseman, Thomas C. O'Laughlin, Cordelia N. Snow, and David M. Brugge, 37–46 (Albuquerque: The Archaeological Society of New Mexico, 2002) (who give several other examples); Marjorie Lambert and J. Richard Ambler, *A Survey and Excavation of Caves in Hidalgo County, New Mexico* (Santa Fe: The School of American Research, 1961), 11–21.

56. Harry J. Winters Jr., *'O'odham Place Names: Meanings, Origins, and Histories, Arizona and Sonora*, 2nd ed. (Tucson: SRI Press, 2020), 249 and 258–59. There is no straightforward English translation for *giwulik*; see further in chapter 7.

57. Ofelia Zepeda, *Where the Clouds Are Formed* (Tucson: University of Arizona Press, 2008), 15, 57–59, 66, 30. Much of "Do'ag Weco" is in O'odham; on Zepeda's use of it, see Angelica Lawson, "Resistance and Resilience in Ofelia Zepeda's *Ocean Power*," *The Kenyon Review* 32 (2010): 180–98. The members of the Tortugas pueblo in Las Cruces, New Mexico, conduct an annual pilgrimage in honor of the Virgin of Guadeloupe to Tortugas Mountain (also called A Mountain) not far east of the campus of New Mexico State University.

58. Luci Tapahonso, *Blue Horses Rush In* (Tucson: University of Arizona Press, 1997), 23.

59. The second two elements in the name may mean "white stand" according to A. L. Kroeber, "Seven Mohave Myths," *University of California Publications: Anthropological Records* 11 (1948), 63n118, but Pamela Munro, Nellie Brown, and Judith G. Crawford, *A Mojave Dictionary* (Los Angeles: Department of Linguistics, University of California, 1992), 148 s.v. nyamatham translate as "tomorrow"; they give nyamasav as "be white" (ibid.). There is no entry for *kuvatše* or anything similar.

60. https://www.blm.gov/Avi Kwa-ame-national-monument, accessed August 25, 2023. Kroeber, "Seven Mojave Myths," 63 I 80; David S. Whitley, *A Guide to Rock Art Sites in Southern California and Southern Nevada* (Missoula: Mountain Press Publishing Co., 1996), 128–31, Site 23. Munro, Brown, and Crawford, *A Mojave Dictionary*, 123, give no translation for kwa'ame, writing only "in Avi Kwa'ame, Saly'ay Kwa'ame," meaning "sandy kwa'ame," a place at the north end of the Chemehuevi Valley (160 s.v.). They give for "spirit" *iimaat kwiisa* (287 s.v.). From a New Age, shamanistic perspective, see Nicholas Clapp, *Old Magic: Lives of the Desert Shamans* (San Diego: Sunbelt Publications, 2017), 125–28.

61. John Peabody Harrington, "A Yuma Account of Origins," *Journal of American Folk-Lore* 21 (1908): 326–27. Harrington identifies the jimson as *Datura meletoides*, but this name is now obsolete. Which species of *Datura* Tsuyukweráu was referring to is impossible now to determine, but all have alkaloids with psychoactive effects. See chapter 8 n69 and chapter 6 n57. For Kumastamxo's birth, Harrington, "Yuma Account," 331, with Harrington's Latin paraphrase of the circumstances of his conception: the woman didn't get how children were conceived, so "[i]n order that the virgin understand well, he himself showed her what must be done. For he lay on the ground with her and copulated four times. The woman, sweating greatly, wiped the sweat off four times with her hands." Harrington transcribes the rough Germanic *ch* sound as "x" whereas Kroeber

used "h." Thus Kumastamxo is Kumastamho; the tie with Mastamho is obvious.

62. Mountains are sacred all over the world. See, for example, Veronica Della Dora, *Mountain: Nature and Culture* (London: Reaktion Books, 2016), 27–71, and Bernbaum, *Sacred Mountains*.

63. Lauren Redniss, *Oak Flat: A Fight for Sacred Land in the American West* (New York: Random House, 2020), 116–20, 122–23. The sacredness of the Colorado River is stressed by the Colorado River Indian Tribes and the Cocopah—the latter especially poignantly—in the otherwise dry 2018 final report on water allocation to Indigenous tribes along the river: United States Bureau of Reclamation and Colorado River Basin Tribes Partnership 2018, 5.8.3, 5.8.5.3, and 5.10.3. The "Cocopah (Kwapa) are known as river people, but there is no river left. They have had a centuries old way of life taken from them." See Formisano, *Tributary Voices*, 178–79.

64. David S. Whitley, "Finding Rain in the Desert: Landscape, Gender, and Far Western North American Rock-Art," in *The Archaeology of Rock-Art*, eds. Christopher Chippendale and Raul S. C. Taçon, 11–29 (Cambridge: Cambridge University Press, 1998), 13.

65. David S. Whitley, Joseph M. Simon, and Ronald I. Dorn, "The Vision Quest in the Coso Range," *American Indian Rock Art* 25 (1999), 17–25; Caroline Boyd, *The White Shaman Mural* (Austin: University of Texas Press, 2016). In her interpretation the central, large white figure is not a shaman but the Moon Goddess (86–89, 139–42). Whitley, *A Guide to Rock Art Sites*, 28–33, largely rejects any explanations for rock art other than the shamanistic. His view has been vigorously disputed by Paul G. Bahn, *Prehistoric Rock Art: Polemics and Progress: The 2006 Rhind Lectures for the Society of Antiquaries of Scotland* (Cambridge: Cambridge University Press, 2010), whose case seems much the better to me.

66. Leslie Spier, *Yuman Tribes of the Gila River* (New York: Dover Publications, 1978), 238.

67. Dean Saxon, Lucille Saxon, and Susie Enos, *Dictionary: Tohono O'odham/Pima to English. English to Tohono O'odham/Pima*, 2nd ed. (Tucson: University of Arizona Press, 1983), 39 s.v. mahkai; Bahr, Gregorio, Lopez, and Alvarez, *Piman Shamanism, passim*; Russell, *The Pima Indians*, 256–57.

68. Laird, *The Chemehuevis*, 31; Whitley, Simon, and Dorn, "Vision Quest," 9. Although Willard Zerbe Park accepts "shamanism" as a reasonable designation for the holding of power among the Indigenous people of the West and canvasses the view that migrants from Asia to North America brought the practice with them, he insists "we are dealing with a locally varying amalgam of historically heterogeneous traits" (Park, *Shamanism*, 2, 8–10 for his definition of the shaman).

69. Jack S. Harris, "The White Knife Shoshoni of Nevada," in *Seven American Indian Tribes*, ed. Ralph Linton (New York: Appleton-Century, 1940), 57, on the White Knife Shoshoni of Nevada. Peter Nabokov, *Where the Lightning Strikes: The Lives of American Indian Sacred Places* (New York: Penguin, 2006), 234, insists "it was in dreams, particularly the all-powerful *Sumach Ahot*, or 'Great Dreams,' that the lower Colorado Indians lived to the fullest."

70. William H. Kelly, *Cocopa Ethnography* (Tucson: University of Arizona Press, 1977), 73–74, 15, Fig. 7 for the location of Mayor Peak. Among the Cahuilla, power could be congenital or passed on by a *puul*, but dreams were the main source: Lowell John Bean, *Mukat's People: The Cahuilla Indians of Southern California* (Berkeley: University of California Press, 1972), 109.

71. See chapter 5 for a more nuanced discussion of gender.

72. Spier, *Yuman Tribes*, 236–41 (dreams generally), 244 (quotation), 243–44 (jimsonweed). On jimsonweed use among the Cahuilla, A. L. Kroeber, *The Ethnography of the Cahuilla Indians* (Berkeley: The University Press, 1908), 65–66. The Piipaash and Halychduum peoples, both of whom originally lived on the Colorado River and migrated later to the Middle Gila River (in the thirteen century CE for the Piipaash, around 1827–1830 for the Halychduum), consolidated as the Maricopa. Both spoke Piipaash Chuukwer, and so I treat the toponyms attested for the Maricopa under both. See Winters, *Maricopa Place Names*, xxxii and xxxv.

73. Polly Schaafsma has been indefatigable in elucidating the history of Tlaloc's migrations: see Polly Schaafsma, "Tlalocs, Kachinas, Sacred Bundles, and Related Symbolism in the Southwest and Mesoamerica," in *The Casas Grandes World*, eds. Curtis Schaafsma and Carroll L. Riley, 164–92 (Salt Lake City: University of Utah Press, 1999) and "Tláloc y las metáforas para hacer llover en el Suroeste de Estados Unidos," *Arqueología Mexicana* 96 (2009): 48–51. Michael Mathiowetz, Polly Schaafsma, Jeremy Coltman, and Karl Taube, "The Darts of Dawn: Tlahuizcalpantecuhtli Venus Complex in the Iconography of Mesoamerica and the American Southwest," *Journal of the Southwest* 57 (2015), 44, note the role of rain-making in the Venus warfare complex that entered the Southwest in the Pueblo IV Period (1300–1598 CE), during "tectonic shifts in social, cultural, and religious life" (see *Religious Transformation in the Late Pre-Hispanic Pueblo World*, eds. Donna M. Glowacki and Scott Van Keuren [Tucson: University of Arizona Press, 2011]). Polly Schaafsma, *Rock Art of New Mexico* (Albuquerque: University of Mexico Press, 1992), 64, on the Tlaloc figure as a "hallmark" of the

Jornada style of southern New Mexico, which started around 1000 CE (60), with 71 Fig. 88. On Mt. Tlaloc, see Richard F. Townsend, "The Renewal of Nature at the Temple of Tlaloc," in *The Ancient Americas: Art from Sacred Landscapes*, ed. Richard F. Townsend, (Chicago: The Art Institute of Chicago, 1992), 173 and 174–75 Fig. 4. On Tlaloc iconography, Schaafsma, "Tlalocs," 177.

74. Tsikomo: Polly Schaafsma and Karl A. Taube, "Bringing the Rain: An Ideology of Rain Making in the Pueblo Southwest and Mesoamerica," in *A Pre-Columbia World: Searching for a Unity Vision of Ancient America*, eds. Jeffrey Quilter and Mary Miller (Washington, DC: Dumbarton Oaks, 2006), 242–45, 265 (Kor'koshi), 262 (Hueco Tanks, which is a Texas state park and historical site: https://tpwd.texas.gov/state-parks/hueco-tanks, accessed August 26, 2022; see also Schaafsma, "Tlalocs," 179, and especially Polly Schaafsma, "Petitions for Rain: Textile and Pottery Designs in Rock Art," *International Letter on Rock Art* 66 (2013), 20), and generally on mountains, 233–35. Kachinas: Schaafsma, "Tlalocs," 171–75. The Pueblo world underwent massive cultural and religious transformations around 1300, a change of which the emergence of *kachinas* was a fundamental part: see Polly Schaafsma, "Visión del mundo e identidad: el arte rupestre en el Suroeste de los Estados Unidos (950–1450 DC)," *Anales de antropología* 44 (2010), 180; Schaafsma and Taube, "Bringing the Rain," 261; Glowacki and Van Keuren, eds., *Religious Transformations*. It seems likely that the Great Drought of 1276–1299 CE, which was one phase of a long period of climatic instability and drought running from 1130 to 1300 CE and precipitated the depopulation of the Four Corners region, would have induced the Ancestral Pueblo population to seek newer and more reliable means of ensuring precipitation for their crops. See Donna M. Glowacki, *Living and Leaving: A Social History of Regional Depopulation in Thirteenth-Century Mesa Verde* (Tucson: University of Arizona Press, 2015), 39–41, on the climate, and especially her observation that the differing responses to the Great Drought and the earlier megadrought of 1130–1180 CE must be explained by "social and cultural differences . . . which in one case allowed people to continue living in the region and in the other prompted widespread emigration" (41).

75. Caves on mountains: Schaafsma, "Tlalocs," 167–71. Greer and Greer, "Dark Zone Pictographs," 38 and 43, Surratt Cave (see also Schaafsma, "Tlalocs," 181); O'Laughlin, "A Possible Dark Area Shrine," 142–43 with Figure 5, Chavez Cave; Lambert and Ambler, *A Survey and Excavation*, 16–17, 83, U-Bar Cave. Mount Taylor: Schaafsma, "Tlalocs," 173.

76. Schaafsma and Taube, "Bringing the Rain," 231.

77. For instance, Greer and Greer, "Dark Zone Pictographs," 39 and 41. For cracks as pathways to the other world in Siberian and Central Asian shamanism, Andrzej Rozwadowski, "Sun Gods or Shamans? Interpreting the 'Solar-Headed' Petroglyphs of Central Asia," in *The Archaeology of Shamanism*, ed. Neil S. Price (London: Routledge, 2001), 74–75, "Disappearing into the Rock: Shamanistic Aspects of Indo-Iranian Mythology as a Context for Interpreting Central Asian Petroglyphs," in *Spirits and Stones: Shamanism and Rock Art in Central Asia and Siberia*, eds. Andrzej Rozwadowski and Maria M. Kośko (Posnań: Instytut Wschodni Uam, 2002), 64–67, for the transformation of an animal as it passes through a crack, and "Crossing the Crack, Flying to the Cloud: Indo-Iranians, Shamanism and Central Asian Rock Art," *Bolletino del Centro Camuno preistorici* 33 (2002), 101–2, and "Disappearing into the Rock." On rock slits representing vulvas, see chapter 5.

78. See Kristina Milnor, *Gender, Domesticity, and the Age of Augustus: Inventing Private Life* (Oxford: Oxford University Press, 2005), 34–36. On the idea that space can have "agency," see chapter 10.

79. Eris Williams Reed, "Environments and Gods: Creating the Sacred Landscape of Mount Kasios," in *Sacred Landscapes in Antiquity: Creation, Manipulation, Transformation*, eds. Ralph Häussler and Gian Franco Chiai (Oxford: Oxbow Books, 2020), 88.

80. J. D. Lewis-Williams and T. A. Dowson, "The Signs of All Times: Entoptic Phenomena in Upper Paleolithic Art," *Current Anthropology* 29 (1988): 201–17; for a recent defense of their approach, Jean Clottes, *What Is Paleolithic Art? Cave Paintings and the Dawn of Human Creativity*, trans. Oliver Y. Martin and Robert D. Martin (Chicago: University of Chicago Press, 2016); also J. David Lewis-Williams, "Rock Art and Shamanism," in *A Companion to Rock Art*, eds. Jo McDonald and Peter Veth (Malden, MA: Wiley-Blackwell, 2012) (with abundant references to earlier literature) and, for another context, place, and time, Boyd, *The White Shaman Mural*. Bahn, *Prehistoric Rock Art*, 76–80 and *passim*.

81. Park, *Shamanism*, is a classic example.

82. Alice Beck Kehoe, *Shamans and Religion: An Anthropological Exploration in Critical Thinking* (Long Grove: Waveland Press, 2000) for an excellent explication. Clapp, *Old Magic* treats the shamanic theory as established; see especially 59, 81–157. His book does provide an abundance of excellent photographs of rock art and Indigenous healers (all called "shamans" by him).

CHAPTER 3

1. Belonging to a wholly different category is Philippe Frey, *America deserta* (Paris: Robert Laffont, 1977), 63–72). His account of his time in Death Valley recounts merely the heat and lack of water; he seems unencumbered by ideological baggage and is far more interested in the lifeways of the Indigenous peoples than Western concepts about the desert. In reading French literature I have usually first consulted translations if available, except for Jean-François Lyotard, *Le mur du Pacifique* (Paris: Éditions Galilée, 1979), available in English as *Pacific Wall*, trans. Bruce Boone (Venice: Lapis, 1989). Yves Berger, *La pierre et le saguaro* (Paris: Bernard Grasset, 1990) has never been translated.

2. On "mediated" and "unmediated" touristic experience, see Gary Reger, "In the Dark without a Light: Understanding Unmediated Sites of Dark Tourism," in *Dark Tourism in the American West*, ed. Jennifer Dawes (London: Palgrave Macmillan, 2020), 183–84.

3. For an overview, see Charles Sowerwine, *France Since 1870: Culture, Politics and Society*, 3rd ed. (London: Red Globe Press, 2018), 216–62, 275–315.

4. Gamila Morcos, "*Mobile* de Butor: typographie et justification," *Australian Journal of French Studies* 18 (1981): 56–76, on Butor's arrangement of text on the page.

5. Lyotard, *Le mur*; for an intellectual biography, see Kiff Bamford, *Jean-François Lyotard* (London: Reaktion Books, 2017).

6. Jean Baudrillard, *America*, trans. Chris Turner (London: Verso, 1988), 28–29; Marco Diani, "The Desert of Democracy, from Tocqueville to Baudrillard," *L'éspirit créateur* 30 (1990), 71: "Baudrillard went [to America] to experience a predetermined social theory." See also Joan Kirby, "'The Noble Savage as Continent': A Review of Baudrillard's *America*," *Australasian Journal of American Studies* 9 (1990), 71. But readings of *America* are all over the place: consider the vastly different commentaries (just by way of example) of Donald Wesling, "The Representational Moment in the Discourse of Nations: Jean Baudrillard's *America*," *Hungarian Journal of English and American Studies* 4 (1998): 9–19, and Élodie Laügt, "America in Time: Aphoristic Writing in Jean Baudrillard's *America*," *Paragraph* 35 (2012): 338–54. *America* as a sort of mirror: what you see in it is what you bring to it, or, as Baudrillard himself warns on the very first page, "Caution: Objects in this mirror may be closer than they appear!"

7. See my treatment of Berger from another angle in chapter 2.

8. Bernard-Henri Lévy, *American Vertigo: Traveling America in the Footsteps of Tocqueville*, trans. Charlotte Mandell (New York: Random House, 2006).

9. On French colonial experience in the Sahara, see Douglas Porch, *Conquest of the Sahara* (New York: Farrar, Straus & Giroux, 1984); Benjamin Claude Brower, *A Desert Named Peace: The Violence of France's Empire in the Algerian Sahara, 1844–1902* (New York: Columbia University Press, 2009) on Algeria, and Michèle Salinas, *Voyages et voyageurs en Algérie, 1830/1930* (Toulouse: Éditions privats, 1989) on French travelers in Algeria. Michel Roux, *Le désert de sable: le Sahara dans l'imaginaire des Français (1900–1994)* (Paris: L'Harmattan, 1996) is excellent on the French desert imaginary.

10. Eugène Fromentin's *Un été dans le Sahara: Voyage dans les oasis au Sud algérien in 1853* (Paris: Éditions France-Empire, 1992) appeared originally in the *Revue de Paris* in the June–December 1854 issues. Fromentin also wrote about his time in the region around Algiers (then called the Sahel, which now refers to the southern edge of the Sahara) in *Une année dans le Sahel* (1859), available in translation as Eugène Fromentin, *Between Sea and Sahara: An Algerian Journal*, trans. Blake Robinson (Athens: Ohio University Press, 1999). Guy Barthélemy, *Fromentin et l'écriture du désert* (Paris: L'Harmattan, 1997) for an analysis of Fromentin's desert writings, and Patrick Tudoret, *Fromentin: le roman d'une vie* (Paris: Les belles lettres, 2018) for a recent study. In Fromentin's time "Sahel" referred to the Mediterranean littoral, not, as today, to the semi-arid belt on the south boundary of the Sahara. "Sahel" comes from the Arabic *sāḥil*, "shore, littoral," so today's Sahel is the southern "shore" of the Sahara Desert.

11. Fromentin, *Un été*, 29. Remo Bodei remarks perceptively that "Less noted is the fact that Eugène Fromentin . . . inaugurated the time of the 'romanticism of the desert'" (Remo Bodei, *Paessagi sublimi: gli uomini davanti alla natura selvaggia* [Milan: Bompiani, 2008], 221n30).

12. See the excellent observation of Anne-Marie Christin, "Space and Convention in Eugène Fromentin: The Algerian Experience," trans. Richard M. Berrong, *The New Literary History* 15 (1984), 566.

13. André Gide, *Amyntas: North African Journals*, trans. Richard Howard (New York: The Echo Press, 1988), 49. For a good review of Gide's desert-related writing, see Uwe Lindemann, *Die Wüste: Terra incognita, Erlebnis, Symbol. Eine Geneaologie der abendlandischen Wüstenvorstellungen in der Literatur von der Antike bis zur Gegenwart* (Heidelberg: C. Winter, 2000), 175–86.

14. David W. Teague, *The Southwest in American Literature and Art: The Rise of a Desert Aesthetic* (Tucson: University of Arizona Press, 1997) was a pioneer.
15. Simone de Beauvoir, *America Day by Day*, trans. Carol Cosman (Berkeley: University of California Press, 1999), 155.
16. Ibid., 155, 152.
17. Ibid., 155–56. Although she does not write about any of the works I discuss in this essay, I have found much evocative of deserts in Hélène Cixous, *Readings: The Poetics of Blanchot, Joyce, Kafka, Keist, Lispector, and Tsvetaeva*, ed. and trans. Verena Anderman Conley (Minneapolis: University of Minnesota Press, 1991), 110–51.
18. On the impact of roadbuilding on desert landscapes, read in a very different way from Beauvoir's happy delight in a reassuring humanness, see Jada Ach, "Desert Roads, 'Construction Men,' and Infrastructural Impulses in Cather's *The Professor's House*," in *Reading Aridity in Western American Literature*, eds. Jada Ach and Gary Reger, 117–40 (Lanham, MD: Lexington Books, 2020).
19. Michel Foucault, *Discipline and Punish: The Birth of the Prison*, trans. Alan Sheridan (New York: Vintage Books, 1995). Baudrillard, *America*, 31, remarks sardonically on "the Californian scholars with monomaniacal passions for things French and Marxist."
20. Simeon Wade, *Foucault in California: [A True Story Wherein the Great French Philosopher Drops Acid in the Valley of Death]* (Berkeley: Heyday, 2019), 31–32.
21. Ibid., 47–48, 41, 53, 54.
22. Ibid., 55.
23. Baudrillard, *America*, 66–67, for all quotations in this paragraph.
24. Berger, *La pierre*, 84–85.
25. Lyotard, *Le mur*, 59–60.
26. Ibid., 3.
27. Berger, *La pierre*, 36.
28. Baudrillard, *America*, 29–30.
29. Berger, *La pierre*, 28.
30. Ibid., 42, 80. Likewise Eugène Fromentin found himself, on his first real experience of the Sahara Desert while camped at an oppressive marsh, "plunged into a singular dejection" due to the country which was "a great formless thing, practically without color, a nothing, an emptiness [*vide*], like something forgotten by the good God" (*Un été*, 54). The 49er William Manly had just the same impression of Death Valley (William L. Manly, *Death Valley in '49: The Autobiography of a Pioneer* [Crabtree: The Narrative Press, 2001], 111); see chapter 4. The trope about the desert as abandoned by God explains its emptiness in part by his retreat; see chapter 1.
31. Lyotard, *Le mur*, 47–49. His feelings for Los Angeles evoke Reyner Banham's "pedestrian litterateur" who visits LA and "stays only long enough to collect material for a hate-novel" (*Los Angeles: The Architecture of Four Ecologies* [New York: Harper Row, Publishers,1971], 243). On the desert "underneath it all" in some writing about Los Angeles, see chapter 6.
32. Beauvoir, *America Day by Day*, 151, both quotations.
33. Lévy, *American Vertigo*, 123, emphasis in the original.
34. Until independence in 1962, however, Algeria was formally a *département* of France. On the gendered contrast between tamed agricultural landscapes and the desert, see chapter 4.
35. Amy Clary, "Mark Twain in the Desert," *Journal of Ecocriticism* 3 (2011): 29–39. See also Bill Kennedy Shaw's racist revulsion at crowded urban Cairo and praise of the empty Sahara in chapter 2.
36. Kyle Bladow and Jennifer Ladino, "Toward an Affective Ecocriticism: Placing Feeling in the Anthropocene," in *Affective Ecocriticism: Emotion, Embodiment, and the Environment*, eds. Kyle Bladow and Jennifer Ladino (Lincoln: University of Nebraska Press, 2018), 1–8.
37. In general, Robert Doran, *The Theory of the Sublime from Longinus to Kant* (Cambridge: Cambridge University Press, 2015); Timothy M. Costelloe, ed., *The Sublime from Antiquity to the Present* (Cambridge: Cambridge University Press, 2012); on desert sublimity, Bodei, *Paessagi sublimi*, 127–41, but he has nothing to say about the American Southwest. For Greek and Roman ideas about the sublime, which served as a basis for the Romantic sublime, see James I. Porter, *The Sublime in Antiquity* (Cambridge: Cambridge University Press, 2016); Kate Rigby, *Topographies of the Sacred: The Poetics of Place in European Romanticism* (Charlottesville: University of Virginia Press, 2004), 156, on the European Romantics and mountain sublime. I discuss the sublime in a very different context in Gary Reger, *First There Is a Mountain* (forthcoming), chapter 8.

38. Berger, *La pierre*, 15, ellipses in original except for the first and second, and 78–79, quoting Lawrence in Berger's French translation. I have not been able to identify the source of this quotation. For a recent exhibition of Western art that evokes the sublime, see Katie Graff, ed., *The Western Sublime: Majestic Landscapes of the American West* (Tucson: Tucson Museum of Art, 2019).

39. Baudrillard, *America*, 71, 68.

40. Butor, *Mobile*, 122, italics in original.

41. Dean MacCannell, *The Ethics of Sightseeing* (Berkeley: University of California Press, 2011), 76.

42. Baudrillard, *America*, 68, 70, 121, and 127 also celebrates the prismatic colors of the desert.

43. Berger, *La pierre*, 25–26 and 34–35 on the mesas of the Hopis.

44. Baudrillard, *America*, 68.

45. Jean-Philippe Mathy, *Extrême-Occident: French Intellectuals and America* (Chicago: University of Chicago Press, 1993), 171. See Richard Slotkin, *Gunfighter Nation: The Myth of the Frontier in Twentieth-Century America* (Norman: University of Oklahoma Press, 1998) and Teague, *The Southwest*, on the desert's role in "purifying" and "restoring" American manhood in the arid West.

46. Kyoko Matsunaga, "Trinitite, Turquoise, and Rattlesnakes: Envisioning the (De)Nuclearized Desert in the Works of Leslie Marmon Silko and Kyoko Hayashi," in *Reading Aridity in Western American Literature*, eds. Jada Ach and Gary Reger, 195–221 (Lanham, MD: Lexington Books, 2020).

47. Berger, *La pierre*, 79–81, for both quotations.

48. Barbara Buhler Lynes, Lesley Poling-Kempes, and Frederick W. Turner, *Georgia O'Keeffe and New Mexico* (Princeton: Princeton University Press, 2004), 11–49. On the sexual imagery in the floral paintings, see Mae Miller Claxton, "'Untameable Texts': The Art of Georgia O'Keeffe and Eudora Welty," *The Mississippi Quarterly* 56 (2003), 319–22, but also the comments and references in Matsunaga, "Trinitite," 216n20. (O'Keeffe herself consistently rejected this reading of her floral paintings.) Berger, *La pierre*, 81–82, for his quoting O'Keeffe.

49. Berger, *La pierre*, 82, is probably referring to "Cow's Skull, Red, White, and Blue" (1931): Barbara Buhler Lynes, *Georgia O'Keeffe: Catalogue raisonné* (New Haven: Yale University Press, 1999), vol. 1, 468–69 no. 773, in the Metropolitan Museum of Art.

50. Lynes, Poling-Kempes, and Turner, *Georgia O'Keeffe*, 20–27; Lynes, *Catalogue raisonné*, vol. 1, 580–81 no. 931 and 2, 630–31 no. 998. Other paintings of O'Keeffe's that illustrate the same themes include "New Mexican Landscape" (1930), "Hill, New Mexico" (1935), "My Backyard" (1937), and "The Cliff Chimneys" (1938): Lynes, *Catalogue raisonné*, vol. 1, 446 no. 732; 1, 540 no. 872; 1, 580–81 no. 932; and 1, 597 no. 955.

51. Matsunaga, "Trinitite," 196 and 199.

52. Berger, *La pierre*, 64–65, first and last ellipses in original. The actual elevation of El Paso is 1,134 meters or 3,720 feet.

53. Beauvoir, *America Day by Day*, 157, 201, 157 (twice).

54. Baudrillard, *America*, 1.

55. Ibid., 56.

56. Ibid., 101. Briefly, Laügt, "America in Time," 342–43.

57. Borrowed from Frey, *America deserta* and Richard Poirier, "America deserta," *London Review of Books* 11, 4 (1989): 3–6, who both no doubt allude to Peter Reyner Banham, *Scenes in America Deserta* (Cambridge: MIT Press, 1982), who in turn lifted his title from Charles M. Doughty, *Travels in Arabia Deserta*, 2 vols. (New York: Dover Publications, 1979), originally published in 1888.

58. Kirby, "The Noble Savage," 71; Baudrillard, *America*, 5 and 7. See Diani, "The Desert of Democracy," 68.

59. Lyotard, *Le mur*, 59–60.

60. Baudrillard, *America*, 50.

61. Lyotard, *Le mur*, 59–60 and 49.

62. Baudrillard, *America*, 6. See also Bruce Begout, *Zeropolis: The Experience of Las Vegas*, trans. Liz Heron (London: Reaktion Books, 2004) and Amy Hamilton, "Imagined Deserts, Planned Communities, and Escape Pods in the American West," in *Reading Aridity in Western American Literature*, eds. Jada Ach and Gary Reger, 21–43 (Lanham, MD: Lexington Books, 2020); Jada Ach, *Sand, Water, Salt: Managing the Elements in Literature of the American West, 1880–1925* (Lubbock: Texas Tech University Press, 2021), 70–71, and "Desert Roads, 'Construction Men,' and Infrastructural Impulses in Cather's *The Professor's House*," in *Reading Aridity in Western American Literature*, eds. Jada Ach and Gary Reger (Lanham, MD: Lexington Books, 2020), 117–40, on another kind of gaze and network of roads—leading only to "the wasteland" made by human beings. Paolo Bacigalupi, *The Water Knife* (New York: Alfred A. Knopf, 2015) conjures up another

vision of Las Vegas cut off from its desert environment, with its arcologies and bubbling fountains.

63. On automobiles and the desert, see Ach, "Desert Roads."

64. See the excellent pages in Tom Lynch, *Xerophilia: Ecocritical Explorations in Southwestern Literature* (Lubbock: Texas Tech University Press, 2008), 177–226, and Celina Osuna, "Color, Place, and Memory in Silko's *Gardens in the Dunes*," in *Reading Aridity in Western American Literature*, eds. Jada Ach and Gary Reger, 223–42 (Lanham, MD: Lexington Books, 2020), which examines the sensuousness of the desert in Leslie Marmon Silko's *Gardens in the Dunes*.

65. Berger, *La pierre*, 14.

66. Ibid., 17.

67. Ibid., 51–52, 79 (emphasis in original because he uses the English word), 109–10. The importance of these pages to Berger is suggested by his decision to include them in an excerpt from his book in the *Revue des deux Mondes* (March 1990), 144–51. Also Baudrillard, *America*, 6.

68. Baudrillard, *America*, 34. On the embodiment of emotions treated with an ecocritical bent, see the essays in Bladow and Ladino, eds., *Affective Ecocriticism*.

69. Butor, *Mobile*, 9–10, quoting Natt N. Dodge and Herbert S. Zim, *The Southwest: A Guide to the Wide Open Spaces* (New York: Golden Press, 1955), 7, italics in original. On desert "vibrancy," an active agency, see Ach, *Sand, Water, Salt*, 2, and chapter 10.

70. For instance, Cecilia Montes-Alcalá, "Code-Switching in US Latino Literature: The Role of Biculturalism," *Language and Literature* 24 (2015): 264–21; Rosina Lozano, *An American Language: The History of Spanish in the United States* (Berkeley: University of California Press, 2018): Spanish as a properly American language, no less than English.

71. Shelley Fisher Fishkin, "Crossroads of Cultures: The Transnational Turn in American Studies—Presidential Address to the American Studies Association, November 12, 2004," *American Quarterly* 57 (2005), 27–28, calling for the embrace of Spanish *and French*. In Anaya 1992 the narrator sometimes translates for the reader—"'Cuídate,' she said. Be careful" (37)—and sometimes— "Qué vida, pero es todo lo que tenemos" (43)—not. See Hamilton, "Imagined Deserts," for discussion of another aspect of *Alburquerque*. And see my brief remarks on Spanish language literature in chapter 1.

72. See Rachel St. John, *Line in the Sand: A History of the Western U.S.-Mexico Border* (Princeton: Princeton University Press, 2011).

73. Fishkin, "Crossroads of Cultures;" Wai Chee Dimock, "Introduction: Planet and America, Set and Subset," in *Shades of the Planet: American Literature as World Literature*, eds. Wai Chee Dimock and Lawrence Buell, 1–16 (Princeton: Princeton University Press, 2007); see also David Rio and Christopher Conway, "Guest Editors' Introduction: The Case for Transnationalism in the American Literary West," *Western American Literature* 54 (2019): ix–xiv. The essays in Ignacio M. Sánchez Prado, ed., *Mexican Literature as World Literature* (New York: Bloomsbury Academic, 2022) make a collective case for Mexican literature as world literature.

74. A Special Forum in volume 9 (2018) examines "Globalization and American Literature," including an article by Lori Merish arguing for the transnational status of Native American literature (Lori Merish, "Mapping the Transnational in Native American Fiction: Silko and Welch," *Journal of Transnational American Studies* 9 [2018]: 339–58). The call for "building cases for various individuals and groups hitherto marginalized by American cultural and political authority to be considered as urgent participants in United States culture-making" (Bryce Traister, "The Object of Study; or, Are We Being Transnational Yet?" *Journal of Transnational American Studies* 2, no. 1 [2010]) could be a call to examine my French writers, too.

75. Susan Weiner, "*Terre à terre*: Tocqueville, Aron, Baudrillard, and the American Way of Life," *Yale French Studies* 100 (2001), 23. And Baudrillard, *America*, 28: "It may be that the truth of America can only be seen by a European, since he alone will discover here the perfect simulacrum—that of immanence and material transcription of all values." See also Kirby, "The Noble Savage," 71: Baudrillard's is a "love affair . . . with America as the absolute anti-Europe."

76. Alexis de Tocqueville, *Democracy in America*, trans. Harvey T. Mansfield (Chicago: University of Chicago Press, 2002), for a recent translation. Harvey C. Mansfield, *Tocqueville: A Very Short Introduction* (Oxford: Oxford University Press, 2010) provides a fine introduction to Tocqueville and pointers to some of the massive bibliography; Hugh Brogan, *Alexis de Tocqueville: A Life* (New Haven: Yale University Press, 2007) for an exhaustive biography.

77. Baudrillard, *America*, 75–76, 88, 95–96, and 108, with Diani, "The Desert of Democracy," 70–71; Lévy, *American Vertigo*, 3–7.

78. Max Lerner, *Tocqueville and American Civilization* (London: Transaction Publishing, 1994), 84.

79. See Quinn Grover, "Aridity, Individualism, and Paradox in Elmer Kelton's *The Time It Never Rained*," in *Reading Aridity in Western American Literature*, eds. Jada Ach and Gary Reger, 45–66 (Lanham, MD: Lexington Books, 2020) and Ach, *Sand, Water, Salt*, 136–55.

80. Lerner, *Tocqueville*, 84 and 88.

81. Traister, "The Object of Study," 2010.

82. A brief overview of French views of the United States can be found in Stephen J. Whitfield, "From Modernization to Post-Modernism: A Century and a Half of French Views of the United States," *Revista española de estudios norteamericanos* 9 (1995); more expansively, Mathy, *Extrême-Occident*, 1993.

CHAPTER 4

1.   Heike Schaefer, *Mary Austin's Regionalism: Reflections on Gender, Genre, and Geography* (Charlottesville: University of Virginia Press, 2004), 48. Some of the research for the paper on which this chapter is based was conducted during a sabbatical leave from my position at Trinity College. I came to the views argued here before I had the benefit of reading Catrin Gersdorf, *The Poetics and Politics of the Desert: Landscape and the Construction of America* (Amsterdam: Rodopi, 2009), whose sharp book's chief aim is to "investigate the cultural and discursive processes of how the desert, once a foreign territory and a topography unfamiliar to America's agrarian imagination, was incorporated into the conceptual borders of America and American nationality" (24).

2.   Annette Kolodny, *The Lay of the Land: Metaphor as Experience and History in American Life and Letters* (Chapel Hill: University of North Carolina Press, 1975), 150: "[T]he experiential reality of a particular object . . . the inherently feminine reality of the vast American landscape. The quality of that experience is variously expressed through an entire range of images, each of which details one of the many elements of that experience, including eroticism, penetration, raping, embrace, enclosure, and nurture. . . . Together, they make up a mutually interrelating and integrated whole, and it is this whole which the phrase 'the land-as-woman' is meant to assert."

3.   Robert Johnson, "Nova Britannia, Offering Most Excellent Fruites by Planting in Virginia," in *Tracts and Other Papers, Relating Principally to the Origin, Settlement and Progress of the Colonies of North America, from the Beginning of the Country to the Year 1776*, vol. 1, ed. Peter Force (Washington, DC: Printed by Peter Force, 1836), 11; Robert Mountgomry, "A Discourse Concerning the Design'd Establishment of a New Colony to the South of Carolina," in *Tracts and Other Papers, Relating Principally to the Origin, Settlement and Progress of the Colonies of North America, from the Beginning of the Country to the Year 1776*, vol. 1, ed. Peter Force (Washington, DC: Printed by Peter Force, 1836), 6; Robert Beverley, *The History and Present State of Virginia*, ed. Louis B. Wright (Chapel Hill: University of North Carolina Press, 1947), 298; Kolodny, *The Lay of the Land*, 10–12. This trope slipped sometimes into pure pornography, as in the essays discussed by Darby Lewes, "Nudes from Nowhere: Pornography, Empire, and Utopia," *Utopian Studies* 4 (1993): 66–73.

4.   Lynn Ross-Bryant, "The Land in American Experience," *Journal of the American Academy of Religion* 58 (1990), 337; Loren Baritz, *City on a Hill* (New York: Wiley, 1964), 261. However, the Puritan response to the land was not unambiguous, as Ross-Bryant argues; for them the New World could also represent the "howling wilderness" in which lurked the devil. This trope was applied likewise to the desert; see below.

5.   F. Scott Fitzgerald, *The Great Gatsby* (New York: Scribner, 2004), 180.

6.   Ralph Waldo Emerson, *The Annotated Emerson*, ed. David Mikics (Cambridge: The Belknap Press, 2012), 39; see Louise H. Westling, *The Green Breast of the New World: Landscape, Gender, and American Fiction* (Athens: University of Georgia Press, 1996), 43. Randolph Stow deploys the same image of Australia as woman, taken by the colonizing male, in his poem "Endymion" (which also inverts the classical myth): Randolph Stow, *Outrider: Poems, 1956–1962* (London: Macdonald Co. [Publishers], 1962), 36.

7.   Simon Ortiz, *Woven Stone* (Tucson: University of Arizona Press, 1992), 117. See below for more examples.

8.   Some further examples of this trope in Carolyn Merchant, *Reinventing Eden: The Fate of Nature in Western Cultures* (New York: Routledge, 2003), 119–23.

9.   Kolodny, *The Lay of the Land*, 4. Central to the working out of this trope in American thought are also Henry Nash Smith, *Virgin Land: The American West as Symbol and Myth* (New York: Vintage Books, 1950) and Leo Marx, *The Machine in the Garden: Technology and the Pastoral Ideal in America* (Oxford: Oxford University Press, 2000).

10. Already in James Fenimore Cooper and Washington Irving the Great American Desert was seen "as far too arid, wild, savage, and intractable a place for agrarian settlement by yeoman farmers. Rather, the territory

exerts its pressure on weaker natures to drive them downward toward savagery": Richard Slotkin, *The Fatal Environment: The Myth of the Frontier in the Age of Industrialization, 1800–1890* (Norman: University of Oklahoma Press, 1985), 119.

11. William L. Manly, *Death Valley in '49: The Autobiography of a Pioneer* (Crabtree: The Narrative Press, 2001), 141; cf. other examples at 65–66, 70 ("the most wonderful picture of grand desolation one could ever see"), 71, 76, 79 ("the most God-forsaken country in the world"), 80 ("The home of the poorest man on earth was preferable to this place"), 84 ("this grand, but worthless landscape"—quoted by Franklin Walker, *A Literary History of Southern California* [Berkeley: University of California Press, 1950], 48), etc. The passage is a favorite quotation: David W. Teague, *The Southwest in American Literature and Art: The Rise of a Desert Aesthetic* (Tucson: University of Arizona Press, 1997), 24, and Patricia Nelson Limerick, *Desert Passages: Encounters with the American Deserts* (Albuquerque: University of New Mexico Press, 1985), 55, for instance.

12. Maria Hargrove Shrode, "Overland by Ox-Train in 1870: From Sulphur Springs, Texas, to San Diego, California," *Quarterly Publication of the Historical Society of Southern California* 26 (1944), 10; Schaefer, *Mary Austin's Regionalism*, 70.

13. Margaret Walker, "Booking West: Tall Tales and 'Books of Every Sort and Size' from Fanny Hill to the Bible," *Overland Journal* 50 (2007), 150–51. On biblical desert tropes, see George H. Williams, *Wilderness and Paradise in Christian Thought: The Biblical Experience of the Desert in the History of Christianity and the Paradise Theme in the Theological Idea of the University* (New York: Harper Brothers, 1962), 3–27; Uwe Lindemann, *Die Wüste: Terra incognita, Erlebnis, Symbol: Eine Geneaologie der abendlandischen Wüstenvorstellungen in der Literatur von der Antike bis zur Gegenwart* (Heidelberg: C. Winter, 2000), 63–79; Laura Feldt, "Wilderness and Hebrew Bible Religion—Fertility, Apostasy and Religious Transformation in the Pentateuch," in *Religion and Society, Wilderness in Mythology and Religion: Approaching Religious Spacialities, Cosmologies, and Ideas of Wild Nature*, eds. Laura Feldt, Gustavo Benavides, and Kocku von Stuckrad, 55–94 (Berlin: De Gruyter, 2012). See chapter 1.

14. Frederick Law Olmstead, *A Journey Through Texas, or, a Saddle Trip on the Southwestern Frontier, with a Statistical Appendix* (New York: Dix, Edwards, & Co., 1857), 450. A view shared by Alfred R. Calhoun, who worked as an agent for the Kansas and Pacific Railroad planning track through the desert: Alfred R. Calhoun, *The Letters of Alfred R. Calhoun: The Mojave Desert, 1867–1868*, ed. John N. Marnell (Goffs: Tales of the Mojave Road Publishing Company, 2011), 77: "For two hundred miles beyond the Colorado the country is a desert and comparatively worthless" (letter originally published in 1868).

15. James Fowler Rusling, *The Great West and Pacific Coast* (New York: Shelton, 1877), 344–46.

16. Josephine Clifford, *Overland Tales* (San Francisco, 1877), 299; Horace Bell, *Reminiscences of a Ranger: Early Times in Southern California* (Norman: University of Oklahoma Press, 1999), 437, 432.

17. John Wesley Powell, *Report on the Lands of the Arid Region of the United States, With a More Detailed Account of the Lands of Utah* (Cambridge: Harvard Commons Press, 1983) is his classic report; on his life, see Donald Worster, *A River Running West: The Life of John Wesley Powell* (New York: Oxford University Press, 2002).

18. The transformation was hardly limited to the desert; as Richard White observes, in but thirty years the transcontinental railroads shifted America's orientation from north-south to east-west. Growth of railroad mileage was spectacular, from 4,461 to 7,961 miles in the five years between 1879 and 1884 in the American West, and to 3,645 miles in northern Mexico by 1885: Richard White, *Railroaded: The Transcontinentals and the Making of Modern America* (New York: W. W. Norton, 2011), xxiv, cf. xxviii–xxxi, 203.

19. On the Southern Pacific expansion across the desert, see Richard Orsi, *Sunset Limited: The Southern Pacific and the Development of the American West* (Berkeley: University of California Press, 2005), 19–22; quotation: Henry T. Williams, ed., *Pacific Tourist: Adams and Bishop's Illustrated Trans-Continental Guide of Travel, from the Atlantic to the Pacific Ocean: A Complete Traveler's Guide of the Union and Central Pacific Railroads* (New York: Adams and Bishop, 1881), 161, 172. And more: Pilot's Peak, near Terrace, was "a noted landmark for many a weary pilgrim across the desert" (172); for Butler Ives, the CP engineer, White, *Railroaded*, 142–43. On Fred Harvey: Steve Fried, *Appetite for America: Fred Harvey and the Business of Civilizing the Wild West—One Meal at a Time* (New York: Random House, 2010); the "Harvey girls" are examined, perhaps a bit romantically, in Lesley Poling-Kempes, *The Harvey Girls: The Women Who Opened the West* (Boston: De Capo Press, 1994); and see Richard Melzer, *Fred Harvey Houses of the Southwest* (Mount Pleasant, SC: Arcadia Publishing, 2008) for historical photographs of Harvey Houses. Even a commentator like Charles F. Lummis who bemoaned the ease of railroad travel across the desert confessed its transformative effects: see Gersdorf, *The Poetics and Politics of the Desert*, 124–25.

20. White, *Railroaded*, 51–54; Daniel Lewis, *Iron Horse Imperialism: The Southern Pacific of Mexico* (Tucson:

University of Arizona Press, 2007) on the Southern Pacific's penetration of Mexico.

21. Richard Lingenfelter, *Bonanzas and Borrascas, Volume 2: The Copper Kings and Stock Frenzies, 1885–1918* (Norman: University of Oklahoma Press, 2012); between 1864 and 1911, forty-one railroads were founded in Arizona alone: G. W. Irvin, "A Sequential History of Arizona Railroad and Mining Development," in *History of Mining in Arizona*, eds. J. M. Canty and M. N. Greeley (Tucson: Mining Club of the Southwest Foundation, 1991), 253–58.

22. The Oatman story was popularized in the exaggerated and partly fictionalized account by R. B. Stratton, *Captivity of the Oatman Girls: Being an Interesting Narrative of Life Among the Apache and Mohave Indians* (New York: Printed for the Author, 1858); one of the girls died in captivity but her sister Olive, "rescued," pined away for her Mohave husband and never readjusted to "civilized life." I recount the Oatman story in chapter 9. For the Apache Wars, see David Roberts, *Once They Moved Like the Wind: Cochise, Geronimo, and the Apache Wars* (New York: Simon and Schuster, 1994), with 141 on the death of Cochise and 306–15 on Geronimo at Fort Sill, Oklahoma; Terry Mort, *The Wrath of Cochise: The Bascom Affair and the Origins of the Apache Wars* (New York: Pegasus Books, 2013); Paul Andrew Hutton, *The Apache Wars: The Hunt for Geronimo, the Apache Kid, and the Boy Who Started the Longest War in American History* (New York: Broadway Books, 2016).

23. James W. Byrkit, "Land, Sky, and People: The Southwest Defined," *Journal of the Southwest* 34 (1992): 342–52, treats all these changes; he sees 1884 as the year of essential transformation. For a response to Byrkit, Michael J. Riley, "Constituting the Southwest, Contesting the Southwest, Reinventing the Southwest," *Journal of the Southwest* 36 (1994): 231–41. This change lay in part behind John C. Van Dyke's revision of the desert imaginary; see chapter 1.

24. It's unsure whether, before the flood that created the Salton Sea, the basin there might have been even lower than Death Valley.

25. The story of Western irrigation has been told many times; to my mind Donald Worster, *Rivers of Empire: Water, Aridity, and the Growth of the American West* (New York: Oxford University Press, 1985) still offers the best account, although his controlling thesis has been pretty universally rejected; see George L. Henderson, *California and the Fictions of Capitalism* (New York: Oxford University Press, 1999), 231n1. Also excellent: Mark Reisner, *Cadillac Desert: The American West and Disappearing Water*, revised and updated (New York: Penguin Books, 1993). One of the earlier proposals appeared in J. P. Widney, "The Colorado Desert," *Overland Monthly and Out West Magazine* 10 (1873): 44–50. I borrow the tagline "the desert disappears" from William T. Vollmann, *Imperial* (New York: Penguin, 2009), 119.

26. Ellen Lloyd Trover, *Birth of the Inland Sea: How the Colorado River Created the Salton Sea* (Coachella: History Trove, 2018), with lots of photos; Traci Brynne Voyles, *The Settler Sea: California's Salton Sea and the Consequences of Colonialism* (Lincoln: University of Nebraska Press, 2021), 55–85; brief discussions appear in Orsi, *Sunset Limited*, 226–32; Henderson, *California*, 176–79. The engine of development was the California Land Company, an outfit in which soon attracted investments from the likes of Harry Chandler.

27. John C. Van Dyke, *The Desert: Further Studies in Natural Appearances* (New York: Charles Scribner's Sons, 1901). Van Dyke dropped Carnegie's name with some frequency: see John C. Van Dyke, *The Open Spaces: Incidents of Nights and Days under the Blue Sky* (New York: C. Scribner's Sons, 1922), 203–8. See chapter 1 for more thorough treatment of Van Dyke and the desert, especially the possible origins of his desert aesthetics.

28. Anonymous, "The Desert" [review of Van Dyke, *The Desert*], *New York Tribune*, February 8, 1902.

29. Walker, *A Literary History*, 185–89; David W. Teague and Peter Wild, *The Secret Life of John C. Van Dyke: Selected Letters* (Reno-Las Vegas: University of Nevada Press, 1997), 3. See also Limerick, *Desert Passages*, 91–94; Teague, *The Southwest*, 127–44. David Jasper, *The Sacred Desert: Religion, Literature, Art, and Culture* (Malden, MA: Blackwell, 2004), 74–75, classes Van Dyke among those who "[i]n the early years of the twentieth century . . . in the United States were beginning to recognize the ecological necessity of preserving the interior desert." But Van Dyke's arguments are aesthetic, not ecological, except perhaps his remark about deserts as the "breathing spaces of the west" (*The Desert*, 59).

30. Frederick Turner, *Genesis: An Epic Poem of Terraforming Mars* (Spokane Valley: Ilium Press, 1988), II, v, 2–10 (p. 123).

31. Teague and Wild, *The Secret Life*, unmask Van Dyke's actual situation and behavior. He left New Jersey in haste because he'd fathered a child on the wife of a faculty colleague. He also may have been in the pay of Andrew Carnegie to track down a union organizer and deliver threats. Again, see chapter 1.

32. Harold Bell Wright, *The Winning of Barbara Worth* (Chicago: Book Supply Co., 1911), 63. William T. Vollmann repeatedly quotes this sentence in mockery: Vollmann, *Imperial*, 161, 162, 186, 1159.

33. Although something of a local hero in Imperial County—the Pioneers Park Museum in Imperial, California, has devoted an entire corner of its second-floor exhibit to a shrine, displaying photographs, Wright's writing desk, manuscript pages from *The Winning of Barbara Worth*, and other memorabilia—and in his own day a well-respected, best-selling writer, Wright has suffered something of an eclipse in literary criticism circles. Many studies focus on his "The Shepherd of the Hills," which attracts attention in part because it has enjoyed a revival in the theaters of Branson, Missouri. Otherwise, the few critical works attending to *Barbara Worth* that I know include Henderson, *California*, 182–95, who offers a subtle reading of sexual politics justified by and in turn justifying capitalist capture of the desert; Lawrence V. Tagg, *Harold Bell Wright* (Boise: Boise State University Press, 1994); Fritz H. Oehlschlager, "Civilization as Emasculation: The Threatening Role of Women in the Frontier Fiction of Harold Bell Wright and Zane Grey," *Midwest Quarterly* 22 (1981): 346–60. Vollmann, *Imperial*, is entirely hostile and often sarcastic; his disdain, unfortunately, has prevented his seeing the value of the book for understanding the social and cultural world of the early twentieth-century Imperial Valley.

34. Wright, *Barbara Worth*, 12. The "rude trail" echoes Olmstead's judgment of the only value that could possibly accrue from the Colorado Desert. Wright, *Barbara Worth*, offers a thorough description of desert desolation at 32–38; more at 46, 48, 50, etc.

35. Wright, *Barbara Worth*, 27, 30.

36. Ibid., 43.

37. Ibid., 64.

38. Compare Mary Austin's explicit evocation of desert-as-woman, "deep-breasted, broad in the hips, tawny, with tawny hair, great masses of it lying smooth along her perfect curves": Mary Austin, *The Land of Little Rain* (New York: Modern Library, 2003), 69; or Terry Tempest Williams, who sees in desert dunes "[s]ensuous curves—the small of a woman's back. Breasts. Buttocks, hips and pelvis. They are the natural shapes of Earth": Terry Tempest Williams, *Refuge: An Unnatural History of Family and Place* (New York: Vintage, 2001), 109. See also Simon Ortiz's poem about the body of his lover quoted in this chapter and Edgar Rice Burroughs's evocation of Dejah Thoris, princess of desert Mars, treated in chapter 9.

39. Wright, *Barbara Worth*, 65, 70, 71–72 (emphasis in original; see also 78), 73–74; Willard too takes one look at her and "felt as did the Seer that somehow she was like the desert" (79).

40. Dale R. Randall, "The 'Seer' and the 'Seen': Themes in Gatsby and Some of their Parallels in Eliot and Wright," *Twentieth Century Literature* 10 (1964): 56–62, explores the theme of the "seer" and the "seen" in Wright's *The Eyes of the World* (1914), a best-seller that influenced F. Scott Fitzgerald, but without any mention of *The Winning of Barbara Worth*. It is notable, however, that Wright treats his main female character, who is drawn with every virtue, as "nothing less than unspoiled Nature incarnate" (58). Wright's expatiation on the theme of "pure nature" in both books points up its importance in his work.

41. William E. Smythe, *The Conquest of Arid America*, new and revised ed. (New York: The Macmillan Company, 1905), the great bible of the reclamationists; Wright, *Barbara Worth*, 82 (emphasis in original).

42. Water evokes "the liquid discharges of sex" (Kolodny, *The Lay of the Land*, 75, 112), of course, but the flood (which is based on the real Colorado flood of 1905–1906 when the river burst a poorly constructed weir and roared into the Imperial Valley; the Salton Sea is its lasting calling card) constitutes in its violent disorder not a fertilization but a rape. The men responsible hate the desert; for them it is only a source of wealth; they lack all understanding. Voyles, *The Settler Sea*, 55–85, on the creation of the sea.

43. Wright, *Barbara Worth*, 508, 509–10 (emphasis in original).

44. Westling, *The Green Breast*, 52.

45. Pat Mora, *Chants* (Houston: Arte Público Press, 1984), 8, and see chapter 10, where the whole stanza this line is in is quoted.

CHAPTER 5

1. Scholarly output on gender has been copious and continues to grow. I benefitted enormously from the advice of Lisa Tatonetti and her *Written by the Body: Gender Expansiveness and Indigenous Non-Cis Masculinities* (Minneapolis: University of Minnesota Press, 2022). A few resources: Charlotte Witt, *The Metaphysics of Gender* (Oxford: Oxford University Press, 2011), Laura Kramer and Ann Beutel, *The Sociology of Gender: A Brief Introduction*, 4th ed. (Oxford: Oxford University Press, 2014), and the wide-ranging collection *Gender in Cross-Cultural Perspective*, eds. Caroline B. Brettell and Carolyn F. Sargent (London: Routledge, 2017).

2. Frances Gillmor, *Fruit Out of Rock* (New York: Duell, Sloan and Pierce, 1940). The canyon is now a wilderness

area under the Bureau of Land Management: https://www.blm.gov/visit/aravaipa-canyon-wilderness, accessed May 11, 2022.

3. Or, as a contemporary reviewer said, their love was "probably intended as the symbol of two conflicting ways of life" (*Saturday Review of Literature*, September 14, 1940, 20). *Fruit Out of Rock* has fallen into a pervasive neglect, it would seem. Aside from a few trenchant pages in Vera Norwood, "Crazy-Quilt Lives: Frontier Sources for Southwestern Women's Literature," in *The Desert Is No Lady: Southwestern Landscapes in Women's Writing and Art*, eds. Vera Norwood and Janice Monk, 74–95 (Tucson: University of Arizona Press, 1987), 88–90, and a short chapter in Whitehill's biography (Sharon Whitehill, *Frances Gillmor: Aztec and Navajo Folklorist* [Lewiston: Edward Mellon Press, 2005], 209–18, without reference to Norwood), I have not found any secondary or critical literature on it. The novel went unmentioned by either the interviewer or Gillmor herself in a 1985 conversation published in 1990 (David Johnson, "Frances Gillmor," in *This Is About Vision: Interviews with Southwestern Writers*, eds. William Balassi, John F. Crawford, and Annie O. Eysturoy, 27–39 [Albuquerque: University of New Mexico Press, 1990]) and was not listed in the bibliography accompanying the interview. Gillmor had begun work on the novel by 1932; a first draft, completed in 1936, was deemed unacceptable by her publisher Houghton Mifflin, an assessment with which she agreed, and she went to work on revision—which she found difficult—during a stay in Mexico City in 1937. Finished the next year, the book was again refused by a series of publishers until her friend Erskine Caldwell suggested at a New Year's party at the end of 1939 that she try Duell, Sloan, and Pearce, who quickly took the book on the condition of a few minor changes which Gillmor gladly accepted. The final version was completed in Mexico City by May and appeared in August 1940; see Whitehill, *Frances Gillmor*, 162, 189, 193, 209–11.

4. As we've seen in chapters 1 and 4.

5. Annette Kolodny, *The Lay of the Land: Metaphor as Experience and History in American Life and Letters* (Chapel Hill: University of North Carolina Press, 1975). Whitehill, *Frances Gillmor*, 143, stresses Gillmor's love of the desert, whose space, remoteness, and distance gave the opportunity to create and act freely. See chapter 4 for another instance of the same theme, and chapter 1 on desert tropes.

6. Gillmor, *Fruit Out of Rock*, 182, 163, 169–70.

7. Ibid., 157, 26–28; this "remarkably sensuous passage" noted also in Whitehill, *Frances Gillmor*, 212–13. For other examples of the link between the canyon and Amanda's sexuality, see Gillmor, *Fruit Out of Rock*, 167–68, 197–99. Compare the less graphic but analogous role of bathing naked in a desert canyon stream for Thea in *The Song of the Lark* (Willa Cather, *The Song of the Lark* [London: John Murray, 1916], 299 and especially 304, with Martha Cutter, *Unruly Tongue: Identity and Voice in Women's Writing, 1850–1930* [Jackson: University of Mississippi Press, 1999], 185: Panther Canyon as a "vulva-like gorge") and, in a desert oasis, Genie in Zane Grey's *Wanderer of the Wasteland* (New York: Harper & Brothers, 1923, 356, with William Bloodworth, "Zane Grey's Western Eroticism," *South Dakota Review* 26 [1985], 6–9). Norwood, "Crazy-Quilt Lives," 89, however, reads this episode as "Amanda seek[ing] self forgetfulness in the natural environment . . . merging with the place, matching her rhythms to those of the canyon": an accomplishment, I would argue, that underlines the sexual identification of Amanda and the canyon. Commenting on some other bathing scenes, Lynch suggests they might "function as baptisms into belonging, as cleansings of the guilt of America's original sin, the theft of Indian land" (Tom Lynch, *Outback and Out West: The Settler-Colonial Environmental Imaginary* [Lincoln: University of Nebraska Press, 2022], 245). Another instance occurs in Sharman Apt Russell's memoir, when she and her companions bathe in a warm spring in the Gila Mountains: Sharman Apt Russell, *Songs of the Fluteplayer: Seasons of Life in the Southwest* (Reading: Addison-Wesley Publishing Company, Inc., 1991), 118–19; see Lynch, *Outback and Out West*, 243–44.

8. The "grotto" proliferates with "maidenhair ferns" (Gillmor, *Fruit Out of Rock*, 187); the visit: Gillmor, *Fruit Out of Rock*, 140.

9. Gillmor, *Fruit Out of Rock*, 193, 195, 65, 206, 164, 110, 118.

10. Willa Cather, *Death Comes for the Archbishop* (Lincoln: University of Nebraska Press, 1999), 32; David Siddel, "Goats, Marginality and the 'Dangerous Other,'" *Environment and History* 15 (2009): 527–31, phrase at 527; on initiation, see Julio Caro Baroja, *The World of Witches* (Chicago: University of Chicago Press, 1987), 85–87. The association of goats with male sexuality is so widespread that it even recurs in Norse mythology: see Kristina Jennbert, "Sheep and Goats in Norse Paganism," in *PECUS: Man and Animal in Antiquity*, ed. Barbro Santillo Frizell (Rome: The Swedish Institute in Rome, 2004), 164. As a folklorist, Gillmor surely knew the reputation of goats.

11. Gillmor, *Fruit Out of Rock*, 93, 95, 164, 206, 227, 102, 167–68, 63, 169–70.

12. Ibid., 208, 102.

13. Ibid., 214 (ditch and fence), 206 (grotto), 213–14 (cutting trees), 73 (desert again).

14. Ibid., 211–14.

15. Austin, *The Land of Little Rain*, 50, with Vera Norwood, *Made from This Earth: American Women and Nature* (Chapel Hill: University of North Carolina Press, 1993), 49, 51.

16. Gillmor, *Fruit Out of Rock*, 12; Whitehill, *Frances Gillmor*, 216.

17. Ibid., 172–95.

18. Ibid., 12, 179. Molybdenum is an interesting choice; not gold, silver, or even copper (see chapter 4 and Fig. 4-5), molybdenum's chief value lies in its ability to temper steel against high temperatures, demanded by use in military applications like aircraft and armor.

19. Gillmor, *Fruit Out of Rock*, 12–13 (Amanda plans to drive herself into town), 32 (John objects; before he'd left he did the driving: 29–30), 130 (Amanda drives anyway), 40–41 (Miguel hired and John's closet cleaned out, place at table), 185 (Tom Dent, whom she kisses at 189, John pronounces "A good guy, Tom—").

20. Gillmor, *Fruit Out of Rock*, 20 (wren and snake), 21 (quotation about trees), 103–11, 114–16, 118–19 (planting), 22–24, 182 (Bane's mining claim), 24, 211 ("up the canyon as far as I could go"). Bane's house-dwelling bull snake recalls the rattlesnakes that live under and around Leslie Marmon Silko's desert house: *The Turquoise Ledge: A Memoir* (New York: Viking, 2010), 82–83. Joan Didion, in stark contrast, grew up under a rule that you kill any rattlesnake you see: see Alice Levick, *Memory and the Built Environment in 20th-Century American Literature: A Reading and Analysis of Spatial Forms* (London: Bloomsbury Academic, 2021), 74–75, 85.

21. Gillmor, *Fruit Out of Rock*, 103–6, 109–11, quotations at 103, 105.

22. Compare the insistence of Howard, the experienced prospector in *The Treasure of the Sierra Madre* (1948), on the responsibility to repair the damage to the mountain he and his companions caused in digging out their gold. See Mark A. Cheetham and Elizabeth D. Harvey, "Obscure Imaginings: Visual Culture and the Anatomy of Caves," *Journal of Visual Culture* 1 (2002), 108.

23. Gillmor, *Fruit Out of Rock*, 19. In 1940 "queer" already carried the implication of "homosexual" in a derogatory sense: see *OED*, s.v. 3, which dates the first such usage in the US to 1914.

24. And we should bear in mind Istvan Csicsery-Ronay Jr.'s remark in his discussion of the female and the grotesque in science fiction: "To identify all interior spaces as exclusively feminine may appear reductive and essentializing, but the reproductive and metamorphic uses to which many caves and grottos are put illustrates the presence of the mythological charge . . . in the grotesque" (*The Seven Beauties of Science Fiction* [Middletown: Wesleyan University Press, 2008], 194).

25. Cather, *Death Comes*, 134; Sandra M. Gilbert and Susan Gubar, "Sexual Linguistics, Gender Language, Sexuality," *New Literary History* 16 (1985), 531–32; Klaus B. Stich, "Cather's 'Midi Romanesque': Missionaries, Myth, and the Grail in *Death Comes for the Archbishop*," *Studies in the Novel* 38 (2006), 65, with Deborah Lindsay Williams, "Losing Nothing, Comprehending Everything: Learning to Read Both the Old World and the New in *Death Comes for the Archbishop*," in *Cather Studies 4: Willa Cather's Canadian Old World Connections*, eds. Robert Thacker and Michael A. Peterman, 80–96 (Lincoln: University of Nebraska Press, 1999), 85 on "the strong, devouring femaleness of the cavities and orifices"; see also John Beck, *Dirty Wars: Landscape, Power, and Waste in Western American Literature* (Lincoln: University of Nebraska Press, 2009), 186.

26. Simon Ortiz, *Woven Stone* (Tucson: University of Arizona Press, 1992), 47, 57. It's not irrelevant that Ortiz's Acoma nation is matrilineal; gender and sexuality play out beyond the confines of a Euro-American duality. I have more to say about this below.

27. The point was made to me in the question-and-answer period after my presentation of the earlier draft of this paper (cited in n. * above) by an audience member whose name I do not know and so cannot properly thank here.

28. Richard Pollay, "'Below the Belt' Cigarette Advertising," *Tobacco Control* 4 (1995): 188–92, reads a Marlboro cigarette advertisement showing a canyon and river as a representation of sexual intercourse.

29. Kessel Schwartz, "Makbara—Metaphysical Metaphor or Goytisolian World Revisited?" *Hispania* 67 (1984), 38; N. Scott Momaday, *House Made of Dawn* (New York: Harper Perennial Modern Classics, 2010), 56–58, 48.

30. Ellen Moers, *Literary Women* (Garden City: Doubleday & Co., Inc., 1976), 254–58, with references. For an interesting commentary on Moers's discussion of female sexual topography, see Ellen Pollak, "'Postlude' to 'Literary Women,'" *Signs* 24 (1999): 739–47; Susan Hawthorne, *The Falling Woman* (North Melbourne: Spinifex, 1992), 251–52, with Tom Lynch, "Literature in the Arid Zone," in *The Littoral Zone: Australian*

Contexts and their Writers, eds. C. A. Cranston and Robert Zeller (Leiden: Brill Academic, 2007), 83.

31. Amanda's love for Stephen is tempered by her disdain for his goats; asked whether "You think maybe they'll [her family] come to love the goats?" she answers sharply, "No—" (Gillmor, *Fruit Out of Rock*, 232–33). Her realization that the baby is what really matters comes at the end of the book, when she tells her mother she's pregnant (the passage is quoted below), 268.

32. Gillmor, *Fruit Out of Rock*, 228.

33. Suzana Sawyer and Arun Agrawal, "Environmental Orientalisms," *Cultural Critique* 45 (2000), 79.

34. Whitehill, *Frances Gillmor*, 202, 219–25, quotation at 213.

35. Ibid., 97–99, quotations at 98.

36. Letter dated April 27, 1930, quoted in Whitehill, *Frances Gillmor*, 146.

37. Whitehill, *Frances Gillmor*, 145–46, for Buzan and Clark's comment. The neighbor who watched their strolls speculated that Joe was the model for Abel Bane (340n560). Whitehill's information comes from personal interviews (see 331nn381 and 382). Is it too literalist (or too Freudian) to suppose that Amanda and Stephen's sex act represents for Gillmor either a memory or a wish?

38. Audre Lorde, *Sister Outsider: Essays and Speeches* (Freedom: Crossing Press, 1984), 88.

39. Gillmor, *Fruit Out of Rock*, 28.

40. Ibid., 91, 92.

41. Ibid., 230, 268.

42. Ibid., 227, for example.

43. Ibid., 32 (working man), 168 (Maren).

44. Ibid., 268.

45. R. W. Connell, *Masculinities*, 2nd ed. (Berkeley: University of California Press, 2005) remains a fine introduction with brief remarks on masculinity and the West at 194–95. He lists concisely the elements of heteronormative Euro-American masculinity at 90; see also 21–27 on the notion of the "masculine role." On gender as a social category, see Ásta, *Categories We Live By: The Construction of Sex, Gender, Race and Other Social Categories* (Oxford: Oxford University Press, 2018).

46. See chapter 2 on neuter space.

47. For an examination of the complexities of gender in Native American societies, see Tatonetti, *Written by the Body*; see also *Indigenous Men and Masculinities: Legacies, Identities, Regeneration*, eds. Robert Alexander Innes and Kim Alexander (Winnipeg: University of Manitoba Press, 2015); Jack Halberstam, *Female Masculinity* (Durham: Duke University Press, 1998); Sabine Lang, "Native American Men-Women, Lesbians, Two-Spirits: Contemporary and Historical Perspectives," *Journal of Lesbian Studies* 20 (2016): 299–323; Deborah A. Miranda, "Extermination of the *Joyas*: Gendercide in Spanish California," *GLQ: A Journal of Lesbian and Gay Studies* 16 (2010): 253–84; Wesley Thomas, "Navajo Cultural Constructions of Gender and Sexuality," in *Two-Spirit People: Native American Gender Identity, Sexuality, and Spirituality*, eds. Sue-Ellen Jacobs, Wesley Thomas, and Sabine Lang, 156–73 (Urbana: University of Illinois Press, 1997).

48. A. H. Grayton, "Yokuts and Western Mono Ethnography," *University of California Anthropological Records* 10 (1948), 58–59; F. Latta, *Handbook of the Yokuts Indians*, 2nd ed. (Santa Cruz: Bear State Books, 1977), 185; David S. Whitley, "Finding Rain in the Desert: Landscape, Gender, and Far Western North American Rock Art," in *The Archaeology of Rock-Art*, eds. Christopher Chippindale and Raul S. C. Taçon, 11–29 (Cambridge: Cambridge University Press, 1998), 18. Among the Mohave, "red" is the female color, "black" the male: George Devereux, "Institutionalized Homosexuality of the Mohave Indians," *Human Biology* 9 (1937), 502.

49. Whitley, "Finding Rain in the Desert," 22–23; Philip Drucker, "Culture Element Distributions XVII: Yuman-Piman," *University of California Anthropological Records* 6 (3) (1941), 163; A. L. Kroeber, "Mojave Clairvoyance: Ethnographic Interpretations 1–6," *University of California Publications in American Archaeology and Ethnography* 47 (2) (1957), 229. Tom Robbins, *Wild Ducks Flying Backward* (New York: Bantam Books, 2005), 7–23, on the "canyon of the vaginas," actually North Canyon in Nye County, Nevada. Ethnographers used the derogatory term "berdache" for this third gender, but the realities are more complicated; see Kylan Mattias de Vries, "Berdache (Two-Spirit)," in *Encyclopedia of Gender and Society*, ed. Jodi O'Brien, 64 (Los Angeles: Sage, 2015) and Tatonetti, *Written by the Body*, 185–86. Will Roscoe, "North American Tribes with Berdache and Alternative Gender Roles," in *Living the Spirit: A Gay American Indian Anthology*, eds. Gay American Indians and Will Roscoe, 217–22 (New York: St. Martin's Press, 1988), 220, and "Bibliography of Berdache and Alternative Gender Roles Among North American Indians," *Journal of Homosexuality* 14 (1987), 100.

50. T. C. Blackburn, *December's Child: A Book of Chumash Oral Narratives* (Berkeley: University of California Press, 1975), 208; David S. Whitley, *A Guide to Rock Art Sites in Southern California and Southern Nevada* (Missoula: Mountain Press Publishing, 1996), 170–74 Site 33 and 1998, 19–20.

51. On the Kumeyaay yonis, see the classic study of Charlotte McGowan, *Ceremonial Fertility Sites in Southern California* (San Diego: San Diego Museum of Man, 1982), 12–15, 20–21, and 30–34, with her map at 3 figure 2, and her analysis of their power at 29–22, and 30–34, and some strikingly naturalistic examples at 41 Plate 1, 43 Plate 5, and 50 Plate 20; the discussion of "The Power of the Vulva" at the Chalfant Petroglyphs in Whitley, *A Guide to Rock Art Sites*, 80–84 Site 10; Galal Gough, "Gender in Stone: Yonis, Phallic Stones, and Male and Female Symbols in Southern California Rock Art," *Proceedings of the Society for California Archaeology* 9 (1996): 73–79, briefly reviews many examples of both vulva ("yoni") and penis formations: 75 Figure 2 reproduces a sketch of a yoni in the Anza Borrego (for pictographs at a boys' initiation site in the Anza-Borrego, see Whitley, *A Guide to Rock Art Sites*, 101–4 Site 16); for vulvas at Grass Valley, Nevada (I presume), Gough, "Gender in Stone," 74 and 79 Figure 17; Whitley, *A Guide to Rock Art Sites*, 80–84 Site 10, Peter Nabokov, *Where the Lightning Strikes: The Lives of American Indian Sacred Places* (New York: Penguin, 2006), 245.

52. "[G]enders also have graphic sexual references in that Woman spreads and Man probes or pierces": Jay Miller, "Basin Religion and Theology: A Comparative Study of Power (*Puha*)," *Journal of California and Great Basin Anthropology* 5 (1983), 77.

53. Frank Russell, *The Pima Indians: Re-edition with Introduction, Citation Sources, and Bibliography by Bernard L. Fontana* (Tucson: University of Arizona Press, 1975), 153; Miller, "Basin Religion," 74, 76. Devereux, "Institutionalized Homosexuality," offers an excellent explication for the Mohave. For Cooley, who works with the Grand Canyon Trust and is a licensed river guide, https://www.grandcanyontrust.org/advocatemag/fall-winter-2020/voices-grand-canyon, accessed September 20, 2023, with Paul A. Formisano, *Tributary Voices: Literary and Rhetorical Explorations of the Colorado River* (Reno: University of Nevada Press, 2022), 183–84.

54. Miller, "Basin Religion," 76–77. On stars, see James A. Goss, "A Basin-Plateau Shoshonean Ecological Model," in *Great Basin Cultural Ecology: A Symposium*, eds. Don D. Fowler, Gladys W. Smith, and C. Melvin Aikens, 123–28 (Reno: Desert Research Institute, 1972), 124. For Ocean Woman as Earth's creator, see Carobeth Laird, *The Chemehuevis* (Banning, CA: Malki Museum, 1976), 45–47, 148–49, 212–13; the Ocean is a "supreme being" in an Akimel O'odham song: Ruth Underhill, Donald M. Bahr, Baptisto Lopez, José Pancho, and David Lopez, *Rainhouse and Ocean: Speeches for the Papago Year* (Tucson: University of Arizona Press, 1979), 38; Ofelia Zepeda, *Ocean Power: Poems from the Desert* (Tucson: University of Arizona Press, 1995), 83–84, fear of the ocean; this poem is treated in more detail in chapter 10.

55. Tatonetti, *Written by the Body*; Devereux, "Institutionalized Homosexuality." Roscoe, "North American Tribes," and for the tribes listed, Roscoe, "Bibliography of Berdache," 97, 112, 101; 96, 112; 112; 107; 106 (as Pima), 105 (as Papago), 100, 111, 110; 102; 103–4 (with the San Juan unit, 107), 108, 110, 99, with extensive bibliography. Roscoe uses the derogatory but then standard term "berdache" to designate persons of other genders. See also Lang, "Native American Men-Women."

56. Devereux, "Institutionalized Homosexuality," provides a detailed and direct account of Mohave practices. Goss, "A Basin-Plateau Shoshonean Ecological Model," 125, 126–27; Whitley, "Finding Rain in the Desert," 15, 18–19; A. L. Kroeber, "The Religion of the Indians of California," *University of California Publications in American Archaeology and Ethnography* 4 (1907), 266–72; Laird, *The Chemehuevis*, 214, and *Mirror and Pattern: George Laird's World of Chemehuevi Mythology* (Banning, CA: Malki Museum Press, 1984), 59; Devereux, "Institutionalized Homosexuality," 500; Pamela Munro, Nellie Brown, and Judith G. Crawford, *A Mojave Dictionary* (Los Angeles: Department of Linguistics, University of California, 1992), 22 s.v. 'alyha, defined as "male transvestite." *Hwame* does not appear in their dictionary.

57. A. L. Kroeber, "A Mohave Historical Epic," *University of California Publications Anthropological Records* 11 (1951), 88 I 92–102 N 166; Arthur T. Hatto, *The Mohave Heroic Epic of Inyo-kutavêre* (Helsinki: Academia Scientiarum Fennica, 1999), 58–70, quotations at 61 and 67. Hatto does not treat the question of gender. Kroeber, "A Mohave Historical Epic," 121–22. Whitley, *A Guide to Rock Art Sites*, 24, on rattlesnakes as guardians of the vagina, and 26, as girls' "spirit helper" since they were "closely associated with women in the Far West." See further on the Mohave Historical Epic in chapters 7 and 10.

58. Kroeber, "A Mohave Historical Epic," 89 I 94, Kroeber's brackets. In Mojave Noise-unruly-night is Tinyãm-nyumêve-kunau (159n17).

59. Detailed in Devereux, "Institutionalized Homosexuality," 500–502, 505–10; Munro, Brown, and Crawford,

Mojave Dictionary, 41 s.v. 'iipa.

60. I'm reminded of Achilles, who tried to escape enrollment in the Greek forces of the Trojan War by disguising himself as a girl. His trick was uncovered when he grasped eagerly at a sword he was offered. On Indigenous women warriors, see Tatonetti, *Written by the Body*, 23–74.

61. Leslie Spier, *Yuman Tribes of the Gila River* (New York: Dover Publications, 1978), 242–43, transcribing the name as *'ialyxa'*; Devereux, "Institutionalized Homosexuality," 526. Harry J. Winters Jr., *Maricopa Place Names* (Tucson: SRI Press, 2018), 23, for the name of the mountain.

62. Roscoe, "North American Tribes," 218; Roscoe, "Bibliography of Berdache," 89; James L. Haley, *Apaches: A History and Culture Portrait* (Norman: University of Oklahoma Press, 1987), 74, quotation; David L. Carmichael, "Places of Power: Mescalero Apache Sacred Sites and Sensitive Areas," in *Sacred Sites, Sacred Places*, eds. David L. Carmichael, Jane Hubert, Brian Reeves, and Audhild Schanche (London: Routledge, 1994), 92–93.

63. Tatonetti, *Written by the Body*, 71–72; Daniel Heath Justice, *Kynship: The Way of Thorn and Thunder* (Wiarton: Kegedonce Press, 2005), 175–82, quotation at 180. *The Way of Thorn and Thunder* is the first volume in a trilogy, completed by *Wyrwood: The Way of Thorn and Thunder, Book 2* (2006) and *Dreyd: The Way of Thorn and Thunder, Book 3* (2007). My thanks to Lisa for directing my attention to this passage.

64. Keith H. Basso, *Wisdom Sits in Places: Landscape and Language Among the Western Apache* (Albuquerque: University of New Mexico Press, 1996), 28, 53, 97–98, 34. Further on Western Apache toponyms in chapter 10, and chapter 7 on the power of names.

65. Karl Jacoby, *Shadows at Dawn: A Borderlands Massacre and the Violence of History* (New York: The Penguin Press, 2008), 104, 131, 156, 166, 2, 139–40, 191–92, 92–93. Edgar Rice Burroughs was stationed at Fort Grant just a few years after the massacre; see chapter 9. For a novel based on the massacre, see Venetia Hobson Lewis, *Changing Woman: A Novel of the Camp Grant Massacre* (Lincoln: University of Nebraska Press, 2023).

66. Gillmor, *Fruit Out of Rock*, 65. On the next page Gillmor remarks, "Even later the Apaches had been gathered into the reservations, and those who had come later into that land fearing them were already an old tale." Earlier, in adumbration, Gillmor writes "that Abel Bane, when he cleared his land, had found stumps cut clean to the ground long before when this was Apache country" (41).

67. For a discussion of agency, see chapter 10.

68. Carolyn Merchant, *Reinventing Eden: The Fate of Nature in Western Culture* (New York: Routledge, 2003), 113–15.

69. The literature on the Hohokam is prodigious. For the canals, Omar A. Turney, *Prehistoric Irrigation in Arizona* (Phoenix: Arizona State Historian, 1929), remains fundamental, especially as urbanization over the following century erased evidence of many of the canals he was able to trace (see his fold-out plan opposite p. 12); a good brief treatment of Hohokam irrigation can be found in David E. Doyel, "Irrigation, Production and Power in Phoenix Basin Hohokam Society," in *The Hohokam Millennium*, eds. Suzanne K. Fish and Paul R. Fish, 83–89 (Santa Fe: School for Advanced Research Press, 2007); on Swilling's canals and subsequent developments, Earl Zarbin, *Two Sides of the River: Salt River Valley Canals, 1867–1902* (Phoenix: Salt River Project, 1997). There is a beautifully produced color map of the Hohokam canal system in William "Bill" H. Doelle, ed., "Love of the Gila: Reflections on Millennia of Life in the Southern Southwest," *Archaeology Southwest Magazine* 36, 1 & 2 (2023), 22–23.

70. On wetness as definitional for the female body in Greek thinking, see Anne Carson, "Putting Her in Her Place: Woman, Dirt, and Desire," in *Before Sexuality: The Construction of Erotic Experience in the Ancient Greek World*, eds. David M. Halperin, John J. Winkler, and Froma I. Zeitlin (Princeton: Princeton University Press, 1990), 137–45. On "Adam as Hero," the active agent operating on the passive land, see Merchant, *Reinventing Eden*, 93–116. A brief treatment of the history of gendering water in Veronica Strang, "Lording It Over the Goddess: Water, Gender, and Human-Environmental Relations," *Journal of Feminist Studies in Religion* 30 (2014): 85–109.

CHAPTER 6

1. Alison Lurie, *The Nowhere City* (New York: Henry Holt and Company, 1997), 12. On *The Nowhere City* in particular and Lurie's fiction in general, see Julie Newman, *Alison Lurie* (Amsterdam: Rodopi, 2000); Arthur Marwick, "Three Alison Lurie Novels of the Long Sixties," in *Windows on the Sixties: Exploring Key Texts of Media and Culture*, eds. Anthony Aldgate, James Chapman, and Arthur Marwick (2000), 123–28; Susan Watkins, "'Women and Wives Mustn't Go Near It': Academia, Language, and Gender in the Novels of Alison Lurie," *Revista canaria de estudios ingleses* 48 (2004): 129–46; Patrick O'Donnell, "Postwar Los

Angeles: Suburban Eden and the Fall into History," in *The Cambridge Companion to the Literature of Los Angeles*, ed. Kevin R. McNamara (Cambridge: Cambridge University Press, 2010), 65–67; Alice Levick, *Memory and Built Environment in 20th-Century American Literature: A Reading and Analysis of Spatial Forms* (London: Bloomsbury Academic, 2021), 96–105. Kevin Starr, *Golden Dreams: California in an Age of Abundance, 1950–1963* (New York: Oxford University Press, 2009), 173, praised *The Nowhere City* as "the best fictive portrait to capture Los Angeles as it made the transition to supercity."

2. In a recent essay, Eric Avila claims *Southern California* "reads like a subtle case for ecological determinism" ("Essaying Los Angeles," in *The Cambridge Companion to the Literature of Los Angeles*, ed. Kevin R. McNamara [Cambridge: Cambridge University Press, 2010], 178), but Carey McWilliams insisted on the mistake of seeing Southern California as wholly determined by its ecology; the cult of climate was, for him, "folklore" (Carey McWilliams, *Southern California: An Island on the Land* [Salt Lake City: Peregrine Books, 2010], 96–112): although McWilliams admits that the climate there does indeed change people, he also insists that "the miraculous qualities of the climate were invented, not by the cynical residents of the region, but by the early tourist" (98).

3. Although some working from smaller circumferences insist on continuing to call it one: most recently Vanessa Friedman, "Dior in the Desert," *The New York Times*, May 12, 2017, https://www.nytimes.com/2017/05/12/fashion/dior-cruise-2018-maria-grazia-chiuri.html?smid=tw-nytfashion&smtyp=cur&_r=0, accessed May 20, 2017.

4. See chapter 1 on the definition of deserts.

5. From data at http://www.laalmanac.com/weather/we13.htm, accessed 19 May 2017. Anton Wagner, *Los Angeles: Werden, Leben und Gestalt der Zweimillionenstadt in Südkalifornie* (Leipzig: Bibliographisches Institut, 1936), 23, gives 379.7 mm (15 in.) as the annual average. On the European settlement-era ecosystems of the Los Angeles Basin, see Paula Schiffman, "The Los Angeles Prairie," in *Land of Sunshine: An Environmental History of Los Angeles*, eds. William Deverell and Greg Hise, 38–51 (Pittsburgh: University of Pittsburgh Press, 2005). D. J. Waldie, *Holy Land: A Suburban Memoir* (New York: W. W. Norton & Company, 1996), 140, rightly writes, "[T]he Los Angeles plain is semiarid. It's not exactly a desert." Of course, with climate change, all bets are off.

6. McWilliams, *Southern California*, 110 (originally 1946). See David Fine, "Introduction," in *Los Angeles in Fiction*, ed. David Fine (Albuquerque: University of New Mexico Press, 1984), 17, characterizing Los Angeles as "a city almost literally carved out of a desert," paraphrasing (I suppose) Richard Lehan, "The Los Angeles Novel and the Idea of the West," in *Los Angeles in Fiction*, ed. David Fine (Albuquerque: University of New Mexico Press, 1984), 30, for whom "Los Angeles was crafted out of the desert."

7. In this chapter I leave aside largely the literature treating Los Angeles as an eco-disaster—greedily gulping water from the Owens Valley, on which see Gary D. Libecap, *Owens Valley Revisited: A Reassessment of the West's First Great Water Transfer* (Palo Alto: Stanford Economics and Finance, 2007), degrading the serene landscape with acres of cheap, ugly houses, inviting deserved eco-obliteration or sheer decay (say, the now clichéd city of the film *Blade Runner*) or the eco-collapse of Claire Vaye Watkins's *Gold Fame Citrus* (New York: Riverhead Books, 2015) or the milder but sadder critique of Waldie's *Holy Land*, on which see Levick, *Memory and the Built Environment*, 26–33. I do examine some of the literature of nuclear annihilation where such disaster evokes or uncovers desert LA.

8. See chapter 1 for a more detailed explication.

9. And see Edgar Rice Burroughs's 1919 *The Moon Maid: Complete and Restored* (Lincoln: University of Nebraska Press, 2002), in which Earth's salvation from Martian domination entails, among other things, the obliteration of Los Angeles; Michael Orth, "Utopia in the Pulps: The Apocalyptic Pastoralism of Edgar Rice Burroughs," *Extrapolation* 27 (1986), 226.

10. Nathalie Vincent-Arnaud, "'To the Land's End' ou 'Farther Out into the Desert': Itinéraires de la négation dans *Less Than Zero* de Bret Easton Ellis," *GRAAT: Groupe des recherches anglo-américaines de Tours* 35 (2006), 179, 188.

11. See many of Joan Didion's essays in *Slouching Towards Bethlehem* (New York: Farrar, Straus and Giroux, 2008) and *The White Album* (New York: Farrar, Straus and Giroux, 1979), and her novel *Play It as It Lays* (New York: Farrar, Straus and Giroux, 2005). On the Imperial Valley, see chapter 4. For Madeline Gottlieb, "Herman Teppis and the Incestuous Fantasy: Exploring Complicated Relationships in Norman Mailer's *The Deer Park*," *The Explicator* 77 (2019), 103: "*The Deer Park* remarkably exposes the truthful ugliness of Hollywood and its tenants through its careful inspection of complicated relationships—including the controversial subject of incest." See briefly Justin Gautreau, *The Last Word: The Hollywood Novel and the Studio System* (New

York: Oxford University Press, 2020), 171, on *The Deer Park* as a critique of the Hollywood industry.

12. Indeed: sixty years ago, Carolyn See catalogued already 500 books set in Hollywood alone and read 300 of them for her dissertation, "The Hollywood Novel: An Historical and Critical Study" (PhD diss., University of California, Los Angeles, 1963), a study more often cited, I suspect, than read (1, for the numbers; 485–516, for the bibliography).

13. For a thorough discussion of the Hebrew biblical tropes, see Laura Feldt, "Wilderness and Hebrew Bible Religion—Fertility, Apostasy and Religious Transformation in the Pentateuch," in *Religion and Society: Wilderness in Mythology and Religion: Approaching Religious Spacialities, Cosmologies, and Ideas of Wild Nature*, eds. Laura Feldt, Gustavo Benavides, and Kocku von Stuckrad, 55–94 (Berlin: De Gruyter, 2012) and Diana K. Davis, *The Arid Lands: History, Power, Knowledge* (Cambridge: MIT Press, 2016), 23–47; also chapter 4 and, on Euro-American desert tropes, chapter 1.

14. So, perhaps, the winds were even responsible for the Watts riots: Eve Babitz, *Eve's Hollywood* (New York: New York Review of Books, 2015), 143–44; Bret Easton Ellis, *Imperial Bedrooms* (New York: Alfred A. Knopf, 2010), 63, and see the drug cartel operatives who killed another character "found shot to death in the desert, not far from where Amanda Flew was last seen" (161).

15. Frank Norris quoted in Fine, "Introduction," 3; Rupert Hughes, *Souls for Sale* (New York: Garland Publishing, 1978), 183 ("blinding blue"), 314 (madcap ride; originally published 1922); Kate Braverman, *Lithium for Medea: A Novel* (New York: Seven Stories Press, 2002), 83; Cynthia Kadohata, *In the Heart of the Valley of Love* (Berkeley: University of California Press, 1997), 1; Hughes, *Souls for Sale*, 340 (William R. Gowen, "Hoo-ray! ri! ro! row! roo! rah! Rupert Hughes and his 'Dozen,'" *Newsboy* [November–December 1995]: 13–16, offers a brief biography; Hughes served with the US Army Mexican Border Service in 1916 [14], perhaps a source for some of the desert images in *Souls for Sale*?); F. Scott Fitzgerald, *The Love of the Last Tycoon*, ed. Matthew J. Bruccoli (New York: Scribner, 2003), 18. See, "The Hollywood Novel," 58–61, alludes to the sense that crossing "the great desert" (58) "often functions as a *rite de passage*" (57), but without developing the analogy to desert purgation in the exodus to the Promised Land; she quotes Dorothy Hughes, *Dread Journey* (New York: Duell, Sloan, and Pierce, 1945), 138, on the three-day trip through a "wasteland." See does, however, argue that the trip west marks "a period of penance" that "divests [the traveler] of his past and all its appurtenances"; he "metaphorically dies and is born again in the long eerie train trip across the Great West to Hollywood." In an ironic twist, the Promised Land into which such travelers are reborn is not a land of milk and honey but the locus of "sins . . . so rarified and vile that in his old life he has perhaps never even heard of them" (See, "The Hollywood Novel," 58).

16. Steve Erickson, *Amnesiascope: A Novel* (New York: Henry Holt and Company, 1996), 80, 217; Braverman, *Lithium for Medea*, 358–62; Hughes, *Souls for Sale*, 372–75; see Gautreau, *The Last Word*, 12–17, on Hughes and his novel, which Gautreau reads as a defense of Hollywood against accusations of immorality. Hughes, however, was wholly owned by Sam Goldwyn. Manly, *Death Valley in '49*, 141, for a classic evocation of the desert as worthless space; see further in chapter 4. For another, but more ironic, escape from a stultifying Midwest to the California desert, see Sheila Ortiz Taylor, *Coachella* (Albuquerque: University of New Mexico Press, 1998).

17. George Pelecanos, "Introduction," in *True Confessions*, by John Gregory Dunne (New York: Thunder Mouth's Press, 2006), v. See Kevin Starr, *Embattled Dreams: California in War and Peace, 1940–1950* (New York: Oxford University Press, 2002), 213–22, for a brief discussion. There have been multiple book-length studies of the case; the most recent known to me is John Gilmore, *Severed: The True Story of the Black Dahlia Murder* (Los Angeles: Amok Books, 2015). Twenty-Nine Palms plays an important role in the UFO contactee experiences of the 1950s: see chapter 8.

18. John Gregory Dunne, *True Confessions* (New York: Thunder Mouth's Press, 2006), 340; see Des's reflections on his fantasies about Mary Ginty, a parishioner whose husband went to prison: "He dreamed about her. That was all. He would awake in a state of arousal, his bedding wet from the nocturnal emission. . . . The impulses of the flesh were the darkest sins in Tommy's canon. How wrong he was. Those impulses could be sublimated. Pride was a substitute. Power. The urge to manipulate. Vices that I have in abundance, Desmond Spellacy thought" (191). See, briefly but cogently, Michael Adams, "Sin and Guilt in the Fiction of John Gregory Dunne," *Critique: Studies in Contemporary Fiction* 25 (1984), 156. Timothy J. Meaghan, "Cops, Priests, and the Decline of Irish America," in *Catholics in the Movies*, ed. Colleen McDannell (New York: Oxford University Press, 2008), 245, sees Des's exile as situating him in "the desert . . . the empty space where relationships can be constructed," but Des's desert space is not in fact empty: it is full of people and preexisting relationships. Christopher P. Wilson, "When Noir Meets Nonfiction," *Twentieth-Century Literature* 61

(2015), 493: "Dunne uses the California desert . . . both as the nexus of suburban spread and, ironically, as the ultimate point of exile." Des "is left in the desert, exempt from further corruption, but now approaching his own death."

19. Husband killer: Phyllis Nirdlinger in James M. Cain, *Double Indemnity* (New York: Vintage, 1989) (original 1936); daughter rapist: Noah Cross (John Huston) in *Chinatown* (1974).

20. Treated in chapter 4.

21. John Fante, *Ask the Dust* (New York: Santa Rosa, Black Sparrow Press, 1980). For "seminal work," Meagan Meylor, "'Sad Flower in the Sand': Camilla Lopez and the Erasure of Memory in *Ask the Dust*," in *John Fante's* Ask the Dust: *A Joining of Voices and Views*, eds. Stephen Cooper and Clorinda Donato (New York: Fordham University Press, 2020), 58. Meylor situates the figure of Camilla within the racial dynamics of 1930s Los Angeles, when Mexicans and Mexican Americans were evicted from the city and "returned" to Mexico in a racist reaction to the Great Depression. Meylor's interpretation adds a depth to Camilla's character in complement to my remarks here. There seems to be an allusion to Camilla in Ellis, *Imperial Bedrooms*, 25, when an actress asks Clay at a party "about a Hispanic girl who disappeared in some desert."

22. Stephen Cooper, *Full of Life: A Biography of John Fante* (New York: North Point Press, 2000), 176 (quotation), 126, 132–33, 155–56, on Marie, 110 and 192 on Audrey, whose last name is apparently unknown, and 192n360; on Fante's Catholic upbringing and schooling, 26, 33–52. My thanks to Meagan Meylor on Camilla. [Sophronios], "Βίος Μαρίας Αἰγυπτίας," in *Patrologia Graeca*, vol. 87, 3, cols. 3697–3726, ed. J.-P. Migne (Paris: Imprimerie Catholique, 1865), 2, 18 and 3, 32. See briefly Veronica Della Dora, *Landscape, Nature, and the Sacred in Byzantium* (Cambridge: Cambridge University Press, 2016), 130–32, quotation at 131. Conferenza episcopale italiana, *Martirologio romano* (Vatican: Librería editrice vaticana, 2004), 295, s.v. 1 aprile no. 3. On the desert-city dichotomy, see James E. Goehring, *Ascetics, Society, and the Desert: Studies in Early Egyptian Monasticism* (Harrisburg: Trinity Press International, 1999), 73–88. [Sophronios] is in brackets because Mary's hagiography, traditionally attributed to him, is in fact not his: Derek Kruger, "Scripture and Liturgy in the Life of Mary of Egypt," in *Education and Religion in Late Antique Christianity: Reflections, Social Contexts, and Genre*, eds. Peter Gemeinhardt, Lieve Van Hoof, and Peter Van Nuffelen (London: Routledge, 2016), 133, with a date of the seventh century CE.

23. Aldous Huxley, *Ape and Essence* (Chicago: Ivan R. Dee, 1992), 62, 123; Nathaniel West, *Miss Lonelyhearts* and *The Day of the Locust* (New York: New Directions Books, 2009), 142; see Gautreau, *The Last Word*, 112–20. Norman Klein, *The History of Forgetting: Los Angeles and the Erasure of Memory* (London: Verso, 2008), 98, suggestively remarks that in the film *Blade Runner* the city invades the desert, LA "smog finally destroying the desert climate itself." Curiously, Hughes, *Souls for Sale*, 70 and 73, refers to a movie being made of Charles Kingsley's novel *Hypatia*, whose climax comes with the vicious assassination of the pagan woman mathematician by an enraged crowd of monks in from the desert.

24. Gavin Lambert, *The Slide Area: Scenes of Hollywood Life* (London: Serpent's Tail, 1998), 56. Wagner, *Los Angeles*, 26, calls the Santa Anas "*föhnartige Wüstenwinde*," which seems about right; also Didion, *Slouching Towards Bethlehem*, 218–19. McWilliams, *Southern California*, 10–11: "desert winds." On the causes of these winds, see Mimi Hughes and Alex Hall, "Local and Synoptic Mechanisms Causing Southern California's Santa Ana Winds," *Climate Dynamics* 34 (2010): 847–57 and Sebastien Conil and Alex Hall, "Local Regimes of Atmospheric Variability: A Case Study of Southern California," *Journal of Climate* 19 (2006): 4308–25.

25. George Randolph Chester and Lilian Chester, *On the Lot and Off* (New York: Harper & Brothers Publishers, 1924), 267. Briefly on Chester's life and career, Jenny E. Robb, "From the Periodical Archives: Winsor McCay, George Randolph Chester, and the Tale of the Jungle Imps," *Periodical Comics and Cartoons* 17 (2007), 249–51. It should be noted that the Chesters' book is saturated with the anti-Semitism so common in Hollywood novels.

26. Chester and Chester, *On the Lot and Off*, 285, 298–99, 275, 268; later, Meyer, Tennyson's father, violates his own business ethics by foreclosing on Luna: "it may have been the enervating wind from the desert" that did it (304).

27. Raymond Chandler, *Stories and Early Novels, Pulp Stories / The Big Sleep / Farewell, My Lovely / The High Window* (New York: The Library of America, 1995), 368 (originally published 1938); Didion, *Slouching Towards Bethlehem*, 218–19; "extraordinary two pages": Klein, *The History of Forgetting*, 239; A. A. Fair [Erle Stanley Gardner], *Double or Quits* (New York: William Morrow and Company, 1941), 21–23. Chandler's famous passage reads: "There was a desert wind blowing that night. It was one of those hot dry Santa Anas that come down through the mountain passes and curl your hair and make your nerves jump and your skin itch. On nights like that every booze party ends in a fight. Meek little wives feel the edge of the carving knife

and study their husbands' necks. Anything can happen. You can even get a full glass of beer at a cocktail lounge." As so often with Chandler, a mocking, ironic deflation at the end.

28. Klein, *The History of Forgetting*, 239, 240. For Joan Didion (*The White Album*, 172), those days when "the wind is coming up" presage the onset of a migraine.

29. Frederick Kohner, *Gidget* (New York: Berkeley Books, 2001), 124, 110 (orgy), 109, 124 and 128, 140–42; Klein, *The History of Forgetting*, 81–83, on LA as "the city burning." Gidget's agonized sexual meditations are pretty blatant: "As I was lying in the darkness I felt real alone and helpless like never before in all my fifteen years. There wasn't enough woman in me yet, and the gidget in me didn't know how to handle it. Will it always be like this, I thought unhappily, will I always be scared of it and scared of being scared?" (140). Ironically, the Kahoona's refusal denies Gidget the "climax" she expected. See Ilana Nash, "'Nowhere Else to Go': Gidget and the Construction of Adolescent Femininity," *Feminist Media Studies* 2 (2002), 348, on the implications of this passage, and in general on the Gidget phenomenon and the patriarchy; but Nash exaggerates when she claims that Gidget never turns to her mother "for support and camaraderie" (352); at least in the first book, Gidget's mother is the one who divines immediately that her daughter's problems stem from sexual desire (see their conversation at Kohner, *Gidget*, 58–60), and her mother sides with her against her father by okaying her date with Moondoggie (91). For a brief account of Kohner's career, Gerhard Mack, "Frederick Kohner," in *Deutsche Exilliteratur seit 1933, Teil I: Kalifornien*, eds. John M. Spalek and Jospeh Strelka, 762–70 (Munich: Franke Verlag, 1976); John M. Spalek, Joseph Strelka, and Sandra H. Hawrylchak, *Deutsche Exilliteratur seit 1933 Band 2: Kalifornien, Teil I* (Munich: Franke Verlag, 1976), 68–71, for a bibliography of Kohner's work (to 1976). Kohner died in 1986. He does not figure in Erhard Bahr, *Weimar on the Pacific: German Exile Culture in Los Angeles and the Crisis of Modernism* (Berkeley: University of California Press, 2007), the most recent study known to me of the German colony in 1930s and 1940s Los Angeles, which included Thomas and Heinrich Mann, Berthold Brecht, Theodor Adorno, and many others; another account in Kevin Starr, *The Dream Endures: California Enters the 1940s* (New York: Oxford University Press, 1997), 342–96 (Kohner and *Gidget*, very briefly, at 388–89); see also now Johannes Evelein, *Literary Exiles from Nazi Germany* (Rochester: Camden House, 2014) on German exile literature more generally. Didion, *The White Album*, 210–11, on a 1975 Santa Ana that blew "in off the Mojave for three weeks and set . . . 69,000 acres of Los Angeles County on fire" and another, in 1978, that fanned a brush fire and "[w]ithin two hours . . . had pushed this fire across 25,000 acres and thirteen miles to the coast, where it jumped the Pacific Coast Highway as a half-mile fire storm generating winds of 100 miles per hour and temperatures up to 2,500 degrees Fahrenheit. Refugees huddled on Zuma Beach. Horses caught fire and were shot on the beach, birds exploded in the air. Houses did not explode but imploded, as in a nuclear strike" (*The White Album*, 222–23).

30. Eve Babitz, *Slow Days, Fast Company: The World, the Flesh, and L.A.* (New York: Alfred A. Knopf, 1977), 71–83. "Tales" from the coyly ambiguous "Tales by Eve Babitz" on the title page: while categorized as "fiction," it is hard to know whether Babitz's narratives are invented at all, or just lightly disguised recountings of her own experiences. For a recent biography, see Lili Anolik, *Hollywood's Eve: Eve Babitz and the Secret History of L.A.* (New York: Scribner, 2019).

31. Babitz, *Slow Days*, 76 (italics in original); 74–75 ("just friends"); 76 (blaming weather); 79; 78 (long quotation, original italics—"it" because William wants the narrator but she's refused to sleep with him; so like a man, to find relief in evidence that it's not *his own* deficiencies that have turned a woman off); 80–81; 83.

32. Kate Flannery, *Strip Tees: A Memoir of Millennial Los Angeles* (New York: Henry Holt and Company, 2023), 7 and 9, Ivy as recruiter at 10–11, Kate decides to take the job and be a "spokesmodel," 12–14.

33. Flannery, *Strip Tees*, 99.

34. In *Less Than Zero*, Clay seems unaware that the winds bear the desert into the city; sitting alone late at night in a coffee shop, he merely observes that "the winds have started and they're blowing so hard the windows are shaking and the sounds of them trembling, about to break, fill the coffee shop" (Bret Easton Ellis, *Less Than Zero* [New York: Vintage Books, 1985], 61).

35. N. Scott Momaday, *House Made of Dawn* (New York: Harper Perennial Modern Classics, 2010), 77–166, for the LA sections; 143–45 (Milly, beach, confidences); 96, 106–7 (lovemaking, drinking, unemployed), 79 (Mission), 96–101 (peyote; quotation at 101).

36. Simon Ortiz, *Woven Stone* (Tucson: University of Arizona Press, 1992), 66.

37. I steal my heading from the title of Traci Lords's autobiography *Underneath It All* (New York: Harper Entertainment, 2003); see further on Lords, chapter 9 n2. Although exploration would take us much too far from Los Angeles and images of the desert, the same trope of "uncovering" the glitz to reveal something

else, usually (but not always) sordid, vapid, arid, and sterile underneath, plays out in analogous ways in the pornography industry. Pornography itself relies literally on "uncovering," by making visible bodies and sexual couplings, but is at the same time a false uncovering, in its meretricious depiction of sex and its urgent need to cover up the abuse, sexism, and violence that accompanies so much of its production. The San Fernando Valley was the epicenter of American pornographic filmmaking in the heydays of the 1970s and 1980s; with the spread of digital photography and cheap, high-quality cameras, the product has been democratized. Still, Laura Pulido, Laura Barraclough, and Wendy Cheng, *A People's Guide to Los Angeles* (Berkeley: University of California Press, 2012), 224, claim that "[a]ccording to one source, 90 percent of all legally distributed pornographic films are made in the San Fernando valley," without, however, citing the "source."

38. Fante, *Ask the Dust*, 120. I'm grateful to Meagan Meylor for reminding me of this passage.

39. Douglas C. Sackman, "A Garden of Worldly Delights," in *Land of Sunshine: An Environmental History of Los Angeles*, eds. William Deverell and Greg Hise (Pittsburgh: University of Pittsburgh Press, 1984), 247, with further references to scholarship of boosterism at 329–30n5; especially notable: Richard Orsi, "Selling the Golden State: A Study of Boosterism in Nineteenth-Century California" (PhD diss., University of Wisconsin-Madison, 1973); Kevin Starr, *Inventing the Dream: California Through the Progressive Era* (New York: Oxford University Press, 1985), 128–75 and *Americans and the California Dream* (New York: Oxford University Press, 1973), 365–414; William Deverell and Douglas Flamming, "Race, Rhetoric, and Regional Identity: Boosting Los Angeles, 1880–1930," in *Power and Place in the North American West*, eds. Richard White and John Findlay, 117–43 (Seattle: University of Washington Press, 1999); and Mike Davis, *Ecology of Fear: Los Angeles and the Imagination of Disaster* (New York: Vintage Books, 1999), 59–91. Bertolt Brecht, *Arbeitsjournal: Zweiter Band, 1942 bis 1955*, ed. Werner Hecht (Frankfurt am Main: Suhrkamp Verlag, 1973), 293, entry for August 9, 1941, and 733, entry for March 20, 1945; see Marcus Wessendorf, "Brecht in Los Angeles—'in this mausoleum of easy *going*,'" *The Germanic Review: Literature, Culture, Theory* 95 (2020), 22–25, on Berthold Brecht's conceptions of "culture" in relation to LA and alienation from nature. This theme comes out especially nicely in Lianha Babener, "Raymond Chandler's City of Lies," in *Los Angeles in Fiction*, ed. David Fine, 109–131 (Albuquerque: University of New Mexico Press, 1984). On Brecht in LA, see Bahr, *Weimar on the Pacific*, 69–147; Babitz, *Slow Days*, 8.

40. See Starr, *Inventing the Dream*, 44–63, for an overview (and *Material Dreams: Southern California Through the 1920s* [New York: Oxford University Press,1990], 90–119, on Los Angeles in particular), and Orsi, "Selling the Golden State," for a detailed study of booster literature. Samuel Storey, *To the Golden Land: Sketches of a Trip to Southern California* (London: Walter Scott, 1889), 30, quoted without attribution in McWilliams, *Southern California*, 98; floral magnificence, 105; enervation, 107.

41. Horace Bell, *Reminiscences of a Ranger: Early Times in Southern California* (Norman: Oklahoma University Press, 1999), 55–57.

42. J. U. Peters, "The Los Angeles Anti-Myth," in *Itinerary: Essays on California Writers*, ed. Charles L. Crow (Bowling Green: Bowling Green State University Press, 1978), 24; see also Babener, "Raymond Chandler's City of Lies," 115, and "*Chinatown*, City of Blight," in *Los Angeles in Fiction*, ed. David Fine (Albuquerque: University of New Mexico Press, 1984), 243–44. Lambert, *Slide Area*, 18, calls Los Angeles "not a city, but a series of suburban approaches to a city that never materializes." Edward Soja, *My Los Angeles: From Urban Restructuring to Regional Urbanization* (Berkeley: University of California Press, 2014), 21–23, argues that this view of Los Angeles is now outdated.

43. Mark Royden Winchell, "Fantasy Seen: Hollywood Fiction Since West," in *Los Angeles in Fiction*, ed. David Fine (Albuquerque: University of New Mexico Press, 1984), 148 with 166n6; Carolyn See, *Golden Days* (Berkeley: University of California Press, 1996), 121 and 6.

44. Dunne, *True Confessions*, 203; Ellis, *Less Than Zero*, 67; See, *Golden Days*, 4 and 7; Aldous Huxley, *After Many a Summer Dies the Swan* (New York: Harper & Row, 1965), 8: the contrasts between "nature" and "urban artifice" that surface in a few passages (see 10, 60, for example) are never developed. The inspiration for *Swan*, "his Hollywood novel" (Peter Munro Jack, "A New Novel by Aldous Huxley," *New York Times Book Review*, January 28, 1940, 2), came from the antics of William Randolph Hearst and Marion Davies: Frank Baldanza, "Huxley and Hearst," in *Itinerary: Essays on California Writers*, ed. David Fine (Bowling Green: Bowling Green State University, 1978), 35–47; David King Dunaway, *Huxley in Hollywood* (New York: Harper & Row, 1989), 106–10, on the writing of *Swan*. J. Ross MacDonald, *The Drowning Pool* (New York: Knopf, 1950), 19; Hughes, *Souls for Sale*, 369. See, "The Hollywood Novel," 178–80, sees artificiality of setting as a fundamental structural feature of the Hollywood novel, though without mentioning the desert (but see also her more extended discussion of the role of climate at 388–402).

45. Lambert, *Slide Area*, 15, 16–17, 35, 94, 15 and 211, 52.
46. See, *Golden Days*, 4, 6, 9, 121, 10–11, 13. When Edith brings her business partner to be, Skip, home for the first time, her house, lights ablaze, looks "*charmed*, with golden light pouring from every window like a just-landed space ship" (21): a flying saucer touched down, appropriately, in the midst of the desert: see chapter 8 on UFOs and the desert. On See's fiction, see Davis, *Ecology of Fear*, 316–18; Fine, *Imagining Los Angeles*, 251–55; O'Donnell, "Postwar Los Angeles," 70–72. In Dunne, *True Confessions*, 82, Tom complains of his wife Mary Margaret, good Catholic girl: "It could be a hundred degrees with a hot dry wind off the desert and still she would wear flannel" to bed.
47. See had already foreshadowed this desert beneath in her dissertation, where she wrote of a "parched" geography, "the constant assumption" in the Hollywood fiction she studied "that Southern California is a desert," indeed a space that, after rain, "as soon as the sun comes out . . . again turns into an incipient desert" ("The Hollywood Novel," 388, 398, 392).
48. Huxley, *Ape and Essence*, 17–18. Kerwin Lee Klein, "Westward, Utopia: Robert V. Hine, Aldous Huxley, and the Future of California History," *Pacific Historical Review* 70 (2001), 474, makes the important observation that *Ape and Essence* "aired Huxley's nostalgia for his lost desert years."
49. Mark Taylor, "Aldous Huxley's *Ape and Essence* and Clashing Discourses of Nature," *Mosaic* 53 (2020), 91–93, argues that *Ape and Essence* stresses that the dangers of nuclear war must not overshadow the broader threat of environmental crises facing the Earth. On the view that responsibility for the condition of California in the novel lies exclusively with nuclear war, see Sanford E. Marovitz, "Aldous Huxley and the Nuclear Age: *Ape and Essence* in Context," in *Critical Essays on Aldous Huxley*, ed. Jerome Meckier, 195–207 (New York: G. K. Hall, 1996) and Patrick Mannix, *The Rhetoric of Anti-Nuclear Fiction: Persuasive Strategies in Novels and Films* (Lewisburg, PA: Bucknell University Press, 1992), 89.
50. Huxley, *Ape and Essence*, 62, 202.
51. On nuclear devastation in Los Angeles's fiction, see David Seed, "Los Angeles' Science Fiction Futures," in *The Cambridge Companion to the Literature of Los Angeles*, ed. Kevin R. McNamara (Cambridge: Cambridge University Press, 2010), 123–34; a brief survey of Los Angeles literature in Davis, *Ecology of Fear*, 311–18, with a focus on See, *Golden Days*. For "The Paradise Crater," see P. D. Smith, *The Doomsday Men: The Real Doctor Strangelove and the Dream of the Superweapon* (New York: St. Martin's Press, 2007), 294. Strangely enough, there was another story that prefigured nuclear weapons: Steve Cartmill's "Deadline," written in 1944 but not published till after the war. In *The Nowhere City*, Paul is awoken at 4 a.m. one morning by terrific noise; "[h]e thought it was, first, a nightmare; then, an atomic war." But it was just another instance of the constant reinvention of LA: a house being moved to make way for a freeway (Lurie, *The Nowhere City*, 256). "For [Raymond] Chandler," observes Liahna K. Babener in a trenchant essay, the "falsity is so prevalent that the truth, if it surfaces at all, is neither redeeming nor ameliorative" ("Raymond Chandler's City of Lies," 111). If the underlying truth of Los Angeles in *Ape and Essence* be desert, then Babener's observation becomes chillingly true. Huxley knew Wylie: see Taylor, "Aldous Huxley's *Ape and Essence*," 89, with reference to a letter from Huxley.
52. Gloria Miklowitz, *After the Bomb* (New York: Scholastic Press, 1985), 2. Note, of course, the patriarchal trope: "Who will rescue me," is the real question in Cara's mind, "when true danger looms?"
53. Lurie, *The Nowhere City*, 285.
54. Babener, "Raymond Chandler's City of Lies," 120–21. "Helen Grayle" summons up "Holy Grail"—the unattainable object of unending search—and Helen of Troy, destroyer of men through sexual allurement and, in the *Odyssey*, memory-erasing drugs; Chandler, *Stories and Early Novels*, 767–984.
55. Note too the misogyny—the woman is false, in metonymy for the city that too is female and false—Los Angeles itself. On the gender of urban space, see chapter 5.
56. Charles L. Crow, "Home and Transcendence in Los Angeles," in *Los Angeles in Fiction*, ed. David Fine (Albuquerque: University of New Mexico Press, 1984), 194–95. The embedded quotation comes from Didion, *Play It as It Lays*, 162. Levick's analysis of *Play It as It Lays* does not engage with the desert (*Memory and the Built Environment*, 82–96), perhaps a missed opportunity, because as for Clay in *Less Than Zero*, Levick sees Los Angeles as a realm of lost memory for Didion's protagonist Maria—so how might she relate to her desert home in Silver Wells, Nevada?
57. As indeed Edward Abbey, writing of what he calls *Datura meteloides*, another desert hazard, remarked: "The correct dosage is said to be spiritually rewarding, but the problem is that a microgram too much may lead to convulsions, paralysis and death—also rewarding, perhaps, but usually considered premature" (*Beyond the Wall: Essays from the Outside* [New York: Henry Holt and Company, 1984], 88). This species name is no

longer used; see chapter 2 n60 and chapter 8 n69.

58. Mike Davis, *City of Quartz: Excavating the Future of Los Angeles* (New York: Vintage Books, 1990), 3–14 (Llano del Rio); 50: "Yet not all Europeans were estranged by either the façade or the desert behind it" (an implicit endorsement, I think); 82–83. Davis, *Ecology of Fear*, 10–14, 17–18 (Mediterranean climate); 25, 23 (quotations); 202 (LA now bordered by deserts and mountains rather than farms). Peter Charles Remondino, *The Mediterranean Shores of America: Southern California: Its Climatic, Physical, and Meteorological Conditions* (Philadelphia: F. A. Davis Co., 1892). I am indebted to *Boom California*'s anonymous reader for reminding me of the importance of this literature. For a discussion of some of the same tropes in a Caribbean context, see Gary Reger, "A New Mediterranean: The Caribbean in the Euro-American Imaginary," in *Turning Tides: Caribbean Intersections in the Americas and Beyond*, eds. Heather Cateau and Milla Cozart Riggio, 36–54 (Kingston-Miami: Ian Randle Publishers, 2019). See Susan Nelson, "Thinking in Ruins: The Rio del Llano Experiment," *LARB Quarterly* 38 (August 2023): 9–19, for a recent contemplation on the Rio del Llano experiment, inspired by a reading of Davis, *City of Quartz*.

59. Glen M. MacDonald, "The Myth of a Desert Metropolis," *Boom: A Journal of California* 3 (Fall 2013), 86–94; see also https://boomcalifornia.com/2017/05/22/the-myth-of-a-desert-metropolis-los-angeles-was-not-built-in-a-desert-but-are-we-making-it-one/, accessed September 20, 2023.

60. Scott Hermanson, "Fear and Loathing in Los Angeles: Mike Davis as Nature Writer," *Western American Literature* 37 (2002), 294, writes, "Davis, however, tackles a landscape that not only has been written over but has been defaced, scarred, and graffitied to the point that its true surface is almost unknowable." Not so: the "true" surface is the desert underneath. Wilson, "When Noir Meets Nonfiction," 489, gets it right: "In Davis's chronicle, Los Angeles was a desert landscape transformed by a group of image-makers, visionaries, and profiteers who constructed a utopian image of California's social order for the middle classes." On Davis's critics, Hermanson, "Fear and Loathing," 314–15.

61. See Patricia Nelson Limerick, *Desert Passages: Encounters with American Deserts* (Albuquerque: University of New Mexico Press, 1985).

62. Reyner Banham, *Los Angeles: The Architecture of Four Ecologies* (New York: Harper Row Publishers, 1971), 235 and 243; perhaps Banham had in mind something like *The Flutter of an Eyelid*, by Myron Brinig (New York: Farrar Rinehart, 1933), or Evelyn Waugh's *The Loved One* (Boston: Little, Brown and Company, 1948). Much the same judgment on Huxley's *After Many a Summer Dies the Swan* in See, "The Hollywood Novel," 39, but of course Huxley never left.

63. For a brief survey of African American expectations about LA, see Shirley Ann Wilson Moore, "No Cold to Grapple With: African-American Expectations of California," *Journal of the West* 44 (2005): 8–15.

64. Richard Slotkin, *Regeneration through Violence: The Mythology of the American Frontier, 1600–1860* (Norman: University of Oklahoma Press, 1973) and *Gunfighter Nation: The Myth of the Frontier in Twentieth-Century America* (Norman: University of Oklahoma Press, 1998); David W. Teague, *The Southwest in American Literature and Art: The Rise of a Desert Aesthetic* (Tucson: University of Arizona Press, 1997); Carolyn Merchant, *Reinventing Eden: The Fate of Nature in Western Culture* (New York: Routledge, 2003). Also useful: Catrin Gersdorf, *The Poetics and Politics of the Desert: Landscape and the Construction of America* (Amsterdam: Rodopi, 2009); Roderick Nash, *Wilderness and the American Mind*, 4th ed. (New Haven: Yale University Press, 2001); William Cronon, "The Trouble with Wilderness, or Getting Back to the Wrong Nature," in *Uncommon Ground: Rethinking the Human Place in Nature*, ed. William Cronon, 69–90 (New York: W. W. Norton & Co., 1995); Jenny Price, "Thirteen Ways of Seeing Nature in L.A.," in *Land of Sunshine: An Environmental History of Los Angeles*, eds. William Deverell and Greg Hise, 220–44 (Pittsburgh: University of Pittsburgh Press, 2010). I explore some of these questions raised whether explicitly or by implication, particularly about "nature," in chapters 2 and 10.

CHAPTER 7

1. Amanda Kearney and John J. Bradley, "'Too strong to ever not be there': Place Names and Emotional Geographies," *Social and Cultural Geography* 10 (2009), 88.

2. Leslie Marmon Silko, *Ceremony* (New York: Penguin Books, 1977), 68.

3. Émile Durkheim, *The Elementary Forms of the Religious Life: A Study in Religious Sociology*, trans. Karen Fields (New York: Free Press, 1995), 134. Durkheim cites Walter Baldwin Spencer and Francis James Gillen, *The Native Tribes of Central Australia* (Macmillan and Co., Limited, 1899), 202. His use of "primitive" reflects anthropological categories of his day. Ernst Cassirer, *The Philosophy of Symbolic Forms, Volume Three: The*

Phenomenology of Knowledge, trans. Ralph Manheim (New Haven: Yale University Press, 1957), 91.

4. In his reflections on the expedition of Lewis and Clark, Dayton Duncan calls the expedition's descent from Lemhi Pass as entrée into "land that was not only unknown [i.e., unnamed], but unowned by any nation" (*Out West: American Journey Along the Lewis and Clark Trail* [New York: Penguin, 1987], 278). See Tom Lynch, *Outback and Out West: The Settler-Colonial Environmental Imaginary* (Lincoln: University of Nebraska Press, 2022), 63–64. Lynch also offers a meditation on naming (105–10) replete with fascinating and evocative observations but looking at the matter through a lens quite different from mine here.

5. Jeff Oliver, "On Mapping and Its Afterlife: Unfolding Landscapes in Northwestern North America," *World Archaeology* 43 (2011), 69–72.

6. James A. Goss, "Traditional Cosmology, Ecology and Language," in *Ute Indian Arts and Culture: From Prehistory to the New Millennium*, ed. William Wroth (Colorado Springs: Taylor Museum of Colorado Springs Fine Arts Center, 2000), 51; Cordelia E. Barrera, *The Haunted Southwest: Towards an Ethics of Place in Borderlands Literature* (Lubbock: Texas Tech University Press, 2022), 31, 33.

7. In an analogous practice, early Christians in the Roman Empire often built churches directly on top of pagan temples both to obliterate the demonic worship that had occurred there and to expropriate the site's preexisting sacrality. On the sacrality of the land, see chapter 2.

8. Aside from the irrigation project in the Imperial Valley examined in chapter 4, several of Zane Grey's Westerns orbit precisely around capitalist projects in the desert: Zane Grey, *Shower of Gold* (New York: Dorchester Publishing Co., Inc., 2007) and *The Light of Western Stars* (Rockville: Phoenix Rider, 2009). Official toponyms in the US can be tracked through the US Board on Geographic Names: https://geonames.usgs.gov/index.html, accessed January 2, 2023. For a critique of the BGN's policies, see Len Beké, "Place Naming and Topographic Silencing in the Sierras of Northern Nuevo México," *Journal of the Southwest* 64 (2022), 501–3.

9. Carobeth Laird, *The Chemehuevis* (Banning, CA: Malki Museum, 1976), 119.

10. Laird, *The Chemehuevis*, 123–24, 126, 127 with 25n14, citing George Devereux, *The Social and Cultural Implications of Incest among the Mohave Indians* (Albany: Psychoanalytic Quarterly, 1939), 360–61.

11. Harry J. Winters Jr., *Maricopa Place Names* (Tucson: SRI Press, 2018), 6–8 (Leslie Spier, *Yuman Tribes of the Gila River* [New York: Dover Publications, 1978], 23, gives *Vi-váva*, but his translation, "solitary mountain," is incorrect), 23 (Spier, *Yuman Tribes*, 6, 242), 20–22 (Spier, *Yuman Tribes*, 23, 131), and 33. Spier, *Yuman Tribes*, 23, gives *xagàvǐcàɷ'*, meaning "water divider," which Winters calls "garbled and mistranslated" (*Maricopa Place Names*, 33). Spier, *Yuman Tribes*, 252–53, 242: but simply dreaming "too much of any one thing" could do it, too. Another mountain near Yuma had the same name; both appeared in dreams as young girls. Spier uses the term "berdache," which, while widely used in earlier ethnographic literature, is derogatory and best avoided; see Kylan Mattias de Vries, "Berdache (Two-Spirit)," in *Encyclopedia of Gender and Society*, ed. Jodi O'Brien (Los Angeles: Sage, 2015), 64; Lisa Tatonetti, *Written by the Body: Gender Expansiveness and Indigenous Non-Cis Masculinities* (Minneapolis: University of Minnesota Press, 2021), 184–85; and for the terminology "woman-man," Sabine Lang, "Native American Men-Women, Lesbians, Two-Spirits: Contemporary and Historical Perspectives," *Journal of Lesbian Studies* 20 (2016): 299–323, and chapter 5. The O'odham insist they are the descendants of the Hohokam, and many ethnographers now accept their view of their origins. Some myths I cite, however, represent the O'odham as expelling the Hohokam.

12. Donald M. Bahr, Juan Smith, William Smith Allison, and Julian Hayden, *Short Swift Time of Gods on Earth: The Hohokam Chronicles* (Berkeley: University of California Press, 1994), 204–5, 239 n. d (*Wonnum*), 245 (*kok chut*), 264 n. d (*komatk*) with Harry J. Winters Jr., *'O'odham Place Names: Meanings, Origins, and Histories, Arizona and Sonora*, 2nd ed. (Tucson: SRI Press, 2020), 436–38; Bahr, Smith, Allison, and Hayden, *Short Swift Time*, 263 (*Ge' Duag*), 269 with n. k (*Wik Akima*), and Dean Saxon, Lucille Saxon, and Susie Enos, *Dictionary: Tohono O'odham/Pima to English: English to Tohono O'odham/Pima*, 2nd ed. (Tucson: University of Arizona Press, 1983), 62 s.v. wegi, "red," Natalie Diaz, *When My Brother Was an Aztec* (Port Townsend: Copper Canyon Press, 2012), 12, with Pamela Munro, Nellie Brown, and Judith G. Crawford, *A Mojave Dictionary* (Los Angeles: Department of Linguistics, University of California, 1992), 15 s.v. 'aha and 77 s.v. haviily; Saxton, Saxton, and Enos, *Dictionary*, 135 with 48 onk ihwagi and onk kui, "saltbush" and "tamarack tree" (literally, "salt tree"). Tamarisks are an invasive exotic: Steven J. Phillips and Patricia Wentworth Comus, *A Natural History of the Sonoran Desert* (Tucson: Arizona-Sonora Museum, 2000), 125. A. L. Kroeber, "Seven Mohave Myths," *University of California Publications: Anthropological Records* 11 (1948), 64 J 82 and 66 M 98 with n. 160. Peter Nabokov, *Where the Lightning Strikes: The Lives of American Indian Sacred Places* (New York: Penguin, 2006), 231, gives *Avi Kwame* as "White-Striped Mountain" and the site of Mastamho's transformation, but the Mastamho myth where this event is narrated clearly sets it on *Avi-kutaparve* and

distinguishes that mountain from *Avi Kwa Ame*. See further in chapter 2. For *Ku'ukchelik*, Winters, *'O'odham Place Names*, 436–38.

13. Julian H. Steward, *Basin-Plateau Aboriginal Sociopolitical Groups* (Washington, DC: United States Government Printing Office, 1938), 71.

14. For further discussion of and more references on the Epic, see chapters 5 and 10. Arthur T. Hatto, *The Mohave Heroic Epic of Inyo-kutavêre* (Helsinki: Academia Scientiarum Fennica, 1999), 99, shows that the majority of the many toponyms recorded in the Epic are "geographically and historically factual." It is possible that some of the toponyms given by Kroeber are in error or mistranslated; Winters, *Maricopa Place Names*, xviii, mentions two trips he took with Lorey Cachorra, a Quechan (Yuma) elder, up and down the Colorado River to identify "places whose names were recorded by Kroeber" (Winters, *Maricopa Place Names*, xviii and 97); he may have corrections, but to the best of my knowledge has not published them (except for one or two mentioned below). Winters mentions a place the Piipaash call Hatay Kw'ii, which is the same as Kroeber's Aha Kwa'a'i (103–4).

15. Munro, Brown, and Crawford, *A Mojave Dictionary*, 23 s.v. 'amat. Transcription and spelling of Mojave words has changed since Kroeber wrote. The ' in front of 'amat stands for a glottal stop, a very common sound in Mojave. When giving toponyms as they appear in the Epic I have abided by Kroeber's practice; in citing entries in Munro, Brown, and Crawford's *A Mojave Dictionary* I have used their spelling. I must note that I have not been able to track down the meanings of every word and every component of words. For the Mojave alphabet, see Pamela Munro, *Mojave Syntax* (New York, Garland, 1976), xiii; Munro, Brown, and Crawford, *A Mojave Dictionary*, 11; a brief discussion of the language in Victor Golla, *California Indian Languages* (Berkeley: University of California Press, 2022), 60 with 307n60; for the structure of the language, Munro, *Mojave Syntax*.

16. A. L. Kroeber, "A Mohave Historical Epic," *University of California Publications: Anthropological Records* 11 (1951), 77 A 2 with 151n12, 84 F 58, F 60, and F 61. Kroeber (156n6 and 10) thinks these names are meaningless, although the latter might embody the word for sleeping, *ismām*, cf. Munro, Brown, and Crawford, *A Mojave Dictionary*, 102, and 23 s.v. 'amat. Dell Hymes, "Lineaments and Approximations," in *Kalevala and the World's Traditional Epics*, ed. Lauri Honko (Helsinki: Finnish Literature Society, 2002), 177, gives a slightly different version of A 2, based on study of Kroeber's field journals, but except for slight orthographic deviations the two new names are the same in both. "Gambling boy" is Kroeber's nickname for Nyîtše-vilye-vave-kwilyêhe derived from his four failed gambling incidents; the nickname does not appear in the Epic.

17. Kroeber, "A Mohave Historical Epic," 144–45 (analysis), 82 E 46–49 (journey out), 83–84 F 57–61 (journey back); Map 2 opposite p. 176 (Fig. 7-2 here). See also the toponyms tracing the track of Apache migrations in Grenville Goodwin, *The Social Organization of the Western Apache* (Chicago: University of Chicago Press, 1942), 608–9, quoted in Karl Jacoby, *Shadows at Dawn: A Borderlands Massacre and the Violence of History* (New York: The Penguin Press, 2008), 147.

18. In her biography of her husband, Theodora Kroeber writes that he took fieldtrips to the region of Parker, Arizona, in February 1953 and 1954 to track the geography "of a Mohave myth" recorded before 1907, "this long ago myth from a man dead many years" (Theodora Kroeber, *Alfred Kroeber: A Personal Configuration* [Berkeley: University of California Press, 1970], 220). This sounds like a reference to the Epic and the detailed map reproduced here as Fig. 7-2, but the dates don't work, as Kroeber published the Epic in 1951. Is Theodora Kroeber referring to something else, or does she have her dates wrong? She makes only this possible, allusive reference to the Epic, whose publication is not included in her bibliography (289–91).

19. Munro, Brown, and Crawford, *A Mojave Dictionary*, 81 s.v. humii.

20. Ibid., 15 s.v. 'aha; 14 s.v. 'achii, "fish;" 15 s.v. 'ah'a, "cottonwood;" 41 s.v. 'iido, "willow;" 198 s.v. vaa i=, "to float;" 41 s.v. 'iikwe, "cloud" (the -*tše* or -*che* is the plural marker). *Ah'a-kuvate* and *Ah'a-θampo* ought to have glottal stop marks at the start, but I have omitted them here because Kroeber does not print them.

21. Winters, *'O'odham Place Names*, 392–402, for the entry; for the features cited: 411 with Figure 76.13; given as ³komal in Saxon, Saxon, and Enos, *Dictionary*, 33 s.v. and translated as "flat, level, thin or shallow (lit. only)" and 11 s.v. chuk; 414–16 with 415 Figure 76.15 and Saxon, Saxon, and Enos, *Dictionary*, 58 s.v. toha; 416 with 60 Figure 10.2, *vashokam* is not in Saxon, Saxon, and Enos, *Dictionary*, who give *pot-lihya* as "pasture" (51 s.v.), a borrowing from the Spanish *potrero*.

22. This formation is marked as Diaz Spire on USGS maps, but this seems wrong to me, since photographs of Diaz Peak and Spire do not resemble this mountain.

23. Winters, *'O'odham Place Names*, 234–40; Saxon, Saxon, and Enos, *Dictionary*, 14 s.v. gakodk, a verb meaning "(be) crooked or bent; (be) curved." The adjective is not included. Winters, *'O'odham Place Names*, 234–35

with Figure 40.1; 239–40 with 238 Figure 40.5 and Saxon, Saxon, and Enos, *Dictionary*, 62 s.v. ²wegi, "(be) red;" 237–38 with 10 Figure 3.2 and, for the meaning of 'a'ai, 8 with Saxon, Saxon, and Enos, *Dictionary*, 2 s.v. aigo, a preposition meaning "across, on the other side of, on each side of," the latter being the denotation here; 241 with 237 Figure 40.4 and Saxon, Saxon, and Enos, *Dictionary*, 64 s.v. wi'ikam.

24. Keith H. Basso, *Wisdom Sits in Places: Landscape and Language among the Western Apache* (Albuquerque: University of New Mexico Press, 1996), 46, 52–53. The failure to perform funeral rites emphasizes the contempt in which the victim was held; incest was strongly condemned by the Western Apache, and relations between step-relatives were counted as incestuous.

25. Basso, *Wisdom Sits in Places*, 55, with an example of the process at work at 56–58.

26. Goss, "Traditional Cosmology," 50. In writing "two major periods of colonization" I omit the intrusion of ancestral Apache into the Southwest.

27. For the impact of colonialism on Native Americans of the Southwest, see the classic analysis of Edward H. Spicer, *Cycles of Conquest: The Impact of Spain, Mexico, and the United States on the Indians of the Southwest, 1533–1960* (Tucson: University of Arizona Press, 1997) (originally published in 1963). I write "post-Columbian" because there were multiple pulses of invasion of the Southwest by Native American groups, notably the Athabaskan-speaking Apache, who came from the north. There is debate among anthropologists and archaeologists about whether the O'odham are descendants of the Hohokam or, as depicted in some O'odham myths, invaders who drove them out, although the O'odham firmly insist they are descended from the Hohokam.

28. Patricia Seed, *Ceremonies of Possession in Europe's Conquest of the New World, 1492–1640* (Cambridge: Cambridge University Press, 1995), 175, 189–90. Lynch, *Outback and Out West*, 106–7, relying on Robert T. Hill, "Descriptive Topographic Terms of Spanish America," *National Geographic Magazine* 7, no. 9 (September 1896): 291–302 (whose argument focuses on the abundance of Spanish words to describe landforms generically), Mary Austin, *The Land of Journey's Ending* (New York: Century, 1924), viii–ix, and Steven L. Driever, "Spanish as a Language for Geographical Expression," *Yearbook (Conference of Latin American Geographers)* 16 (1990): 3–14 (italics in original), who suggests that "because Spain is more arid than England, the Spanish language, especially with its extensive Arabic influence, inevitably *evolved* to be better suited for describing the features of arid landscapes" like those of the Southwest (Lynch, *Outback and Out West*, 107). While true enough, the actual toponyms assigned by Spanish colonists tend to be derived from other sources, as I discuss below. None of the descriptive terms Lynch cites are Arabic derivations.

29. Fray Silvestre Vélez de Escalante, *The Domínguez-Escalante Journal: Their Expedition through Colorado, Utah, Arizona, and New Mexico in 1776*, ed. Ted J. Warner and trans. Fray Angelico Chavez (Salt Lake City: University of Utah Press, 1995), 8 (Santo Domingo, today flooded under Heron Lake, 8n29), 9, 11, 12–13, 21, 24, 26, 29, 32, and 148–49 for a glossary of names. George English Brooks, "The Business of Heaven and Earth: Toponymy and the Imperial Idyll in the Domínguez-Escalante Journal of 1776," in *Before the West Was West: Critical Essays on Pre-1800 Literature of the American Frontiers*, eds. Amy T. Hamilton and Tom J. Hillard (Lincoln: University of Nebraska Press, 2014), 267–68.

30. Vélez de Escalante, *Journal*, 20, 9, 28 with n. 118; Robert Julyan, *The Place Names of New Mexico*, revised ed. (Albuquerque: University of New Mexico Press, 1998), 301.

31. Pedro de Castañeda de Nájera, "The Relación de la Jornada de Cíbola: Pedro de Castañeda de Nájera's Narrative, 1560s (copy, 1596)," in *Documents of the Coronado Expedition, 1539–1542: "They Were Not Familiar with His Majesty, Nor Did They Wish to Be His Subjects,"* eds. and trans. Richard Flint and Shirley Cushing Flint (Albuquerque: University of New Mexico Press, 2005), 412 (chapter 22; Pedro de Castañeda, *The Journey of Coronado*, trans. George Parker Winship [New York: Dover Publications, Inc., 1990], 44, with 138n4 on first part: chapter xxii, 57) with 598 s.v. Brava, Uraba, Yuraba, Valladolid; 421 (chapter 6).

32. Vélez de Escalante, *Journal*, 10, 21, 19 with n. 75, 28.

33. Father Eusebio Francisco Kino, *Kino's Historical Memoir of Pimería Alta: A Contemporary Account of the Beginnings of California, Sonora, and Arizona*, trans. and ed. Herbert Eugene Bolton (Cleveland: The Arthur H. Clark Company, 1919), vol. 1, 249–55. I have excerpted only part of the journey and some of the toponyms.

34. Brooks, "The Business of Heaven and Earth," 264–65.

35. Ibid., 268, cites Maureen Ahern, "'Llevando el norte sobre el ojo izquierdo': Mapping, Measuring, and Naming in Castañedo's *Relación de la jornada de Cíbola*," in *Mapping Colonial Spanish America: Places and Commonplaces in Identity, Culture, and Experience*, eds. Santa Arias and Mariselle Meléndez (2002), 34, who very briefly compares this to Roman colonization practice of renaming; more broadly, see Gary Reger,

"Romans in the Egyptian Desert: From Desert Space to Roman Place," in *Économie et inégalité: Ressources, échanges et pouvoir dans l'antiquité classique*, eds. Sitta von Reden and Pascal Derron, 115–49 (Vandoevres: Fondation Hardt, 2017) and "Greeks and Romans in the Sahara Desert: Ideology and Experience," *Global Environment* 12 (2019): 22–55, on Greek and Roman efforts to "normalize" the Egyptian desert; Brooks, "The Business of Heaven and Earth," 269, on erasure, 271 on the change, 273.

36. A brief notice of the practice in Australia of Governor Lachlan Macquarie (1810–1821) "spreading his own and other old country names across the map" of New South Wales appears in Russel Ward, *The Australian Legend*, 3rd ed. (Melbourne: Oxford University Press, 1987), 82. Another instance of renaming linked to colonialism.

37. Will C. Barnes, *Arizona Place Names: Revised and Enlarged by Byrd H. Granger* (Tucson: University of Arizona Press, 1982), 177 (the cattleman is also the author of the first edition of the collection), 189–90 (see chapter 4), 258 (s.v. Amole Peak), 265, 266, 300; David V. Alexander, *Arizona Frontier Military Place Names, 1846–1912*, revised ed. (Las Cruces: Yucca Tree Press, 2002), 11; Bill Broyles, Luke Evans, Richard Stephen Felger, and Gary Paul Nabhan, "Our Grand Desert: A Gazetteer for Northwestern Sonora, Southwestern Arizona, and Northeastern Baja California," in *Dry Borders: Great Natural Reserves of the Sonoran Desert*, eds. Richard Stephen Felger and Bill Broyles (Salt Lake City: University of Utah Press, 2007), 593 (Baker), 623 (Growler). On the Oatmans, see chapter 9.

38. Barnes, *Arizona Place Names*, 372.

39. Julyan, *The Place Names of New Mexico*, 77 and 306–7, 94 and 222, 111. It strikes me, skimming through Julyan, that New Mexico also preserves a very large number of Spanish-derived names.

40. Barnes, *Arizona Place Names*, 267 (see also Broyles, Evans, Felger, and Nabhan, "Our Grand Desert," 624), 308, 192; Julyan, *The Place Names of New Mexico*, 18, 55. And then there are the bizarros. Pasadena, California, is part of a supposed translation of "Key (or Crown) of the Valley" into Chippewa, *Tá-pe-ká-e-gun Pá-sá-de-na*: George R. Stewart, *Names on the Land: A Historical Account of Place-Naming in the United States* (New York: New York Review of Books, 2008), 349.

41. However, as JM Arthur insists in her study of colonial naming in Australia, when colonists choose to use an Indigenous name, this naming "remains a colonial naming. The 'Aboriginal' or 'native name' is *chosen* by the colonist and *applied* by the colonist. The 'Aboriginal name' operates as an artefact, passed into use, divorced from its social, cultural and geographical context" (*The Default Country: A Lexical Geography of Twentieth-Century Australia* [Sydney: New South Wales University Press, 2003], 75, italics in original).

42. Sabina Sestigiani, *Writing Colonisation: Violence, Landscape, and the Act of Naming in Modern Italian and Australian Literature* (New York: Peter Lang, 2014), 65–123, with her discussion of Benjamin and Blanchot at 69–79; Walter Benjamin, *Gesammelte Schriften, II-1*, eds. Rolf Tiedemann and Hermann Schweppenhäuser (Frankfurt am Main: Suhrkamp Verlag, 1977), 148, 153, 155. She appeals also to Martin Heidegger's idea of colonialist "enframing," "by which things are rendered as objects to be looked at. . . . [T]he world represented as a picture and the act of containing it inside a frame" (76; see Martin Heidegger, *The Question Concerning Technology and Other Essays*, trans. William Lovin [New York: Garland Press, 1977], 115–54). The same resorting to seeing the landscape as a picture, and so becoming "picturesque," is explored in Simon Ryan, *The Cartographic Eye: How Explorers Saw Australia* (Cambridge: Cambridge University Press, 1999), 60–76.

43. Maurice Blanchot, *The Gaze of Orpheus and Other Literary Essays*, ed. Geoffrey Hartman and trans. Lydia Davis (Barryton: Station Hill Press, 1981), 42, 41, 53.

44. Sestigiani, *Writing Colonisation*, 75, and at 174 naming is "annihilation."

45. Blanchot, *The Gaze of Orpheus*, 42, where, after using "woman" as a word that obliterates the real, living, woman, an utterance by which "I must somehow take her flesh and blood reality away from her, cause her to be absent, annihilate her" (strong language indeed!), he adds, "Of course my language does not kill anyone." And then he cuts the ground from under this concession: "And yet: when I say, 'This woman,' real death has been announced and is already present in my language . . . this person, who is here right now, can be detached from herself, removed from her existence and her presence and suddenly plunged into a nothingness in which there is no existence or presence." The concern with death, announced in the title, is wrapped up in Blanchot's claim that language, writing, and death are inextricably intertwined. So in a way he has slipped out of his own apparent conundrum here.

46. Sestigiani, *Writing Colonisation*, 72. She erases Jacobs's (primary) coauthor Gelder in her references to *Uncanny Australia*; her quotations from this book here come from 205n57 and 60, which reverse the page reference (n57 should be to Ken Gelder and Jane M. Jacobs, *Uncanny Australia: Sacredness and Identity in a Postcolonial Nation* [Melbourne: Melbourne University Press, 1998], 50, and n60 to 49); the intervening

come from Howard Morphy and Frances Morphy, "The Spirit of the Plains Kangaroo," in *Words for Country: Landscape and Language in Australia*, eds. Tim Bonyhady and Tom Griffiths (Sydney: University of South Wales Press, 2002), 115–17. The Muecke quotations are from his *Textual Spaces: Aboriginality and Cultural Studies* (Sydney: New South Wales University Press, 1992), 9.

47. Arthur, *The Default Country*, 72–78, quotation at 72. *Gulaga* is now a national park: see https://www.nationalparks.nsw.gov.au/visit-a-park/parks/gulaga-national-park, accessed September 10, 2022. See also Dale Kerwin, *Aboriginal Dreaming Paths and Trading Routes: The Colonisation of the Australian Economic Landscape* (Brighton: Sussex Academic Press, 2012), 2–3, for like comments on the impact of colonial renaming in Australia.

48. Arthur, *The Default Country*, 54.

49. Paul Kavanagh, "With Breath Just Condensing on It: An Interview with David Malouf," *Southerly* 46, 3 (1986), 252.

50. Basso, *Wisdom Sits in Places*, 111–20, with 115 Figure 8, a photograph of the cottonwood.

51. Shakespeare, *Romeo and Juliet*, Act 2, Scene 2.

52. Lois Rudnick, "Re-Naming the Land: Anglo Expatriate Women in the Southwest," in *The Desert Is No Lady: Southwestern Landscapes in Women's Writing and Art*, eds. Vera Norwood and Janice Monk (Tucson: University of Arizona Press, 1987), 16. On reflections of naming in Mary Austin's work, see both Rudnick's essay and Seth D. Horton, "Critical Regionality and (Mis-)Translation: The Modernist Elision of Pueblo Source Material in Mary Austin's Later Career," *Western American Literature* 58 (2023), 123–28.

53. Basso, *Wisdom Sits in Places*, 10.

54. Barnes, *Arizona Place Names*, 276, 191.

55. For a critique of the term "cultural landscape," see chapter 10.

56. Ahern, "Llevando el norte," 33, 34, 36 on erasure of Indigenous names by the renaming process; Barbara Mundy, *The Mapping of New Spain: Indigenous Cartography and the Maps of the Relaciones Geográficas* (Chicago: University of Chicago Press, 1996), 138. De Castañeda, "The Relación," 414–24 (translation), 469–81 (Spanish). On Cibola, see William K. Hartmann, *Searching for Golden Empires: Epic Cultural Collisions in Sixteenth-Century America* (Tucson: University of Arizona Press, 2014). For a couple of instances where indigenous names have been attached to physical features in translation, see Moon Mountain—Vii Hly'a— and Mesquite Mountain—Vii 'Iish—in Winters, *Maricopa Place Names*, 108 and 112, both near the Colorado River.

57. See Sestigiani, *Writing Colonisation*, 91: "[In] a colonial context, language is vital to the act of rendering spaces available to humans, turning territories into 'areas of action,'" quoting Amanda Nettlebeck, *Reading David Malouf*, ed. Pamela Gay (Sydney: Sydney University Press, 1995), 33. Sestigiani, however, also notes the inability of the protagonist of Ennio Flaiano's *A Time to Kill*, trans. Stuart Hood (London: Quartet, 1992) to give names to all the strange landscapes and creatures he encounters in Africa (*Writing Colonisation*, 137, 143).

58. Tzvetan Todorov, *The Conquest of America: The Question of the Other*, trans. Richard Howard (Norman: University of Oklahoma Press, 1999), 27, italics in original.

59. Only "apparent" because the deserts were interlaced with trails used for centuries by Indigenous groups for travel and trade; some can still be traced quite easily on the desert pavement. See the fine photograph of a Cahuilla trail in Nicholas Clapp, *Old Magic: Lives of the Desert Shamans* (San Diego: Sunbelt Publications, 2017), 125.

CHAPTER 8

1. Gregory L. Reece, *UFO Religion: Inside Flying Saucer Cults and Culture* (London-New York: I. B. Tauris, 2007), 52.

2. Hüsker Dü, "Books about UFOs" (1985).

3. J. Gordon Melton, "The Contactees: A Survey," in *The Gods Have Landed: New Religions from Other Worlds*, ed. James Lewis, 1–13 (Albany: State University of New York Press, 1995) offers a brief survey; David Michael Jacobs, *The UFO Controversy in America* (Bloomington: Indiana University Press, 1975), 108–28, remains a good brief, if somewhat selective, introduction. Mark Probert, who was connected with the Borderland Sciences Research Foundation (BSRF) established in 1945 by Meade Layne, is sometimes said to have been the first attested contactee: see Diana Tumminia, *When Prophecy Never Fails: Myth and Religion in a Flying Saucer Group* (Oxford: Oxford University Press, 2005), 3, 38, and 54. The first report of one of Probert's séances seems to be in the BSRF *Round Robin* 3, no. 2 (February 1947), https://borderlandsciences.

org/journal/vol/03/n02/Probert_Seance_Report.html, accessed April 21, 2017. For the BSRF: https://borderlandsciences.org/, accessed April 21, 2017. Since 1954 there has been an outpouring of publications by contactees and their champions, detractors, and academics: J. Gordon Melton and George M. Eberhard, "The Flying Saucer Contactee Movement, 1950–1994: A Bibliography," in *The Gods Have Landed: New Religions from Other Worlds*, ed. James Lewis, 251–332 (Albany: State University of New York Press, 1995) counted 619 entries in a bibliography that has only grown in the subsequent three decades. It is easy to mock the contactees, especially at the distance of six decades, when many of their pronouncements read as utter nonsense. But I prefer to follow Hilary Evans, who argues that their experiences are both *real*, in the sense that something happened to them (even if surely not as they interpret them), and *purposeful*, that is, that their experiences did something meaningful to or for the contactee (*Gods, Spirits, Cosmic Guardians: A Comparative Study of the Encounter Experience* [Wellingborough: Aquarian Press, 1987], 197); see also the very sympathetic treatment of Robert Plank, *The Emotional Significance of Imaginary Beings: A Study of the Interaction between Psychopathology, Literature, and Reality in the Modern World* (Springfield: Charles C. Thomas, 1968) and Jacobs, *The UFO Controversy*, 127: because the aliens were clearly highly moral, "the contactee followers' logic dictated that the contactee was telling the truth. The key is the sincerity of the contactees; all the major ones seemed to have had more than the required amount. Serious investigators were always struck by the contactees' sincerity and how people seemed to *want* to believe them" (italics in original); see also Clay Routledge, Andrew A. Abeyta, and Christina Roylance, "We Are Not Alone: The Meaning Motive, Religiosity, and the Belief in Extraterrestrial Intelligence," *Motivation and Emotion* 41 (2017): 135–46. In what follows I write ingenuously about their reports. Of course, fraud and purposeful deception always linger in the shadows.

4. So Nick Redfern, *Contactees: A History of Alien-Human Interactions* (Franklin Lakes: New Page Books, 2010) in his chapter title on Adamski (25).

5. George Adamski, "George Adamski," in *Flying Saucers Have Landed*, eds. Desmond Leslie and George Adamski, 9–22 (London: Werner Laurie, 1953) in general and George Adamski, *Inside the Space Ships* (New York: Abelard-Schuman, Inc., 1955), 184 (171: Adamski admits he always had believed in inhabitants of other planets); George Adamski, "The Memorable November Twentieth," in *Flying Saucers Have Landed*, ed. Desmond Leslie and George Adamski (London: Werner Laurie, 1953), 185. As the most famous of the contactees, Adamski has accumulated a long bibliography. Some examples: Aaron John Gulyas, *Extraterrestrials and the American Zeitgeist: Alien Contact Tales Since the 1950s* (Jefferson: McFarland Company, Publishers, 2013), 42–48, 60–82; Evans, *Gods, Spirits, Cosmic Guardians*, 131–35; David Stupple, "The Man Who Talked with Venusians," in *Proceedings of the First International UFO Congress*, eds. Curtis G. Fuller, Mary Margaret Fuller, Jerome Clark, and Betty Lou White, 261–71 (New York: Warner Books, 1980); C. G. Jung, *Flying Saucers: A Modern Myth of Things Seen in the Sky*, trans. R. F. C. Hull (Princeton: Princeton University Press, 1978), 16. He served in the Thirteenth Cavalry on the Mexican border 1913–1919; perhaps this service affected his desert interests (see Charlotte Blodget, "Introduction," in *Inside the Space Ships* by George Adamski, 9–20 [New York: Abelard-Schuman, 1955], and at 254). Charlotte Blodget was Adamski's ghost writer. Peter Reyner Banham, *Scenes in America Deserta* (Cambridge: MIT Press, 1982), 44, on the importance of the Mojave as the first site of contact.

6. Adamski, "The Memorable November Twentieth," 185–86 (trips, companions), 187 (sand, rocks, plants, wind, etc.), 188 ("The sky"). Also in Adamski, *Inside the Space Ships*, 23–54.

7. Adamski, *Inside the Space Ships*, 26–53, "The Memorable November Twentieth," 194, capitals in original (reprinted as George Adamski, *Inside the Space Ships*, revised ed. (Vista: The George Adamski Foundation, 2001). His companions consisted of Al and Betty Bailey, Alice Wells (who made the sketch), Lucy McGinnis, Adamski's secretary, and George Williamson and his wife. Williamson and Bailey later tried to contact aliens via Ouija board and short-wave radio, reporting their efforts in George Hunt Williamson and Brother Philip, *The Saucers Speak: Calling All Occupants of Interplanetary Craft*, ed. Timothy Green Beckley (Global Communications, 2012), perhaps alluded to in Reverend George King, *You Are Responsible!* (London: The Aetherius Press, 1961), 125. See also George Hunt Williamson, *Other Tongues, Other Flesh* (Amherst: Amherst Press, 1957). For communication with aliens by signs, see also in chapter 9. In Ernest Favenc, *The Secret of the Australian Desert* (London: Blackie & Son, 1894), explorers must exchange information with the Indigenes they meet by signs: 50, 51, 54, 57, 58, 80.

8. Not, Adamski insists, the visitor's real name: Adamski, *Inside the Space Ships*, 43. He's mentioned by name in King, *You Are Responsible!*, 126, and 127 for Oriel.

9. Adamski, *Inside the Space Ships*, 37 and 40; the same procedure, 113, 174, 191, 255–56 (drive to a desert spot), and elsewhere. John A. Saliba, "Religious Dimensions of UFO Phenomena," in *The Gods Have Landed: New*

Religions from Other Worlds, ed. James Lewis (Albany: State University of New York, 1995), 38–39, reads Adamski's interpretation of his Venusians as essentially biblical angels sent to help humankind; in this view, Adamski has simply reconfigured a traditional Christianity to account for his experiences with aliens; there are also elements of Mormonism. See further below. For a curious assessment of Adamski's psychological response to contact, see R. M. Decker, *35 Minutes to Mars* (Lakeville: Glade Press, Inc., 2004), 179–83.

10. See Lillian Makeda, "Visions of a Liminal Landscape: Mythmaking on the Rainbow Plateau," *Journal of the Southwest* 58 (2016), 633–46, for an excellent evocation of these same tropes concerning the Rainbow Plateau of the Navajo (Diné) Reservation. Daniel Fry's aliens, however, chose "the 'Great American Desert'" because White Sands Proving Ground was the locus of space technology (*The White Sands Incident Including an Extraterrestrial Statement* [Madison: Horus House Press, 1992], 27).

11. George W. Van Tassel, *The Council of Seven Lights* (Clarksburg: Saucerian Publisher, 2020), *I Rode a Flying Saucer* (Clarksburg: Saucerian Publisher, 2020), 10. Redfern, *Contactees*, 69–83. James Mosley in Greg Bishop, "Interview: James Mosley *Saucer Smear* 'Commander' and Publisher," in *Wake Up Down There! The Excluded Middle Collection*, ed. Greg Bishop (Kempton: Adventures Unlimited Press, 2000), 114; Mosley must have misremembered the date of his attendance. Robert Short, *Out of the Stars: A Message from Extraterrestrial Intelligence* (Haverford: Infinity Publishing, 2010), 8–9.

12. Van Tassel, *I Rode a Flying Saucer*, 13, 16, 21, 24, 22. All italics in original.

13. www.integratron.com, accessed September 20, 2023.

14. Gulyas, *Extraterrestrials and the American Zeitgeist*, 89–94, 204–6; Redfern, *Contactees*, 47–55; Reece, *UFO Religion*, 116–17; Evans, *Gods, Spirits, Cosmic Guardians*, 145–47; Jacobs, *The UFO Controversy*, 111–12. Truman Bethurum, *Aboard a Flying Saucer: A Non-Fiction True Story of Personal Experience* (Los Angeles: DeVorss & Co., Publishers, 1954), 31, 168; visits occurred on the nights of July 27–28, 33 (but July 20–21 at p. 159); August 3–4, 53; August 18, 66; August 25, 78; September 5, 100; September 6–7, 109; September 16, 132; September 23, 142; October 2, 153; October 12, 159; November 2–3, 168.

15. Bethurum, *Aboard a Flying Saucer*, 43, 44, 153, 184, etc.; 165: landing near Glendale. Bethurum is a slightly slippery character. There is a 12-page booklet, published in 1961 and titled *Fighting Communism with Common Sense: Is America Being "Sold Down the River?"* under the name "Truman Betherum"; is this the same person (see n44)? His *Personal Scrapbook* (see n17 below) isn't listed in WorldCat, although several other books, some published after his death, are. In some cases below I have had to rely on others' references to work of his that I have not been able to obtain.

16. Bethurum, *Aboard a Flying Saucer*, 45.

17. Ibid., 40 ("smooth skin"), 155 ("slack outfit"), 51 ("dame"); Aura gives her name at 68. Bubbling barely below the surface in Bethurum's account is an obvious but veiled sexual attraction to the splendid Aura Rhanes. At one point he admits to her, "'It seems hard to believe that I am out in the middle of a great desert, sitting across from a beautiful woman who should actually be said is from out of this world." She noticed, Bethurum supposes, "that I eyed her flesh quite a bit" and so "told me to feel of her arm and shoulder and convince myself that she was a real woman." As he placed his hands on her shoulders, she warned him: "Please use restraint. Else you might guess something that isn't so" (Bethurum, *Aboard a Flying Saucer*, 69–70; and see his poem on Aura in his *Personal Scrapbook* (Scotia: Arcturus, 1982); extracts can be found at http://www.xdream.freeserve.co.uk/Space%20People/TrumanB.htm, accessed April 6, 2022); I have not been able to obtain a copy. Bethurum is hardly alone. Angelucci has Lyra, "dazzlingly beautiful," whose "beauty was breath-taking." Later, he became suddenly "fully aware for the first time of all her exquisite feminine beauty and loveliness. Involuntarily, a wave of desire for her swept over me." But never fear: when they were "enfolded in an embrace of the spirit untouched by sensuality or carnality" he pitied his earthly brothers who "know mostly only the counterfeit embrace of sexual desire and animal passion" for "sexual desire is merely another of the erroneous manifestations of materiality"; it does not exist in "higher spiritual worlds" (Orfeo Angelucci, *Son of the Sun: The Secret of the Saucers*, ed. Timothy Green Beckley [New Brunswick: Global Communications/Conspiracy Journal, 2008], 54–55; see Evans, *Gods, Spirits, Cosmic Guardians*, 137–38, and Jung, *Flying Saucers*, 112–20). Angelucci's later friend Adam is tempted by not one but three gorgeous Space Sisters; his trip with Eve—and note their names—reads very like a thinly disguised metaphor for sexual intercourse, with a big orgasm as the climax (*Son of the Sun*, 48, 54–55; cf. 73; 122, 128, 149, on Lily: Adam "saw her body as the gateway to her shining soul"; 216–27). At age 10 in 1932 (!) Howard Menger met a Space Sister who "was the most exquisite woman my young eyes had ever beheld!" She boasted "long golden hair . . . [and] the curves of her lovely body were delicately contoured—revealed through the translucent material of clothing. . . . [T]he feeling I received was unmistakable . . . a tremendous surge of warmth, love and physical attraction." The same sexual appeal

recurs whenever he meets a Space Sister, and sometimes they express the same attraction to him (Howard Menger, *From Outer Space to You* [Clarksburg: Saucerian Books, 1959], 26, 36; see Evans, *Gods, Spirits, Cosmic Guardians*, 142). In 1957 the Brazilian farmer Antonio Vallejo Boas experienced plain old direct sex with a "space woman." Abducted, he was shut up in a room where a beautiful, naked woman appeared; she had strange eyes, though, and barked like a dog as they copulated. Boas averred he was repulsed, attributing his double bout of intercourse to a drug presumably infused through his skin by an ointment the aliens daubed him with (Redfern, *Contactees*, 109–15). Boas's partner sported red pubic hair; red hair, we are assured, seems characteristic of at least some female "Star Travelers" (*The Dulce Wars: Underground Alien Bases & the Battle for Planet Earth*, ed. Branton [New Brunswick: Inner Light/Global Communications, 1999], 113; see chapter 9 n16). Budd Hopkins has claimed that "hundreds of cases" offer "evidence of the profound interest of UFO occupants . . . in basic human sexuality" ("Abduction and Deception," *International UFO Reporter* [September–October 1990], 16), but for contactees, this was a two-way street. Adamski introduces a pair of stunning women, one each from Venus and Mars (Adamski, *Inside the Space Ships*, 61–63). His descriptions of these women, while not as fulsome as Bethurum's, are clearly of a piece: their "loose, flowing gowns revealed merely a suggestion of the perfect symmetry of their bodies" until "they changed into close-fitting uniforms" and "the beauty and grace with which all were formed was clearly apparent" (Adamski, *Inside the Space Ships*, 133; see also "pilot suits" at 140 and 141). Elizabeth Klarer, in contrast to the shift from body to spirit, celebrated her own very carnal sexual encounters with Akon of Meton: "I surrendered in ecstasy to the magic of his love making. Our bodies merged in magnetic union as the divine essence of our spirits became one. . . . I found the true meaning of love in mating with a man from another planet" (Elizabeth Klarer, *Beyond the Light Barrier: The Autobiography of Elizabeth Klarer* [Flagstaff: Light Technology Publishing, 2009], 88). Their "magnetic union" produced a child, who was raised on Meton. Whitley Strieber's "woman" (who sometimes appears like a praying mantis) is not physically attractive, but "she" too "created states of sexual arousal." In one encounter, "She asked if I was as hard as I could get. . . . 'I guess I am,'" he replied. She persisted: "'Can you be harder?' 'Can I be harder?' Oh, Lord, didn't know I was hard like that. 'No, not with you around I can't be harder.'" Immediately she asked, "'What would you like me to be?'" While this conversation is going on, Strieber is being penetrated anally by "a big gray thing with what looked like a little cage on the end of it, a little round nubbin about the size of your thumb" (Whitley Strieber, *Communion: A True Story* [New York: William Morrow, 1987], 105, see also 151; 84–85; brief discussion: Bridget Brown, *They Know Us Better Than We Know Ourselves: The History and Politics of Alien Abduction* (New York: New York University Press, 2007), 54–55, who likely based her book's title on Angelucci, *Son of the Sun*, 5: "We know you as you do not know yourselves"). The psychoanalysis performs itself. See chapter 9 n6 for an early instance of naked Martians on a visit to Earth.

18. Bethurum, *Aboard a Flying Saucer*, 54 ("hit out," "bright"), 62 ("In the west"), 53 ("nuts"), 44 ("She mentioned"), 69 ("We talked").

19. Bethurum, *Aboard a Flying Saucer*, 146 ("like heaven"), 74–75 ("what is right" and following), 136–37 (later rumination). George King's contacts too promised "to help you [humankind] by teaching you how you can irrigate and cultivate your deserts, so that they can again become as fertile as when the Great Pyramids were built" (King, *You Are Responsible!*, 72).

20. Dana Howard, *Diane: She Came from Venus* (London: Regency Press, n.d. [1956]), 9–10 (quotation at 10 and 9, respectively) and *My Flight to Venus: A True Mystical Experience—Long Before the Advent of the Flying Saucer—Heralding the Coming of Interplanetary Spacecraft* (Clarksburg: New Saucerian Press, 2017); Redfern, *Contactees*, 97–100. After this second manifestation Diane usually prefers to appear in the desert (see below), but occasionally she chooses other venues, like Howard's bedroom or Pine Cove, a small settlement in the San Jacinto Mountains (Howard, *Diane*, 69, 73, 61).Women contactees have often been ignored in favor of their more famous male fellows, partly no doubt due to simple sexism, but perhaps also because they tended to make contact not physically but psychically. In addition to Howard, there were Gloria Lee, supporter of Adamski and founder of the Cosmon Research Foundation, through which she promoted her psychic contact with J.W. of Jupiter; Frances Swan, who lived in Maine and communicated by automatic writing with Affa of Uranus and Ponnar, commanders of Earth-circling spaceships; and Dorothy Martin, who seems to have been inspired by Truman Bethurum to seek contact with Clarion and later, as Sister Thedra, founded the Association of Sananda and Sanat Kumara, headquartered in the famous cosmic vortex site of Sedona, Arizona. See https://web2.ph.utexas.edu/~coker2/calbum/calbum.html, accessed May 1, 2017, for brief discussion of these figures.

21. Howard, *Diane*, 10–16 (Diane in church séance), 38, 8 (driving in desert, quoting 1954, 87); 1957, 81.

22. Howard, *Diane*, 80 ("high in the beautiful valley"), ("one of those mid-March"), 71 ("It was high noon"), n.d. [1956], 53.

23. Howard, *Diane*, 53 ("[I]t is", "the same clean", and "Out where"), her emphasis; 65 ("balmy summer" and "starry"), 81, for the rest of the quotations.

24. Howard, *Diane*, 27 ("perhaps" through "Day by day"), 81 ("Altar" through "plot"). Even as Howard and Diane were conferring at the Altar in the Wilderness Shrine, Palm Springs was booming as a Hollywood resort just below: see Lawrence Culver, *The Frontier of Leisure: Southern California and the Shaping of Modern America* (New York: Oxford University Press, 2010), 170–93. The aliens' preference for this desert setting affected even the stars who vacationed there. Bob Hope, upon seeing the design for his Palm Springs home (built in 1979), is reported to have remarked: "[A]t least when they come down from Mars they'll know where to go" (Culver, *Frontier of Leisure*, 186). Akhenaton figures in other UFO cults too. Ernest Norman, founder with his wife Ruth of the Unarius cult, learned from Mark Probert (see n3) that he had been that pharaoh in an earlier life (R. George Kirkpatrick and Diana Tumminia, "California Space Goddess: The Mystagogue in a Flying Saucer Cult," in *Twentieth-Century World Religious Movements in Neo-Weberian Perspective*, ed. William H. Swatos Jr. [Lewiston: Mellen, 1992], 303). For Moses in the desert, see chapter 1.

25. Howard, *Diane*, 82.

26. Dana Howard, *Over the Threshold* (Los Angeles: Llewellyn Publications, Ltd., 1957), 74 ("[t]he desert's"), 72 ("the sunshine"); n.d. [1956], 36, for the rest. Regan Lee, "The Mystical Contactee Encounters of Dana Howard: Parallels to the Marian Apparitions?" *UFO Digest* (2007), http://www.ufodigest.com/news/1207/danahoward.html, accessed April 27, 2017, and "From the Desert Sands, Cauldrons of Magic Will Spring," in *Secrets of Death Valley: Mysteries and Haunts of the Mohave Desert*, ed. Timothy Green Beckley, 15–19 (New Brunswick: Global Communications, 2010). The idea that visions of aliens compare to visions of Mary is not new: see Hilary Evans, *Visions, Apparitions, Alien Visitors* (Wellingborough: Aquarian Press, 1984, 147, 150, 157, and *Gods, Spirits, Cosmic Guardians*, 51–57.

27. Saliba, "Religious Dimensions," 43. See, for instance, Howard, *Diane*, 34–35.

28. An important text in the development of this notion is Charles Berlitz and William Moore, *The Roswell Incident* (New York: Berkeley Books, 1980), who revived the Roswell crash. A recent credulous review of the literature and evidence for Roswell as a genuine UFO crash can be found in Kevin D. Randle, *Roswell in the 21st Century: The Evidence as It Exists Today* (Naples: Speaking Volumes, LLC, 2016), but see the scholarly approach of B. Saler, C. Ziegler, and C. Moore, *UFO Crash at Roswell: The Genesis of a Modern Myth* (Washington, DC: Smithsonian Institution Press, 1997). D. W. Pasulka, *American Cosmic: UFOs, Religion, Technology* (New York: Oxford University Press, 2019), 17–24, 47–50, 73–80, relates a visit to a UFO crash site with a couple of "investigators": the site isn't named, but the details suggest Roswell.

29. Howard, *Over the Threshold*, 39 ("Our deserts," the block quotation, whose ellipsis is Howard's, and "hallowed," (my ellipsis). There are dozens of similar and sometimes more evocative passages throughout Howard's writing: "Slipping from my sandals, I buried my feet in the desert sand. In a few moments my thoughts began to soar, bounding over the broad expanse of unspoiled, cactus-studded sandy waste" (Howard, *Over the Threshold*, 53); Howard sometimes falls into such clichés as "desert wastes," but the tenor of her writing makes it quite clear that she does not regard the desert as a "wasteland" in the usual manner. Nor does she wholly romanticize the desert; she remarks on "a night of desert violence" when "winds lashed with fury . . . terrifying in no small degree" or "when the rains came they were torrential" for "[t]he desert knew no moderation"; but still, "with it all, when the desert was in one's blood, it was there forever" (Howard, *Over the Threshold*, 39 and 81 ["desert wastes"], 63, rest of quotations).

30. Fry, *The White Sands Incident*, 37–115, quotation at 115; Redfern, *Contactees*, 18–22. Sumathi Ramaswamy, *The Lost Land of Lemuria: Fabulous Geographies, Catastrophic Histories* (Berkeley: University of California Press, 2004), 256n102, for the thermonuclear war between Lemuria and Atlantis, in David L. Manley, *Aros of Atlantis* (Philadelphia: Dorrance, 1972), xiii–xvii.

31. Angelucci, *Son of the Sun*, 92–232; Redfern, *Contactees*, 65–66. According to Greg Bishop, Angelucci later admitted he suffered hallucinations that "came back through his subconscious to his consciousness as visions" (Bishop, "Interview," 115). King, *You Are Responsible!*, 124, seems to allude to Angelucci's Adam, whose story occupies the whole of 1959's version of *Son of the Sun* (*Sun of the Son*, 88–232).

32. Redfern, *Contactees*, 118.

33. Angelucci, *Son of the Sun*, 95.

34. Gulyas, *Extraterrestrials and the American Zeitgeist*, 131–75; John Rimmer, *The Evidence for Alien Abductions* (Wellingborough: The Aquarian Press, 1984); see also Brown, *They Know Us Better* and MJ Banias, *The*

UFO People: A Curious Culture (n.p.: August Night Books, 2019). For the striking parallels between alien abduction and Indian captivity narratives, see A. Panay, "From *Little Big Man* to Little Green Men: The Captivity Scenario in American Culture," *European Journal of American Culture* 23 (2004): 201–16, and Michael Sturma, "Aliens and Indians: A Comparison of Abduction and Captivity Narratives," *Journal of Popular Culture* 36 (2002): 318–34; further references below in n39.

35.   Not all contactees by any means had physical contact in a desert. The South African Elizabeth Klarer, who claimed her first encounter occurred in 1956 (see for the first report of her experiences Anonymous, "Landing in South Africa," *Flying Saucer Review* [December 1956]: 2–5, but she did not tell her own story until 1980, and then in a radically different form [Klarer, *Beyond the Light Barrier* with Gulyas, *Extraterrestrials and the American Zeitgeist*, 118 and 213–23]), met her Venusian, or later Akon the Metonian, in the Drakensberg Mountains (today a national park); for the climate, see Werner Nel, "Rainfall Trends in the KwaZulu-Natal Draksenberg Region of South Africa in the Twentieth Century," *International Journal of Climatology* 29 (2009): 1634–1641. Betty and Helen Mitchell, whose story appeared as *We Met the Space People* in 1959, struck up their acquaintance with Martians in a drugstore in St. Louis (Gulyas, *Extraterrestrials and the American Zeitgeist*, 207; their account can be found at http://sacred-texts.com/ufo/wmsp/wmsp01.htm, accessed April 21, 2017). Bethurum's Aura Rhanes also strolled around Overton, Nevada, in disguise, once ducking into a drugstore herself (Bethurum, *Aboard a Flying Saucer*, 111).

36.   Hatonn's organization: see Gyeorgos C. Hatonn, *Space-Gate: The Veil Removed*, 3rd ed. (Las Vegas: Phoenix Source, 1993), 1.

37.   Betty and Barney Hill were taken while driving late one night in rural New Hampshire (see John Fuller, *The Interrupted Journey: Two Lost Hours "Aboard a Flying Saucer"* [New York: Penguin-Random House, 2022]), originally published in 1966; for two recent takes, one credulous, one skeptical and far-ranging, Stanton T. Friedman and Kathleen Marden, *Captured! The Betty and Barney Hill UFO Experience: The True Story of the First Documented Alien Abduction* (Newburyport: New Page Books, 2021); Matthew Bowman, *The Abduction of Betty and Barney Hill: Alien Encounters, Civil Rights, and the New Age in America* (New Haven: Yale University Press, 2023); Brown, *They Know Us Better*, 72–73 (also 232n10), suggests their experiences might have been prompted by 1950s science fiction films; later instances that attracted considerable attention were recounted by Budd Hopkins (*Missing Time* [New York: Ballantine, 1981] and *Intruders: The Incredible Visitations at Copley Woods* [New York: Ballantine Books, 1987]) and, perhaps most prominently, Whitley Strieber (*Communion*). Ed Walters and Frances Walters, *The Gulf Breeze Sightings: The Most Astounding Multiple Sightings of UFOs in U.S. History* (New York: William Morrow and Company, Inc., 1990), 26–35, describe a failed abduction attempt at the start of a "flap" of UFO sightings at Gulf Breeze, Florida, in 1987. On the phenomenon in general, see Susan A. Clancy, *Abducted: How People Come to Believe They Were Kidnapped by Aliens* (Cambridge: Harvard University Press, 2005); Terry Matheson, *Alien Abductions: Creating a Modern Phenomenon* (Amherst: Prometheus Books, 1998); Evans, *Gods, Spirits, Cosmic Guardians*, 154–71, and, for a recent (credulous) review, Preston Dennett, *Inside UFOs: True Accounts of Contacts with Extraterrestrials* (Scotts Valley: Create Space Independent Publishing Platform, 2017). Michael Shermer, *The Believing Brain: From Ghosts and Gods to Politics and Conspiracies—How We Construct Beliefs and Reinforce Them as Truths* (New York: St. Martin's Griffin, 2011), 190–95, offers a neuro-psychological explanation for the experiences of abductees. Brown, *They Know Us Better* sets abduction within multiple contexts: diversion of trauma memories into an abduction experience; nervousness about the trajectory of the US in the 1970s and 1980s; conspiracy theorizing. See further Jodi Dean, *Aliens in America: Conspiracy Theories from Outerspace to Cyberspace* (Ithaca: Cornell University Press, 1998) and Matheson, *Alien Abductions*, for a good history of the development of the abduction narrative.

38.   Neatly summarized by James Mosley in Bishop, "Interview," 111. Brown, *They Know Us Better*, 4, lists three categories of interpretation of abductions by outside observers: "[T]he New Age argument that alien abduction is a mode of spiritual transformation; the so-called 'realist' argument that alien abduction is simply physical and emotional victimization to be treated therapeutically; and the conspiracy theory argument that alien abduction is the product of human-alien conspiracy and government deception." For abductees themselves there is no question the experiences are real, and often motivated by an alien-human hybrid breeding program. On psychological woundedness, 58–65. As Brown shows (*They Know Us Better*, 152–59), the earliest abduction accounts continue to deploy warnings about the dangers of nuclear war and, now, environmental destruction, combined with kidnapping, as opposed to the voluntarism of Adamski and his ilk.

39.   Fuller, *The Interrupted Journey*; Strieber, *Communion*, who however insists that he cannot say for certain that his experiences were "alien abduction," although many of the people with similar tales whom he interviews

have little doubt. In general, see Hopkins, *Missing Time* and *Intruders*, who first popularized the abduction experience after the shock of Betty and Barney Hill faded. On fear and pain: one abductee Strieber interviewed stated, "Most of the time I was angry or terrified" (257). On abduction, see n37 above and in addition David M. Jacobs, *Secret Life: Firsthand Documented Accounts of UFO Abductions* (New York: Simon, 1992), John E. Mack, *Abduction: Human Encounters with Aliens* (New York: Ballantine, 1994), Patricia Felisa Barbeito, "'He's Making Me Feel Things in My Body That I Don't Feel': The Body as Battleground in Accounts of Alien Abduction," *Journal of American Culture* 28 (2005): 201–15, Brown, *They Know Us Better*, and Susan Lepselter, "The Resonance of Captivity: Aliens and Conquest," *Hau: Journal of Ethnographic Theory* 2 (2012) with 94–97 on the Hills; Barbeito and Lepselter explore the intersections between classic Native American abduction narratives and alien abduction. Brown, *They Know Us Better*, who briefly notes the differences between 1950s and later alien encounters (145–52), offers perhaps the best and most nuanced account of the abduction phenomenon (in which she does not believe); 54–56 on sexual violation. Notable also are the racial stereotypes: in the 1950s the aliens are fully human in appearance; the abductors of the 1960s–1970s are, first, the short "Grays" and then reptilians and insectoids; later "Nordic" or "tall whites" who are "good" show up (Brown, *They Know Us Better*, 188).

40. Branton, ed., *The Dulce Wars*, *passim*, with a sketch of the layout of the Archuleta facility at 151. The copyright date on the book is 1999, but there are references in it to events of 2008.

41. Adamski, "The Memorable November Twentieth," 198–99. This trope likely bled into the more malevolent views of abductees, with underground UFO bases (especially the so-called Dulce base in New Mexico) with Fig. 8-5, alien-government conspiracy, and continuing fear of radioactivity and the bomb: Brown, *They Know Us Better*, 106–16, 128–35. For a credulous account of Dulce, see Branton, ed., *The Dulce Wars*. Fry's aliens, however, admit their motives are not entirely "philanthropic": they want some "materials" Earth has that are rare elsewhere (1992, 62–63).

42. Howard, *Diane*, 70; Adamski, "The Memorable November Twentieth," 198 (emphasis in original); Adamski, *Inside the Space Ships*, 153, 136 (his emphasis); King, *You Are Responsible!*, 86–103, quotation at 94, 143: "Abandon [nuclear energy] completely.... [It] should not be touched at all by you because on the whole the motives of the Governments of Terra are quite wrong." Angelucci, *Son of the Sun*, 16.

43. Howard, *Diane*, 58; Adamski, "The Memorable November Twentieth," 201; Adamski, *Inside the Space Ships*, 178.

44. Adamski, *Inside the Space Ships*, 137, 116 (identity with divine), 154 ("force"), 165 (Master's comments); Howard, *Diane*, 46, see also 56 (same idea, more detail). Angelucci's contacts are also worried about Communism: *Son of the Sun*, 24, 66; Betherum ([*sic*]; presumably the same person as our Bethurum) also wrote a pamphlet about the communist threat: see above n15.

45. Gulyas, *Extraterrestrials and the American Zeitgeist*, 42–43 and 85 (citing Benjamin Creme, *The Gathering Forces of Light: The UFOs and Their Spiritual Mission* [Amsterdam-London: Share International Foundation, 2010]); Reece, *UFO Religion*, 104–7; Christopher Partridge, "Alien Demonology: The Christian Roots of the Malevolent Extraterrestrial in UFO Religions and Abduction Spiritualities," *Religion* 34 (2004), 174–75; Saliba, "Religious Dimensions," 22–30. Helena Blavatsky (1831–1891), founder of Theosophy along with Henry Olcott, described her "pseudo-religion" (so René Guénon, *Le théosophisme: histoire d'une pseudo-religion* [n.p.: Éditions Dervy, 1921], his take-down of Theosophy) in multiple books, starting with *Isis Revealed* (1877) and most thoroughly expounded in *The Secret Doctrine* (1888–1889). Theosophy came to America when Blavatsky, Olcott, and others formed the Theosophical Society in New York City in 1875. Robert Crosbie established the first United Lodge of Theosophists in Los Angeles in 1909, a locale perhaps not irrelevant to the spate of contactees four and a half decades later; see below. See also the famous spiritualist visits to Mars of "Hélène Smith" (actually Catherine-Elise Müller) in the 1890s: Théodore Flournoy, *From India to the Planet Mars: A Case of Multiple Personality with Imaginary Languages*, trans. Daniel B. Vermilye (Princeton: Princeton University Press, 1994), 87–164, with the extensive analysis of Waldemar Deonna, *De la planète Mars en terre sainte: art et subconscient: un medium peintre: Hélène Smith* (Paris: De Boccard, 1932), focusing on her post-Martian experiences. For a somewhat dated but still useful general introduction to the history of theosophy, see Bruce F. Campbell, *Ancient Wisdom Revived: A History of the Theosophical Movement* (Berkeley: University of California Press, 1980).

46. C. S. Lewis, *Out of the Silent Planet* (New York: Scribner, 2003). Ironically (if that's the right word), Lewis himself played the central role in a spiritualist encounter: the theologian J. B. Phillips saw the dead Lewis twice in 1964: *Journal of the Society for Psychical Research* 45, no. 746 (December 1970); Evans, *Gods, Spirits, Cosmic Guardians*, 84–85. Darko Suvin, *Metamorphoses of Science Fiction: On the Poetics and History of a Literary*

Genre (New Haven: Yale University Press, 1979), 26, denigrates Lewis's science fiction trilogy as "attempts to transplant the metaphysical orientation of mythology and religion into SF, in a crudely overt way."

47. Percival Lowell, *Mars* (New York, Houghton Mifflin, 1895), *Mars and Its Canals* (New York: The Macmillan Company, 1906), and *Mars as an Abode of Life* (New York: The Macmillan Company, 1908). David Strauss, *Percival Lowell: The Culture and Science of a Boston Brahmin* (Cambridge: Harvard University Press, 2001) on Lowell's life (and the "Boston Brahmin"). Arthur Powell Davis, "What Irrigation Is Doing for Arizona," *National Magazine: An Illustrated Monthly* 15 (1901–1902), 642, makes explicit the analogy between Martian canals and those of Arizona.

48. C. S. Lewis, *Of Other Worlds: Essays and Stories*, ed. Walter Hooper (London: Geoffrey Bles, 1966), 69. For Martian canals as an optical illusion, see already Nathaniel E. Greene, "Observations on Mars, at Madeira, in August and September 1877," *Memoirs of the Royal Astronomical Society* 44 (1877–1879), 124–25, and 130–31; Simon Newcomb, "Problems of Astronomy," *Science* 5, issue 125 (May 21, 1897), 783–84, argued against Lowell's canals; the death blow came finally in 1910: Eugène-Michel Antoniadi, "Mars Section Sixth Interim Report for 1909, Dealing with Some Further Notes on the So-Called 'Canals,'" *Journal of the British Astronomical Association* 20 (1910), 189. For scientific reaction to Lowell, William Graves Hoyt, *Lowell and Mars* (Tucson: University of Arizona Press, 1976), 163–72. See chapter 5 on the emergent canal system in the Phoenix region in the later nineteenth century.

49. Angelucci, *Son of the Sun*, 23.

50. Adamski, *Inside the Space Ships*, 177–89. See also King, *You Are Responsible!*, 110: "You [people of Earth] are not alone in your struggles—you have never been alone in your struggles for Spiritual supremacy." For centuries there has been a "tremendous battle . . . raging on Terra—a battle between basic materialism . . . and Spirituality and enlightenment." It will not escape the perspicacious observer that Adamski's account displays echoes of the more or less "secret" doctrines of the Church of Jesus Christ of Latter-day Saints: especially the view that good Mormons will, upon death, be assigned planets over which they will rule like deities.

51. King, *You Are Responsible!*, 142.

52. However, as will be clear in chapter 9, there isn't necessarily any reason to suppose the inhabitants of other planets know anything about, or need the salvatory intervention of, Jesus.

53. Flournoy, *From India to the Planet Mars*, 91, 99, 123–64, 89.

54. Albert de Rochas d'Aiglun, *Les vies successives: documents pour l'étude de cette question*, 2nd ed. (Paris: Librairie P. Lemaire, 1924), 277. "Mireille" is a pseudonym.

55. Camille Flammarion, "Les satellites d'Uranus et les ésprits," *Annales des sciences psychiques* 18 (1908): 16–23, but he rejected the reality of these visions. From early youth he was convinced that life existed on other planets; see his *La pluralité des mondes habités: étude où on expose les conditions d'habitabilité des terres* (Paris: Marpon et Flammarion, 1862), published when he was only 19; his Mars book: Camille Flammarion, *La planète Mars et ses conditions d'habitabilité: encyclopédie générale des observations martiennes*, 2 vols. (Paris: Gauthier-Villars, 1892–1909). Mrs. Smead, a pseudonym for Mrs. Willis M. Cleaveland (I have not been able to trace her given name): James H. Hyslop, "The Smead Case," *The Annals of Psychical Science* 4 (1906), 70–85, who rejects the credibility of her Martian visions but entertains that of others; Flournoy, *From India to the Planet Mars*, 223–68; Charles Richet, *Traité de métapsychique* (Paris: Librairie Félix Alcan, 1922), 93n1 and 272, asserts she simply copied Hélène Smith, and poorly. Machner: Anonymous, "Les dessins médiumiques de Machner," *Annales des sciences psychiques* 17 (1908): 86–88, with vegetation from Mars and Saturn (87); the painting with saucers or lenticular clouds is reproduced at 86, but the art critic Ludwig Peitsch (1824–1911) commented in the *Vossische Zeitung* for November 12, 1901, on houses "under a sky full of golden clouds" (88), perhaps in reference to the same painting. "Stellar songs": Jules Bois, *Le miracle moderne: la métapsychique—la surnâme et le surhomme—la télépathie et les fantômes des vivants—rayons humains—maisons hantées—aventures d'un revenant—un chapelet de voyantes—le mystère des tables tornantes éclairci—le mécanisme du miracle de Lourdes—les professeurs de volante—le miracle est en nous—création d'une humanité supérieure* (Paris: P. Ollendorff, 1907), 254–55. Desmoulin: Bois, *Le miracle moderne*, 154. Sardou: Bois, *Le miracle moderne*, 13, 145, and 255 with Anonymous, "Victorien Sardou, le doyen des spirites de France," *Annales des sciences psychiques* 18 (1908): 335–39. For all this, see Deonna, *De la planète Mars*, 11–12. The efflorescence of spiritualist communication with Mars and other planets in the late nineteenth and early twentieth centuries is remarkable. To my knowledge no one has offered an explanation.

56. There was a spate of "UFO" reports in the United States in the late nineteenth century, in which dirigible-shaped vessels hovered over Midwestern and Western towns, sometimes tossing out anchors that caught on locals' chimneys, but I doubt very much whether these accounts—which were certainly all hoaxes—penetrated the

consciousness of European mediums. On these early sightings, see Jacobs, *The UFO Controversy*, 5–34, and Robert E. Bartholomew, "The Airship Hysteria of 1896–97," *Skeptical Inquirer* 14 (1990): 171–81.

57. H. G. Wells, *A Critical Edition of the War of the Worlds: H. G. Wells's Scientific Romance*, eds. David Y. Hughes and Harry M. Geduld (Bloomington: Indiana University Press, 1993); Kurd Lasswitz, *Auf zwei Planeten*, 2 vols. (Berlin: Verlag von Emil Felber, 1897).

58. Ardy Sixkiller Clarke, *Space Age Indians: Their Encounters with the Blue Men, Reptilians, and Other Star People* (San Antonio: Anomalist Books, 2019), 22, see also 15–28, 31–38; healing, 85–89; levitated car, 83; warmongering, 12; peaceful and anti-war, 17; 40, 42; healing: 2014, 2, 127, 47 (healing a dog). See also Richard Boylan, "Native Elders Reveal Centuries of E.T. Contact Lore," *Contact Forum* 4 (1996): 1–6, accessed March 29, 2022, https://www.drboylan.com/strknrpt2.html, B. Raynes, *Visitors from Hidden Realms: The Origin and Destiny of Humanity as Told by Our Star Elders, Shamen, and UFO Visitors* (Memphis: Eagle Wing Books Incorporated, 2004), and N. Red Star, *Star Ancestors: Indian Wisdomkeepers Share the Teachings of the Extraterrestrials* (Rochester: Inner Traditions International, 2000).

59. Clarke, *Space Age Indians*, 3–4, 19, 20 (quotation), 122, 134, 138, 144, 146, 179, 187, 223.

60. Ardy Sixkiller Clarke, *Sky People: Untold Stories of Alien Encounters in Mesoamerica* (Franklin Lakes: Red Wheel Weiser, 2014), 59, emphasis in original; Mayas remember Lemuria, or "Lemurlia," 97.

61. Clarke, *Space Age Indians*, 121 (quotation), 134, 144.

62. Ibid., 138–39, 144.

63. Clarke, *Space Age Indians*, 157–65, underground bases: 231–36, 255–60, in the Panamint Mountains of the Mojave Desert, 275–84; cattle mutilation: 240; bad Grays: Clarke, *Sky People*, 111–12.

64. Mark Harrington, "'Little Devil So High,'" *The Masterkey* 24 (1950): 170; David S. Whitley, "Ways of Knowing and Seeing: Spiritual Agents and the Origins of Native American Rock Art," in *Working with Rock Art: Presenting and Understanding Rock Art Using Indigenous Knowledge*, eds. Benjamin Smith, Knut Arne Heiskog, and David Morris (Johannesburg: Wits University Press, 2012), 184–85, with references.

65. See George Devereux, "On Mojave Beliefs Concerning the Twins," *American Anthropologist* 43 (1941), 573–74, citing A. L. Kroeber, *The Handbook of the Indians of California* (Washington, DC: Bureau of American Ethnology, 1925). Devereux documents two interpretations. I give the primary one in the text; the second, obtained from one informant, regards twins as reincarnations (584–87). I return to the Mojave Twins in chapter 10.

66. Christopher Roth, "Ufology as Anthropology: Race, Extraterrestrials, and the Occult," in *E. T. Culture: Anthropology in Outerspaces*, ed. Deborah Battaglia (Durham: Duke University Press, 2006), 129, 154, 130, 178, 122, 128–29.

67. Leslie Marmon Silko, *The Turquoise Ledge: A Memoir* (New York: Viking, 2010), 129 (she does not cite her "reading," unfortunately), 130. See Kyoko Matsunaga, "Trinitite, Turquoise, and Rattlesnakes: Envisioning the (De)Nuclearized Desert in the Works of Leslie Marmon Silko," in *Reading Aridity in Western American Literature*, eds. Jada Ach and Gary Reger (Lanham, MD: Lexington Books, 2020), 206–13, on aspects of Silko's memoir.

68. Silko, *The Turquoise Ledge*, 132, 134, 137, 135, 140–41, 138–39.

69. On Tlaloc, see further in chapter 2. For Hueco Tanks, see chapter 2 and n73 there. *Datura*, jimsonweed, contains a toxic narcotic used in many desert Native America rituals: see A. H. Grayton, "Yokuts and Western Mono Ethnography," *University of California Anthropological Records* 10 (1948), 38–39, 173–74, 211, 281–84 (Yokuts people of California, only marginally desert-dwelling, for the most part); Leslie Spier, *Yuman Tribes of the Gila River* (New York: Dover Publications, Inc., 1933), 243–44; Frank Russell, *The Pima Indians: Re-edition with Introduction, Citation Sources, and Bibliography by Bernard L. Fontana* (Tucson: University of Arizona Press, 1975), 300, as "thornapple" in an Akimel O'odham hunting song; on the hawk moth and *Datura*, Caroline Boyd, *The White Shaman Mural* (Austin: University of Texas Press, 2016), 93–96; chapter 2, n60, and chapter 6, n57.

70. Silko, *The Turquoise Ledge*, 181–82 (*Datura*), 135 on Tlaloc, 132 (summer rains), 137 (money troubles).

71. Nuclear tests endanger Earth: Clarke, *Sky People*, 132–33; lost secrets: 89; domestic violence: 13: Hoagland: 33–35. Hoagland is a conspiracy theorist with no formal scientific training who has made many wild and unfounded claims about his own expertise and NASA's alleged "cover-up" of evidence for advanced civilization on Mars; see Richard C. Hoagland, *The Monuments on Mars: A City on the Edge of Forever*, 5th ed. (Berkeley: Frog Ltd., 2002) and Richard C. Hoagland and Mike Bara, *Dark Mission: The Secret History of NASA*, revised and expanded ed. (Port Townsend: Feral House, 2009). Covenant: Clarke, *Sky People*, 115; Grays created: 139; manipulation: 133; galactic war and quotation: 135.

72. Clarke, *Sky People*, 164–65 (soul abduction), 178–79 (benign), 142 (sperm, eggs, incubation, Rapture, Tribulation); 110–11 (Revelation); xiv (imminent return); 122: Venus, see Immanuel Velikovsky, *Worlds in Collison* (London: Paradigma Ltd., 2009).

73. Lepselter, "The Resonance of Captivity," 99, italics in original.

74. Jung, *Flying Saucers*, 34–37. Rimmer, *The Evidence for Alien Abductions*, 121–22, notes the strong influence of Jung's "collective unconscious" and "archetypes" on a "New Ufology" that emerged in the 1970s and promoted psychological explanations for UFO abduction narratives. It strikes me as intriguing that other "new" versions of old fields also emerged at the same time, like the New Archaeology and the New Science Fiction. The phenomenon is worth study.

75. Belden C. Lane, *The Solace of Fierce Landscapes: Exploring Desert and Mountain Spirituality* (Oxford: Oxford University Press, 1998), offers a wide-ranging treatment of deserts and spirituality embedded, however, in an insistent Christianity that undermines its appeal to readers not sharing his commitments. Evans, *Visions, Apparitions, Alien Visitors*, 155, notes the problematics of the choice of the Space Brothers and Sisters to deliver their messages in remote places, at night, at enormous length, to persons with no political influence. But as we have seen, there are good reasons for deserts to serve them as points of contact.

76. Angelucci, *Son of the Sun*, 16.

77. Van Tassel, *I Rode a Flying Saucer*, 11–12, italics in original; Laura Feldt, "Wilderness and Hebrew Bible Religion—Fertility, Apostasy and Religious Transformation in the Pentateuch," in *Religion and Society: Wilderness in Mythology and Religion: Approaching Religious Spacialities, Cosmologies, and Ideas of Wild Nature*, eds. Laura Feldt, Gustavo Benavides, and Kocku von Stuckrad (Berlin: De Gruyter, 2012). See chapter 1.

78. The bibliography is enormous, as always, but see Kevin Starr, *Material Dreams: Southern California Through the 1920s* (New York: Oxford University Press, 1990), 139–44, on Amy Semple McPherson; Mike Davis, *City of Quartz: Excavating the Future of Los Angeles* (New York: Vintage Books, 1990), 59–60, on Parsons; on Scientology, see the essays in *Scientology*, ed. James R. Lewis (Oxford: Oxford University Press, 2009), and on Hollywood and Scientology, Lawrence Wright, *Going Clear: Scientology, Hollywood, and the Prison of Belief* (New York: Alfred A. Knopf, 2013).

79. For discussion of one aspect of this trope see chapter 6.

80. Saliba, "Religious Dimensions," 51. On the other hand, Bethurum's experiences contributed to his divorce. Much more rarely later abductees felt an analogous positive transformation; most, however, suffered: Brown, *They Know Us Better*, 70–99.

81. Evans, *Gods, Spirits, Cosmic Guardians*, 239–40, following ideas from Mircea Eliade, *Rites and Symbols of Initiation: The Mysteries of Birth and Rebirth*, trans. Willard R. Taske (New York: Harper and Row, 1975) by way of Rimmer, *The Evidence for Alien Abduction*, 139; cf. Saliba, "Religious Dimensions," 51. Howard, *Diane*, 57 ("morning light").

82. An ironic, and surely completely unconscious, reversal of *Auf zwei Planeten*, where benevolence turns ugly when the colonized fail to appreciate the gifts the colonial power is bestowing.

CHAPTER 9

1. Edgar Rice Burroughs, *The Martian Tales Trilogy: A Princess of Mars, The Gods of Mars, The Warlord of Mars* (New York: Barnes and Noble, 2004), 56; her nakedness again remarked at 91 (on her career, Clark A. Brady, *The Burroughs Cyclopaedia: Characters, Places, Fauna, Flora, Technologies, Languages, Ideas and Terminologies Found in the Works of Edgar Rice Burroughs* [Jefferson: McFarland & Company, Inc., 1996], 88); for Thuvia, 250, cf. Edgar Rice Burroughs, *More Martian Tales: Thuvia, Maid of Mars, The Chessmen of Mars* (New York: Barnes and Noble, 2006), 65 (Brady, *The Burroughs Cyclopaedia*, 336–37). The nonhuman, six-legged Tharks, the first "race" Carter meets on Mars (see Brady, *The Burroughs Cyclopaedia*, 332), are likewise "[w]ith the exception of their ornaments . . . naked" (Burroughs, *The Martian Tales Trilogy*, 28); briefly, Brady, *The Burroughs Cyclopaedia*, 239, s.v. "nudity": "Barsoomians go almost completely naked all the time, wearing only a harness. . . . Women tend to wear even less than men." "Barsoom" is Burroughs's Martians' name for Mars. K. Maria Lane, *Geographies of Mars: Seeing and Knowing the Red Planet* (Chicago: University of Chicago Press, 2011), 211, reads exposure of breasts as "an essentialized visual trope to convey the vulnerability and inferiority of the Other"; I will argue that it is rather more complicated. In this study I look mostly at the trilogy of Mars novels Burroughs produced between 1912 and 1914 and which were later issued in book form by McClurg: see Richard Lupoff, *Master of Adventure: The Worlds of Edgar Rice Burroughs* (Lincoln: University

of Nebraska Press, 2005), 263–65 for a checklist of book (but not magazine) publication dates. "Under the Moons of Mars" is conveniently reprinted in *Under the Moons of Mars: A History and Anthology of "The Scientific Romance" in the Munsey Magazines, 1912–1920*, ed. Sam Moskowitz (New York: Holt, Rinehart and Winston, 1970), 3–52; this original version is considerably shorter than the book. A couple of caveats: I use here the pairs "naked/nude" and "nakedness/nudity" interchangeably, in contrast to the distinction drawn (but not invented) by Kenneth Clark (*The Nude: A Study in Ideal Form* [Princeton: Princeton University Press, 1972], 3) between "naked" as a bodily state of being "deprived of our clothes, and . . . implying some of the embarrassment most of us feel in that condition," while "the word 'nude,' on the other hand, carries, in educated usage, no uncomfortable overtones." See, for instance, Larissa Bonafonte, "Nudity as Costume in Classical Art," *American Journal of Archaeology* 93 (1989): 543–70. For a good summary of critique of Clark, see Ruth Barcan, *Nudity: A Cultural Anatomy* (Oxford: Berg, 2004), 30–47, who rejects the distinction and uses nude and naked interchangeably (46). The inability to decide whether performers on the 1890s London stage in *tableaux vivants* were "nude" or "naked" contributed to the failure of reformers to ban them; see Brenda Assael, "Art or Indecency? Tableaux Vivants on the London Stage and the Failure of Late Victorian Moral Reform," *Journal of British Studies* 45 (2006), 745, 756–57. Throughout my discussion, sexuality refers to heteronormative sexuality, the only form explicit in the material I am studying. I mean no judgment.

2. Burroughs, *The Martian Tales Trilogy*, 246, 76–77; Thuvia (Fig. 9-1), too, is "the perfect type of that remarkably beautiful race whose outward appearance is identical with the more god-like races of Earth men" (Burroughs, *The Martian Tales Trilogy*, 246). Green Martian women are also "naked" (Burroughs, *The Martian Tales Trilogy*, 28). For Frazetta's work, see http://www.frankfrazetta.net (the official website) and http://www.frankfrazetta.org (an approved fan site). Frazetta remarked in an interview on his Burroughs work, "Why are bigger tits worse than smaller tits?" (Russ Cochran, *The Edgar Rice Burroughs Library of Illustration: Volume Three* [West Plains: Russ Cochran, 1984], 238)—the "Woman Warrior" illustrates nicely the principle. In his treatment of Martian customs, John Flint Roy remains silent on Martian women's nudity: John Flint Roy, *A Guide to Barsoom: Eleven Sections of References in One Volume Dealing with the Martian Stories Written by Edgar Rice Burroughs* (New York: Ballantine Books, 1976), 131–40. Film versions have been no truer: neither the 2009 direct-to-DVD *Princess of Mars*, with Antonio Sabato Jr. as Carter and Traci Lords as Dejah, nor the 2012 *John Carter*, starring Taylor Kitsch as Carter and Lynn Collins as Dejah, dared to depict the characters naked (for a rare positive appreciation of this version, see Tony Williams, "Authorship and Utopia: The Case of *John Carter*," *Film International* 11 [2013]: 44–54). In *Princess of Mars* Carter does arrive naked, but close-ups show only his torso or legs, while whole-body shots are taken at a great distance. Lords, whose career as a pornographic actress was driven by childhood sexual abuse, rape, alcohol, and drugs, last performed nude in the starring role in the Roger Corman B-movie *Not of This Earth* (1988), and refused Corman's offer of more work on the condition she agree to further nude scenes. She has never appeared nude in a film since; see her autobiography, Traci Lords, *Underneath It All* (New York: Harper Entertainment, 2003), 137–43, 199 (and chapter 6 n37). For a very different view of Lords's early career, see Christy Canyon, *Lights, Camera, Sex!* (Sherman Oaks: Christy Canyon, 2003), 90–115.

3. In his treatment of Martian customs, John Flint Roy remains silent on Martian women's nudity: Roy, *A Guide to Barsoom*, 131–40.

4. *National Geographic* 7, no. 11, October 1896, 357.

5. See Sharon DeGraw, *The Subject of Race in American Science Fiction* (New York: Routledge, 2007), 1–9, on the development of the genre of science fiction and its audience. Edward James remarked that in Britain Burroughs's fiction was regarded as "suitable for boys and Americans, but not for British adults. . . . [F]ew young males can resist . . . helping [John Carter] search (once more) for his beautiful (and generally nude) wife, Dejah Thoris" (Edward James, *Science Fiction in the Twentieth Century* [New York: Oxford University Press, 1994], 46–47). Robert Crossley, *Imagining Mars: A Literary History* (Middletown: Wesleyan University Press, 2011), 149–67, reads *Princess of Mars* in a tradition of "masculinist fantasy" set on Mars; he refers only briefly to Martian nakedness (160). Likewise, Robert Markley, in an excellent study, mentions Martian nakedness only once (*Dying Planet: Mars in Science and Imagination* [Durham: Duke University Press, 2005], 192); Benjamin S. Lawson, "The Time and Place of Edgar Rice Burroughs's Early Martian Trilogy," *Extrapolation* 27 (1986): 208–20, offers a suggestive analysis of the social framework of American society into which the Mars novels fit. Harry Stecopoulos, "The World According to Normal Bean: Edgar Rice Burroughs's Popular Culture," in *Race and the Subject of Masculinities*, eds. Harry Stecopoulos and Michael Uebel (Durham: Duke University Press, 1997), 170–91, teases out the psychological implications of Burroughs's failed pseudonym—he had submitted his story under the name "Normal Bean," changed by an editor or typesetter to

"Norman" on the assumption it was a typo—which Stecopoulos sees as representative of the tension around white male racial and sexual identity Burroughs experienced as a result of his decision to write disreputable science fiction stories.

6. Burroughs, *The Martian Tales Trilogy*, 56. This passage is unchanged from the original publication: Burroughs 1970, 27; see briefly on Burroughs in *All-Story* Mike Ashley, *The Time Machines: The Story of the Science-Fiction Pulp Magazines from the Beginning to 1950* (Liverpool: Liverpool University Press, 2000), 36. On April 19, 1897, the *St. Louis Post-Dispatch* published on page 1 (with a continuation on page 2) a letter from one W. H. Hopkins, who reported stumbling on an airship resting on the ground outside Springfield, Missouri, one of whose occupants was a golden-haired woman: "She was rather under medium size," Hopkins averred, "but of the most exquisite form and features such as would put to shame the forms as sculptured by the ancient Greeks. She was dressed in nature's garb and her golden hair, wavy and glossy, hung to her waist, unconfined excepting by a band of glistening jewels that bound it back from her forehead. The jewels threw out rays of light as she moved her head. She was plucking the little flowers that were just blossoming from the soil with exclamations of delight and in a language I could not understand. Her voice was like low, silvery bells and her laughing rang out like chimes. In one hand she held a fan of curious design that she fanned herself vigorously with, though to me the air was not warm and I wore an overcoat." A man with a full beard lay in the shade of the airship, likewise fanning himself. "I wondered if Adam and Eve had come to earth again, or was I dreaming?" When Hopkins moved, the woman heard him and ran in fear to the man, who gave off a threatening look. After a while Hopkins persuaded the man to come forward; they shook hands; the man gestured for the woman to approach, and "[s]he came hesitatingly forward, her form undulating with exquisite grace." Hopkins kissed her hand, she blushed and withdrew. As Hopkins tried to get the man to say where he was from, he "pointed upwards, pronouncing a word which, in my imagination, sounded like Mars." After Hopkins got a tour of the ship, the couple entered it and it "rose as lightly as a bird, and shot away like an arrow." Another example of naked Martians in the tale of Samuel Thompson: Nick Redfern, *Contactees: A History of Alien-Human Interactions* (Franklin Lakes: New Page Books, 2010), 22.

7. Jennifer Putzi, *Identifying Marks: Race, Gender, and the Marked Body in Nineteenth-Century America* (Athens: University of Georgia Press, 2006), 32–33.

8. Richard Dale Mullen, "The Prudish Prurience of H. Rider Haggard and Edgar Rice Burroughs," *Riverside Quarterly* 5 (1973): 4–19.

9. Burroughs, *The Martian Tales Trilogy*, 90–91; Diane Newell and Victoria Lamont, "Savagery on Mars: Representations of the Primitive in Brackett and Burroughs," in *Visions of Mars: Essays on the Red Planet in Fiction and Science*, eds. H. V. Hendrix, G. Slusser, and E. S. Rabkin (Jefferson: McFarland & Company, 2011), 75. More or less the same analysis at David Mogen, *The Western Theme in Science Fiction Literature* (San Bernardino: The Borgo Press, 1993, 86, not cited by Newell and Lamont).

10. Tim Whitmarsh, *Beyond the Second Sophistic: Adventures in Greek Postclassicism* (Berkeley: University of California Press, 2013), 123. Richard Kyle, "Out of Time's Abyss: The Martian Stories of Edgard Rice Burroughs, A Speculation," *Riverside Quarterly* 4 (1970), 121, maintains that on Mars "men and women exult in their naked bodies," but this misreads the practice; there's no "exultation," for nudity is as normal for them as clothing for us.

11. Richard Slotkin, *Gunfighter Nation: The Myth of the Frontier in Twentieth-Century America* (Norman: University of Oklahoma Press, 1998), 206–7, argues that Dejah embodies and perfects the "tragic mulatto" first limned by James Fenimore Cooper as Cora Munro in *The Last of the Mohicans*; Slotkin suspects direct borrowing.

12. Burroughs, *The Martian Tales Trilogy*, 56, 89–90 (ignorance); "Love-Making on Mars" is the title of chapter XIII; 93, 161 (marriage to another), 197.

13. It is important to remember that she is *always* naked. T. J. Glenn, "A Fighting Manual of Mars," in *Edgar Rice Burroughs' Fantastic Worlds: Essays and Examinations of the Science Fiction Universe Spawned by the Man Who Created Tarzan*, ed. James Van Hise (Yucca Valley: James Van Hise, 1996), 27–28, has stressed that in our first encounter with her "she is literally naked and alone among the green barbarians, having seen her escort ship and crew slaughtered, yet she faces her captors with dignity and not a shred of fear," but her nakedness here is irrelevant, since both she and the Tharks who capture her are by custom naked. *We* construct nudity in such a situation as vulnerability, but neither Dejah nor her captors do. James Van Hise, "The Power of Burroughs' Mars Trilogy," in *Edgar Rice Burroughs' Fantastic Worlds: Essays and Examinations of the Science Fiction Universe Spawned by the Man Who Created Tarzan*, ed. James Van Hise (Yucca Valley: James Van Hise, 1996), 12–13, chides Burroughs for infecting his women characters with "the Dale Arden syndrome,"

by which they "are portrayed as helpless hand-wringers who stand back while men do all the fighting." Only in Tavia, who appears in *A Fighting Man of Mars*, does Burroughs create a "sword-wielding female," according to Van Hise's reading. But this is a misapprehension of Dejah's character.

14. Burroughs, *The Martian Tales Trilogy*, 122, see Richard Mullen (the Elder), "Edgar Rice Burroughs and the Fate Worse Than Death," *Riverside Quarterly* 1 (1970), 187n22, in his fulsome catalogue of rape threats.

15. Burroughs, *The Martian Tales Trilogy*, 64, 66. Note the hostility to communism, a view shared by many Space Brothers and Sisters of the 1950s (see chapter 8).

16. Red, of course, is the appropriate color for the Red Planet. William Ferguson's Martians were all redheads (William Ferguson, *My Trip to Mars* [London: Forgotten Books, 2008], 9), and Antonio Villejo Boas attested of the naked woman he had sex with on a UFO in Brazil in 1958 that "her hair in her armpits and in another place [pubes] was very red, almost the color of blood" (Redfern, *Contactees*, 111), and chapter 8 n17. See Branton, ed., *The Dulce Wars: Underground Alien Bases & the Battle for Planet Earth* (New Brunswick: Inner Light/Global Communications, 1999), 113, on red-headed aliens, and chapter 8 n17. Perhaps not irrelevant is the stereotype that redheads are especially sexually hot? See Marion Roach, *The Roots of Desire: The Myth, Meaning, and Sexual Power of Red Hair* (New York: Bloomsbury USA, 2005), esp. 145.

17. Thomas Dixon, *The Sins of the Father: A Romance of the South* (Lexington: The University Press of Kentucky, 2004), 30. Diana Rebekkah Paulin, *Imperfect Unions: Staging Miscegenation in U.S. Drama and Fiction* (Minneapolis: University of Minneapolis Press, 2012), 187–227. Markley, *Dying Planet*, 182–97, offers an excellent discussion of the whole problem of race in Burroughs's novels. Slotkin, *Gunfighter Nation*, 207, encapsulates Dejah's situation neatly: "Dejah Thoris is the perfect reconciliation of the values attached to women in the Frontier Myth. Her Indian qualities make her an appropriate object for the indulgence of erotic fantasies, while her aristocratic lineage and status both as a virgin and Indian captive identify her as a 'redemptive' White woman and an appropriate mate for the White hero." Burroughs, *The Martian Tales Trilogy*, 333, on racial "amalgamation" on Mars. Slotkin, *Gunfighter Nation*, 197–202, traces Burroughs's racism, but the influences cited—Madison Grant and Theodore Lothrop Stoddard—in fact published their screeds *after* the Mars stories appeared. The same idea appears in the 1891 Australian novel *The Golden Lake*, in which a mixed-race individual—white and Indigenous—is described as wholly repulsive and defective, a "marvellous [*sic*] mixture of white and black vice" (W. Carlton Dawe, *The Golden Lake: or, the Marvellous History of a Journey through the Great Lone Land of Australia* [Melbourne: E. A. Petherick & Co., 1891], 164–65). This fellow happens to be a man, so there's no question of sexual appeal to the male narrator. Later, a white woman expresses her horror at the thought of interracial sex (185).

18. See Rosemary Barrow, "Toga Plays and Tableaux Vivants: Theatre and Painting on London's Late-Victorian and Edwardian Popular Stage," *Theatre Journal* 62 (2010): 209–26, and Tracy C. Davis, "The Spectacle of the Absent Costume: Nudity on the Victorian Stage," *New Theater Quarterly* 5 (1989), 328–30; a good short history of the *tableau vivant* in Assael, "Art or Indecency?", 746–47.

19. George Arnold, *The Sociable; or, One Thousand and One Home Amusements* (New York: Dick and Fitzgerald, 1858), iii; he treats tableaux at 153–69.

20. Mary Chapman, "'Living Pictures': Women and *Tableaux Vivants* in Nineteenth-Century American Fiction and Culture," *Wide Angle* 18, no. 3 (1996), 31. The first three quotations come from *tableaux vivants* manuals: Joseph Vila Prichard, *Tableaux Vivants Arranged for Amateur Representation* (New York: Samuel French, n.d.) (*non vidi*), 28; Tony Denier, *Parlor Tableaux; or Animated Pictures* (New York: Samuel French: 1869) (*non vidi*), 66; and Arnold, *The Sociable*, 157.

21. Arnold, *The Sociable* recommends in various *tableaux* a female model with "bare arms, and . . . arrayed in a loose, flowing white garment" (157); or "a young girl, extremely pale, in a long, sweeping, white robe, with her hands crossed upon her bosom, and her eyes turned upwards" (162); or, in a *tableau* called "The Music Lesson," set in "a lady's boudoir," where her music teacher takes advantage of his position to kiss her hand as he kneels before her and an older man looks on from behind wearing an expression of "comical horror and surprise," sheet music and the teacher's gloves and hat scattered on the floor, "[t]he young lady should be in an easy, elegant position, with her face a little averted, but her eyes turned toward her suitor. A little rouge may be effectively used on her cheeks, for producing the blush which is supposed to be natural upon such occasions" (169). Voyeurism as parlor entertainment.

22. Davis, "The Spectacle of the Absent Costume," 321 (quoting Ryan), 330 ("actual nudity"), 327 (quoting Phillips); "exposed breasts," etc.: Assael, "Art or Indecency?", 756.

23. Louisa May Alcott, *Behind a Mask: The Unknown Thrillers of Louisa May Alcott*, ed. Madeleine B. Stern (New York: Morrow, 1975), 47, 51 with Chapman, "'Living Pictures,'" 1996, 39–43.

24. Céline Renooz, *Psychologie comparée de l'homme et de la femme* (Paris: Bibliothèque de la Nouvelle Encyclopédie, 1898), 85–86, italics in the original. The discrepancy by one year here is because I have used a re-edition of the 1897 original, which was self-published. On the author, see James Smith Allen, "The Gendered Politics of Correspondence: The Curious Case of Céline Renooz," in *Gender and Politics in the Age of Letter Writing, 1750-2000*, eds. Caroline Bland and Máire Cross (Burlington: Ashgate, 2004), 161–71. Jack S. Harris, "The White Knife Shoshoni of Nevada," in *Seven American Indian Tribes*, ed. Ralph Linton (New York: Appleton-Century, 1940), 62, 104, reports the power of the vulva among the White Knife Shoshoni of Nevada: the sight of a vulva could render a man ill or sick; the same was not true of women. (See on desert vulvas chapter 2.) And already in ancient Sumer, the goddess Inana boasted about her vulva: "her genitals were remarkable . . . her genitals were remarkable. She praised herself, full of delight at her genitals, she praised herself, full of delight at her genitals," in *Inana and Enki* c.1.3.1, https://etcsl.orinst.ox.ac.uk/section1/tr131.htm, accessed June 11, 2024. (The Sumerian word *gala* translated here, slightly coyly, as "genitals" really means "vulva.") It would be fun but take us very far from the desert to explore the history of the psychoanalyst Karen Horney's contentions about men's fear of vaginas: see Karen Horney, "The Dread of Woman: Observations on a Specific Difference in the Dread Felt by Men and Women Respectively for the Opposite Sex," in *Female Sexuality: The Early Psychoanalytic Controversies*, eds. Russell Grigg, Dominique Hecq, and Craig Smith, 241–52 (Abingdon: Routledge, 2018), published originally in 1932.
25. John Williams, *The Samoan Journals of John Williams, 1830 and 1832*, ed. Richard M. Moyle Jr. (Bloomington: Indiana University Press, 1984), quoted in Nicholas Thomas, "Colonizing Cloth: Interpreting Material Culture of Nineteenth-Century Oceania," in *The Archaeology of Colonialism*, eds. C. L. Lyons and J. K. Papadopoulos (Los Angeles: Getty Research Institute, 2002), 191–93.
26. Barcan, *Nudity*, 136–38, 150–65, on nakedness and the primitive, with references to the abundant literature.
27. The classic study of the topos, Mogen, *The Western Theme*, 12, dismisses Burroughs in a few contemptuous lines but offers a good analysis of the formula (23–38), which frames my discussion here. Also Fred G. See, "'Writing So As Not to Die': Edgard Rice Burroughs and the West Beyond the West," *Melus* 11 (1984), 62–64, and the excellent study of DeGraw, *The Subject of Race*, who looks in detail at race and the Western trope in Burroughs's Mars books (2–52); note also the brief remarks of Jason Haslam, *Gender, Race and American Science Fiction: Reflections on Fantastic Identities* (New York: Routledge, 2015), 100n13.
28. Mogen, *The Western Theme*, 28.
29. Mogen, *The Western Theme*, 27; Slotkin, *Gunfighter Nation*, 197, 202. Once, by the end of the third book in Burroughs's Martian trilogy, Carter is declared "Jeddak of Jeddaks," ruler of all Mars (Burroughs, *The Martian Tales Trilogy*, 613)—the Martian frontier, really, is gone; Carter now brings peace, law, and civilization, and there is no role for him anymore. It becomes the duty of his son now to find a new Martian frontier where he can be the western hero.
30. Kyle, "Out of Time's Abyss," 116, identifies a possible source for Carter's translation to Mars. Adam Roberts, *The History of Science Fiction*, 2nd ed. (London: Palgrave Macmillan, 2016, 264), sees Carter's translation as an act of "virile will," which underlies all of Carter's actions on Mars. See also Théodore Flournoy, *From India to the Planet Mars: A Case of Multiple Personality with Imaginary Languages*, trans. Daniel B. Vermilye (Princeton: Princeton University Press, 1994), 108, for another version of translation. Perhaps Angelucci's translation to another world was inspired by Carter's (Orfeo Angelucci, *Son of the Sun: The Secret of the Saucers*, ed. Timothy Green Beckley [New Brunswick: Global Communications/Conspiracy Journal, 2008], 47)?
31. See David W. Teague, *The Southwest in American Literature and Art: The Rise of a Desert Aesthetic* (Tucson: University of Arizona Press, 1997), 101–3. Richard Dale Mullen, "The Undisciplined Imagination: Edgar Rice Burroughs and Lowellian Mars," in *The Other Side of Realism: Essays on Modern Fantasy and Science Fiction*, ed. Thomas D. Carlson, 229–47 (Bowling Green: Bowling Green University Popular Press, 1971) catalogues all the details in which Barsoom deviates from the Lowellian Mars, but the details don't, in my view, outweigh the obvious indications that Burroughs had Lowell in mind: see, for instance, the canals (Burroughs, *The Martian Tales Trilogy*, 49, 110; Brady, *The Burroughs Cyclopaedia*, 57–58), and, of course, the desert setting.
32. Burroughs, *The Martian Tales Trilogy*, 81, 49, 118, 155.
33. On this figure, see Paul Andrew Hutton, *The Apache Wars: The Hunt for Geronimo, the Apache Kid, and the Boy Captive Who Started the Longest War in American History* (New York: Broadway Books, 2016), 391–425, and 117–29 on Camp Grant; Jesse G. Hayes and Horace T. Pierce, *Apache Vengeance: True Story of the Apache Kid* (n.p.: Literary Licensing LLC, 2011).
34. Burroughs's Western experience: John Taliaferro, *Tarzan Forever: The Life of Edgar Rice Burroughs, the Creator*

of Tarzan (New York: Scribner, 1999), 30–39. On his Apache novels, see Robert E. Morsberger, "Edgar Rice Burroughs' Apache Epic," *Journal of Popular Culture* 6 (1973): 200–287. Burroughs also published two other books set in the West: *The Bandit of Hell's Bend* (1926) and *The Deputy Sheriff of Comanche County* (1940).

35. George W. B. Evans, *Mexican Gold Trail: The Journal of a Forty-Niner*, ed. Glenn S. Dumke (San Marino: Huntington Library, 2006), 22 and 44; cf. also 41, noting women's "small, naked feet, pendulous breasts, and naked arms"; James Pattie, *The Personal Narrative of James O. Pattie of Kentucky* (Santa Barbara: The Narrative Press, 2001), 184, 198–99; Franklin Walker, *A Literary History of Southern California* (Berkeley: University of California Press, 1950), 16–17, on the possible role of Flint in cleaning up Pattie's text. Other comments on women's dress and appearance: Pattie, *Personal Narrative*, 60, 153.

36. Zane Grey, *Heritage of the Desert* (New York: Grosset & Dunlap, 1938), 228; and see the unashamed nudity of Genie in Zane Grey, *Wanderer of the Wasteland* (New York: Harper & Brothers, 1923), 356, with William Bloodworth, "Zane Grey's Western Eroticism," *South Dakota Review* 26 (1985), 6–8; Zane Grey, *Wildfire* (New York: Harper & Brothers, 1917), 180–81, with Jane Tompkins, *West of Everything: The Inner Life of Westerns* (New York: Oxford University Press, 1992), 94–95.

37. Frederick Monsen, "The Primitive Folk of the Desert: Splendid Physical Development That Yet Shows Many of the Characteristics of an Earlier Race Than Our Own," *The Craftsman* 12 (1907), 164, 173. See Martin Padget, *Indian Country: Travels in the American Southwest, 1840–1935* (Albuquerque: University of New Mexico Press, 2004), 183–87.

38. Burroughs, *The Martian Tales Trilogy*, 56.

39. Adeline Masquelier, "Dirt, Undress, and Difference: An Introduction," in *Dirt, Undress, and Difference: Critical Perspectives on the Body's Surface*, ed. Adeline Masquelier (Bloomington: Indiana University Press, 2005), 1, writes: "British travelers to India in the nineteenth century were similarly impressed by the 'naked-ness' of most Indians, although they eventually adjusted, 'owing to the dark color of the skin, which as it is unusual to European eyes has the effect of a dress'" (quoting a colonial commentator). Or on Bali, where a visitor in 1933 remarked that "after a few days of seeing these bronzed natives . . . entirely unconscious of their bared beautiful breasts, you no longer notice them. Their dark skin seems like a garment" (Helen Eva Yates, *Bali, Enchanted Isle: A Travel Book* [Boston: Houghton Mifflin, 1933], 76–77, quoted in Margaret Wiener, "Breasts, (un)Dress, and Modernist Desires in the Balinese-Tourist Encounter," in *Dirt, Undress, and Difference: Critical Perspectives on the Body's Surface*, ed. Adeline Masquelier [Bloomington: Indiana University Press, 2005], 61). See also Ellen Strain, "Exotic Bodies, Distant Landscapes: Tourist Viewing and Popularized Anthropology in the Nineteenth Century," *Wide Angle* 18 (1996): 70–100. Helen Yates's visit to Bali came as Dutch colonial officials and, especially, Western artists and anthropologists (including Margaret Mead) were constructing Bali as a tourist paradise; see Shinji Yamashita, *Bali and Beyond: Explorations in the Anthropology of Tourism*, trans. S. Eades (New York: Berghahn Books, 2003), 25–41. Body-painting may achieve the same effect today: Philip Carr-Gomm, *A Brief History of Nakedness* (London: Reaktion Books, 2010), 245.

40. Excellent treatment of the whole problem in Philippa Levine, "States of Undress: Nakedness and the Colonial Imagination," *Victorian Studies* 50 (2008): 189–219. And, as Suzana Sawyer and Arun Agrawal, "Environmental Orientalisms," *Cultural Critiques* 45 (2000), 79, stress, "The obsession [of colonialists] with native female nudity and sexuality was not a mere innocent male fantasy. The female body, both literally and metaphorically, was a primary terrain on which European colonialism asserted its power." This isn't, however, quite how things play out on Mars, as the natives' nudity is never rebarbative.

41. David Martínez, "Hiding in the Shadows of History: Revitalizing the Hia-Ced O'odham Peoplehood," *Journal of the Southwest* 55 (2013), 135–38 (quotation at 135), 145; Pedro de Castañeda, *The Journey of Coronado*, trans. George Parker Winship (New York: Dover Publications, Inc., 1990), 56; the translation in Pedro de Castañeda de Nájera, "La Relación de la Jornada de Cíbola, Pedro de Castañeda de Nájera's Narrative, 160s (Copy 1596)," in *Documents of the Coronado Expedition, 1539–1542: "They Were Not Familiar with His Majesty, nor Did They Wish to Be His Subjects,"* eds. Richard Flint and Shirley Cushing Flint (Albuquerque: University of New Mexico Press, 2005), 420, follows the Spanish of Flint and Flint's transcription, which reads "preguntandole yo po que causa en aquella provincia andaban las mugeres moças en cueros haçiendo tam gran frio dixome que las donçellas havian de andar ansi hasta que tomasen maridos y que en co(g)noçiendo varon se cubrian trayan los hombres" (476; note that spelling and italics follow the source), i.e., "When I asked him [an Indian who'd spent a year there] why the young women in that *provincial* went about naked, even when it was so very cold, he told me the virgins must go about that way until they take husbands. Once they had carnal relations with a young man, they covered themselves" (420). There are several other passages

in the documents collected in Flint and Flint, *Documents*, that mention female nudity.

42. Charles Sturt, *Narrative of an Expedition into Central Australia, Performed under the Authority of Her Majesty's Government, during the Years 1844, 5, and 6* (London: T. and W. Boone, 1849), vol. 1, 274, 298, 340, 349; Dixon Denham, Hugh Clapperton, and Walter Oudney, *Narrative of Travels and Discoveries in Northern and Central Africa in the Years 1822, 1823, and 1824* (London: John Murray, 1828), vol. 1, 384. In Dawe, *The Golden Lake*, 85, nudity among Indigenous Australians is attributed to "the excessive heat of the weather" rather than simple primitiveness; later, though, the Indigenes are called "so low in the scale of humanity . . . that they seem to value life not one jot" (93; see also 206–7). Indigenous clothing decisions in Australia, however, depended on season and ritual: sometimes people went naked, sometimes clothed; see Peter Sutton and Keryn Walshe, *Farmers or Hunter-Gatherers? The* Dark Emu *Debate* (Melbourne: Melbourne University Press, 2021), 93–100.

43. Burroughs, *The Martian Tales Trilogy*, 73 and *More Martian Tales*, 60; Burroughs reminds us, soon after Cathoris and Thuvia meet the Lotharians, that she is naked and her state surprises their hosts: Burroughs, *More Martian Tales*, 65. See Newell and Lamont, "Savagery on Mars," 76.

44. Herman Melville, *Typee: A Peep at Polynesian Life* (Evanston: Northwestern University Press, 2003), 87; Charles Roberts Anderson, *Melville in the South Seas* (New York: Dover Publications, 1966), 117–95, remains an excellent guide to Melville's "experiences" in the Marquesas Islands, especially his mining of travelers' reports. European observers (no surprise) completely misunderstood the meanings of female nakedness and apparent sexual freedom in Polynesia: see Serge Tcherkézoff, *"First Contacts" in Polynesia: The Samoan Case (1722–1848): Western Misunderstandings about Sexuality and Divinity* (Canberra: The Australian National University Press, 2008), 6–11, 29–50, 61–65, 75–76, 109–10, 168–77, on Samoa; for the same problem on Tahiti, see Anne Salmond, *Aphrodite's Island: The European Discovery of Tahiti* (Berkeley: University of California Press, 2009); on Bali, Wiener, "Breasts, (Un)Dress, and Modernist Desires."

45. See Levine, "States of Undress," 191. The "natives," of course, had their own ideas; see, for instance, the Tswana chief from Southern Africa who had made for himself a Western-style suit out of leopard skin: the combination of foreign style and indigenous material, both potent markers of status, served only to enhance his prestige and authority: Jean L. Comaroff and John Comaroff, *Of Revelation and Revolution, Vol. 2: The Dialectics of Modernity on a South African Frontier* (Chicago: University of Chicago Press, 1997), 244–45.

46. R. B. Stratton, *Captivity of the Oatman Girls: Being an Interesting Narrative of Life among the Apache and Mohave Indians* (New York: Printed for the Author, 1858), 271.

47. Putzi, *Identifying Marks*, 32–33, contrasts Stratton's attention to the sartorial barbarity of his Indians— "needlessly and shockingly indecent," referring to Stratton, *Captivity*, 135; see also 160–67 on Mohave "primitiveness"—to his demur silence on Olive and Mary till Olive's return to Fort Yuma; Putzi also notes that never "during her [Olive's] captivity . . . does [Olive] Oatman appear to be in danger of losing her white, Christian sense of propriety," which, however, is gainsaid by the illustrations (32–33). Salaciousness and sex were at play too. See Brian McGinty, *The Oatman Massacre: A Tale of Desert Captivity and Survival* (Norman: University of Oklahoma Press, 2005), 163; Margot Mifflin quoted in Deborah Lawrence and Jon Lawrence, *Violent Encounters: Interviews on Western Massacres* (Norman: University of Oklahoma Press, 2011), 27; and Margot Mifflin, *The Blue Tattoo: The Life of Olive Oatman*, with a new postscript by the author (Lincoln: University of Nebraska Press, 2011), 203–6, for later uses of Olive's sexuality. The drawings for the first edition of *Captivity* were probably done by Charles and Arthur Nahl of San Francisco, but were redrawn, anonymously, for the second and third editions; McGinty, *The Oatman Massacre*, 163, 167, and 170. On the publication history, McGinty, *The Oatman Massacre*, 163–70; see also Kathryn Zabelle Derounian-Stodola, "The Captive and her Editor: The Ciphering of Olive Oatman and Royal B. Stratton," *Prospects: An Annual of American Studies* 23 (1998), 180–83. The woodcuts of the Oatman girls in Indian dress echo illustrations of Yuma, Cocopah, and "Pimo" (Akimel O'odham) women accompanying N. Michler's contribution to the 1857 report of the United States and Mexican Boundary Survey. See Dawn Hall, ed., *Drawing the Borderland: Artist-Explorers and the U.S.-Mexico Boundary Survey* (Albuquerque: University of New Mexico Press, 1996) on the artists who worked on the Commission. On the identity of the attacking Indians as likely Tolkepayas, McGinty, *The Oatman Massacre*, 81–83.

48. Edgar Rice Burroughs, *The War Chief* (New York: Ballantine Books, 1964), 7, 14, 22, 25, 27, etc.

49. Burroughs, *The Martian Tales Trilogy*, 17, 20, 28; at 57 Carter finally acquires his "arms" or "trappings," but the harness of the warrior does not serve as anything we would regard as clothing (*contra*, perhaps, Mullen, "The Prudish Prurience," 5).

50. Burroughs, *The Martian Tales Trilogy*, 56. Later Dejah explains that the Martians have devices that allow

them to see Earth in detail, so that she is perfectly aware that "Earth men, almost without exception, cover their bodies with strange, unsightly pieces of cloth . . . grotesque coverings" (76); see Mullen, "The Prudish Prurience," 5, and the remarks of Van Hise, "the Power," 16: "[T]he fact that John Carter can mate with Dejah Thoris shows that human males on Mars must be virtually identical in important respects with human males on Earth. There is no reference in the first novel to Dejah Thoris screaming when she sees John Carter naked, so we can pretty much accept the similarity of males as a given." Also Glenn, "A Fighting Manual," 21.

51. Applied explicitly to Carter: Slotkin, *Gunfighter Nation*, 203.

52. See Slotkin, *Gunfighter Nation*, 14–16. Richard Slotkin, *Regeneration through Violence: The Mythology of the American Frontier, 1600–1860* (Norman: University of Oklahoma Press, 1973), 488–508, especially 500–502, for his initial analysis of the Leatherstocking tales. I give here only the barest sketch of a complex phenomenon, treated in great detail and with considerable subtlety in the last volume of Slotkin's trilogy on the myth of the frontier. Slotkin's analysis of Burroughs appears in *Gunfighter Nation*, 195–211.

53. Carter's single combats: Burroughs, *The Martian Tales Trilogy*, 32 and 67–69, 36, 34, 37–38, 40–44, 64.

54. Burroughs, *The Martian Tales Trilogy*, 139–43; Richard A. Lupoff, *Edgar Rice Burroughs: Master of Adventure* (New York: Canaveral Press, 1965), 14. Brady, *The Burroughs Cyclopaedia*, 109 (airships), 274 (radium), 28 (atmosphere plant). This "plant," overseen by two red Martians, the older of whom had been on duty 800 years, concentrates a mysterious "ninth ray" which, once separated from the other rays, "is then treated electronically, or rather certain proportions of refined electric vibrations are incorporated with it, and the result is then pumped to the five principal air centers of the planet where, as it is released, contact with the ether of space transforms it into atmosphere" (141).

55. Giorgio Agamben, *Nudities*, trans. David Kishik and Stefan Pedatella (Stanford: Stanford University Press, 2011), 60–65, quotation at 62.

56. Already suggested by Slotkin, *Gunfighter Nation*, 202.

57. Walker, *A Literary History*, 17.

58. Burroughs's anxiety about this "shame" peeks through when, mulling over Thuvia's offer to be his concubine, Carter reflects: "While I was quite familiar with the Martian custom which allows female slaves to Martian men, whose high and chivalrous honour is always ample protection for every woman in his household, yet I had never myself chosen other than men as my body servants." Is Carter (or Burroughs?) completely oblivious to the contradictions here? Thuvia had almost "thrown her arms about my neck and smothered me with caresses" (Burroughs, *The Martian Tales Trilogy*, 355, 354). It's sex Thuvia's offering—why else "body servants"?—and claims to "chivalrous honour" as protection for female slaves simply a diversion.

59. Carter's "naked limbs"; Talu, prince of Marentina, is naked except when cold forces him to wear furs; Carter naked (Burroughs, *The Martian Tales Trilogy*, 264, 539, 597; Brady, *The Burroughs Cyclopaedia*, 312–13).

60. No doubt there are obscure instances that I've missed; for instance, like the story "Shut the Door When You Go Out," by George Turner, where humans have evolved into genital-less creatures of Gaia (George Turner, "Shut the Door When You Go Out," *Void* no. 4 [1986]: 13–15), and the typically naked waitresses in an exclusive nightclub—which turns out to be a spaceship—in Pamela Vincent's "I Wanna Go Home!" (Pamela Vincent, "I Wanna Go Home!" *Far Out* 3 [1985]: 42–44). Leigh Brackett, who devoured Burroughs as a youth, depicted her Martian women nude from the waist up and wearing skirts slit above the thigh; a servant is said to possess "impudent breasts bare above a jeweled girdle" (Leigh Brackett, *Eric John Stark: Outlaw of Mars* [New York: Ballantine Books, 1964], 10–11; *The Coming of the Terrans* [New York: Ace Books, 1967], 25; Newell and Lamont, "Savagery on Mars," 73). The rampant nudity in William S. Burroughs's *Cities of the Red Night* (1981) belongs to a completely different category.

61. There is considerable literature on Delany in general and *Triton* in particular: Wendy Gay Pearson, "Born to be Bron: Destiny and *Destinerrance* in Samuel R. Delany's *Trouble on Triton*," *Science Fiction Studies* 36 (2009): 461–47, is just one example. The notion of "heterotopia" goes back to the work on Michel Foucault, including a short but fundamental essay (Michel Foucault, "Of Other Spaces," trans. Jay Miskowiec, *Diacritics* 16 [1968]: 22–27); again, there is a long bibliography, but I have found Edward Soja, *Thirdspace: Journeys to Los Angeles and Other Real-and-Imagined Places* (Oxford: Blackwell, 1996), 145–63, especially helpful. For *Nude on the Moon*, see its Internet Movie Database entry and Chase Winstead, "Two Faces of Voyeurism: *Nude on the Moon* and *'X'—The Man with the X-Ray Eyes*, in *Science Fiction America: Essays on SF Cinema*, ed. David J. Hogan, 176–87 (Jefferson: McFarland & Company, 2006).

CHAPTER 10

1. Herrmann Diels and Walther Krantz, *Die Fragmente der Vorsokratiker: Griechisch und Deutsch* (Dublin: Weidmann, 1967–1969), chap. 31, B103. *Tyche* is sometimes translated as "Providence," but that word carries too many Christian overtones to be used here, although it does nicely capture the sense.

2. Jane Bennett, *Vibrant Matter: A Political Ecology of Things* (Durham: Duke University Press, 2010); Mel Y. Chen, *Animacies: Biopolitics, Racial Mattering, and Queer Affect* (Durham: Duke University Press, 2012); see chapter 8.

3. Pat Mora, *Chants* (Houston: Arte Público Press, 1984), 8.

4. Ibid., 11, 26.

5. Garrison Allen, *Desert Cat* (New York: Zebra Books, 1994).

6. Ron Felber, *Mojave Incident: Inspired by a Chilling Story of Alien Abduction* (Fort Lee: Barricade Books, 2015), 5 (buck), 3 (cave), 22–23 (late arrival), 26–28 (Table Top campsite), 17, 30 (apprehension), 36–40 (multiple craft), 43, 44, 47, 98 (red-eyed gremlins), 47–49 (monitors), 102–3, 214–15 (ghostly figure, comforter), 51 (mother ship), 100–101 (bodily violation), 105 (fear of lost time), 37–38, 59 (earlier encounter), 93–94 (Elise's rape), 109 (sensations), 54–59, 60–66, 77–82, 85–91, 133–34 (mind invasion), 71–72, 204 (emotions), 172, 203 (sex while watched), 118, 149 (invisible watchers), 101, 121, 156 (ovary theft, pregnant), 123, 142 (demand answers), 159, 198, 209 (probed), 110, 196, 198–200 (implant), 200 (anal probe), 173–212 (hypnosis sessions), 183 (daughter). These citations comprise only a selection of mentions in the book. In her rather credulous research on UFOs, D. W. Pasulka, *Encounters: Experiences with Nonhuman Intelligences* (New York: St. Martin's Essentials, 2023), 84–93, 95–96, 113–149 (a "black demon"), relates some recent analogous unpleasant encounters in the bedroom (or elsewhere).

7. Susan A. Clancy, *Abducted: How People Come to Believe They Were Kidnapped by Aliens* (Cambridge: Harvard University Press, 2005), 35–36.

8. Jodi Dean, *Aliens in America: Conspiracy Theories from Outerspace to Cyberspace* (Ithaca: Cornell University Press, 1998), 23, 122 (sexual experimentation), 174 (watchers); Budd Hopkins, *Intruders: The Incredible Visitations at Copley Woods* (New York: Ballantine Books, 1987), 18 (medical experiments); Bridget Brown, *They Know Us Better Than We Know Ourselves: The History and Politics of Alien Abduction* (New York: New York University Press, 2007), 57 (loss of control), 62–63, 80, 49–56 (sexual experimentation), missing time and hypnosis (Budd Hopkins, *Missing Time* [New York Ballantine Books, 1981]). Orfeo Angelucci, *Son of the Sun: The Secret of the Saucers*, ed. Timothy Green Beckley (New Brunswick: Global Communications/Conspiracy Journal, 2008), 159. A pre-abduction instance of a few of these themes in Angelucci, *Son of the Sun*, 45–46. See L. S. Newman and R. F. Baumeister, "Toward an Explanation of the UFO Abduction Phenomenon: Hypnotic Elaboration, Extraterrestrial Sadomasochism, and Spurious Memories," *Psychological Inquiry* 7 (1996): 99–126, for a discussion, from a psychological viewpoint, of the features of the abduction narrative.

9. John Fuller, *The Interrupted Journey: Two Lost Hours "Aboard a Flying Saucer"* (New York: Penguin-Random House, 2022). Every study of abduction cites the Hills' experience as seminal: Dean, *Aliens in America*, 48–50; Terry Matheson, *Alien Abductions: Creating a Modern Phenomenon* (Amherst: Prometheus Books, 1998), 47–76; Clancy, *Abducted*, 94–99; Gregory L. Reece, *UFO Religion: Inside Flying Saucer Cults and Culture* (London-New York: I. B. Tauris, 2007), 79–82; Brown, *They Know Us Better*, 25–32, 56–57. See also chapter 8.

10. To give a few examples: Betty Andreason in Indiana (Matheson, *Alien Abductions*, 77–106), Travis Walton in an Arizona national forest (108–14), two women in Tujunga Canyon north of Los Angeles (114–30); Whitley Strieber in New York City and an upstate cabin (Whitney Strieber, *Communion: A True Story* [New York: William Morrow, 1987]). There are many more.

11. Felber, *Mojave Incident*, 17, 33, 75, 132. *Mystic Places* presumably refers to *Mystic Places (Mysteries of the Unknown)*, ed. George Constable (New York: Time Life Books, 1987).

12. On the Mojave Twins, who were indeed believed to come for a visit from the sky, see George Devereux, "On Mojave Beliefs Concerning the Twins," *American Anthropologist* 43 (1941): 573–92; David S. Whitley, *A Guide to Rock Art Sites in Southern California and Southern Nevada* (Missoula: Mountain Press Publishing Co., 1996), 124–27 Site 22, with a nice aerial photograph (125 Photo 28); Peter Nabokov, *Where the Lightning Strikes: The Lives of American Indian Sacred Places* (New York: Penguin, 2006), 238–40, and, briefly, chapter 8. Harry Casey and Anne Morgan, *Geoglyphs of the Desert Southwest: Earthen Art as Viewed from Above* (El Cajon: Sunbelt Publications, Inc., 2019) provide a beautiful compilation of pioneering aerial photos of the geoglyphs; the "Fort Mojave Twins" are illustrated at 46. The bulbous head of one twin could easily be seen

as a "space helmet." There are many other large-scale desert figures along the Colorado. Boma Johnson, *Earth Figures of the Lower Colorado and Gila River Deserts: A Functional Analysis* (Yuma: Bureau of Land Management, Yuma District Office, 1985) documented 144 geoglyphs or intaglios along the Colorado and Gila Rivers, mapped at 48. He notes, drily, the notion that "space travelers made the long-lined figures as guides for landing on earth," citing Erich von Dänikan's preposterous *Chariots of the Gods* (15), and demolishes the idea in a few sentences; on the Twins, 32–33; for geoglyph and intaglio, 6–7.

13. A. L. Kroeber, "A Mohave Historical Epic," *University of California Publications: Anthropological Records* 11 (1951), 71 for the background; Lauri Honko, "On the Difficulty of Documenting Oral Epics," in *Die heutige Bedeutung oraler Traditionen: Ihre Archivierung, Publikation und Index-Erschließ / The Present-Day Importance of Oral Traditions: Their Preservation, Publication and Indexing*, eds. Walther Heissig and Rüdiger Schott, 185–94 (Wiesbaden: Verlag für Sozialwissenschaften Wiesbaden, 1998); *Surviving through the Days: Translations of Native California Stories*, ed. Herbert W. Luthin (Berkeley: University of California Press, 2002), 443–60, for the excerpt, part of Hipahipa's episode. See Dell Hymes's "Lineaments and Approximations," in *Kalevala and the World's Traditional Epics*, ed. Lauri Honko (Helsinki: Finnish Literature Society, 2002), 164, apposite warning: A normalized translation into "English can misrepresent the actual relations of a narrative, especially a narrative in another language." Hymes offers a somewhat different version of A 1 through A 10 ("Lineaments and Approximations," 176–80), based on Kroeber's field journals, and restructured to reflect his view of the epic structure of the language. Arthur T. Hatto, *The Mohave Heroic Epic of Inyo-kutavêre* (Helsinki: Academia Scientiarum Fennica, 1999), 185–88 (the monograph), discusses the possible losses in Kroeber's transcription of the Epic. The Epic is not mentioned in Lorraine M. Sherer with Frances Stillman, *The Bitterness Road: The Mojave, 1604–1860*, eds. Sylvia Brakke Vane and Lowell John Bean (Menlo Park: Ballena Press, 1994). Other aspects of the Epic are treated in chapters 5 and 7. A fine photograph of Jack Jones, whose Mohave name was Kwaknialka, is published in Theodora Kroeber and Robert F. Heizer, *Almost Ancestors: The First Californians* (San Francisco: Sierra Club, 1968), 50 Photograph 21. (Probably the same photograph, though less well reproduced, forms the frontispiece to Kroeber, "A Mohave Historical Epic.")

14. Kroeber, "A Mohave Historical Epic," 78 C 16, 79 C 30.

15. Ibid., 90 I 95–96.

16. Ibid., 82 D 45, 129 (quotation), 85 F 65. On Nyĭtše-vilye-vave-kwilyêhe, see Hatto, *The Mohave Heroic Epic*, 75–84.

17. Kroeber, "A Mohave Historical Epic," 82–83 E 50–54.

18. Ibid., 82 E 47–48.

19. Kroeber, "A Mohave Historical Epic," 88 I 92–93. On Hipahipa, whose name Arthur T. Hatto thinks may mean *"abundance of cholla"* (*The Mohave Heroic Epic*, 60, italics in original), see Hatto, *The Mohave Heroic Epic*, 58–70, and chapter 5 on his possibly ambiguous gender. *Hipa* appears in Pamela Munro, Nellie Brown, and Judith D. Crawford, *A Mojave Dictionary* (Los Angeles: Department of Linguistics, University of California, 1992), 78 s.v. Hiipa only as a clan name, "Coyote," first attested in John G. Bourke, "Notes on the Cosmogony and Theogony of the Mojave Indians of the Rio Colorado, Arizona," *Journal of American Folk-Lore* 6 (1889), 180.

20. Kroeber, "A Mohave Historical Epic," 87 G 81 with 146, 87 H 86, 88 H 90–91, 147–48; itineraries G1–G8 and H1–H5 at Fig. 7-2.

21. Kevin Honold, *Molly* (Pittsburgh: Autumn House Press, 2022), 10, 17. On desert roadbuilding and masculinity, a trope that erases nonhuman agency, and the land's resistance, see Jada Ach, "Desert Roads, 'Construction Men,' and Infrastructural Impulses in Cather's *The Professor's House*," in *Reading Aridity in Western American Literature*, eds. Jada Ach and Gary Reger (Lanham, MD: Lexington Books, 2020), 120–34.

22. Cordelia E. Barrera, *The Haunted Southwest: Towards an Ethics of Place in Borderlands Literature* (Lubbock: Texas Tech University Press, 2022), 92–105, quotations at 94; and "Desert Haunting: A Gothic Reading of Arturo Islas' *The Rain God*," in *Reading Aridity in Western American Literature*, eds. Jada Ach and Gary Reger (Lanham, MD: Lexington Books, 2020), 69–71.

23. Arturo Islas, *The Rain God* (New York: Avon Books, 1984), 6, 8, 102, 114, 113.

24. Barrera, *The Haunted Southwest*, 93, 100.

25. Margo Neale and Lynne Kelly, *Songlines: The Power and the Promise* (Port Melbourne: Thames Hudson Australia Pty Ltd., 2020), 1. "Country"—always capitalized—refers to one's homeland, that part of Australia curated and cared for by its Traditional Owners.

26. George English Brooks, "The Business of Heaven and Earth: Toponymy and the Imperial Idyll in the

Domínguez-Escalante Journal of 1776," in *Before the West Was West: Critical Essays on Pre-1800 Literature of the American Frontiers*, eds. Amy T. Hamilton and Tom J. Hillard (Lincoln: University of Nebraska Press, 2014), 264.

27.   Christa Grewe-Volpp, "Nature 'Out There' and as a 'Social Player': Some Basic Consequences for a Literary Ecocritical Analysis, in *Nature in Literary and Cultural Studies: Transatlantic Conversations*, eds. Catrin Gersdorf and Sylvia Mayer (New York: Rodopi, 2006), 79.

28.   D. H. Lawrence, *Studies in Classic American Literature* (London: Penguin Books, 1977), 83–84, italics in original.

29.   Chen, *Animacies*, 159–221, quotations at 159, 166, 203. David J. Alworth seems also to edge toward a non-human agency when he argues that sites (settings in fiction) are "themselves mediators engaging in 'active participation' capable of transforming and modifying meaning themselves, not just providing the setting for this [a narrative drama] to take place" (Alice Levick, *Memory and the Built Environment in 20th-Century American Literature: A Reading and Analysis of Spatial Forms* [London: Bloomsbury Academic, 2021], 87; internal quotation: David J. Alworth, *Site Reading: Fiction, Art, Social Form* [Princeton: Princeton University Press, 2015], 11). Istvan Csicsery-Ronay Jr. seems to impute a general agency to nonhuman objects when he writes, "In a surprising parody of the anthropomorphic cosmology of the ancients, the scientific universe becomes populated with bodies, all of them capable of transformations that disturb the human sense of its place in the world" (*The Seven Beauties of Science Fiction* [Middletown: Wesleyan University Press, 2008], 185). Although I would object to the disparagement inherent in "parody" and the gross overgeneralization of "the ancients," the sentiment seems right.

30.   Bennett, *Vibrant Matter*, viii–ix, italics in original.

31.   Ibid., 23–24, italics in original.

32.   Val Plumwood, "The Concept of a Cultural Landscape: Nature, Culture and Agency in the Land," *Ethics & the Environment* 11 (2006), 116–17, 119–22 (cultural landscape), 125, italics in original. Her use of "services," however, undercuts her position by smuggling through the backdoor the notion of nature as subordinated to humans. David K. Heckerl, "Critical Theory, Causality, and the Emancipation of Nature," in *Re-Naming the Landscape*, eds. Jürgen Kleist and Bruce A. Butterfield (New York: Peter Lang, 1994), 243–46 and 250–51, offers a similar critique of nature as a cultural construct in an argument that, however, does not go as far as Plumwood's. Nor do I find convincing his argument that "causality" frees nature from anthropocentric domination.

33.   Plumwood, "The Concept of a Cultural Landscape," 146.

34.   Bruno Latour, *Facing Gaia: Eight Lectures on the New Climatic Regime* (London: Polity, 2017), 68, emphasis in original.

35.   Ibid., 40–74. Perhaps surprisingly, given the astounding range of Latour's reading, Bennett, *Vibrant Matter*, does not appear in his references (294).

36.   Latour, *Facing Gaia*, 70. The earlier essays are Bruno Latour, "Agency in the Time of the Anthropocene," *New Literary History* 45 (2014): 1–18, and "How Better to Register the Agency of Things," in *The Tanner Lectures on Human Values*, vol. 34, ed. Mark Matheson, 9–117 (Salt Lake City: University of Utah Press, 2016). Latour has a love of *italics*, which I fear has infected me in this paragraph.

37.   Ofelia Zepeda, *Ocean Power: Poems from the Desert* (Tucson: University of Arizona Press, 1995, 83–84). See too already Émile Durkheim, citing an ethnography of the Sioux: "The whole of life comes from it ['"it" being "wakan"] . . . and by the word 'life' must be understood all that acts and reacts and all that moves and is moved, as much in the mineral kingdom as the biological one" (*The Elementary Forms of the Religious Life: A Study in Religious Sociology*, trans. Karen Fields [New York: Free Press, 1995], 205).

38.   Song, rainmaking, running, and sexual power are typical of the gifts desert Native Americans sought when they wanted power: a Piipaash and Halychduum (Maricopa) seeker of wealth, abundant crops, being a good runner, or to "have many girls about him" retreated to a certain cave in the Painted Rock Mountains to attain that power; the ability to make rain acquired through a spirit, Leslie Spier, *Yuman Tribes of the Gila River* (New York: Dover Publications, 1978), 244, 251; also Lowell John Bean, *Mukat's People: The Cahuilla Indians of Southern California* (Berkeley: University of California Press, 1972), 111. On "thing-power," Bennett, *Vibrant Matter*, xvi: "Thing-power gestures toward the strange ability of ordinary, man-made items to exceed their status as objects and to manifest traces of independence or aliveness." I would extend her thing-power to non-artificial things like the ocean.

39.   Paul A. Formisano, *Tributary Voices: Literary and Rhetorical Explorations of the Colorado River* (Reno: University of Nevada Press, 2022), 170–72, alludes to material agencies, but his focus is on the responsibilities

of the Tohono O'odham to the natural world Zepeda invokes in her poetry.

40. https://pwccc.wordpress.com/programa, Articles 1 (1) and 4 (1), accessed September 24, 2023; Joni Adamson and Salma Monani, "Introduction: Cosmovisions, Ecocriticism, and Indigenous Studies," in *Ecocriticism and Indigenous Studies: Conversations from Earth to Cosmos*, eds. Salma Monani and Joni Adamson (London: Routledge, 2017), 2, 4. For an Australian example, see Simone Bignall, Steve Hemming, and Daryle Rigney, "Three Ecosophies for the Anthropocene: Environmental Governance, Continental Posthumanism, and Indigenous Expressivism," *Deleuze Studies* 10, 4 (2016), 456–74.

41. Mary Douglas, *Purity and Danger: An Analysis of the Concept of Pollution and Taboo* (London-New York: Routledge, 2002), xii.

42. Polly Schaafsma, "Petitions for Rain: Textile and Pottery Designs in Rock Art," *International Letter on Rock Art* 66 (2013), 24.

43. Keith H. Basso, *Wisdom Sits in Places: Landscape and Language among the Western Apache* (Albuquerque: University of New Mexico Press, 1996), 107–8. He adds in a note, where he acknowledges a debt to Martin Heidegger, Jean-Paul Sartre, and Edward S. Casey, "that place is a crucial element in many forms of social experience" (158n2).

44. Basso, *Wisdom Sits in Places*, 108.

45. Bennett, *Vibrant Matter*, 99. Latour, *Facing Gaia*, 66, offers his own defense of anthropomorphism, based on Isaac Newton's project of finding a ground for gravity's action at a distance in the attributes of angels.

46. T. H. White, *The Sword in the Stone* (New York: Bantam Doubleday Dell Books for Young Readers, 1963), 232–33, 230. This episode was excised from the omnibus edition of T. H. White, *The Once and Future King* (New York: G. P. Putnam's Sons, 1958). On the "Earth language" sought by Iya Whiteley (who works in the Department of Space & Climate Physics at University College London), "of which Western science is not aware, but according to most indigenous cultures, the Earth and land are sentient, along with the plants and animals that populated" it, see D. W. Pasulka, *Encounters: Experiences with Nonhuman Intelligences* (New York: St. Martin's Essentials, 2023), 54; see also Tim Ingold, "The Temporality of the Landscape," *World Archaeology* 25 (1993), 164, on the endless, interconnected movement and change of everything, agency over time.

47. This objection was already articulated by David Hume in his "Natural History of Religion," *On Religion*, ed. Richard Wollheim (Cleveland: Meridian Books—The World Publishing Company, 1964), 40–41 (chapter III).

48. J. E. Lovelock, *Gaia: A New Look at Life on Earth* (Oxford: Oxford University Press, 1987), 116, 119, and 2007.

49. Latour, *Facing Gaia*.

50. Plumwood, "The Concept of a Cultural Landscape," 125, italics in original. Lovelock, *Gaia*, 115–32, considers the ways we as humans can interact with Gaia, either supporting her or undermining her, though in the end Gaia will always win: she is a system far beyond our capacity to ruin, even if one imagines a situation in which we become the custodians of Earth.

51. Stanislaw Lem, *Solaris*, trans. Joanna Kilmartin and Steve Cox (New York: Mariner, 2002); Csicsery-Ronay Jr., *The Seven Beauties*, 203–6, for a discussion of *Solaris* as a literary grotesque.

52. Lem, *Solaris*, 24 (all quotations), 111–25 for the tour de force.

53. Ibid., 124.

54. Ibid., 164–75 on the theories, 199 for Snow's new theory that the ocean is just a child. Carl Freedman, *Critical Theory and Science Fiction* (Hanover: Wesleyan University Press, 2000), 96–111, however, argues that Kelvin may have achieved communication with Solaris at the novel's end; Freedman's interpretation rests on the application of Jacques Lacan's Freudian ideas about the Other. Melody Jue, "Churning Up the Depths: Nonhuman Ecologies of Metaphor in *Solaris* and 'Oceanic,'" in *Ecology and Science Fiction*, eds. Gerry Canavan and Kim Stanley Robinson (Middletown: Wesleyan University Press, 2014), 227, has no doubt that the Solaris ocean is sentient; she also definitely sees it as "active and agential" (231); so too Frederick Jameson, *Archaeologies of the Future: The Desire Called Utopia and Other Science Fictions* (New York: Verso Books, 2007), 111, writing, "It is proven to everyone's satisfaction that the ocean is not only sentient" but the creator of Rheya and other apparitions. But to accept the ocean's sentience as "proven" ignores Lem's repeated warning that *all* notions about it are uncertain, unproven, and deeply problematic. In *The Invincible*, Lem imagines swarming crystals—which Jameson, *Archaeologies of the Future*, 114, characterizes as "a new form of alien: the intelligent non-organic"—in which he sees "a persistent equilibrium . . . active and a form of agency" (Stanislaw Lem, *The Invincible* [New York: Seabury Press, 1973], 183). (The new 2020 translation omits "form of agency," replacing it with the phrase "active survival": Stanislaw Lem, *The Invincible* [Cambridge: MIT Press, 2020], 170. The 1973 version was translated from the German

translation. My ignorance of Polish precludes my checking the original.) Andrew Milner, *Locating Science Fiction* (Middletown: Wesleyan University Press, 2012), 170–72, reads *Solaris* as a reflection of the limits of science: all efforts, even bombarding the ocean with X-rays, "fail to discover anything of significance about the conscious planetary intelligence they attempt to understand and contact" (171). *Solaris* presents a bevy of complex philosophical conundrums around sentience, intelligence, and reading the other; a fine introduction to these problematics, far too involved to enter into here, can be found in Pawel Grabarczyk, "What Does the Silent Planet Tell Us? The Analysis of Selected Philosophical Themes Found in Stanislaw Lem's *Solaris*," *Acta Universitatis Lodziensis: Folia Litteraria Polonica* 4 (59) (2020): 69–80.

55. Ezra Klein, "Kim Stanley Robinson on Climate Change, Dropping Acid and 'Psychogeology': The Sci-Fi Giant Explains Why He Is Feeling More Hopeful about the Planet," *New York Times*, July 15, 2022. All quotations attributed to Robinson come from the transcript of this podcast.

56. Kim Stanley Robinson, *The High Sierra: A Love Story* (New York: Little, Brown and Company, 2022). I'm reminded, reading Robinson, of Kate Rigby's remark on the "experience of the greater ecocosmic self that today's deep ecologists still seek up mountains" (*Topographies of the Sacred: The Poetics of Place in European Romanticism* [Charlottesville: University of Virgina Press, 2004], 166).

57. The Ionian Basin is a high bowl in Kings Canyon National Park, at the head of the Enchanted Gorge and dominated by Mount Goddard. It is one of the most remote places in the Sierra Nevada Mountains.

58. See Bruno Latour, *Reassembling the Social: An Introduction to Actor-Network Theory* (Oxford: Oxford University Press, 2005) for an introduction. His writings on Actor-Network Theory are voluminous; many can be traced through his webpage: www.bruno-latour.fr.

59. Jeffrey Jerome Cohen, *Stone: An Ecology of the Inhuman* (Minneapolis: University of Minnesota Press, 2015), see for instance 39–47.

60. A stroll into the voluminous philosophical literature exploring the differences between fictional worlds and the "real" world we inhabit would take us far beyond the framework of this book and my competence. I have found Thomas G. Pavel, *Fictional Worlds* (Cambridge: Harvard University Press, 1986) a useful, if old and rather awkwardly written, guide, with which I also have my disagreements.

61. In *The Great Derangement: Climate Change and the Unthinkable* (Chicago: University of Chicago Press, 2016), Amitav Ghosh constructs a powerful case for seeing agency of the natural expressed in climate change— and as a view long held, and still held, by people all over the world.

62. Timothy Clark, *The Value of Ecocriticism* (Cambridge: Cambridge University Press, 2019), 128, italics in original.

63. Orlando Patterson, *Slavery and Social Death: A Comparative Study*, with a new preface, (Cambridge: Harvard University Press, 2018). I grossly generalize in this paragraph; in particular, many societies and individuals regard the restriction of some groups—women, Blacks, etc.—as an unalloyed, necessary good.

64. An exploration of what we might call the "prehistory" of new ideas like posthumanism and the new materialism, which turn out to have deep antecedents, even though they may be unknown to practitioners today, would burst the binding of this book. For a good discussion of Greek thought and posthumanism, see Simon Goldhill, "Conclusions," in *Classical Literature and Posthumanism*, eds. Giulia Maria Chesi and Francesca Spiegel, 331–41 (London: Bloomsbury Academic, 2020), who cites Philippe Descola, *Beyond Nature and Culture*, trans. Janet Lloyd (Chicago: University of Chicago Press, 2014) at 335, from whom I have borrowed my summary of Descola's argument. As for agency, again, examples of agency attributed to natural features can be found in Greek, Roman, and Mesopotamian antiquity. For instance, in "Aetna," a poem about the volcano falsely attributed to Vergil, the lava of the erupting volcano is consuming the greedy inhabitants of the town of Katania in Sicily but spares two brothers who, instead of grabbing their property, carried their parents out of town; the fire is described as "pius" (625–35, 606); see Jarrett T. Welsh, "How To Read a Volcano," *Transactions of the American Philological Association* 144 (2014): 97–132, for a discussion of this text. In a Sumerian myth, the goddess Inana is outraged when the mountain Ebiḫ refuses to show her respect; in her anger she attacks it with battering rams and other weapons: "Inana and Ebih," in Jeremy A. Black, Graham Cunningham, Eleanor Robson, and Gábor Zóyomi, *The Literature of Ancient Sumer* (Oxford: Oxford University Press, 2006), 335 lines 25–48.

BIBLIOGRAPHY

Abbey, Edward. *Beyond the Wall: Essays from the Outside*. New York: Henry Holt and Company, 1984.

———. *Desert Solitaire: A Season in the Wilderness*. New York: Simon and Schuster, 1968.

Ach, Jada. "Desert Roads, 'Construction Men,' and Infrastructural Impulses in Cather's *The Professor's House*." In *Reading Aridity in Western American Literature*, edited by Jada Ach and Gary Reger, 117–40. Lanham, MD: Lexington Books, 2020.

———. *Sand, Water, Salt: Managing the Elements in Literature of the American West, 1880–1925*. Lubbock: Texas Tech University Press, 2021.

Ach, Jada, and Gary Reger, eds. *Reading Aridity in Western American Literature*. Lanham, MD: Lexington Books, 2020.

Adams, Michael. "Sin and Guilt in the Fiction of John Gregory Dunne." *Critique: Studies in Contemporary Fiction* 25 (1984): 154–59.

Adamski, George. "December Thirteenth: The Return Visit." In *Flying Saucers Have Landed*, Desmond Leslie and George Adamski, 217–22. London: Werner Laurie, 1953. (And in *Inside the Space Ships*, George Adamski, 55–60. New York: Abelard-Schuman, Inc., 1955.)

———. "George Adamski." In *Flying Saucers Have Landed*, Desmond Leslie and George Adamski, 171–84. London: Werner Laurie, 1953. (And in *Inside the Space Ships*, George Adamski, 9–22. New York: Abelard-Schuman, Inc., 1955.)

———. *Inside the Space Ships*. New York: Abelard-Schuman, Inc., 1955.

———. *Inside the Spaceships*, revised ed. Vista, CA: The George Adamski Foundation, 2001.

———. "The Memorable November Twentieth." In *Flying Saucers Have Landed*, Desmond Leslie and George Adamski, 185–216. London: Werner Laurie, 1953. (And in *Inside the Space Ships*, George Adamski, 23–54. New York: Abelard-Schuman, Inc., 1955.)

Adamson, Joni, and Salma Monani. "Introduction: Cosmovisions, Ecocriticism, and Indigenous Studies." In *Ecocriticism and Indigenous Studies: Conversations from Earth to Cosmos*, edited by Salma Monani and Joni Adamson, 1–19. London: Routledge, 2017.

Agamben, Giorgio. *Nudities*, translated by David Kishik and Stefan Pedatella. Stanford: Stanford University Press, 2011.

Ahern, Maureen. "'Llevando el norte sobre el ojo izquierdo': Mapping, Measuring, and Naming in Castañedo's *Relación de la jornada de Cíbola*." In *Mapping Colonial Spanish America: Places and Commonplaces of Identity, Culture, and Experience*, edited by Santa Arias and Mariselle Meléndez, 24–50. Lewisburg, PA: Bucknell University Press, 2002.

Ainsworth, Edward Maddin. *Beckoning Desert*. Englewood Cliffs: Prentice Hall, 1962.

Alcott, Louisa May. *Behind a Mask: The Unknown Thrillers of Louisa May Alcott*, edited by Madeleine B. Stern. New York: Morrow, 1975.

Aldgate, Anthony, James Chapman, and Arthur Marwick, eds. *Windows on the Sixties: Exploring Key Texts of Media and Culture*. London: I. B. Tauris, 2000.

Alexander, David V. *Arizona Frontier Military Place Names, 1846–1912*, revised ed. Las Cruces: Yucca Tree Press, 2002.

Allen, Garrison. *Desert Cat.* New York: Zebra Books, 1994.

Allen, James Smith. "The Gendered Politics of Correspondence: The Curious Case of Céline Renooz." In *Gender and Politics in the Age of Letter Writing, 1750–2000,* edited by Caroline Bland and Máire Cross, 161–71. Burlington: Ashgate, 2004.

Alworth, David J. *Site Reading: Fiction, Art, Social Form.* Princeton: Princeton University Press, 2015.

Anaya, Rudolfo. *Alburquerque.* Albuquerque: University of New Mexico Press, 1992.

Anderson, Charles Roberts. *Melville in the South Seas.* New York: Dover Publications, 1966.

Angelucci, Orfeo. *Son of the Sun: The Secret of the Saucers,* edited by Timothy Green Beckley. New Brunswick: Global Communications/Conspiracy Journal, 2008.

Annerino, John. *Desert Survivor: An Adventurer's Guide to Exploring the Great American Desert.* New York: Four Walls Eight Windows, 2001.

Anolik, Lili. *Hollywood's Eve: Eve Babitz and the Secret History of L.A.* New York: Scribner, 2019.

Anonymous. "The Desert" [review of Van Dyke 1901]. *New York Tribune,* February 8, 1902, 10.

Anonymous. "Les dessins médiumiques de Machner." *Annales des Sciences Psychiques* 17 (1908): 86–88.

Anonymous. "Landing in South Africa." *Flying Saucer Review,* December 1956, 2–5.

Anonymous. "Victorien Sardou, le doyen des spirites de France." *Annales des Sciences Psychiques* 18 (1908): 335–39.

Antoniadi, Eugène-Michel. "Mars Section Sixth Interim Report for 1909, Dealing with Some Further Notes on the So-Called 'Canals.'" *Journal of the British Astronomical Association* 20 (1910): 189–92.

Arias, Santa, and Mariselle Meléndez, eds. *Mapping Colonial Spanish America: Places and Commonplaces of Identity, Culture, and Experience.* Lewisburg, PA: Bucknell University Press, 2002.

Arnold, George. *The Sociable; or One Thousand and One Home Amusements.* New York: Dick and Fitzgerald, 1858.

Arthur, JM. *The Default Country: A Lexical Geography of Twentieth-Century Australia.* Sydney: New South Wales University Press, 2003.

Ashley, Mike. *The Time Machines: The Story of the Science-Fiction Pulp Magazines from the Beginning to 1950.* Liverpool: Liverpool University Press, 2000.

Assael, Brenda. "Art or Indecency? Tableaux Vivants on the London Stage and the Failure of Late Victorian Moral Reform." *Journal of British Studies* 45 (2006): 744–58.

Ásta. *Categories We Live By: The Construction of Sex, Gender, Race and Other Social Categories.* Oxford: Oxford University Press, 2018.

Austin, Mary. *The Land of Journey's Ending.* New York: Century, 1924.

———. *The Land of Little Rain.* New York: Modern Library, 2003.

Avila, Eric. "Essaying Los Angeles." In *The Cambridge Companion to the Literature of Los Angeles,* edited by Kevin R. McNamara, 177–90. Cambridge: Cambridge University Press, 2010.

Babener, Lianha. "*Chinatown,* City of Blight." In *Los Angeles in Fiction,* edited by David Fine, 273–85. Albuquerque: University of New Mexico Press, 1984.

———. "Raymond Chandler's City of Lies." In *Los Angeles in Fiction,* edited by David Fine, 109–31. Albuquerque: University of New Mexico Press, 1984.

Babitz, Eve. *Eve's Hollywood.* New York: New York Review of Books, 2015.

———. *Slow Days, Fast Company: The World, the Flesh, and L.A.* New York: Alfred A. Knopf, 1977.

Bacigalupi, Paolo. *The Water Knife.* New York: Alfred A. Knopf, 2015.

Bahn, Paul G. *Prehistoric Rock Art, Polemics and Progress: The 2006 Rhind Lectures for the Society of Antiquaries of Scotland.* Cambridge: Cambridge University Press, 2010.

Bahr, Donald M., Juan Gregorio, David I. Lopez, and Albert Alvarez. *Piman Shamanism and Staying Sickness (Ká:cim Múmkidag).* Tucson: University of Arizona Press, 1974.

Bahr, Donald M., Juan Smith, William Smith Allison, and Julian Hayden. *Short Swift Time of Gods on Earth: The Hohokam Chronicles.* Berkeley: University of California Press, 1994.

Bahr, Erhard. *Weimar on the Pacific: German Exile Culture in Los Angeles and the Crisis of Modernism.* Berkeley: University of California Press, 2007.

Balassi, William, John F. Crawford, and Annie O. Eysturoy, eds. *This Is About Vision: Interviews with Southwestern Writers.* Albuquerque: University of New Mexico Press, 1990.

Baldanza, Frank. "Huxley and Hearst." In *Itinerary: Essays on California Writers,* edited by Charles L. Crow, 35–47. Bowling Green: Bowling Green State University Press, 1978.

Bamford, Kiff. *Jean-François Lyotard.* London: Reaktion Books, 2017.

Banham, Peter Reyner. *Scenes in America Deserta.* Cambridge: MIT Press, 1982.

Banham, Reyner. *Los Angeles: The Architecture of Four Ecologies.* New York: Harper & Row, 1971.

Banias, MJ. *The UFO People: A Curious Culture.* N.p.: August Night Books, 2019.

Barbeito, Patricia Felisa. "'He's Making Me Feel Things in My Body That I Don't Feel': The Body as Battleground in Accounts of Alien Abduction." *Journal of American Culture* 28 (2005): 201–15.

Barcan, Ruth. *Nudity: A Cultural Anatomy.* Oxford: Berg, 2004.

Baritz, Loren. *City on a Hill.* New York: Wiley, 1964

Barnes, Will C. *Arizona Place Names,* revised and enlarged by Byrd H. Granger. Tucson: University of Arizona Press, 1982.

Barrera, Cordelia E. "Desert Haunting: A Gothic Reading of Arturo Islas' *The Rain God.*" In *Reading Aridity in Western American Literature,* edited by Jada Ach and Gary Reger, 69–86. Lanham, MD: Lexington Books, 2020.

———. *The Haunted Southwest: Towards an Ethics of Place in Borderlands Literature.* Lubbock: Texas Tech University Press, 2022.

Barrow, Rosemary. "Toga Plays and Tableaux Vivants: Theatre and Painting on London's Late-Victorian and Edwardian Popular Stage." *Theatre Journal* 62 (2010): 209–26.

Barthélemy, Guy. *Fromentin et l'écriture du désert.* Paris: L'Harmattan, 1997.

Bartholomew, Robert E. "The Airship Hysteria of 1896–97." *Skeptical Inquirer* 14 (1990): 171–81.

———. "The Quest for Transcendence: An Ethnography of UFOs in America." *The Anthropology of Consciousness* 2, 1–2 (1991): 1–12.

Basso, Keith H. *Wisdom Sits in Places: Landscape and Language among the Western Apache.* Albuquerque: University of New Mexico Press, 1996.

Battaglia, Debbora, ed. *E.T. Culture: Anthropology in Outerspaces.* Durham: Duke University Press, 2003.

Baudrillard, Jean. *America,* translated by Chris Turner. London: Verso, 1988.

Bean, Lowell John. *Mukat's People: The Cahuilla Indians of Southern California.* Berkeley: University of California Press, 1972.

Beauvoir, Simone de. *America Day by Day,* translated by Carol Cosman. Berkeley: University of California Press, 1999.

Beck, John. *Dirty Wars: Landscape, Power, and Waste in Western American Literature.* Lincoln: University of Nebraska Press, 2009.

Beckley, Timothy Green, ed. *Secrets of Death Valley: Mysteries and Haunts of the Mojave Desert.* New Brunswick: Global Communications, 2010.

Begout, Bruce. *Zeropolis: The Experience of Las Vegas,* translated by Liz Heron. London: Reaktion Books, 2004.

Beké, Len. "Place Naming and Toponymic Silencing in the Sierras of Northern Nuevo México." *Journal of the Southwest* 64 (2022): 495–528.

Bell, Horace. *Reminiscences of a Ranger: Early Times in Southern California.* Norman: University of Oklahoma Press, 1999.

Benjamin, Walter. *Gesammelte Schriften, II-1,* edited by Rolf Tiedemann and Hermann Schweppenhäuser. Frankfurt am Main: Suhrkamp Verlag, 1977.

Bennett, Jane. *Vibrant Matter: A Political Ecology of Things.* Durham: Duke University Press, 2010.

Berger, Yves. "The Burial of Edward Abbey." *Journal of the Southwest* 35 (1993): 357–62.

———. *La pierre et le saguaro.* Paris: Bernard Grasset, 1990.

Bergon, Frank. *The Temptations of St. Ed and Brother S.* Reno: University of Nevada Press, 1993.

Berlitz, Charles, and William Moore. *The Roswell Incident.* New York: Berkeley Books, 1980.

Bernbaum, Edwin. *Sacred Mountains of the World,* 2nd ed. Cambridge: Cambridge University Press, 2022.

Bethurum, Truman. *Aboard a Flying Saucer: A Non-fiction True Story of Personal Experience.* Los Angeles: DeVorss & Co., 1954.

———. *Personal Scrapbook.* Scotia: Arcturus, 1982.

Beverley, Robert. *The History and Present State of Virginia,* edited by Louis B. Wright. Chapel Hill: University of North Carolina Press, 1947.

Bignall, Simone, Steve Hemming, and Daryle Rigney. "Three Ecosophies for the Anthropocene: Environmental Governance, Continental Posthumanism, and Indigenous Expressivism." *Deleuze Studies* 10, 4 (2016): 455–78.

Bishop, Greg. "Interview: James Mosley *Saucer Smear* 'Commander' and Publisher." In *Wake Up Down There! The Excluded Middle Collection,* edited by Greg Bishop, 107–17. Kempton: Adventures Unlimited Press, 2000.

———, ed. *Wake Up Down There! The Excluded Middle Collection.* Kempton: Adventures Unlimited Press, 2000.

Black, Jeremy A., Graham Cunningham, Eleanor Robson, and Gábor Zóyomi. *The Literature of Ancient Sumer.* Oxford: Oxford University Press, 2006.

Blackburn, T. C. *December's Child: A Book of Chumash Oral Narratives*. Berkeley: University of California Press, 1975.

Bladow, Kyle, and Jennifer Ladino, eds. *Affective Ecocriticism: Emotion, Embodiment, and the Environment*. Lincoln: University of Nebraska Press, 2018.

———. "Toward an Affective Ecocriticism: Placing Feeling in the Anthropocene." In *Affective Ecocriticism: Emotion, Embodiment, and the Environment*, edited by Kyle Bladow and Jennifer Ladino, 1–22. Lincoln: University of Nebraska Press, 2018.

Blanchot, Maurice. *The Gaze of Orpheus and Other Literary Essays*, edited by Geoffrey Hartman and translated by Lydia Davis. Barryton: Station Hill Press, 1981.

Bland, Caroline, and Máire Cross, eds. *Gender and Politics in the Age of Letter Writing, 1750–2000*. Burlington: Ashgate, 2004.

Blodget, Charlotte. "Introduction." In *Inside the Space Ships*, George Adamski, 9–20. New York: Abelard-Schuman, Inc., 1955.

Bloodworth, William. "Zane Grey's Western Eroticism." *South Dakota Review* 26 (1985): 5–14.

Bodei, Remo. *Paesaggi sublimi: gli uomini davanti alla natura selvaggia*. Milan: Bompiani, 2008.

Bois, Jules. *Le miracle moderne: la métapsychique—la surâme et le surhomme—la télépathie et les fantômes des vivants—rayons humains—maisons hantées—aventures d'un revenant—un chapelet de voyantes—le mystère des tables tournantes éclairci—le mécanisme du miracle de Lourdes—les professeurs de volante—le miracle est en nous—création d'une humanité supérieure*. Paris: P. Ollendorff, 1907.

Bonafante, Larissa. "Nudity as Costume in Classical Art." *American Journal of Archaeology* 93 (1989): 543–70.

Bonyhady, Tim, and Tom Griffiths, eds. *Words for Country: Landscape and Language in Australia*. Sydney: University of South Wales Press, 2002.

Bourke, John G. "Notes on the Cosmogony and Theogony of the Mojave Indians of the Rio Colorado, Arizona." *Journal of American Folk-Lore* 6 (1889): 169–89.

Bowman, Matthew. *The Abduction of Betty and Barney Hill: Alien Encounters, Civil Rights, and the New Age in America*. New Haven: Yale University Press. 2023.

Boyd, Caroline. "Pictographs, Patterns, and Peyote in the Lower Pecos Canyonlands of Texas." In *A Companion to Rock Art*, edited by Jo McDonald and Peter Veth, 34–50. Malden, MA: Wiley-Blackwell, 2012.

———. *The White Shaman Mural*. Austin: University of Texas Press, 2016.

Boylan, Richard. "Native Elders Reveal Centuries of E.T. Contact Lore." *Contact Forum* 4 (1996): 1–6. Accessed March 29, 2022. https://www.drboylan.com/strknrpt2.html.

Brackett, Leigh. *The Coming of the Terrans*. New York: Ace Books, 1967.

———. *Eric John Stark: Outlaw of Mars*. New York: Ballantine Books, 1964.

Brady, Clark A. *The Burroughs Cyclopaedia: Characters, Places, Fauna, Flora, Technologies, Languages, Ideas and Terminologies Found in the Works of Edgar Rice Burroughs*. Jefferson: McFarland & Company, Inc., 1996.

Branton, ed. *The Dulce Wars: Underground Alien Bases & the Battle for Planet Earth*. New Brunswick: Inner Light/Global Communications, 1999.

Braverman, Kate. *Lithium for Medea: A Novel*. New York: Seven Stories Press, 2002.

Brecht, Bertolt. *Arbeitsjournal: Zweiter Band, 1942 bis 1955*, edited by Werner Hecht. Frankfurt am Main: Suhrkamp Verlag, 1973.

Brettell, Caroline B., and Carolyn F. Sargent. *Gender in Cross-Cultural Perspective*. London: Routledge, 2017.

Brinig, Myron. *The Flutter of an Eyelid*. New York: Farrar & Rinehart, 1933.

Broder, Melissa. *Death Valley: A Novel*. New York: Scribner, 2023.

Brogan, Hugh. *Alexis de Tocqueville: A Life*. New Haven: Yale University Press, 2007.

Brooks, George English. "The Business of Heaven and Earth: Toponymy and the Imperial Idyll in the Domínguez-Escalante Journal of 1776." In *Before the West Was West: Critical Essays on Pre-1800 Literature of the American Frontiers*, edited by Amy T. Hamilton and Tom J. Hillard, 263–90. Lincoln: University of Nebraska Press, 2014.

Brossard, Nicole. *Le désert mauve*. Montreal: Typo, 2010.

Brower, Benjamin Claude. *A Desert Named Peace: The Violence of France's Empire in the Algerian Sahara, 1844–1902*. New York: Columbia University Press, 2009.

Brown, Bridget. *They Know Us Better Than We Know Ourselves: The History and Politics of Alien Abduction*. New York: New York University Press, 2007.

Broyles, Bill, Luke Evans, Richard Stephen Felger, and Gary Paul Nabhan. "Our Grand Desert: A Gazetteer for Northwestern Sonora, Southwestern Arizona, and Northeastern Baja California." In *Dry Borders: Great*

Natural Reserves of the Sonoran Desert, edited by Richard Stephen Felger and Bill Broyles, 581–79 and 737–48. Salt Lake City: University of Utah Press, 2007.

Burroughs, Edgar Rice. *The Martian Tales Trilogy: A Princess of Mars, The Gods of Mars, The Warlord of Mars.* New York: Barnes and Noble, 2004.

———. *The Moon Maid*, complete and restored. Lincoln: University of Nebraska Press, 2002.

———. *More Martian Tales: Thuvia, Maid of Mars, The Chessmen of Mars.* New York: Barnes and Noble, 2006.

———. "Under the Moons of Mars." In *Under the Moons of Mars: A History and Anthology of "The Scientific Romance" in the Munsey Magazines, 1912–1920*, edited by Sam Moskowitz, 1–52. New York: Holt, Rinehart and Winston, 1970.

———. *The War Chief.* New York: Ballantine Books, 1964.

Butor, Michel. *Mobile*, translated by Richard Howard. Bloomington: Dalkey Archive Press, 2004.

Byrkit, James W. "Land, Sky, and People: The Southwest Defined." *Journal of the Southwest* 34 (1992): 342–52.

Cain, James M. *Double Indemnity.* New York: Vintage, 1989.

Calhoun, Alfred R. *The Letters of Alfred R. Calhoun: The Mojave Desert, 1867–1868*, edited by John N. Marnell. Goffs: Tales of the Mojave Road Publishing Company, 2011.

Campbell, Bruce F. *Ancient Wisdom Revived: A History of the Theosophical Movement.* Berkeley: University of California Press, 1980.

Canavan, Gerry, and Kim Stanley Robinson, eds. *Ecology and Science Fiction.* Middletown: Wesleyan University Press, 2014.

Canty, J. M., and M. N. Greeley, eds. *History of Mining in Arizona.* Tucson: Mining Club of the Southwest Foundation, 1991.

Canyon, Christy. *Lights, Camera, Sex!* Sherman Oaks: Christy Canyon, 2003.

Carlson, Thomas D., ed. *The Other Side of Realism: Essays on Modern Fantasy and Science Fiction.* Bowling Green: Bowling Green University Popular Press, 1971.

Carmichael, David L. 1994. "Places of Power: Mescalero Apache Sacred Sites and Sensitive Areas." In *Sacred Sites, Sacred Places*, edited by David L. Carmichael, Jane Hubert, Brian Reeves, and Audhild Schanche, 89–98. London: Routledge, 1994.

Carmichael, David L., Jane Hubert, and Brian Reeves. "Introduction." In *Sacred Sites, Sacred Places*, edited by David L. Carmichael, Jane Hubert, Brian Reeves, and Audhild Schanche, 1–8. London: Routledge, 1994.

Carmichael, David L., Jane Hubert, Brian Reeves, and Audhild Schanche, eds. *Sacred Sites, Sacred Places.* London: Routledge, 1994.

Caro Baroja, Julio. *The World of Witches.* Chicago: University of Chicago Press, 1987.

Carr-Gomm, Philip. *A Brief History of Nakedness.* London: Reaktion Books, 2010.

Carson, Anne. "Putting Her in Her Place: Woman, Dirt, and Desire." In *Before Sexuality: The Construction of Erotic Experience in the Ancient Greek World*, edited by David M. Halperin, John J. Winkler, and Froma I. Zeitlin, 135–69. Princeton: Princeton University Press, 1990.

Casey, Harry, and Anne Morgan. *Geoglyphs of the Desert Southwest: Earthen Art as Viewed from Above.* El Cajon: Sunbelt Publications, Inc., 2019.

Cassirer, Ernst. *The Philosophy of Symbolic Forms, Volume Three: The Phenomenology of Knowledge*, translated by Ralph Manheim. New Haven: Yale University Press, 1957.

Cateau, Heather, and Milla Cozart Riggio, eds. *Turning Tides: Caribbean Intersections in the Americas and Beyond.* Kingston-Miami: Ian Randle Publishers, 2019.

Cather, Willa. *Death Comes for the Archbishop.* Lincoln: University of Nebraska Press, 1999.

———. *The Song of the Lark.* London: John Murray, 1916.

Chandler, M. A. "Depiction of Modern and Pangean Deserts: Evaluation of GCM Hydrological Diagnostics for Paleoclimate Studies." In *Pangea: Paleoclimate, Tectonics, and Sedimentation during Accretion, Zenith, and Breakup of a Supercontinent*, edited by George D. Klein, 117–38. Boulder: Geological Society of America, 1994.

Chandler, Raymond. *Stories and Early Novels, Pulp Stories / The Big Sleep / Farewell, My Lovely / The High Window.* New York: The Library of America, 1995.

Chapman, Mary. "'Living Pictures': Women and *Tableaux Vivants* in Nineteenth-Century American Fiction and Culture." *Wide Angle* 18, no. 3 (1996): 22–52.

Cheetham, Mark A., and Elizabeth D. Harvey. "Obscure Imaginings: Visual Culture and the Anatomy of Caves." *Journal of Visual Culture* 1 (2002): 105–26.

Chen, Mel Y. *Animacies: Biopolitics, Racial Mattering, and Queer Affect.* Durham: Duke University Press, 2012.

Chesi, Giula Maria, and Francesca Spiegel, eds. *Classical Literature and Posthumanism.* London: Bloomsbury

Academic, 2020.

Chester, George Randolph, and Lilian Chester. *On the Lot and Off.* New York: Harper & Brothers Publishers, 1924.

Chippindale, Christopher, and Raul S. C. Taçon, eds. *The Archaeology of Rock-Art.* Cambridge: Cambridge University Press, 1998.

Christin, Anne-Marie. "Space and Convention in Eugène Fromentin: The Algerian Experience," translated by Richard M. Berrong. *The New Literary History* 15 (1984): 559–74.

Cixous, Hélène. *Readings: The Poetics of Blanchot, Joyce, Kafka, Keist, Lispector, and Tsvetaeva*, edited and translated by Verena Andermatt Conley. Minneapolis: University of Minnesota Press, 1991.

Clancy, Susan A. *Abducted: How People Come to Believe They Were Kidnapped by Aliens.* Cambridge: Harvard University Press, 2005.

Clapp, Nicholas. *Old Magic: Lives of the Desert Shamans.* San Diego: Sunbelt Publications, 2017.

Clark, Kenneth. *The Nude: A Study in Ideal Form.* Princeton: Princeton University Press, 1972.

Clark, Timothy. *The Value of Ecocriticism.* Cambridge: Cambridge University Press, 2019.

Clarke, Ardy Sixkiller. *More Encounters with Star People: Urban American Indians Tell Their Stories.* San Antonio: Anomalist Books, 2016.

———. *Sky People: Untold Stories of Alien Encounters in Mesoamerica.* Franklin Lakes: Red Wheel Weiser, 2014.

———. *Space Age Indians: Their Encounters with the Blue Men, Reptilians, and Other Star People.* San Antonio: Anomalist Books, 2019.

Clary, Amy. "Mark Twain in the Desert." *Journal of Ecocriticism* 3 (2011): 29–39.

Claxton, Mae Miller. "'Untameable Texts': The Art of Georgia O'Keeffe and Eudora Welty." *The Mississippi Quarterly* 56 (2003): 315–30.

Clifford, Josephine. *Overland Tales.* San Francisco: A. L. Bancroft, 1877.

Clottes, Jean. *What Is Paleolithic Art? Cave Paintings and the Dawn of Human Creativity*, translated by Oliver Y. Martin and Robert D. Martin. Chicago: University of Chicago Press, 2016.

Cochran, Russ. *The Edgar Rice Burroughs Library of Illustration*, vol. 3. West Plains: Russ Cochran, 1984.

Cohen, Jeffrey Jerome. *Stone: An Ecology of the Inhuman.* Minneapolis: University of Minnesota Press, 2015.

Colby, Georgina. *Bret Easton Ellis: Underwriting the Contemporary.* New York: Palgrave Macmillan, 2011.

Comaroff, Jean L., and John Comaroff. *Of Revelation and Revolution, Vol. 2: The Dialectics of Modernity on a South African Frontier.* Chicago: University of Chicago Press, 1997.

Conferenza episcopale italiana. *Martirologio romana.* Vatican: Libreria editrice vaticana, 2004.

Conil, Sebastien, and Alex Hall. "Local Regimes of Atmospheric Variability: A Case Study of Southern California." *Journal of Climate* 19 (2006): 4308–25.

Connell, R. W. *Masculinities*, 2nd ed. Berkeley: University of California Press, 2005.

Cooper, Stephen. *Full of Life: A Biography of John Fante.* New York: North Point Press, 2000.

Cooper, Stephen, and Clorinda Donato, eds. *John Fante's Ask the Dust: A Joining of Voices and Views.* New York: Fordham University Press, 2020.

Costelloe, Timothy M., ed. *The Sublime from Antiquity to the Present.* Cambridge: Cambridge University Press, 2012.

Cranston, C. A., and Robert Zellers, eds. *The Littoral Zone: Australian Contexts and their Writers.* Leiden: Brill Academic, 2007.

Creme, Benjamin. *The Gathering of the Forces of Light: The UFOs and their Spiritual Mission.* Amsterdam-London: Share International Foundation, 2010.

Cronon, William. "The Trouble with Wilderness, or, Getting Back to the Wrong Nature." In *Uncommon Ground: Rethinking the Human Place in Nature*, edited by William Cronon, 69–90. New York: W. W. Norton & Co, 1995.

———. *Uncommon Ground: Rethinking the Human Place in Nature.* New York: W.W. Norton & Co, 1995.

Crossley, Robert. *Imagining Mars: A Literary History.* Middletown: Wesleyan University Press, 2011.

Crow, Charles L. "Home and Transcendence in Los Angeles." In *Los Angeles in Fiction*, edited by David Fine, 207–23. Albuquerque: University of New Mexico Press, 1984.

———, ed. *Itinerary: Essays on California Writers.* Bowling Green: Bowling Green State University Press, 1978.

Csicsery-Ronay, Istvan, Jr. *The Seven Beauties of Science Fiction.* Middletown: Wesleyan University Press, 2008.

Culver, Lawrence. *The Frontier of Leisure: Southern California and the Shaping of Modern America.* New York: Oxford University Press, 2010.

Cutter, Martha. *Unruly Tongue: Identity and Voice in American Women's Writing, 1850–1930.* Jackson: University of Mississippi Press, 1999.

Davis, Arthur Powell. "What Irrigation Is Doing for Arizona." *National Magazine: An Illustrated Monthly* 15

(1901–1902): 642–44.

Davis, Diana K. *The Arid Lands: History, Power, Knowledge.* Cambridge: MIT Press, 2016.

Davis, Mike. *City of Quartz: Excavating the Future of Los Angeles.* New York: Vintage Books, 1990.

———. *Ecology of Fear: Los Angeles and the Imagination of Disaster.* New York: Vintage Books, 1999.

Davis, Tracy C. "The Spectacle of the Absent Costume: Nudity on the Victorian Stage." *New Theater Quarterly* 5 (1989): 321–33.

Dawe, W. Carlton. *The Golden Lake: or, the Marvellous History of a Journey through the Great Lone Land of Australia.* Melbourne: E. A. Petherick & Co., 1891.

Dawes, Jennifer, ed. *Dark Tourism in the American West.* London: Palgrave Macmillan, 2020.

De Castañeda, Pedro. *The Journey of Coronado,* translated by George Parker Winship. New York: Dover Publications, Inc., 1990.

De Castañeda de Nájera, Pedro. "The Relación de la Jornada de Cíbola, Pedro de Castañeda de Nájera's Narrative, 1560s (copy, 1596)." In *Documents of the Coronado Expedition, 1539–1542: "They Were Not Familiar with His Majesty, nor Did They Wish to Be His Subjects,"* edited and translated by Richard Flint and Shirley Cushing Flint, 378–496. Albuquerque: University of New Mexico Press, 2005.

De Vries, Kylan Mattias. "Berdache (Two-Spirit)." In *Encyclopedia of Gender and Society,* edited by Jodi O'Brien, 64. Los Angeles: Sage, 2015.

Dean, Jodi. *Aliens in America: Conspiracy Theories from Outerspace to Cyberspace.* Ithaca: Cornell University Press, 1998.

Decker, R. M. *35 Minutes to Mars.* Lakeville: Glade Press, Inc., 2004.

DeGraw, Sharon. *The Subject of Race in American Science Fiction.* New York: Routledge, 2007.

Delany, Samuel R. *Trouble on Triton: An Ambiguous Heterotopia.* Middletown: Wesleyan University Press, 1996.

Della Dora, Veronica. *Landscape, Nature, and the Sacred in Byzantium.* Cambridge: Cambridge University Press, 2016.

———. *Mountain: Nature and Culture.* London: Reaktion Books, 2016.

Denham, Dixon, Hugh Clapperton, and Walter Oudney. *Narrative of Travels and Discoveries in Northern and Central Africa in the Years 1822, 1823, and 1824,* 2 vols. London: John Murray, 1828.

Denier, Tony. *Parlor Tableaux; or Animated Pictures.* New York: Samuel French, 1869.

Dennett, Preston. *Inside UFOs: True Accounts of Contacts with Extraterrestrials.* Scotts Valley: CreateSpace Independent Publishing Platform, 2017.

Deonna, Waldemar. *De la planète Mars en terre sainte: art et subconscient: un medium peintre: Hélène Smith.* Paris: De Boccard, 1932.

Derounian-Stodola, Kathryn Zabelle. "The Captive and her Editor: The Ciphering of Olive Oatman and Royal B. Stratton." *Prospects: An Annual of American Studies* 23 (1998): 171–92.

Descola, Philippe. *Beyond Nature and Culture,* translated by Janet Lloyd. Chicago: University of Chicago Press, 2014.

Deverell, William, and Douglas Flamming. "Race, Rhetoric, and Regional Identity: Boosting Los Angeles, 1880–1930." In *Power and Place in the North American West,* edited by Richard White and John Findlay, 117–43. Seattle: University of Washington Press, 1999.

Deverell, William, and Greg Hise, eds. *Land of Sunshine: An Environmental History of Los Angeles.* Pittsburgh: University of Pittsburgh Press, 2005.

Devereux, George. "Institutionalized Homosexuality of the Mohave Indians." *Human Biology* 9 (1937): 498–527.

———. "On Mojave Beliefs Concerning the Twins." *American Anthropologists* 43 (1941): 573–92.

———. *The Social and Cultural Implications of Incest among the Mohave Indians.* Albany: Psychoanalytic Quarterly, 1939.

Diani, Marco. "The Desert of Democracy, from Tocqueville to Baudrillard." *L'Éspirit créateur* 30 (1990): 67–80.

Diaz, Natalie. *When My Brother Was an Aztec.* Port Townsend: Copper Canyon Press, 2012.

Didion, Joan. *Play It as It Lays.* New York: Farrar, Straus and Giroux, 2005.

———. *Slouching Towards Bethlehem.* New York: Farrar, Straus and Giroux, 2008.

———. *The White Album.* New York: Farrar, Straus and Giroux, 1979.

Diels, Hermann, and Walther Krantz. *Die Fragmente der Vorsokratiker: Griechisch und Deutsch.* Dublin: Weidmann, 1967–1969.

Dimock, Wai Chee. "Introduction: Planet and America, Set and Subset." In *Shades of the Planet: American Literature as World Literature,* edited by Wai Chee Dimock and Lawrence Buell, 1–16. Princeton: Princeton University Press, 2007.

Dimock, Wai Chee, and Lawrence Buell, eds. *Shades of the Planet: American Literature as World Literature.*

Princeton: Princeton University Press, 2007.

Dixon, Thomas. *The Sins of the Father: A Romance of the South.* Lexington: The University Press of Kentucky, 2004.

Dodge, Natt N., and Herbert S. Zim. *The Southwest: A Guide to the Wide Open Spaces.* New York: Golden Press, 1955.

Doelle, William "Bill" H., ed. "Love of the Gila: Reflections on Millennia of Life in the Southern Southwest." *Archaeology Southwest Magazine* 36, 1 & 2 (2023): 3–59.

Dolujanoff, Emma. *Cuentos del desierto.* Hermosillo: Gobierno del Estado Sonora. Instituto Sonorense de Cultura, 2016.

Donne, John. *Metaphysical Poetry.* London: Penguin, 2006.

Dorab, Robert. *The Theory of the Sublime from Longinus to Kant.* Cambridge: Cambridge University Press.

Doughty, Charles M. *Travels in Arabia Deserta,* 2 vols. New York: Dover Publications, Inc., 1979.

Douglas, Mary. *Purity and Danger: An Analysis of the Concept of Pollution and Taboo.* London-New York: Routledge, 2002.

Dowling, Terry. *The Complete Rynosseros,* 3 vols. Hornsea: PS Publishing Ltd., 2022.

Doyel, David E. "Irrigation, Production, and Power in Phoenix Basin Hohokam Society." In *The Hohokam Millennium,* edited by Suzanne K. Fish and Paul R. Fish, 83–89. Santa Fe: School for Advanced Research Press, 2007.

Driever, Steven L. "Spanish as a Language for Geographical Expression." *Yearbook (Conference of Latin American Geographers)* 16 (1990): 3–14.

Drucker, Philip. "Culture Element Distributions XVII: Yuman-Piman." *University of California Anthropological Records* 6, no. 3 (1941): 91–230.

Dunaway, David King. *Huxley in Hollywood.* New York: Harper & Row, 1989.

Duncan, Dayton. *Out West: American Journey Along the Lewis and Clark Trail.* New York: Penguin, 1987.

Dunne, John Gregory. *True Confessions.* New York: Thunder Mouth's Press, 2006.

Durkheim, Émile. *The Elementary Forms of the Religious Life: A Study in Religious Sociology,* translated by Karen Fields. New York: Free Press, 1995.

Ehret, Christopher. *Ancient Africa: A Global History, to 300 CE.* Princeton: Princeton University Press, 2023.

Eliade, Mircea. *Rites and Symbols of Initiation: The Mysteries of Birth and Rebirth,* translated by Willard R. Taske. New York: Harper and Row, 1975.

———. *The Sacred and the Profane: The Nature of Religion,* translated by Willard R. Trask. New York: Harcourt, Brace & World, 1nc., 1987.

Ellis, Bret Easton. *Imperial Bedrooms.* New York: Alfred A. Knopf, 2010.

———. *Less Than Zero.* New York: Vintage Books, 1985.

Emerson, Ralph Waldo. *The Annotated Emerson,* edited by David Mikics. Cambridge: The Belknap Press, 2012.

Emory, William H. *Report of the United States and Mexican Boundary Survey, Made Under the Direction of the Secretary of the Interior.* Washington, DC: Cornelius Wendell, 1857.

Enger, Philipp. "Eine Wüstenwanderung mit Israel." In *Was Ist eine Wüste? Interdisziplinäre Annäherungen an einen interkulturellen Topos,* edited by Uwe Lindemann and Monika Schwitz-Emans, 29–43. Würzberg: Verlag Königshausen & Neumann, 2000.

Erickson, Steve. *Amnesiascope: A Novel.* New York: Henry Holt and Company, 1996.

Evans, George W. B. *Mexican Gold Trail: The Journal of a Forty-Niner,* edited by Glenn S. Dumke. San Marino: Huntington Library, 2006.

Evans, Hilary. *Gods, Spirits, Cosmic Guardians: A Comparative Study of the Encounter Experience.* Wellingborough: Aquarian Press, 1987.

———. *Visions, Apparitions, Alien Visitors.* Wellingborough: Aquarian Press, 1984.

Evelein, Johannes. *Literary Exiles from Nazi Germany.* Rochester: Camden House, 2014.

Eyre, Edward John. *Journals of Expeditions of Discovery into Central Australia and Overland from Adelaide to King George's Sound, in the Years 1840–1,* 2 vols. London: T. &W. Boone, 1845.

Fair, A. A. *Double or Quits.* New York: William Morrow and Company, 1941.

Fante, John. *Ask the Dust.* New York: Black Sparrow Press, 1980.

Favenc, Ernest. *The Secret of the Australian Desert.* London: Blackie & Son, 1894.

Felber, Ron. *Mojave Incident: Inspired by a Chilling Story of Alien Abduction.* Fort Lee: Barricade Books, 2015.

Feldt, Laura. "Wilderness and Hebrew Bible Religion—Fertility, Apostasy and Religious Transformation in the Pentateuch." In *Religion and Society, Wilderness in Mythology and Religion: Approaching Religious Spatialities, Cosmologies, and Ideas of Wild Nature,* edited by Laura Feldt, Gustavo Benavides, and Kocku von Stuckrad, 55–94. Berlin: De Gruyter, 2012.

Feldt, Laura, Gustavo Benavides, and Kocku von Stuckrad, eds. *Religion and Society, Wilderness in Mythology and Religion: Approaching Religious Spatialities, Cosmologies, and Ideas of Wild Nature*. Berlin: De Gruyter, 2012.

Felger, Richard Stephen, and Bill Broyles, eds. *Dry Borders: Great Natural Reserves of the Sonoran Desert*. Salt Lake City: University of Utah Press, 2007.

Ferguson, William. *My Trip to Mars*. London: Forgotten Books, 2008.

Fine, David. *Imagining Los Angeles: A City in Fiction*. Albuquerque: University of New Mexico Press, 2000.

———. "Introduction." In *Los Angeles in Fiction*, edited by David Fine, 1–26. Albuquerque: University of New Mexico Press, 1984.

———, ed. *Los Angeles in Fiction*. Albuquerque: University of New Mexico Press, 1984.

Fish, Suzanne K., and Paul R. Fish, eds. *The Hohokam Millennium*. Santa Fe: School for Advanced Research Press, 2007.

Fishkin, Shelley Fisher. "Crossroads of Cultures: The Transnational Turn in American Studies—Presidential Address to the American Studies Association, November 12, 2004." *American Quarterly* 57 (2005): 17–57.

Fitzgerald, F. Scott. *The Great Gatsby*. New York: Scribner, 2004.

———. *The Love of the Last Tycoon*, edited by Matthew J. Bruccoli. New York: Scribner, 2003.

Flammarion, Camille. *La planète Mars et ses conditions d'habitabilité: Encyclopédie générale des observations martiennes*, 2 vols. Paris: Gauthier-Villars, 1892–1909.

———. *La pluralité des mondes habités: Étude où on expose les conditions d'habitabilité des terres*. Paris: Marpon et Flammarion, 1862.

———. "Les satellites d'Uranus et les ésprits." *Annales des sciences psychiques* 18 (1908): 16–23.

Flannery, Kate. *Strip Tees: A Memoir of Millennial Los Angeles*. New York: Henry Holt and Company, 2023.

Flint, Richard, and Shirley Cushing Flint, eds. and trans. *Documents of the Coronado Expedition, 1539–1542: "They Were Not Familiar with His Majesty, nor Did They Wish to Be His Subjects."* Albuquerque: University of New Mexico Press, 2005.

Flournoy, Théodore. *From India to the Planet Mars: A Case of Multiple Personality with Imaginary Languages*, translated by Daniel B. Vermilye. Princeton: Princeton University Press, 1994.

Force, Peter, ed. *Tracts and Other Papers, Relating Principally to the Origin, Settlement, and Progress of the Colonies of North America, from the Beginning of the Country to the Year 1776*, vol. 1. Washington, DC: Printed by Peter Force, 1836.

Formisano, Paul A. *Tributary Voices: Literary and Rhetorical Explorations of the Colorado River*. Reno: University of Nevada Press, 2022.

Foucault, Michel. *Discipline and Punish: The Birth of the Prison*, translated by Alan Sheridan. New York: Vintage Books, 1995.

———. "Of Other Spaces," translated by Jay Miskowiec. *Diacritics* 16 (1968): 22–27.

Fowler, Don D., Gladys W. Smith, and C. Melvin Aikens, eds. *Great Basin Cultural Ecology: A Symposium*. Reno: Desert Research Institute, University of Nevada, 1972.

Francaviglia, Richard. *Believing in Place: A Spiritual Geography of the Great Basin*. Reno: University of Nevada Press, 2003.

Freedman, Carl. *Critical Theory and Science Fiction*. Hanover: Wesleyan University Press, 2000.

Frey, Philippe. *America deserta*. Paris: Robert Laffont, 1998.

Fried, Steve. *Appetite for America: Fred Harvey and the Business of Civilizing the Wild West—One Meal at a Time*. New York: Random House, 2010.

Friedman, Stanton T., and Kathleen Marden. *Captured! The Betty and Barney Hill UFO Experience: The True Story of the First Documented Alien Abduction*. Newburyport: New Page Books, 2021.

Friedman, Vanessa. "Dior in the Desert." *New York Times*, May 12, 2017.

Fromentin, Eugène. *Between Sea and Sahara: An Algerian Journal*, translated by Blake Robinson. Athens: Ohio University Press, 1999.

———. *Un été dans le Sahara: voyage dans les oasis au Sud algérien en 1853*. Paris: Éditions France-Empire, 1992.

Fry, Daniel. *The White Sands Incident Including an Extraterrestrial Statement*. Madison: Horus House Press, Inc., 1992.

Fuller, Curtis G., Mary Margaret Fuller, Jerome Clark, and Betty Lou White, eds. *Proceedings of the First International UFO Congress*. New York: Warner Books, 1980.

Fuller, John. *The Interrupted Journey: Two Lost Hours "Aboard a Flying Saucer."* New York: Penguin-Random House, 2022.

Gardea, Jesús. *Stripping Away the Sorrows from this World*, translated by Mark Schafer. Colonia del Valle: Editorial

Aldus, S. A., 1998.

Gautreau, Justin. *The Last Word: The Hollywood Novel and the Studio System.* New York: Oxford University Press, 2020.

Gay American Indians and Will Roscoe, eds. *Living the Spirit: A Gay American Indian Anthology.* New York: St. Martin's Press, 1988.

Gelder, Ken, and Jane M. Jacobs. *Uncanny Australia: Sacredness and Identity in a Postcolonial Nation.* Melbourne: Melbourne University Press, 1998.

Gemeinhardt, Peter, Lieve Van Hoof, and Peter Van Nuffelen, eds. *Education and Religion in Late Antique Christianity: Reflections, Social Contexts, and Genres.* London: Routledge, 2016.

Gersdorf, Catrin. *The Poetics and Politics of the Desert: Landscape and the Construction of America.* Amsterdam: Rodopi, 2009.

Gersdorf, Catrin, and Sylvia Mayer, eds. *Nature in Literary and Cultural Studies: Transatlantic Conversations.* New York: Rodopi, 2006.

Ghosh, Amitav. *The Great Derangement: Climate Change and the Unthinkable.* Chicago: University of Chicago Press, 2016.

Gide, André. *Amyntas: North African Journals,* translated by Richard Howard. New York: The Echo Press, 1988.

Gilbert, Sandra M., and Susan Gubar. "Sexual Linguistics, Gender Language, Sexuality." *New Literary History* 16 (1985): 515–43.

Gillette, Donna L., and Mavis Greer. "Spirituality in Rock Art Yesterday and Today: Reflections from the Northern Plains and Far Western United States." In *Rock Art and Sacred Landscapes,* edited by Donna L. Gillette, Mavis Greer, Michele Helene Hayward, and William Breen Murray, 253–73. New York: Springer, 2014.

Gillette, Donna L., Mavis Greer, Michele Helene Hayward, and William Breen Murray, eds. *Rock Art and Sacred Landscapes.* New York: Springer, 2014.

Gillmor, Frances. *Fruit Out of Rock.* New York: Duell, Sloan and Pierce, 1940.

Gilmore, John. *Severed: The True Story of the Black Dahlia Murder.* Los Angeles: Amok Books, 2015.

Glenn, T. J. "A Fighting Manual of Mars." In *Edgar Rice Burroughs' Fantastic Worlds: Essays and Examinations of the Science Fiction Universe Spawned by the Man who Created Tarzan,* edited by James Van Hise, 20–28. Yucca Valley: James Van Hise, 1996.

Glowacki, Donna M. *Living and Leaving: A Social History of Regional Depopulation in Thirteenth-Century Mesa Verde.* Tucson: University of Arizona Press, 2015.

Glowacki, Donna M., and Scott Van Keuren, eds. *Religious Transformation in the Late Pre-Hispanic Pueblo World.* Tucson: University of Arizona Press, 2011.

Goehring, James E. *Ascetics, Society, and the Desert: Studies in Early Egyptian Monasticism.* Harrisburg: Trinity Press International, 1999.

Goldhill, Simon. "Conclusions." In *Classical Literature and Posthumanism,* edited by Giulia Maria Chesi and Francesca Spiegel, 331–41. London: Bloomsbury Academic, 2020.

Golla, Victor. *California Indian Languages.* Berkeley: University of California Press, 2022.

Goodwin, Grenville. *The Social Organization of the Western Apache.* Chicago: University of Chicago Press, 1942.

Goss, James A. "A Basin-Plateau Shoshonean Ecological Model." In *Great Basin Cultural Ecology: A Symposium,* edited by Don D. Fowler, Gladys W. Smith, and C. Melvin Aikens, 123–28. Reno: Desert Research Institute, University of Nevada, 1972.

———. "Traditional Cosmology, Ecology and Language." In *Ute Indian Arts and Culture: From Prehistory to the New Millennium,* edited by William Wroth, 27–52. Colorado Springs: Taylor Museum of Colorado Springs Fine Arts Center, 2000.

Gottlieb, Madeline. "Herman Teppis and the Incestuous Fantasy: Exploring Complicated Relationships in Norman Mailer's *The Deer Park." The Explicator* 77 (2019): 103–6.

Gough, Galal. "Gender in Stone: Yonis, Phallic Stones, and Male and Female Symbols in Southern California Rock Art." *Proceedings of the Society for California Archaeology* 9 (1996): 73–79.

Gowen, William R. "Hoo-ray! ri! ro! row! roo! rah! Rupert Hughes and his 'Dozen.'" *Newsboy:* November–December 1995, 13–16.

Grabarczyk, Pawel. "What Does the Silent Planet Tell Us? The Analysis of Selected Philosophical Themes Found in Stanisław Lem's *Solaris." Acta Universitatis Lodziensis: Folia Litteraria Polonica* 4, no. 59 (2020): 69–80.

Graff, Katie, ed. *The Western Sublime: Majestic Landscapes of the American West.* Tucson: Tucson Museum of Art, 2019.

Grayton, A. H. "Yokuts and Western Mono Ethnography." *University of California Anthropological Records* 10

(1948): 1–290.

Greene, Nathaniel E. "Observations of Mars, at Madeira, in August and September 1877." *Memoirs of the Royal Astronomical Society* 44 (1877–1879): 123–40.

Greer, John, and Mavis Greer. "Dark Zone Pictographs at Surratt Cave, Central New Mexico." In *Forward into the Past: Papers in Honor of Teddy Lou and Francis Stickney*, edited by Regge N. Wiseman, Thomas C. O'Laughlin, Cordelia T. Snow, and David M. Brugge, 37–46. Albuquerque: The Archaeological Society of New Mexico, 2002.

Grewe-Volpp, Christa. "Nature 'Out There' and as a 'Social Player': Some Basic Consequences for a Literary Ecocritical Analysis." In *Nature in Literary and Cultural Studies: Transatlantic Conversations*, edited by Catrin Gersdorf and Sylvia Mayer, 71–86. New York: Rodopi, 2006.

Grey, Zane. *The Heritage of the Desert*. New York: Grosset & Dunlap, 1938.

———. *The Light of Western Stars*. Rockville: Phoenix Rider, 2009.

———. *Shower of Gold*. New York: Dorchester Publishing Co., Inc., 2007.

———. *Wanderer of the Wasteland*. New York: Harper & Brothers, 1923.

———. *Wildfire*. New York: Harper & Brothers, 1917.

Grigg, Russell, Dominique Hecq, and Craig Smith, eds. *Female Sexuality: The Early Psychoanalytic Controversies*. Abingdon: Routledge, 2018.

Grove, Richard H. *Green Imperialism: Colonial Expansion, Tropical Island Edens, and the Origins of Environmentalism, 1600–1860*. Cambridge: Cambridge University Press, 1995.

Grover, Quinn. "Aridity, Individualism, and Paradox in Elmer Kelton's *The Time It Never Rained*." In *Reading Aridity in Western American Literature*, edited by Jada Ach and Gary Reger, 45–66. Lanham, MD: Lexington Books, 2020.

Gueldry, Michel. "Yves Berger: de la quête poétique à la disparition du roman." *French Review* 68 (1995): 615–25.

Guénon, René. *Le théosophisme: histoire d'une pseudo-religion*. N.p.: Éditions Dervy, 2021.

Gulyas, Aaron John. *Extraterrestrials and the American Zeitgeist: Alien Contact Tales Since the 1950s*. Jefferson: McFarland & Company, Publishers, 2013.

Halberstam, Jack. *Female Masculinity*. Durham: Duke University Press, 1998.

Haley, James L. *Apaches: A History and Culture Portrait*. Norman: University of Oklahoma Press, 1987.

Hall, Dawn, ed. *Drawing the Borderland: Artist-Explorers and the U.S.-Mexico Boundary Survey*. Albuquerque: University of New Mexico Press, 1996.

Halperin, David M., John J. Winkler, and Froma I. Zeitlin, eds. *Before Sexuality: The Construction of Erotic Experience in the Ancient Greek World*. Princeton: Princeton University Press, 1990.

Hamilton, Amy. "Imagined Deserts, Planned Communities, and Escape Pods in the American West." In *Reading Aridity in Western American Literature*, edited by Jada Ach and Gary Reger, 21–43. Lanham, MD: Lexington Books, 2020.

Hamilton, Amy T., and Tom J. Hillard, eds. *Before the West Was West: Critical Essays on Pre-1800 Literature of the American Frontiers*. Lincoln: University of Nebraska Press, 2014.

Hamilton, William F., III. *Cosmic Top Secret: America's Secret UFO Program*. New Brunswick: Inner Light, 1991.

Hareuveni, Nogah. *Desert and Shepherd in Our Biblical Heritage*, translated by Helen Frenkley. Keot Kedumim: The Biblical Landscape Reserve in Israel, 1991.

Harrington, John Peabody. "A Yuma Account of Origins." *Journal of American Folk-Lore* 21 (1908): 324–47.

Harrington, Mark. "'Little Devil So High.'" *The Masterkey* 24 (1950): 170.

Harris, Jack S. "The White Knife Shoshoni of Nevada." In *Seven American Indian Tribes*, edited by Ralph Linton, 39–166. New York: Appleton-Century, 1940.

Hartmann, William K. *Searching for Golden Empires: Epic Cultural Collisions in Sixteenth-Century America*. Tucson: University of Arizona Press, 2014.

Haslam, Jason. *Gender, Race and American Science Fiction: Reflections on Fantastic Identities*. New York: Routledge, 2015.

Hatonn, Gyeorgos C. *Space-Gate: The Veil Removed*, 3rd ed. Las Vegas: Phoenix Source, 1993.

Hatto, Arthur T. *The Mohave Heroic Epic of Inyo-kutavêre*. Helsinki: Academia Scientiarum Fennica, 1999.

Hawthorne, Susan. *The Falling Woman*. North Melbourne: Spinifex, 1992.

Hayes, Jesse G., and Horace T. Pierce. *Apache Vengeance: True Story of the Apache Kid*. N.p.: Literary Licensing LLC, 2011.

Haynes, Roslynn D. *Seeking the Centre: The Australian Desert in Literature, Art, and Film*. Cambridge: Cambridge University Press, 1998.

Heckerl, David K. "Critical Theory, Causality, and the Emancipation of Nature." In *Re-Naming the Landscape*, edited by Jürgen Kleist and Bruce A. Butterfield, 239–58. New York: Peter Lang, 1994.

Heidegger, Martin. *The Question Concerning Technology and Other Essays*, translated by William Lovitt. New York: Garland Press, 1977.

Heissig, Walther, and Rüdiger Schott, eds. *Die heutige Bedeutung oraler Traditionen: Ihre Archivierung, Publikation und Index-Erschließung / The Present-Day Importance of Oral Traditions: Their Preservation, Publication and Indexing*. Wiesbaden: Verlag für Sozialwissenschaften Wiesbaden, 1998.

Henderson, George L. *California and the Fictions of Capitalism*. New York: Oxford University Press, 1999.

Hendrix, H. V., G. Slusser, and E. S. Rabkin, eds. *Visions of Mars: Essays on the Red Planet in Fiction and Science*. Jefferson: McFarland & Company, 2011.

Hermanson, Scott. "Fear and Loathing in Los Angeles: Mike Davis as Nature Writer." *Western American Literature* 37 (2002): 293–317.

Hill, Barry. *The Rock: Travelling to Uluru*. St. Leonards: Allen & Unwin Pty Ltd., 1994.

Hill, Robert T. "Descriptive Topographic Terms of Spanish America." *National Geographic Magazine* 7, no. 9, September 1896, 291–302.

Hoagland, Richard C. *The Monuments on Mars: A City on the Edge of Forever*, 5th ed. Berkeley: Frog Ltd., 2002.

Hoagland, Richard C., and Mike Bara. *Dark Mission: The Secret History of NASA*. Rev. and exp. ed. Port Townsend: Feral House, 2009.

Hogan, David J., ed. *Science Fiction America: Essays on SF Cinema*. Jefferson: McFarland & Company, 2006.

Honko, Lauri, ed. *Kalevala and the World's Traditional Epics*. Helsinki: Finnish Literature Society, 2002.

———. "On the Difficulty of Documenting Oral Epics." In *Die heutige Bedeutung oraler Traditionen: Ihre Archivierung, Publikation und Index-Erschließung / The Present-Day Importance of Oral Traditions: Their Preservation, Publication and Indexing*, edited by Walther Heissig and Rüdiger Schott, 185–94. Wiesbaden: Verlag für Sozialwissenschaften Wiesbaden, 1998.

Honold, Kevin. *Molly*. Pittsburgh: Autumn House Press, 2022.

Hopkins, Budd. "Abduction and Deception." *International UFO Reporter*, September/October 1990, 15–17, 22.

———. *Intruders: The Incredible Visitations at Copley Woods*. New York: Ballantine Books, 1987.

———. *Missing Time*. New York: Ballantine, 1981.

Horney, Karen. "The Dread of Woman: Observations on a Specific Difference in the Dread Felt by Men and Women Respectively for the Opposite Sex." In *Female Sexuality: The Early Psychoanalytic Controversies*, edited by Russell Grigg, Dominique Hecq, and Craig Smith, 241–52. Abingdon: Routledge, 2018.

Horton, D. Seth. "Critical Regionality and (Mis-)Translation: The Modernist Elision of Pueblo Source Material in Mary Austin's Later Career." *Western American Literature* 58 (2023): 121–42.

Howard, Dana. *Diane: She Came from Venus*. London: Regency Press, n.d. [1956].

———. *My Flight to Venus: A True Mystical Experience—Long Before the Advent of the Flying Saucer—Heralding the Coming of Interplanetary Spacecraft*. Clarksburg: New Saucerian Press, 2017.

———. *Over the Threshold*. Los Angeles: Llewellyn Publications, Ltd., 1957.

Hoyt, William Graves. *Lowell and Mars*. Tucson: University of Arizona Press, 1976.

Hubert, Jane. "Sacred Beliefs and Beliefs of Sacredness." In *Sacred Sites, Sacred Places*, edited by David L. Carmichael, Jane Hubert, Brian Reeves, and Audhild Schanche, 9–19. London: Routledge, 1994.

Hughes, Dorothy. *Dread Journey*. New York: Duell, Sloan, and Pierce, 1945.

Hughes, Mimi, and Alex Hall. "Local and Synoptic Mechanisms Causing Southern California's Santa Ana Winds." *Climate Dynamics* 34 (2010): 847–57.

Hughes, Rupert. *Souls for Sale*. New York: Garland Publishing, Inc., 1978.

Hume, David. *On Religion*, edited by Richard Wollheim. Cleveland: Meridian Books–The World Publishing Company, 1964.

Hutton, Paul Andrew. *The Apache Wars: The Hunt for Geronimo, the Apache Kid, and the Boy Captive Who Started the Longest War in American History*. New York: Broadway Books, 2016.

Huxley, Aldous. *After Many a Summer Dies the Swan*. New York: Harper & Row, 1965.

———. *Ape and Essence*. Chicago: Ivan R. Dee, 1992.

Hymes, Dell. "Lineaments and Approximations." In *Kalevala and the World's Traditional Epics*, edited by Lauri Honko, 163–81. Helsinki: Finnish Literature Society, 2002.

Hyslop, James H. "The Smead Case." *The Annals of Psychical Science* 4 (1906): 69–105.

Ingold, Tim. "The Temporality of the Landscape." *World Archaeology* 25 (1993): 152–74.

Innes, Robert Alexander, and Kim Alexander, eds. *Indigenous Men and Masculinities: Legacies, Identities,*

Regeneration. Winnipeg: University of Manitoba Press, 2015.

Irvin, G. W. "A Sequential History of Arizona Railroad and Mining Development." In *History of Mining in Arizona*, edited by J. M Canty and M. N. Greeley, 253–78. Tucson: Mining Club of the Southwest Foundation, 1991.

Islas, Arturo. *The Rain God.* New York: Avon Books, 1984.

Jack, Peter Munro. "A New Novel by Aldous Huxley." *New York Times Book Review*, January 28, 1940, 2.

Jackson, John Brinckerhoff. *A Sense of Place, a Sense of Time.* New Haven: Yale University Press, 1994.

Jackson, Richard H., and Roger Henrie. "Perception of Sacred Space." *Journal of Cultural Geography* 3 (1983): 94–107.

Jacobs, David M. *Secret Life: Firsthand Documented Accounts of UFO Abductions.* New York: Simon, 1992.

Jacobs, David Michael. *The UFO Controversy in America.* Bloomington: Indiana University Press, 1975.

Jacobs, Sue-Ellen, Wesley Thomas, and Sabine Lang, eds. *Two-Spirit People: Native American Gender Identity, Sexuality, and Spirituality.* Urbana: University of Illinois Press, 1997.

Jacoby, Karl. *Shadows at Dawn: A Borderlands Massacre and the Violence of History.* New York: The Penguin Press, 2008.

James, Edward. *Science Fiction in the Twentieth Century.* New York: Oxford University Press, 1994.

Jameson, Frederick. *Archaeologies of the Future: The Desire Called Utopia and Other Science Fictions.* New York: Verso Books, 2007.

Jasper, David. *The Sacred Desert: Religion, Literature, Art, and Culture.* Malden, MA: Blackwell, 2004.

Jennbert, Kristina. "Sheep and Goats in Norse Paganism." In *PECUS: Man and Animal in Antiquity*, edited by Barbro Santillo Frizell, 160–66. Rome: The Swedish Institute in Rome, 2004.

Johnson, Boma. *Earth Figures of the Lower Colorado and Gila River Deserts: A Functional Analysis.* Yuma: Bureau of Land Management, Yuma District Office, 1985.

Johnson, David. "Frances Gillmor." In *This Is About Vision: Interviews with Southwestern Writers*, edited by William Balassi, John F. Crawford, and Annie O. Eysturoy, 27–39. Albuquerque: University of New Mexico Press, 1990.

Johnson, Robert. "Nova Britannia: Offering Most Excellent Fruites by Planting in Virginia, etc." In *Tracts and Other Papers, Relating Principally to the Origin, Settlement, and Progress of the Colonies of North America, from the Beginning of the Country to the Year 1776*, vol. 1, edited by Peter Force, no pagination. Washington, DC: Printed by Peter Force, 1836.

Johnston, Alison M. *Is the Sacred for Sale? Tourism and Indigenous Peoples.* London: Earthscan, 2006.

Jue, Melody. "Churning Up the Depths: Nonhuman Ecologies of Metaphor in *Solaris* and 'Oceanic.'" In *Ecology and Science Fiction*, edited by Gerry Canavan and Kim Stanley Robinson, 226–41. Middletown: Wesleyan University Press, 2014.

Julyan, Robert. *The Place Names of New Mexico*, revised ed. Albuquerque: University of New Mexico Press, 1998.

Jung, C. G. *Flying Saucers: A Modern Myth of Things Seen in the Sky*, translated by R. F. C. Hull. Princeton: Princeton University Press, 1978.

Justice, Daniel Heath. *Kynship: The Way of Thorn and Thunder.* Wiarton: Kegedonce Press, 2005.

Kadohata, Cynthia. *In the Heart of the Valley of Love.* Berkeley: University of California Press, 1997.

Kavanagh, Paul. "With Breath Just Condensing on It: An Interview with David Malouf." *Southerly* 46, no. 3 (1986): 247–59.

Kearney, Amanda, and John J. Bradley. "'Too strong to ever not be there': Place Names and Emotional Geographies." *Social & Cultural Geography* 10 (2009): 77–94.

Kehoe, Alice Beck. *Shamans and Religion: An Anthropological Exploration in Critical Thinking.* Long Grove: Waveland Press, Inc., 2000.

Kelly, Isabel T. *Southern Paiute Ethnography.* Anthropological Papers 69. Salt Lake City: University of Utah Department of Anthropology, 1971.

Kelly, Saul. *The Lost Oasis: The Desert War and the Hunt for Zerzura.* Boulder: Westview Press, 2000.

Kelly, William H. *Cocopa Ethnography.* Tucson: University of Arizona Press, 1977.

Kelton, Elmer. *The Time It Never Rained.* Fort Worth: TCU Press, 1984.

Kerwin, Dale. *Aboriginal Dreaming Paths and Trading Routes: The Colonisation of the Australian Economic Landscape.* Brighton: Sussex Academic Press, 2010.

King, Reverend George. *You Are Responsible!* London: The Aetherius Press, 1961.

Kino, Father Eusebio Francisco. *Kino's Historical Memoir of Pimería Alta: A Contemporary Account of the Beginnings of California, Sonora, and Arizona*, translated and edited by Herbert Eugene Bolton, 2 vols. Cleveland: The Arthur H. Clark Company, 1919.

Kirby, Joan. "'The Noble Savage as Continent': A Review of Jean Baudrillard's *America*." *Australasian Journal of*

American Studies 9 (1990): 70–74.

Kirkpatrick, R. George, and Diana Tumminia. "California Space Goddess: The Mystagogue in a Flying Saucer Cult." In *Twentieth-Century World Religious Movements in Neo-Weberian Perspective*, edited by William H. Swatos Jr., 299–311. Lewiston: Mellen, 1992.

———. "Space Magic, Techno-Animism, and the Cult of the Goddess in a Southern Californian UFO Contactee Group: A Case Study of Millenarianism." *Syzygy: Journal of Alternative Religion and Culture* 1 (1992): 159–72.

Klarer, Elizabeth. *Beyond the Light Barrier: The Autobiography of Elizabeth Klarer*. Flagstaff: Light Technology Publishing LLC, 2009.

Klein, Ezra. "Kim Stanley Robinson on Climate Change, Dropping Acid and 'Psychogeology': The Sci-Fi Giant Explains Why He Is Feeling More Hopeful about the Planet." *New York Times*, July 15, 2022. Accessed October 1, 2023. https://www.nytimes.com/2022/07/15/opinion/ezra-klein-podcast-kim-stanley-robinson.html?showTranscript=1.

Klein, George D., ed. *Pangea: Paleoclimate, Tectonics, and Sedimentation during Accretion, Zenith, and Breakup of a Supercontinent*. Boulder: Geological Society of America, 1994.

Klein, Kerwin Lee. "Westward, Utopia: Robert V. Hine, Aldous Huxley, and the Future of California History." *Pacific Historical Review* 70 (2001): 465–76.

Klein, Norman. *The History of Forgetting: Los Angeles and the Erasure of Memory*. London: Verso, 2008.

Kleist, Jürgen, and Bruce A. Butterfield, eds. *Re-Naming the Landscape*. New York: Peter Lang, 1994.

Kohner, Frederick. *Gidget*. New York: Berkeley Books, 2001.

Kolodny, Annette. *The Lay of the Land: Metaphor as Experience and History in American Life and Letters*. Durham: University of North Carolina Press, 1975.

Kramer, Laura, and Ann Beutel. *The Sociology of Gender: A Brief Introduction*, 4th ed. Oxford: Oxford University Press, 2014.

Kroeber, A. L. *The Ethnography of the Cahuilla Indians*. Berkeley: The University Press, 1908.

———. "Mojave Clairvoyance: Ethnographic Interpretations 1–6." *University of California Publications in American Archaeology and Ethnology* 47, no. 2 (1957): 226–33.

———. "A Mohave Historical Epic." *University of California Publications: Anthropological Records* 11 (1951): 71–176.

———. "The Religion of the Indians of California." *University of California Publications in American Archaeology and Ethnology* 4 (1907): 319–56.

———. "Seven Mohave Myths." *University of California Publications: Anthropological Records* 11 (1948): 1–70.

Kroeber, Theodora. *Alfred Kroeber: A Personal Configuration*. Berkeley: University of California Press, 1970.

Kroeber, Theodora, and Robert F. Heizer. *Almost Ancestors: The First Californians*. San Francisco: Sierra Club, 1968.

Kruger, Derek. "Scripture and Liturgy in the Life of Mary of Egypt." In *Education and Religion in Late Antique Christianity: Reflections, Social Contexts, and Genres*, edited by Peter Gemeinhardt, Lieve Van Hoof, and Peter Van Nuffelen, 131–41. London: Routledge, 2016.

Kuletz, Valerie. *The Tainted Desert: Environmental and Social Ruin in the American West*. New York: Routledge, 1998.

Kunzru, Hari. *Gods Without Men*. New York: Alfred A. Knopf, 2012.

Kyle, Richard. "Out of Time's Abyss: The Martian Stories of Edgar Rice Burroughs, A Speculation," *Riverside Quarterly* 4 (1970): 110–23.

Laird, Carobeth. *The Chemehuevis*. Banning, CA: Malki Museum, 1976.

———. *Mirror and Pattern: George Laird's World of Chemehuevi Mythology*. Banning, CA: Malki Museum Press, 1984.

Laity, Julie. *Deserts and Desert Environments*. Oxford: Wiley-Blackwell, 2008.

Lambert, Gavin. *The Slide Area: Scenes of Hollywood Life*. London: Serpent's Tail, 1998.

Lambert, Marjorie, and J. Richard Ambler. *A Survey and Excavation of Caves in Hidalgo County, New Mexico*. Santa Fe: The School of American Research, 1961.

Lane, Belden C. *The Solace of Fierce Landscapes: Exploring Desert and Mountain Spirituality*. Oxford: Oxford University Press, 1998.

Lane, K. Maria. *Geographies of Mars: Seeing and Knowing the Red Planet*. Chicago: University of Chicago Press, 2011.

Lang, Sabine. "Native American Men-Women, Lesbians, Two-Spirits: Contemporary and Historical Perspectives." *Journal of Lesbian Studies* 20 (2016): 299–323.

Lasswitz, Kurd. *Auf zwei Planeten*, 2 vols. Berlin: Verlag von Emil Felber, 1897.

Latour, Bruno. "Agency at the Time of the Anthropocene." *New Literary History* 45 (2014): 1–18.

———. *Facing Gaia: Eight Lectures on the New Climatic Regime*. London: Polity, 2017.

———. "How Better to Register the Agency of Things." In *The Tanner Lectures on Human Values*, vol. 34, edited by Mark Matheson, Mark, 79–117. Salt Lake City: University of Utah Press, 2016.

———. *Reassembling the Social: An Introduction to Actor-Network-Theory*. Oxford: Oxford University Press, 2005.

Latta, F. *Handbook of the Yokuts Indians*, 2nd ed. Santa Cruz: Bear State Books, 1977.

Laügt, Élodie. "America in Time: Aphoristic Writing in Jean Baudrillard's *America*." *Paragraph* 35 (2012): 338–54.

Lawrence, D. H. *Studies in Classic American Literature*. London: Penguin Books, 1977.

Lawrence, Deborah, and Jon Lawrence. *Violent Encounters: Interviews on Western Massacres*. Norman: University of Oklahoma Press, 2011.

Lawson, Angelica. "Resistance and Resilience in Ofelia Zepeda's *Ocean Power*." *The Kenyon Review* 32 (2010): 180–98.

Lawson, Benjamin S. "The Time and Place of Edgar Ricer Burroughs's Early Martian Trilogy." *Extrapolation* 27 (1986): 208–20.

Lazarus, N., ed. *Postcolonial Literary Studies*. Cambridge: Cambridge University Press, 2004.

Lee, Regan. "'From the Desert Sands, Cauldrons of Magic Will Spring.'" In *Secrets of Death Valley: Mysteries and Haunts of the Mojave Desert*, edited by Timothy Green Beckley, 15–19. New Brunswick: Global Communications, 2010.

———. "The Mystical Contactee Encounters of Dana Howard: Parallels to the Marian Apparitions?" *UFO Digest*, 2007. Accessed April 17, 2017. http://www.ufodigest.com/news/1207/danahoward.html.

Lehan, Richard. "The Los Angeles Novel and the Idea of the West." In *Los Angeles in Fiction*, edited by David Fine, 29–41. Albuquerque: University of New Mexico Press, 1984.

Lem, Stanislaw. *The Invincible*. Cambridge: MIT Press, 2020.

———. *The Invincible*. New York: Seabury Press, 1973.

———. *Solaris*, translated by Joanna Kilmartin and Steve Cox. New York: Mariner, 2002.

Lepselter, Susan. "The Resonance of Captivity: Aliens and Conquest." *Hau: Journal of Ethnographic Theory* 2 (2012): 84–104.

Lerner, Max. *Tocqueville and American Civilization*. London: Transaction Publishers, 1994.

Leslie, Desmond, and George Adamski. *Flying Saucers Have Landed*. London: Werner Laurie, 1953.

Levick, Alice. *Memory and the Built Environment in 20th-Century American Literature: A Reading and Analysis of Spatial Forms*. London: Bloomsbury Academic, 2021.

Levine, Philippa. "States of Undress: Nakedness and the Colonial Imagination." *Victorian Studies* 50 (2008): 189–219.

Lévy, Bernard-Henri. *American Vertigo: Traveling America in the Footsteps of Tocqueville*, translated by Charlotte Mandell. New York: Random House, 2006.

Lewes, Darby. "Nudes from Nowhere: Pornography, Empire, and Utopia." *Utopian Studies* 4 (1993): 66–73.

Lewis, C. S. *Of Other Worlds: Essays and Stories*, edited by Walter Hooper. London: Geoffrey Bles, 1966.

———. *Out of the Silent Planet*. New York: Scribner, 2003.

———. *Perelandra*. New York: Macmillan Company, 1965.

———. *That Hideous Strength*. New York: Macmillan Company, 1974.

Lewis, Daniel. *Iron Horse Imperialism: The Southern Pacific of Mexico*. Tucson: University of Arizona Press, 2007.

Lewis, James, ed. *The Gods Have Landed: New Religions from Other Worlds*. Albany: State University of New York Press, 1995.

Lewis, James R., ed. *Scientology*. Oxford: Oxford University Press, 2009.

Lewis, Venetia Hobson. *Changing Woman: A Novel of the Camp Grant Massacre*. Lincoln: University of Nebraska Press, 2023.

Lewis-Williams, J. D., and T. A. Dowson. "The Signs of All Times: Entoptic Phenomena in Upper Paleolithic Art." *Current Anthropology* 29 (1988): 201–17.

Lewis-Williams, J. David. "Rock Art and Shamanism." In *A Companion to Rock Art*, edited by Jo McDonald and Peter Veth, 17–33. Malden, MA: Wiley-Blackwell, 2012.

Libecap, Gary D. *Owens Valley Revisited: A Reassessment of the West's First Great Water Transfer*. Palo Alto: Stanford Economics and Finance, 2007.

Limerick, Patricia Nelson. *Desert Passages: Encounters with the American Deserts*. Albuquerque: University of New Mexico Press, 1985.

Lindemann, Uwe. *Die Wüste: Terra incognita, Erlebnis, Symbol: Eine Genealogie der abendländischen*

Wüstenvorstellungen in der Literatur von der Antike bis zur Gegenwart. Heidelberg: C. Winter, 2000.

Lindemann, Uwe, and Monika Schwitz-Emans, eds. *Was Ist eine Wüste? Interdisziplinäre Annäherungen an einen interkulturellen Topos.* Würzberg: Verlag Königshausen & Neumann, 2000.

Lingenfelter, Richard. *Bonanzas and Borrascas, Volume 2: The Copper Kings and Stock Frenzies, 1885–1918.* Norman: University of Oklahoma Press, 2012.

Linton, Ralph, ed. *Seven American Indian Tribes.* New York: Appleton-Century, 1940.

Lorde, Audre. *Sister Outsider: Essays and Speeches.* Freedom: Crossing Press, 1984.

Lords, Traci. *Underneath It All.* New York: Harper Entertainment, 2003.

Louv, Richard. *Last Child in the Woods: Saving Our Children from Nature-Deficit Disorder.* Chapel Hill: Algonquin Books, 2008.

Lovelock, J. E. *Gaia: A New Look at Life on Earth.* Oxford: Oxford University Press, 1987.

Lovelock, James. *The Revenge of Gaia: Earth's Climate Crisis & the Fate of Humanity.* New York: Basic Books, 2007.

Lowell, Percival. *Mars.* New York: Houghton Mifflin, 1895.

———. *Mars and its Canals.* New York: The Macmillan Company, 1906.

———. *Mars as an Abode of Life.* New York: The Macmillan Company, 1908.

Lozano, Rosina. *An American Language: The History of Spanish in the United States.* Berkeley: University of California Press, 2018.

Lupoff, Richard. *Master of Adventure: The Worlds of Edgar Rice Burroughs.* Lincoln: University of Nebraska Press, 2005.

Lupoff, Richard A. *Edgar Rice Burroughs: Master of Adventure.* New York: Canaveral Press, 1965.

Lurie, Alison. *The Nowhere City.* New York: Henry Holt and Company, 1997.

Luthin, Herbert W., ed. *Surviving through the Days: Translations of Native California Stories.* Berkeley: University of California Press, 2002.

Lynch, Tom. "From Handback to Landback: Lessons from Uluru." In *Storied Deserts: Reimagining Global Arid Lands,* edited by Celina Osuna and Aidan Tynan, 195–213. London: Routledge, 2024.

———. "Literature in the Arid Zone." In *The Littoral Zone: Australian Contexts and Their Writers,* edited by C. A. Cranston and Robert Zellers, 71–92. Leiden: Brill Academic, 2007.

———. *Outback and Out West: The Settler-Colonial Environmental Imaginary.* Lincoln. University of Nebraska Press, 2022.

———. *Xerophilia: Ecocritical Explorations in Southwestern Literature.* Lubbock: Texas Tech University Press, 2008.

Lynes, Barbara Buhler. *Georgia O'Keeffe: Catalogue raisonné,* 2 vols. New Haven: Yale University Press, 1999.

Lynes, Barbara Buhler, Lesley Poling-Kempes, and Frederick W. Turner. *Georgia O'Keeffe and New Mexico.* Princeton: Princeton University Press, 2004.

Lyons, C. L., and J. K. Papadopoulos, eds. *The Archaeology of Colonialism.* Los Angeles: Getty Research Institute, 2002.

Lyotard, Jean-François. *Le mur du Pacifique.* Paris: Éditions Galilée, 1979.

———. *Pacific Wall,* translated by Bruce Boone. Venice: Lapis, 1989.

MacCannell, Dean. *The Ethics of Sightseeing.* Berkeley: University of California Press, 2011.

MacDonald, Alexander. *The Lost Explorers: A Story of the Trackless Desert.* London: Blackie and Son Limited, 1907.

MacDonald, Glen M. "The Myth of a Desert Metropolis." *Boom: A Journal of California* 3 (Fall 2013): 86–94.

MacDonald, J. Ross. *The Drowning Pool.* New York: Knopf, 1950.

Mack, Gerhard. "Frederick Kohner." In *Deutsche Exilliteratur seit 1933, Teil I: Kalifornien,* edited by John M. Spalek and Joseph Strelka, 762–70 Munich: Franke Verlag, 1976.

Mack, John E. *Abduction: Human Encounters with Aliens.* New York: Ballantine, 1994.

———. *Passport to the Cosmos: Human Transformation and Alien Encounters.* New York: Crown, 1999.

Mailer, Norman. *The Deer Park.* New York: Vintage Books, 1983.

Makeda, Lillian. "Visions of a Liminal Landscape: Mythmaking on the Rainbow Plateau." *Journal of the Southwest* 58 (2016): 633–96.

Manley, David L. *Aros of Atlantis.* Philadelphia: Dorrance, 1972.

Manly, William L. *Death Valley in '49: The Autobiography of a Pioneer.* Crabtree: The Narrative Press, 2001.

Mannix, Patrick. *The Rhetoric of Anti-Nuclear Fiction: Persuasive Strategies in Novels and Films.* Lewisburg, PA: Bucknell University Press, 1992.

Mansfield, Harvey C. *Tocqueville: A Very Short Introduction.* Oxford: Oxford University Press, 2010.

Markley, Robert. *Dying Planet: Mars in Science and Imagination.* Durham: Duke University Press, 2005.

Marovitz, Sanford E. "Aldous Huxley and the Nuclear Age: Ape and Essence in Context." In *Critical Essays on*

Aldous Huxley, edited by Jerome Meckier, 195–207. New York: G. K. Hall, 1996.

Marsh, George Perkins. *Man and Nature: Or, Physical Geography as Modified by Human Action*, edited by David Lowenthal. Cambridge, MA: The Belnap Press of Harvard University Press, 1965.

Martínez, David. "Hiding in the Shadows of History: Revitalizing the Hia-Ced O'odham Peoplehood." *Journal of the Southwest* 55 (2013): 131–71.

Marwick, Arthur. "Three Alison Lurie Novels of the Long Sixties." In *Windows on the Sixties: Exploring Key Texts of Media and Culture*, edited by Anthony Aldgate, James Chapman, and Arthur Marwick, 114–38. London: I. B. Tauris, 2000.

Marx, Leo. *The Machine in the Garden: Technology and the Pastoral Ideal in America*. Oxford: Oxford University Press, 2000.

Masquelier, Adeline. "Dirt, Undress, and Difference: An Introduction." In *Dirt, Undress, and Difference: Critical Perspectives on the Body's Surface*, edited by Adeline Masquelier, 1–33. Bloomington: Indiana University Press, 2005.

———, ed. *Dirt, Undress, and Difference: Critical Perspectives on the Body's Surface*. Bloomington: Indiana University Press, 2005.

Mathé, Sylvie. "Méditation sur le désert: figures et voix." In *Mythes ruraux et urbains dans la culture américaine*, edited by Serge Ricard, 135–56. Aix-en-Provence: Publications de l'U de Provence, 1990.

Matheson, Mark, ed. *The Tanner Lectures on Human Values*, vol. 34. Salt Lake City: University of Utah Press, 2016.

Matheson, Terry. *Alien Abductions: Creating a Modern Phenomenon*. Amherst: Prometheus Books, 1998.

Mathiowetz, Michael, Polly Schaafsma, Jeremy Coltman, and Karl Taube. "The Darts of Dawn: Tlahuizcalpantecuhtli Venus Complex in the Iconography of Mesoamerica and the American Southwest." *Journal of the Southwest* 57 (2015): 1–102.

Mathy, Jean-Philippe. *Extrême-Occident: French Intellectuals and America*. Chicago: University of Chicago Press, 1993.

Matsunaga, Kyoko. "Trinitite, Turquoise, and Rattlesnakes: Envisioning the (De)Nuclearized Desert in the Works of Leslie Marmon Silko and Kyoko Hayashi." In *Reading Aridity in Western American Literature*, edited by Jada Ach and Gary Reger, 195–221. Lanham, MD: Lexington Books, 2020.

McDannell, Colleen, ed. *Catholics in the Movies*. New York: Oxford University Press, 2008.

McDonald, Jo, and Peter Veth, eds. *A Companion to Rock Art*. Malden, MA: Wiley-Blackwell, 2012.

McGinty, Brian. *The Oatman Massacre: A Tale of Desert Captivity and Survival*. Norman: University of Oklahoma Press, 2005.

McGowan, Charlotte. *Ceremonial Fertility Sites in Southern California*. San Diego: San Diego Museum of Man, 1982.

McGrath, Melanie. *Motel Nirvana: Dreaming of the New Age in the American Desert*. New York: Picador, 1995.

McNamara, Kevin R., ed. *The Cambridge Companion to the Literature of Los Angeles*. Cambridge: Cambridge University Press, 2010.

McPherson, R. S. *Sacred Land, Sacred View: Navajo Perceptions of the Four Corners Region*. Provo: Brigham Young University, 1992.

McWilliams, Carey. *Southern California: An Island on the Land*. Salt Lake City: Peregrine Books, 2010.

Meaghan, Timothy J. "Cops, Priests, and the Decline of Irish America: True Confessions (1981)." In *Catholics in the Movies*, edited by Colleen McDannell, 227–49. New York: Oxford University Press, 2008.

Meckier, Jerome, ed. *Critical Essays on Aldous Huxley*. New York: G. K. Hall, 1996.

Melton, J. Gordon. "The Contactees: A Survey." In *The Gods Have Landed: New Religions from Other Worlds*, edited by James Lewis, 1–13. Albany: State University of New York Press, 1995.

———. "UFO Contactees—A Report on Work in Progress." In *Proceedings of the First International UFO Congress*, edited by Curtis G. Fuller, Mary Margaret Fuller, Jerome Clark, and Betty Lou White, 378–95. New York: Warner Books, 1980.

Melton, J. Gordon, and George M. Eberhart. "The Flying Saucer Contactee Movement, 1950–1994: A Bibliography." In *The Gods Have Landed: New Religions from Other Worlds*, edited by James Lewis, 251–332. Albany: State University of New York Press, 1995.

Melville, Herman. *Typee: A Peep at Polynesian Life*. Evanston: Northwestern University Press, 2003.

Melzer, Richard. *Fred Harvey Houses of the Southwest*. Mount Pleasant, SC: Arcadia Publishing, 2008.

Menger, Howard. *From Outer Space to You*. Clarksburg: Saucerian Books, 1959.

Merchant, Carolyn. *Reinventing Eden: The Fate of Nature in Western Culture*. New York: Routledge, 2003.

Merish, Lori. "Mapping the Transnational in Contemporary Native American Fiction: Silko and Welch." *Journal of Transnational American Studies* 9 (2018): 339–58.

Meylor, Meagan. "'Sad Flower in the Sand': Camilla Lopez and the Erasure of Memory in *Ask the Dust*." In *John Fante's* Ask the Dust: *A Joining of Voices and Views*, edited by Stephen Cooper and Clorinda Donato, 58–82. New York: Fordham University Press, 2020.

Michler, N. "From the 111th Meridian of Longitude to the Pacific Ocean." In *Report of the United States and Mexican Boundary Survey, Made Under the Direction of the Secretary of the Interior*, William H. Emory, 101–25. Washington, DC: Cornelius Wendell, 1857.

Mifflin, Margot. *The Blue Tattoo: The Life of Olive Oatman*, with a new postscript by the author. Lincoln: University of Nebraska Press, 2011.

Miklowitz, Gloria. *After the Bomb*. New York: Scholastic Press, Inc., 1985.

Miller, Jay. "Basin Religion and Theology: A Comparative Study of Power (Puha)." *Journal of California and Great Basin Anthropology* 5 (1983): 66–86.

Milner, Andrew. *Locating Science Fiction*. Middletown: Wesleyan University Press, 2012.

Milnor, Kristina. *Gender, Domesticity, and the Age of Augustus: Inventing Private Life*. Oxford: Oxford University Press, 2005.

Miranda, Deborah A. "Extermination of the Joyas: Gendercide in Spanish California." *GLQ: A Journal of Lesbian and Gay Studies* 16 (2010): 253–84.

Misrach, Richard. *Bravo 20: The Bombing of the American West*. Baltimore: Johns Hopkins University Press, 1990.

Mitchell, Helen, and Betty Mitchell. "We Met the Space People." Accessed July 17, 2017. http://sacred-texts.com/ufo/wmsp/wmsp01.htm and http://sacred-texts.com/ufo/wmsp/wmsp02.htm.

Moers, Ellen. *Literary Women*. Garden City: Doubleday & Co., Inc., 1976.

Mogen, David. *The Western Theme in Science Fiction Literature*. San Bernardino: The Borgo Press, 1993.

Momaday, N. Scott. *House Made of Dawn*. New York: Harper Perennial Modern Classics, 2010.

Monani, Salma, and Joni Adamson, eds. *Ecocriticism and Indigenous Studies: Conversations from Earth to Cosmos*. London: Routledge, 2017.

Monsen, Frederick. "The Primitive Folk of the Desert: Splendid Physical Development That Yet Shows Many of the Characteristics of an Earlier Race Than Our Own." *The Craftsman* 12 (1907): 164–78.

Montes-Alcalá, Cecilia. "Code-Switching in US Latino Literature: The Role of Biculturalism." *Language and Literature* 24 (2015): 264–81.

Montrie, Chad. *The Myth of Silent Spring: Rethinking the Origins of American Environmentalism*. Berkeley: University of California Press, 2018.

Mora, Pat. *Chants*. Houston: Arte Público Press, 1984.

Morcos, Gamila. "*Mobile* de Butor: typographie et justification." *Australian Journal of French Studies* 18 (1981): 56–76.

Morphy, Howard, and Frances Morphy. "The Spirit of the Plains Kangaroo." In *Words for Country: Landscape and Language in Australia*, edited by Tim Bonyhady and Tom Griffiths, 102–23. Sydney: University of South Wales Press, 2002.

Morsberger, Robert E. "Edgar Rice Burroughs' Apache Epic." *Journal of Popular Culture* 6 (1973): 280–87.

Mort, Terry. *The Wrath of Cochise: The Bascom Affair and the Origins of the Apache Wars*. New York: Pegasus Books, 2013.

Moskowitz, Sam, ed. *Under the Moons of Mars: A History and Anthology of "The Scientific Romance" in the Munsey Magazines, 1912–1920*. New York: Holt, Rinehart and Winston, 1970.

Mountgomry, Robert. "A Discourse Concerning the Design'd Establishment of a New Colony to the South of Carolina, in the Most Delightful Country of the Universe." In *Tracts and Other Papers, Relating Principally to the Origin, Settlement, and Progress of the Colonies of North America, from the Beginning of the Country to the Year 1776*, vol. 1, edited by Peter Force, 1–24. Washington, DC: Printed by Peter Force, 1836.

Muecke, Stephen. *Textual Spaces: Aboriginality and Cultural Studies*. Sydney: New South Wales University Press, 1992.

Mullen, Richard Dale. "The Prudish Prurience of H. Rider Haggard and Edgar Rice Burroughs." *Riverside Quarterly* 5 (1973): 4–19.

———. "The Undisciplined Imagination: Edgar Rice Burroughs and Lowellian Mars." In *The Other Side of Realism: Essays on Modern Fantasy and Science Fiction*, edited by Thomas D. Carlson, 229–47. Bowling Green: Bowling Green University Popular Press, 1971.

Mullen, Richard (the Elder). "Edgar Rice Burroughs and the Fate Worse Than Death." *Riverside Quarterly* 1 (1970): 186–91.

Mundy, Barbara. *The Mapping of New Spain: Indigenous Cartography and the Maps of the Relaciones Geográphicas.* Chicago: University of Chicago Press, 2000.

Munro, Pamela. *Mojave Syntax.* New York: Garland, 1976.

Munro, Pamela, Nellie Brown, and Judith G. Crawford. *A Mojave Dictionary.* Los Angeles: Department of Linguistics, University of California, 1992.

Nabokov, Peter. *Where the Lightning Strikes: The Lives of American Indian Sacred Places.* New York: Penguin, 2006.

Nash, Ilana. "'Nowhere Else to Go': Gidget and the Construction of Adolescent Femininity." *Feminist Media Studies* 2 (2002): 341–56.

Nash, Roderick. *Wilderness and the American Mind*, 4th ed. New Haven: Yale University Press, 2001.

Neale, Margo, and Lynne Kelly. *Songlines: The Power and the Promise.* Port Melbourne: Thames & Hudson Australia Pty Ltd, 2020.

Nel, Werner. "Rainfall Trends in the KwaZulu-Natal Draksenberg Region of South Africa in the Twentieth Century." *International Journal of Climatology* 29 (2009): 1634–41.

Nelson, Susan. "Thinking in Ruins: The Rio del Llano Experiment." *LARB Quarterly* 38 (August 2023): 9–19.

Nettlebeck, Amanda. *Reading David Malouf*, edited by Pamela Gay. Sydney: Sydney University Press, 1995.

Newcomb, Simon. "The Problems of Astronomy." *Science* 5, no. 125 (May 21, 1897): 777–85.

Newell, Diane, and Victoria Lamont. "Savagery on Mars: Representations of the Primitive in Brackett and Burroughs." In *Visions of Mars: Essays on the Red Planet in Fiction and Science*, edited by H. V. Hendrix, G. Slusser, and E. S. Rabkin, 73–79. Jefferson: McFarland & Company, 2011.

Newman, Julie. *Alison Lurie: A Critical Study.* Amsterdam: Rodopi, 2000.

Newman, L. S., and R. F. Baumeister. "Toward an Explanation of the UFO Abduction Phenomenon: Hypnotic Elaboration, Extraterrestrial Sadomasochism, and Spurious Memories." *Psychological Inquiry* 7 (1996): 99–126.

Norwood, Vera. "Crazy-Quilt Lives: Frontier Sources for Southwestern Women's Literature." In *The Desert Is No Lady: Southwestern Landscapes in Women's Writing and Art*, edited by Vera Norwood and Janice Monks, 74–95. Tucson: University of Arizona Press, 1987.

Norwood, Vera. *Made from This Earth: American Women and Nature.* Chapel Hill: University of North Carolina Press, 1993.

Norwood, Vera, and Janice Monk, eds. *The Desert Is No Lady: Southwestern Landscapes in Women's Writing and Art.* Tucson: University of Arizona Press, 1987.

O'Brien, Jodi, ed. *Encyclopedia of Gender and Society.* Los Angeles: Sage, 2015.

O'Donnell, Patrick. "Postwar Los Angeles: Suburban Eden and the Fall into History." In *The Cambridge Companion to the Literature of Los Angeles*, edited by Kevin R. McNamara, 59–74. Cambridge: Cambridge University Press, 2010.

Oehlschlaeger, Fritz H. "Civilization as Emasculation: The Threatening Role of Women in the Frontier Fiction of Harold Bell Wright and Zane Grey." *Midwest Quarterly* 22 (1981): 346–60.

O'Laughlin, Thomas C. "A Possible Dark Area Shrine in Chavez Cave, Doña Ana County, New Mexico." In *Climbing the Rocks: Papers in Honor of Helen and Jay Crotty*, edited by Regge N. Wiseman, Thomas C. O'Laughlin, Cordelia N. Snow, Helen K. Crotty, and Jay Crotty, 137–46. Albuquerque: The Archaeological Society of New Mexico, 2003.

Oliver, Jeff. "On Mapping and Its Afterlife: Unfolding Landscapes in Northwestern North America." *World Archaeology* 43 (2011): 66–85.

Olmstead, Frederick Law. *A Journey Through Texas, or, a Saddle Trip on the Southwestern Frontier, with a Statistical Appendix.* New York: Dix, Edwards, & Co, 1857.

Orsi, Richard. "Selling the Golden State: A Study of Boosterism in Nineteenth-Century California." PhD diss., University of Wisconsin, 1973.

———. *Sunset Limited: The Southern Pacific and the Development of the American West, 1850–1930.* Berkeley: University of California Press, 2005.

Orth, Michael. "Utopia in the Pulps: The Apocalyptic Pastoralism of Edgar Rice Burroughs." *Extrapolation* 27 (1986): 221–33.

Ortiz, Simon. *Woven Stone.* Tucson: University of Arizona Press, 1992.

Osuna, Celina. "Color, Place, and Memory in Silko's Gardens in the Dunes." In *Reading Aridity in Western American Literature*, edited by Jada Ach and Gary Reger, 223–42. Lanham, MD: Lexington Books, 2020.

Osuna, Celina, and Aidan Tynan, eds. *Storied Deserts: Reimagining Global Arid Lands.* London: Routledge, 2024.

Padget, Martin. *Indian Country: Travels in the American Southwest, 1840–1935.* Albuquerque: University of New Mexico Press, 2004.

Panay, A. "From Little Big Man to Little Green Men: The Captivity Scenario in American Culture." *European Journal of American Culture* 23 (2004): 201–16.

Park, Willard Z. *Shamanism in Western North America: A Study in Cultural Relationships.* Evanston: Northwestern University Press, 1938.

Partridge, Christopher. "Alien Demonology: The Christian Roots of the Malevolent Extraterrestrial in UFO Religions and Abduction Spiritualties." *Religion* 34 (2004): 163–89.

Pasulka, D. W. *American Cosmic: UFOs, Religion, Technology.* New York: Oxford University Press, 2019.

———. *Encounters: Experiences with Nonhuman Intelligences.* New York: St. Martin's Essentials, 2023.

Patterson, Orlando. *Slavery and Social Death: A Comparative Study,* with a new preface. Cambridge: Harvard University Press, 2018.

Pattie, James. *The Personal Narrative of James O. Pattie of Kentucky.* Santa Barbara: The Narrative Press, 2001.

Paulin, Diana Rebekkah. *Imperfect Unions: Staging Miscegenation in U.S. Drama and Fiction.* Minneapolis: University of Minnesota Press, 2012.

Pavel, Thomas G. *Fictional Worlds.* Cambridge: Harvard University Press, 1986.

Pearson, Wendy Gay. "Born to Be Bron: Destiny and Destinerrance in Samuel R. Delany's *Trouble on Triton.*" *Science Fiction Studies* 36 (2009): 461–77.

Pelecanos, George. "Introduction." In *True Confessions,* John Gregory Dunne, v–ix. New York: Thunder Mouth's Press, 2006.

Peters, J. U. "The Los Angeles Anti-Myth." In *Itinerary: Essays on California Writers,* edited by Charles L. Crow, 21–32. Bowling Green: Bowling Green State University Press, 1978.

Phillips, Steven J., and Patricia Wentworth Comus, eds. *A Natural History of the Sonoran Desert.* Tucson: Arizona-Sonora Desert Museum Press, 2000.

Plank, Robert. *The Emotional Significance of Imaginary Beings: A Study of the Interaction between Psychopathology, Literature, and Reality in the Modern World.* Springfield, IL: Charles C. Thomas, 1968.

Plumwood, Val. "The Concept of a Cultural Landscape: Nature, Culture and Agency in the Land." *Ethics & the Environment* 11 (2006): 115–50.

Poirier, Richard. "America deserta." *London Review of Books* 11, no. 4 (February 16, 1989): 3–6.

Poling-Kempes, Lesley. *The Harvey Girls: The Women Who Opened the West.* Boston: De Capo Press, 1994.

Pollak, Ellen. "'Postlude' to 'Literary Women.'" *Signs* 24 (1999): 739–47.

Pollay, Richard. "'Below the Belt' Cigarette Advertising." *Tobacco Control* 4 (1995): 188–92.

Porch, Douglas. *Conquest of the Sahara.* New York: Farrar, Straus & Giroux, 1984.

Porter, James I. *The Sublime in Antiquity.* Cambridge: Cambridge University Press, 2016.

Powell, John Wesley. *Report on the Lands of the Arid Region of the United States, With a More Detailed Account of the Lands of Utah.* Cambridge: Harvard Commons Press, 1983.

Powell, Lawrence Clark. *El Morro.* Santa Barbara: Capra Press, 1984.

Press, Margaret L. *Chemehuevi: A Grammar and Lexicon.* Berkeley: University of California Press, 1979.

Prettejohn, Elizabeth. *Art for Art's Sake: Aestheticism in Victorian Painting.* New Haven: Yale University Press, 2008.

Price, Jenny. "Thirteen Ways of Seeing Nature in L.A." In *Land of Sunshine: An Environmental History of Los Angeles,* edited by William Deverell and Greg Hise, 220–44. Pittsburgh: University of Pittsburgh Press, 2005.

Price, Neil S., ed. *The Archaeology of Shamanism.* London: Routledge, 2001.

Prichard, Joseph Vila. *Tableaux Vivants Arranged for Amateur Representation.* New York: Samuel French, n.d.

Pritzer, G. M. "The Only Good Alien Is a Dead Alien: Science Fiction and the Metaphysics of Indian-Hating on the High Frontier." *Journal of American Culture* 18 (1995): 51–67.

Pulido, Laura, Laura Barraclough, and Wendy Cheng. *A People's Guide to Los Angeles.* Berkeley: University of California Press, 2012.

Putzi, Jennifer. *Identifying Marks: Race, Gender, and the Marked Body in Nineteenth-Century America.* Athens: University of Georgia Press, 2006.

Quilter, Jeffrey, and Mary Miler, eds. *A Pre-Columbian World: Searching for a Unity Vision of Ancient America.* Washington, DC: Dumbarton Oaks, 2006.

Ramaswamy, Sumathi. *The Lost Land of Lemuria: Fabulous Geographies, Catastrophic Histories.* Berkeley: University of California Press, 2004.

Randall, Dale R. "The 'Seer' and the 'Seen': Themes in Gatsby and Some of Their Parallels in Eliot and Wright." *Twentieth Century Literature* 10 (1964): 56–62.

Randle, Kevin D. *Roswell in the 21st Century: The Evidence as It Exists Today.* Naples: Speaking Volumes, LLC, 2016.

Raynes, B. *Visitors from Hidden Realms: The Origin and Destiny of Humanity as Told by Our Star Elders, Shamen, and UFO Visitors*. Memphis: Eagle Wing Books Incorporated, 2004.

Red Star, N. *Star Ancestors: Indian Wisdomkeepers Share the Teachings of the Extraterrestrials*. Rochester: Inner Traditions International, 2000.

Redfern, Nick. *Contactees: A History of Alien-Human Interactions*. Franklin Lakes: New Page Books, 2010.

Redniss, Lauren. *Oak Flat: A Fight for Sacred Land in the American West*. New York: Random House, 2020.

Reece, Gregory L. *UFO Religion: Inside Flying Saucer Cults and Culture*. London-New York: I. B. Tauris, 2007.

Reger, Gary. *First There Is a Mountain*. Ann Arbor: University of Michigan Press, forthcoming.

———. "Greeks and Romans in the Sahara Desert: Ideology and Experience." *Global Environment* 12 (2019): 22–55.

———. "In the Dark without a Light: Understanding Unmediated Sites of Dark Tourism." In *Dark Tourism in the American West*, edited by Jennifer Dawes, 181–201. London: Palgrave Macmillan, 2020.

———. "A New Mediterranean: The Caribbean in the Euro-American Imaginary." In *Turning Tides: Caribbean Intersections in the Americas and Beyond*, edited by Heather Cateau and Milla Cozart Riggio, 36–54. Kingston-Miami: Ian Randle Publishers, 2019.

———. "Romans in the Egyptian Desert: From Desert Space to Roman Place." In *Économie et inégalité: Ressources, échanges et pouvoir dans l'antiquité classique*, edited by Sitta Von Reden and Pascale Derron, 115–49. Vandoevres: Fondation Hardt, 2017.

Reisner, Mark. *Cadillac Desert: The American West and Disappearing Water*, revised and updated. New York: Penguin Books, 1993.

Remondino, Peter Charles. *The Mediterranean Shores of America: Southern California: Its Climatic, Physical, and Meteorological Conditions*. Philadelphia: F. A. Davis Co, 1892.

Renooz, Céline. *Psychologie comparée de l'homme et de la femme*. Paris: Bibliothèque de la Nouvelle Encyclopédie, 1898.

Ricard, Serge, ed. *Mythes ruraux et urbains dans la culture américaine*. Aix-en-Provence: Publications de l'U de Provence, 1990.

Richet, Charles. *Traité de métapsychique*. Paris: Librairie Félix Alcan, 1922.

Rigby, Kate. *Topographies of the Sacred: The Poetics of Place in European Romanticism*. Charlottesville: University of Virgina Press, 2004.

Riley, Michael J. "Constituting the Southwest, Contesting the Southwest, Reinventing the Southwest." *Journal of the Southwest* 36 (1994): 231–41.

Rimmer, John. *The Evidence for Alien Abductions*. Wellingborough: The Aquarian Press, 1984.

Rio, David, and Christopher Conway. "Guest Editors' Introduction: The Case for Transnationalism in the American Literary West." *Western American Literature* 54 (2019): ix–xiv.

Roach, Marion. *The Roots of Desire: The Myth, Meaning, and Sexual Power of Red Hair*. New York: Bloomsbury USA, 2005.

Robb, Jenny E. "From the Periodical Archives: Winsor McCay, George Randolph Chester, and the Tale of the Jungle Imps." *Periodical Comics and Cartoons* 17 (2007): 245–59.

Robbins, Tom. *Wild Ducks Flying Backward*. New York: Bantam Books, 2005.

Roberts, Adam. *The History of Science Fiction*, 2nd ed. London: Palgrave Macmillan, 2016.

Roberts, David. *Once They Moved Like the Wind: Cochise, Geronimo, and the Apache Wars*. New York: Simon and Schuster, 1994.

Robinson, Kim Stanley. *The High Sierra: A Love Story*. New York: Little, Brown and Company, 2022.

Rochas d'Aiglun, Albert de. *Les vies successives: Documents pour l'étude de cette question*, 2nd ed. Paris: Librairie P. Lemaire, 1924.

Ronald, Ann. *The New West of Edward Abbey*, 2nd ed. Reno: University of Nevada Press, 2000.

Roscoe, Will. "Bibliography of Berdache and Alternative Gender Roles Among North American Indians." *Journal of Homosexuality* 14 (1987): 81–172.

———. "North American Tribes with Berdache and Alternative Gender Roles." In *Living the Spirit: A Gay American Indian Anthology*, edited by Gay American Indians and Will Roscoe, 217–22. New York: St. Martin's Press, 1988.

Ross, Andrew. *Bird on Fire: Lessons from the World's Least Sustainable City*. New York: Oxford University Press, 2011.

Ross-Bryant, Lynn. "The Land in American Experience." *Journal of the American Academy of Religion* 58 (1990): 333–55.

Roth, Christopher. "Ufology as Anthropology: Race, Extraterrestrials, and the Occult." In *E.T. Culture: Anthropology in Outerspaces*, edited by Debbora Battaglia, 38–93. Durham: Duke University Press, 2003.

Roth, John E. *American Elves: An Encyclopedia of Little People from the Lore of 380 Ethnic Groups of the Western Hemisphere.* Jefferson: McFarland & Co., Inc., Publishers, 1997.

Routledge, Clay, Andrew A. Abeyta, and Christina Roylance. "We Are Not Alone: The Meaning Motive, Religiosity, and the Belief in Extraterrestrial Intelligence." *Motivation and Emotion* 41 (2017): 135–46.

Roux, Michel. *Le désert de sable: le Sahara dans l'imaginaire des Français (1900–1994).* Paris: L'Harmattan, 1996.

Roy, John Flint. *A Guide to Barsoom: Eleven Sections of References in One Volume Dealing with the Martian Stories Written by Edgar Rice Burroughs.* New York: Ballantine Books, 1976.

Rozwadowski, Andrzej. "Crossing the Crack, Flying to the Cloud: Indo-Iranians, Shamanism and Central Asian Rock Art." *Bolletino del Centro Camuno preistorici* 33 (2002): 97–105.

———. "Disappearing into the Rock: Shamanistic Aspects of Indo-Iranian Mythology as a Context for Interpreting Central Asian Petroglyphs." In *Spirits and Stones: Shamanism and Rock Art in Central Asia and Siberia,* edited by Andrzej Rozwadowski and Maria M. Kośko, 49–79. Posnań: Instytut Wschodni Uam, 2002.

———. "Sun Gods or Shamans? Interpreting the 'Solar-Headed' Petroglyphs of Central Asia." In *The Archaeology of Shamanism,* edited by Neil S. Price, 65–86. London: Routledge, 2001.

Rozwadowski, Andrzej, and Maria M. Kośko, eds. *Spirits and Stones: Shamanism and Rock Art in Central Asia and Siberia.* Posnań: Instytut Wschodni Uam, 2002.

Rudnick, Lois. "Re-Naming the Land: Anglo Expatriate Women in the Southwest." In *The Desert Is No Lady: Southwestern Landscapes in Women's Writing and Art,* edited by Vera Norwood and Janice Monk, 10–26. Tucson: University of Arizona Press, 1987.

Rusling, James Fowler. *The Great West and Pacific Coast.* New York: Shelton, 1877.

Russell, Frank. *The Pima Indians.* Re-edition with introduction, citation sources, and bibliography by Bernard L. Fontana. Tucson: University of Arizona Press, 1975.

Russell, Sharman Apt. *Songs of the Fluteplayer: Seasons of Life in the Southwest.* Reading: Addison-Wesley Publishing Company, Inc., 1991.

Ryan, Simon. *The Cartographic Eye: How Explorers Saw Australia.* Cambridge: Cambridge University Press, 1996.

Sackman, Douglas C. "A Garden of Worldly Delights." In *Land of Sunshine: An Environmental History of Los Angeles,* edited by William Deverell and Greg Hise, 245–66. Pittsburgh: University of Pittsburgh Press, 2005.

Saler, B., C. Ziegler, and C. Moore. *UFO Crash at Roswell: The Genesis of a Modern Myth.* Washington: Smithsonian Institution Press, 1997.

Saliba, John A. "Religious Dimensions of UFO Phenomena." In *The Gods Have Landed: New Religions from Other Worlds,* edited by James Lewis, 15–64. Albany: State University of New York Press, 1995.

Salinas, Michèle. *Voyages et voyageurs en Algérie, 1830/1930.* Toulouse: Éditions Privat, 1989.

Salmond, Anne. *Aphrodite's Island: The European Discovery of Tahiti.* Berkeley: University of California Press, 2009.

Sánchez Prado, Ignacio M., ed. *Mexican Literature as World Literature.* New York: Bloomsbury Academic, 2022.

Santillo Frizell, Barbro, ed. *PECUS: Man and Animal in Antiquity.* Rome: The Swedish Institute in Rome, 2004.

Sawyer, Suzana, and Arun Agrawal. "Environmental Orientalisms." *Cultural Critique* 45 (2000): 71–108.

Saxon, Dean, Lucille Saxon, and Susie Enos. *Dictionary: Tohono O'odham/Pima to English, English to Tohono O'odham/Pima,* 2nd ed. Tucson: University of Arizona Press, 1983.

Schaafsma, Curtis, and Carroll L. Riley, eds. *The Casas Grandes World.* Salt Lake City: University of Utah Press, 1999.

Schaafsma, Polly. "Petitions for Rain: Textile and Pottery Designs in Rock Art." *International Letter on Rock Art* 66 (2013): 17–27.

———. *Rock Art of New Mexico.* Albuquerque: University of Mexico Press, 1992.

———. "Tláloc y las metáforas para hacer llover en el Suroeste de Estados Unidos." *Arqueología mexicana* 96 (2009): 48–51.

———. "Tlalocs, Kachinas, Sacred Bundles, and Related Symbolism in the Southwest and Mesoamerica." In *The Casas Grandes World,* edited by Curtis Schaafsma and Carroll L. Riley, 164–92. Salt Lake City: University of Utah Press, 1999.

———. "Visión del mundo e identidad: el arte rupestre en el Suroeste de los Estados Unidos (950–1450 DC)." *Anales de antropología* 44 (2010): 159–93.

Schaafsma, Polly, and Karl A. Taube. "Bringing the Rain: An Ideology of Rain Making in the Pueblo Southwest and Mesoamerica." In *A Pre-Columbian World: Searching for a Unity Vision of Ancient America,* edited by Jeffrey Quilter and Mary Miler, 231–85. Washington, DC: Dumbarton Oaks, 2006.

Schaefer, Heike. *Mary Austin's Regionalism: Reflections on Gender, Genre, and Geography.* Charlottesville: University of Virginia Press, 2004.

Schechter, Alex. "'The Place Where Shamans Dream': Safeguarding Spirit Mountain." *New York Times*, January 24, 2023.

Schiffman, Paula M. "The Los Angeles Prairie." In *Land of Sunshine: An Environmental History of Los Angeles*, edited by William Deverell and Greg Hise, 38–51. Pittsburgh: University of Pittsburgh Press, 2005.

Schwartz, Kessel. "Makbara—Metaphysical Metaphor or Goytisolian World Revisited?" *Hispania* 67 (1984): 36–42.

See, Carolyn. *Golden Days*. Berkeley: University of California Press, 1996.

———. "The Hollywood Novel: An Historical and Critical Study." PhD diss., University of California, Los Angeles, 1963.

See, Fred G. "'Writing So as Not to Die': Edgar Rice Burroughs and the West Beyond the West." *Melus* 11 (1984): 59–72.

Seed, David. "Los Angeles' Science Fiction Futures." In *The Cambridge Companion to the Literature of Los Angeles*, edited by Kevin R. McNamara, 123–34. Cambridge: Cambridge University Press, 2010.

Seed, Patricia. *Ceremonies of Possession in Europe's Conquest of the New World, 1492–1640*. Cambridge: Cambridge University Press, 1995.

Sencindiver, Susan Yi. "New Materialism." *Oxford Bibliographies*. Accessed August 15, 2023. https://www.oxford-bibliographies.com/display/document/obo-9780190221911/obo-9780190221911-0016.xml.

Sestigiani, Sabina. *Writing Colonisation: Violence, Landscape, and the Act of Naming in Modern Italian and Australian Literature*. New York: Peter Lang, 2014.

Sherer, Lorraine M., with Frances Stillman. *The Bitterness Road: The Mojave, 1604–1860*, edited by Sylvia Brakke Vane and Lowell John Bean. Menlo Park: Ballena Press, 1994.

Shermer, Michael. *The Believing Brain: From Ghosts and Gods to Politics and Conspiracies—How We Construct Beliefs and Reinforce Them as Truths*. New York: St. Martin's Griffin, 2011.

Short, Robert. *Out of the Stars: A Message from Extraterrestrial Intelligence*. Haverford: Infinity Publishing, 2010.

Shrode, Maria Hargrove. "Overland by Ox-Train in 1870: From Sulphur Springs, Texas, to San Diego, California." *Quarterly Publication of the Historical Society of Southern California* 26 (1944): 8–37.

Siddel, David. "Goats, Marginality and the 'Dangerous Other.'" *Environment and History* 15 (2009): 521–36.

Silko, Leslie Marmon. *Ceremony*. New York: Penguin Books, 1977.

———. *The Turquoise Ledge: A Memoir*. New York: Viking, 2010.

Slotkin, Richard. *The Fatal Environment: The Myth of the Frontier in the Age of Industrialization, 1800–1890*. Norman: University of Oklahoma Press, 1985.

———. *Gunfighter Nation: The Myth of the Frontier in Twentieth-Century America*. Norman: University of Oklahoma Press, 1998.

———. *Regeneration Through Violence: The Mythology of the American Frontier, 1600–1860*. Norman: University of Oklahoma Press, 1973.

Smith, Benjamin, Knut Arne Heiskog, and David Morris, eds. *Working with Rock Art: Presenting and Understanding Rock Art Using Indigenous Knowledge*. Johannesburg: Wits University Press, 2012.

Smith, Henry Nash. *Virgin Land: The American West as Symbol and Myth*. New York: Vintage Books, 1950.

Smith, Laura. "Resurrection after the 'Blue Death': Literature, Politics, and Ecological Redemption at Glen Canyon." *Western American Literature* 51 (2016): 39–69.

Smith, P. D. *The Doomsday Men: The Real Doctor Strangelove and the Dream of the Superweapon*. New York: St. Martin's Press, 2007.

Smythe, William E. *The Conquest of Arid America*, new and revised ed. New York: The Macmillan Company, 1905.

Soja, Edward. *My Los Angeles: From Urban Restructuring to Regional Urbanization*. Berkeley: University of California Press, 2014.

———. *Thirdspace: Journeys to Los Angeles and Other Real-and-Imagined Places*. Oxford: Blackwell, 1996.

Sole, T., and K. Woods. "Protection of Indigenous Sacred Places: The New Zealand Experience." In *Sacred Sites, Sacred Places*, edited by David L. Carmichael, Jane Hubert, Brian Reeves, and Audhild Schanche, 339–51. London: Routledge, 1994.

[Sophronios] 1865. "Βίος Μαρίας Αἰγυπτίας, *Patrologia Graeca*, edited by J.-P. Migne, vol. 87, 3, cols. 3697–3726. Paris: Imprimerie Catholique.

Sowerwine, Charles. *France Since 1870: Culture, Politics and Society*, 3rd ed. London: Red Globe Press, 2018.

Spalek, John M., and Joseph Strelka, eds. *Deutsche Exilliteratur seit 1933, Teil I: Kalifornien*. Munich: Franke Verlag, 1976.

Spalek, John M., Joseph Strelka, and Sandra H. Hawrylchak, eds. *Deutsche Exilliteratur seit 1933, Band 2: Kalifornien. Teil 1*. Munich: Franke Verlag, 1976.

Spencer, Walter Baldwin, and Francis James Gillen. *The Native Tribes of Central Australia*. London: Macmillan and Co. Limited, 1899.

———. *The Northern Tribes of Central Australia*. London: Macmillan and Company, Limited, 1904.

Spicer, Edward H. *Cycles of Conquest: The Impact of Spain, Mexico, and the United States on the Indians of the Southwest, 1533–1960*. Tucson: University of Arizona Press, 1997.

Spier, Leslie. *Yuman Tribes of the Gila River*. New York: Dover Publications, Inc., 1978.

St. John, Rachel. *Line in the Sand: A History of the Western U.S.-Mexico Border*. Princeton: Princeton University Press, 2011.

Starr, Kevin. *Americans and the California Dream, 1850–1914*. New York: Oxford University Press, 1973.

———. *The Dream Endures: California Enters the 1940s*. New York: Oxford University Press, 1997.

———. *Embattled Dreams: California in War and Peace, 1940–1950*. New York: Oxford University Press, 2002.

———. *Golden Dreams: California in an Age of Abundance, 1950–1963*. New York: Oxford University Press, 2009.

———. *Inventing the Dream: California Through the Progressive Era*. New York: Oxford University Press, 1985.

———. *Material Dreams: Southern California Through the 1920s*. New York: Oxford University Press, 1990.

Stecopoulos, Harry. "The World According to Normal Bean: Edgar Rice Burroughs' Popular Culture." In *Race and the Subject of Masculinities*, edited by Harry Stecopoulos and Michael Uebel, 170–91. Durham: Duke University Press, 1997.

Stecopoulos, Harry, and Michael Uebel, eds. *Race and the Subject of Masculinities*. Durham: Duke University Press, 1997.

Steward, Julian H. *Basin-Plateau Aboriginal Sociopolitical Groups*. Washington, DC: United States Government Printing Office, 1938.

Stewart, George R. *Names on the Land: A Historical Account of Place-Naming in the United States*. New York: New York Review of Books, 2008.

Stewart, Kenneth M. "A Brief History of the Chemehuevi Indians." *Kiva* 34 (1968): 9–27.

Stich, Klaus B. "Cather's 'Midi Romanesque': Missionaries, Myth, and the Grail in *Death Comes for the Archbishop*." *Studies in the Novel* 38 (2006): 57–73.

Storey, Samuel. *To the Golden Land: Sketches of a Trip to Southern California*. London: Walter Scott, 1889.

Stow, Randolph. *Outrider: Poems, 1956–1962*. London: Macdonald & Co. (Publishers), Ltd., 1962.

Strain, Ellen. "Exotic Bodies, Distant Landscapes: Tourist Viewing and Popularized Anthropology in the Nineteenth Century." *Wide Angle* 18 (1996): 70–100.

Strang, Veronica. "Lording It Over the Goddess: Water, Gender, and Human-Environmental Relations." *Journal of Feminist Studies in Religion* 30 (2014): 85–109.

Stratton, R. B. *Captivity of the Oatman Girls: Being an Interesting Narrative of Life among the Apache and Mohave Indians*. New York: Printed for the Author, 1858.

Strauss, David. *Percival Lowell: The Culture and Science of a Boston Brahmin*. Cambridge: Harvard University Press, 2001.

Strieber, Whitley. *Communion: A True Story*. New York: William Morrow, 1987.

Stupple, David. "The Man Who Talked with Venusians." In *Proceedings of the First International UFO Congress*, edited by Curtis G. Fuller, Mary Margaret Fuller, Jerome Clark, and Betty Lou White, 261–71. New York: Warner Books, 1980.

Sturma, Michael. "Aliens and Indians: A Comparison of Abduction and Captivity Narratives." *Journal of Popular Culture* 36 (2002): 318–34.

Sturt, Charles. *Narrative of an Expedition into Central Australia, Performed under the Authority of Her Majesty's Government, during the Years 1844, 5, and 6*, 2 vols. London: T. and W. Boone, 1849.

Sutton, Peter, and Keryn Walshe. *Farmers or Hunter-Gatherers? The* Dark Emu *Debate*. Melbourne: Melbourne University Press, 2021.

Suvin, Darko. *Metamorphoses of Science Fiction: On the Poetics and History of a Literary Genre*. New Haven: Yale University Press, 1979.

Swatos, William H., Jr., ed. *Twentieth-Century World Religious Movements in Neo-Weberian Perspective*. Lewiston: Mellen, 1992.

Tagg, Lawrence V. *Harold Bell Wright*. Boise: Boise State University Press, 1994.

Taliaferro, John. *Tarzan Forever: The Life of Edgar Rice Burroughs, the Creator of Tarzan*. New York: Scribner, 1999.

Tapahonso, Luci. *Blue Horses Rush In*. Tucson: University of Arizona Press, 1997.

Tatonetti, Lisa. *Written by the Body: Gender Expansiveness and Indigenous Non-Cis Masculinities*. Minneapolis: University of Minnesota Press, 2021.

Taylor, Mark. "Aldous Huxley's *Ape and Essence* and Clashing Discourses of Nature." *Mosaic* 53 (2020): 87–102.

Taylor, Sheila Ortiz. *Coachella*. Albuquerque: University of New Mexico Press, 1998.

Tcherkézoff, Serge. *"First Contacts" in Polynesia: The Samoan Case (1722–1848): Western Misunderstandings about Sexuality and Divinity*. Canberra: The Australian National University Press, 2008.

Teague, David W. *The Southwest in American Literature and Art: The Rise of a Desert Aesthetic*. Tucson: University of Arizona Press, 1997.

Teague, David W., and Peter Wild. *The Secret Life of John C. Van Dyke: Selected Letters*. Reno-Las Vegas: University of Nevada Press, 1997.

Thacker, Robert, and Michael A. Peterman, eds. *Cather Studies 4: Willa Cather's Canadian & Old World Connections*. Lincoln: University of Nebraska Press, 1999.

Thomas, Nicholas. "Colonizing Cloth: Interpreting the Material Culture of Nineteenth-Century Oceania." In *The Archaeology of Colonialism*, edited by C. L. Lyons and J. K. Papadopoulos, 182–98. Los Angeles: Getty Research Institute, 2002.

Thomas, Wesley. "Navajo Cultural Constructions of Gender and Sexuality." In *Two-Spirit People: Native American Gender Identity, Sexuality, and Spirituality*, edited by Sue-Ellen Jacobs, Wesley Thomas, and Sabine Lang, 156–73. Urbana: University of Illinois Press, 1997.

Tocqueville, Alexis de. *Democracy in America*, translated by Harvey C. Mansfield. Chicago: University of Chicago Press, 2002.

Todorov, Tzvetan. *The Conquest of America: The Question of the Other*, translated by Richard Howard. Norman: University of Oklahoma Press, 1999.

Tompkins, Jane. *West of Everything: The Inner Life of Westerns*. New York: Oxford University Press, 1992.

Townsend, Richard F., ed. *The Ancient Americas: Art from Sacred Landscapes*. Chicago: The Art Institute of Chicago, 1992.

———. "The Renewal of Nature at the Temple of Tlaloc." In *The Ancient Americas: Art from Sacred Landscapes*, edited by Richard F. Townsend, 171–86. Chicago: The Art Institute of Chicago, 1992.

Trafzer, Clifford E. *A Chemehuevi Song: The Resilience of a Southern Paiute Tribe*. Seattle: University of Washington Press, 2015.

Traister, Bryce. "The Object of Study; or, Are We Being Transnational Yet?" *Journal of Transnational American Studies* 2, no. 1 (2010). Accessed May 25, 2019. https/scholarship.org/uc/item/864843hs.

Trover, Ellen Lloyd. *Birth of the Inland Sea: How the Colorado River Created the Salton Sea*. Coachella: History Trove, 2018.

Tuan, Yi-Fu. *Topophilia: A Study of Environmental Perception, Attitudes, and Values* (with a new preface by the author). New York: Columbia University Press, 1990.

Tudoret, Patrick. *Fromentin: le roman d'une vie*. Paris: Les belles lettres, 2018.

Tumminia, Diana. *When Prophecy Never Fails: Myth and Religion in a Flying Saucer Group*. Oxford: Oxford University Press, 2005.

Turner, Frederick. *Genesis: An Epic Poem of Terraforming Mars*. Spokane Valley: Ilium Press, 1988.

Turner, George. "Shut the Door When You Go Out." *Void* no. 4 (1986): 13–15.

Turney, Omar A. *Prehistoric Irrigation in Arizona*. Phoenix: Arizona State Historian, 1929.

Tynan, Aidan. *The Desert in Modern Literature and Philosophy: Wasteland Aesthetics*. Edinburgh: Edinburgh University Press, 2022.

Underhill, Ruth, Donald M. Bahr, Baptisto Lopez, José Panco, and David Lopez. *Rainhouse and Ocean: Speeches for the Papago Year*. Tucson: University of Arizona Press, 1979.

United States Bureau of Reclamation and Colorado River Basin Tribes Partnership. *Colorado River Basin Ten Tribes Partnership Tribal Water Study Report: Final Report*. Denver: U.S. Department of the Interior, Bureau of Reclamation, 2018. Accessed September 21, 2023. https://usbr.gov/lc/region/programs/crbstudy/tws/finalreport.html.

Urrea, Luis Alberto. *The Devil's Highway: A True Story*. New York: Back Bay Books, 2004.

Valley of Love. Dir. Guillaume Nicloux. Perf. Isabelle Huppert, Gérard Depardieu, Dan Warner. Strand Releasing, 2016.

Van Dyke, Dix. *Daggett: Life in a Mojave Frontier Town*, edited by Peter Wild. Baltimore-London: Johns Hopkins University Press, 1997.

Van Dyke, John C. *Art for Art's Sake: Seven University Lectures on the Technical Beauties of Painting*. New York: Charles Scribner's Sons, 1893.

———. *The Desert: Further Studies in Natural Appearances*. New York: Charles Scribner's Sons, 1901.

———. *The Open Spaces: Incidents of Nights and Days under the Blue Sky.* New York: C. Scribner's Sons, 1922.

Van Hise, James, ed. *Edgar Rice Burroughs' Fantastic Worlds: Essays and Examinations of the Science Fiction Universe Spawned by the Man who Created Tarzan.* Yucca Valley: James Van Hise, 1996.

———. "The Power of Burroughs' Mars Trilogy." In *Edgar Rice Burroughs' Fantastic Worlds: Essays and Examinations of the Science Fiction Universe Spawned by the Man Who Created Tarzan,* edited by James Van Hise, 11–19. Yucca Valley: James Van Hise, 1996.

Van Tassel, George W. *The Council of Seven Lights.* Clarksburg: Saucerian Publisher, 2020.

———. *I Rode a Flying Saucer: The Mystery of the Flying Saucers Revealed.* Clarksburg: Saucerian Publisher, 2020.

Vecsey, Christopher, ed. *Handbook of American Indian Religious Freedom.* New York: Crossroads, 1993.

Vélez de Escalante, Fray Silvestre. *The Domínguez-Escalante Journal: Their Expedition through Colorado, Utah, Arizona, and New Mexico in 1776,* edited by Ted J. Warner and translated by Fray Angelico Chavez. Salt Lake City: University of Utah Press, 1995.

Velikovsky, Immanuel. *Worlds in Collision.* London: Paradigma Ltd., 2009.

Vincent, Pamela. "I Wanna Go Home!" *Far Out* 3 (1985): 42–44.

Vincent-Arnaud, Nathalie. "'To the Land's End' ou 'Farther Out into the Desert': Itinéraires de la négation dans *Less Than Zero* de Bret Easton Ellis." *GRAAT: Groupe des recherches anglo-américaines de Tours* 35 (2006): 179–89, 530–31.

Vollmann, William T. *Imperial.* New York: Penguin Books, 2010.

Von Reden, Sitta, and Pascale Derron, eds. *Économie et inégalité: Ressources, échanges et pouvoir dans l'antiquité classique.* Vandoevres: Fondation Hardt, 2017.

Voyles, Traci Brynne. *The Settler Sea: California's Salton Sea and the Consequences of Colonialism.* Lincoln: University of Nebraska Press, 2021.

Wade, Simeon. *Foucault in California: [A True Story Wherein the Great French Philosopher Drops Acid in the Valley of Death].* Berkeley: Heyday, 2019.

Wagner, Anton. *Los Angeles: Werden, Leben und Gestalt der Zweimillionenstadt in Südkalifornie.* Leipzig: Bibliographisches Institut, 1936.

Waldie, D. J. *Holy Land: A Suburban Memoir.* New York: W. W. Norton & Company, 1996.

Walker, Deward E., Jr. "Protection of American Indian Sacred Geography." In *Handbook of American Indian Religious Freedom,* edited by Christopher Vecsey, 100–115. New York: Crossroads, 1993.

Walker, Franklin. *A Literary History of Southern California.* Berkeley: University of California Press, 1950.

Walker, Margaret. "Booking West: Tall Tales and 'Books of Every Sort and Size' from Fanny Hill to the Bible." *Overland Journal* 50 (2007): 148–67.

Walters, Ed, and Frances Walters. *The Gulf Breeze Sightings: The Most Astounding Multiple Sightings of UFOs in U.S. History.* New York: William Morrow and Company, Inc., 1990.

Ward, Russel. *The Australian Legend,* 3rd ed. Melbourne: Oxford University Press, 1987.

Warner, Thomas T. *Desert Meteorology.* Cambridge: Cambridge University Press, 2004.

Warnke, Georgia. *Debating Sex and Gender.* Oxford: Oxford University Press, 2010.

Watkins, Claire Vaye. *Gold Fame Citrus.* New York: Riverhead Books, 2015.

Watkins, Susan. "'Women and Wives Mustn't Go Near It': Academia, Language, and Gender in the Novels of Alison Lurie." *Revista canaria de estudios ingleses* 48 (2004): 129–46.

Waugh, Evelyn. *The Loved One.* Boston: Little, Brown and Company, 1948.

Weiner, Susan. "*Terre à terre*: Tocqueville, Aron, Baudrillard, and the American Way of Life." *Yale French Studies* 100 (2001): 13–24.

Wells, H. G. *A Critical Edition of* The War of the Worlds*: H. G. Wells's Scientific Romance,* edited by David Y. Hughes and Harry M. Geduld. Bloomington: Indiana University Press, 1993.

Welsh, Jarrett T. "How to Read a Volcano." *Transactions of the American Philological Association* 144 (2014): 97–132.

Wesling, Donald. "The Representational Moment in the Discourse of Nations: Jean Baudrillard's *America.*" *Hungarian Journal of English and American Studies* 4 (1998): 9–19.

Wessendorf, Markus. "Brecht in Los Angeles—'in this mausoleum of *easy going.*'" *The Germanic Review: Literature, Culture, Theory* 95 (2020): 21–34.

West, Nathaniel. *Miss Lonelyhearts* and *The Day of the Locust.* New York: New Directions Books, 2009.

Westling, Louise H. *The Green Breast of the New World: Landscape, Gender, and American Fiction.* Athens: University of Georgia Press, 1996.

White, Richard. *Railroaded: The Transcontinentals and the Making of Modern America.* New York: W. W. Norton, 2011.

White, Richard, and John Findlay, eds. *Power and Place in the North American West.* Seattle: University of Washington Press, 1999.

White, T. H. *The Once and Future King.* New York: G. P. Putnam's Sons, 1958.

———. *The Sword in the Stone.* New York: Bantam Doubleday Dell Books for Young Readers, 1963.

Whitehill, Sharon. *Frances Gillmor: Aztec and Navajo Folklorist.* Lewiston: Edward Mellon Press, 2005.

Whitfield, Stephen J. "From Modernization to Post-Modernism: A Century and a Half of French Views of the United States." *Revista española de estudios norteamericanos* 9 (1995): 77–89.

Whitley, David S. "Finding Rain in the Desert: Landscape, Gender, and Far Western North American Rock-Art." In *The Archaeology of Rock-Art*, edited by Christopher Chippindale and Raul S. C. Taçon, 11–29. Cambridge: Cambridge University Press, 1998.

———. *A Guide to Rock Art Sites in Southern California and Southern Nevada.* Missoula: Mountain Press Publishing Co., 1996.

———. "Ways of Knowing and Seeing: Spiritual Agents and the Origins of Native American Rock Art." In *Working with Rock Art: Presenting and Understanding Rock Art Using Indigenous* Knowledge, edited by Benjamin Smith, Knut Arne Heiskog, and David Morris, 179–92. Johannesburg: Wits University Press, 2012.

Whitley, David S., Joseph M. Simon, and Ronald I. Dorn. "The Vision Quest in the Coso Range." *American Indian Rock Art* 25 (1999): 1–31.

Whitmarsh, Tim. *Beyond the Second Sophistic: Adventures in Greek Postclassicism.* Berkeley: University of California Press, 2013.

Widney, J. P. "The Colorado Desert." *Overland Monthly and Out West Magazine* 10 (1873): 44–50.

Wiener, Margaret. "Breasts, (Un)Dress, and Modernist Desires in the Balinese-Tourist Encounter." In *Dirt, Undress, and Difference: Critical Perspectives on the Body's Surface*, edited by Adeline Masquelier, 61–95. Bloomington: Indiana University Press, 2005.

Wild, Peter. "Introduction." In *Daggett: Life in a Mojave Frontier Town*, Dix Van Dyke, edited by Peter Wild, 1–19. Baltimore-London: Johns Hopkins University Press, 1997.

Wild, Peter, and Neil Carmony. "The Trip Not Taken: John C. Van Dyke, Heroic Doer or Armchair Seer?" *Journal of Arizona History* 34 (1993): 65–80.

Williams, Deborah Lindsay. "Losing Nothing, Comprehending Everything: Learning to Read Both the Old World and the New in *Death Comes for the Archbishop*." In *Cather Studies 4: Willa Cather's Canadian & Old World Connections*, edited by Robert Thacker and Michael A. Peterman, 80–96. Lincoln: University of Nebraska Press, 1999.

Williams, George H. *Wilderness and Paradise in Christian Thought: The Biblical Experience of the Desert in the History of Christianity and the Paradise Theme in the Theological Idea of the University.* New York: Harper Brothers, 1962.

Williams, Henry T., ed. *Pacific Tourist: Adams and Bishop's Illustrated Trans-Continental Guide of Travel, from the Atlantic to the Pacific Ocean: A Complete Traveler's Guide of the Union and Central Pacific Railroads.* New York: Adams and Bishop, 1881.

Williams, John. *The Samoan Journals of John Williams, 1830 and 1832*, edited by Richard M. Moyle Jr. Bloomington: Indiana University Press, 1984.

Williams, Terry Tempest. *Refuge: An Unnatural History of Family and Place.* New York: Vintage, 2001.

Williams, Tony. "Authorship and Utopia: The Case of *John Carter*." *Film International* 11 (2013): 44–54.

Williams Reed, Eris. "Environments and Gods: Creating the Sacred Landscape of Mount Kasios." In *Sacred Landscapes in Antiquity. Creation, Manipulation, Transformation*, edited by Ralph Häussler and Gian Franco Chiaia, 87–94. Oxford: Oxbow Books, 2020.

Williamson, George Hunt. *Other Tongues, Other Flesh.* Amherst: Amherst Press, 1957.

Williamson, George Hunt, and Brother Philip. *The Saucers Speak: Calling All Occupants of Interplanetary Craft*, edited by Timothy Green Beckley. Global Communications, 2012.

Wilson, Christopher P. "When Noir Meets Nonfiction." *Twentieth-Century Literature* 61 (2015): 484–510.

Wilson Moore, Shirley Ann. "No Cold to Grapple With: African-American Expectations of California." *Journal of the West* 44 (2005): 8–15.

Winchell, Mark Royden. "Fantasy Seen: Hollywood Fiction Since West." In *Los Angeles in Fiction*, edited by David Fine, 165–85. Albuquerque: University of New Mexico Press, 1984.

Winstead, Chase. "Two Faces of Voyeurism: *Nude on the Moon* and '*X*'—*The Man with the X-Ray Eyes*." In *Science Fiction America: Essays on SF Cinema*, edited by David J. Hogan, 176–87. Jefferson: McFarland & Company, 2006.

Winters, Harry, Jr. *Maricopa Place Names*. Tucson: SRI Press, 2018.

Winters, Harry J., Jr. *'O'odham Place Names: Meanings, Origins, and Histories, Arizona and Sonora*, 2nd ed. Tucson: SRI Press, 2020.

Wiseman, Regge N., Thomas C. O'Laughlin, Cordelia T. Snow, and David M. Brugge, eds. *Forward into the Past: Papers in Honor of Teddy Lou and Francis Stickney*. Albuquerque: The Archaeological Society of New Mexico, 2002.

Wiseman, Regge N., Thomas C. O'Laughlin, Cordelia N. Snow, Helen K. Crotty, and Jay Crotty, eds. *Climbing the Rocks: Papers in Honor of Helen and Jay Crotty*. Albuquerque: The Archaeological Society of New Mexico, 2003.

Witt, Charlotte. *The Metaphysics of Gender*. Oxford: Oxford University Press, 2011.

Worster, Donald. *A River Running West: The Life of John Wesley Powell*. New York: Oxford University Press, 2002.

Worster, Donald. *Rivers of Empire: Water, Aridity, and the Growth of the American West*. New York: Oxford University Press, 1985.

Wozencraft, Oliver M. "Through Northern Mexico in '49." *Californian* 6 (1882): 421–26.

Wright, Harold Bell. *Eyes of the World*. Chicago: Book Supply Co., 1914.

———. *The Winning of Barbara Worth*. New York: A. L. Burt Company, 1911.

Wright, Lawrence. *Going Clear: Scientology, Hollywood, and the Prison of Belief*. New York: Alfred A. Knopf, 2013.

Wroth, William, ed. *Ute Indian Arts and Culture: From Prehistory to the New Millennium*. Colorado Springs: Taylor Museum of Colorado Springs Fine Arts Center, 2000.

Yamashita, Shinji. *Bali and Beyond: Explorations in the Anthropology of Tourism*, translated by J. S. Eades. New York: Berghahn Books, 2003.

Yates, Helen Eva. *Bali, Enchanted Isle: A Travel Book*. Boston: Houghton Mifflin, 1933.

Zarbin, Earl. *Two Sides of the River: Salt River Valley Canals, 1867–1902*. Phoenix: Salt River Project, 1997.

Zepeda, Ofelia. *Ocean Power: Poems from the Desert*. Tucson: University of Arizona Press, 1995.

———. *Where Clouds Are Formed*. Tucson: University of Arizona Press, 2008.

INDEX

[Created with TExtract / www.TExtract.com]

ABOUT THE AUTHOR

Gary Reger's work has focused on two arenas: the economy of the Greek and Roman world and the history of human interaction with deserts. He has published widely in both fields, and he has served as the epigrapher for an excavation in Turkey. Reger has been a Hyde Fellow in the Classics Department at the University of Pennsylvania and a National Endowment for the Humanities Fellow and in 2023 undertook a Fulbright Fellowship to study deserts at the University of Western Australia. Now retired from his professorship at Trinity College in Hartford, Connecticut, he currently lives in Las Cruces, New Mexico.